The Mobilization of Political Islam in Turkey

The Mobilization of Political Islam in Turkey explains why political Islam, which has been part of Turkish politics since the 1970s but on the rise only since the 1990s, has now achieved governing power. Drawing on social movement theory, the book focuses on the dominant form of Islamist activism in Turkey by analyzing the increasing electoral strength of four successive Islamist political parties: the Welfare Party; its successor, the Virtue Party; and the successors of the Virtue Party, the Felicity Party and the Justice and Development Party. This book, which is based on extensive primary and secondary sources as well as in-depth interviews, provides the most comprehensive analysis available regarding the Islamist political mobilization in Turkey.

Banu Eligür has written extensively on Turkish domestic and foreign policy and taught courses on Political Islam and Civil Society in the Middle East at Brandeis University as a visiting assistant professor. The recipient of numerous awards and fellowships, she now lives in Turkey and conducts field research on Turkish nationalism.

To
my best friend,
my father Özcan Eligür

The Mobilization of Political Islam in Turkey

BANU ELIGÜR

CAMBRIDGE
UNIVERSITY PRESS

CAMBRIDGE UNIVERSITY PRESS
Cambridge, New York, Melbourne, Madrid, Cape Town, Singapore,
São Paulo, Delhi, Dubai, Tokyo

Cambridge University Press
32 Avenue of the Americas, New York, NY 10013-2473, USA

www.cambridge.org
Information on this title: www.cambridge.org/9780521760218

© Banu Eligür 2010

This publication is in copyright. Subject to statutory exception
and to the provisions of relevant collective licensing agreements,
no reproduction of any part may take place without the written
permission of Cambridge University Press.

First published 2010

Printed in the United States of America

A catalog record for this publication is available from the British Library.

Library of Congress Cataloging in Publication Data

Eligür, Banu, 1974–
  The mobilization of political Islam in Turkey / Banu Eligür.
    p. cm.
  Includes bibliographical references and index.
  ISBN 978-0-521-76021-8 (hardback)
  1. Islam and politics – Turkey. 2. Turkey – Politics and government – 1980– I. Title.

BP173.7.E45 2010
322′.109561–dc22   2009014154

ISBN 978-0-521-76021-8 Hardback

Cambridge University Press has no responsibility for the persistence or accuracy of URLS
for external or third-party Internet Web sites referred to in this publication and does not
guarantee that any content on such Web sites is, or will remain, accurate or appropriate.

Contents

List of Tables		page vii
List of Diagrams, Charts, and Boxes		ix
List of Acronyms		xi
Acknowledgments		xiii
Preface		xvii
1	Introduction	1
	Theoretical Approaches to Islamist Mobilization	4
	The Social Movement Literature	9
	The Political Process Model	12
2	Emergence of the Islamist Social Movement in Turkey	37
	Islam in the Ottoman Empire	37
	Ottomanism, Islamism, and Turkism	39
	The Turkish Revolution	41
	An Overview of Turkish Politics (1946–1960)	48
	From the Liberal 1961 Constitution to the 1971 Military Intervention	59
	The 1980 Military Intervention and Its Aftermath	76
	Conclusion	84
3	The Turkish-Islamic Synthesis and the Islamist Social Movement	85
	Turkey on the Brink of Civil War	85
	Turkey under Military Rule (1980–1983): The Military and the Islamists	88
	Adoption of the Turkish-Islamic Synthesis	93
	Turkey under Motherland Party Rule (1983–1991)	118
	Conclusion	135

4	The Malfunctioning State and Consolidation of the Islamist Social Movement	136
	Origins of the Malfunctioning State	137
	Framing the Political Opportunity Structure: The Welfare Party and the Just Order (Adil Düzen)	144
	The Welfare Party Becomes a Party of the Masses	154
	Municipal Governance as Political Opportunity Structure	164
	Conclusion	181
5	Organizational Dynamics of the Islamist Social Movement	182
	Islamist Party Organizational Networks: The Welfare Party and Virtue Party	183
	Party Mobilizational Efforts	189
	The Emergence of "Reformists"	198
	The Parallel Islamic Sector	200
	Conclusion	213
6	The Soft Intervention of 1997 and the Islamist Social Movement	214
	The Welfare Party Comes to Power	215
	The "Soft" Intervention of 1997 and the End of the Welfare Party	220
	The Virtue Party	234
	After "Virtue": Justice and Development	243
	The Justice and Development Party Tests the Limits	248
	The July 2007 General Elections	254
	The Justice and Development Party Mobilizes against the Secular-Democratic State	261
	Conclusion	275
7	The Islamist Social Movement Today and Prospects for the Future	276

Bibliography	285
Index	303

List of Tables

2.1	Reasons for NSP Support among Potential NSP Voters, 1973 Election Poll	*page* 71
2.2	Percentage of Votes Won by Parties in General Elections, 1950–2002	72
2.3	Seats Won in Parliament, 1950–2002	74
2.4	Party Choice of the Fully Employed, 1988 (percent)	79
2.5	Vote Share (percent) of Islamist Political Parties in General Elections in Major Cities, 1987–2002	80
2.6	Vote Share (percent) of Islamist Political Parties in Municipal Elections, 1984–2004	81
2.7	Approval of the *Sharia* Rule in Turkey (percent)	82
2.8	Religiosity, Nationalism, and Voter Preference (percent)	83
3.1	Methods of Teaching Quranic Verses and Prayers	110
3.2	Methods of Teaching the *Hadiths*	111
3.3	*İmam-Hatip* High School Students as a Proportion of Total Number of High School Students in Secondary (*Ortaöğretim*) Education, by Academic Year	127
3.4	Investment and Development Banks and Special Finance Houses in Turkey (as of November 2000)	133
4.1	Shantytown Housing in Turkey, 1950–1990	141
4.2	Party Support by Type of Urban Community (percent of total vote in community), 1973 General Elections	143
4.3	Party Support in Major Cities in General Elections, 1969–1977 (percent)	143
4.4	Party Support in Major Cities in General Elections, 1983–1999 (percent)	144

4.5	Rates of Increase in Cost-of-Living Index for Wage-Earners in Istanbul (percent)	168
4.6	Party Vote in Municipal Elections, 1984–1999 (percent)	170
6.1	Percentage of Votes and Seats Won by Parties in 1995 General Elections	216
6.2	Comparison of Attitudes of İmam-Hatip High School Students and WP Voters	223
6.3	Perceptions of the Function of İmam-Hatip High Schools	224
6.4	Sectors that İmam-Hatip High Schools Students Want to Work in the Future (percent)	224
6.5	Number of Companies Owned by Islamic Brotherhoods	231
6.6	Public Poll, 1997	233
6.7	Public Poll, 1997	233
6.8	Results of the July 2007 Turkish General Elections	255

List of Diagrams, Charts, and Boxes

DIAGRAMS

1.1	The Dynamics of Preconsolidation (1980–1991)	*page* 24
1.2	The Dynamics of Consolidation (1991–1997)	28
1.3	The Dynamics of Divergence and Reconsolidation (1997–2007)	34
5.1	The Welfare Party's Organizational Network	186

CHART

1.1	The Mobilization of Political Islam in Turkey (1980–2007)	22

BOXES

2.1	Political Parties in Turkey	53
2.2	Genealogy of Islamic and Islamist Political Parties in Turkey (1946–2007)	55

List of Acronyms

AMGT	European National View Organization (*Avrupa Milli Görüş Teşkilâtı*)
ASKON	Anatolian Tigers (*Anadolu Kaplanları*)
COMCEC	Standing Committee for Economic and Commercial Cooperation
D-8	Developing 8
DİSK	Confederation of Revolutionary Trade Unions (*Devrimci İşçi Sendikaları Konfederasyonu*)
DLP	Democratic Left Party (*Demokratik Sol Parti*, DSP)
DP	Democrat Party (*Demokrat Parti*, DP)
DPP	Democratic People's Party (*Demokratik Halk Partisi*, DEHAP)
DSP	Democratic Society Party (*Demokratik Toplum Partisi*, DTP)
FP	Felicity Party (*Saadet Partisi*, SP)
GMEI	Greater Middle East Initiative
GUP	Great Unity Party (*Büyük Birlik Partisi*, BBP)
IH	Intellectuals' Hearth (*Aydınlar Ocağı*)
IsDB	Islamic Development Bank
İTMGT	National View Organization of Muslim Community (*İslam Toplumu Milli Görüş Teşkilâtı*)
JDP	Justice and Development Party (*Adalet ve Kalkınma Partisi*, AKP)
JP	Justice Party (*Adalet Partisi*, AP)
LPT	Labor Party of Turkey (*Türkiye İşçi Partisi*, TİP)
MİSK	Confederation of Nationalist Trade Unions (*Milliyetçi İşçi Sendikaları Konfederasyonu*)
MP	Motherland Party (*Anavatan Partisi*, ANAP)
MÜSİAD	Independent Industrialists' and Businessmen's Association
NAP	Nationalist Action Party (*Milliyetçi Hareket Partisi*, MHP)
NCR	National Culture Report

NDP	Nationalist Democracy Party (*Milliyetçi Demokrasi Partisi*, MDP)
NOP	National Order Party (*Milli Nizam Partisi*, MNP)
NP	Nation Party (*Millet Partisi*, MP)
NSC	National Security Council
NSP	National Salvation Party (*Milli Selamet Partisi*, MSP)
NWP	Nationalist Work Party (*Milliyetçi Çalışma Partisi*, MÇP)
PDP	People's Democracy Party (*Halkın Demokrasi Partisi*, HADEP)
PEP	People's Endeavor Party (*Halkın Emek Partisi*, HEP)
PKK	Kurdistan Workers' Party
POS	Political Opportunity Structure
PP	Populist Party (*Halkçı Parti*, HP)
PPM	Political Process Model
RDP	Reformist Democracy Party (*Islahatçı Demokrasi Partisi*, IDP)
RNP	Republican Nation Party (*Cumhuriyetçi Millet Partisi*, CMP)
RPNP	Republican Peasants Nation Party (*Cumhuriyetçi Köylü Millet Partisi*, CKMP)
RPP	Republican People's Party (*Cumhuriyet Halk Partisi*, CHP)
SDPP	Social Democratic Populist Party (*Sosyal Demokrat Halkçı Parti*, SHP)
TIS	Turkish-Islamic Synthesis (*Türk İslam Sentezi*)
TPP	True Path Party (*Doğru Yol Partisi*, DYP)
TÜSİAD	Turkish Industrialists' and Businessmen's Association
VP	Virtue Party (*Fazilet Partisi*, FP)
WP	Welfare Party (*Refah Partisi*, RP)
WWG	West Working Group (*Batı Çalışma Grubu*)

Acknowledgments

This book, which is based on my PhD dissertation, has been a work in progress since 2003. First of all, I would like to express my deepest gratitude to my dissertation adviser, Professor Steven Burg, in the Politics Department at Brandeis University, for his invaluable guidance, comments, and support. I am indebted to him for believing in this project since its inception. It was a privilege and real education for me to work under his guidance. Without his invaluable comments and support, I could not have finished this book.

I am grateful to Professor Steven Teles, who is now at the Johns Hopkins University, for his invaluable support and guidance for this book. He has been a mentor and friend since my arrival at Brandeis University in 2000. I wish to thank him for broadening my academic approach through our interdisciplinary discussions and for always being there for me when I needed guidance.

I would like to express my gratitude to Professor Jack A. Goldstone and Professor Barry Rubin for their enthusiasm and support for this book.

I would like to acknowledge my gratitude to a number of institutions for supporting me as I wrote my dissertation and revised it into a book. Brandeis University Politics Department doctoral fellowship, Benjamin fellowship, and the Morris Abrams Award in International Relations enabled me to conduct my dissertation field research in Turkey between 2003 and 2004. Koret dissertation fellowship and Grand fellowship enabled me to write my dissertation between 2004 and 2005. Crown Center for Middle East Studies postdoctoral fellowship at Brandeis University between 2005 and 2007, Crown Center research fellowship, and Madeleine Haas Russell Visiting Assistant Professorship in Islamic and Middle Eastern Studies in the Near Eastern and Judaic Studies Department at Brandeis University between 2007 and 2008 enabled me to revise my dissertation into a book. Without the generous financial support of the Crown Center for Middle East Studies and the Near Eastern Judaic Studies Department, I could not have completed this book. Special thanks to Professor Shai Feldman, director of the Crown Center, and Kristina Cherniahivsky, the center's associate director, for their financial support for this book. I am particularly grateful to Professor David Wright, Near Eastern and Judaic Studies Department chair, Professor Avigdor Levy, Professor Jonathan Sarna, and Dean Adam B. Jaffe for providing me this invaluable opportunity for teaching and writing at an early stage of my career. I also thank Professor Asher Susser for our intellectual discussions on Turkish politics at the Crown Center during the 2007 and 2008 academic years. I wish to thank my dissertation committee members Professor David Cunningham in the Sociology Department at Brandeis University and Professor Shai Feldman. I also thank Professor Robert Art, Professor Daniel Kryder, Professor George Ross, and Professor Ralph Thaxton, in the Politics Department at Brandeis University, for their enthusiasm for this book.

This book is based on extensive primary and secondary sources (party programs, speeches, newspapers – Islamist, liberal, and leftist), as well as in-depth interviews conducted in Turkey in 2003 and 2004. I interviewed Islamist politicians (former and current parliamentarians) and party workers, Islamist foundation members, military officers and retired generals, center-right and center-left parliamentarians, sociology professors, divinity professors, members of the directorate of religious affairs, and Turkish nationalists. These interviews provide important insights into the thinking of key members of the Islamist movement regarding Turkish society and its future, and of key secular actors, as well. I would like to thank a number of Turkish scholars that I interviewed for this book: Professor Oya Akgönenç, Professor Sencer Ayata, Professor Nahide Bozkurt, Professor Hasan Onat, and Professor Binnaz Toprak. Although I cannot mention all people that I interviewed for this book, I would like to thank the following people who kindly agreed to be interviewed and provided research assistance: Şevket Kazan, the vice-chair of the Felicity Party; Ayşenur Tekdal, the chair of the Felicity Party Women Commission; Felicity Party Women Commission workers; Hüseyin Kansu, then the Justice and Development Party parliamentarian; Hüseyin Besli, the Justice and Development Party parliamentarian; Selma Kavaf, then chair of the Justice and Development Party Women Commission and current State Minister for Women and Family Affairs; Zelkif Kazdal, then chair and current founding chair of the Justice and Development Party Youth Commission; Nevzat Kösoğlu, the former Nationalist Action Party parliamentarian; Ayvaz Gökdemir, the former Minister of State and parliamentarian from the True Path Party (TPP); Mehmet Ağar, then the TPP chair; Uluç Gürkan, the former Democratic Left Party parliamentarian; Yakup Kepenek, the Republican People's Party parliamentarian; Nuri Gürgür, the Turkish Hearths chair; Galip Tamur, the prominent Turkish Hearths member; and Retired General Çevik Bir and Retired General Aytekin Ziylan. I would like to acknowledge my debt to all, who generously shared their time and views with me and patiently answered my questions during my interviews. Without their invaluable input, this book could not have been as profound.

I wish to thank Brandeis Library Interlibrary Loan Borrowing Coordinator Dzintra Lacis and her staff as well as the Turkish Grand National Library staff for processing my endless research material requests.

Acknowledgments

I would like to thank Cambridge University Press for bringing this book to print. Many thanks to Lewis Bateman, the Press's senior editor, for his enthusiasm and support for this book and to Emily Spangler, senior editorial assistant, for kindly answering my questions and making the publication process smooth. I would like to thank two anonymous readers that Cambridge University Press solicited for this book for the valuable comments.

Finally, I would like to thank my parents Aylâ and Özcan Eligür; without their encouragement and support I could not have completed this book. They have been part of my journey from beginning to end. I am particularly grateful to my father for his friendship and invaluable contributions to my field research. I also thank Kurgu, my good friend and "assistant," for accompanying me while I wrote this book.

Preface

This book explains why political Islam, which has been part of Turkish politics since the 1970s but on the rise only since the 1990s, has now achieved governing power. The book focuses on the dominant form of Islamist activism in Turkey by analyzing the increasing electoral strength of four successive Islamist political parties: the Welfare Party; its successor, the Virtue Party; and the successors of the Virtue Party, the Felicity Party and the Justice and Development Party. The Justice and Development Party is now the party of government in Turkey. Drawing upon social movement theory, and the political process model variant of this theory, this book argues that the rise of political Islam in Turkey can be attributed to three factors: first, the emergence of a political opportunity structure, created primarily by the adoption of the Turkish-Islamic Synthesis by the military regime in the aftermath of the 1980 intervention; second, the presence of movement entrepreneurs with significant organizational, financial, and human resources; and, third, the successful framing of issues by entrepreneurs to expand the appeal of the Islamist social movement beyond the population of Islamists to secular but socioeconomically aggrieved voters.

While the successful mobilization of political Islam can be attributed in part to the malfunctioning state and the structural conditions that it created, particularly since the 1990s, these factors alone do not explain how the Islamist movement could establish the well-organized and resource-rich networks that enabled it to address the ills of the state since the 1990s. For grievances to lead to successful social movement mobilization, two additional conditions must exist: a political opportunity and successful framing of that opportunity by movement entrepreneurs. Movement entrepreneurs must establish a dynamic relationship between movement networks, framing processes, grievances, and the political opportunity structure. These four factors, while necessary for social movement mobilization, are insufficient by themselves. Movement entrepreneurs are also necessary for success.

1

Introduction

Turkey is the only Muslim secular-democratic state: the Atatürk Revolution (1923–38) relegated Islam to the private sphere; yet Islam has remained an active force in Turkish society, manifest both in the articulated views of some intellectual elites and in the activities of secretive, grassroots Islamic religious brotherhoods or orders (*tarikats*).[1] But repeated attempts to establish an Islamic political party in the period following World War II ended in failure until the foundation of the National Order Party (NOP) in 1970. An Islamist social movement has achieved unqualified success only since the 1990s. An Islamist successor to the NOP, the Welfare Party (WP) entered the government by securing the highest vote share (21.4%) in the 1995 general elections along with 158 seats in the 550-seat parliament. The most recent in a series of successive Islamist parties, the Justice and Development Party (JDP), is now the party of government as a result of its securing 34.3 percent of the popular vote in the 2002 general elections, entitling it to 363 seats in parliament. The party further increased its support in the 2007 general elections by securing 46.6 percent of the popular vote and 341 seats in parliament, and following the elections, placed its candidate into the presidency of Turkey.

What accounts for the relatively sudden increase, after seventy years, in the political salience of Islam and the success of an Islamist social movement in Turkish politics? The research question of this book, "Why has political Islam, which has been part of Turkish politics since the 1970s, been on the rise only

[1] The Islamic brotherhoods, as the main institutions of Sufism, originally aimed at searching for divine truth and purification of the soul, thus enabling the achievement of the status of *insan-ı kâmil* (perfect human being). See Mustafa Kara, *Tasavvuf ve Tarikatlar Tarihi* [History of Sufism and Islamic Brotherhoods], 5th ed. (Istanbul: Dergâh Yayınları, 1999), 18–19. Yet, Ünver Günay, a divinity professor, argues that the Islamic orders were not immune from the institutional decline of the Ottoman Empire – as a result of which they turned out to be centers of exploitation of the public's religious sentiments for *tarikat* leaders' personal economic gains. See Ünver Günay, "Türkiye'de Toplumsal Değişme ve Tarikatler" [Social Change and Islamic Brotherhoods in Turkey], *İslâmiyât* V, no. 4 (2002): 141–62.

since the 1990s, but not before?" is an important one, and a review of the existing literature on Turkey reveals that there is a gap in adequately addressing it. The existing literature offers very rich and detailed analyses regarding the components of political Islam in Turkey such as Islamic brotherhoods,[2] the role of Islamist women in political Islam,[3] Islamism in shantytowns,[4] Islamist intellectuals,[5] and Islamism as identity politics.[6] But this literature provides only a partial answer to the research question.[7]

This book views the Islamist mobilization in Turkey as a social movement and uses the political process model (PPM) variant of the theory advanced by Sidney Tarrow, Doug McAdam, Charles Tilly, and others to explain the puzzle.

---

[2] Sencer Ayata, "Traditional Sufi Orders on the Periphery: Kadiri and Nakşibendi Islam in Konya and Trabzon," in *Islam in Modern Turkey: Religion, Politics and Literature in a Secular State*, ed. Richard Tapper (London: I. B. Tauris, 1991), 223–53; Şerif Mardin, "The Nakshibendi Order of Turkey," in *Fundamentalisms and the State: Remaking Polities, Economies, and Militance*, eds. Martin E. Marty and R. Scott Appleby (Chicago: University of Chicago Press, 1993), 204–32.

[3] Yeşim Arat, *Political Islam in Turkey and Women's Organizations* (Istanbul: TESEV Yayınları, 1999); Feride Acar, "Women in the Ideology of Islamic Revivalism in Turkey: Three Islamic Women's Journals," in Tapper, *Islam in Modern Turkey*, 280–303.

[4] Jenny B. White, *Islamist Mobilization in Turkey: A Study of Vernacular Politics* (Seattle: University of Washington Press, 2002).

[5] Michael E. Meeker, "The New Muslim Intellectuals in the Republic of Turkey," in Tapper, *Islam in Modern Turkey*, 189–219; Binnaz Toprak, "Islamist Intellectuals of the 1980s in Turkey," *Current Turkish Thought* 62 (Spring 1987): 2–19; Nilüfer Göle, "Secularism and Islamism in Turkey: The Making of Elites and Counter-elites," *Middle East Journal* 51, no. 1 (Winter 1997): 46–58.

[6] M. Hakan Yavuz, *Islamic Political Identity in Turkey* (New York: Oxford University Press, 2003); Nilüfer Göle, "Islam in Public: New Visibilities and New Imaginaries," *Public Culture* 14, no. 1 (2002): 173–90; and Haldun Gülalp, *Kimlikler Siyaseti: Türkiye'de Siyasal İslam'ın Temelleri* [Politics of Identities: The Bases of Political Islam in Turkey] (Istanbul: Metis Yayınları, 2003).

[7] Sencer Ayata's, Binnaz Toprak's, and Birol Yeşilada's articles and chapters provide in-depth analyses of the rise of political Islam in Turkey. Binnaz Toprak and Ali Yaşar Sarıbay provide rich analyses of the Islamist movement in the 1970s. However, none of these scholars examined the Islamist mobilization in Turkey within the framework of social movement theory. Sencer Ayata, "Patronage, Party, and State: The Politicization of Islam in Turkey," *The Middle East Journal* 50, no. 1 (Winter 1996): 41–57; Sencer Ayata, "The Rise of Islamic Fundamentalism and Its Institutional Framework," in *The Political and Socioeconomic Transformation of Turkey*, eds. Atila Eralp, Muharrem Tünay, and Birol Yeşilada (Westport, CT: Praeger, 1993), 51–68; Birol Yeşilada, "The Virtue Party," *Turkish Studies* 3, no. 1 (Spring 2002): 62–81; Birol Yeşilada, "Realignment and Party Adaptation: The Case of the Refah and Fazilet Parties," in *Politics, Parties, and Elections in Turkey*, eds. Sabri Sayarı and Yılmaz Esmer (Boulder, CO: Lynne Rienner Publishers, 2002), 157–77; Binnaz Toprak, *Islam and Political Development in Turkey* (Leiden, the Netherlands: E. J. Brill, 1981); Binnaz Toprak, "Religion as State Ideology in a Secular Setting: The Turkish-Islamic Synthesis," in *Aspects of Religion in Secular Turkey*, ed. Malcolm Wagstaff, Occasional Paper Series no. 40 (Durham, UK: University of Durham, Center for Middle East and Islamic Studies, 1990), 10–15; and Ali Yaşar Sarıbay, *Türkiye'de Modernleşme, Din ve Parti Politikası: MSP Örnek Olayı* [Modernism, Religion, and Party Politics: The Case of the National Salvation Party] (Istanbul: Alan Yayıncılık, 1985). Yavuz's book *Islamic Political Identity in Turkey* is a comprehensive analysis of the relationship between Islamic brotherhoods and Islamism in Turkey within the framework of social movement theory. Yet, his generalization of Islamists' grievances against the secular Turkish state to the entire public is problematic on the following grounds: first, there were no massive public protests against Atatürk's reforms; and second, an Islamist social movement has achieved unqualified success only since the 1990s. This shows that, in the pre-1990 period, the electorate was attracted by appeals to religion-based grievances only to a very limited degree.

Tarrow defines social movements as "collective challenges, based on common purposes and social solidarities, in sustained interaction with elites, opponents, and authorities."[8] The PPM proposes that movement entrepreneurs do not determine their goals, strategies, and tactics with respect to mobilization in a vacuum. Rather, the political context – that is, the presence of a favorable political opportunity for mobilization, along with the movement's organizational dynamics and the framing of movement activists – plays a crucial role. Drawing upon the PPM, this study argues that the rise of political Islam in Turkey can be attributed to specific actions: the introduction by the military regime in power from 1980 to 1983 of the Turkish-Islamic Synthesis (TIS – *Türk İslam Sentezi*), a mixture of Sunni Islam and nationalism, as a state policy to counter the leftist movement in Turkey. The TIS was maintained by the center-right Motherland Party (MP), which ruled from 1983 to 1991, and created the first political opportunity structure (POS 1) that was framed by Islamic forces to establish strong organizational networks. This constituted *the first phase of the mobilization of political Islam in Turkey (1980–91)*.

The Islamists, having established strong organizational networks and framed a viable political rhetoric of a "Just Order," then successfully seized upon the malfunctioning of the state since the 1990s as the second political opportunity structure (POS 2). This constituted *the second phase of the movement's mobilization*, from 1991 to the present. In the 1990s, the Islamists, unlike the mainstream political parties, exploited this POS 2 to compete successfully in democratic elections.

Movement activists ("entrepreneurs") may engage in institutional/conventional activities (peaceful protests, lobbying, forming new political parties, petitioning government bodies, or engaging in legal battles) or noninstitutional/unconventional activity, ranging from terrorism to civil disobedience.[9] Political context determines movement entrepreneurs' framing activities. As David Meyer and Debra Minkoff argue, "a polity that provides openness to one kind of participation may be closed to others."[10] The political context – the existence in Turkey of a secular-democratic polity and its acceptance by the majority of its citizens – determined the movement entrepreneurs' strategies. Thus, the Islamist movement in Turkey is a good example of how movement entrepreneurs frame their strategies according to the existing political context. The Islamists, while utilizing social networks (such as charitable organizations, foundations, economic enterprises, media, Quran courses, dormitories, and schools that belong to Islamic brotherhoods [*tarikats*]) to Islamize the society from below – by changing individual habits and social relations,[11] thus mobilizing by developing

---

[8] Sidney Tarrow, *Power in Movement: Social Movements and Contentious Politics*, 2nd ed. (New York: Cambridge University Press, 1998), 4.
[9] Edwin Amenta and Michael P. Young, "Democratic States and Social Movements: Theoretical Arguments and Hypotheses," *Social Problems* 46, no. 2 (1999): 155.
[10] David S. Meyer and Debra C. Minkoff, "Conceptualizing Political Opportunity," *Social Forces* 82, no. 4 (June 2004): 1463.
[11] I adopt the term *Islamizing the society from below* from Sheri Berman, "Islamism, Revolution, and Civil Society," *APSA, Perspectives on Politics* 1, no. 2 (June 2003): 257–72.

an Islamist collective identity – have at the same time managed to increase their political power by founding a political party (in 1970) under the leadership of Necmettin Erbakan, the NOP. This book focuses on the dominant form of Islamic activism in Turkey – mobilization through a political party – by analyzing four Islamist political parties (the WP; its successor, the Virtue Party (VP); and *its* successors, the Felicity Party (FP) and the JDP).

Political Islamists, though differing in their means (violent and nonviolent), regard the individual and collective return to the *Asr-ı Saadet* – the age of happiness during the Prophet Muhammad's era – as the solution to the political and socioeconomic problems of Muslim societies. Islamist terrorist organizations continue to exist in Turkey (e.g., *Hizbullah*, the *İBDA-C* [Islamic Great Orient Fighters Front], the *Hizbu't-Tahrir*, and the Islamic Jihad). These seek to bring the rule of Islamic law (*Sharia*) to Turkey by initiating an Iranian-style, top-down revolution. Beginning in the 1990s, a number of prominent professors (Muammer Aksoy, Bahriye Üçok, Ahmet Taner Kışlalı, and Necip Hablemitoğlu) and journalists (Uğur Mumcu and Çetin Emeç), who wrote and spoke openly about the dangers of an Islamist threat to secularism in Turkey, were assassinated. Yet, the existence of a secular-democratic state structure and the acceptance of secularism by the majority of citizens[12] have marginalized these terrorist groups in Turkish society. More mainstream political Islamists in Turkey therefore have been pursuing a more cautious and effective strategy to challenge secularism and democracy in the country.

THEORETICAL APPROACHES TO ISLAMIST MOBILIZATION

The existing literature on political Islam in the Muslim world focuses on cultural[13] and socioeconomic factors[14] underlying the movement's mobilization. Furthermore, as Quintan Wiktorowicz notes, most publications on the Islamist

---

[12] According to a comprehensive survey that was conducted in 1999, 77.3% of the Turkish people support Atatürk's reforms and the present secular character of the state. See Ali Çarkoğlu and Binnaz Toprak, *Türkiye'de Din, Toplum ve Siyaset* [Religion, Society, and Politics in Turkey] (Istanbul: TESEV Yayınları, 2000), 16–17.

[13] Bassam Tibi, *Islam between Culture and Politics* (New York: Palgrave, 2001); François Burgat and William Dowell, "Islamism as the Language of Political Reaction to Western Cultural Domination," in *The Islamic Movement in North Africa*, eds. François Burgat and William Dowell (Austin: Center for Middle Eastern Studies, University of Texas, 1993), 63–85; and Leila Hessini, "Wearing the Hijab in Contemporary Morocco: Choice and Identity," in *Reconstructing Gender in the Middle East: Tradition, Identity, and Power*, eds. Fatma Müge Göçek and Shiva Balaghi (New York: Columbia University Press, 1994), 40–56.

[14] Mark Juergensmeyer, *The New Cold War? Religious Nationalism Confronts the Secular State* (Berkeley: University of California Press, 1993); Philip S. Khoury, "Islamic Revivalism and the Crisis of the Secular State in the Arab World: An Historical Appraisal," in *Arab Resources: The Transformation of a Society*, ed. Ibrahim Ibrahim (Washington, DC: Center for Contemporary Arab Studies, Georgetown University, 1983), 213–36; and Mark Tessler, "The Origins of Popular Support for Islamist Movements: A Political Economy Analysis," in *Islam, Democracy, and the State in North Africa*, ed. John P. Entelis (Bloomington: Indiana University Press, 1997), 93–126.

movement do not go beyond descriptive analyses of the ideology, structure, and goals of various Islamic actors or the histories of particular movements.[15] From the perspective of social movement theory, however, grievances – the existence of social strains or relative deprivation, giving rise to claims against the existing social and political order – are "a necessary but not a sufficient condition of social protest."[16] Herbert Kitschelt, in his analysis of the mobilization of antinuclear movements in four democracies (France, Sweden, the United States, and West Germany), finds that even though citizens of these countries expressed similar grievances, the mobilization of the antinuclear movement in these countries developed in distinct ways, shaped by the overall political structure: that is, whether the political *input* structure was open or closed and whether the political *output* structure was weak or strong. From this perspective, grievances by themselves cannot explain variations in the mobilization of social movements.[17]

Along the same lines as Kitschelt, Eric Hobsbawm finds that Peruvian peasants' age-old land grievances did not lead to collective action against landlords; rather, it was the struggles for power between elites seeking the support of subaltern classes – what Tarrow calls unstable elite alignments – that led to the peasants' collective action.[18] Social movement theory suggests the mobilization of citizens suffering from grievances is contingent on two factors: people must perceive that their situation is amenable to change; and, more importantly, movement entrepreneurs must successfully generate motivation, resources, and political opportunities for collective action.[19] "Even under the most extreme conditions of human misery and exploitation," Carry Rosefsky Wickham notes, "the emergence of collective protest is not assured."[20]

This book argues that grievance-based explanations alone cannot explain the mobilization of political Islam in Turkey. Cultural explanations, which are based on grievances, regard political Islam as a protest movement against modernity and Western colonial domination. As will be argued in Chapter 2, this, too, is inadequate in the Turkish case. Atatürk established the secular

---

[15] Quintan Wiktorowicz, "Introduction: Islamic Activism and Social Movement Theory," in *Islamic Activism: A Social Movement Theory Approach*, ed. Quintan Wiktorowicz (Bloomington: Indiana University Press, 2004), 3–4.

[16] Herbert P. Kitschelt, "Political Opportunity Structures and Political Protest: Anti-Nuclear Movements in Four Democracies," *British Journal of Political Science* 16, no. 1 (January 1986): 59.

[17] Kitschelt finds that "political opportunity structures functioned as 'filters' between the mobilization of the movement and its choice of strategies and its capacity to change the social environment." In ibid.

[18] Sidney Tarrow, "States and Opportunities: The Political Structuring of Social Movements," in *Comparative Perspectives on Social Movements: Political Opportunities, Mobilizing Structures, and Cultural Framings*, eds. Doug McAdam, John D. McCarthy, and Mayer N. Zald (New York: Cambridge University Press, 1996), 55. See Eric J. Hobsbawm, "Peasant Land Occupations," *Past and Present* 62 (February 1974): 120–52.

[19] Carrie Rosefsky Wickham, *Mobilizing Islam: Religion, Activism, and Political Change in Egypt* (New York: Columbia University Press, 2002), 7–8.

[20] Ibid., 7.

state in Turkey in the aftermath of the War of Independence (1923). The goal of infusing Turks with Western liberal ideas was to create a new type of citizenship, and hence a modern society, rather than an *umma* (Islamic community of believers), where there would be no room for individualism. It should be noted that the Turkish experiment in secularism represented not a gradual change but a drastic one, which also included a degree of forceful state imposition. The revolutionary movement headed by Atatürk aimed at removing Islam from public affairs and relegating religion to the private sphere through state control; thus, religious institutions were not just separated from the state, but became subservient to it. The dismantling of the sultanate, the caliphate, the *ulema* (the religious class), and the Islamic brotherhoods disestablished institutional Islam in Turkey.

Despite this forced expulsion of Islam from public life and its restriction to the private realm – and the subsequent introduction of a series of reforms aimed at modernizing and Westernizing the country – there was no popular Islamist mobilization in Turkey. Rather, political Islamists were reduced to a marginal group. The Islamic brotherhoods that were antithetical to secularism in the country were forced underground, in the form of Quran courses beyond state control.[21] As Verta Taylor argues, movements that are confronted with a nonreceptive political and social environment do not disappear; they develop "abeyance structures." According to Taylor, when a movement loses support, its activists become isolated to establish alternative structures in order to keep the movement fresh. A "movement in abeyance" develops, in the form of a group of activists who find a niche for themselves and who ensure the continuance of the movement by maintaining activist networks, goals, and tactics along with a collective identity. Thus, abeyance structures maintain the movement and play a crucial role in later rounds of movement mobilization.[22]

The Islamic brotherhoods and the illegal Quran courses they organized played an important role as abeyance structures in maintaining the Islamist movement in Turkey in the form of an Islamist collective identity. As abeyance structures, the Islamic brotherhoods sustained Islamist perspectives and aspirations. Thus, they served as the breeding grounds for the creation of an Islamic elite that later not only seized upon existing POSs, but also created new ones. Since the transition to a multiparty system in Turkey, the Islamic brotherhoods have pursued three basic strategies vis-à-vis political parties: they have supported by electoral means the leading center-right parties,[23] voted for the

---

[21] Toprak, *Islam and Political Development in Turkey*, 1–2; Niyazi Berkes, *Türkiye'de Çağdaşlaşma* [Modernization in Turkey], 3rd ed. (Istanbul: Yapı Kredi Yayınları, 2002), 532–52; Feroz Ahmad, *The Turkish Experiment in Democracy, 1950–1975* (Boulder, CO: Westview Press, 1977), 2; and Erik J. Zürcher, *Turkey: A Modern History* (New York: I. B. Tauris, 1994), 173–203.

[22] Verta Taylor, "Social Movement Continuity: The Women's Movement in Abeyance," *American Sociological Review* 54, no. 5 (October 1989): 761–75.

[23] Taylor suggests that movements in abeyance structures "may have little impact in their own time and may contribute, however unwillingly, to maintenance of the status quo." In ibid., 762.

political Islamist parties,[24] and provided the organizational basis for the formation of political Islamist parties, beginning with the NOP.

Cultural explanations that regard political Islam as a protest movement against Western colonial domination are inappropriate in the Turkish case. Turkey was never subjected to Western colonial domination. The Turkish Revolution, which introduced a secular state, was a successful struggle to forestall Western imperialism and domination.[25] Thus, unlike the case of Arab countries, where there was simultaneously Western colonial domination and endeavors to install a Western type of state, in Turkey there was both independence and secularism. The Turkish Revolution's goal was achieving secularism for the sake of preventing any future Western domination. Furthermore, there were no massive social demonstrations against modernization attempts in the country.

If the secular Turkish state cannot be regarded as a political remnant of colonialism, then what *are* the factors that have led to the rise of political Islam in Turkey? Analyses that focus on socioeconomic factors, which emphasize the absence of economic prosperity, provide only a partial explanation in the Turkish case. Turkish citizens who regard political Islam as offering them an effective vehicle for the expression of their anger at the government, and as a way to exert pressure for political and economic change, do support political Islam.[26] To a certain degree, the rise of political Islam is therefore a response to the malfunctioning state in Turkey. But the Turkish state began to malfunction long before the rise of political Islam. Moreover, the malfunctioning state by itself cannot explain how the Islamist movement could establish the well-organized and resource-rich networks, formal and informal, that enabled it to address the ills of the secular state in the 1990s.

A malfunctioning state creates inequalities and a sense of relative deprivation that are structural conditions providing a basis for grievances. But for a successful movement mobilization, movement entrepreneurs must turn these conditions into popular grievances by framing a viable political rhetoric that encourages a sense of unfairness. In the Turkish case, the WP entrepreneurs successfully framed the "Just Order," which created a perception of unfairness in the minds of the electorate. Thus, for grievances to lead to a successful social movement mobilization, there must be present both a POS and movement entrepreneurs who successfully frame an existing POS by establishing a dynamic relationship among movement networks, framing processes (movement entrepreneurs'

---

[24] Ayata, "The Rise of Islamic Fundamentalism and Its Institutional Framework," 61.
[25] Ernest Gellner also notes that Turkish achievement of political modernity was not an alien imposition, but was a result of endogenous development. See Ernest Gellner, *Encounters with Nationalism* (Oxford: Blackwell Publishing, 1994), 81–91.
[26] Mark Tessler makes this argument for Arab states. This book demonstrates that it is equally true of Turkey. See Mark Tessler, "Democratic Concern and Islamic Resurgence: Converging Dimensions of the Arab World's Political Agenda," in *Democracy and Its Limits: Lessons from Asia, Latin America, and the Middle East*, eds. Howard Handelman and Mark Tessler (Notre Dame, IN: University of Notre Dame Press, 1999), 280.

shared understandings, goals, and tactics), grievances, and the POS. Both grievances *and* a social movement must exist in order for a successful social movement mobilization to occur.

The social movement literature focuses on the impact on movement mobilization of shifts in POSs, movement organizations, ideational factors such as culture, and social interaction. Such inquiry yields explanations that provide a more comprehensive framework for the analysis of the rise of political Islam in Turkey than grievance-based explanations alone. But social movement scholarship has focused on analyzing cases from Western Europe and the United States. The literature presents cases about civil rights movements operating in the context of civil states, where such movements have goals compatible with the values and norms of the state. McAdam, Tarrow, and Tilly note that there is a gap between studies of social movements in liberal democratic polities and those of social movements in the rest of the world.[27] Along the same lines, Bert Klandermans, Suzanne Staggenborg, and Tarrow point out the lacuna in studies of social movements, by using similar methods and theoretical concepts, outside the range of Western democracies.[28]

The Muslim world is almost entirely absent from the social movement literature. It provides a few analyses from the Iranian Revolution and pays some attention to the mobilization of political Islam in Egypt, Jordan, and Yemen.[29] This book applies social movement theory to a non-Western case. The Turkish case also presents a unique example of the mobilization of a social religious movement – that is, a noncivil movement – that challenges to the very definition of the state, which in the Turkish case is civil and secular. Analyses of

---

[27] Doug McAdam, Sidney Tarrow, and Charles Tilly, "Toward an Integrated Perspective on Social Movements and Revolution," in *Comparative Politics: Rationality, Culture, and Structure*, eds. Mark Irving Lichbach and Alan S. Zuckerman (Cambridge: Cambridge University Press, 1997), 142.

[28] Bert Klandermans, Suzanne Staggenborg, and Sidney Tarrow, "Conclusion: Blending Methods and Building Theories in Social Movement Research," in *Methods of Social Movement Research*, eds. Bert Klandermans and Suzanne Staggenborg (Minneapolis: University of Minnesota Press, 2002), 320.

[29] Charles Kurzman, "A Dynamic View of Resources: Evidence from the Iranian Revolution," *Research in Social Movements, Conflict and Change* 17 (1994): 53–84; Misagh Parsa, "Conversion or Coalition? Ideology in the Iranian and Nicaraguan Revolutions," *Political Power and Social Theory* 9 (1995): 23–60; Mohammed Amjad, "Rural Migrants, Islam and Revolution in Iran," *Research in Social Movements, Conflict and Change* 16 (1993): 35–50; Carrie Rosefsky Wickham, *Mobilizing Islam: Religion, Activism, and Political Change in Egypt* (New York: Columbia University Press, 2002); Sheri Berman, "Islamism, Revolution, and Civil Society," APSA, *Perspectives on Politics* 1, no. 2 (June 2003): 257–72; Janine A. Clark, "Islamist Women in Yemen: Informal Nodes of Activism," in Wiktorowicz, *Islamic Activism*, 164–84; Jillian Schwedler, "The Islah Party in Yemen: Political Opportunities and Coalition Building in a Transitional Polity," in Wiktorowicz, *Islamic Activism*, 205–28; Jillian Schwedler, *Faith in Moderation: Islamist Parties in Jordan and Yemen* (New York: Cambridge University Press, 2006); Quintan Wiktorowicz, *The Management of Islamic Activism: Salafis, the Muslim Brotherhood, and State in Jordan* (New York: SUNY Press, 2001); and Janine A. Clark, *Islam, Charity, and Activism: Middle-Class Networks and Social Welfare in Egypt, Jordan, and Yemen* (Bloomington: Indiana University Press, 2004).

Islamist mobilization in the Muslim world (such as those relating to Iran, Egypt, Jordan, and Yemen) provide examples of the mobilization of a noncivil movement in the context of noncivil states: the Turkish case thus not only analyzes the applicability of the PPM to the non-Western world, but also presents a valuable test-case examining the impact of a civil context on a noncivil movement. Expanding the research agenda on social movements by applying the literature to a majority Muslim country with a secular-democratic structure permits a better understanding of the mobilization of political Islam in the Muslim world – a movement that is likely to remain strong in the region for years to come.

THE SOCIAL MOVEMENT LITERATURE

Because the social movement literature has been developed by analyzing cases from Western liberal democracies, it exhibits some important deficiencies with regard to explaining the mobilization of political Islam in Turkey, and hence needs to be amended in certain ways. First, with a few exceptions,[30] the literature equates mobilization of a social movement with social protest activity – that is, moving the masses to challenge the authorities through demonstrations, boycotts, or other actions aiming at changing a specific policy. Hanspeter Kriesi argues that "the crucial element of a social movement is its overt challenge to authorities."[31] Similarly, William Gamson regards movement participation – which, he argues, is riskier than more conventional types of political action – as consisting of actions aimed at achieving political goals that are undertaken when conventional and institutionalized means such as voting are not available.[32] This approach neglects the possibility that social movements may also utilize conventional means to enable or enhance mobilization.

The second deficiency of the literature is that it usually regards social movements as institutions separate from political parties. In this view, social

---

[30] Hans De Witte and Bert Klandermans, "Political Racism in Flanders and the Netherlands: Explaining Differences in the Electoral Success of Extreme Right-Wing Parties," *Journal of Ethnic and Migration Studies* 26, no. 4 (October 2000): 699–717; Schwedler, "The Islah Party in Yemen," 205–28; Helmut Anheier, "Movement Development and Organizational Networks: The Role of 'Single Members' in the German Nazi Party, 1925–30," in *Social Movements and Networks: Relational Approaches to Collective Action*, eds. Mario Diani and Doug McAdam (New York: Oxford University Press, 2003), 49–74; Ronald Aminzade, "Between Movement and Party: The Transformation of Mid-Nineteenth-Century French Republicanism," in *The Politics of Social Protest: Comparative Perspectives on States and Social Movements*, eds. J. Craig Jenkins and Bert Klandermans (Minneapolis: University of Minnesota Press, 1995), 39–62; and Wiktorowicz, "Introduction," 1–33.
[31] Hanspeter Kriesi, "The Political Opportunity Structure of New Social Movements: Its Impact on Their Mobilization," in Jenkins and Klandermans, *The Politics of Social Protest*, 196.
[32] William A. Gamson, *The Strategy of Social Protest*, 2nd ed. (Belmont, CA: Wadsworth, 1990). See also Paul Burstein, Rachel L. Einwohner, and Jocelyn A. Hollander, "The Success of Political Movements: A Bargaining Perspective," in Jenkins and Klandermans, *The Politics of Social Protest*, 275–95.

movements try to realize their goals by *influencing* political parties.[33] Craig Jenkins and Klandermans focus on the three-way struggle between social movements, political parties, and the state. Political parties, not social movements, according to this analysis, are the agents that deal directly with the state.[34] This line of reasoning also excludes noncivil social movements that mobilize *in the form of* political parties with the goal of transforming a civil state into a noncivil one. McAdam is, accordingly, correct when he argues that the role social movements play in reshaping the institutional structure and political alignments of a given polity is an underdeveloped area of research.[35] As will be shown in the following text, the Islamist movement in Turkey is a clear example of a social movement utilizing conventional means, in the form of a political party, to mobilize against a civil state – in this case, to replace a secular-democratic state structure with an Islamist one.

Third, most of the literature examines social movements that take place in the context of Western liberal democracies (such as feminism, environmentalism, and civil rights) and social movements for democratization in the former communist states.[36] There is also an overwhelming emphasis on civil movements operating in the context of civil states. This has resulted in a tendency toward a positive normative bias in the literature: all social movements are assumed to share goals compatible with Western liberal ideas. Wiktorowicz notes, "Dominated by empirical research on the United States and Western Europe, social movement theory building has been heavily contextualized by liberal democratic polities and Western societies, thus narrowing the generalizability of findings and conclusions."[37] In the social movement literature analyzing mobilization by Islamist movements, there seems to be tendency to focus primarily on the political context (democratic, semidemocratic, or authoritarian).

---

[33] There are a few studies that examine the mobilization of a social movement in the form of a political party. For these studies see Paul Lucardie, "Prophets, Purifiers, and Prolocutors: Towards a Theory on the Emergence of New Parties," *Party Politics* 6, no. 2 (April 2000): 175–85; Kent Redding and Jocelyn S. Viterna, "Political Demands, Political Opportunities: Explaining the Differential Success of Left-Libertarian Parties," *Social Forces* 78, no. 2 (December 1999): 491–510; De Witte and Klandermans, "Political Racism in Flanders and the Netherlands," 699–717; John K. Glenn, "Parties Out of Movements: Party Emergence in PostCommunist Eastern Europe," in *States, Parties, and Social Movements*, ed. Jack A. Goldstone (New York: Cambridge University Press, 2003), 147–69; and Manali Desai, "From Movement to Party to Government: Why Social Policies in Kerala and West Bengal are so Different," in Goldstone, *States, Parties, and Social Movements*, 170–96.

[34] J. Craig Jenkins and Bert Klandermans, "The Politics of Social Protest," in Jenkins and Klandermans, *The Politics of Social Protest*, 3–13. See also Diarmuid Maguire, "Opposition Movements and Opposition Parties: Equal Partners or Dependent Relations in the Struggle for Power and Reform?" in Jenkins and Klandermans, *The Politics of Social Protest*, 199–228.

[35] Doug McAdam, "Conceptual Origins, Current Problems, Future Directions," in McAdam, McCarthy, and Zald, *Comparative Perspectives on Social Movements*, 35–6.

[36] Regarding the normative bias in the social movement literature, an analogous issue is the underemphasis on left-wing movements and their analyses by employing theories to understand right-wing protest.

[37] Wiktorowicz, "Introduction," 4.

Accordingly, Islamist movements are seen as a reaction against the lack of democracy in the Muslim world.[38]

This view, however, ignores the specific nature and goals of the Islamist movements. While not denying the impact of an authoritarian setting triggering countermobilization in such repressive political contexts, one should not forget the presence of religious fundamentalist and racist movements in Western liberal democratic settings. As a variable, it is not the regime *type*, but its *openness* that enables a social movement mobilization. It is the presence of a POS, and of movement entrepreneurs who exploit the POS and create new ones, that lead to the mobilization of social movements. Grievance-based explanations alone are inadequate in explaining the mobilization of social movements. Whether a regime is authoritarian or democratic determines movement entrepreneurs' strategies, rather than being a causal factor for movement mobilization. As Jenkins and Klandermans note, "Social movements develop in the context defined by the state and the representation system, which afford opportunities for mobilization and set limits on the effectiveness of movement strategies."[39]

As discussed earlier, the existing literature mostly examines cases from the Western world, where civil movements mobilize in the context of civil states. One example of this is Ronald Aminzade's study of the transformation of mid-nineteenth-century French Republicanism from a movement to a party, which he attributes to "the establishment of a liberal-democratic political culture and an institutional setting that embodied a distinctive understanding of the meaning of political representation."[40] He presents an example of how a social movement can transform itself into a political party. The present study of Turkish Islamists demonstrates that a noncivil, peripheral, and resource-poor movement opposed to democracy can nonetheless exploit the opportunities available under a democratic system to become a political party, compete in elections, and, in the Turkish case, mobilize the population in support of redefining a secular-democratic structure in accordance with a politicized form of Islam. Since the Turkish state has a secular-democratic character that is contradictory to the Islamist state model, the Islamist movement targets the civil state itself.

The Islamist movement in Turkey framed its strategies according to the existing political setting: namely, democracy. Furthermore, as will be explained in the following text, the presence of an inadvertent elite ally (the secular military) in the aftermath of the 1980 coup played a crucial role in the mobilization of the Islamist movement in Turkey. Thus, while the Islamists continued to determine their strategies in ways compatible with democratic rules in the aftermath of the transition to democracy in 1983, between the years 1980 and 1983 there was military rule, which opened up a POS for the movement's mobilization. This POS played a crucial role during the first phase of the movement's mobilization (1980–91).

---

[38] See Diane Singerman, "The Networked World of Islamist Social Movements," in Wiktorowicz, *Islamic Activism*, 143–63.
[39] Jenkins and Klandermans, "The Politics of Social Protest," 7.
[40] Aminzade, "Between Movement and Party," 61.

The fourth deficiency of the social movement literature is its relative neglect of the important contribution that *religion* plays in social movement mobilization. As Christian Smith observes, religion, with its organizational resources, enabling of a shared identity, motivational and moral systems, and public legitimacy, has a great potential to mobilize masses. "Religion *can* help to keep everything in its place," Smith argues, "But it can *also* turn the world upside-down."[41] This study aims at filling this void in the literature by analyzing how Islamist entrepreneurs have utilized Islam to challenge the secular-democratic order in Turkey.

Finally, social movement scholarship that focuses on one or another of the factors that lead to the emergence and outcome of a given movement overlooks possible interactions among opportunities, organizational dynamics, and framing processes in the mobilization phase. The PPM proposed by McAdam, Tarrow, and Tilly, focuses directly on the dynamic relationships among political opportunities,[42] mobilizing structures, and framing processes in the course of mobilization.[43] Thus, the PPM is a more viable analytical framework for analyzing mobilization of a social movement. Turkey is an important case for the PPM because, given the political role of the secular military, Turkey is a conservative-secular state. It is a hard test for Islamism as a social movement.

THE POLITICAL PROCESS MODEL

The PPM explains social movement mobilization by positing a dynamic relationship among three factors: POSs, organizational dynamics, and framing processes. Political opportunities are defined in terms of the relative openness of the institutionalized political system; presence or absence of elite allies; the stability or instability of elite alignments; and the state's capacity and propensity for repression. Organizational dynamics are defined by the level of organization within the movement, along with its goals and tactics. Framing processes are defined as the shared meanings and definitions proffered by movement actors that lead to collective action. Political opportunities play a critical role during the emergence phase of a social movement. Thereafter, the movement itself (its organizational structure) comes to occupy center stage. Framing processes help shape outcomes at each stage of a movement's development.[44]

---

[41] Christian Smith, "Correcting a Curious Neglect, or Bringing Religion Back In," in *Disruptive Religion: The Force of Faith in Social Movement Activism*, ed. Christian Smith (New York: Routledge, 1996), 1 (emphasis in original).

[42] The political opportunity argument suggests that movement mobilization can take place only under favorable political conditions.

[43] Doug McAdam, John D. McCarthy, and Mayer N. Zald, "Introduction: Opportunities, Mobilizing Structures, and Framing Processes – Toward a Synthetic, Comparative Perspective on Social Movements," in McAdam, McCarthy, and Zald, *Comparative Perspectives on Social Movements*, 7–8.

[44] Ibid., 10, 12–13, 15, 17; Doug McAdam, "'Initiator' and 'Spin-off' Movements: Diffusion Processes in Protest Cycles," in *Repertoires and Cycles of Collective Action*, ed. Mark Traugott (Durham, NC: Duke University Press, 1995), 220–2.

The Political Process Model

The POS at the core of Islamist mobilization in Turkey was created by the TIS adopted by the military in the aftermath of the third intervention (1980) and the malfunctioning of the Turkish state, on the one hand, and the exploitation of that opportunity made possible by the Islamist political parties' strong organizational networks (both formal and informal), on the other. The first phase of the movement's mobilization (1980–91) was a result of the exploitation of political opportunities; the second phase (since 1991) is the product of a combination of political opportunities and organizational dynamics. Framing processes played an important role in both phases.

The concept of POS is the central explanatory variable of the PPM in analyzing the emergence, mobilization, and outcome of social movements. Yet, as Kriesi notes, "The concept of political opportunity structure (POS) needs some clarification and specification in order to be useful for the analysis of the development of social movements."[45] Along the same lines, William Gamson and David Meyer remark that "The concept of political opportunity structure is . . . in danger of becoming a sponge that soaks up every aspect of the social movement environment – political institutions and culture, crises of various sorts, political alliances, and policy shifts."[46] Meyer and Debra Minkoff suggest that scholars need to pay much more systematic attention to operationalizing the concept of POS and to specifying of political opportunity models.[47]

The term *political opportunity structure* was first introduced by Peter Eisinger to explain variations in "riot behavior" in American cities. I adopt Eisenger's definition: "the degree to which groups are likely to be able to gain access to power and to manipulate the political system."[48] Later, social movement scholars (e.g., Jenkins and Perrow; Tilly, McAdam, and Tarrow)[49] developed the PPM, which views "the timing and fate of movements as largely dependent upon the opportunities afforded insurgents by the shifting institutional structure and ideological disposition of those in power."[50] Several social movement

---

[45] Kriesi, "Political Opportunity Structure of New Social Movements," 168.
[46] William A. Gamson and David S. Meyer, "Framing Political Opportunity," in McAdam, McCarthy, and Zald, *Comparative Perspectives on Social Movements*, 275.
[47] Meyer and Minkoff, "Conceptualizing Political Opportunity," 1458.
[48] Peter K. Eisinger, "The Conditions of Protest Behavior in American Cities," *American Political Science Review* 67, no. 1 (March 1973): 25.
[49] J. Craig Jenkins and Charles Perrow, "Insurgency of the Powerless: Farm Worker Movements (1946–1972)," *American Sociological Review* 42, no. 2 (April 1977): 249–68; Charles Tilly, *From Mobilization to Revolution* (Reading, MA: Addison-Wesley, 1978); Doug McAdam, *Political Process and the Development of Black Insurgency, 1930–1970* (Chicago: University of Chicago Press, 1982); and Sidney Tarrow, *Struggling to Reform: Social Movements and Policy Change during Cycles of Protest*, Western Societies Program Occasional Paper no. 15 (Ithaca: Cornell University New York Center for International Studies, 1983).
[50] McAdam, "Conceptual Origins, Current Problems, Future Directions," 23.

scholars (Brockett, Kriesi et al., Rucht, and Tarrow)[51] conceptualized the POS mainly in terms of two elements: "the formal legal and institutional structure of a given polity" and "the informal structure of power relations characteristic of a given system."[52] McAdam developed the PPM by combining different scholars' elaborations of the core components of the POS. He articulated four criteria for identifying a POS: "the relative openness or closure of the institutionalized political system," "the stability or instability of that broad set of elite alignments that typically under-gird a polity," "the presence or absence of elite allies," and "the state's capacity and propensity for repression."[53] While the first element is an aspect of the formal legal and institutional structure of a state, the second and third elements describe the informal structure of power relations in a state.[54] In sum, the relative openness of the institutionalized political system, the presence of elite allies, instability in elite alignments, and a decline in the state's capacity and propensity for repression lead to the mobilization of a social movement.[55]

There is a fundamental deficiency in the literature regarding how political opportunities trigger the mobilization of a social movement mobilization. As Meyer and Minkoff observe, "Although changes in political opportunity correlate with changes in the volume and tactics of social mobilization, we know less about how opportunities translate into collective action."[56] They suggest that understanding the relationship between opportunities and mobilization is crucial, "to tackling the larger theoretical question of the relationship between structure and agency."[57] A POS always exists; the crucial question, according to the PPM, is whether a given POS is favorable for a particular social movement or not. The four criteria enumerated by McAdam are the closest the literature has come to specifying the presence of a favorable POS. The PPM assumes that social movement mobilization mainly requires political opportunities. Meyer suggests that political process theorists identify social movements and then read back to find expanding political opportunities, which risks conflating opportunities with mobilization.[58] This deficiency

---

[51] Charles D. Brockett, "The Structure of Political Opportunities and Peasant Mobilization in Central America," *Comparative Politics* 23, no. 3 (April 1991): 253–74; Hanspeter Kriesi et al., "New Social Movements and Political Opportunities in Western Europe," *European Journal of Political Research* 22 (1992): 219–44; Dieter Rupert, "The Impact of National Contexts on Social Movement Structures: A Cross-Movement and Cross-National Comparison," in McAdam, McCarthy, and Zald, *Comparative Perspectives on Social Movements*, 185–204; and Tarrow, *Power in Movement*.

[52] McAdam, "Conceptual Origins, Current Problems, Future Directions," 27.

[53] McAdam adds the fourth dimension of the POS by borrowing from Brockett. In ibid., 28.

[54] Ibid., 27.

[55] See McAdam, "Conceptual Origins, Current Problems, Future Directions," 27; McAdam, McCarthy, and Zald, "Introduction," 1–20; and Tarrow, *Power in Movement*.

[56] Meyer and Minkoff, "Conceptualizing Political Opportunity," 1463.

[57] Ibid.

[58] David S. Meyer, "Tending the Vineyard: Cultivating Political Process Research," in *Rethinking Social Movements: Structure, Meaning, and Emotion*, eds. Jeff Goodwin and James Jasper (Lanham: Rowman and Littlefield Publishers, 2004), 55.

The Political Process Model

creates a danger that POS becomes a tautology. As Jeff Goodwin and James Jasper explain, "political opportunity is built into the definition of a social movement."[59]

Goodwin and Jasper astutely convey the political process theorists' dilemma: "The more broadly one defines political opportunities, the more trivial (and, ultimately, tautological) the political opportunity thesis becomes; conversely, the more narrowly one defines political opportunities, the more inadequate or implausible the political opportunity thesis becomes as an explanation for the rise of any particular social movement."[60] Yet they overgeneralize the problem with POS by identifying the PPM, which they call "tautological, trivial, inadequate, or just plain wrong,"[61] as the source of the problem. Meyer convincingly argues that their critique is "unfair and untrue."[62] Contrary to what Goodwin and Jasper suggest, political process theorists make an effort to separate opportunities from mobilization. In an earlier work, for example, Meyer suggested that "Movements . . . are the product of more than opportunity; they represent the efforts of groups and individuals not only to take advantage of opportunity but also to alter the subsequent opportunity structure. . . . A breakdown in the functioning of the state or society increases the political space available for dissident social movements. It does not, however, create these movements, nor does it ensure their success. . . . A movement's success in mobilizing or achieving policy goals is a function of how well it and its competitors . . . respond to that limited opportunity and the extent to which they fill or expand the available political space."[63]

The social movement scholars are divided into culturalists and structuralists.[64] Culturalists recognize the role of agency more explicitly than structuralists. Culturalists criticize the PPM on the following grounds: first, the PPM emphasizes structural factors – that is, factors that are relatively stable over time and outside the control of movement entrepreneurs (e.g., wars, economic crises, industrialization, and widespread demographic shifts)[65] – at the expense of nonstructural elements (agency and strategy). Second, nonstructural factors, which were added to political opportunities, are not accurately theorized as nonstructural.[66]

---

[59] Jeff Goodwin and James M. Jasper, "Caught in a Winding, Snarling Vine: The Structural Bias of Political Process Theory," in Goodwin and Jasper, *Rethinking Social Movements*, 6.
[60] Ibid.
[61] Ibid., 4.
[62] Meyer, "Tending the Vineyard," 55.
[63] David S. Meyer, *A Winter of Discontent: The Nuclear Freeze and American Politics* (New York: Praeger, 1990), 8.
[64] Goodwin, Jasper, and Marshall Ganz represent the culturalist paradigm, whereas the political process theorists represent the structuralist paradigm. See responses of Tilly, Tarrow, Meyer, and Ruud Koopmans to the critiques of Goodwin and Jasper in Goodwin and Jasper, *Rethinking Social Movements*, 3–93.
[65] See Doug McAdam, "Revisiting the U.S. Civil Rights Movement: Toward a More Synthetic Understanding of the Origins of Contention," in Goodwin and Jasper, *Rethinking Social Movements*, 203.
[66] Goodwin and Jasper, "Caught in a Winding, Snarling Vine," 4.

Goodwin and Jasper assign an important role to agency by arguing that "Political opportunities and mobilizing structures are also heavily shaped by strategic considerations, by the choices movement leaders and activists make," that is, "activists can sometimes create their own opportunities and mobilizing structures. Strategic decisions depend heavily on interaction between movements and other players (especially, but not exclusively, their opponents and the state), and this interaction is strongly shaped by the expectations that each side has of the other. Each side tries to surprise, undermine, and discredit the other."[67] In a similar vein, Marshall Ganz suggests that "Changing environments generate opportunities and resources, but the significance of those opportunities or resources – and even what constitutes them – emerges from the hearts, heads, and hands of the actors who develop the means of putting them to work."[68]

Meyer convincingly argues that "Meaningful understanding of agency can only come with attention to structure"[69] – that is, we need to understand the role external factors (structure) play in movement activists' choices with respect to strategies and tactics. Meyer and Minkoff recognize the fact that the literature is unclear on the relationship between agency and structure. They argue that some studies focus on factors completely outside the control of movement activists, while others emphasize how movement entrepreneurs perceive opportunities. They suggest that the literature needs a robust theory that will allow scholars to distinguish between the relative impact of the strategic choices of movement activists, on the one hand, and that of contextual constraints, on the other.[70]

This book argues that *the dynamic relationship between structure (the POS) and agency (movement entrepreneurs)* deserves greater attention in the analysis of a social movement mobilization. As will be discussed later, the Turkish case is an instructive example of how movement entrepreneurs both exploited existing political opportunities and created new ones. Sometimes they were constrained by context, as the PPM predicts. At other times, they were active agents and created new political opportunities for mobilization. As the culturalists expect, the Islamist mobilization in Turkey shows that movement entrepreneurs played an active role in the movement's mobilization by creating new political opportunities. Yet, as the PPM predicts, movement activists were also constrained by the existing political opportunities and developed strategies according to those constraints, resorting to successful framing efforts and availing themselves of the movement's strong organizational networks. When the POS narrows down, movement entrepreneurs' successful framing efforts and the movement's strong organizational networks play a crucial role for the movement's mobilization.

---

[67] Ibid., 28.
[68] Marshall Ganz, "Why David Sometimes Wins: Strategic Capacity in Social Movements," in Goodwin and Jasper, *Rethinking Social Movements*, 196–7.
[69] Meyer, "Tending the Vineyard," 54.
[70] Meyer and Minkoff, "Conceptualizing Political Opportunity," 1463.

A social movement mobilization, then, depends on the existence of a POS, *and* the presence of movement entrepreneurs, *along with* the availability of organizational resources and grievances that can be created or exploited by movement activists. The analysis of the Turkish case presented here demonstrates the importance of movement entrepreneurs who seize upon an existing POS. Islamist entrepreneurs, who did not come on the scene until the 1970s, made choices with goals in mind: first, to develop abeyance structures into a movement in the 1970s, and then to exploit and even create a POS, which became possible in the 1980s and 1990s.

The problem of tautology in the concept of a POS can be avoided by separating the elements of a movement mobilization (the POS, movement entrepreneurs, organizational resources, and grievances) from each other. This allows examination of the causal sequence among these elements. The mere presence of a favorable POS does not guarantee a successful movement mobilization; rather, a POS is a set of structural conditions, a political and social environment that movement entrepreneurs face over time that can lead to a social movement mobilization given the presence of such entrepreneurial agents of mobilization, the availability of organizational resources, and the marshaling of suitable grievances. Political opportunities can be missed if there are no movement entrepreneurs to frame them, or no organizational resources for entrepreneurs to mobilize. A POS is a battlefield on which movements can gain advantage – if there is an effective entrepreneurial leadership and effective organization.

The PPM recognizes the dynamic relationship among political opportunities, organizational dynamics, and the framing activities of movement entrepreneurs. As McAdam notes, the availability of organizational resources enables movement activists to exploit a political opportunity for mobilization. Framing processes mediate between political opportunities and organizational resources. Without framing processes, political opportunities and organizational structures are insufficient for movement mobilization.[71]

The relationship between grievances and movement mobilization is a central focus of the social movement literature. Inequalities cannot lead to mobilization unless movement entrepreneurs are present. Yet, the existence of movement entrepreneurs without grievances is not sufficient for movement mobilization either. A grievance is a claim against the existing social and political order. Movement entrepreneurs as well as organizational resources are essential for converting grievances into a movement.

Theorists are divided regarding whether their focus should be on the formal and legal institutional structures of a state, or on how *changes* in states lead to movement mobilization. Tarrow, in his analysis of the statist paradigm,[72] proposes that "there are two major ways of specifying political structures in

---

[71] McAdam, "Revisiting the U.S. Civil Rights Movement," 204.
[72] The statist paradigm focuses on the question of "how political institutions and processes structure collective action." In Tarrow, "States and Opportunities," 43.

relation to collective action: as cross-sectional and static structures of opportunity and as intrasystemic and dynamic ones."[73] In the former, the focus is on cross-national variations,[74] whereas in the latter, it is on how states *change*, and how these changes affect POS. A static approach involves taking a snapshot, as it were, of one point in time. This misses the central issue, which is the process of change and the likelihood of the emergence of a POS. Assessing a POS involves assessing a direction of change in different characteristics of a state. A dynamic model allows observation of changes over time in key state institutions, processes, and ideologies and is much more sophisticated and sensitive with respect to whether a favorable POS exists or not. The question is how much change has occurred. An accumulation of changes in several key state institutions over time creates sufficient momentum to enable change in a state's regime. Thus, while static models are just pictures, dynamic models enable observation of changes over time.

Kitschelt, in analyzing the antinuclear movement in France, Sweden, the United States, and West Germany, applies "cross-national statism."[75] He distinguishes between two kinds of domestic POSs – political *input* structures, which are defined by the openness of political regimes to new demands, and political *output* structures, which are defined as the (strong or weak) capacity of political systems to implement policies – in order to explain the variations in strategies on the part of the antinuclear movements in these four countries. Kitschelt finds that in the openness of the Swedish state, for example, led the antinuclear movement there to pursue an assimilative strategy; whereas the closed French state resulted in a confrontational movement strategy.[76] Yet, Tarrow, by comparing the success of the temperance movement in nineteenth-century America with the repression of the labor movement in that period, finds that the formal and legal institutional structure of states is open or closed; by itself this is inadequate to explain variations in movement mobilization. He notes that "Although some national political opportunity structures are clearly more 'open' than others, state elites are far from neutral between different social actors and movements."[77] Thus, Tarrow argues, "National opportunity structures may be the basic grids within which movements operate, but the grid is seldom neutral between social actors."[78] Even this observation is inadequate. The structure alone is insufficient to explain different outcomes. Agency, or choices made by entrepreneurs, is also important.

Along the same lines as Tarrow, Edwin Amenta and Michael Young challenge the idea that weak-open states lead to movement mobilization, whereas strong-closed ones do not. Instead, they suggest, "scholars need to go beyond the distinction between weak and strong states and instead examine different

---

[73] Ibid., 41.
[74] Tarrow uses the terms *cross-sectional* and *cross-national* interchangeably.
[75] Kitschelt, "Political Opportunity Structures and Political Protest," 57–85.
[76] Ibid.
[77] Tarrow, "States and Opportunities," 51.
[78] Ibid.

The Political Process Model

important aspects of states."⁷⁹ They give the unsuccessful mobilization of politically disadvantaged people in the United States as an example of a weak state (with divided political authority and a weak state bureaucracy) dampening movement mobilization. This occurs because in polities with divided political authority, it is easier for members of the polity to block the collective activism of relatively excluded groups. Furthermore, weak-underprofessionalized state bureaucracies are susceptible to the influence of polity members.

Amenta and Young emphasize the presence of elite allies rather than the formal institutional structure of states, to explain successful movement mobilization. They note that "Although strong bureaucracies that oppose the missions of challengers are likely to dampen social mobilization, state bureaucracies with missions that are consistent with those of challengers are likely to encourage challengers."⁸⁰ Amenta and Young do not deny the impact of state structures on the form of mobilization. Yet, their finding is contrary to what the literature suggests. Movement mobilization is varied and smaller in scale and scope in federal political systems like that of the United States. This diminishes the influence of movements vis-à-vis the state.⁸¹

Kriesi proposes three broad sets of properties of a political system within the POS domain: "its formal institutional structure, its informal procedures and prevailing strategies with regard to challengers, and the configuration of power relevant for the confrontation with the challengers."⁸² This book focuses on the first two factors. Kriesi defines the formal institutional structure of a state according to four characteristics: the degree of territorial centralization (federal or central); the degree of functional concentration of state power in the executive, legislative, or judiciary branches of government (or, alternatively, the degree to which there is a separation of powers among these branches); the relative coherence or fragmentation of the public administration; and the degree to which direct democratic procedures are institutionalized (e.g., in referenda).⁸³ Kriesi defines states as either weak or strong in terms of these four aspects of their formal institutional structure. A weak state provides a more favorable setting for mobilization. A strong state provides a less favorable setting.⁸⁴

Besides a state's formal institutional structure, Kriesi considers the effects of informal procedures, and the prevailing strategies employed by the authorities with respect to challengers. These strategies will typically be either exclusive (repressive, confrontational, polarizing) or integrative (facilitative, cooperative, assimilative).⁸⁵

Kriesi does not find a correlation between the weak or strong formal institutional structure of a state and the dominant strategy of the authorities with

---

[79] Amenta and Young, "Democratic States and Social Movements," 163.
[80] Ibid.
[81] Ibid., 163-4.
[82] Kriesi, "Political Opportunity Structure of New Social Movements," 168.
[83] Ibid., 171.
[84] Ibid., 171-3.
[85] Ibid., 173-4.

respect to challengers; rather, the key variables determining the dominant strategy of the authorities are whether there is an informal facilitation of access and whether there is a weak repression of challengers. The greater the informal facilitation of access and the less the state's resort to repression, the more successful challengers will be. Kriesi calls the combination of a strong state and an exclusive strategy vis-à-vis challengers, a situation of "full exclusion." An example is France, where there is strong repression of challengers, neither formal nor informal facilitation of access, and the possibility of neither veto nor substantive concessions.[86]

In terms of its formal institutional structure, Turkey, like France, is a strong state; thus, one would expect full exclusion of the Islamist movement in Turkey. In terms of informal procedures with respect to challengers – in the Turkish case, the influence of a secular military – one would not expect a successful Islamist mobilization either. Yet, as will be shown in Chapter 3, the successful mobilization of political Islam in Turkey actually began under military rule in the aftermath of the 1980 coup. Thus, I argue that *the availability of elite allies, not the strong or weak formal institutional structure of a state, is the key to a successful movement mobilization*. According to Kriesi, Turkey is an example of informal cooptation (a combination of a strong state and an inclusive dominant strategy with respect to challengers). Whereas the degree of openness or closure of formal political access by challengers is determined by whether a state is strong or weak, successful social movement mobilization is contingent on the availability of elite allies. In the Turkish case, the Islamist movement not only enjoyed informal access to the state, but also experienced weak repression as a result of the availability of the secular military's serving as an inadvertent elite ally. As Tarrow notes, "Allies can act as a friend in court, as guarantors against brutal repression, or as acceptable negotiators on behalf of constituencies which – if left a free hand – might be far more difficult for authorities to deal with."[87]

Tarrow finds the cross-national statist paradigm useful in linking "the political opportunities of social movements to a national grid of institutional regularities" – and, hence, in analyzing the relationship between POS and social movement mobilization. Yet, he also adds that this model risks, among other problems, underspecifying subnational and subgroup variations in movement opportunities, underplaying the dynamic of protest cycles, and excluding

---

[86] According to Kriesi, "Integrative strategies are typical for two types of countries. On the one hand, they are the hallmark of countries with a long history of coexistence of different religions, such as the Netherlands and Switzerland. On the other hand, they also prevail in Catholic countries that have experienced a split between religious and laic subcultures but have not experienced a prominent split between communists and social democrats; Austria and Belgium are the typical examples. Moreover, integrative strategies seem to be facilitated by the small size of a polity and its openness with regard to the world market; all the countries mentioned are among the small Western European nation-states." In Kriesi, "Political Opportunity Structure of New Social Movements," 175.

[87] Tarrow, "States and Opportunities," 55.

The Political Process Model

transnational influences on social movement mobilization.[88] Thus, Tarrow argues for dynamic statism in analyzing the relationship between POS and social movement mobilization. The main idea in dynamic statism is that *"entire political systems undergo changes which modify the environment of social actors sufficiently to influence the initiation, forms, and outcomes of collective action."*[89] Dynamic statism, Tarrow argues, "allows us to specify political opportunity for different actors and sectors, to track its changes over time, and to place the analysis of social movements in their increasingly transnational setting."[90] The Turkish case is a viable example of dynamic statism in the analysis of POS. This book applies Tarrow's dynamic statist paradigm to analyze the relationship between POS and the mobilization of political Islam in Turkey.

Social movement scholars argue that movement entrepreneurs take political opportunities as a given in their short-term strategic calculations. But movements also *create* opportunities. Indeed, movement entrepreneurs can themselves *create* political opportunities. Tarrow asserts that changing opportunities and constraints provide openings that lead resource-poor actors to engage in contentious politics.[91] Gamson and Meyer argue that in order to understand dynamic processes of mobilization and demobilization (e.g., changes in alliances, breakdowns of social control and elite unity, and shifts in public policy), one must pay attention to the interaction between structure and agency – to the ways in which opportunity and movement strategy influence each other.[92] Along the same lines, McAdam, Tarrow, and Tilly note two conditions for an opportunity to lead to mobilization: the opportunity's visibility to potential challengers and its perception *as* an opportunity.[93] The Turkish case is an example of how "opportunities both *exist* and are *made*."[94] Tarrow observes that the volatility evident in the history of collective action suggests that "we cannot hope to understand the dynamics and the impact of movements by 'placing' them in a static grid of cleavages, conflicts, and state institutions; we must watch them as a moving target, much as we study ordinary politics."[95]

As displayed in Chart 1.1 and Diagram 1.1, during the first phase of the mobilization of political Islam in Turkey (1980–91), the presence of the secular military as an inadvertent elite ally was the key POS. Between 1980 and 1983, Turkey was ruled by a military regime. Even after the transition to democracy and until recently, the military continued to exercise – as it always had exercised – a

---

[88] Ibid., 45.
[89] Ibid., 44 (emphasis in original).
[90] Ibid., 45.
[91] Tarrow, *Power in Movement*, 20.
[92] Gamson and Meyer, "Framing Political Opportunity," 278.
[93] Doug McAdam, Sidney Tarrow, and Charles Tilly, *Dynamics of Contention* (New York: Cambridge University Press, 2001), 43.
[94] Jenkins and Klandermans, "The Politics of Social Protest," 7 (emphasis in original). See also McAdam, "Conceptual Origins, Current Problems, Future Directions," 35–6; Gamson and Meyer, "Framing Political Opportunity," 276.
[95] Tarrow, "States and Opportunities," 61.

CHART 1.1. *The Mobilization of Political Islam in Turkey (1980–2007)*

	Preconditions and Emergence (1970–80)	Preconsolidation (1980–91)	Consolidation (1991–97)	Divergence and Reconsolidation (1997–2007)
Political Opportunity Structures				
A. Electoral and Party Politics	The NOP and its successor, the NSP enter in electoral politics	Local and national elections (1983–)	Local and national elections (1983–)	The Constitutional Court closes down the WP (1998) and the VP (2001)
	1980 coup closes down all political parties	The WP (1983) enters in electoral politics (1984) MP becomes an elite ally (1983–91)		
B. State Structure	No available elite allies	The secular military introduces the TIS and becomes an inadvertent elite ally	The malfunctioning state	The malfunctioning state continues the soft military intervention (1997)
C. International Context	Ongoing threat of communism	The military regime establishes close economic relations with Saudi Arabia (1980–3)	The global wave of democratization	Islamists reframe Turkey's quest for EU membership

Framing Processes	Islamists advance the "National View," which failed as it was not wide enough	Saudi capital helps create a wealthy Turkish Islamist business class. Islamist entrepreneurs exploit the TIS to strengthen the WP's organizational networks (1980–91)	Islamist entrepreneurs advance the "Just Order". Islamist entrepreneurs adopt face-to-face contacts and create selective and soft incentives	The Islamist movement splits into two political parties: the JDP and the FP
Organizational Dynamics	Weak Islamist organizational networks	Islamist organizational networks are strengthened under the TIS	Islamists further strengthen organizational networks. Islamists win municipal elections and succeed in government	Strong organizational networks of the JDP and moderately strong organizational networks of the FP
Outcome	Marginal success in local and national elections	Increasing vote share in national elections	Islamists become the largest party (1995)	The JDP becomes the party of government (2002 and 2007)

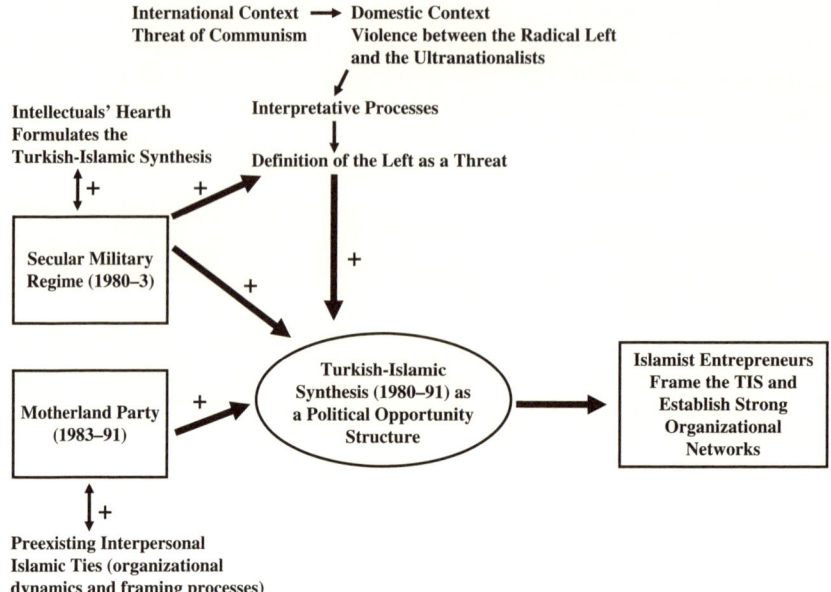

DIAGRAM 1.1. *The Dynamics of Preconsolidation (1980–1991)*

decisive influence in Turkish politics. The secular military, facing the rise of communism in the country, first adopted elements of the ideological framework of the Intellectuals' Hearth (*Aydınlar Ocağı*), a right-wing organization of scholars and intellectuals that was then in the process of Islamization. The military then introduced the TIS as the official state ideology in the aftermath of the 1980 coup. The military promoted Sunni Islam by introducing it as a mandatory course in public schools and permitting the enrollment of *imam-hatip* graduates' (prayer leader and preacher) in all departments of universities, rather than restricting them only to the divinity faculties. At the same time, the military eliminated the leftist movement and repressed the rightist ultranationalists.

Unlike the radical left-wing and ultranationalist groups, the Islamists did not engage in violence in the period before the 1980 coup. As a result, even though the military had the capacity to repress the Islamists as well, it did not do so. In this way, the military tactically opened up a social and political space for Islamist mobilization in Turkey. The military's decision suggests a parallel to Israel's decision to pursue a new policy toward Hamas in the 1970s, which led to the mobilization of Hamas in the 1980s. Glenn Robinson, in his analysis of that mobilization, argues that Israel tactically chose to afford political space to the Muslim Brotherhood (and subsequently to Hamas) in order to counterbalance the Palestine Liberation Organization (PLO). Hamas seized upon this political opportunity to advance its organizational development and mobilization.[96]

---

[96] Glenn E. Robinson, "Hamas as Social Movement," in Wiktorowicz, *Islamic Activism*, 123–4.

The Political Process Model

In addition, because of the shortage of foreign currency in Turkey, the military regime established close economic relations with Saudi Arabia. Under MP rule (1983–91), those relations would be exploited by the Islamist activists so as to strengthen the Islamist business class.

The military, while it sought to increase the religiosity of Turkish citizens by promoting Sunni Islam as a bulwark against communism, remained suspicious of the Islamists. Both Eisenger and Tarrow, in their analyses of the relationship between protest activity and POS, argue that "partially opened access to participation"[97] – that is, "systems characterized by a mix of open and closed factors"[98] – encourages protest. The Turkish case supports their findings. The military permitted the establishment of the WP, which showed that it was committed to democracy. But the party was barred from the 1983 general elections. Although the political system was thus only "partially open" to the WP, the Islamists identified and exploited a POS in the postcoup regime: middle- and lower-tier cadres from the National Salvation Party (NSP), the predecessor to the WP that had been banned by the military in 1980, entered Turgut Özal's MP, which became the ruling party between 1983 and 1991. As Jenkins and Klandermans argue, "Some social movements become third parties while others permeate the existing parties, operating as 'special interests' within party chambers."[99] Özal had ties to the *Nakşibendi* brotherhood and had been a parliamentary candidate on the NSP ticket in the 1970s.

The presence of interpersonal ties and preexisting social networks[100] based in part on the *Nakşibendi* brotherhood facilitated the permeation of the MP by former NSP members. They eventually became a major wing of the MP. Under MP rule, Saudi and Kuwaiti finance houses were established in Turkey, and Saudi capital flowed into the country, facilitated by key members of the *Nakşibendi* order and influential members of Özal's government.

The MP also pursued a strategy of establishing *imam-hatip* schools, Quran courses, and mosques. Part of the Islamist movement in Turkey proselytizes an Islamic way of life, in the belief that the spread of Islamic piety will lead to an Islamic society and the transformation of the country into an Islamic state. Hakan Yavuz, a professor of political science, in his analysis of the

---

[97] Tarrow, "States and Opportunities," 54. Tarrow gives the example of liberation and democratization movements in the former Soviet Union and Eastern Europe in the late 1980s.
[98] Eisenger, "The Conditions of Protest Behavior in American Cities," 15. Eisenger finds that "the relationship between protest and political opportunity is neither negative nor positive but curvilinear: Neither full access nor its absence encourages the greatest amount of protest." In Tarrow, "States and Opportunities," 54.
[99] Jenkins and Klandermans, "The Politics of Social Protest," 7.
[100] Mustafa Emirbayer and Jeff Goodwin define a social network as follows: "A social network is one of many possible sets of social relations of a specific content – for example, communicative, power, affectual, or exchange relations – that link actors within a larger social structure (or network of networks)." In Emirbayer and Goodwin, "Network Analysis, Culture, and the Problem of Agency," *American Journal of Sociology* 99, no. 6 (May 1994): 1417.

"society-oriented Islamic movements" in Turkey,[101] notes that the Islamic orders (which he calls "the Nur faith movement and Sufi orders") regard personal redemption as the key to societal change, which they believe will be achieved by engaging in pious activism (praying, fasting, reading the Quran, and giving alms to the needy). "Society-oriented Islamic movements," Yavuz argues, "seek to transform society from within by utilizing new societal opportunity spaces in the market, education, and media to change individual habits and social relations."[102] Jenkins and Klandermans argue that social movements, by shaping the attitudes and actions of citizens, can have indirect effects on the political system.[103]

There seems to be a correlation between the increased number of Quran courses, *imam-hatip* schools, and mosques (religious social networks that are deeply embedded in the society) and the mobilization of the Islamist movement in Turkey. The social movement literature regards social networks as the primary source of both membership and financial support for formal movement organizations. Janine Clark, in her analysis of the Yemeni Islamists' utilization of *nadwas* (Quranic study groups) to recruit women into the Islamist movement, notes that preexisting social networks provide the glue that holds a movement together. "Solidarity to the movement and its cause," she writes, "is strengthened by preexisting ties of friendship and loyalty."[104] John McCarthy defines family units, friendship networks, voluntary associations, work units, and elements of the state structure as "everyday life micromobilization structural social locations that are not aimed primarily at movement mobilization, but where mobilization may be generated."[105]

There is a need for more analyses of the role of social networks in the identity construction of targeted persons or groups as a means of mobilizing a social movement. Carrie Rosefsky Wickham, in her analysis of the mobilization of Islamism in Egypt, finds informal, dispersed, and small-size groups and associations – like local mosques, community associations, informal study groups, and peer networks – serve as prime locations for Islamists to reach out to potential recruits.[106] Similarly, Diane Singerman asserts that heterogeneous, informal networks (familial, mosque-based, occupational, educational, clerical, and village networks of activists) "must be considered in any assessment of the phenomenon of Islamist movements, since they provide a vehicle for recruitment, facilitate the consolidation of their material and social bases, and offer general support and solidarity."[107]

---

[101] M. Hakan Yavuz, "Opportunity Spaces, Identity, and Islamic Meaning in Turkey," in Wiktorowicz, *Islamic Activism*, 276.
[102] Ibid.
[103] Jenkins and Klandermans, "The Politics of Social Protest," 7.
[104] Clark, "Islamist Women in Yemen," 164.
[105] John D. McCarthy, "Constraints and Opportunities in Adopting, Adapting, and Inventing," in McAdam, McCarthy, and Zald, *Comparative Perspectives on Social Movements*, 141.
[106] Wickham, *Mobilizing Islam*, 16.
[107] Singerman, "The Networked World of Islamist Social Movements," 155.

Sheri Berman further expands the literature on the role of social networks by noting that the Islamist movement in Egypt utilized its network of civil society organizations not only for propagating the movement's ideas, creating support networks, and showing that Islamic values could be implemented in the modern world, but also for reshaping everyday life by Islamizing the entire society – the poor and uneducated as well as the secular elite – from below.[108] The successful civil society–based strategy of the Islamist movement in Egypt aims at transforming the society from the bottom up by permeating almost all sectors of society affecting gender roles, consumption habits, governance, and education – with Islamic values and norms.[109] Like Berman, Wiktorowicz argues that the ultimate goal of Islamist movements is to create a society that is governed and guided by the *Sharia*. Thus, controlling and reconstructing state institutions is a means (and only one of the means) for realizing this goal, not the end.[110]

This book regards mosques, *imam-hatip* schools, Quran courses, and civil society organizations as potential social networks facilitating the Islamist recruitment process not only by providing a web of preexisting relationships, but also by reshaping the identities of the targeted people and groups according to the Islamists' politicized interpretation of Islam. In the long run, as in the case of Egypt, societal and cultural transformation may precede political change in Turkey rather than Islamists capturing the state and trying to construct a top-down new political order.

During the first phase of the mobilization of political Islam in Turkey, the Islamists, having the secular military as an inadvertent elite ally (providing the key POS), framed democracy and MP rule as a POS for strengthening the Islamist business class. The Islamist movement exploited this POS thereafter – Islamist social networks (foundations, associations, media, dormitories, the *imam-hatip* schools, private schools, and Quran courses) – in an effort to Islamize the society from below. At the same time, the Islamist business class backed the WP's organizational network, building the WP's capacity to respond to the ills of the malfunctioning state starting in the 1990s. The first phase of the mobilization of the Islamist movement played a crucial role in strengthening social networks that empowered the WP's and its successors' organizational networks and increased its electoral support base.

The malfunctioning state, which was characterized by massive corruption, unequal distribution of wealth, unemployment, and a decay in moral values as well as in law and order, became a POS in the second phase (since 1991) of the mobilization of political Islam in Turkey (Chart 1.1 and Diagram 1.2). Robert Benford and David Snow point to framing processes, alongside POSs and organizational dynamics,[111] "as a central dynamic in understanding the character

---

[108] Berman, "Islamism, Revolution, and Civil Society," 263.
[109] Ibid., 265.
[110] Wiktorowicz, "Introduction," 16.
[111] I adopt the term *meaning construction* from Robert D. Benford and David A. Snow, "Framing Processes and Social Movements: An Overview and Assessment," *Annual Review of Sociology* 26 (2000): 614.

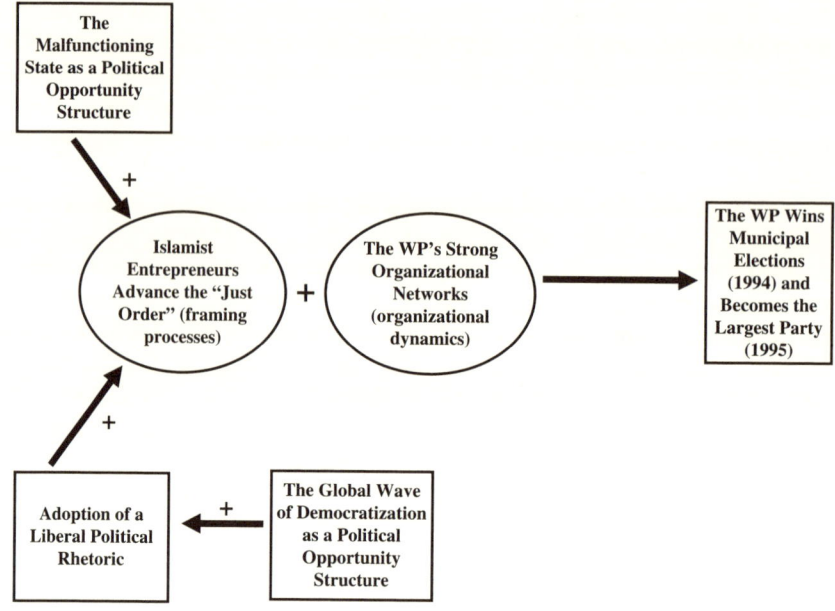

DIAGRAM 1.2. *The Dynamics of Consolidation (1991–1997)*

and course of social movements."[112] Chapter 4 provides an analysis of the dynamic relationship between political opportunity and framing processes, which encompasses movement entrepreneurs first framing a POS to mobilize a movement, then framing the movement's strategies and tactics according to the POS. Thus, opportunities or openings in a POS are not directly created or shaped by movements, but they are exploited by movement entrepreneurs in accordance with their particular strategies and frames.

Political Islam utilizes religion, which is a cultural element in the definition of self of the majority in Turkish society, to propose an Islamic political and socioeconomic order. Necmettin Erbakan, the founder of the first Islamist party in Turkey, the NOP, was already proposing that Turkey become an Islamic state in the 1970s. But it was not until the 1990s that the WP's message achieved significant appeal to Turkish citizens.

The Turkish public's cultural affinity to Islam alone was not enough to increase the party's vote. WP elites needed to frame a POS to construct a meaning that, when expressed in the party's political rhetoric, would appeal to the electorate. The WP's primary emphasis on the adverse impacts of Westernization (especially, religious and moral decay in Turkish society) and Western imperialism, and on the "suppressive" character of the Turkish state, received support from the Islamist segment of the electorate in the 1980s. But it was impossible to become the ruling party by securing only the traditional Islamist vote. Thus,

[112] Ibid., 612.

beginning with the 1991 general election campaign, the WP, while retaining its Islamist staff and goals, shifted the emphasis of its political rhetoric to socioeconomic problems: corruption, unemployment, injustice, atomization of the individual, and decay in moral values. This new framing of the POS was reflected in the party's adoption of the "Just Order" as its slogan, which attracted the secular disaffected votes. Thus, the party constructed a definition of the POS in terms that made it more meaningful and attractive to voters.

"[M]ovement scholars," notes McAdam, "have, to date, grossly undervalued the impact of *global* political and economic pressures in structuring the *domestic* possibilities for successful collective action."[113] The WP, while seizing on the malfunctioning state as a domestic POS, successfully framed another POS in an international context – specifically, the global wave of democratization, freedom, and human rights in the aftermath of the cold war – which enabled it to present its illiberal political agenda as a quest for "real" democracy, secularism, and liberalism. In this way, the party presented its Islamist political agenda by utilizing a liberal tool kit. As Tarrow notes, "Social movements not only seize opportunities; they make them, both for themselves and for others who may not share their interests or values."[114] In the Turkish case, the global quest for democratization and freedom was exploited by an Islamist political party in an attempt to disestablish a secular-democratic system.

The WP/VP gained legitimacy through positive performance in local office: it seized upon the malfunctioning state as a POS by – unlike the mainstream parties – providing social services to the citizens it governed in municipalities, thereby expanding its base of electoral support. As Gamson and Meyer argue, "An opportunity unrecognized is no opportunity at all."[115] The existence of such successfully governed municipalities convinced the electorate that the "Just Order" project was not an empty slogan, but a viable alternative model to the malfunctioning state.

The PPM suggests that because there are different electoral levels (local and national) in the Turkish political system, that system is relatively susceptible to exploitation. Islamists began to exploit the system because of these multiple levels: for example, the military cannot take over local governments. The WP, by seizing on the malfunctioning state, the global quest for democratization, and the availability of local/municipal elections as POSs, tried to frame new interpretations of what a state should be like, and what constituted the good life, and how real democracy and secularism were supposed to be in the minds of the public. Klandermans and Bernd Simon suggest three stages leading to a politicized collective identity: "awareness of shared grievances, adversarial attributions to blame opponents, and the involvement of society at large."[116]

---

[113] McAdam, "Conceptual Origins, Current Problems, Future Directions," 34 (emphasis in original).
[114] Tarrow, "States and Opportunities," 58.
[115] Gamson and Meyer, "Framing Political Opportunity," 283.
[116] Bert Klandermans and Bernd Simon, "Politicized Collective Identity: A Social Psychological Analysis," *American Psychologist* 56, no. 4 (April 2001): 319, 324.

There is a bidirectional causal relationship, they note, between collective identity and awareness of shared grievances.[117] The mobilization of the Islamist movement in Turkey exemplifies Klandermans and Simon's model of how movement entrepreneurs frame such an identity. The WP activists, by utilizing the grievances of the public, tried to convince the electorate that the source of their socioeconomic problems was the present secular-democratic character of the state – although the electorate's main concern was the problems arising out of the poor performance *of* the state. The secular-democratic system as an external enemy was blamed for socioeconomic problems. An Islamic lifestyle and an Islamic state model – the Just Order – was proposed as the solution to those problems. The WP activists tried to create an Islamic politicized collective identity that would mobilize citizens against the secular state by electoral means. A "politicized collective identity," note Klandermans and Simon, "affects how people perceive the social world and act on and in it."[118]

The Just Order reflected the three core framing tasks identified by Benford and Snow: diagnostic framing, comprising identifying the problem and attributing blame; prognostic framing, incorporating the articulation of a solution to the problem; and motivational framing, or a call to collective action. The "Just Order" thus enabled party activists to achieve both "consensus mobilization" and "action mobilization."[119] The realization of the second phase of the mobilization of political Islam in Turkey, partly as a result of the malfunctioning state, is a clear example of "agency," of how movement activists can frame an opportunity so as to expand their goals.

According to the PPM, once a movement is underway, organizational dynamics come to occupy center stage, while framing processes continue to shape the development of the movement. Dieter Rucht criticizes the political opportunity and resource mobilization approaches: in his view, the former ignores the structural basis for resource mobilization, whereas the latter largely neglects the broader political environments in which social movement organizations are embedded. Thus, Rucht suggests that the two research strands should be linked in order to achieve a comprehensive understanding of the factors underlying movement mobilization.[120] Chapter 5 focuses on the organizational networks (formal and informal) surrounding the WP/VP, while regarding the relationship between POS, organizational dynamics, and framing processes as dynamic. The WP/VP would not be able to exploit the malfunctioning state as a POS if it did not have a strong organizational network, which was established during the first phase of the movement's mobilization.

Florence Passy asserts that social networks fulfill three functions in the mobilization of a social movement: they participate in the socialization and

---

[117] Ibid., 325.
[118] Ibid., 327.
[119] Benford and Snow, "Framing Processes and Social Movements," 615–18.
[120] Dieter Rucht, "The Impact of National Contexts on Social Movement Structures," in McAdam, McCarthy, and Zald, *Comparative Perspectives on Social Movements*, 185.

The Political Process Model

construction of identities, connect potential participants to a social movement organization, and influence the individual perceptions that enable potential participants to decide on their involvement and its intensity.[121] The presence of a strong Islamist social network (parallel Islamic sector) alongside the WP party apparatus – comprising the Islamist business class, the Independent Industrialists' and Businessmen's Association (MÜSİAD), the National View Organization of Muslim Community (İTMGT) in Europe, the National Youth Foundation, the Association of *İmam-Hatip* Graduates, the media, publishing houses, periodicals, newspapers, and an Islamic labor union (Hak-İş) – has played a crucial role in strengthening the party's organizational capacity, and hence the movement's mobilization.

Berman criticizes the literature for establishing a positive correlation between the expansion of civil society activity and political liberalization and democratization, without analyzing what the civil society advocates. She notes that the expansion of civil society in Egypt was both a reflection and a cause of local states' declining effectiveness and legitimacy, which served as a basis for Islamist revolutionaries' launching of a challenge to the status quo.[122] In the case of Turkey, the presence of Islamist social networks led to an expansion of the party's electoral support base in a malfunctioning state; the electoral success of the WP/VP came after its organizational development. Starting in 1987, the WP established a hierarchically organized network down to the level of electoral precincts (ballot boxes). The precinct observers maintained a database of information on everyone living in the area, including the details of each family unit, so that the party staff determined who was in need of help. The aim was to convince the electorate that political Islam would be a more efficient and more humane system of governance than the secular state.

As Tarrow notes, organized movements "engage in a variety of ... actions ranging from providing 'selective incentives' to members, building consensus among current or prospective supporters, lobbying and negotiating with authorities, to challenging cultural codes through new religious or personal practices."[123] In the Turkish case, the WP/VP provided selective incentives in the form of material benefits to the electorate in order to become a governing party that would challenge the existing secular-democracy. The change in the WP's propaganda style starting in the 1990s – in the content of its framing processes – should be noted in accounting for the increase in its electoral support. The party embraced all segments of the society: Islamist, leftist, Alevi,

---

[121] Florence Passy, "Social Networks Matter. But How?" in Diani and McAdam, *Social Movements and Networks*, 23–7.
[122] Berman, "Islamism, Revolution, and Civil Society," 259. According to Berman civil society refers to "all voluntary institutions and associations that exist below the level of the state but above the level of the family: churches, clubs, civic groups, professional organizations, nongovernmental organizations, and so forth." In ibid. See Helmut Anheier on the role of local activists and political entrepreneurs in the spread and development of an authoritarian movement. Anheier, "Movement Development and Organizational Networks," 49–74.
[123] Tarrow, *Power in Movement*, 5.

Kurd, liberal, and conservative. By the mid-1990s, the WP was no longer a marginal party of the Islamist segment of the society, but a party of the masses.

The social movement literature generally accepts the role that *conversational* settings play in a movement's mobilization.[124] Clark elaborates on this theme by defining the process of recruitment as "a conscious effort by movement activists to selectively target prospective participants in sympathetic social networks and communities."[125] WP activists, by having face-to-face contacts with the electorate (including household chats, panels, and point visits to public places), established close, friendly relationships with their constituents, especially those who resided in shantytowns. And because the faith of Islam plays a crucial role in Turkish society, Islamists could utilize religion as a cultural resource in approaching the electorate. Tarrow argues that "leaders can only create a social movement when they tap more deep-rooted feelings of solidarity or identity." He regards religion and ethnicity as reliable bases of movement organization.[126]

It should be noted that in addition to selective material incentives such as food, clothing, and jobs, soft incentives – for example, the psychological and emotional rewards afforded by feelings of solidarity and belongingness – also play a crucial role in a movement's mobilization. Karl-Dieter Opp, in his analysis of participation in the antinuclear movement in Germany, asserts that soft incentives such as concern about the welfare of the public good played an important role leading to collective action.[127]

Islamists propose a comprehensive political and societal project for the sake of the public good. The atomization of the individual is a persisting problem among the migrant urban poor in shantytowns. Furthermore, as a result of the decay in moral values in the Turkish society, conservative-minded people regard Islamists as something of a protective shield resisting that decline. Thus, selective incentives can be the starting point for the Islamists to establish a relationship with the electorate. Yet, during the recruitment process, ideational and intangible factors seem to play the foremost role. As Roy Baumeister, Karen Dale, and Mark Muraven assert, people join movements as a way of satisfying their need to belong.[128]

The WP party activists, through conversational settings, tried to reconstruct the identity of those contacted for strengthening the movement's

---

[124] Ann Mische, "Cross-talk in Movements: Reconceiving the Culture-Network Link," in Diani and McAdam, *Social Movements and Networks*, 258–80.
[125] Clark, "Islamist Women in Yemen," 166. On the role of social ties in movement recruitment see Doug McAdam and Ronnelle Paulsen, "Specifying the Relationship between Social Ties and Activism," *American Journal of Sociology* 99, no. 3 (November 1993): 640–67.
[126] Tarrow, *Power in Movement*, 6.
[127] Karl-Dieter Opp, "Soft Incentives and Collective Action: Participation in the Anti-Nuclear Movement," *British Journal of Political Science* 16, no. 1 (January 1986): 87–112.
[128] Roy F. Baumeister, Karen L. Dale, and Mark Muraven, "Volition and Belongingness: Social Movements, Volition, Self-Esteem, and the Need to Belong," in *Self, Identity, and Social Movements*, eds. Sheldon Stryker, Timothy J. Owens, and Robert W. White (Minneapolis: University of Minnesota Press, 2000), 241.

support base. As Clark argues, "friendship networks emerge from recruitment efforts."[129] By instilling a sense of faith-based community and collective identity, the WP's establishment of close contacts in conversational settings such as household chats usually leads to identity formation on the part of those contacted. Islamists' utilization of nonpolitical, informal social gatherings for political purposes plays a crucial role in this process of identity reconstruction.

Unlike the mainstream political parties, the WP had ideologically motivated party workers who framed political participation and activism as a religious duty. Recruited people join the movement and start to work for the *da'wa* (propagation of the faith) as a vital component of practicing Islam. As Clark notes, "The act of da'wa itself promotes an environment in which Islam and Muslims can flourish."[130] In the case of Turkey, passive agents' identities are shaped by the Islamists. In turn, they either remain passive supporters or become active participants in the movement. A "politicized collective identity," note Klandermans and Simon, "affects how people perceive the social world and act on and in it."[131] And they identify three stages leading to politicized collective identity: "awareness of shared grievances, adversarial attributions, and involvement of society at large."[132]

As will be argued in Chapter 6, the WP became the party of government in Turkey by receiving the highest vote share (21.4%, or 6,012,450 votes) in the 1995 general elections. This led movement entrepreneurs to overestimate the movement's power vis-à-vis the secular-democratic structure. The contradictory statements and activities on the part of the WP's leader and members of parliament[133] vis-à-vis the secular establishment resulted in tension between the party and the military (Chart 1.1 and Diagram 1.3). Charles Kurzman, in his analysis of the Iranian Revolution, finds that perceived political opportunities

---

[129] Clark, "Islamist Women in Yemen," 180.
[130] Ibid., 169.
[131] Klandermans and Simon, "Politicized Collective Identity," 327.
[132] Ibid., 319.
[133] Erbakan already asked in a speech in 1994 whether the change in the social order when the WP came to power would be "peaceful or violent" and would be achieved "harmoniously or bloodshed": "The sixty million must make up their minds on that point." Erbakan hosted representatives of Palestinian Hamas, Egypt's Muslim Brothers, and Algeria's FIS at the WP's political convention after his premiership. The WP parliamentarian, Abdullah Gül, denied the existence of Islamic fundamentalist organizations in Turkey. According to Gül, most of the crimes in Turkey blamed on the Islamic movement were "international operations" and "plots of the West" against Turkey. The breaking point was the "Jerusalem Night" incident in January 1997, when the WP mayor of Sincan (a suburb of Ankara) organized a gathering with the support of Iranian diplomats. He displayed large posters of the leaders of Islamic terrorist organizations, such as Hamas and the Lebanese Hizbullah, and stated that he would "infuse the shari'a into the intellectual sector" in Turkey. See European Court of Human Rights, *Case of Refah Partisi (the Welfare Party) and Others v. Turkey* (Applications nos. 41340/98, 41342/98, 41343/98, and 41344/98); Ely Karmon, "The Demise of Radical Islam in Turkey," (International Center for Counter-Terrorism) http://www.ict.org.il (June 3, 2000): 7, 11 (Internet ed.) (accessed January 30, 2003).

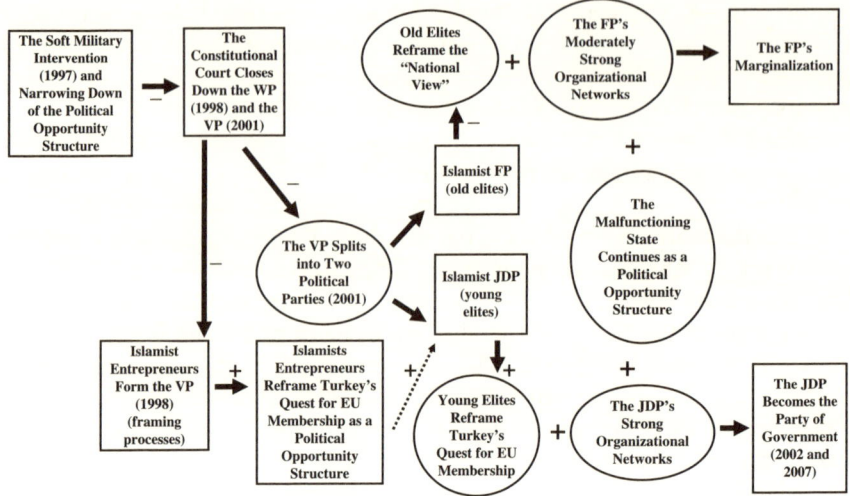

DIAGRAM 1.3. *The Dynamics of Divergence and Reconsolidation (1997–2007)*

as a result of the growth in the opposition movement there outweighed structural opportunities, which led to a successful outcome. Kurzman regards Iran as a deviant case for social movement theory, as it suggests that "perceived opportunities may affect the outcome of revolutionary protest independent of structural opportunities."[134] The case of Turkey is a contrary example, in that perceived opportunities of the movement participants led to a strong counter-mobilization of the structure (the soft military coup of 1997).

The closure of the WP (1998) and the VP (2001) narrowed down the POS and led to a sharp division among Islamist movement leaders over how to define and respond to the changed opportunity structure. This division led the movement to split into two parties in 2001: the "traditionalists" under the leadership of Recai Kutan established the FP, while the "reformists" under the leadership of Recep Tayyip Erdoğan (the former founding member of the WP/VP and the mayor of Istanbul) founded the JDP.[135] This lends support to

---

[134] Charles Kurzman, "Structural Opportunity and Perceived Opportunity in Social-Movement Theory: The Iranian Revolution of 1979," *American Sociological Review* 61, no. 1 (February 1996): 165. According to Kurzman, the Iranian monarchy was not structurally vulnerable. However, the Iranians perceived opportunities for successful protest, basing their perceptions on a shift in the opposition movement, not on a shift in the structural opposition of the state. In ibid., 153. See also Charles Kurzman, *The Unthinkable Revolution in Iran* (Cambridge, MA: Harvard University Press, 2004).

[135] Erdoğan previously made antisecular statements. In 1996, Tayyip Erdoğan, in a newspaper interview, "admitted that democracy is not the goal but is an instrument for the WP. Similarly, Erbakan stated that democracy is an instrument, not the aim; the aim is to establish *saadet nizamı* (order of happiness)." In *Milliyet*, July 14, 1996. See also interview with Recep Tayyip Erdoğan, in 2. *Cumhuriyet Tartışmaları* [The Second Republic Discussions], eds. Metin Sever and Cem Dizdar (Ankara: Başak Yayınları, 1993), 419–32. In another interview in 1994, Erdoğan stated, "Elhamdulillah [thank God] we are for the Sharia." In *Milliyet*, November 21, 1994.

Gamson and Meyer's suggestion that it is more useful to regard "framing as an internal process of contention within movements with different actors taking different positions."[136] In this case, the narrowing down of the POS in the aftermath of the soft military intervention, while ending the "framing consensus"[137] among movement activists, led to their innovation of new strategies – and despite the state's strong countermobilization, led by the military, the movement not only survived, but also became stronger than ever.[138] This was because the Islamist movement had firmly established itself in the country since 1980. A "reformist group" led by Recep Tayyip Erdoğan saw that there was no opportunity for change (futility) and insisting on changing the system might risk all the achievements already won (pervasive effects)[139] by maintaining the movement by the same political rhetoric and cadres.

The JDP became the governing party in Turkey by securing 34.3 percent of the votes in the 2002 general elections and 363 out of 550 seats in parliament, whereas the FP was marginalized by gaining only 2.5 percent of the votes. The JDP further increased its support in the 2007 general elections by securing 46.6 percent of the popular vote and 341 seats in parliament, whereas the FP gained only 2.3 percent of the votes. "[A]s opportunities narrow," Tarrow notes, "even the strong grow weak and movements are forced to change their forms of action and their strategies."[140] Many secular military, academic, media, cultural, and political figures in Turkish society, many of whom have been interviewed for this book and are cited in later chapters, regard establishment of the JDP as constituting merely a tactic of the Islamist entrepreneurs, rather than a change in the movement activists' strategy.

The JDP as governing party following the 2002 general elections seemed to be in the process of adopting a more moderate line. However, following the 2007 general elections, the JDP as the party of government seems to be in the process of abandoning its moderate line. It is possible to see policies that challenge the secular state structure, on the one hand, and policies that can be pursued by a mainstream party, on the other. The impact on the Islamist movement of the European Union (EU) reform packages introducing more democratization in Turkey remains to be seen. McAdam notes that regional ethnic mobilizations – for example, those of the Basque and Catalan separatists in

---

[136] Gamson and Meyer, "Framing Political Opportunity," 283.
[137] Framing consensus is the movement activists' definition of what an opportunity refers to.
[138] See Kim Voss's analysis of the collapse of a social movement when it cannot innovate new strategies facing a countermobilization. Kim Voss, "The Collapse of a Social Movement: The Interplay of Mobilizing Structures, Framing, and Political Opportunities in the Knights of Labor," in McAdam, McCarthy, and Zald, *Comparative Perspectives on Social Movements*, 227–58.
[139] See Albert Hirschman, *The Rhetoric of Reaction* (Cambridge, MA: Harvard University Press, 1991), 1–10.
[140] Tarrow, "States and Opportunities," 54.

Spain and the Welsh nationalists in the United Kingdom – have benefited from the expansion in political opportunities introduced by the EU.[141] Another question that remains to be seen is whether the JDP will be able to sustain the consensus among party cadres and be a center-right party in the future, or it will split between moderates and hard-liners. As of this writing, the JDP has successfully become a people's party.

---

[141] McAdam, "Conceptual Origins, Current Problems, Future Directions," 34–5.

2

Emergence of the Islamist Social Movement in Turkey

In establishing the Turkish state in 1923, Atatürk aimed at eliminating Islam from official public life. Yet, instead of relegating religion to the private sphere, the state assumed responsibility for supervising and controlling religious activity, thus maintaining organizational links between religious institutions and the state bureaucracy. The Turkish version of separation of church and state took a different form from what is generally understood by this term in the United States: religious institutions were not separated from the state, but rather became subservient to it. For example, when the caliphate and the Chief Religious Office of the State were abolished, the Grand National Assembly created a Directorate of Religious Affairs under the direct supervision of the prime minister. The agency manages Islam and controls mosques and mausoleums in the country.[1] In order to understand the reason why the state has been controlling Islam in Turkey, one has to analyze the Ottoman Empire's state structure and the failure of the modernization attempts started in that era.

ISLAM IN THE OTTOMAN EMPIRE

Islam was the dominant force in all areas of the Ottoman Empire. The sultan (ruler of the empire) was at the same time the caliph (religious leader of the Muslim world). Thus, the sultan was not considered the representative of the people, but of God. Political obedience to the ruler on the part of the community was the duty of every Muslim, since the political order had divine sanction. As Binnaz Toprak, a professor of political science, argues, "the sultan-caliph symbolized the Islamic ideal of a political community based on religious legitimacy. That

---

[1] Toprak, *Islam and Political Development in Turkey*, 1–2; Zürcher, *Turkey*, 173–203; John L. Esposito, *Islam and Politics*, 3rd ed. (New York: Syracuse University Press, 1991), 96; and Paul Dumont, "The Origins of Kemalist Ideology," in *Atatürk and the Modernization of Turkey*, ed. Jacob M. Landau (Boulder, CO: Westview Press, 1984), 38.

ideal was elevated into a political doctrine through the Ottoman concept of *din u devlet*, that is to say, the unity of religion and the state."[2]

The well-organized and powerful *ulema* class (religious clergy) within the administrative structure of the empire should also be emphasized. The *ulema* primarily controlled educational and judicial processes; but through the institution of the *fetva* (religious orders), the *ulema* also had the power to sanction or condemn policy decisions of the sultan and his government as well as programs of reform and innovation within the empire.[3] The *ulema*, by utilizing the institution of the *fetva*, and the Janissaries (*Yeni Çeri* – New Army) by using their military power, started to exert political pressure over the sultan.[4] The conservative interpretation of Islam by the *ulema* thereby inhibited modernization attempts in the empire. However, the *ulema* and the Janissaries were not immune from the decay of the empire by the eighteenth century. The first modernization attempts could start only in the early eighteenth century in the military realm, after the defeats of the Ottoman armies by the European armies.[5]

During the Tanzimat era (1839–76), modernization was extended to the political and social areas of the empire – but a nation-state based on the notions of Western liberalism and citizenship was still not achieved. Niyazi Berkes, a professor of sociology, argued that as a result of the Tanzimat era's Westernizing social and political changes, the empire, while keeping its technology and social structure from the Middle Ages, became dependent on the support of Western powers for its survival. Berkes summarizes the failure of the Tanzimat era by remarking of the Ottoman Empire that it "was neither an Islam state, nor a Turkish state, nor a modernized secular state."[6]

Society in the Ottoman Empire was based on the *millet* system of religious community, according to which subjects of the empire were defined according to their religion (Muslim and non-Muslim). Each *millet* was recognized as a legal community under its own religious leadership. For example, there was a Muslim *millet*, but there were neither Turkish nor Arab *millets*; any national identity was regarded as a threat to the empire's unity. For this reason, a Turkish national idea could not emerge until the mid-nineteenth century.[7]

---

[2] Toprak, *Islam and Political Development in Turkey*, 26.
[3] Ibid., 26, 29; S. N. Eisenstadt, "The Kemalist Regime and Modernization: Some Comparative and Analytical Remarks," in Landau, *Atatürk and the Modernization of Turkey*, 13. E.g., the *fetvas* of the *Şeyh-ül İslam* (the head of the hierarchy of the *ulema* in the Ottoman Empire) led to the depositions of the Sultans Ibrahim (1648), Mehmed IV (1687), Ahmed III (1730), and Selim III (1807). See Khurshid Ahmad, "Islam and Democracy: Some Conceptual and Contemporary Dimensions," *The Muslim World* 90, no. 1/2 (Spring 2000): 6.
[4] Nevzat Kösoğlu, *Devlet: Eski Türkler'de, İslam'da ve Osmanlı'da* [The State: In Ancient Turks, Islam, and Ottomans] (Istanbul: Ötüken Neşriyât, 1997), 269–70.
[5] Bernard Lewis, *The Emergence of Modern Turkey*, 3rd ed. (New York: Oxford University Press, 2002), 40–64; Niyazi Berkes, *Türk Düşününde Batı Sorunu* [The Question of the West in Turkish Thinking] (Ankara: Bilgi Yayınevi, 1975), 21.
[6] Berkes, *Türk Düşününde Batı Sorunu*, 37.
[7] Lewis, *The Emergence of Modern Turkey*, 2, 335; Bozkurt Güvenç, *Türk Kimliği: Kültür Tarihinin Kaynakları* [Turkish Identity: The Source of Cultural History], 5th ed. (Istanbul: Remzi Kitabevi, 1997), 22–3, 32.

"According to the Christian West," argues Bozkurt Güvenç, a professor of anthropology, "the Ottoman Sultanate was Turkish. But, according to the Ottomans, Muslim Turks were subjects of the Empire. In Ottoman thinking, there was a division between the governing state (the military) and the governed public (the subjects/peasants), instead of between being Turkish and non-Turkish."[8]

Until the mid-nineteenth century, the Turks identified themselves with Islam, and their loyalty belonged to Islam and to the Ottoman sultanate. This led to the submergence of the concept of Turkish nationality. As both Bernard Lewis and the ideologue of Turkish nationalism, Ziya Gökalp (1876–1924), assert, the ethnic term *Turk* was little used in the empire and then mainly in a derogatory sense, to refer to the Turcoman nomads, or the ignorant and uneducated Turkish-speaking peasants in Anatolia.[9]

Society was organized into religious communities, or *millets*, rather than ethnic or national communities. The sultan-caliph was a religious figure for society and a military leader for the state, in which the military was dominant. The concept of a Turkish *nation* was not central to the self-identification of the sultan-caliph, the ruling elites, or even the masses, among whom religious identification (Muslim and non-Muslim) was dominant. It was not until the Westernizing influences of the Tanzimat era that the idea of a Turkish *nation*, and a national state, began to emerge.

OTTOMANISM, ISLAMISM, AND TURKISM

Following the decline of the Ottoman Empire, three ideas emerged with the goal of preserving the empire's unity: Ottomanism, Islamism, and Turkism. Ottomanism aimed at providing equal political rights and duties, including freedom of thought and faith, to both Muslims and non-Muslims, thus creating an Ottoman nation in order to preserve the empire's unity. But Western powers quickly exploited the freedom and rights that Ottomanism provided to non-Muslims in order to weaken the empire. As Hasan Kayalı, a professor of history, explains,

the Western powers quickly made use of their newly strengthened extraterritorial rights, known as the capitulations, to promote Christian merchants as their protégés and secure for them tax exemptions and immunity from the due process to Ottoman law. In the predominantly Christian-populated Balkan Peninsula the centralizing measures of the Tanzimat, particularly in the sphere of taxation, contributed to social unrest and nationalist movements.[10]

---

[8] Güvenç, *Türk Kimliği*, 167.
[9] Lewis, *The Emergence of Modern Turkey*, 1–2; Ziya Gökalp, *Türkçülüğün Esasları* [The Principles of Turkism] (prepared by Prof. Mehmet Kaplan) (Ankara: Kültür Bakanlığı Yayınları, 1990), 43 (Gökalp's book was first published in 1923).
[10] Hasan Kayalı, *Arabs and Young Turks: Ottomanism, Arabism, and Islamism in the Ottoman Empire, 1908–1918* (Berkeley: University of California Press, 1997), 18.

Thus, the subsequent wave of nationalism, which extended to southeastern Europe in the late nineteenth century, proved the failure of the idea of Ottomanism to curb the dismemberment of the empire.[11]

Following the failure of Ottomanism, Islamism emerged as a way to preserve the unity of the empire. Islamists, who equated religion and nation, proposed that all of the empire's Muslims should be united around the faith of Islam. Thus, following the decline of the empire, Islam gained an ideological component.[12] Sultan Abdülhamid II (1876–1909) seized on the Islamist reaction to Western imperialism in an effort to strengthen the empire by unifying Ottoman Muslims under the umbrella of Islam. It should be noted that the sultan, while pursuing Islamism, was "a firm believer in modernization."[13] As Kemal Karpat, a professor of history, notes, "Abdülhamid preserved all the reforms introduced by his predecessors and opened new avenues of change, including the letters and sciences, that greatly widened the intellectual horizons of Ottoman modernization and, paradoxically, brought the elites closer to European culture."[14] In the end, Islamism, following the rise of Arab nationalism at the expense of the empire, proved to be a failure.[15]

Yusuf Akçura (1876–1939),[16] a prominent ideologue of Turkish nationalism, explained the reason why both Ottomanism and pan-Islamism were bound to fail in an article "Three Kinds of Policy" ("*Üç Tarz-ı Siyaset*"). Akçura, while criticizing Ottomanism for minimizing the rights of the Turks in the empire, rejected pan-Islamism because it antagonized non-Muslim groups in the empire. Akçura argued in the article published in 1904 that Turkism was the only way to maintain the unity of the empire. The rise of Arab nationalism, which led to Arab opposition and revolt against Ottoman rule during World War I and to Arabs' separation from the empire, along with the military defeat of the Ottoman Empire in Libya and the Balkans, left Turkism as an ideology of last resort.[17] Thus, Turkism emerged following the failure of both Ottomanism and Islamism.

---

[11] Yusuf Akçura, *Üç Tarz-ı Siyaset* [Three Kinds of Policy], 3rd ed. (Ankara: Türk Tarih Kurumu Basımevi, 1991), 19–21 (Akçura's article was first published in 1904); Jacob M. Landau, *Pan-Turkism: From Irredentism to Cooperation* (Bloomington: Indiana University Press, 1995), 46–7; and Lewis, *The Emergence of Modern Turkey*, 326.

[12] Şerif Mardin, "XIX. Yüzyılda Düşünce Akımları ve Osmanlı Devleti," [Ideologies in the 19th century and the Ottoman State] in *Türk Modernleşmesi: Makaleler*, vol. 4 [Turkish Modernization: Essays], ed. Şerif Mardin (Istanbul: İletişim Yayınları, 1991), 89, 93–5; Taner Timur, *Türk Devrimi: Tarihi Anlamı ve Felsefi Temeli* [The Turkish Revolution: Its Historical Meaning and Philosophical Basis] (Ankara: Sevinç Matbaası, 1968), 11–12.

[13] Kemal H. Karpat, *The Politicization of Islam: Reconstructing Identity, State, Faith, and Community in the Late Ottoman State* (New York: Oxford University Press, 2001), 15.

[14] Ibid., 15–16.

[15] Kösoğlu, *Devlet*, 94.

[16] Akçura was an emigrant Tatar from the Russian Empire to Turkey. See Lewis, *The Emergence of Modern Turkey*, 326.

[17] Landau, *Pan-Turkism*, 32–3; Lewis, *The Emergence of Modern Turkey*, 349.

Turkish nationalism in its origins is a nonracialist and secular ideology. Gökalp suggested that "one became a part of the nation through education in its values, not through 'blood' and 'spirit.'"[18] Gökalp and his followers advocated the Turkification of the language (by expunging Arabic and Persian words) and the adoption of customs from the Turkish past. Justin McCarthy notes that those customs reflected "real democracy and political participation, completely secular courts, equality for women, including an end to polygamy, and a nationalized Islam reduced to basic principles and then merged with Turkish customs and language."[19] Yet, during the Ottoman era, Gökalp's idea of unifying around the idea of Turkish language and culture did not receive much attention or support. Instead, Turkism, which turned out to be nonterritorial by virtue of its ambition of uniting all Turks, gave way to pan-Turkism/Turanism (*Turancılık*).[20] For example, Enver Pasha's (1881–1922) passion for pan-Turkism was the main drive behind the Ottoman Empire's entrance into World War I on the side of the Central Powers.[21] The defeat and dismantling of the Ottoman Empire by the Entente Powers proved not only the failure of pan-Turkism to save the empire, but also that of Ottomanism and Islamism.[22]

THE TURKISH REVOLUTION

The idea "of a territorial nation-state based on the Turkish nation in Turkey" appeared first in the early days of the War of Independence (1919–22) led by Mustafa Kemal Atatürk.[23] Atatürk successfully created a new conception of Turkish nationalism, which rejected irredentist claims of pan-Turkism and united the people in the defense of the land against the invaders.[24] "Neither Islamic union nor Turanism," argued Atatürk in a 1921 speech, "may constitute a doctrine, or logical policy for us. Henceforth the Government policy of the new Turkey is to consist in living independently, relying on Turkey's own sovereignty within her national frontiers."[25]

The Turkish nationalism proposed by Atatürk became the state ideology of the republic. Prominent pan-Turkists such as Mehmet Emin Yurdakul, Ahmet Ağaoğlu, Yusuf Akçura, and Tekin Alp abandoned pan-Turkism and adopted the Kemalist strand of Turkish nationalism.[26] During the Atatürk era, "the glorious past of the Turks since their earliest origins" was studied, focusing on language, literature, history, and geography.[27] Yet, while arguing the Turkish

---

[18] Justin McCarthy, *The Ottoman Peoples and the End of Empire*, 2nd ed. (London: Arnold, 2004), 75.
[19] Ibid., 75–6.
[20] Güvenç, *Türk Kimliği*, 33.
[21] Landau, *Pan-Turkism*, 51–2.
[22] Ibid., 74.
[23] Lewis, *The Emergence of Modern Turkey*, 352.
[24] Landau, *Pan-Turkism*, 74.
[25] Ibid.
[26] Ibid., 75–6.
[27] Ibid., 78.

nation had a glorious past of its own it could be proud of, Kemalism rejected racism. The republican regime conducted a Turkification policy based partly on the ideas of Gökalp and Akçura as well as on the crucial experience of the War of Independence, which resulted in the establishment of a territorial Turkish nation-state that greatly contributed to establishing the Turkish identity.[28]

Following the War of Independence, Atatürk's foremost goal as the founder of the Turkish Republic was to establish an independent secular nation-state based on the European model. The collapse of the empire suggested that it was not possible to achieve modernization within the existing traditional Islamic-Ottoman structure; successful modernization required establishment of a secular nation-state.[29] Replacement of the sultanate-caliphate regime (a protectorate of European invading powers)[30] with a nation-state based on the Turkish nation's sovereignty, Atatürk believed, would be the source of the legitimacy of the War of Independence.[31]

The modernization efforts of the Turkish Republic were quite different from those of the Ottoman era. As Berkes notes, what makes the Turkish Revolution a significant one is the replacement of a remnant regime from the Middle Ages with a Turkish nation-state.[32] Atatürk saw the necessity of adopting not only Western technology but also Western political, economic, judicial, and social structures as well as Western culture. The lack of any one of these factors would have resulted in failure, as was the case in the Ottoman era. Modernization during the Tanzimat era could not go beyond imitation of the West because there was an attempt to retain the traditional Islamic-Ottoman state structure. Thus, Tanzimat modernization did not result in the establishment of an independent nation-state based on national sovereignty.[33] Westernization during the Tanzimat era, which further accelerated the weakening of the empire vis-à-vis the European powers, was a total failure; rather than saving the

---

[28] Karpat, *The Politicization of Islam*, 419.
[29] Oral Sander, *Türkiye'nin Dış Politikası* [Foreign Policy of Turkey] (Ankara: İmge Yayınevi, 1998), 76–7.
[30] During the War of Independence, both the sultan-caliph and the *Şeyh-ül İslam* (the head of the religious institution) sided with the invading European states, mainly Great Britain. On April 5, 1920, the *Şeyh-ül İslam*, Dürrizade Abdullah Efendi, issued a *fetva* declaring that the killing of rebels, on the orders of the caliph, was a religious duty. Hence, he ordered an unconditional surrender and put an end to the national resistance movement under the leadership of Mustafa Kemal against the invading forces. On April 18, 1920, the sultan and his government formed the Disciplinary Forces (*Kuvva-i İnzibatiye*) to fight against the Kemalists' National Forces (*Kuvva-i Milliye*). On May 11, 1920, Mustafa Kemal and other nationalist leaders were sentenced to death, in absentia, by a court-martial in Istanbul. Dürrizade Abdullah Efendi's *fetva* led to local revolts against the Kemalists, who were simultaneously fighting against the European invading forces. See Ahmad, *The Turkish Experiment in Democracy, 1950–1975*, 363; Lewis, *The Emergence of Modern Turkey*, 252; and Cemal Kutay, *Cumhuriyet'in 75. Yılında Onlara Saygı: Kurtuluşun "Kuvvacı" Din Adamları* [A Respect to Them in the 75th Year of the Republic: The Kemalist Men of Religion during the War of Independence] (Istanbul: Aksoy Yayıncılık, 1998), 202.
[31] Berkes, *Türk Düşününde Batı Sorunu*, 86.
[32] Ibid.
[33] Ibid., 36–7; Berkes, *Türkiye'de Çağdaşlaşma*, 522.

empire, the Tanzimat modernization expedited its dissolution. The Western powers, with the collaboration of minorities in the empire, actually achieved a strengthened control over the empire's economy.[34] As Lewis argues,

> the men of the *Tanzimat* had thrown the country wide open to foreign influence and interference of every kind. Foreigners had been given the right to own land in Turkey, and were acquiring positions of control in every branch of the economic and public life of the Empire. To domestic tyranny, the men of the *Tanzimat* had added foreign exploitation. A direct result of these policies was the economic ruination of the Empire.[35]

Atatürk's goal, unlike that of the Tanzimat era modernizers, was to create a modern Turkish nation that would be independent of any possible future Western dominance. The creation of a modern nation-state based on the nation's sovereignty inevitably required the principle of secularism.[36] The goal of the Turkish society according to Atatürk, should be to attain the level of contemporary civilization (*muasır medeniyet seviyesi*) – and that meant a Turkish society guided by reason and science in the fashion of Western societies.[37] "We do not adapt Western civilization for the sake of imitation," Atatürk stated, "We take it [Western civilization] because we find good sides in it that are compatible with our structure, [and] for attaining a world civilization level."[38]

With the establishment of the Turkish Republic, the historical connection between Islam and the state was broken off. Atatürk's reforms (1923–38) aimed at bringing Western culture to the Islamic society. To accomplish this goal, a series of reforms was initiated that were designed to weaken both the institutional and the functional strength of Islam in Turkish society.[39] The main reforms were as follows: the sultanate, the caliphate, the Chief Religious Office of the State, the *Şeyh-ül Islam*, and the *Sharia* courts were abolished in 1924.[40] Through the passage of the Law on the Unification of Education (*Tevhid-i Tedrisat Kanunu*) in the same year, all education was made secular, which eliminated the traditional Islamic educational system in Turkey. The Latin alphabet, Gregorian calendar, and a new dress code were adopted in 1925. The constitutional article adopting Islam as the state religion was nullified in 1928. Islamic laws were abolished, and the Swiss civil code, the Italian penal code, and the German

---

[34] Sarıbay, *Türkiye'de Modernleşme, Din ve Parti Politikası*, 59, 65.

[35] Lewis, *The Emergence of Modern Turkey*, 171–2 (emphasis in original).

[36] Niyazi Berkes, *Teokrasi ve Laiklik* [Theocracy and Secularism] (Istanbul: Adam Yayıncılık, 1984), 97.

[37] Atilla İlhan, *Hangi Batı: Anılar ve Acılar* [Which West: Memoirs and Pains] (Ankara: Bilgi Yayınevi, 2001), 80–1; Tımur, *Türk Devrimi*, 98–9.

[38] Arı İnan, ed., *Düşünceleriyle Atatürk* [Atatürk with His Thoughts], 3rd ed. (Ankara: Türk Tarih Kurumu Basımevi, 1999), 120

[39] Toprak, *Islam and Political Development in Turkey*, 1; Berkes, *Türkiye'de Çağdaşlaşma*, 521–52.

[40] Suna Kili, *Türk Devrim Tarihi* [History of the Turkish Revolution] (Istanbul: Türkiye İş Bankası Kültür Yayınları, 2002), 271–5, 279–89; and Suna Kili, *Atatürk Devrimi: Bir Çağdaşlaşma Modeli* [The Atatürk Revolution: A Modernization Model] (Ankara: Türkiye İş Bankası Kültür Yayınları, 2000), 268.

commercial code were adopted between 1926 and 1930; rights were granted to women in 1934. Finally, the Turkish state was defined as secular in the constitution in 1937. Thus, the aim was to achieve secularism at all levels of the state.[41]

Members of the Turkish national independence movement (secular intellectuals, men of religion,[42] radical reformers, political conservatives, and a few members with communist leanings), who were represented by the First Grand National Assembly (1920–3), were deeply divided both ideologically and socially.[43] Ergun Özbudun, a professor of political science, argues that the Turkish Revolution, which combined features of a war of national liberation and a political revolution, was not a social revolution in its initial years. The revolution was directed against European invading powers and their internal collaborators – that is, the Sultan Mehmet VI Vahidettin[44] – instead of at a particular social class.[45]

---

[41] Osman Okyar, "Atatürk's Quest for Modernism," in Landau, *Atatürk and Modernization of Turkey*, 51; John Esposito, "Muslim Societies Today," in *Islam: The Religious and Political Life of a World Community*, ed. Marjorie Kelly (New York: Praeger, 1984), 199; and Ahmad, *The Turkish Experiment in Democracy, 1950–1975*, 2.

[42] During the War of Independence, men of religion in Anatolia played a crucial role in mobilizing the people to fight on the side of the Kemalists. The *Şeyh-ül Islam* Dürrizade Abdullah Efendi's *fetva*, which ordered an unconditional surrender of the nation and killing members of the national resistance movement under the leadership of Mustafa Kemal, led to a counter-*fetva* of the Anatolian men of religion. On May 5, 1920, the *mufti* of Ankara Mehmet Rıfat Efendi issued a *fetva*, supported by 152 other Anatolian *muftis*, declaring that a *fetva* issued under foreign occupation was invalid and ordering that the Muslims had to liberate their caliph from captivity. On June 15, 1920, Mehmet Rıfat Efendi was sentenced to death, in absentia, by a court of martial in Istanbul. See Lewis, *The Emergence of Modern Turkey*, 252; Kutay, *Cumhuriyet'in 75. Yılında Onlara Saygı*, 194–5. On the role of men of religion in Anatolia see also Recep Çelik, *Milli Mücadelede Din Adamları* [The Men of Religion during the War of Independence] (Istanbul: Emre Yayınları, 1999).

[43] Ergun Özbudun, "The Nature of the Kemalist Political Regime," in *Atatürk: Founder of a Modern State*, eds. Ergun Özbudun and Ali Kazancıgil (Hamden, CT: Archon Books, 1981), 80–1; Tarık Zafer Tunaya, *Islamcılık Akımı* [The Islamist Movement] (Istanbul: Bilgi Üniversitesi Yayınları, 2003), 132–3.

[44] The last Ottoman Sultan Vahidettin pursued policies with the goal of appeasing the Entente Powers, particularly Great Britain, in order to get a favorable peace treaty. But the Entente Powers' imposition of the extremely severe Sèvres Treaty (1920) proved the sultan's failure in his endeavors. According to the treaty, Eastern Thrace and the region around Izmir (a city in the Aegean region) were given to Greece, and the Straits were internationalized. France set up mandates in Syria and Lebanon and had a sphere of influence in southern Anatolia. An independent Armenian republic was to be founded in eastern Anatolia. Italy controlled the southwestern part of Anatolia as a sphere of influence. Great Britain established mandates in Palestine, southern Syria, and Iraq. In the north of Mosul province Kurdistan was to receive autonomy and the right to appeal for independence to the League of Nations within a year. Thus, as Zürcher argues, the treaty created a rump state in northern Asia Minor with Istanbul as its capital. See Zürcher, *Turkey*, 153. Zürcher describes the sultan as follows: "What mattered for him was the preservation of the dynasty, of Istanbul, as the seat of the caliphate and of his own authority over the Muslim population of the Middle East, for which he felt a strong responsibility. He was not a nationalist... and he cared little for the complete independence of Anatolia or any other region." In Zürcher, *Turkey*, 142.

[45] Özbudun, "The Nature of the Kemalist Political Regime," 83.

During the War of Independence, Atatürk did not declare his real intention of establishing a secular nation-state.[46] Following the establishment of the Turkish Republic, both the Islamic brotherhoods and the communists were suppressed by the Kemalist regime.[47] The creation of a new republic based on the Western state model was a big disappointment for Islamic-oriented people. As Şevket Kazan, the vice-chair of the Felicity Party (FP), argued in an interview with the author in June 2004, "the faith caused us to win the war of independence. Yet, it was the faith, which was betrayed in the end."[48] Kazan also asserted that during the Lausanne Peace Conference[49] (November 20, 1922–July 24, 1923), the Entente Powers, mainly Great Britain, granted Turkey independence on the condition that Turkey would give up the Quranic order in its governance and instead it would adopt the Western order. According to Kazan, the aim of the Western powers was to weaken the nation's ability to challenge the West by eliminating the power of the Quran.[50]

It should be noted that only Islamists in Turkey express a feeling of disappointment at the establishment of a secular state. Non-Islamist conservatives, in contrast, value the establishment of the secular state even when they recognize the importance of Islam to Turkish society. For example, Galip Tamur, a prominent member of the Turkish Hearths (*Türk Ocakları* – a leading Turkish nationalist association), in an interview with the author in February 2004, while emphasizing the importance of the faith of Islam in Turkish society, described Atatürk as a leader who wanted the Turkish nation to learn the faith of Islam in its fullest sense.[51] Nevzat Kösoğlu, a former prominent right-wing Nationalist Action Party (NAP– *Milliyetçi Hareket Partisi*) parliamentarian, remarked during an interview with the author in February 2004 that there is no command in the Quran regarding how a political regime should be constituted.[52] He criticized the Islamists in Turkey for exploiting Islam and Islamic religious culture for political purposes. For example, the Islamists praise the Ottoman Empire period; but Kösoğlu suggested in the interview that "the Islamists utilize the Ottoman era as a tool only. They just utilize it as nostalgia. They are not frank. The Islamists want a political system based on Islam, while rejecting the notion of Turkishness."[53]

Ioanna Kuçuradi emphasizes that Atatürk's revolution was a cultural revolution carried out politically, through the modernization of the legal system

---

[46] Mustafa Kemal Atatürk, *Nutuk* [The Speech], vol. 2 (Istanbul: Milli Eğitim Basımevi, 1980), 468.
[47] Özbudun, "The Nature of the Kemalist Political Regime," 96.
[48] Author's interview with Şevket Kazan, the vice-chair of the FP, Ankara, June 10, 2004.
[49] The Lausanne Treaty recognized the reestablishment of complete and undivided Turkish sovereignty. Lewis, *The Emergence of Modern Turkey*, 254.
[50] Author's interview with Şevket Kazan, the vice-chair of the FP, Ankara, June 10, 2004.
[51] Author's interview with Galip Tamur, a prominent Turkish Hearths member, Ankara, February 14, 2004.
[52] For a detailed analysis of the relationship between Islam and state see Kösoğlu, *Devlet*, 68–71, 185–7.
[53] Author's interview with Nevzat Kösoğlu, the former NAP parliamentarian, Ankara, February 17, 2004.

and of social institutions.⁵⁴ By attempting to infuse Turks with Western liberal ideas, the aim was to create a new type of citizenship and thus a modern society rather than an *umma*, in which there was no room for individualism. The emphasis was on the potentialities of the Turkish people; sovereignty that was taken away from the sultan-caliph was invested unconditionally in the nation by creating the Grand National Assembly.⁵⁵ But because the masses were not familiar with Western notion of liberalism, having lived for centuries under an Islamic system dominated by the conservative *ulema* and Islamic brotherhoods, the newly established state was required to play a paternalistic role vis-à-vis its citizens, with the goal of removing religion from public affairs through state control. Thus, the Turkish experience with separation of church and state has not been in conformity with the Western conception. Furthermore, the Turkish adoption of secularism represented not a gradual change but a drastic one, which also contained a measure of coercion. All reforms were made under the one-party rule (between 1923 and 1946) of the Republican People's Party (RPP – *Cumhuriyet Halk Partisi*).⁵⁶

The secular state sought to restrict Islam to the private sphere of life in society, where Islam had dominated almost every aspect of life for centuries. Lewis notes that Turkish Islam always functioned on two levels: the formal, legal, and dogmatic religion of the state represented by the *ulema*; and the popular, mystical, intuitive faith of the masses represented by Islamic brotherhoods (*tarikats*).⁵⁷ The Islamic brotherhood leaders, who remained part of the people, exerted more influence on the masses than the wealthy *ulema*.⁵⁸ As Lewis argues,

> By the eighteenth century the brotherhoods had established themselves in almost every town and village in Turkey. Through their close links with the guilds and corporations, they were able to dominate the professional and social, as well as the religious life of the artisan and much of the merchant classes.⁵⁹

Atatürk, by implementing a series of secularizing reforms, eliminated the power of the *ulema*. Yet the most persistent resistance to secularism came from the Islamic brotherhoods – because they, unlike the *ulema*, were used to

---

⁵⁴ Ioanna Kuçuradi, "Secularization in Turkey," in *Averroes and the Enlightenment*, eds. Mourad Wahba and Mona Abousenna (New York: Prometheus Books, 1996), 173.
⁵⁵ Ahmad, *The Turkish Experiment in Democracy, 1950–1975*, 2.
⁵⁶ Esposito, "Muslim Societies Today," 200; Kili, *Atatürk Devrimi*, 111; Tarık Zafer Tunaya, *Devrim Hareketleri İçinde Atatürk ve Atatürkçülük* [Atatürk and Atatürkism in Revolutionary Movements] (Istanbul: Bilgi Üniversitesi Yayınları, 2002), 324, 334–5; Toprak, *Islam and Political Development in Turkey*, 2, 28; and Ahmad, *The Turkish Experiment in Democracy, 1950–1975*, 1. It should be emphasized that Atatürk's initial aim was not to have a one-party rule. Yet, the concern for counterrevolutionary movements, like the antisecular Kurdish rebellion of 1925, led to the outlawing of the Progressive Republican Party and the dissolution of the Free Republican Party in 1930. See Ahmad, *The Turkish Experiment in Democracy, 1950–1975*, 3.
⁵⁷ Lewis, *The Emergence of Modern Turkey*, 404–5.
⁵⁸ Ibid., 406.
⁵⁹ Ibid., 407.

independence and being in opposition. The *ulema*, which was part of the Ottoman state apparatus, was reincorporated into the public bureaucracy, this time in a weaker form, through the establishment of the Directorate of Religious Affairs. But the Islamic brotherhoods, which had their roots in folk culture, were not tied to the state structure.[60] Furthermore, some of the Islamic brotherhoods sided with the Kemalists during the War of Independence, whereas the *ulema* sided with the caliphate's army, and hence with the European invading forces. Thus, unlike the *ulema*, the Islamic brotherhood leaders "enjoyed the confidence and loyalty of the common people."[61]

Atatürk's aim was not to encourage atheism, but to liberate the Turkish people from the political, social, cultural, economic, and psychological constraints of the Islamic system established by the conservative *ulema* and the Islamic brotherhoods.[62] In a public speech in 1925, Atatürk defined bringing "the people of the Turkish Republic into a state of society entirely modern and completely civilized in spirit and form" as the central aim of the Turkish Revolution.[63] Atatürk stated,

I flatly refuse to believe that today, in the luminous presence of science, knowledge, and civilization in all its aspects, there exist, in the civilized community of Turkey, men so primitive as to seek their material and moral well-being from the guidance of one or another *şeyh*. Gentlemen, you and the whole nation must know, and know well, that the Republic of Turkey cannot be the land of *şeyhs*, dervishes, disciplines, and lay brothers. The straightest, truest Way (tarikat) is the way of civilization. To be a man, it is enough to do what civilization requires. The heads of brotherhoods will understand this truth that I have uttered in all its clarity, and will of their own accord at once close their convents, and accept the fact that their disciplines have at last come of age.[64]

The Kemalists reduced Islam to the role of religion in a modern, Western nation-state.[65] Under the Turkish Republic, the Turkification of Islam began. As Paul Stirling has argued, the goal was to replace Arab Islam, which was viewed as conservative, backward, and more interested in a romanticized past than in the present, with a modern, scientific, Turkish Islam.[66] Within this framework, Turkish replaced Arabic as the language of religion – the Quran was translated into Turkish, and Turkish replaced Arabic in the five daily calls to prayer as well as in the Friday sermon in mosques, so that the masses could understand.[67]

---

[60] Özbudun, "The Nature of the Kemalist Political Regime," 96.
[61] Lewis, *The Emergence of Modern Turkey*, 409.
[62] Kili, *Atatürk Devrimi*, 268–9.
[63] Lewis, *The Emergence of Modern Turkey*, 410.
[64] Ibid., 410–11 (emphasis in original).
[65] Ibid., 412.
[66] See Paul Stirling, "Religious Change in Republican Turkey," *Middle East Journal* 12, no. 4 (Autumn 1958): 400.
[67] Ibid. Years before the state's decision, Ziya Gökalp, the theoretician of Turkish nationalism, suggested that the call to prayer in the country should be uttered in the Turkish language. See Lewis, *The Emergence of Modern Turkey*, 415. Gökalp, *Türkçülüğün Esasları*, 170–1.

The state's secularization policies did not lead to widespread public protest. Hasan Onat, a professor of divinity, observed during an interview with the author in February 2004, that the public at that time were subjects who had been transferred from Ottoman rule to the republic. Thus, unlike the alienated Islamic-oriented people, the public as a whole did not have a problem with the republic.[68] Attempts on the part of Islamic circles to initiate local revolts were suppressed during the period of one-party rule (1923–46).[69] Two serious revolts occurred. The first one was led by Şeyh (sheik) Sait (1925), a leading member of the Nakşibendi order and of Kurdish origin. The second revolt occurred in 1930, when a young Kemalist officer named Kubilay was beheaded by a local Nakşibendi leader and his followers.[70] The state suppressed all rebellions, as a result of which the Islamic brotherhoods were forced underground.[71] The Islamic orders, which were very influential in the countryside, were outlawed in 1925; yet they have continued to exist as underground movements. The Progressive Republican Party in 1924 and the Free Republican Party in 1930 were allowed to be established as official opposition parties; but because these parties carried strong religious elements, both were closed down within their first year.[72]

AN OVERVIEW OF TURKISH POLITICS (1946–1960)

Despite Turkey's formal secularization, the reforms penetrated the countryside only to a limited degree.[73] Moreover, during the initial years of the Turkish Republic, the public's educational level was insufficient to grasp the meaning of Atatürk's reforms.[74] In 1935, the population was 76.5 percent rural, and 80.8 percent of the population was illiterate.[75] In order to better communicate to the citizens, People's Homes (*Halk Evleri*) were established in cities in 1932, and People's Chambers (*Halk Odaları*) were founded in towns and villages, followed in 1940 by Village

---

[68] Author's interview with Professor Hasan Onat, Ankara, February 19, 2004.
[69] See Neşet Çağatay, *Türkiye'de Gerici Eylemler (1923'ten Buyana)* [Reactionary Attempts in Turkey since 1923] (Ankara: Ankara Üniversitesi Basımevi, 1972) for a detailed analysis of Islamist revolts in Turkey.
[70] After both revolts, the independence tribunals (*istiklâl mahkemeleri*) were established and imposed the death penalty on the leaders of the rebellions. See Lewis, *The Emergence of Modern Turkey*, 410, 417.
[71] Gareth Jenkins, "Muslim Democrats in Turkey?" *Survival* 45, no. 1 (Spring 2003): 48.
[72] Ronnie Margulies and Ergin Yıldızoğlu, "The Resurgence of Islam and the Welfare Party in Turkey," in *Political Islam: Essays from Middle East Report*, eds. Joel Beinin and Joe Stork (Berkeley: University of California Press, 1997), 152.
[73] Okyar, "Atatürk's Quest for Modernism," 53; Sabri M. Akural, "Kemalist Views on Social Change," in Landau, *Atatürk and Modernization of Turkey*, 126; Bernard Lewis, "Islam and Liberal Democracy: A Historical Overview," *Journal of Democracy* 7, no. 2 (April 1996): 62; Jacob M. Landau, *Radical Politics in Modern Turkey* (Leiden, the Netherlands: E. J. Brill 1974), 171; and Güvenç, *Türk Kimliği*, 42.
[74] Author's interviews with Galip Tamur, the prominent Turkish Hearths member, Ankara, February 14, 2004; and with Retired General Çevik Bir, Istanbul, February 27, 2004.
[75] Devlet İstatistik Enstitüsü (DİE, State Statistics Institute), *Statistical Yearbook of Turkey, 2001* (Ankara: DİE, 2002), 48, 65.

Institutes (*Köy Enstitüleri*).⁷⁶ Activities in those institutions encompassed the study of language and literature, fine arts, and drama; other adult education programs; sports; and social work and village welfare programs. These establishments also incorporated libraries, museums, and cultural exhibits.⁷⁷ Nahide Bozkurt, a professor of divinity, noted in an interview with the author in February 2004 that while village institutions were quite effective in educating the people, they were guided by positivism and underestimated the role of Islam among the rural population, and thus were not fully accepted by the villagers.⁷⁸

In the aftermath of Atatürk's death in 1938, the ruling RPP continued the Kemalist legacy, but did so in a more elitist manner. Even though there was one-party rule during the Atatürk period (1923–38), Atatürk, as the liberator of the country from foreign invasion, was a national hero in the eyes of the public. Unlike RPP Chair İsmet İnönü, Atatürk always emphasized communicating with the public during his visits to various cities and villages in order to learn their demands.⁷⁹ Atatürk declared that "the villager as the real owner of the country and the very essence of the nation" (*heyeti içtimaiyemizin unsuru esasisi*).⁸⁰ He also argued that the gap between the (urban-intellectual) elite and the (rural-uneducated) masses had to be overcome if the country was to attain the level of modern (*muasır*) civilization; accordingly, it was the responsibility of the intellectuals to educate the public.⁸¹ Yet, the RPP under İnönü overlooked the problem of the urban-rural gap. As Toprak notes, "The military-bureaucratic elite of the Republican governments had largely overlooked the economic and cultural interests of a large sector of the peasantry."⁸² Instead, the party focused on raising a future generation of middle- and upper-class urban elites who would protect and advance the Westernizing reforms initiated by Atatürk.⁸³ Along the same lines as Toprak, Özbudun observes that "The RPP remained largely a cadre party, an elite organization, dominated by the official elite and local notables. The RPP leadership made no notable effort to broaden the party's popular base and to enlist the support of the peasant masses; instead, it concentrated its attention on the small westernized elite."⁸⁴ As a result, the rural population did not welcome the RPP's policy of secularism, which was based on suppressing expressions of popular faith. Lewis summarizes the difference between Atatürk's rule and that of the RPP under İnönü as follows:

---

⁷⁶ Kili, *Türk Devrim Tarihi*, 315–16, 347–9.
⁷⁷ Özbudun, "The Nature of the Kemalist Political Regime," 94.
⁷⁸ Author's interview with Professor Nahide Bozkurt, Ankara, February 17, 2004.
⁷⁹ Author's interviews with Professor Oya Akgönenç, the Founding Council and the General Governing Council member of the FP and a former parliamentarian from the VP, Ankara, February 12, 2004; and with Professor Binnaz Toprak, Istanbul, February 26, 2004.
⁸⁰ Atatürk, "1 Mart 1922 Meclis açılış nutkundan" [March 1, 1922: From the parliamentary opening speech], in *Atatürk'ün Maarife Ait Direktifleri* [Atatürk's Directives on Education], Maarif Bakanlığı [Ministry of Education] (Istanbul: Maarif Matbaası, 1939), 6.
⁸¹ Atatürk's speech from İlhan, *Hangi Batı*, 192–3.
⁸² Toprak, *Islam and Political Development in Turkey*, 76.
⁸³ Ibid., 88.
⁸⁴ Özbudun, "The Nature of the Kemalist Political Regime," 93.

After the death of Atatürk there was some deterioration. In the hands of lesser men than himself, his authoritarian and paternalist mode of government degenerated into something nearer to dictatorship as the word is commonly understood. The disappearance of Atatürk's own dominating personality and the rise of a new generation influenced by the constitutional ideas of the victorious West undermined the popular acceptance of authoritarian government inherited from the past, and forced the regime to rely more and more on simple repression.[85]

It was not only the RPP's elitist understanding of secularism but also, even more importantly, its economic policies that made the government deeply unpopular among the large majority of Turkish citizens by the end of World War II. The rural population did not see any great improvement in their standard of living (with respect, e.g., to health, education, infrastructure, or communications). Even though Turkey did not participate in World War II, it carried out a partial mobilization as a precaution, and this mobilization was sustained economically by having the Central Bank simply print more money, thus leading to inflation. This led to a sharp decline in the purchasing power of wage and salary earners. Large landowners, for their part, were already discontent with the government's "Tax on Agricultural Produce," which was an artificially low pricing of agricultural produce intended to combat inflation during the war. They were further alienated by the government's proposing the "Law on Giving Land to the Farmer"[86] in January 1945. In fact, it was not the RPP's policy of secularism but its land distribution bill that led to the formation of a political opposition.

Because of domestic and external pressures,[87] the RPP government decided to transform the country into a multiparty system in early 1946. This led a group of dissident RPP parliamentarians to form the Democrat Party (DP – *Demokrat Parti*) in January 1946. The RPP parliamentarian Adnan Menderes, a large landowner from Aydın (a province in the Aegean region), became the spokesman for some of the RPP parliamentarians with landowning connections.[88] Menderes, along with three other RPP parliamentarians – Celal Bayar (the former prime

---

[85] Lewis, *The Emergence of Modern Turkey*, 303–4.
[86] The land distribution law aimed at providing adequate land for farmers who had little or none by distributing unused state lands, lands from pious endowments, reclaimed land, land without clear ownership, and land expropriated from landowners who owned more than 500 acres. See Zürcher, *Turkey*, 219.
[87] One of the external factors leading Turkey's transformation to the multiparty politics was the foundation of the UN in June 1945. Turkey, as a founding UN member, had to comply with the UN Charter, which is based on democratic principles. See Ali Eşref Turan, *Türkiye'de Seçmen Davranışı: Önceki Kırılmalar ve 2002 Seçimi* [Electorate Behavior in Turkey: Previous Breakdowns and the 2002 Elections] (Istanbul: Istanbul Bilgi Üniversitesi Yayınları, 2004), 13; Lewis, *The Emergence of Modern Turkey*, 304.
[88] Zürcher, *Turkey*, 216–17, 220–1; Cem Eroğul, *Demokrat Parti: Tarihi ve Ideolojisi* [The Democrat Party: Its History and Ideology] (Ankara: Sevinç Matbaası, 1970), 9–12. The first opposition party, the National Development Party, was formed in July 1945 by a rich industrialist, before the DP was founded. Yet, the National Development Party attracted little attention. See Ergun Özbudun, *Contemporary Turkish Politics: Challenges to Democratic Consolidation* (Boulder, CO: Lynne Rienner Publishers, 2000), 15.

minister), Refik Koraltan, and Fuat Köprülü – while maintaining their opposition to the land reform bill, submitted a proposal demanding that the Turkish Constitution be implemented in full and democracy established.[89] The RPP parliamentary group rejected the proposal. When the dissident parliamentarians continued their criticism in the press, three were expelled from the party, and the fourth, Bayar, resigned from the party and gave up his parliamentary seat.[90]

There was not a great ideological difference between the DP and the RPP. The main difference was in their attitude toward the proper roles of the state, the bureaucracy, private enterprise, peasant participation in politics, and secularism. Whereas the RPP wanted to maintain direct state control over the economy and to guard secularism, the DP advocated less state intervention in economics and religious affairs and a greater respect for religion.[91]

The introduction of the multiparty system led to Islam becoming a political issue in the competition for votes. As Kazan suggested in an interview with the author in February 2004, the RPP leadership, having realized that DP would capitalize on the religion issue in order to gain electoral support in the coming elections, decided to reappraise the party's secularization policies in the aftermath of its Seventh General Congress in 1947. In 1948, pilgrimage to Mecca was allowed. This was followed a year later by the reopening of the sacred tombs (*türbe*), which had been closed down in 1925. In 1949, religious instruction, which had been withdrawn from the public schools curriculum in 1932, was restored in primary schools as an elective course for two hours a week with the prerequisite of a written approval by parents. Also in 1949, the Ministry of Education set up the prayer leader and preacher courses and the faculty of divinity was founded at the University of Ankara.[92]

Despite the RPP's conciliatory policies toward Islam, the DP became the governing party following the 1950 general elections by securing 55.2 percent of the votes and 415 seats in parliament, against the RPP's 39.6 percent and 69 seats (see Tables 2.2 and 2.3).[93] The DP came to power by winning the electoral support of four sectors of society: the rising petty bourgeoisie (merchants), who were trying to increase their power vis-à-vis the state bureaucracy and etatism;[94] the rural population, who were ignored by the RPP elite; religious people (conservative Muslims), who were alienated by the RPP's secularist policies;[95] and the Islamic brotherhoods,[96] to whom the secular state, symbolized

---

[89] Zürcher, *Turkey*, 220.
[90] Özbudun, *Contemporary Turkish Politics*, 14–15.
[91] Ibid., 30; Margulies and Yıldızoğlu, "The Resurgence of Islam and the Welfare Party in Turkey," 146.
[92] Author's interview with Şevket Kazan, the vice-chair of the FP, Ankara, February 16, 2004; Toprak, *Islam and Political Development in Turkey*, 76–8; and Landau, *Radical Politics in Modern Turkey*, 172.
[93] Zürcher, *Turkey*, 227.
[94] Merchants wanted to invest freely and circulate their capital.
[95] Sarıbay, *Türkiye'de Modernleşme, Din ve Parti Politikası*, 92; Margulies and Yıldızoğlu, "The Resurgence of Islam and the Welfare Party in Turkey," 146.
[96] Ali Said Özkan, "Nurculuk ve siyaset" [Nurculuk and politics], *Yeni Şafak*, December 4, 1995, 2.

by the RPP, was antithetical. It is a paradox that the Islamic orders started to exert an indirect influence on politics as a result of the freedom they gained in the transition to democracy. Under Ottoman rule, in contrast, the Islamic orders were controlled by the *Meclisi Mesayih* (an institution, in turn, controlled by the head of the *ulema*, the *Şeyh-ül Islam*) for their appointments, promotions, and salaries, and thus could not exercise independent political influence.[97] The DP retained its hold on government by increasing its vote share vis-à-vis the RPP in the 1954 and 1957 general elections (see Tables 2.2 and 2.3). The military intervention in May 1960 ended the DP's decade-long rule (1950–60) (see Boxes 2.1 and 2.2).[98]

Despite Turkey's formally achieved secularization, Islam has remained as an important cultural force in Turkey. The secularizing reforms were absorbed by the countryside only to a limited degree.[99] Until the end of the 1960s, however, there was no movement of political Islam in Turkey. As Kazan argued in an interview with the author in February 2004, "the DP period was an era of Quran course and mosque construction. Yet, there was no consciousness of political Islam [at that time]."[100]

With the introduction of multiparty politics in 1946, the Islamic brotherhoods (*Nakşibendilik*, *Nurculuk*, and *Süleymancılık*) started to have an impact on Turkish politics by providing conservative votes from the countryside to center-right parties in the elections. However, while the majority of the Turkish people might have been religious in their private lives, they did not equate religion with the project of political Islam at this time. With the transition to democracy, a number of political parties based on Islamic themes emerged. Between the years 1945 and 1950, twenty-four political parties were founded, and at least eight had explicit references in their party programs to Islamic themes. The Nation Party (NP – *Millet Partisi*), which was founded in 1948 by a group of dissident DP members who were expelled from the party for breaching party discipline, was the most important religious party at the time. The NP affirmed "the need for religious reform," and demanded "greater emphasis on Islamic mores and values in social life, greater respect for Islamic institutions, an end to state control of religious organization, and the inclusion of courses on religion in the primary and secondary

---

[97] See Mehmet Demirci, "Türkiye'nin Çağdaşlaşma Sürecinde Tarikatler" [Tarikats in the Process of Turkey's Modernization], in *Türkiye'nin Çağdaşlaşma Problemi ve İslam* [Turkey's Modernization Problem and Islam], ed. Mehmet Demirci (Sempozyum [Conference]: May 3–4, 1997, Izmir) (Ankara: Türkiye Diyanet Vakfı Yayınları, 2000), 163–8; and Şaban Sitembölükbaşı, "Türkiye'de İslam ve Siyasal Sisteme Yönelik Olumsuz Tutumlar" [Islam in Turkey and Negative Attitudes toward the Political System], in *İslam ve Demokrasi Kutlu Doğum Sempozyumu* [Islam and Democracy], ed. Ömer Turan (Ankara: Türkiye Diyanet Vakfı Yayınları, 1998), 274, 277–82.

[98] In the 1954 general elections, the DP received 58.4% of the votes, while the RPP got 35.1%. In the 1957 general elections, the DP won 48.6%, while the RPP received 41.1% of the votes.

[99] Akural, "Kemalist Views on Social Change," 126; Lewis, "Islam and Liberal Democracy," 62; and Landau, *Radical Politics in Modern Turkey*, 171.

[100] Author's interview with Şevket Kazan, the vice-chair of the FP, Ankara, February 16, 2004.

An Overview of Turkish Politics 53

BOX 2.1. *Political Parties in Turkey*

Democrat Party (DP, 1946–60) (*Demokrat Parti*, DP), a center-right party, succeeded by the Justice Party, which was in turn succeeded by the True Path Party in 1983.
Democratic Left Party (DLP, 1985–) (*Demokratik Sol Parti*, DSP), a center-left party. Following the 1999 general elections, the party became the senior partner of the coalition government.
Democratic People's Party (DPP, 1997–2005) (*Demokratik Halk Partisi*, DEHAP), a Kurdish nationalist party with separatist goals.
Democratic Society Party (DSP, 2005–) (*Demokratik Toplum Partisi*, DTP), a Kurdish nationalist party with separatist goals. It is the successor to the People's Democracy Party and the Democratic People's Party.
Felicity Party (FP, 2001–) (*Saadet Partisi*, SP), an Islamist party. It is the successor to the Virtue Party.
Great Unity Party (GUP, 1993–) (*Büyük Birlik Partisi*, BBP), a party that combined elements of Turkish nationalism and Islamism. The party was formed as a result of a factional split from the right-wing Nationalist Action Party.
Justice Party (JP, 1961–80) (*Adalet Partisi*, AP), a center-right party. The successor to the Democrat Party. In the 1960s and 1970s, the party headed a number of coalition governments. The JP was banned in the aftermath of the 1980 military intervention.
Justice and Development Party (JDP, 2001–) (*Adalet ve Kalkınma Partisi*, AKP), an Islamist party. It is the successor to the Virtue Party. The JDP became the party of government following the 2002 and 2007 general elections.
Labor Party of Turkey (LPT, 1961–71, 1975–80) (*Türkiye İşçi Partisi*, TİP), a Marxist party.
Motherland Party (MP, 1983–) (*Anavatan Partisi*, ANAP), a center-right party. The MP ruled Turkey as the party of government between 1983 and 1991. Between 1996 and 1999, the party participated in a number of coalition governments.
Nation Party (NP, 1948–53) (*Millet Partisi*, MP), a party based on Islamic themes. The party was succeeded by the Republican Nation Party, a conservative party on the right, in 1954. The NP reappeared on the Turkish political scene in 1962 after a factional split from the Republican Peasants Nation Party.
National Order Party (NOP, 1970–1) (*Milli Nizam Partisi*, MNP), an Islamist party. The party was banned by the Constitutional Court in 1971.
National Salvation Party (NSP, 1972–80) (*Milli Selamet Partisi*, MSP), an Islamist party. It was the successor to the National Order Party. Between 1974 and 1978, the party participated in coalitions that were formed by the center-left Republican People's Party and the center-right Justice Party. The NSP was banned in the aftermath of the 1980 military intervention.

(continued)

BOX 2.1. *(continued)*

Nationalist Action Party (NAP, 1969–80, 1983–) (*Milliyetçi Hareket Partisi*, MHP), a Turkish nationalist party. Between the years 1983 and 1993, the party's name was the Nationalist Work Party. In 1993, the party returned to its original name.

Nationalist Democracy Party (NDP, 1983–5) (*Milliyetçi Demokrasi Partisi*, MDP), a center-right party. In 1985, the party merged with the Motherland Party.

Nationalist Work Party (NWP, 1983–93) (*Milliyetçi Çalışma Partisi*, MÇP), a Turkish nationalist party. The party adopted its original name, the Nationalist Action Party, in 1993.

People's Democracy Party (PDP, 1994–2003) (*Halkın Demokrasi Partisi*, HADEP), a Kurdish nationalist party with separatist goals. The party was banned by the Constitutional Court in 2003.

Populist Party (PP, 1983–5) (*Halkçı Parti*, HP), a center-left party. In 1985, the party merged with the Social Democracy Party to create the Social Democratic Populist Party.

Republican Nation Party (RNP, 1954–7) (*Cumhuriyetçi Millet Partisi*, CMP), a conservative party on the right. It was the successor to the Nation Party.

Republican Peasants Nation Party (RPNP, 1957–69) (*Cumhuriyetçi Köylü Millet Partisi*, CKMP), a minor nationalist party on the right. The party was formed following a merger between the Republican Nation Party and the Peasants Party. Later the RPNP was taken over by ultranationalists and renamed itself the Nationalist Action Party in 1969.

Republican People's Party (RPP, 1923–80, 1992–) (*Cumhuriyet Halk Partisi*, CHP), a center-left party. The party was founded by Atatürk in 1923. The RPP was banned in the aftermath of the 1980 military intervention. In 1992, the party reemerged on the Turkish political scene.

Social Democratic Populist Party (SDPP, 1985–95) (*Sosyal Demokrat Halkçı Parti*, SHP), a center-left party. The party was formed in 1985 following a merger between the Populist Party and the Social Democracy Party. In 1995, the party merged with the Republican People's Party.

True Path Party (TPP, 1983–) (*Doğru Yol Partisi*, DYP), a center-right party. It was the successor to the Justice Party. Between 1991 and 1997, the party participated in a number of coalition governments. The party renamed itself the Democrat Party in 2007.

Virtue Party (VP, 1998–2001) (*Fazilet Partisi*, FP), an Islamist party. It was the successor to the Welfare Party. The party was banned by the Constitutional Court in 2001.

Welfare Party (WP, 1983–98) (*Refah Partisi*, RP), an Islamist party. It was the successor to the National Salvation Party. The party was banned by the Constitutional Court in 1998.

> BOX 2.2. *Genealogy of Islamic and Islamist Political Parties in Turkey (1946–2007)*
>
> **Nation Party** (1948–53), a party based on Islamic themes. The party was closed down because of its political use of religion.
> **National Order Party** (1970–1), an Islamist party. It was outlawed in the aftermath of the 1971 military coup and was succeeded by the **National Salvation Party** (1972–80). The NSP was closed down in the aftermath of the 1980 military intervention and was succeeded by the **Welfare Party** (1983–98), which was outlawed by the Constitutional Court after the soft military intervention of 1997. The **Virtue Party** (1998–2001) succeeded the WP, but was outlawed by the Constitutional Court in 2001, whereupon the Islamist movement split into two groups: reformists founded the **Justice and Development Party** (2001–), while traditionalists founded the **Felicity Party** (2001–).

school curricula."[101] The party included Marshal Fevzi Çakmak, War Minister and chief of the General Staff during the Ottoman Empire, and later chief of the General Staff of the republic until his retirement in 1944,[102] and enjoyed some support in the press, such as the daily *Kudret* and the periodicals *Millet* and *Sebilürreşad*. Yet, the party could not mobilize the electorate in the 1950 general elections. It won only a single seat in parliament, receiving 4.6 percent of the votes.[103]

This electoral result demonstrated that religion, by itself, was not a crucial factor in determining the Turkish electorate's votes. Furthermore, it also showed that modernization in the context of an initially Muslim culture was insufficient to turn Islam into a political movement. Appeals to religion-based (or cultural) grievances attracted only a small percentage of the electorate. While the majority of the electorate supported a relaxation of the RPP's secularist policies, the electorate's major concern was their socioeconomic interests.[104]

In July 1953, the NP was banned because of its political use of religion. The party was soon reconstituted in the form of the conservative Republican Nation Party (RNP – *Cumhuriyetçi Millet Partisi*). The RNP had limited success in the 1954 general elections, receiving only 5.3 percent of the votes and sending only five deputies to the parliament, all from the same province (Kırşehir, a province in central Anatolia). In the 1957 general elections the party increased its vote

---

[101] Toprak, *Islam and Political Development in Turkey*, 75.
[102] In 1946, Çakmak joined the Democrat Party opposition against the Republican People's Party. In 1948, he left the Democrat Party and joined the Nation Party.
[103] Toprak, "Islam and the Secular State in Turkey," in *Turkey: Political, Social, and Economic Challenges in the 1990s*, eds. Çiğdem Balım et al. (Leiden, the Netherlands: E. J. Brill, 1995), 92; DİE, *Statistical Yearbook of Turkey, 2001*, 199.
[104] Toprak, *Islam and Political Development in Turkey*, 76.

share to 6.5 percent. Following the elections, the party merged with the small Peasants Party and became the Republican Peasants Nation Party (RPNP – *Cumhuriyetçi Köylü Millet Partisi*). In the 1961 general elections, the RPNP increased its vote share to 14 percent and fifty-four seats in parliament.[105] Nonetheless, in the 1950s and 1960s, the vast majority of the Turkish electorate preferred to vote for parties associated with either the center-right (the DP, 1946–60, or the Justice Party [JP – *Adalet Partisi*], 1961–80) or the center-left (the RPP, 1923–80).[106] Since political parties with Islamic themes were unable to mobilize the electorate against the secular state, the Islamic brotherhoods supported the leading center-right parties – that is, the DP and its successor, the JP – until the formation of Necmettin Erbakan's political Islamist National Order Party (NOP – *Milli Nizam Partisi*) in 1970.[107]

The Islamic brotherhoods, as "abeyance structures," focused on raising an Islamic youth through the illegal Quran courses under their control. Some Islamic brotherhood followers became civil servants at the Directorate of Religious Affairs and utilized state-owned mosques to keep Islamic collective identity alive. Yavuz argues that "these orders took refuge in the mosques and 'covered' themselves as the 'mosque community.'"[108] The leader of the *Nurcu* brotherhood, Said-i Nursi (1876–1960), believed "there is no such thing in between faith and *küfür* (impiety)" (*imanla küfrün ortası yoktur*). Working within the limits of his era, Nursi focused on saving the faith from atheism, masons, and communism. Nursi advised that Islamists should not get involved in politics until 60 or 70 percent of the nation became really religious. Until there were faithful cadres, he argued, it was improper to attempt to govern the state. He emphasized raising Muslim consciousness at the individual level, which would be followed by the collective adoption of an Islamic way of life. Nursi predicted that *Sharia* rule would be established and Islam would be the dominant force in the country in the future: one day, a faithfully raised generation would take control of the state.[109]

Professor İrfan Gündüz, a student of *Nakşibendi* leader Mehmet Zahit Kotku (1897–1980),[110] argues that Kotku always argued for "Muslims" to

---

[105] Zürcher, *Turkey*, 234, 243.
[106] "In the three elections held in 1950, 1954, and 1957, the two major parties collectively received more than 90 percent of the total votes and controlled 98 percent of the parliamentary seats." In Sabri Sayarı, "The Changing Party System," in *Politics, Parties and Elections in Turkey*, eds. Sabri Sayarı and Yılmaz Esmer (Boulder, CO: Lynne Rienner Publishers, 2002), 11.
[107] See also Birol Yeşilada, "The Virtue Party," *Turkish Studies* 3, no. 1 (Spring 2002): 71.
[108] Yavuz, *Islamic Political Identity in Turkey*, 140.
[109] Mehmet Gümüş, "Bediüzzaman ve DP" [Bediüzzaman (Nursi) and the DP], *Milli Gazete*, January 7, 2000, 2; Bekir Berk, "İslam sevgisini ekebiliriz" [We can plant the liking of Islam], *Milli Gazete*, October 4, 1991, 9. According to 1996 figures, Yavuz estimates that the number of *Nurcus* in Turkey ranges between five and six million. Yavuz, *Islamic Political Identity in Turkey*, 11. *Nurcus* such as A. Tevfik Paksu, Hüsamettin Akmumcu, Sudi Reşat Saruhan, and Gündüz Sevilgen played an important role in the formation of the National Salvation Party. Yavuz, *Islamic Political Identity in Turkey*, 174.
[110] Kotku was the leader of the *İskenderpaşa* congregation of the *Nakşibendi* order between the years 1952 and 1980.

An Overview of Turkish Politics

govern the state.[111] In fact, the *Nakşibendi* brotherhood under the leadership of Kotku played a crucial role in the founding by Necmettin Erbakan, a follower of Kotku, of the NOP in 1970.[112] Süleyman Hilmi Tunahan (1888–1959), another *Nakşibendi* sheik and the leader of the *Süleymancı* order, educated youth in his Quran courses beyond the state control. These youth later became prayer leaders and preachers all over Turkey. It is estimated that there are more than two million *Süleymancıs* in Turkey.[113]

The DP forged an alliance with the Islamic brotherhoods, mainly with the *Nurcus* and the *Nakşibendis*, in exchange for their electoral support. This led to a resurgence of the Islamic brotherhoods, their increased influence on politics, and a relaxation of DP policy toward secularism.[114] For example, after a twenty-three year apolitical life, *Nurcu* leader Said-i Nursi renewed his interest in politics with the DP's coming into power. He stated publicly that he would vote for the DP, and ordered his followers to do the same.[115] By doing this, Nursi aimed at "showing the politicians the right path and leading them to serve for the religion."[116]

Under DP rule, religious instruction in public schools was made virtually compulsory. It was made obligatory to furnish a letter for parents, who did not wish their children to receive such an instruction. Article 526 of the penal code, which forbade the call for prayer being made in any language other than Turkish, was amended. Arabic replaced Turkish in five daily calls for prayer and in sermons in mosques, and broadcasts of the Quran over state-owned radio started.[117] The DP also turned a blind eye toward the Quran courses of the Islamic brotherhoods. For example, *Süleymancıs* facing legal measures were released by orders of some DP parliamentarians and of Prime Minister Adnan

---

[111] İ. Selim, Ü. Oğuz, and S. Ömeroğlu, "Doç. Dr. İrfan Gündüz 'Hocaefendi'yi anlatıyor: Bizi devlete talip olmaya yönlendirirdi" [Prof. İrfan Gündüz tells Kotku: He directed us to compete for the state], *Milli Gazete*, November 14, 1991, 12.

[112] Selami Çalışkan's interview with a student of Kotku, Professor Cevat Akşit, *Milli Gazete*, November 21, 2005. Necmettin Erbakan, Fehim Adak, Lütfü Doğan, Cevat Ayhan, Temel Karamollaoğlu, Turgut Özal, Korkut Özal, Hilmi Güler, Recep Tayyip Erdoğan, and many other followers of Kotku became prominent figures in Turkish politics. Yavuz, *Islamic Political Identity in Turkey*, 141.

[113] M. Fatih Saraç, "Hatıralarla Süleyman Hilmi Tunahan Efendi 1–4" [Süleyman Hilmi Tunahan with Memories], *Milli Gazete*, September, 4–7, 1992, 9; Numan Turhal, "Süleymancılığın Doğuşu ve Gelişmesi" [The Emergence and Development of *Süleymancılık*] (unpublished B.A. thesis: Ankara Üniversitesi İlâhiyat Fakültesi, 1997).

[114] Esposito, "Muslim Societies Today," 201; Yavuz, *Islamic Political Identity in Turkey*, 62; Jenkins, "Muslim Democrats in Turkey?" 48; Özkan, "Nurculuk ve siyaset," *Yeni Şafak*, December 4, 1995, 2; and author's interview with Professor Binnaz Toprak, Istanbul, February 26, 2004.

[115] Margulies and Yıldızoğlu, "The Resurgence of Islam and the Welfare Party in Turkey," 147; Şerif Mardin, *Religion and Social Change in Modern Turkey: The Case of Bediüzzaman Said Nursi* (New York: State University of New York Press, 1989), 40, 98.

[116] Gümüş, "Bediüzzaman ve DP," *Milli Gazete*, January 7, 2000, 2.

[117] Ahmad, *The Turkish Experiment in Democracy, 1950–1975*, 365; Landau, *Radical Politics in Modern Turkey*, 174; and Zürcher, *Turkey*, 244.

Menderes;[118] in 1956, the case against Nursi and his followers, which had continued for eight years, was closed. The *Nurcus* freely printed copies of Nursi's book *Risale-i Nur* (The Epistles of Light) and distributed them throughout the country.[119]

While the DP co-opted the Islamic brotherhoods for electoral gain, it also passed a Law to Penalize Anti-Atatürk Criminal Conduct in July 1951. By doing so, the party aimed at putting an end to attacks by the *Tijani* Sufi order on Atatürk's busts and statues. Kemal Pilavoğlu, the leader of the *Tijani* order, was sentenced to fifteen years for his actions against Atatürk's memory.[120] The DP closed down People's Homes and People's Chambers in 1951 and Village Institutes in 1954, bringing an end to the enlightenment program of the Kemalist Revolution. The masses could not absorb the reforms, which stayed at the elite level.[121] Erik Zürcher argues that the People's Homes and People's Chambers were closely linked to the RPP. By closing down these institutions and turning their assets over to the treasury, the DP aimed at diminishing the RPP's organizational power.[122]

The DP came to power with the promise of bringing more liberalism and democracy to Turkish politics. Yet the party increasingly became a source of authoritarianism, with its resort to repressive measures against the opposition such as tightening the press law, jailing scores of journalists, using the state radio in a one sided-manner, banning political meetings and demonstrations except during election campaigns, barring judicial review of acts forcing civil servants to take early retirement, and changing the rules of procedure of the parliament so as to stifle opposition criticisms.[123] Having secured the majority of the votes in a series of general elections, the party concluded that it had received a mandate from the public, and hence had the right to monopolize and use for its own purposes all the institutions of the state.[124]

The DP also launched the *Vatan Cephesi* (Fatherland Front) campaign, which consisted of the daily reading on state-controlled radio of endless lists of people who had joined the front; babies, deceased people, and even fictitious names were included in the front's list. The DP thereby aimed at expanding its support base in the country.[125] In April 1960, the DP formed a parliamentary committee of inquiry, with extraordinary judicial and administrative powers, to investigate "subversive" activities of the RPP and some of the press.[126]

---

[118] Turhal, "Süleymancılığın Doğuşu ve Gelişmesi," 93.
[119] Gümüş, "Bediüzzaman ve DP," *Milli Gazete*, January 7, 2000, 2; Kıyasettin Koçoğlu, "Said Nursi ve Nurculuk" [Said Nursi and *Nurculuk*] (unpublished B.A. thesis: Ankara Üniversitesi İlâhiyat Fakültesi, 1996), 12.
[120] Yavuz, *Islamic Political Identity in Turkey*, 62.
[121] In 1951, there were 478 People's Homes and 4,322 People's Chambers. See Sina Akşin, "The Nature of the Kemalist Revolution," in *The Turkish Republic at Seventy-Five Years*, ed. David Shankland (Cambridgeshire, UK: The Eothen Press, 1999), 26; Zürcher, *Turkey*, 233.
[122] Zürcher, *Turkey*, 233.
[123] Özbudun, *Contemporary Turkish Politics*, 30.
[124] Ahmad, *The Turkish Experiment in Democracy, 1950–1975*, 44–5.
[125] Zürcher, *Turkey*, 250–1.
[126] Özbudun, *Contemporary Turkish Politics*, 31.

The DP regarded the state bureaucracy (civilian and military) as the main pillar of the single-party regime. The fact that many state functionaries maintained their RPP loyalties under multiparty politics was considered by the DP to be an obstacle to consolidating its political power. The bureaucrats, for their part, regarded it as their duty to protect the public interest against the DP's efforts to use state funds for political patronage purposes. They also viewed the DP's permissive policies toward religious activities as a betrayal of secularism.[127] Under DP rule, the bureaucrats' social status and political power vis-à-vis the rising petty bourgeoisie diminished. Furthermore, the DP's economic policy was based on foreign debt and inflation rather than industrialization, and the government's inflationary economic policies resulted in a deterioration in the living standards of the wage- and salary-earning classes, especially civil servants and military officers.[128] Thus, while the economic situation of the entrepreneurial class improved, discontent started to rise among the wage and salary earners.[129]

The DP's policies toward the Islamist movement, and its repressive policies toward freedom of the press and freedom of expression, led to the military intervention of May 27, 1960, which suspended electoral politics in Turkey until October 1961. The DP was outlawed, and its leadership was tried by a mixed civilian-military tribunal. Prime Minister Menderes, Minister of Foreign Affairs Fatin Rüştü Zorlu, and Minister of Finance Hasan Polatkan were sentenced to death.

In February 1961, the JP was founded, which inherited the legacy of the DP as a party representing rural interests against the military-bureaucratic alliance. The party also advertised itself as the "champion of Islam."[130] The Islamic brotherhoods maintained their electoral support for the center-right, now represented by the JP. A high-ranking officer in the Directorate of Religious Affairs argued in an interview with the author in June 2004 that the 1960 military intervention could retard the politicization of Islam in Turkey for ten years only.[131]

FROM THE LIBERAL 1961 CONSTITUTION TO THE 1971 MILITARY INTERVENTION

The aim of the 1960 coup was to preserve the secular Turkish state from a variety of ideological threats: leftist, ultranationalist, and Islamist. Under military rule, a Constituent Assembly was formed; it prepared a draft of the liberal

---

[127] Ibid., 31–2.
[128] "The DP's economic policies consisted of rapid import substitution-based industrialization and the modernization of agriculture, largely through external borrowing and inflationary financing. Although a relatively high rate of economic growth was achieved in the 1950s, income distribution became much more inequitable, with salaried groups hit particularly hard by the inflationary policies." In ibid., 32.
[129] Zürcher, *Turkey*, 236–7, 241; Sarıbay, *Türkiye'de Modernleşme, Din ve Parti Politikası*, 92–3.
[130] Toprak, *Islam and Political Development in Turkey*, 92.
[131] Author's interview with a high-ranking Directorate of Religious Affairs officer, Ankara, June 7, 2004.

1961 Constitution, which was ratified by a referendum in the same year. The 1961 Constitution guaranteed civil liberties, such as freedom of association and the press, worship and religious belief, and education, along with the right to collective bargaining and the right to strike. At the same time, the constitution threatened with criminal prosecution and penalties any misuse of religion for political purposes.[132] According to Article 19 of the constitution, "No individual can exploit religion in order to change the social, economic, political, or legal structure of the state according to religious principles, neither can he use religion to further his personal or political interests."[133]

The postcoup period also brought about institutional changes, beginning with the establishment of a Constitutional Court, with the power of judicial review over the decisions of the parliament and the cabinet. In addition, a National Security Council (NSC) was constituted, consisting of the commanders of Land, Air, Naval, and Gendarme Forces, the chief of the General Staff, and the secretary of the NSC, who had been a three-star general. The NSC assists the cabinet in making national security decisions. Under the 1961 Constitution, both the judiciary and the military gained greater autonomy.[134] Government oversight of the military was reduced by removing the military from control by a civilian Minister of Defense and placing it under the control of the prime ministry.[135] The judiciary was empowered by the establishment of a Constitutional Court. The military also encouraged freedom of associational life among citizens, in anticipation that it would have a limiting effect on the parliament.[136]

In the 1961 general elections, the RPP secured 36.7 percent of the votes and 173 seats in parliament (see Tables 2.2 and 2.3). The RPP led four different coalition governments between 1961 and the 1965 general elections. The coalition governments continued the DP policy of allocating substantial state resources for religious institutions (mosques) and prayer leader and preacher (*imam-hatip*) schools. In the aftermath of the 1960 coup, the military continued the Kemalist tradition of distinguishing between enlightened and reactionary Islam. The state implemented a number of policies designed to propagate and maintain enlightened Islam: the Directorate of Religious Affairs started publication of enlightened sermons to be delivered in mosques; the Quran was published in Turkish translation; and sociology, economics, and law courses

---

[132] Landau, *Radical Politics in Modern Turkey*, 175; Bilge Criss, "Mercenaries of Ideology: Turkey's Terrorism War," in *Terrorism and Politics*, ed. Barry Rubin (New York: St. Martin's Press, 1991), 125. "The prohibition of the political use of religion, which had been incorporated into the High Treason Law in 1925 and into the penal code in 1949, was now made an article in the new constitution." In Zürcher, *Turkey*, 260.

[133] Toprak, *Islam and Political Development in Turkey*, 91.

[134] Yavuz, *Islamic Political Identity in Turkey*, 63.

[135] Yavuz reports only that "The constitution also recognized the autonomy of the Turkish military by removing the chief of Staff from the supervision of the civilian Ministry of Defense." In ibid., 63. However, the role of the prime minister is widely acknowledged in the Turkish media and other reporting.

[136] Yavuz, *Islamic Political Identity in Turkey*, 64.

were added to the curriculum of the prayer leader and preacher schools in order to educate progressive and secular *imams*.[137] "Enrollments in imam-hatip schools more than doubled during the four years following the military intervention of 1960."[138] Ümit Cizre Sakallıoğlu, a professor of political science, notes that in the 1960s, "Enlightened Islam was regarded as the best bulwark against communism and religious fanaticism."[139]

Before the 1961 liberal constitution, Marxist (leftist), ultranationalist, and Islamist groups were suppressed by the state, and hence kept a low profile. These groups exploited the postcoup wave of liberalism in Turkish politics – and the liberalism of the constitution – as a political opportunity to establish their organizational networks. As Şevket Kazan noted, "before the 1961 Constitution, there were no ideological political parties."[140] Similarly, Nuri Gürgür, the Turkish Hearths (*Türk Ocakları*) chair; Uluç Gürkan, a former prominent Democratic Left Party (DLP – *Demokratik Sol Parti*) parliamentarian; and Professor Binnaz Toprak, during separate interviews with the author in February and June 2004, noted that ideological groups on the left and the right enhanced their organizational skills after the adoption of the 1961 Constitution.[141]

Leftist groups with varying interpretations of Marxism mushroomed, and the Labor Party of Turkey (LPT – *Türkiye İşçi Partisi*) was formed in 1961.[142] In 1965, the conservative RPNP, the successor to the NP, which advocated Islamic themes in the 1940s, was taken over by ultranationalists, thereupon adopting pan-Turkism as one of the party's official tenets.[143] Islamists also began organizing. They were influenced by the wave of Islamism in the Muslim world, which gained prominence starting by the late 1960s only.[144] Tarrow suggests that contemporary social movements have a transnational character by both crossing national boundaries and transcending state structures.[145] In the mid-1960s, the wave of political Islam in the Muslim world affected the ideas of Turkish Islamists. Translations into Turkish of the works of the twentieth-century political Islamists Hassan al-Banna (1906–49), Sayyid Qutb (1906–64),

---

[137] Zürcher, *Turkey*, 259–60; Yavuz, *Islamic Political Identity in Turkey*, 64.
[138] Toprak, *Islam and Political Development in Turkey*, 92.
[139] Ümit Cizre Sakallıoğlu, "Parameters and Strategies of Islam-State Interaction in Republican Turkey," *International Journal of Middle East Studies* 28, no. 2 (May 1996): 239.
[140] Author's interview with Şevket Kazan, the vice-chair of the FP, Ankara, February 16, 2004.
[141] Author's interviews with Nuri Gürgür, the chair of the Turkish Hearths, Ankara, February 20, 2004; with Professor Binnaz Toprak, Istanbul, February 26, 2004; and with Uluç Gürkan, the former DLP parliamentarian, Ankara, June 10, 2004.
[142] Jacob M. Landau, "The Nationalist Action Party in Turkey," *Journal of Contemporary History* 17, no. 4 (October 1982): 588.
[143] Jacob M. Landau, *Pan-Turkism in Turkey: A Study of Irredentism* (Hamden, CT: Archon Books, 1981), 145.
[144] Gilles Kepel, *Jihad: The Political Trial of Islam* (Cambridge, MA: Harvard University Press, 2002), 343; author's interview with Nuri Gürgür, the chair of the Turkish Hearths, Ankara, February 20, 2004.
[145] Tarrow, "States and Opportunities," 61.

and Abu-l-'Ala' Mawdudi (1903–79) played an important role in the reframing of the Islamists' political rhetoric in Turkey. But unlike the leftists and the ultranationalists, the Islamists did not form a political party until 1970. Instead, as Kazan pointed out, the Islamists entered existing political parties and acted individually.[146]

The Islamic Revolution in Iran in 1979 also became an admired model among Islamists in Turkey.[147] Ayvaz Gökdemir, the former Minister of State and prominent parliamentarian from the True Path Party (TPP – *Doğru Yol Partisi*), observed in an interview with the author in June 2004 that the Islamists in Turkey, despite sectarian differences, were very affected by the doctrines and implementations of the Iranian Revolution in 1979. The Islamists in Turkey admired Khomeini's establishment of a state based on Islam.[148] While the Islamists were reframing their ideology, the Islamic brotherhoods started to get strengthened. Sencer Ayata, a professor of sociology, noted in an interview with the author in February 2004 that as a result of rapid urbanization in Turkey in the 1960s and 1970s, the Islamic brotherhoods began to exercise a prominent influence over Turkish society by strengthening ideologically, financially, and organizationally.[149]

Even though the LPT had never received more than 3 percent of the votes,[150] under cold war conditions the state's main concern was the leftist movement in the country. This threat perception, alongside the U.S. cold war strategy, led Islam to acquire a new ideological dimension in the mid-1960s, according to which Islam was defined as an "antidote of communism."[151] Former Central Intelligence Agency (CIA) Middle East Policy Chair Graham Fuller argues that "there was a very strong leftist movement in Turkey at that time. And the Turks regarded communism as a greater threat than Islam.... The USA always pursued a double-track policy: On the one hand, we wanted the strengthening of democracy in Turkey; on the other hand, we tried to weaken communism. I guess we behaved contradictory at those times."[152] Thus, from the mid-1940s until the mid-1960s, the relationship between Islam and secularism was an issue that was exploited by center-right parties for electoral gain only. By the mid-1960s, while Islam was still a useful tool for electoral gain,

---

[146] Author's interview with Şevket Kazan, the vice-chair of the FP, Ankara, June 9, 2004.
[147] Hasan Onat, *Türkiye'de Din Anlayışında Değişim Süreci* [The Process of Change in the Understanding of Religion in Turkey] (Ankara: Ankara Okulu Yayınları, 2003), 93–4.
[148] Author's interview with Ayvaz Gökdemir, the former Minister of State and parliamentarian from the TPP, Ankara, June 11, 2004.
[149] Author's interview with Professor Sencer Ayata, Ankara, February 21, 2004.
[150] The Labor Party of Turkey, which was supported by young leftist intellectuals, received 3% of the votes in the 1965 general elections and 2.7% of the votes in the 1969 general elections. The party was outlawed in the aftermath of the 1971 military intervention.
[151] Ahmad, *The Turkish Experiment in Democracy, 1950–1975*, 376; Heinz Kramer, *A Changing Turkey: The Challenge to Europe and the United States* (Washington, DC: Brookings Institution Press, 2001), 64. See also Yavuz, *Islamic Political Identity in Turkey*, 62.
[152] "Tarihi İtiraf" [A historical confession], Devrim Sevimay's interview with Graham Fuller, *Vatan*, November 1, 2004.

"it was now an instrument to be used against the radical Left and on behalf of the NATO alliance."[153] For example, during the 1965 general election campaign the JP under the leadership of Süleyman Demirel chose the slogan "We are right of center and on the path of Allah," (*Ortanın Sağındayız, Allah'ın Yolundayız*), while accusing the RPP of being a communist party with the slogan "Left of the center is the road to Moscow" (*Ortanın Solu Moskova Yolu*).[154]

In the 1965 and the 1969 general elections the center-right JP became the governing party by securing 52.9 percent and 46.6 percent of the vote, respectively, and 240 seats and 256 seats in parliament (see Tables 2.2 and 2.3). The party maintained its alliance with leaders of influential Islamic brotherhoods, the *Nurcus* and the *Nakşibendis*, in order to cultivate rural conservative votes.[155] In turn, the Islamic brotherhoods tried to infiltrate into the state bureaucracy. Heinz Kramer notes that in the 1960s followers of the influential İskender Pasha congregation of the *Nakşibendi* order, under the leadership of Mehmet Zahit Kotku, systematically tried to infiltrate into the state bureaucracy, such as the State Planning Organization and the Ministries of Education and Internal Affairs. The *Nurcus*, who established a lasting relationship with the DP in the 1950s, maintained their ties with its successor, the JP, in the 1960s. The *Süleymancıs* also managed to establish connections with various bureaucrats and center-right parties.[156] The JP governments supported the construction of mosques and establishment of *imam-hatip* schools and Quran courses in order to court rural conservative voters.[157]

In the 1970s, some radical leftists decided that agitation was not enough; an "armed propaganda and an armed guerilla struggle" were needed to bring about a socialist revolution by destabilizing the country. The leftist movement started to resort to terrorism, perpetuated by the Maoist splinter group, the Turkish Communist Party-Marxist/Leninist (*Türkiye Komünist Partisi-Marksist/Leninist*, TKP-ML). The TKP-ML, in turn, spawned the Turkish Labor Peasant Liberation Army (*Türkiye İşçi Köylü Kurtuluş Ordusu*, TİKKO); the Turkish People's Liberation Army (*Türkiye Halk Kurtuluş Ordusu*, THKO); and the Turkish People's Liberation Party-Front (*Türkiye Halk Kurtuluş Partisi-Cephesi*, THKP-C).[158]

In the 1970s, ultranationalists organized themselves as a counterforce to the radical leftists. In the process, there was an important change in some ultranationalists' understanding of Islam. By the end of World War II, Turkism, rather than having a narrow approach based on Turkishness, focused on the threat of

---

[153] Ahmad, *The Turkish Experiment in Democracy, 1950–1975*, 382.
[154] Ibid., 377; Zürcher, *Turkey*, 263.
[155] Zürcher, *Turkey*, 264; Sakallıoğlu, "Parameters and Strategies of Islam-State Interaction in Republican Turkey," 240.
[156] Kramer, *A Changing Turkey*, 63–4.
[157] Jenkins, "Muslim Democrats in Turkey?" 48.
[158] Zürcher, *Turkey*, 268–9.

communism, and searched for potential allies against communism.[159] In the 1950s and 1960s, the ultranationalists were actively involved in antileftist organizations such as the Association for Struggling Against Communism in Turkey (*Komünizmle Mücadele Derneği*).[160] Such anticommunist associations enjoyed support from antileftist Islamist circles.

A division started to emerge among the ultranationalists in the 1960s. Because Turkish nationalism is a secular ideology, it was as opposed to Islamism as to communism. But this started to change in the 1960s: some ultranationalists began to add a Sunni Islam component to their ideology. In the pre-1960 period, the ultranationalists were clearly secular and regarded Islam as just one of the cultural components of the making of the Turkish nation. To value Islam as anything more than that was regarded as incompatible with the ideology of Turkish nationalism. Alparslan Türkeş,[161] who was elected chair of the RPNP in August 1965, was an outspoken supporter of secularism. Yet, he changed his tune before the 1969 general elections, when he started to emphasize Islam as a cultural component of the Turkish national heritage in order to attract conservative-religious votes for the party.

The party was renamed the NAP in 1969. In the aftermath of the party's Third General Convention in 1969, an ideological clash developed between the party leadership, which regarded Turkism as only one of several major tenets, and ultranationalists who regarded Turkism as the party's definitive principle. This difference became obvious during the discussion over the selection of the party emblem. While the ultranationalists wanted the grey wolf, symbol of the ancient Turks, the party leadership chose the three crescents, which represented a switch toward Islam. As a result, a number of ultranationalists left the party.[162] Tanıl Bora, a researcher on Turkish nationalism, argues that the NAP leadership's aim was to turn the marginal and elitist Turkish nationalist movement into a popular one. The integration of Sunni Islam into the Turkish nationalist ideology was completed in the 1970s with the slogans "Islam is our spirit, Turkishness is our body" and "Conscious and proud of Turkishness, ethics, and the virtue of Islam."[163] Jacob Landau explains the division in the ideology of Turkish nationalism as follows:

---

[159] Landau, *Pan-Turkism in Turkey*, 122.
[160] Ibid., 145.
[161] Türkeş, who made a career in the military, was one of the chief initiators of the 1960 military intervention. Yet, "he and a minority group of officers ('The Fourteen') were expelled by the majority of the officers' Council for National Unity which then governed Turkey and, in October 1960, were posted to various Turkish missions abroad. In February 1963, Türkeş returned to Turkey, resigned his military commission and entered politics. In 1965, he joined the conservative RPNP." In Landau, "The Nationalist Action Party in Turkey," 589.
[162] Ibid., 594; Zürcher, *Turkey*, 270.
[163] Tanıl Bora, *Türk Sağının Üç Hali: Milliyetçilik, Muhafazakârlık, İslâmcılık* [Three Situations of the Turkish Right: Nationalism, Conservatism, Islamism], 2nd ed. (Istanbul: Birikim Yayınları, 1999), 128–9.

Pan-Turkists were prepared to combat the leftists, but maintained a certain ambivalence towards Islamists, as their own sympathizers included some who were committed to a secular type of Pan-Turkism and others who were committed to a secular type of Pan-Turanism and others who had inscribed on village walls such slogans as Rehber Kuran-Hedef Turan (Our guide is the Koran; our aim is the Turan).[164]

In the mid-1970s, the Intellectuals' Hearth, in order to counter the leftist movement, formulated the Turkish-Islamic Synthesis (TIS – *Türk İslam Sentezi*) by combining elements of Turkish nationalism and Sunni Islam.[165] The TIS would be adopted and implemented by the military as a state policy in the aftermath of the 1980 coup.

The Islamist movement, which did not have a political party of its own as a counterweight to the leftist movement, was represented mainly within the nationalist-conservative wing of the JP. In the 1960s, the Islamic-oriented parliamentarians first tried to unite small conservative right-wing parties such as the New Turkey Party, the New Nation Party, and the RPNP. When this failed the Islamists tried to control the JP under the leadership of the JP parliamentarian Professor Osman Turan.[166] At the JP's Third General Convention in November 1966, the religious-nationalist dissidents (in Turkish, *milliyetçi-mukaddesatçı* – literally, nationalist-sacredentist) led by Professor Turan tried to eliminate the liberal wing within the party by removing Süleyman Demirel from the party's leadership. Their attempt failed: Demirel was reelected as party chair by receiving 1,239 votes against 175 for his rival Kadri Eroğan. As a result, the JP started to lose its ultraconservative and religious character.[167]

The JP, as the party of "industrialists, small traders and artisans, peasants and large landowners, religious reactionaries and Western-oriented liberals," had little ideological coherence.[168] The JP's emphasis on large-scale modern capitalist development created a small group of rich industrialists like Vehbi Koç and Sakıp Sabancı. The Anatolian petty bourgeoisie (small merchants and craftsmen) found it difficult to survive the competition from this modern sector. The political and economic power of large landowners and the petty bourgeoisie started to decline, while the state bureaucracy, to a great extent, lost its autonomy vis-à-vis both bourgeoisie classes. The JP's pro–big business policies led the petty bourgeoisie to search for a political platform that would articulate

---

[164] Landau, *Pan-Turkism in Turkey*, 144.
[165] Bora, *Türk Sağının Üç Hali*, 127.
[166] Süleyman Arif Emre, *Siyasette 35 Yıl*, vol. 1 [35 Years in Politics] (Ankara: Keşif Yayınları, 2002), 157–9.
[167] Ahmad, *The Turkish Experiment in Democracy, 1950–1975*, 242. Turan continued to accuse Demirel of sliding to the left by suppressing the nationalists, while not repressing the left sufficiently; serving vested interest groups rather than the mass of the people; and pursuing the RPP's secularist policies. In October 1967, Turan was expelled from the JP for violating the party discipline. In ibid., 242–3.
[168] Zürcher, *Turkey*, 263.

their demands. This need would be exploited by the Islamists as a political opportunity to create an electoral base for their future political party.[169]

By the late 1960s, Islamist JP parliamentarians Ahmet Tevfik Paksu, Hasan Aksay, and Arif Hikmet Güner; New Turkey Party parliamentarian Süleyman Arif Emre; and Professor Nevzat Yalçıntaş, chair of the Intellectuals' Hearth, started efforts to represent the Islamist movement in the form of a political party. Necmettin Erbakan, who was then general secretary of the Union of Chambers of Commerce and Industry, joined this group.[170] Erbakan became chair of the Union of Chambers of Commerce and Industry in 1968 and the defender of the interests of the Anatolian petty bourgeoisie against the big industrialists and traders in big cities. This led to the opposition of big businessmen in Istanbul and Izmir, which resulted in Erbakan's expulsion from his post by the JP Minister of Trade. The JP also vetoed Erbakan's parliamentary candidacy in the 1969 general elections. However, Erbakan won the elections as an independent candidate from the province of Konya (a province in central Anatolia) and became an independent parliamentarian.[171]

"Political Islam," which Şevket Kazan defined as "retuning to our core/identity (öz) and not imitating the West," emerged in 1969.[172] Erbakan founded the National View Movement (*Milli Görüş Hareketi*), which Kazan called the "(*iman, inanç*) faith," and formed the NOP in January 1970 with the support of the leading figure of the *Nakşibendi* brotherhood and the head of the related İskender Pasha congregation, Mehmet Zahit Kotku. The followers of the *Nakşibendi* and *Nurcu* orders also played an active role in the party's establishment.[173] Kotku gave his blessing to the establishment of the party by stating,

> In the aftermath of the deposition of the Sultan Abdülhamid II, the country's governance has been taken over by masons, who are imitating the west. They are a minority. They cannot represent our nation. It is a historical duty to give the governance of the country to the real representatives of our nation by establishing a political party. Join this already belated endeavor.[174]

Erbakan's National View Movement proposed a national culture and education, industrialization, and social justice based on the principles of Islam.[175] Because it is illegal to use religious symbols for political purposes, the party

---

[169] Sarıbay, *Türkiye'de Modernleşme, Din ve Parti Politikası*, 96–7, 105; Ahmad, *The Turkish Experiment in Democracy, 1950–1975*, 243; Marguiles and Yıldızoğlu, "The Resurgence of Islam and the Welfare Party in Turkey," 147–8; and author's interview with Yakup Kepenek, the RPP parliamentarian, Ankara, June 11, 2004.
[170] Emre, *Siyasette 35 Yıl*, vol. 1, 162–3.
[171] Ibid., 162–71; Sarıbay, *Türkiye'de Modernleşme, Din ve Parti Politikası*, 98.
[172] Author's interview with Şevket Kazan, the vice-chair of the FP, Ankara, February 16, 2004.
[173] Ruşen Çakır, *Ne Şeriat Ne Demokrasi: Refah Partisini Anlamak* [Neither the Sharia nor Democracy: Understanding the Welfare Party] (Istanbul: Metis Yayınları, 1994), 21; Yavuz, *Islamic Political Identity in Turkey*, 209; and Özkan, "Nurculuk ve siyaset," *Yeni Şafak*, December 4, 1995, 2.
[174] Emre, *Siyasette 35 Yıl*, vol. 1, 173.
[175] Necmettin Erbakan, *Milli Görüş* [The National View] (Istanbul: Dergâh Yayınları, 1975).

used the code words *national* and *culture* to refer to Islam, and *National View* to refer to the project of political Islam. As a prominent FP member stated in an interview with the author, "the National View cannot say that the laws are [should be] based on Islam. But it tells its [the idea's or ideology's] roots."[176] Erbakan argued that the Ottoman Empire, which established its dominance over three continents for six hundred years, was a successful experience; accordingly, Turkey had nothing to learn from the West regarding state governance. He regarded all political parties on both the right and the left as imitators of the West.[177] Erbakan declared that his party was open to membership for everybody, except masons, communists, and Zionists.[178]

Süleyman Arif Emre, a follower of the İskender Pasha congregation of the *Nakşibendi* order and one of the founding members of the NOP, reports that for a while party members thought the public would not support their movement.[179] Emre also notes that because the center-right and center-left parties already dominated Turkish politics, the NOP established its networks with some difficulty – a task it began after convening its First General Congress in February 1971.[180] Because the mainstream press ignored the party's activities, the NOP utilized the events surrounding the inauguration of its branch offices throughout the country for propaganda purposes. It also founded its own newspaper, *Milli Gazete* (National Newspaper).[181] By February 1971, the party had successfully established its networks in sixty provinces (*il*) and more than forty districts (*ilçe*).[182] In the 1970s, the party received electoral and financial support from culturally alienated and economically deprived conservative Muslims (petty bourgeoisie) in small towns and villages.[183]

By the end of the 1960s, the JP government was unable to deal with the worsening political polarization of the radical left and the ultranationalists and the growing political violence – including murders, kidnappings, bank robberies, and bombings – between the two groups.[184] Furthermore, there was also a polarization within the military between the left and the right, which led to the second military intervention on March 12, 1971. Özbudun explains the 1971 coup as a preemptive action by conservative officers in the military against radical (leftist) colleagues:

---

[176] Author's interview with a prominent FP member, Ankara, February 16, 2004.
[177] Author's interview with Şevket Kazan, the vice-chair of the FP, Ankara, February 16, 2004.
[178] Sarıbay, *Türkiye'de Modernleşme, Din ve Parti Politikası*, 99.
[179] Emre, *Siyasette 35 Yıl*, vol. 1, 182.
[180] Ibid., 191–2.
[181] Ibid., 183.
[182] Ibid., 192.
[183] Jacob M. Landau, "The National Salvation Party in Turkey," *Asian and African Studies* 11, no. 1 (1976): 5; Sakallıoğlu, "Parameters and Strategies of Islam-State Interaction in Republican Turkey," 241; and Çakır, *Ne Şeriat Ne Demokrasi*, 22. The NOP was closed down by the Constitutional Court on May 20, 1971 on the grounds that it sought to restore a theocratic order in Turkey.
[184] Özbudun, *Contemporary Turkish Politics*, 33.

radical officers, frustrated by the successive electoral victories of the conservative JP, aimed to establish a long-term military regime, ostensibly to carry out radical social reforms. In fact, the military memorandum of 12 March 1971 that forced the JP government to resign was a last-minute move by top military commanders to forestall a radical coup. Once the high command of the armed forces established control, it quickly forced the leading radical officers to retire – including five generals, one admiral, and thirty-five colonels on 17 March.[185]

The 1971 coup was thus a big disappointment for the leftists, who at first interpreted it as a 1960-type military intervention against a center-right government, and greeted it accordingly. Yet, as Zürcher puts it, "This soon proved to be a dreadful mistake. It was a 'coup' by the high command, not by a radical group of officers and the high command by this time was mesmerized by the specter of a communist threat."[186]

An interim technocratic government led by veteran RPP politician Nihat Erim was formed, which stayed in power until the 1973 general elections. In the aftermath of the 1971 coup, both the Islamist NOP and the leftist LPT were closed down by the Constitutional Court. Erbakan fled to Switzerland to avoid prosecution and stayed there until 1972.[187] But the military pursued only a mild policy toward the Islamist movement because of the rise of the radical left; it permitted the reestablishment of the NOP, contingent only on a change in name. Thus, the National Salvation Party (NSP – *Milli Selamet Partisi*) was formed as the successor to the NOP in October 1972. In a similar spirit, the leadership of the LPT was brought to court but, not that of the NOP.[188] Süleyman Arif Emre, a prominent NOP parliamentarian, remarked on the change in the military's approach toward Islam as follows:

Then the General Secretary of the National Security Council, General Refet Ülgenalp, was against closure of the NOP. Nuri Emre [an agent at the Turkish National Intelligence Service and relative of Süleyman Arif Emre] showed me the report of Refet Pasha. In this report, Refet Pasha was arguing that it was necessary to emphasize religious education in order to counter increased leftist anarchy. He even sent an army official to the National Education convention to prevent a decision against religious education.[189]

This was a conscious action by the military, which created a political opportunity that was seized on by Islamists entrepreneurs. The NSP's founders denied any connection between the new party and the NOP. None of the NSP founders were from the NOP. The NSP's chair until after the 1973 general elections was Süleyman Arif Emre. But, even though Erbakan called himself an

---

[185] Ibid. Radical officers represented the leftist faction in the military.
[186] Zürcher, *Turkey*, 271.
[187] Yavuz, *Islamic Political Identity in Turkey*, 209; Landau, "The National Salvation Party in Turkey," 5.
[188] Sarıbay, *Türkiye'de Modernleşme, Din ve Parti Politikası*, 108. See also Çakır, *Ne Şeriat Ne Demokrasi*, 22.
[189] Emre, *Siyasette 35 Yıl*, vol. 1, 221.

independent member of parliament, he was the party's shadow chair. He joined the NSP officially in May 1973 together with two former members of both the JP and the NOP, Hüsamettin Akmumcu and Hüseyin Abbas.

The NSP, in order not to be outlawed like its predecessor, kept a low profile. Within this framework, the party held its meetings at party headquarters rather than in public places. Erbakan's speeches were distributed to villages and towns in the form of audiocassettes.[190] The party's administrative board appointed Erbakan as party chair following the 1973 general elections.[191] Kazan argued, "the NSP had a living, that is, faith side" and reported the party aimed at three targets: "First, the priority of morals and spirituality leading to a spiritual development, which would lead to material development in the end. Second, equal distribution of wealth among the citizens. Third, a national, rapid, and widespread development, that is, the heavy industry leap forward (*ağır sanayi hamlesi*)."[192] The NSP "opposed secularism to the extent allowable under the law and strongly attacked communism, freemasonry, and Zionism."[193] The party criticized Turkey's endeavors to enter the European Economic Community, an institution that Erbakan defined as "a product of a new crusade mentality."[194] The NSP rejected capitalism, which it regarded as representing the rule of big capital, and socialism, which it viewed as limiting individual freedom, on the grounds that both were "materialist and selfish" and lacked a "moral basis."[195]

The party also emphasized the development of a strong organizational network. In January 1973, the NSP established its networks in forty-two provinces and three hundred districts. By early April 1973, the party had branches in fifty-two out of the sixty-seven Turkish provinces. A month later, the party had branches in four hundred districts in sixty-three provinces; and by July 1977, the party was organized in sixty-five provinces and in more than four hundred districts.[196]

In 1976, Erbakan founded the European National View Organization (AMGT – *Avrupa Milli Görüş Teşkilâtı*) for the purpose of creating a financial support base for his party among Turkish migrant workers in Western Europe. An Islamist organization called *Akıncılar* (Raiders), which was linked to the NSP, also emerged in the 1970s. The NSP's Raiders Network can be divided into three groups: first, legal organizations, which included *Akıncılar Derneği*

---

[190] Sarıbay, *Türkiye'de Modernleşme, Din ve Parti Politikası*, 109; Emre, *Siyasette 35 Yıl*, vol. 1, 186.
[191] Yavuz, *Islamic Political Identity in Turkey*, 210.
[192] Author's interview with Şevket Kazan, the vice-chair of the FP, Ankara, February 16, 2004.
[193] Marguiles and Yıldızoğlu, "The Resurgence of Islam and the Welfare Party in Turkey," 148.
[194] Ibid.
[195] Landau, "The National Salvation Party in Turkey," 11.
[196] Ibid., 6–7. *Milli Gazete*, April 6, 1973; *Milli Gazete*, May 30, 1973; Sarıbay, *Türkiye'de Modernleşme, Din ve Parti Politikası*, 109; and MSP Genel Başkanı Süleyman Arif Emre'nin I. Fevkalade Büyük Kongre Açış Konuşması [The NSP Chair Süleyman Arif Emre's Opening Speech at the First Great Convention] (Ankara, 1977).

(AK-DER – Raiders Association), *Akıncı Memurlar* (AK-MEM – Raider Civil Servants), *Akıncı İşçiler* (AK-İŞ – Raider Workers), and *Akıncı Sporcular* (AK-SPOR – Raider Athletes); second, illegal organizations, which included *Akıncı Liseliler* (Raider High School Students), *Türkiye İslam Kurtuluş Ordusu* (TİKO – Islamic Freedom Army of Turkey), *Türkiye İslam Kurtuluş Cephesi* (TİK/C – Islamic Freedom Front of Turkey), *İslam Devriminin Acil Mücahitleri* (İDAM – Rapid Freedom Fighters of Islamic Revolution), *Dünya Şeriat Kurtuluş Ordusu* (DŞKO – Sharia Liberation Army of the World), *Evrensel Kardeşlik Cephesi Şeriatçı İntihar Mangası* (EKC/ŞİM – Global Brotherhood Front Suicide Squad of Sharia), and *Evrensel İslam Kurtuluş Savaşının Türkiye Mücahitleri* (EİKS/TM – Turkey's Fighters of the Universal Islamic War of Liberation); and third, organizations that broke away from the NSP after 1977 including AK-GÜÇ (Pure Force), which changed its name to *İslam Kurtuluş Partisi Cephesi* (İKP/C – Islamic Freedom Party Front), *Türkiye İslam Mücahitleri Ordusu* (TİMO – Army of the Islamic Freedom Fighters), and *İslam Kültür Ocağı İslam Kurtuluş Ordusu* (İKO – Islamic Freedom Army of Islamic Hearth of Culture).[197] Despite the highly combative, revolutionary, or at least militant names of many of these organizations, there is little evidence they engaged in any actual political violence. They may have been merely empty shells, or only in the preliminary stages of preparation for later action.

In the 1973 general elections, the NSP won 11.8 percent of the votes and forty-eight seats in parliament, making it the third-largest party, after the RPP and the JP (see Tables 2.2 and 2.3). The NSP secured its electoral support mainly from small merchants; craftsmen; conservative, deeply religious Muslims; and people of low income in the semi- and underdeveloped central and eastern Anatolian provinces.[198] Yavuz argues that many voters were attracted by the party's promise of "rapid industrialization" rather than "Islamization."[199] However, data on the motivations of NSP voters presented by Toprak presented in the table in the following text (Table 2.1), suggests that the religious appeal of the party played a very important role in the mobilization of electoral support.

The NSP became a key party in the formation of coalition governments in the 1970s. The RPP formed a coalition with the NSP in January 1974, which lasted until March 1975.[200] Erbakan became deputy prime minister, and his party controlled the Ministries of Interior, Justice, Trade, Food and Agriculture, and Industry and Technology, along with the State Ministry of Religious Affairs. In March 1975, the JP Chair Demirel formed the First Nationalist Front with the NSP, the NAP, and the Republican Reliance Party.

---

[197] Yeşilada, "The Virtue Party," 66.
[198] Landau, "The National Salvation Party in Turkey," 20; Marguiles and Yıldızoğlu, "The Resurgence of Islam and the Welfare Party in Turkey," 148.
[199] Yavuz, *Islamic Political Identity in Turkey*, 210.
[200] In March 1975, the JP Chair Demirel formed the First Nationalist Front with the NSP, the Nationalist Action Party, and the Republican Reliance Party.

TABLE 2.1. *Reasons for NSP Support among Potential NSP Voters, 1973 Election Poll*

Reason	Percentage of Potential NSP Voters
Because it is a religious party	42.5
Because the Justice Party changed its goals and became a party of Freemasons	12.3
Because of Erbakan's leadership	9.4
Because of the influence of close friends or relatives	6.6
Because it expresses the respondent's own political outlook	5.7
Because the Justice Party has failed during its tenure in office	5.7
Because of rising prices	2.8
Do not know	0.9
Other	27.4

Source: Binnaz Toprak, *Islam and Political Development in Turkey* (Leiden, the Netherlands: E. J. Brill, 1981), 97. Copyright © 1981 by Binnaz Toprak. Reproduced courtesy of the author.

In the 1977 general elections, the NSP's vote share declined to 8.6 percent and twenty-four seats in parliament (see Tables 2.2 and 2.3). But the party participated in the Second Nationalist Front government with the JP and the NAP, which lasted from July 1977 until January 1978. Islamists infiltrated into the state bureaucracy when the NSP was part of the governments in the 1970s.[201] Furthermore, Ergin Yıldızoğlu, a Turkish scholar, notes that "While the NSP became the organized Islamist expression of popular discontent, an unofficial Islamist movement also grew alongside it," in the form of illegal courses, associations, youth clubs, and charitable associations.[202]

The results of both the 1973 and 1977 general elections suggest that the NSP's electoral support base was in rural areas. In the 1973 elections, the party received 67.2 percent of its votes from rural areas. In the 1977 elections, 63.2 percent of its votes were from rural areas. The party had a strong electoral base in the Kurdish-populated provinces in eastern Anatolia, such as Bingöl and Elazığ, and in Alevi-Sunni-populated provinces[203] in central and eastern Anatolia, such as Sivas, Erzurum, Kahramanmaraş, and Malatya.[204]

---

[201] Çakır, *Ne Şeriat Ne Demokrasi*, 22–4; Nilüfer Narlı, "The Rise of the Islamist Movement in Turkey," *MERIA Journal* 3, no. 3 (September 1999): 39.
[202] Marguiles and Yıldızoğlu, "The Resurgence of Islam and the Welfare Party in Turkey," 148.
[203] There is a traditional conflict between the Alevis and Sunnis; the former is identified as the electoral base of the Kemalist RPP.
[204] Yavuz, *Islamic Political Identity in Turkey*, 210–11.

TABLE 2.2. *Percentage of Votes Won by Parties in General Elections, 1950–2002*

Party	1950	1954	1957	1961	1965	1969	1973	1977	1983	1987	1991	1995	1999	2002
Center-Left														
Republican People's Party	39.6	35.1	41.4	36.7	28.7	27.4	33.3	41.4	—	—	—	10.7	8.7	19.4
Populist Party	—	—	—	—	—	—	—	—	30.5	—	—	—	—	—
Social Democratic Populist Party	—	—	—	—	—	—	—	—	—	24.8	20.8	—	—	—
Democratic Left Party	—	—	—	—	—	—	—	—	—	8.5	10.8	14.6	22.2	1.2
Center-Right														
Democrat Party	55.2	58.4	48.6	—	—	—	—	—	—	—	—	—	—	—
Justice Party	—	—	—	34.8	52.9	46.6	29.8	36.9	—	—	—	—	—	—
Nationalist Democracy Party	—	—	—	—	—	—	—	—	23.3	—	—	—	—	—
Motherland Party	—	—	—	—	—	—	—	—	45.1	36.3	24.0	19.6	13.2	5.1
True Path Party	—	—	—	—	—	—	—	—	—	19.1	27.0	19.2	12.0	9.5
Nationalist														
Nationalist Work Party	—	—	—	—	—	—	—	—	—	2.9	—	—	—	—

Party																
Nationalist Action Party	–	–	–	–	3.0	3.4	6.4	–	–	–	–	–	–	8.2	18.0	8.4
Kurdish																
People's Democracy Party	–	–	–	–	–	–	–	–	–	–	–	–	–	4.2	4.7	–
Democratic People's Party	–	–	–	–	–	–	–	–	–	–	–	–	–	–	–	6.2
Islamist																
National Order Party	–	–	–	–	–	–	–	–	–	–	–	–	–	–	–	–
National Salvation Party	–	–	–	–	–	–	11.8	8.6	–	–	–	–	–	–	–	–
Welfare Party	–	–	–	–	–	–	–	–	–	7.2	16.9[a]	21.4	–	–	–	–
Virtue Party	–	–	–	–	–	–	–	–	–	–	–	–	–	–	15.4	–
Felicity Party	–	–	–	–	–	–	–	–	–	–	–	–	–	–	–	2.5
Justice and Development Party	–	–	–	–	–	–	–	–	–	–	–	–	–	–	–	34.3

[a] The WP, NWP, and the conservative Reformist Democracy Party formed an alliance in order to meet the 10 percent threshold required to enter parliament. The coalition was disestablished following the 1991 general elections.

Source: DİE, *Statistical Yearbook of Turkey, 2002* (Ankara: DİE, 2003).

TABLE 2.3. *Seats Won in Parliament, 1950–2002*

Party	1950	1954	1957	1961	1965	1969	1973	1977	1983	1987	1991	1995	1999	2002
Center-Left														
Republican People's Party	69	31	178	173	134	143	185	213	–	–	–	49	–	178
Populist Party	–	–	–	–	–	–	–	–	117	–	–	–	–	–
Social Democratic Populist Party	–	–	–	–	–	–	–	–	–	99	88	–	–	–
Democratic Left Party	–	–	–	–	–	–	–	–	–	–	7	76	136	–
Center-Right														
Democrat Party	415	503	424	–	–	–	–	–	–	–	–	–	–	–
Justice Party	–	–	–	158	240	256	149	189	–	–	–	–	–	–
Nationalist Democracy Party	–	–	–	–	–	–	–	–	71	–	–	–	–	–
Motherland Party	–	–	–	–	–	–	–	–	211	292	115	132	86	–
True Path Party	–	–	–	–	–	–	–	–	–	59	178	135	85	1[a]
Nationalist														
Nationalist Work Party	–	–	–	–	–	–	–	–	–	–	–	–	–	–

Party										
Nationalist Action Party	–	–	–	–	–	129	–	–	–	–
Kurdish										
People's Democracy Party	–	–	1	–	–	–	–	–	–	–
Democratic People's Party	–	–	3	16	–	–	–	–	–	–
Islamist										
National Order Party	–	–	–	–	–	–	–	–	–	–
National Salvation Party	–	–	–	48	24	–	–	–	–	–
Welfare Party	–	–	–	–	–	62	158	–	–	–
Virtue Party	–	–	–	–	–	–	–	111	–	–
Felicity Party	–	–	–	–	–	–	–	–	–	–
Justice and Development Party	–	–	–	–	–	–	–	–	–	363

[a] The chair of the TPP, Mehmet Ağar, was elected as an independent member of parliament in the 2002 general elections.

Source: DİE, *Statistical Yearbook of Turkey*, 2002.

THE 1980 MILITARY INTERVENTION AND ITS AFTERMATH

The late 1970s was a period of "short-lived and ideologically incompatible coalition governments,"[205] which were unable to curb the political violence of the radical leftist and the ultranationalist groups. By late 1979 the growing political violence, inability or unwillingness of the RPP and the JP to reach a compromise to save the democratic regime, as well as an economic crisis led to the third military intervention on September 12, 1980.[206] From September 1980 to November 1983, the military regime that governed Turkey – the NSC – outlawed all existing political parties. The military, having realized that the increased ideological polarization of the 1970s had led to the political instability and terrorism, manipulated the electoral laws in order to eliminate ideological minor parties and transform the party system into a manageable two- or three-party system. A new electoral law passed in 1983, while maintaining proportional representation, introduced a 10 percent national threshold.[207]

Retired General Sabri Yirmibeşoğlu argues that the military regime's outlawing of all political parties and the introduction of new electoral laws did not result in a stable democracy in Turkey. On the contrary, it led to the partition of both the center-right and center-left, which was seized on as a political opportunity by the Welfare Party (WP – *Refah Partisi*).[208] Along the same lines, Retired General Doğu Silahçıoğlu notes that the 1980 coup, while eliminating the left in Turkey, increased the power of the proponents of the TIS and depoliticized Turkish society (the youth in particular), which in the end empowered political Islam in the country. Following the elimination of the left, the urban poor, who had been voting for left-wing political parties in the pre-1980 coup period, started to vote for the political Islamist parties.[209]

Turkey returned to civilian rule by holding general elections in 1983. But the military allowed only three political parties to contest the elections: the Populist Party (PP – *Halkçı Parti*), the Nationalist Democracy Party (NDP – *Milliyetçi Demokrasi Partisi*), and the center-right Motherland Party (MP – *Anavatan Partisi*). The MP became the governing party by winning 45.1 percent of the votes and 211 seats in parliament in the 1983 general elections, and 36.3 percent and 292 seats in parliament in the 1987 general elections (see Tables 2.2 and 2.3). The MP ruled the country for almost a decade (1983–91) until the 1991 general elections. Turgut Özal, the party leader, argued that his party represented four different ideological strands: conservatism (Sunni Islam),

---

[205] Ergun Özbudun, "The Institutional Decline of Parties in Turkey," in *Political Parties and Democracy*, eds. Larry Diamond and Richard Gunther (Baltimore, MD: The Johns Hopkins University Press, 2001), 240.
[206] Sayarı, "The Changing Party System," 14–15.
[207] Özbudun, "The Institutional Decline of Parties in Turkey," 240–1.
[208] Sabri Yirmibeşoğlu, *Askeri ve Siyasi Anılarım, 1965–1999*, vol. 2 [My Military and Political Memoirs, 1965–1999] (Istanbul: Zafer Matbaası, 1999), 215; Sabri Yirmibeşoğlu, *Askeri ve Siyasi Anılarım, 1928–1956*, vol. 1 [My Military and Political Memoirs, 1928–1956] (Istanbul: Zafer Matbaası, 1999), 281–2.
[209] Derya Sazak's interview with Retired General Doğu Silahçıoğlu, *Milliyet*, October 31, 2005.

nationalism, economic liberalism, and social democracy.[210] Thus, the party received electoral support from various groups: upwardly mobile, entrepreneurially minded, pragmatic, modernized groups that were predominantly urban and living in the developed areas of Turkey; occupational groups like the urban self-employed, businessmen, and upwardly mobile urban workers; urban migrants; former NSP and NAP supporters; and various Islamic brotherhoods (the *Nakşibendi*, the *Fetullahçı* [a leading *Nurcu* group that follow Fetullah Gülen], the *Süleymancı*, and the *Kadiri*).[211] The MP also received the votes of the electorate that would have voted for the political parties that were not allowed to enter the elections. The social democrats were already disillusioned by the 1980 coup, "while the traditional liberals had long been looking for an integrating leadership to take them out of ideological crisis."[212]

Özal's experience in economics as the deputy prime minister during military rule, along with his future-oriented policies, created an impression of being responsive to the demands of the people. For example, the MP received support from two major social democratic strongholds of the 1970s, securing 51.4 percent of the vote in Istanbul and 45.5 percent of the vote in Ankara.[213] In the 1980s and 1990s, the MP and the successor to the JP, the TPP, represented the center-right. The return of the banned political leaders (Süleyman Demirel, Necmettin Erbakan, Bülent Ecevit, and Alparslan Türkeş) to politics following the 1987 referendum, which lifted the ban, along with rising economic problems, led to a decline in the MP's vote share starting in the mid-1980s.

In the 1980s, the TPP's electoral base was drawn from the less-educated rural population of farmers and the traditional Anatolian petty bourgeoisie. In the mid-1990s, the party was supported by secular pro-Western middle-class voters as well.[214] Ultranationalism had been represented by the Nationalist Work Party (NWP – *Milliyetçi Çalışma Partisi*), which was renamed the NAP in 1983, while political Islam was represented by the WP (1983–98), the successor to the NSP.[215]

---

[210] Ersin Kalaycıoğlu, "The Motherland Party: The Challenge of Institutionalization in a Charismatic Leader Party," in *Political Parties in Turkey*, eds. Barry Rubin and Metin Heper (London: Frank Cass, 2002), 45.

[211] Ayata, "The Rise of Islamic Fundamentalism and Its Institutional Framework," 55, 62; Ruşen Çakır, *Ayet ve Slogan: Türkiye'de İslamcı Oluşumlar* [Verse and Slogan: Islamic Emergences in Turkey], 9th ed. (Istanbul: Metis Yayınları, 2002), 141; and Sakallıoğlu, "Parameters and Strategies of Islam-State Interaction in Republican Turkey," 243.

[212] Muharrem Tünay, "The Turkish New Right's Attempt at Hegemony," in Eralp, Tünay, and Yeşilada, *The Political and Socioeconomic Transformation of Turkey*, 21.

[213] Ayşe Ayata, "Ideology, Social Bases, and Organizational Structure of the Post-1980 Political Parties," in Eralp, Tünay, and Yeşilada, *The Political and Socioeconomic Transformation of Turkey*, 34–5.

[214] Ayşe Güneş-Ayata and Sencer Ayata, "Turkey's Mainstream Political Parties on the Center-Right and Center-Left," in *Turkey since 1970: Politics, Economics, and Society*, ed. Debbie Lovatt (New York: Palgrave, 2000), 96.

[215] Kalaycıoğlu, "The Motherland Party," 45.

The center-left had been represented by the RPP until its dissolution by the military in 1980. In the 1980s and 1990s, the center-left was represented mainly by two political parties: the Social Democratic Populist Party (SDPP – *Sosyal Demokrat Halkçı Parti*), which merged with the PP in 1985 and with the RPP in 1995, and the DLP. Both center-left parties defended secularism, although the DLP has adopted a critical stance vis-à-vis the RPP's elitist understanding of secularism.[216] While the RPP's voters had come from the university-educated urban professional middle class, the DLP's electoral base had been drawn from the poorer and less-educated sectors of the population.[217] Not surprisingly, the former DLP parliamentarian Uluç Gürkan commented in an interview with the author in June 2004 that "the DLP leader Ecevit argued for secularism, while being respectful to all faiths."[218] Table 2.4 shows party choice of the fully employed in Turkey.

Following the 1991 general elections, the center-right TPP, which received 27 percent of the votes and 178 seats in parliament, formed a coalition government with the center-left SDPP, which secured 20.8 percent of the votes and 88 seats in parliament. The TPP-SDPP coalition government lasted until the 1995 general elections, when the WP became the largest party, securing 21.4 percent of the vote and 158 seats in parliament. This was a great success for the party, which received only 4.4 percent of the vote in the 1984 local elections and 7.2 percent in the 1987 general elections (see Tables 2.2 and 2.3).

The WP's successful performance in the municipalities under its governance attracted electorate to vote for the party. By receiving 19.1 percent of the votes in the 1994 local elections, the WP was no longer a party of the rural and semi-developed areas, as had been the case in the 1970s. In the 1994 local elections, the party not only captured twenty-eight out of seventy-six provincial mayorships and leadership of 327 local governments, but also six major metropolitan centers, including Istanbul and Ankara. As displayed in Tables 2.5 and 2.6, by the 1990s, while the center-right and center-left vote share was declining, that of the Islamist WP was increasing, to the point where it became the main actor in Turkish politics.[219]

In the 1980s and 1990s, the WP and its successors continued to draw on the Kurdish-populated provinces in eastern Anatolia and provinces with divided Alevi-Sunni populations as their strong electoral base. These rural areas are characterized by more traditional populations, and Kurds in particular are not sympathetic to right-wing nationalists, viewing Islam as more inclusive. Yet, it was the successful increase in the party's votes in three major

---

[216] Ayata-Güneş and Ayata, "Turkey's Mainstream Political Parties on the Center-Right and Center-Left," 100.
[217] Ibid., 101–2.
[218] Author's interview with Uluç Gürkan, the former DLP parliamentarian, Ankara, June 10, 2004.
[219] Narlı, "The Rise of Islamist Movement in Turkey," 42.

TABLE 2.4. *Party Choice of the Fully Employed, 1988 (percent)*

		Employees						
Party	Public Sector	Private Sector	Professionals	Workers	Businessmen	Shop Owners	Farmers	Others
Motherland Party	20.4	26.2	15.1	13.2	29.5	26.6	18.6	20.5
Social Democratic Populist Party	41.6	41.9	58.6	38.5	25.2	27.3	32.9	32.0
True Path Party	10.7	7.9	10.6	24.1	22.1	22.9	27.9	20.8
Democratic Left Party	2.5	5.1	2.2	9.8	2.4	4.5	3.9	4.0
Welfare Party	6.0	2.2	–	2.1	10.4	4.0	1.6	4.9
Nationalist Work Party	0.3	–	–	0.4	–	2.5	0.6	–
Others	5.3	–	–	–	–	–	–	4.1
Nonvoting	9.5	–	7.8	3.8	–	2.8	2.1	5.8

Source: Ayşe Ayata, "Ideology, Social Bases, and Organizational Structure of the Post-1980 Political Parties," in *The Political and Socioeconomic Transformation of Turkey*, eds. Atila Eralp, Muharrem Tünay, and Birol Yeşilada (Westport, CT: Praeger, 1993), 35. Copyright © 1993 by Praeger. Reproduced with permission of Greenwood Publishing Group, Inc., Westport, CT.

TABLE 2.5. *Vote Share (percent) of Islamist Political Parties in General Elections in Major Cities, 1987–2002*

Party	1987			1991			1995			1999			2002		
	Istanbul	Ankara	Izmir	Istanbul	Ankara	Izmir	Istanbul	Ankara	Izmir	Istanbul	Ankara	Izmir	Istanbul	Ankara	Izmir
Welfare Party	6.9	4.2	2.3	16.7	17.6	6.0	23.9	20.9	8.4	–	–	–	–	–	–
Virtue Party	–	–	–	–	–	–	–	–	–	21.3	17.1	4.9	–	–	–
Felicity Party	–	–	–	–	–	–	–	–	–	–	–	–	3.7	1.1	0.8
Justice and Development Party	–	–	–	–	–	–	–	–	–	–	–	–	37.2	38.1	17.1

Source: DİE, *Results of General Election of Representatives 18.04.1999* (Ankara: DİE, 2001), xvi–xvii, xxx–xxxi; TÜİK, *Results of General Election of Representatives, 2002* (Internet ed.), http://www.tuik.gov.tr/secimdagitimapp/secim.zul (accessed November 25, 2005).

TABLE 2.6. *Vote Share (percent) of Islamist Political Parties in Municipal Elections, 1984–2004*

Party	1984	1989	1994	1999	2004
Welfare Party	4.4	9.8	19.1	–	–
Virtue Party	–	–	–	16.5	–
Felicity Party	–	–	–	–	4.0
Justice and Development Party	–	–	–	–	41.7

Source: DİE, *Results of Elections of Local Administrations, 18.04.1999* (Ankara: DİE, 2000), 2–3; TÜİK, *Statistical Indicators (1923–2004)* (Ankara: TÜİK, n.d.), 143.

cities – Ankara, Istanbul, and Izmir – that carried the party to the parliament in the 1990s. These cities comprised 26 to 30 percent of the electorate in the 1990s.[220]

As noted by Ali Çarkoğlu, a political science professor, the increasing Islamist vote in the 1990s must also be attributed to a striking change in the Turkish electorate during the mid-1990s. The data presented by Çarkoğlu, shown in the following text, demonstrates that between the years 1995 and 1999, at least one in five voters expressed their approval of the establishment of *Sharia* rule in Turkey (see Table 2.7).[221]

According to the World Values Survey that was conducted in 1997, the military was viewed as the most trustworthy institution in Turkey, while political parties were the least trustworthy. Only 6 percent of the respondents indicated that they had trust in political parties, while only 2.2 percent of the respondents indicated that they do not have trust in the army. The survey also showed that the religiosity of the Turkish people, which was 63 percent in 1991, increased to 83 percent in 1997. The respondents, who declared that everything was determined by faith, increased from 28 percent in 1991 to 37 percent in 1997.[222] The malfunctioning state has created a deep pessimism among the majority of voters (voter alienation) who believe that no political party deserves their vote. Thus, they choose "the least evil" among them.[223]

In the 1990s, while there was an erosion in the center-right and center-left political parties' vote share, that of political Islamist and ethnically based nationalist (Turkish and Kurdish) parties increased. Yet, compared to the nationalist

---

[220] DİE, *Statistical Yearbook of Turkey*, 2002, 200–1; DİE, *Results of General Election of Representatives 18.04.1999*, xiv–xv.
[221] Ali Çarkoğlu, "Religiosity, Support for Şeriat and Evaluations of Secularist Public Policies in Turkey," *Middle Eastern Studies* 40, no. 2 (March 2004): 117–18.
[222] "Toplumsal gidişatımız iyi" [Our societal future is good], *Zaman*, March 8, 1997, 9.
[223] Özbudun, *Contemporary Turkish Politics*, 79; Ayata-Güneş and Ayata, "Turkey's Mainstream Political Parties on the Center-Right and Center-Left," 91.

TABLE 2.7. *Approval of the* Sharia *Rule in Turkey (percent)*

	June 1995	March 1996	May 1998	February 1999
Approve	19.9	26.7	19.8	21.0
Do not approve	61.8	58.1	59.9	67.9
Do not know/no opinion	18.4	15.2	20.2	11.1

Source: TÜSES Foundation, *Türkiye'de Siyasi Parti Seçmenleri ve Toplum Düzeni* [Political Party Constituencies and Social Order in Turkey] (Ankara: TÜSES Yayınları, 1999), 68–9; Ali Çarkoğlu, "Religiosity, Support for Şeriat and Evaluations of Secularist Public Policies in Turkey," *Middle Eastern Studies* 40, no. 2 (March 2004): 118–19.

parties, the political Islamist WP was the only party that received the highest and steady electoral support. The 1995 general elections marked one of the lowest points for the mainstream political parties: the combined vote share of the two center-right parties (the MP and the TPP) was 38.8 percent, while that of the two social democratic parties (the RPP and the DLP) was 25.3 percent. The WP received the highest single-party vote share (21.4%). There was an increase in the votes cast for the right-wing NAP to 8.2 percent; the Kurdish separatist People's Democracy Party (PDP – *Halkın Demokrasi Partisi*) won 4.2 percent. Thus, the total vote share for these three parties in 1995 was 33.8 percent (see Tables 2.2 and 2.3).[224]

In the 1999 general elections, Ecevit's DLP ranked first by receiving 22.2 percent of the votes, followed by the right-wing NAP, with 18 percent of the votes. Frank Tachau notes the severe fragmentation of the Turkish political scene in the aftermath of the 1999 general elections. Three roughly equal groupings emerged: the center-right, the center-left, and the Islamist and nationalist right.[225] It is interesting to note that according to a survey that was conducted following the 1999 general elections, only 8.6 percent of the surveyed voters who voted for the Virtue Party (VP – *Fazilet Partisi*) believed the press should give first priority to human rights and democracy, a smaller proportion than for any other party. A much higher proportion of VP voters, 32.9 percent, said the press should give first priority to religious values. Although 18.7 percent of VP voters gave priority to traditions and moral values, this was not larger than the proportions of NAP and DLP voters, and not much larger than the proportion of even MP voters (Table 2.8).[226]

Yılmaz Esmer, a political science professor, notes the increase in the value of religion in the eyes of the Turkish public in the 1990s. In 1991, 63 percent of

---

[224] Özbudun, *Contemporary Turkish Politics*, 78.
[225] Frank Tachau, "An Overview of Electoral Behavior: Toward Protest or Consolidation of Democracy?" in Sayarı and Esmer, *Politics, Parties, and Elections in Turkey*, 38.
[226] Yılmaz Esmer, "At the Ballot Box: Determinants of Voting Behavior," in Sayarı and Esmer, *Politics, Parties, and Elections in Turkey*, 102.

TABLE 2.8. *Religiosity, Nationalism, and Voter Preference (percent)*

The Press Should Give First Priority To	Motherland Party	Republican People's Party	Democratic Left Party	True Path Party	Virtue Party	Nationalist Action Party
Nationalist values	10.5	4.3	15.1	15.1	13.6	31.8
Religious values	11.0	0.7	9.9	13.4	32.9	20.2
Traditions and moral values	17.4	3.2	20.0	12.9	18.7	25.2
Human rights and democracy	15.6	14.0	29.1	9.3	8.6	10.6
Secularism	12.8	18.1	32.2	16.1	4.0	12.8

Source: Yılmaz Esmer, "At the Ballot Box: Determinants of Voting Behavior," in *Politics, Parties and Elections in Turkey*, eds. Sabri Sayarı and Yılmaz Esmer (Boulder, CO: Lynne Rienner Publishers, 2002), 102. Copyright © 2002 by Lynne Rienner Publishers, Inc. Used with permission of the publisher.

those interviewed stated that "for me religion is very important." In 1997, 83 percent agreed with this statement.[227]

Following the 1995 general elections, a WP-TPP coalition government was formed in June 1996, and it lasted one year. The entry of the WP into government, Erbakan's actions as the prime minister, and increased Islamist activism led to the soft military intervention of February 28, 1997. As a result of pressures from the secular state, mainly the military, and from the secular segment of the society, the coalition government was dissolved in June 1997. An interim government composed of the MP, the DLP, and the Democratic Turkey Party (which was founded by a group of former TPP members) was formed, and it lasted until the 1999 general elections.

The WP was banned by the Constitutional Court in 1998; it was succeeded by the VP, which was outlawed in 2001. The Islamist movement then split into two political parties: the Felicity Party (FP – *Saadet Partisi*) and the Justice and Development Party (JDP – *Adalet ve Kalkınma Partisi*). Following the 1999 general elections, the DLP, the NAP, and the MP formed a coalition government, which lasted until the 2002 general elections. In the 2002 general elections, the JDP became the governing party by securing 34.3 percent of the vote and 363 seats in parliament. Both the JDP and the FP increased their vote share in the 2004 local elections: the former received 41.7 percent of the vote, while the latter received 4 percent.

---

[227] "Dine yöneliş hızlandı" [Leaning toward religion has increased], *Akit*, April 10, 1997, 7.

CONCLUSION

The rise of political Islam thus can be divided into two distinct periods. During the 1980s, the WP enjoyed only limited electoral support, and the movement focused largely on exploiting the military's adoption of the TIS to engage in grassroots organization building. It was during the early 1990s that the movement gained significant electoral strength, first at the level of provincial elections and, after 1995, at the national level, positioning itself to take power in 2002. The next two chapters examine these two periods in the development of the political Islamist movement in Turkey.

3

The Turkish-Islamic Synthesis and the Islamist Social Movement

This chapter analyzes the first phase of the mobilization of political Islam in Turkey (1980–91). The political opportunity structure (POS) exploited by Islamist political forces in the 1990s had its origins in a crucial policy choice made by the military government that took power on September 12, 1980. The coup was aimed at putting an end to an extraordinary outbreak of extremist politics and to the attendant political violence between radical leftists and ultranationalists. The coup was initiated primarily against the leftists.

The military's strategy for legitimizing the Turkish state and securing popular support for it involved a radical departure from the Kemalist secularism that had defined Turkey until then. The Turkish-Islamic Synthesis (TIS, a mixture of Sunni Islam and Turkish nationalism), adopted and implemented by the military and maintained by the center-right Motherland Party (MP) rule (1983–91), opened the door to organizational and framing activities by Islamist forces – activities reinforced by such external factors as the Islamic Revolution in Iran and the financial support of Saudi capital, and supported by an emerging Islamist business class in Turkey. These activities laid the foundation for the entry of political Islam into electoral competition and its eventually successful bid for power in the 1990s.

TURKEY ON THE BRINK OF CIVIL WAR

In the late 1970s, the Turkish political scene was characterized by a thorough ideological polarization between right-wing ultranationalists (*ülkücüs* – idealists) and radical left-wing groups, along with a lack of decisive authority on the part of the government. Polarization was manifest not only among political parties, but also in important social sectors, such as labor unions, the state bureaucracy, student organizations, teachers, and the civil police. Even though martial law was in effect in much of the country since December 1978, it could not contain the violence unfolding between the left and the right, partly because the police forces were themselves divided into two rival associations, right-wing

(POL-BİR) and left-wing (POL-DER). Economic problems including high inflation, industrial slowdowns, and shortages of consumer and imported goods[1] further exacerbated the political turmoil.[2]

Violence between extreme right-wing and left-wing groups was a daily occurrence. Among the victims of political assassinations were parliament members, university professors, prominent journalists, and a former prime minister. Traditional interethnic (Turkish-Kurdish) and sectarian (Sunni-Alevi) cleavages were exploited by political extremists in several provincial cities. In 1978, for example, Abdullah Öcalan, who was a student at Ankara University, founded the neo-Marxist Kurdistan Workers' Party, known as the PKK. Öcalan's aim had been the establishment of an independent Kurdish state in the southeast part of Turkey.

In the 1970s, the distinct identity of Alevis[3] was strengthened through rapid urbanization, and many Alevis adopted revolutionary leftist ideologies in contradistinction to the Sunni right.[4] In December 1978, the *ülkücüs* carried out a series of gruesome pogroms against Alevis in Kahramanmaraş (a province in southeast Turkey) that left more than a hundred Alevis dead.[5] In September 1979, the chief of the General Staff, General Kenan Evren, established a study group in the military under the leadership of General Haydar Saltık to determine the ripeness of the country for a coup. The Saltık report concluded that the country was heading toward a civil war, and, if military intervention was delayed, the military itself might split into two groups.[6] In response to the ongoing

---

[1] The growth rate of GNP, which was 3.9% in 1977 declined to 0.4% in 1979, while inflation rose from 24.5% in 1977 to 71.1% in 1979. Sübidey Togan, Hasan Olgun, and Halis Akder, *Report on Developments in External Economic Relations of Turkey*, 2nd ed. (Ankara: Foreign Trade Association of Turkey, 1988), 10.

[2] Frank Tachau and Metin Heper, "The State, Politics, and the Military in Turkey," *Comparative Politics* 16, no. 1 (October 1983): 24–5; Birol Yeşilada, "Islamic Fundamentalism and the Saudi Connection," *UFSI* no. 18 (1988–9): 1; Milli Güvenlik Kurulu Genel Sekreterliği [The General Secretariat of the National Security Council], *12 Eylül Öncesi ve Sonrası* [September 12th in Turkey: Before and After] (Ankara: Türk Tarih Kurumu Basımevi, 1981), 215–18; Kenan Evren, *Unutulan Gerçekler* [The Forgotten Realities] (Ankara: Tisamat Basım, 1995), 108; and Zürcher, *Turkey*, 277.

[3] Alevis belong to the Shi'a tradition and live mainly in Central and Eastern Anatolia. They combine pre-Islamic Turkic religions and traditions with the Shiism. For this reason, they are often referred to as a secular segment of the Turkish society. It is estimated that the Alevis represent approximately 15 to 20% (nearly 10–12 million) of the population. For further information on the Alevis see David Shankland, *Alevis in Turkey: The Emergence of a Secular Islamic Tradition* (London: RoutledgeCurzon, 2003); Tord Olsson, Elisabeth Özdalga, and Catharina Raudvere eds., *Alevi Identity: Cultural, Religious, and Social Perspectives* (Richmond, UK: Curzon Press, 1998).

[4] Meliha Benli Altunışık and Özlem Tür, *Turkey: Challenges of Continuity and Change* (London: RoutledgeCurzon, 2005), 41.

[5] A similar incident took place in Çorum in July 1980, when the *ülkücüs* attacked an Alevi neighborhood and left fifty people dead. Another similar event occurred in Sivas in July 1993, when the Islamists, who were provoked by atheist writer Aziz Nesin's contradictory remarks on Islam, set fire to the hotel hosting the participants of an Alevi cultural festival (the Pir Sultan Abdal festival). This was an indication of hostility, potential violence, and depth of conflict between the Islamists and others.

[6] Mehmet Barlas, *Turgut Özal'ın Anıları* [Turgut Özal's Memoirs] (Istanbul: Sabah Kitapları, 1994), 20.

political crisis, the Turkish Armed Forces sent a letter to President Fahri Koruturk on December 27, 1979, stating:

> Our nation no longer has the patience for people who sing the communist international instead of our National Anthem; who invite the sharia; who want to bring all sorts of fascism by replacing the democratic regime; and who want anarchy, destruction, and separatism by misusing freedoms that are provided by our Constitution.[7]

Between the years 1975 and 1980, more than five thousand people died and three times as many were wounded. Violence on the part of radical groups, which included assassinations, bank robberies, kidnappings, and bombings, became intense between the years 1978 and 1980. A total of 822,632 arms were confiscated – including infantry and automatic rifles, submachine guns, mortars, and rocket launchers – along with 5,454,925 rounds of ammunition. By the summer of 1980, the rate of political killings reached an average of more than twenty per day. Because the security forces were unable to restore order, neighborhoods came under the control of one or the other clashing groups and were declared "liberated areas."[8]

By September 1980, Turkey faced a civil war. There were forty-nine radical leftist groups involved in terrorism. At the same time, "right-wing terrorism was concentrated in the 'idealist' organizations with unofficial links to the Nationalist Action Party (NAP)"[9] (*ülkücü gençlik teşkilâtı* – the idealist youth organization). In contrast to the *ülkücüs* and left-wing groups, the Islamist National Salvation Party's (NSP's) Raiders organization (*akıncılar teşkilâtı*) was not involved in violence.[10] But the party's political Islamist themes represented a challenge to the legitimacy of the secular character of the regime.

The NSP organized an antisecular Islamic "Saving Jerusalem" rally in the city of Konya (September 6, 1980), where NSP supporters openly called for the destruction of the secular Turkish state.[11] The rally was organized to protest Israel's decision to proclaim Jerusalem as its capital city. During the rally, the demonstrators, while marching in long robes and fez and carrying green flags, called for the restoration of a *Sharia* order in Turkey by shouting such slogans as "Sharia will come, brutality will end," "Sovereignty belongs to Allah," "The Constitution is the Quran," "Secularism is atheism," "Government with Allah's rules," "We are ready for jihad," "We want [an] unlimited, classless Islamic state," and "Sharia or death."[12] The Islamists refused to sing the

---

[7] Kenan Evren, 12 *Eylülden Önce ve Sonra . . . Ne Demişlerdi? Ne Dediler? Ne Diyorlar?* [Before and After September 12 . . . What had they said? What did they say? What do they say?] (Istanbul: AD Yayıncılık A.Ş., 1997), 13.

[8] Tachau and Heper, "The State, Politics, and the Military in Turkey," 24–5; Özbudun, *Contemporary Turkish Politics*, 35; Zürcher, *Turkey*, 277; and Criss, "Mercenaries of Ideology," 143.

[9] Özbudun, *Contemporary Turkish Politics*, 5. See also Evren, *Unutulan Gerçekler*, 27–8.

[10] Yeşilada, "The Virtue Party," 66–7.

[11] Özbudun, *Contemporary Turkish Politics*, 36; Jeremy Salt, "Nationalism and the Rise of Muslim Sentiment in Turkey," *Middle Eastern Studies* 31, no. 1 (January 1995): 3 (Internet ed.).

[12] *Milliyet*, September 7, 1980; The General Secretariat of the National Security Council, *12 Eylül Öncesi ve Sonrası*, 187.

national anthem, instead declaring "Rebellion to the system," "The Sharia is the *hak* [God's order; a just order]; [an] unbeliever is [a] traitor," and "We want the call of prayer (*ezan*); we do not sing this anthem."

In his speech at the rally, NSP leader Necmettin Erbakan declared that his National View (*Milli Görüş*) Movement, rather than the "Western club," would save and strengthen Turkey. His speech was frequently interrupted by the Islamists' slogan "Tell us to shoot, we will shoot; tell us to die, we will die."[13] Turkish Islamists who had migrated to West European countries also organized marches calling for a *Sharia* order in Turkey. In September 1980, such marches took place in Bonn and Munich, where the Islamists proclaimed "The Great Jihad March," "Muslim Turkey – Islam is the only way," and "Today Iran – Tomorrow Turkey."[14] The "Saving Jerusalem" rally in Konya was the last straw that finally led the military to act. The third military intervention in Turkish politics was carried out in September 1980 and aimed at bringing an end to the violence of extreme right-wing and left-wing groups, as well as to the threat of political Islam embodied in the NSP.

It may also have been a preemptive strike against efforts to undermine the military. The polarization within the Turkish Armed Forces anticipated by General Saltık and the General Staff appeared to be underway. On October 30, 1980, Chief of the General Staff General Evren reminded the public:

> the Turkish Armed Forces would never allow the Turkish Republic, which they inherited from Atatürk, to be taken over by traitors. No one should attempt, for evil purposes, to take advantage of the patience of the military and their seriousness of purpose concerning this issue. But they did not understand me. Instead, *they made the mistake of thinking they could infiltrate the Armed Forces, divide them, and so realize their detestable goals.* For them the most important thing was not the general welfare of the nation, but the particular interests of their political parties. The sole *raison d'etre* of the Turkish Armed Forces is to defend this great country as an indivisible whole against its internal as well as external enemies, and of seeing to it that this country will always be secure and its citizens happy and well cared for.[15]

TURKEY UNDER MILITARY RULE (1980–1983): THE MILITARY AND THE ISLAMISTS

The Turkish Armed Forces declared that they had taken over political power because state organs had ceased to function. The parliament was dissolved, immunity of parliamentarians was lifted, and all political parties, along with two extremist trade union confederations (the socialist DİSK – *Devrimci İşçi Sendikaları Konfederasyonu* [Confederation of Revolutionary Trade Unions] and the ultranationalist MİSK – *Milliyetçi İşçi Sendikaları Konfederasyonu*

---

[13] The General Secretariat of the National Security Council, *12 Eylül Öncesi ve Sonrası*, 187.
[14] Ibid., 188.
[15] *Milliyet*, October 30, 1980, 5 from Tachau and Heper, "The State, Politics, and the Military in Turkey," 28 (emphasis added).

[Confederation of Nationalist Trade Unions]), were suspended.[16] All mayors and municipal councils were dismissed.[17] The autonomy of universities was abolished. The National Security Council (NSC), which was headed by General Evren, appointed a mixed civilian-military cabinet[18] led by a retired admiral, Bülent Ulusu, which governed Turkey from September 1980 until November 1983. The cabinet's only function was to advise the NSC and execute its decisions, while the NSC reserved the right to fire individual ministers. In addition to the cabinet, the NSC also acted through regional and local commanders who, under martial law, were given very wide-ranging powers; for example, the commanders were put in charge of education, the press, chambers of commerce, and trade unions.[19] The military regime's primary goal was the elimination of anarchy and terror in the country.[20]

Both Feroz Ahmad and Kemal Karpat note that there were two factions within the military under the ideological umbrella of Kemalism. The moderates wanted a less harsh regime and an earlier restoration of power to civilians by forming an alliance with second-layer politicians from the old political parties. The hard-liners favored a stronger military rule and wanted a thorough restructuring of the political system, in order to eliminate pre-1980 coup politicians once and for all, and the creation of a new political party when the country was ready to return to democracy. The decision to close down all political parties, including the center-right Justice Party (JP) and the center-left Republican People's Party (RPP) came after the hard-line faction gained the upper hand.[21] General Evren made it clear that former politicians would not be allowed to return to politics again. On September 17, 1980, General Evren commented to his colleagues,

All my trust in the politicians has been rubbed away. If they are all asking their leaders what to do, it means that in practice they will go on doing the same thing. We need people who really believe in us and will stick with us. Let's give up the idea of forming a government made up of the RPP and JP moderates.[22]

The military, in addition to former politicians, prohibited all public discussion of political matters.[23]

---

[16] Feroz Ahmad notes that even though MİSK members never went on strike, the military suspended the labor union in order to create the impression that it was impartial between the left and the right: "of the 51,000 striking workers in September 1980, 47,319 belonged to DISK and the remainder to Türk-İş." In Ahmad, *The Making of Modern Turkey* (London: Routledge, 1993), 182.

[17] Zürcher, *Turkey*, 293.

[18] The cabinet of 27 was composed of 6 retired generals and the remainder were bureaucrats and academicians. None of the cabinet members were active or former politicians.

[19] Zürcher, *Turkey*, 293.

[20] Evren, *Unutulan Gerçekler*, 75; Zürcher, *Turkey*, 292–3.

[21] Ahmad, *The Making of Modern Turkey*, 182; Kemal Karpat, "Military Interventions: Army-Civilian Relations in Turkey before and after 1980," in *State, Democracy, and the Military: Turkey in the 1980s*, eds. Metin Heper and Ahmet Evin (New York: Walter de Gruyter, 1988), 153.

[22] William Hale, "Transition to Civilian Governments in Turkey," in Heper and Evin, *State, Democracy, and the Military in Turkey in the 1980s*, 167.

[23] Zürcher, *Turkey*, 293.

There were also personnel shifts within the military after the hard-liners gained the upper hand. Retired General Nevzat Bölügiray notes that proright personnel were promoted and proleft personnel were eliminated.[24] Karpat reports, for example, that "General Necdet Üruğ became the Secretary and Coordinator of the NSC, while General Haydar Saltık, rumored to have demanded lenient treatment for leftists not involved in violence, was sent to complete his field duty as Commander of the First Army in control of Istanbul, the Straits, and Thrace."[25] Thus, General Saltık would no longer have an influence on the NSC's decisions.

In the aftermath of the 1980 coup, 650,000 people were arrested, 1,683,000 prosecutions were prepared, and 517 people were sentenced to death; 49 of the death sentences were carried out. Furthermore, 30,000 people were fired from their jobs for holding political views incompatible with the state, 14,000 had their Turkish citizenship revoked, and 667 associations and foundations were banned.[26] The coup leader, General Evren, explained the takeover as follows:

The aim of the operation is to safeguard the integrity of the country, to provide for national unity and fraternity, to prevent the existence and the possibility of a civil war and internecine struggle, to reestablish the existence and the authority of the state, and to eliminate the factors that hinder the smooth working of the democratic order.[27]

In the aftermath of the coup, both JP Chair Süleyman Demirel and RPP Chair Bülent Ecevit were held in protective custody. Both leaders were released on October 11, 1980, as there were no legal grounds for prosecuting them. Both the right-wing NAP and the Islamist NSP leaders, however, were prosecuted for breaking the law and violating the constitution. The NSP's Erbakan was charged with undermining the principle of secularism. The NAP's Türkeş was charged, along with 585 members of his party, with instigating civil war and murdering about six hundred people between 1974 and 1980.[28] Erbakan was subsequently acquitted, and Türkeş was released for medical reasons in 1985.[29]

The military regime eliminated the leftists and diminished the power of the ultranationalists. But even though the NSP was closed down for a second time,

---

[24] Nevzat Bölügiray, 28 Şubat Süreci, vol. 2 [The February 28th Process] (Istanbul: Tekin Yayınevi, 2000), 20. Retired General Bölügiray was the Turkish General Staff, Martial Order Coordination chair between December 10, 1980 and September 2, 1983.
[25] Karpat, "Military Interventions," 153.
[26] Yavuz, Islamic Political Identity in Turkey, 69; Milliyet, September 12, 1998.
[27] The General Secretariat of the National Security Council, 12 Eylül: Öncesi ve Sonrası, 229 from Tachau and Heper, "The State, Politics, and the Military in Turkey," 26.
[28] Hale, "Transition to Civilian Governments in Turkey," 167–8.
[29] Erbakan and his party members received a formal acquittal in September 1985. Türkeş was convicted, but released for medical reasons in April 1985. Hale, "Transition to Civilian Governments in Turkey," 168.

the Islamist movement was not eliminated under military rule (1980–3).[30] Because of the ongoing global threat of communism, the military's foremost concern was the rise of radical leftism and the anarchy that it created in the country. In an interview with the author in February 2004, a retired general pointed out that "on the eve of September 12th the Islamists, unlike the radical leftists and *ülkücüs* (idealists, or ultranationalists), were not involved in street violence; thus, they hid themselves well."[31] Retired General Bölügiray makes a similar argument by noting that in the pre-1980 coup period, even though political Islam had a presence in the country, unlike the radical left and the ultranationalists, it was an unorganized movement at that time. Unlike the numerous organizations of the radical left and ultranationalists, there was only the *Akıncılar* (Raiders) organization, tied to the NSP representing the Islamist movement, which was not involved in violence.[32] The fact that the NSP was not involved in violence led the military not to view political Islam as an imminent threat. While breaking the backbone of the NAP and its paramilitary organizations, the military focused primarily on the left-wing groups. Even though the Islamist Iranian Revolution took place in Iran in 1979, which gave inspiration to the Turkish Islamists at that time, the military defined communism as the number-one threat. In separate interviews with the author, Retired General Çevik Bir, who had a high-ranking position during the 1980 coup, and the vice-chair of the Felicity Party (FP), Şevket Kazan, both suggested that "September 12th was initiated primarily against the left."[33] Kazan also argued that "the military supported the American green belt project (*yeşil kuşak projesi*)."[34] Graham Fuller, the former CIA Middle East Policy chair, while noting that "he was one of the most outspoken individuals in this project," explained the aim of the U.S. green belt project in an interview with the Turkish press in November 2004: "It was for containing Soviet expansion toward the south during the Cold War. I guess the idea was ours. But at that time all Muslim states understood that Islam was a very strong wall against communism."[35] Turkey was included in the green belt project, Fuller notes, "Because there was a very strong left in Turkey. The same was true for Iran. . . . In the 1950s, 1960s, and 1970s, communism was a very strong movement. And, in Turkey, Islam was not so effective against communism. Islam was weak, but leftism

---

[30] Karmon, "The Demise of Radical Islam in Turkey," 1. Nevzat Bölügiray, *Sokaktaki Askerin Dönüşü: 12 Eylül Yönetimi Dönemi* [Return of the Soldier on Street: The September 12th Governance Period] (Istanbul: Tekin Yayınevi, 1991), 198. Retired General Bölügiray notes that civil servants who participated in left-wing political gatherings were expelled from their positions. But civil servants (*muftis* and prayer leaders) (except 3 or 5), who participated in the NSP's "Saving Jerusalem" rally, continued to hold their positions under the military regime. In ibid., 200–3.

[31] Author's interview with a retired general, Istanbul, February 27, 2004.

[32] Bölügiray, *Sokaktaki Askerin Dönüşü*, 197–8.

[33] Author's interview with Retired General Çevik Bir, Istanbul, February 27, 2004; author's interview with Şevket Kazan, the vice-chair of the FP, Ankara, February 16, 2004.

[34] Author's interview with Şevket Kazan, the vice-chair of the FP, Ankara, February 16, 2004.

[35] "Tarihi İtiraf," Devrim Sevimay's interview with Graham Fuller, *Vatan*, November 1, 2004.

was strong."[36] Yet, even though he regards this project as "a very correct thesis," on the grounds that "Islam was a real wall against communism,"[37] Kazan noted, "The USA supported Turkey for this job. Yet, it [the United States] could not predict what kind of a result it would lead to in the end. When the Americans realized this, [the rise of political Islam in Turkey] they started to reject it."[38] Along the same lines as Kazan, Retired General Güven Erkaya, who was the commander of Navy Forces during the 1997 soft military intervention, noted that during the cold war the United States regarded Islam as a counterforce against communism in Turkey. Yet, upon realizing that this was a big mistake, as a result of the rise of political Islam in Turkey in the 1990s, the United States started to declare totally different views.[39]

In the aftermath of the coup, General Evren argued that the military gave priority to struggling against anarchy and providing stability in the country.[40] It is important to note that the military, while eliminating the left-wing groups, also diminished the power of the right-wing ultranationalists. This was a reversal of its earlier approach to the latter. In the late 1960s and 1970s, the military considered the ultranationalists to be both a useful tool against communists and a force that should and could be controlled. The *ülkücüs* were claiming that they were fighting against communists as a civil force alongside the state. Indeed, the NAP supported the second military intervention of March 12, 1971 to such an extent that in its 1973 general election pamphlet it declared that as a result of the intervention, "the *ülkücü* youth transferred its duty to the honorable armed forces."[41] In the aftermath of the 1971 coup, the military closed down the *ülkü ocakları* (ideas hearths – organizations attached to the NAP, and not to be confused with the Intellectuals' Hearth [IH – *Aydınlar Ocağı*]) as a way to control the movement. Yet, the *ülkücü* movement, which was still useful against the communists, continued to exist.

In the 1970s, the *ülkücüs* were trained with the mission of fighting against communism to assist the state when it was weak. The NAP leadership knew that there were followers of their anticommunist stance in the military and the state.[42] The suppression of the *ülkücüs* in the aftermath of the 1980 coup,

---

[36] Ibid.
[37] Ibid.
[38] Author's interview with Şevket Kazan, the vice-chair of the FP, Ankara, February 16, 2004.
[39] Taner Baytok, *Bir Asker Bir Diplomat: Güven Erkaya-Taner Baytok Söyleşi* [One Soldier One Diplomat: Güven Erkaya-Taner Baytok Conversation], 3rd ed. (Istanbul: Doğan Kitapçılık, 2001), 238.
[40] T.C. Başbakanlık [Turkish Republic Prime Ministry], *T.C. Devlet Başkanı Orgeneral Kenan Evren'in Söylev ve Demeçleri (12 Eylül 1980–12 Eylül 1981)* [The Turkish Republic Head of the State General Kenan Evren's Speeches (12 September 1980–12 September 1981)] (Ankara: Başbakanlık Basımevi, 1981), 398.
[41] Tanıl Bora and Kemal Can, *Devlet, Ocak, Dergâh: 12 Eylül'den 1990'lara Ülkücü Hareket* [State, Hearth, Dergâh: The Idealist Movement from September 12th to the 1990s], 6th ed. (Istanbul: İletişim Yayınları, 2000), 59.
[42] Ibid., 101. Retired General Bölügiray notes that there were high-ranking military officers who were praising the ultranationalists' siding with the state in the fight against the communists. Bölügiray, *Sokaktaki Askerin Dönüşü*, 23.

nearly to the same extent as that of the communists, came as a great shock to the ultranationalists. Tanıl Bora and Kemal Can, researchers on Turkish nationalism, argue that the NAP leadership could not comprehend the fact that the military had never regarded the party as a serious element of a future leadership, but rather as a useful tool to be utilized only in "emergency situations."[43] Many of the disappointed *ülkücüs* imprisoned as a result of the 1980 coup turned to Islam as a political alternative.[44]

The reaction of one such *ülkücü*, Sebahattin Civelek, to the military's policy of putting the *ülkücüs* in the same cells with communists captures the psychological dynamic of this shift in allegiance from nationalism to Islamism: "among the eyes of the dominant forces, there was no difference between an atheist, unfaithful, traitor communist and a patriot *ülkücü* who recognizes Allah [and] the Quran. Moreover, with the command of the USA our ideas and bodies were tried to be imprisoned."[45] The retired general cited earlier confirmed that "the *ülkücüs* started to get Islamized in the aftermath of the 1980 military intervention." He emphasized that "in the post-1980 era, the Islamists founded a high number of associations, dormitories, and food houses and provided an Islamist consciousness to the *ülkücü* youth."[46] This suggests that Islamist entrepreneurs undertook a conscious effort to mobilize disaffected youth recruits into newly established institutions.

ADOPTION OF THE TURKISH-ISLAMIC SYNTHESIS

In the aftermath of the 1980 coup, the military regarded Sunni Islam as a counterweight to the power of radical left-wing groups in Turkey, particularly Kurdish separatist and Alevi activist groups that were ideologically allied with Marxism.[47] According to Ruşen Çakır, a journalist and researcher, the military regarded Sunni Islam as a useful tool for creating citizens who would be respectful and loyal to the state. The military faced two types of Muslim communities: ordinary Muslims who had more or less absorbed the idea of secularism, and more religious people who were members of traditional Sunni Islamic orders (*cemaat*, or congregations). Çakır argues that the military established a special relationship with the second group. The military would not create difficulties for this group – who, in turn, would be expected to support the military's policies. The Islamic orders/congregations, for their part, were not deeply opposed to the coup, which ended the anarchy and weakened the movement of communism and atheism in Turkey.

---

[43] Bora and Can, *Devlet, Ocak, Dergâh*, 97.
[44] Ibid., 134.
[45] Ibid.
[46] Author's interview with the retired general, Istanbul, February 27, 2004.
[47] Zürcher, *Turkey*, 303; Yasemin Çelik, *Contemporary Turkish Foreign Policy* (Westport, CT: Praeger, 1999), 92; and Anat Lapidot, "Islamic Activism in Turkey since the 1980 Military Takeover," in *Religious Radicalism in the Greater Middle East*, eds. Bruce Maddy-Weizman and Efraim Inbar (London: Frank Cass, 1997), 62–74.

The Islamists and the military thus came to a tacit agreement,[48] which was reflected in the regime's treatment of the NSP. NSP leaders were prosecuted for violating Article 163 of the penal code, which prohibits "the exploitation of religion for political purposes."[49] Unlike the trial of the ultranationalist NAP leaders, however, no death sentences were demanded. Furthermore, the NSP leader Erbakan was released while awaiting trial.[50] General Evren even established a close relationship with a prominent leader of the *Nurcu* brotherhood leader in Erzurum (a province in eastern Anatolia), Mehmet Kırkıncı.[51] During the military regime, Retired General Bölügiray prepared a proposal called "Directive of Reactionism" (*İrtica Direktifi*) that would bring all Quran courses and student dormitories that belonged to the Islamic brotherhoods and their associations under state supervision. Despite his endeavors, however, the military-backed Bülent Ulusu government did not implement his proposal.[52]

The military rulers, while viewing Islam and Islamist groups with suspicion, regarded Sunni Islam both as a legitimizing force for its policies and as a unifying instrument against anarchy. For this reason, they tried to create a sense of community among those who shared Islam as their faith, while attempting to control the Islamist groups. The military imposed state control over Quran courses, which had been abandoned under MP rule starting in 1983. The military also dictated the content of all sermons delivered in mosques, and occasionally banned fundamentalist organizations. The contradictory policies of the military toward Islamism were criticized by both secular intellectuals and Islamists. The former viewed these policies as permissive and as the main cause of the resurgence of fundamentalist Islam in Turkey. The latter condemned the military regime for attempting to define "what the true religion is."[53]

Anat Lapidot describes the strategy that was pursued by the military in the post-1980 coup era as follows:

After the military coup of September 1980, the generals' attitude towards Islam was ambiguous, on the one hand opposing Islamic radicalism and on the other promoting Islamic activities. Even though the fear of Islamic *irtica* (reaction) was one of the reasons for the military takeover, ironically it was the generals who introduced Islam and adopted it as part of the state ideology.[54]

Muharrem Tünay, a political science professor, characterizes the military's pragmatic strategy of the early 1980s as "Caesarism," and notes that it paved

---

[48] Çakır, *Ayet ve Slogan*, 292–3.
[49] Margulies and Yıldızoğlu, "The Resurgence of Islam and the Welfare Party in Turkey," 149.
[50] Binnaz Toprak, "Religion as State Ideology in a Secular Setting: The Turkish-Islamic Synthesis," in *Aspects of Religion in Secular Turkey*, ed. Malcolm Wagstaff, Occasional Paper Series, no. 40 (Durham, UK: University of Durham, Center for Middle East and Islamic Studies, 1990), 11; Tachau and Heper, "The State, Politics, and the Military," 30.
[51] Yavuz, *Islamic Political Identity in Turkey*, 70.
[52] Bölügiray, *Sokaktaki Askerin Dönüşü*, 212–18. Bölügiray was informed that the General Secretary of the Turkish General Staff, General Necdet Üruğ, did not find his proposal appropriate. In ibid., 217.
[53] Ayata, "The Rise of Islamic Fundamentalism and Its Institutional Framework," 64.
[54] Lapidot, "Islamic Activism in Turkey since the 1980 Military Takeover," 68.

Adoption of the Turkish-Islamic Synthesis 95

the way for a crucial change in the balance of political forces favoring the political Islamists in Turkey. According to Tünay, the military, despite its rhetoric of maintaining and expanding secularism in Turkey, tolerated the Islamist movement (by not targeting Islamic forces) in order to counterbalance the radical left-wing groups. As a result, while all sorts of left-wing movements (both revolutionary and moderate social democratic) were weakened, the Islamists united their forces with the remnants of pan-Turkist nationalism and assumed a central position in the formation and ideology of the "new right" of the 1980s. In his evaluation of the ambiguous strategy of the military, Tünay argues,

> even the top leaders of the military regime at the time were incapable of predicting the implications of this strategy. In actuality, it would soon prepare the ground for the revival of militant Islamic fundamentalism, a real threat posed against the very existence of the republic.[55]

As the evidence in Chapters 1 and 6 demonstrates, Tünay was correct regarding the revival of militant Islamic fundamentalism in Turkey. The military's strategy resulted in an even more powerful threat to the secular state: the resurgence and consolidation of the Islamic brotherhoods, which sought to replace Turkey's secular regime with an Islamic one by pursuing a cautious strategy of Islamizing the society from below. As a result of the military's strategy, the process of Islamization in society grew stronger than ever. Richard Tapper describes the change in the military's understanding of secularism in Turkey as follows:

> Without abandoning the basic principle of secularism, the generals, as well as the powerful intellectual elite of judges, professors, and administrators who controlled the media, adopted a new approach to protecting it. A tacit admission of the failure of the ideology and forms of Kemalist republicanism led to a reassessment of its elements and a perception of the need for reinforcing an unchanging national culture and eliminating foreign influences. A departure from strict traditional secularism was supported by the newly active tarikats and substantial Islamic funding from abroad, channeled into educational facilities and huge budget increases for the Directorate of Religious Affairs.[56]

In the aftermath of the coup, the generals introduced the TIS, which represented a fundamental shift in state ideology away from Kemalist secularism. The Kemalist understanding of secularism, which relegated religion to the private sphere through state control, was replaced by a new state policy (the TIS), according to which Turkish-Islamic history was reinterpreted and Islam was incorporated into the nationalist credo, with the goal of creating an Islamic sense of national community and preventing a recurrence of ideological clashes and the political violence of the 1970s.[57] Thus, in the post-1980 period, the

---

[55] Muharrem Tünay, "The Turkish New Right's Attempt at Hegemony," in Eralp, Tünay, and Yeşilada, *The Political and Socioeconomic Transformation of Turkey*, 20.

[56] Tapper, "Introduction," in Tapper, *Islam in Modern Turkey*, 10.

[57] Toprak, "Religion as a State Ideology in a Secular Setting," 10.

military no longer saw Islam as a force to be contained. On the contrary, it was a useful tool that was to be encouraged in order to counter the leftist threat.

The TIS was originally formulated by the first chair of the IH, Professor İbrahim Kafesoğlu, in May 1972 and became the Hearth's official policy thereafter. The Hearth was founded by a group of right-wing nationalist intellectuals, mostly university professors, who founded a club in the late 1960s as a reaction to the rise of the leftist movement in Turkey.[58]

While the club's name includes the word *intellectuals*, in the words of Professor Süleyman Yalçın, IH chair, "It is true that the Intellectuals' Hearth does not have pure academic and scientific concerns. The Hearth has not been founded just to carry out an ideological exercise. On the contrary, it emerged by being loyal to the core values [of the Turkish nation], to find a solution to problems of the Turkish people, its nation and state."[59] The Hearth, with its pragmatic slogan of the "Turkish-Islamic Synthesis," aimed at integrating Turkish Islamists and nationalists in an effort to end the rise of radical left-wing groups, and especially of communism.[60] Yalçın explained the establishment of the club as follows:

the May 27, 1960 coup and the political situation as a result of the 1961 constitution resulted in a serious ideological clash and instability in Turkey in the 1960s and 1970s. In particular, the radical left ideology was enhancing its influence, despite the disapproval of the nation's majority.... This arrogance of the left that opposed all root values of the Turks, brought together intellectuals who have values ... and defend them.[61]

Another IH member, Professor Abdülkadir Donuk, asserted:

"the idea of the Turkish-Islamic Synthesis" arose in response to "an attack on Turkishness:" The attack on our language, history, arts, music, customs, and traditions continues. There is also an attack on Islam. Even though both of them are Allah's gift to us. What should be done in such a situation? Should we do anything? Be silent? Thus, our valuable intellectuals rightly felt the necessity to stop this misleading direction and they argued loudly within the framework of the Intellectuals' Hearth, that was founded by them as their struggle, and the law.[62]

The former prominent NAP parliamentarian Nevzat Kösoğlu, in an interview with the author in February 2004, defined the TIS "not as a systematic

---

[58] Bora and Can, *Devlet, Ocak, Dergâh*, 170.
[59] *2000'e Doğru*, January 25, 1987.
[60] Muharrem Ergin, Aydın Bolak, and Süleyman Yalçın, *Yeni Bir Yüzyıla Girerken Türk-İslam Sentezi Görüşünde Meselelerimiz: Milliyetçiler IV. Büyük İlmi Kurultayı*, vol. 1 [Our Views on Turkish-Islamic Synthesis, While Entering a New Century: The Fourth Great Scientific Convention of Nationalists] (Istanbul: Aydınlar Ocağı; Taşangil Matbaacılık, 1988), 23, 30; Süleyman Yalçın, "Aydınlar Ocağı ve Türk-İslam Sentezi" [The Intellectuals' Hearth and the Turkish-Islamic Synthesis] (Istanbul: Uğur Ofset, 1988), 4; and Toprak, "Religion as State Ideology in a Secular Setting," 10.
[61] Yalçın, "Aydınlar Ocağı ve Türk-İslam Sentezi," 4.
[62] Abdülkadir Donuk, "Kültürümüzde Türk-İslam Sentezi'nin Yeri" [Place of the Turkish-Islamic Synthesis in Our Culture], in Ergin, Bolak, and Yalçın, *Yeni Bir Yüzyıla Girerken Türk-İslam Sentezi Görüşünde Meselelerimiz*, vol. 3, 28.

and lasting ideology, but just as an interpretation of Turkish history by Professor Kafesoğlu."⁶³ According to Kafesoğlu, the pre-Islamic culture of the Turkish people in Central Asia was based on a social structure wherein the family and the military were the two important institutions. When the Turkish nation settled in Anatolia, they already had a certain belief system and cultural accumulation based on morality and virtue, love of country, fear of God, obedience to state authority, and the sanctity of custom that was compatible with Islam. Thus, Turkish culture was based on two sources: Turkishness and Islam. The Turkish Islamic cultural heritage resulted in the establishment of two great empires, the Selçukian and the Ottoman. Yet, because Turkish intellectuals started to imitate the West beginning in the eighteenth century, the balance between the family, the mosque, and the barracks was disturbed, which led to the dissolution of the Ottoman Empire. It was again an imitation of the West, which was leading to the political instability of the country in the 1970s.⁶⁴

Bozkurt Güvenç, a professor of anthropology, argues that initially the Hearth adopted Ziya Gökalp's assumption that "Islam was the essence of the Turkish nation and its culture."⁶⁵ Later, the Hearth placed more emphasis on Peyami Safa's East-West synthesis, which criticized the Turkish Revolution and proposed a Turkish-Islamic synthesis, replacing Gökalp's cultural nationalism (*kültür milliyetçiliği*). According to the Hearth's new interpretation of history, "Islam was the starting point of the Turkish culture."⁶⁶ According to Professor Yalçın, Kafesoğlu, who had initially adopted Ziya Gökalp's ideas of romantic Turkish nationalism, came to believe that Islam was indispensable to the ideology of pan-Turkism in the 1970s.⁶⁷

Thus, a shift occurred in the 1970s in the ultranationalists' understanding of Turkish nationalism. What had previously been defined according to nationality (Turkishness) was now regarded as a mixture of Turkishness and Sunni Islam. Unlike the nationalists, for the Hearth, the religious component would dominate its ideology for years to come. The Hearth had close ties to the Islamist Society to Disseminate Science (*İlim Yayma Cemiyeti*). A number of prominent Hearth members were also members of that society.⁶⁸ The NAP Chair Alparslan Türkeş and his close circle had good relations with the Hearth.⁶⁹ However, in

---

⁶³ Author's interview with Nevzat Kösoğlu, the former NAP parliamentarian, Ankara, February 17, 2004.

⁶⁴ İbrahim Kafesoğlu, *Türk İslam Sentezi* [The Turkish Islamic Synthesis], 2nd ed. (Istanbul: Ötüken Neşriyât, 1996); author's interview with Nevzat Kösoğlu, the former NAP parliamentarian, Ankara, February 17, 2004.

⁶⁵ Güvenç, *Türk Kimliği*, 28.

⁶⁶ Ibid., 30.

⁶⁷ Bozkurt Güvenç, Gencay Şaylan, İlhan Tekeli, and Şerafettin Turan, *Dosya: Türk-İslam Sentezi* [The File: The Turkish-Islamic Synthesis] (Istanbul: Sarmal Yayınevi, 1991), 188.

⁶⁸ Mehmet Aydın, İbrahim Bodur, Professor Mustafa Köseoğlu, Aydın Bolak, Dr. Asım Taşer, Professor Salih Tuğ, Professor Süleyman Yalçın, Professor Nevzat Yalçıntaş, and Professor Sabahattin Zaim were members of both associations. Güvenç et al., *Dosya*, 189.

⁶⁹ Gencay Şaylan, "İslamcı Akımlar Ne Istiyor? 4: Türk-İslam Sentezi" [What do the Islamic currents want? The Turkish-Islamic Synthesis], *Cumhuriyet*, January 14, 1987; Tünay, "The Turkish New Right's Attempt at Hegemony," 21.

the 1970s the *ülkücü* movement's supporters did not have close relations with the Hearth. The *ülkücüs*' opposition to the Hearth had even resulted in the *ülkücü* youth's burning of the Hearth's newspaper, *Ortadoğu* (the Middle East), in the late 1970s.[70] It was not until the great disappointment among the *ülkücüs* at the 1980 coup that their mass membership turned to political Islam.

The Hearth rejected the pre-Islamic history and culture of the Turkish people. By focusing on the last twelve hundred years of Turkish history, the Hearth defined Turkish civilization and culture as a mixture of being Muslim and being Turkish. Yalçın defined a Turk as "a Muslim who speaks Turkish. By this definition, the Hearth emphasizes that our people are aware of pursuing a life that is full of being responsible and to be subjects of Allah in our secular-democratic system."[71] The Hearth regarded Islam as the essence of Turkish culture; from its architecture and fine arts to its customs, Islam had played a primary role.[72]

Nevzat Kösoğlu argues that at first glance, almost all Turkish nationalists regarded the TIS as a positive development. This led to the misinterpretation that all Turkish nationalists who were against the leftist movement were a part of the TIS. But as a nationalist, Kösoğlu criticizes the TIS for defining Turkish culture by focusing only on the Turkish people's experiences in Central Asia and in Islam. By not taking into account their cultural accumulation in Anatolia (both among ancient Anatolian civilizations and in the Byzantine Empire), the architects of the TIS committed what Kösoğlu calls "a mistake." For this reason, he argues that "because Kafesoğlu's interpretation of Turkish history ignores the cultural accumulation in Anatolia, it would be proper to call the TIS not a synthesis, but just an idea."[73] Güvenç also criticizes the TIS for ignoring the pre-Turkish Anatolian cultural heritage.

In effect, the Hearth intellectuals were opposing those intellectuals called Anatolianists (*Anadolucular*), who argued that the pre-Turkish Anatolian civilizations had become a part of the Turkish cultural heritage – a view that was shared by Atatürk. In September 1924, for example, Atatürk expounded on the roots of Turkish history in a public speech: "If we think about the essence of our nation, it leads us from six hundred and seven hundred year-long Ottoman Turkishness to many centuries-long Selçuki Turks and to the great Turkish era, a period that comes before and is equal to each of the eras stated above."[74] According to the Anatolianists, "while the Turkish-speaking Oguzes started to become Anatolian (*Anadolulaşmak*), the inhabitants of Anatolia started to

---

[70] Bora and Can, *Devlet, Ocak, Dergâh*, 153–4.
[71] Ergin, Bolak, and Yalçın, *Yeni Bir Yüzyıla Girerken Türk-İslam Sentezi Görüşünde Meselelerimiz*, vol. 1, 23.
[72] T.C. Başbakanlık Devlet Planlama Teşkilâtı (DPT) [The Turkish Republic Prime Ministry State Planning Organization], *Milli Kültür: Özel İhtisas Komisyon Raporu* [The National Culture: The Special Commission's Report] (Ankara: Devlet Planlama Teşkilâtı, 1983), 514–17.
[73] Author's interview with Nevzat Kösoğlu, the former NAP parliamentarian, Ankara, February 17, 2004.
[74] Afet İnan, *Türkiye Cumhuriyeti ve Türk Devrimi* [The Turkish Republic and the Turkish Revolution], 4th ed. (Ankara: Türk Tarih Kurumu Basımevi, 1998), 193.

become Turkish by accepting the faith of Islam."[75] As a school of thought, Anatolianism (*Anadoluculuk*) faded away in time, when the idea's two prominent intellectual representatives Azra Erhat (1915–82) and Halikarnas Balıkçısı (1890–1973) passed away.[76]

According to Güvenç, the roots of Turkish history are manifold: the people and cultures of Anatolia (Little Asia) before the Turkish people arrived; Central Asian Turkish communities (*boyları*) that did not migrate to Anatolia; Muslims, Turkomans, and Oguzes (*Oğuzlar*) who invaded and settled in Anatolia; inhabitants (*yerliler*) who were invaded and became Turkish by converting to the faith of Islam; and Western, contemporary (*çağdaş*), and secular Turks. Güvenç argues that asking what particular historical period and culture the Turkish people belong to is an unnecessary question – because the Turkish people's cultural history is a combination, an amalgam, of all of those factors rather than a reflection of just one.[77]

The nationalist intellectuals associated with the Hearth viewed Islam not only as a crucial part of Turkish culture, but also as part of the ideological context of society: Islam contributed to maintaining political, cultural, and economic order. Religious terms were linked in Hearth thinking to national ones. For example, the existing social, political, and economic order was legitimate because it was God-given.[78] Tapper argues that "Proponents of the Turkish-Islamic Synthesis wanted an authoritarian but not an Islamic state: religion, the essence of culture and social control, must be fostered in schools, but it must not be politicized."[79] In the interview cited above, Nevzat Kösoğlu distinguished the TIS from Erbakan's National View Movement: unlike the proponents of the TIS associated with the Hearth, Islamists do not take into account the element of Turkishness. "The National View Movement," Kösoğlu argued, "which emerged as a political movement, regards Islam as the essence of the Turkish nation. According to this view, all elements other than Islam can be disregarded, even omitted. They [the Islamists] are not interested in the pre-Islamic Turkish history, but focus on the history of the Prophet, Islam, the Emevis, the Abbasids, the Selçukis, and the Ottomans."[80] For this reason, the former NAP nationalist politician Kösoğlu called the Islamists' interpretation of the Turkish history "an approach that is not related to the [Turkish] nation's existence and reality."[81]

Even though the ultranationalists were Islamized in the post-1980 period, a distinction between them and the Islamists still exists, with the latter disregarding any kind of ethnic definition of Turkish identity. The ultranationalists'

---

[75] Güvenç, *Türk Kimliği*, 49.
[76] Author's interview with Nevzat Kösoğlu, the former NAP parliamentarian, Ankara, February 17, 2004.
[77] Güvenç, *Türk Kimliği*, 47–9.
[78] Lapidot, "Islamic Activism in Turkey since the 1980 Military Takeover," 68–9.
[79] Tapper, "Introduction," 11.
[80] Author's interview with Nevzat Kösoğlu, the former NAP parliamentarian, Ankara, February 17, 2004.
[81] Ibid.

understanding of Islam also differed from that of the Islamists. The NSP rejected any kind of nationalism based on ethnicity by according a hegemonic role to Islam, whereas the ultranationalists constructed a synthesis of Turkishness and Islam. In an interview with the author conducted in February 2004, Galip Tamur, the prominent Turkish Hearths (*Türk Ocakları*) member, argued that according to "the idea of the TIS, one cannot separate ethnic Turkishness from Islam. There has to be a Muslim Turk. Think like a Turk, live like Islam."[82] In contrast, the vice-chair of the Islamist FP, Şevket Kazan, in another interview with the author, criticized "the TIS for taking Turkishness first and Muslimness afterwards." According to Kazan, "Islam is just used in the TIS."[83]

Bora and Can, in their widely read study of nationalism and Islamism in Turkey, note that, while the Islamists' and ultranationalists' understandings with regard to whether Islam or Turkishness should be dominant conflict, both groups criticize Kemalism. The Intellectuals' Hearth attempted to bridge the gap between NSP and NAP supporters by proposing an ambiguous TIS.[84] The chair of the Hearth, Süleyman Yalçın stated,

In the beginning, the nationalists had differences in their understanding of [Turkish] nationalism. Yet, as a result of a collaborative work, thinking, and research they agreed on the same essential point, which was that the Turkish nation's source of life, existence, and character have been based on a combination of Turkish consciousness and Islamic worship and world view.[85]

The Hearth was not only against communism, but also against the idea of adopting Western civilization in its entirety in Turkey. In a way, the foremost goal of the Hearth was to establish an ideology that would be an alternative to Kemalism, "which was blamed for the confusion that was affecting Turkey's younger generation."[86] Communism and humanism were regarded as ideologies having a "cosmopolitan" nature, and the intellectuals of the Hearth identified both of them as major factors in the destruction of "national cultures" throughout the world. They regarded communism as a political threat to Turkish independence, and humanism as a tool of Western cultural imperialism. Imperialism and rapid urbanization were seen as having weakened the national culture, the dissolution of which led to the 1980 coup. Yalçın concluded that when Turks lose their faith in Islam, they disappear.[87] According to the Hearth, Turkey was under cultural attack by its internal and external foes, Western imperialism tried to destroy the Turkish national culture, and the

---

[82] Author's interview with Galip Tamur, the prominent Turkish Hearths member, Ankara, February 14, 2004.
[83] Author's interview with Şevket Kazan, the vice-chair of the FP, Ankara, February 16, 2004.
[84] Bora and Can, *Devlet, Ocak, Dergâh*, 160–1.
[85] Ergin, Bolak, and Yalçın, *Yeni Bir Yüzyıla Girerken Türk-İslam Sentezi Görüşünde Meselelerimiz*, vol. 1, 23.
[86] Lapidot, "Islamic Activism in Turkey since the 1980 Military Takeover," 68.
[87] Toprak, "Religion as State Ideology in a Secular Setting," 11–12; "Prof. Yalçın: İslam'da reform gerekmez" [Professor Yalçın: There is no need for reform in Islam], *Cumhuriyet*, April 21, 1987, 8.

Westernization policy that was pursued in the post-Atatürk era did not preserve it.[88] According to the Hearth, rapid Westernization in Turkey was a mistake, which led to the alienation of the Turkish people from themselves. Westernization emphasized materialism rather than moral values. As a result of alienation and materialism, Turkish youth decided to seek "ideologies from alien sources" (such as communism) and started anarchy in Turkey.[89]

The military cadres who initiated the 1980 coup adopted, implemented, and defended the Hearth's policy in its entirety.[90] Even though the TIS does not appear in any official documents, interviews conducted by the author with retired generals, Turkish nationalists, Islamists, and both center-right and center-left politicians confirm that the TIS was adopted as a new set of values guiding policy choices about education, religion, and culture in the post-1980 period. Hearth members began to hold prominent positions in the state bureaucracy. The Hearth played an important role in the preparation of the 1982 Constitution, the Higher Education Law, and various official documents such as the National Culture Report on the state's role in cultural engineering.[91]

In the aftermath of the 1980 coup, for the first time a chief of the General Staff, while praising secularism and Atatürk's reforms and emphasizing the importance of secularism in his speeches, also mentioned Islam and its unifying and progressive role for Turkish citizens. Yet, General Evren's statements did not directly contradict the Kemalist understanding of secularism. For example, General Evren included verses from the Quran and the Prophet Muhammad's *hadiths* (sayings) in his speeches to the public in order to convince the public to send their children to schools, thus overcoming the problem of illiteracy in the country. General Evren stated, "Both great (*yüce*) Allah and Hz. Muhammad commands us this," he stated, "Muhammad in one of his hadits commands, 'Science (*ilim*) is a sine qua non for all Muslims.' Can a person who is illiterate be knowledgeable? Thus, first of all, we should be literate."[92] In another speech, General Evren asserted that "There is no sectarianism in our religion. All of us believe in Allah, we have one Prophet, we read the same Quran. Then why is this separation?"[93]

Unlike the Hearth, General Evren did not criticize Kemalism. Yet, it is still opaque why the military accorded the Hearth so much influence in determining

---

[88] The Hearth defined culture as "a public's belief system from birth to death, from morning to evening, and even during sleeping, an entire lifestyle, and a nation's behavior style that passes from generations to generations." In Mim Kemal Öke, "Kültür Komisyonu Sonuç Raporu" [The Culture Commission's Conclusion Report], in Ergin, Bolak, and Yalçın, *Yeni Bir Yüzyıla Girerken Türk-İslam Sentezi Görüşünde Meselelerimiz*, vol. 1, 356.

[89] Ergin, Bolak, and Yalçın, *Yeni Bir Yüzyıla Girerken Türk-İslam Sentezi Görüşünde Meselelerimiz*, vol. 1, 23; Tahsin Banguoğlu, in ibid., 21–2.

[90] Güvenç, *Türk Kimliği*, 47.

[91] Toprak, "Religion as State Ideology in a Secular Setting," 10–11.

[92] Milli Eğitim Bakanlığı [Ministry of Education], *Cumhurbaşkanı Kenan Evren'in Milli Eğitime Ait Direktif ve Sözleri* [President Kenan Evren's Directives and Speeches on National Education] (Ankara: MEB, 1984), 6. See also Evren's various speeches to the public in ibid., 8–25.

[93] "Kahramanmaraş'ta halka hitaben yaptıkları konuşma (17 Ocak 1981)" [General Evren's public speech in Kahramanmaraş (January 17, 1981)], in T. C. Başbakanlık, *T. C. Devlet Başkanı Orgeneral Kenan Evren'in Söylev ve Demeçleri (12 Eylül 1980–12 Eylül 1981)*, 162.

the country's educational, religious, and cultural policies in the post-1980 period. After the 1980 coup, the Hearth clearly supported the military and established close relations with it. Thus, even though the military banned making any suggestions to the state in 1982, the Hearth proposed a new constitution directly to the NSC. Şener Akyol and Yılmaz Altuğ, members of the Constitution Council (*Anayasa Komisyonu*) that was created at the Consultation Assembly (*Danışma Meclisi*), were already affiliated with the Hearth. Other high-ranking members of the Hearth argued that nearly 80 percent of the 1982 Constitution was the same as the constitution proposal prepared by the Hearth.[94]

In the post-1980 coup era, the primary institutions of Turkish political and cultural life were restructured along the lines advocated by the Hearth. In 1987, Yalçın asserted that the TIS had become an official state ideology after the coup:

Yes, our Turkish-Islamic Synthesis has been accepted and respected at the state level in the post-1980 period. Because, this event [TIS] was an outcome of mind and science. Thus, we are pleased by the fact that the Atatürk High Institute accepted the Turkish-Islamic Synthesis. Why does this happen? They look around, when they cannot find an outlet, they come to this idea.[95]

Hasan Celal Güzel, then the Minister of State from the Motherland Party, acknowledged the role of the Hearth and its ideology during the fourth general meeting of the Intellectuals' Hearth in 1987. He declared that

the Intellectuals' Hearth has an incredible sacred place in the Turkish cultural, scientific, and intellectual life. And reported that the results of a scientific meeting, which was held nearly nine years ago, became a guide for the governments and various official works; universities and various academic institutions utilized these scientific works. Turkish nationalism is the official doctrine of the Republic of Turkey. I want to strongly emphasize this with pride.[96]

Adoption of the TIS as a de facto official ideology represented an important shift in the POS for Islamists in the 1980s. The military leadership, faced with the challenge of ending the civil war between left and right and stabilizing Turkish society, made a conscious choice to utilize Islam for this purpose. In doing so, they opened the door to participation, influence, and organizational activity by Islamist intellectuals, clergy, lay activists, and politicians – in other words, to the organizational and mobilization activities of a social movement.

Introduction of Mandatory Religious Education in Public Schools

One of the ambiguous actions undertaken under military rule was to change the status of religious education in Turkish public schools from optional to mandatory in 1982. The Intellectuals' Hearth played an important role in this

---

[94] Bora and Can, *Devlet, Ocak, Dergâh*, 156. See also Mehmet Umur and Tanıl Bora, "Türk-İslam 'Masonları'" [Turkish-Islamic masons], *Yeni Gündem*, February 22, 1987, 10–18.
[95] *Nokta*, February 22, 1987.
[96] Hasan Celal Güzel, in Ergin, Bolak, and Yalçın, *Yeni Bir Yüzyıla Girerken Türk-İslam Sentezi Görüşünde Meselelerimiz*, vol. 1, 36–7.

process. On May 9 and 10, 1981, a seminar entitled "National Education and Religious Education," organized by the Hearth, was held in Ankara. The primary emphasis of the seminar participants was on the essence of religious education (Sunni Islam) and making it widespread in Turkey. Accordingly, religious education had to be offered as a compulsory course in kindergartens; in primary, secondary, and high schools; and in the army. Turgut Özal, the deputy prime minister under the military regime (who would later become prime minister of the postintervention civilian government led by the MP); Tayyar Altıkulaç, the chair of the Religious Affairs Directorate; Necati Öztürk, the chair of Religious Education; and Salih Tuğ, the chair of the Intellectuals' Hearth were among the participants in the seminar. The seminar played an influential "positive" role in certain circles.[97]

In addition to the Hearth, the dean of the Ankara University Divinity Faculty, Hüseyin Atay, and another faculty member, Professor Beyza Bilgin were also influential in convincing the military to introduce compulsory religious education in public schools. In November 1980, Dean Atay submitted a report to the NSC arguing for compulsory religious education in public schools. Education without religion, he argued, would not produce loyal citizens; even though the ideas of Atatürk and the Turkish Republic were being taught in public schools, he argued, the youth were still not loyal to the state, because of their lack of religious knowledge. Atay argued that there was no contradiction between secularism and mandatory religious education.

Atay's report was criticized by the Ministry of Education's Commission on Religious Education, which pointed out that a course on ethics (*ahlâk*) was already mandatory in the public schools. Making religious education compulsory, the commission argued, would contradict the principle of secularism. In response, Atay wrote a second report, once again emphasizing the role of religion in providing national unity. In the second report, he argued that the rate of participation in religious education was low, as the course was optional and this was leading to an ideological polarization among students. Furthermore, instruction in the mandatory course on ethics was based on philosophy, which he argued was above the capacity of students. For Atay, the Unity of Education Law would be implemented by introducing a mandatory religion course in public schools. As a result of Atay's second report, in May 1981 the Ministry of Education's commission agreed that there was no contradiction between secularism and mandatory religious education in public schools.[98]

General Evren, the leader of the military government, established a Religious Education Counseling Commission under the chairmanship of the head

---

[97] Halis Ayhan, *Türkiye'de Din Eğitimi (1920–1998)* [Religious Education in Turkey (1920–1998)] (Istanbul: Marmara Üniversitesi İlâhiyat Fakültesi Vakfı Yayınları, 1999), 256.

[98] Beyza Bilgin, "1980 Sonrası Türkiye'de Din Kültürü ve Ahlâk Bilgisi Dersinin Zorunlu Oluşu ve Program Anlayışları" [The Introduction of Mandatory Religious Culture and Ethics Course and Program Understandings in Turkey after 1980], in T. C. MEB Din Öğretimi Genel Müdürlüğü [Ministry of Education, General Directorate of Religious Education], *New Methodological Approaches in Religious Education International Symposium Papers and Discussions (March 28–30, 2001, Istanbul)* (Ankara: MEB Yayınları, 2003), 673–7.

of the Turkish General Staff Education Department, General Osman Feyzoğlu. On May 28, 1981, this commission met and discussed the Ministry of Education's report on religious education in Turkey. During the meeting, the commission agreed that religious education (*din kültürü ve ahlâk öğretimi*) should be made compulsory in public schools, starting from elementary level until the last year of high school. Once more, the views of Dean Atay and Professor Bilgin played an important role in the commission's decision. During the meeting, Atay downplayed the existence of differences between Islamic sects in Turkey by arguing that Turkish civil law made the existence of sects unnecessary. He offered to a return to the first implication of the Unity of Education Law. What he understood from the law was that religious education (Islam) should be made compulsory for all students without exception from elementary school up to the highest grade of high school.[99] Like Atay, Bilgin made an ambiguous argument by noting that an optional religious education was contradictory to Atatürk's directives, the Unity of Education Law, and the religion of Islam.[100] What Atay and Bilgin were arguing, however, was inconsistent with the history of religious instruction in Turkey. Under Atatürk, religious instruction was optional in elementary schools (1930) and eliminated from secondary schools (1927), city elementary schools (1931), and, finally, village elementary schools (1938).[101]

Atay framed his arguments to fit the constraints on politics imposed by the military, and argued that making the religion course compulsory would have a number of positive effects. First, unity between right-wing and left-wing groups would be achieved; nobody would initiate terrorist activities against the state; and youth would be loyal to the state. Second, clashes between different sects would be reduced to a minimum. Third, youth would not learn Islam from antisecular people, and Islam would thus not be taught from a perspective hostile to the state. Finally, parents would not be sending their children to the *imam-hatip* schools, thereby further reducing exposure of youth to potentially antistate perspectives. Atay also argued that people did not speak Turkish in the eastern parts of Turkey because religious education was not compulsory – and because atheism was promoted in the region. Compulsory religious education would rectify this situation.

Only two commission members, İbrahim Ağah Çubukçu and Neda Armaner, voted against the report. They argued that compulsory religious education in public schools was contradictory to secularism and was incompatible with the

---

[99] It is important to note that in the first implication of the Unity of Education Law (1924), a religion course was not taught in high schools. It was taught in elementary schools starting from the second degree to the last year (5th grade) and in secondary schools for the 1st and 2nd grades. The course on religion experienced numerous changes.
[100] Bilgin, "1980 Sonrası Türkiye'de Din Kültürü ve Ahlâk Bilgisi Dersinin Zorunlu Oluşu ve Program Anlayışları," 685.
[101] Recai Doğan, "1980'e Kadar Türkiye'de Din Öğretimi Programı Anlayışları (1924–1980)" [Understandings of Religious Education Program in Turkey until 1980 (1924–1980)], in T. C. MEB Din Öğretimi Genel Müdürlüğü, *New Methodological Approaches in Religious Education International Symposium Papers and Discussions*, 612–17.

essence of the Unity of Education (*Tevhid-i Tedrisat*), and warned that it would have adverse impacts on the Alevis and on non-Muslim citizens of Turkey. They emphasized that making the religion course compulsory would not solve any problems, if anti-Kemalist teachers were retained. An extensive compulsory religious education had been offered in the *imam-hatip* schools, and the students that attended these schools were not loyal to Atatürk and the republic. Çubukçu and Armaner argued that educating the teachers of the religion course should be the primary concern, rather than making the religion course compulsory.[102]

Nonetheless, the commission agreed to make religious education (Sunni Islam) mandatory in public schools. The commission also approved the Higher Islam Institute's (*Yüksek İslam Enstitüsü*) report on religious education. Accordingly, the prayer leader and preacher (*imam-hatip*) schools would continue to pursue their dual function: educating prayer leaders and preachers for the future and, as secondary education institutions, preparing *imam-hatip* students to enter universities.[103]

The military regime also established a new Department of Propagation (*İrşad Dairesi*) within the Directorate of Religious Affairs (*Diyanet*) in 1981 as a countermeasure to the Kurdish separatist movement, the PKK, in the southeastern part of Turkey. The department had regularly organized conferences and lectures regarding the dangers of the PKK and of Marxism.[104]

The National Culture Report

The TIS became the state's official cultural policy as a result of the State Planning Organization's National Culture Report (NCR) of October 18, 1982, which was mostly prepared by members of the Hearth.[105] General Evren regarded the protection, development, and spread of a national culture based on Sunni Islam as a solution to the threat of communism in Turkey. Evren viewed Sunni Islam as the source of the Turkish nation's moral life, which would strengthen the society's integrity in the face of communism.[106] According to the NCR, the Kemalist republican educational system, by imitating the West, neglected the values intrinsic to the Turkish national culture, which had been a guiding force behind the major achievements of the Turkish-Islamic civilization in statecraft, military power, the arts, and literature.

As a result of the Western impact on education, positivism[107] was accepted in raising a new generation. Positivism, by representing itself as "a new

---

[102] Bilgin, "1980 Sonrası Türkiye'de Din Kültürü ve Ahlâk Bilgisi Dersinin Zorunlu Oluşu ve Program Anlayışları," 684, 689.
[103] Ayhan, *Türkiye'de Din Eğitimi (1920–1998)*, 251–2.
[104] Yavuz, *Islamic Political Identity in Turkey*, 69–70; Mehmet Kırkıncı, *Mektuplar, Hatıralar* [Letters, Memories] (Istanbul: Zafer Yayınları, 1992), 84–93.
[105] The National Culture Report was prepared by the National Culture Special Working Commission on the orders of General Evren.
[106] DPT, *Milli Kültür*, 23, 141.
[107] Positivism is the rejection of metaphysics and acceptance of human reason and scientific experiments in defining the source of knowledge.

religion,"[108] led to a materialist view of life. As a result of a decline in the attractiveness of Islam, materialism had become increasingly dominant in social relations. The NCR defined Marxism, Darwinism, Freudianism, pragmatism, and humanism as "variants" of positivism, all of which had led to spiritual decline and decadence of both Western societies and Turkey.[109] By criticizing positivism, the report represented an implicit critique of Atatürk and of the origins of Turkish nationalism. For example, the report criticized the republican education system for teaching Auguste Comte, Durkheim, and Ziya Gökalp, whose positivist outlook, it argued, had led to a decline in the nation's core values.

> Durkheim's ideas and sociological views were represented by Ziya Gökalp in our country . . . and were put into the curriculum for half a century in schools as the state view. . . . Durkheim's ideas . . . caused the decline of our real values [and] this led positivism to be regarded as a religion in our country.[110]

"[A]ll of those materialistic philosophies," stated the NCR, "led to a great moral deterioration in the West."[111]

The report focused on the negative impact of these philosophies on Turkish society and called for restoring the moral role of the state.

> Because a human being has too much difficulty in disciplining his spiritual side, strengthening his will, and controlling his instincts; law, state, education, family, religious and moral principles should support the individual in this respect.[112]

The report argued that republican education had destroyed the respect for authority and moral discipline that had been important elements of the national culture and had been transmitted to new generations through family, tradition, custom, and religious faith. The republican education system, it argued, had sowed the seeds of the anarchist generation of the 1960s and 1970s by creating a youth that was alienated from the national culture, ignorant of its own history, drawn to foreign ideologies, rebellious of authority, rootless, confused, and without hope.[113] The report recommended that "a faithful, knowledgeable, and moral" generation had to be brought up in order to rectify this situation.[114] Religion would play a crucial role in this effort. "Science without religion," the report stated, "causes a disaster."[115]

The commission's foremost goal was to raise a "model human being" by utilizing Sunni Islam in order to solve the problem of anarchy in Turkey.[116] By comparing the numbers of literates and illiterates in the country who were

---

[108] DPT, *Milli Kültür*, 536.
[109] Ibid., 535–43; see also Toprak, "Religion as State Ideology in a Secular Setting," 11.
[110] DPT, *Milli Kültür*, 537.
[111] Ibid., 540.
[112] Ibid., 541.
[113] Ibid., 542–3.
[114] Ibid., 541–2.
[115] Ibid., 527.
[116] Ibid., 542.

sentenced to prison in the years 1965 and 1969, the commission concluded that the education system was actually having a negative effect on students. Because the current education system "does not care about spirituality, illiterates, who are more respectful to the state and authority, commit crime to a lesser extent than the literates."[117] The report viewed Islam as a tool that would play a historical role in connecting the individual to the state, thus serving as a unifying force between various classes and the state. The state was expected to revive Sunni Islam in order to provide this unity. The idea of re-creating an Islamic *umma* (a unified community of believers) seems to have had the most appeal for policy makers of the post-1980 period, including both the military regime (1980–3) and the civilian governments under MP rule (1983–91).

In addition to providing stability to Turkish society, the TIS was also presented as a formula for achieving economic development. It was suggested that Turkey should pursue a new path of development that would emphasize the priority of a spiritual Islamic awakening as a prerequisite for economic growth. This would minimize social conflicts that might occur as a result of rapid industrialization and fierce competition in the market.

In the end, religious education (Sunni Islam) was made mandatory in public schools in Turkey with a clause in the new constitution. Article 24 of the constitution of 1982, on "Freedom of Religion and Conscience," states,

> Education and instruction in religion and ethics shall be conducted under State supervision and control. Instruction in religious culture and moral education shall be compulsory in the curricula of primary and secondary schools. Other religious education and instruction shall be subject to the individual's own desire, and in the case of minors, to the request of their legal representatives.[118]

The official explanation of the 1982 Constitution states,

> Religious and moral education and instruction have been placed under state supervision and control in order to prevent exploitation and abuse. This education is compulsory in primary and secondary schools. Naturally, the scope of this compulsory education does not extend to non-Muslims.[119]

At the same time, however, Article 2 of the 1982 Constitution continued to define Turkey as a secular state.

The decision by the military leadership to introduce religious instruction ("religion and ethics course" – Sunni Islam) as compulsory from the fourth grade in primary school through the highest grade of high school represented a fundamental contradiction of the principles guiding the military, which up to this point had been the primary institutional guardian of secularism.

General Evren, by asserting that secularism did not refer to atheism, argued that 90 percent of secondary school students and 75 percent of high school

---

[117] Ibid., 543.
[118] Prime Ministry, Directorate General of Press and Information, *The Constitution of the Republic of Turkey* (Ankara: Başbakanlık Basımevi, 1982), 16.
[119] Kani Ekşioğlu, *Gerekçeli Anayasa 1982* (Istanbul: Yasa Yayınları, 1982), 41.

students already chose to attend the religion class and that what the military did was to make all students take it.[120] General Evren defended the military's decision by arguing that children should learn Islam in public schools rather than in illegal Quran courses controlled by antisecular Islamic brotherhoods.[121] However, the Islamic brotherhoods also continued to exist under military rule. Perhaps even more important, the military also modified the National Education Law (*milli eğitim temel kanunu*) to allow *imam-hatip* graduates, heretofore limited to enrollment in divinity faculties, to enter all departments of universities. This action further widened the opportunity created for Islamists to enter universities. The law was introduced in 1975 under JP rule, when the NSP and the NAP were coalition members. This action created a clear "opportunity" for Islamists for it widened the scope of their potential employment in the state and the professions, from which positions it would be possible to exercise even greater influence.

General Evren, in his public speeches, quoted verses from the Quran to justify both secularism in Turkey and the necessity of offering mandatory religious education in public schools. According to Evren, "a person who does not have religious knowledge can easily be influenced; [but] he will not be misled, if he reads and knows. Each family provides a different knowledge [to a child], the right place to learn this [religious] knowledge is a school."[122] Evren, while emphasizing that "secularism is not atheism,"[123] noted the dangers of Islamic reaction (*irtica*) for Turkey and how Islam is compatible with science and reason.[124] Ümit Cizre Sakallıoğlu, a professor of political science, evaluates General Evren's use of Islam as follows:

> Gen. Evren ... was particularly adept at using Islam to rationalize his new program of restructuring the Turkish political system on more authoritarian principles. However, his references to Islam and the Quran were used to support concepts such as "literacy," "science-knowledge," "civilization," "positivism," and "secularism" and highlighted his attempt to support the fundamental secular goals of the regime through Islam, but without changing the position the state held in its relationship with society.[125]

Thus, the military junta, while viewing Islamist groups with suspicion, regarded Sunni Islam both as a legitimizing force for its policies and as a unifying

---

[120] T. C. Başbakanlık, *T. C. Devlet Başkanı Orgeneral Kenan Evren'in Söylev ve Demeçleri (12 Eylül 1981–12 Eylül 1982)* [The Turkish Republic Head of the State General Kenan Evren's Speeches (September 12, 1981–September 12, 1982)] (Ankara: Başbakanlık Basımevi, 1982), 57.
[121] Ibid.; Milli Eğitim Bakanlığı, *Cumhurbaşkanı Kenan Evren'in Milli Eğitime Ait Direktif ve Sözleri*.
[122] "Evren: Gene imzalardım" [Evren: I would sign it again], *Cumhuriyet*, March 28, 1987, 7.
[123] T. C. Başbakanlık, *T. C. Devlet Başkanı Orgeneral Kenan Evren'in Söylev ve Demeçleri (12 Eylül 1980–12 Eylül 1981)*, 50, 56.
[124] Ibid., 50, 56, 120.
[125] Sakallıoğlu, "Parameters and Strategies of Islam-State Interaction in Republican Turkey," 246.

Adoption of the Turkish-Islamic Synthesis

instrument against anarchy in the country.[126] William Hale evaluates General Evren's ambiguous approach toward secularism as follows:

> It is difficult to be categorical about the position of President Evren on the vexed question of religion and politics, however, since it contained elements of ambiguity, which reflected important changes in the nature of the debate in Turkey. Certainly, the contest was not now a straightforward clash between strict secularism (represented by the army) on the one hand and radical Islamic fundamentalism (represented by civilian political groups) on the other, since the lines of distinction were frequently blurred, and there were many intermediate positions.[127]

Contrary to the expectations or, at least, the arguments of military leaders, the introduction of mandatory Sunni Islamic religious education in public schools did not lead to the teaching of Islam in an enlightened fashion. A divinity professor, Nevzat Aşıkoğlu, conducted a time-series survey for the years 1995, 1996, and 1997 among 240 teachers in public schools and *imam-hatip* high schools who offered the religion course (Table 3.1). The teachers were asked what method they used to teach the Quran (verses and prayers) and the *hadiths* to their students. With respect to the teaching of verses and prayers, 73.76 percent of the teachers said that they were making their students memorize the content by repeating and writing it. Only 12.50 percent claimed they were making the students memorize it, while emphasizing the meaning and interpretation of a verse. Only 5.83 percent of the teachers reported that they were teaching both the meaning of a verse and its relation to today's world.[128]

A greater proportion of *imam-hatip* high school teachers claimed to rely on memorization than did teachers in other schools (Table 3.2). Among primary school teachers, 78.57 percent used the method of memorizing, while only 17.14 percent claimed that they were providing the meaning of a verse. Among high school teachers, 85.19 percent chose memorization,

---

[126] Ayata, "The Rise of Islamic Fundamentalism and Its Institutional Framework," 60; Bahriye Üçok, *Atatürk'ün İzinde Bir Arpa Boyu* [A Short Advancement in Atatürk's Path] (Istanbul: Cem Yayınevi, 2000), 145, 228–31; Erik Cornell, *Turkey in the 21st Century: Opportunities, Challenges, Threats* (Richmond, UK: Curzon Press, 2001), 112; Paul J. Magnarella, "Desecularization, State Corporatism, and Development in Turkey," *Journal of Third World Studies* 6 (Fall 1989): 37; and Esposito, "Muslim Societies Today," 201.

[127] William Hale, "Generals and Politicians in Turkey, 1983–1990," *The Turkish Yearbook of International Relations* XXV (1995): 14.

[128] Nevzat Y. Aşıkoğlu, "Günümüzde Kur'an ve Hadis Öğretimi Üzerine" [On Today's Quran and Hadith Education], in *Ankara Üniversitesi İlâhiyat Fakültesi ve TÖMER Dil Öğretim Merkezi, Almanya, Fransa, İngiltere, İtalya, Japonya, ABD ve Türkiye'de Uluslararası Din Eğitimi Sempozyumu (20–21 Kasım 1997)* [Ankara University Divinity Faculty and TÖMER Language Learning Center, International Symposium on Religious Education in Germany, France, Great Britain, Italy, Japan, the United States, and Turkey (November 20–21, 1997)], 172–81. Among the informants (teachers who were teaching the religion course) 47.92% were from the *imam-hatip* high schools, 29.16% were from primary schools, 22.50% were from high schools. In terms of their experience, 50.83% had 1–10 years, 38.34% had 11–20 years, 5% had 21–30 years of teaching experience. In ibid., 174.

TABLE 3.1. *Methods of Teaching Quranic Verses and Prayers*

Method Reported	All Teachers		İmam-Hatip High School Teachers	
	Number	Percent	Number	Percent
I have the content to be memorized by having it repeated (and by having it written)	177	73.76	75	65.22
I have the content being memorized, while emphasizing its meaning and interpretation	30	12.50	15	13.04
I explain the meaning (and emphasize its meaning today)	14	5.83	12	10.43
Other (I have it to be read in Arabic; I have it to be prepared by students; etc.)	5	2.08	5	4.35
Unanswered	14	5.83	8	6.96
TOTAL	240	100.00	115	100.00

Source: Nevzat Y. Aşıkoğlu, "Günümüzde Kur'an ve Hadis Öğretimi Üzerine" [On Today's Quran and Hadith Education], in *Ankara Üniversitesi İlâhiyat Fakültesi ve TÖMER Dil Öğretim Merkezi, Almanya, Fransa, İngiltere, İtalya, Japonya, ABD ve Türkiye'de Uluslararası Din Eğitimi Sempozyumu (20–21 Kasım 1997)* [Ankara University Divinity Faculty and TÖMER Language Learning Center, International Symposium on Religious Education in Germany, France, Great Britain, Italy, Japan, the United States, and Turkey (November 20–1, 1997)], 175–6.

while only 9.26 percent were explaining its meaning. Among *imam-hatip* high school teachers, in contrast, 65.22 reported their method was memorizing, while 23.47 percent claimed that they were explaining the meaning of a verse.[129]

With respect to the teaching of *hadiths*, 52.92 percent of all teachers claimed that they emphasized explaining the meaning of the *hadiths*. This rate increased to 60.87 percent among *imam-hatip* high school teachers.[130]

This survey shows that religious education in Turkey in the 1990s was based largely on memorization; it did not explain the meaning of Islam or how Islam should be interpreted by students. Memorization without thinking about the meaning of verses and *hadiths* was widespread among the *imam-hatip* students who would go on to become *imams* (preachers).

Ahmet Akbulut, a divinity professor, has identified the dilemma inherent in providing religious education in Turkey. The traditional understanding of the religion is dominated by the Islamic brotherhoods' (*tarikats*') interpretation of Islam. If state education is based on the traditional interpretation of Islam, then the secular and democratic character of the state is endangered. If the state does not provide any religious education, then such education, provided by unauthorized people and institutions, although still illegal, will operate unopposed. This will

[129] Ibid., 175–6.
[130] Ibid., 176.

TABLE 3.2. *Methods of Teaching the* Hadiths

	All Teachers		İmam-Hatip High School Teachers	
Method Reported	Number	Percent	Number	Percent
Repetition by saying (and memorizing)	32	13.33	18	15.65
Explanation of some of them (and emphasizing its meaning today)	45	18.75	22	19.13
Emphasis on the meaning (and memorizing)	82	34.17	48	41.74
Determining some *hadiths* from the book and ask during the exam	10	4.17	–	–
Knowing our Prophet and learning lessons from him	4	1.67	–	–
Unanswered	67	27.91	27	23.48
TOTAL	240	100.00	115	100.00

Source: Aşıkoğlu, "Günümüzde Kur'an ve Hadis Öğretimi Üzerine," 177.

create a greater threat to the state in the long term. Akbulut suggests a change in the traditional interpretation of Islam and its replacement with an enlightened interpretation of the religion, one based on questioning and discussion. Yet, the *tarikats'* understanding of Islam is the greatest obstacle to raising the type of free individual who is able to understand and interpret Islam on his own. The Islamic brotherhoods are opposed to religious education that is based on discussion and freedom of interpretation of the religion. According to Akbulut, *tarikats* do not want freedom of thought, reasoning, and faith. Thus, Akbulut suggests that teachers and *imams* should be selected and educated carefully.[131] The survey data presented in the preceding text suggest that to the extent explanations of meaning are being offered to students, they are provided by teachers who are unlikely to be teaching the enlightened form of Islam anticipated or hoped for by the military. They are more likely to be offering meanings consistent with the efforts of Islamist elites to exploit the opportunities created by the military's concessions to Islam by framing their explanations in a manner that contributes to Islamist mobilization.

The Flow of Saudi Capital into Turkey

Another ambiguous policy that was pursued during the military regime was the establishment of close relations with Saudi Arabia – a policy that can be attributed to the military's interest in securing access to additional capital.[132]

---

[131] Akbulut also notes that the so-called secularists in the country that want people to become atheists are helping the Islamists by generating public resentment toward secularism. Ahmet Akbulut, "Laiklik ve Din Öğretimi" [Secularism and Religious Education], in *Ankara Üniversitesi İlâhiyat Fakültesi ve TÖMER Dil Öğretim Merkezi, Almanya, Fransa, İngiltere, İtalya, Japonya, ABD ve Türkiye'de Uluslararası Din Eğitimi Sempozyumu*, 155–60.

[132] *Cumhuriyet*, March 21, 1987; interview with Turgut Özal, March 21, 1987, in Uğur Mumcu, *Rabıta* [Rabitat], 24th ed. (Ankara: Uğur Mumcu Araştırmacı Gazetecilik Vakfı, 2000), 200–1.

The military sought Saudi capital to finance its program of economic development. However, the flow of Saudi capital into Turkey also played a crucial role in the mobilization of political Islam in the country by financially strengthening the Islamist business class backing the Welfare Party (WP).

Turkey had experienced economic difficulties starting with the 1973 oil crisis, which led to a drastic increase in petroleum import expenditures. Beginning in 1974, Turkish statesmen tried to finance the budget deficit with short-term commercial credits. By 1979, a decline in export earnings revealed the inadequacy of that policy. Two International Monetary Fund (IMF)–based economic stabilization programs were adopted in 1978 and 1979. Due to increasing political violence in Turkey, both programs failed to implement several IMF resolutions to devalue the national currency and institute tight monetary policies. As a measure to rectify the economic situation, a new IMF austerity package, known as the January 24 Measures, was adopted in 1980. As a result of these measures, Turkey started to pursue a new economic policy aimed at achieving economic stabilization and reorienting itself toward the global market economy (market forces, foreign competition, and foreign investments).[133] The results of the January 24 Measures were encouraging. Between the years 1954 and 1980 the cumulative foreign capital inflow into Turkey was $228 million; the amount for the years between 1980 and 1986 was $874.1 million. Between 1980 and 1985, merchandise export volume tripled, as did its share of gross national product (GNP). Turkey increased its share of exports from non-oil-developing countries to industrial countries, and dramatically increased its share of exports to the Middle East.[134] It was during this period that the inflow of Saudi capital into Turkey started.[135]

The idea of bringing the oil-exporting countries' capital into Turkey dates back to the precoup period, when Turgut Özal suggested that Turkey should take advantage of this resource.[136] Özal became deputy prime minister responsible for finance during the military regime. The 1980 military regime, unlike that in 1971, realized there was no practical alternative to shifting toward a liberal market economy and integration into international markets. Even though Özal was, in his own words, "the right-hand of then Prime Minister Süleyman Demirel," whose failure in government prompted the 1980 intervention, the post-1980 military regime nonetheless promoted Özal to the position of deputy prime minister. Because Özal was familiar with the sources of external financial support, the military had no option but to fulfill Özal's demand of "providing all powers to him" in finance. Yet, Özal also notes the

---

[133] Yeşilada, "Islamic Fundamentalism in Turkey and the Saudi Connection," 1.
[134] Togan, Olgun, and Akder, *Report on Developments in External Economic Relations of Turkey*, 105–6.
[135] Yeşilada, "Islamic Fundamentalism in Turkey and the Saudi Connection," 2.
[136] "Devlet Bakanı ve Başbakan Yardımcısı Turgut Özal'ın II. İzmir İktisat Kongresi Kapanış Oturumu Konuşmaları 'Geleceğe Bakış' (Izmir, 2–7 Kasım 1981)" [Deputy Prime Minister Turgut Özal's Closing Speech at the Second Izmir Economics Congress (Izmir, November 2–7, 1981)], in *Değişim Belgeleri, 1979–1992* [Documents of Change] (Istanbul: Kazancı Matbaacılık, 1993), 69.

fact that the military was suspicious toward him, because of his affinity to the previous leadership.[137]

Özal had ties to the underground *Nakşibendi* order and was a parliamentary candidate on the NSP ticket in the 1977 general elections.[138] Turgut Özal's brother Korkut Özal, who was an NSP member of parliament and a member of the *Nakşibendi* order, explains how he convinced General Evren to leave the management of economics to his brother.

> General Evren was worried about the economy. [I said] In my opinion Turgut Özal can manage the economy. If you receive a briefing from him, he can tell you how he will solve the problem. . . . Later I learned that General Evren took my advice.[139]

Turgut Özal delivered two briefings at the Turkish General Staff in Ankara, and the military was very satisfied with his economic plans. In the aftermath of the coup, the military wanted Özal to keep his position as the state minister responsible for the economy.[140] The military regime contacted Prince Muhammed al-Faisal, the Kuwait Finance House in 1981, and Saudi billionaire Sheik Salih Abdallah Kamil in 1982.[141]

The flow of Saudi capital into Turkey after the 1980 coup played a crucial role in the mobilization of political Islam. As Birol Yeşilada, a professor of political science, notes, "the flow of the Saudi capital into Turkey did not aim simply at economic payoffs. Rather, it brought with it some crucial political and social goals that could threaten the secular nature of the Turkish republic."[142] Saudi interest in Turkish politics dated back to the 1970s. In 1976, an Islamic conference, also known as the First *Siret-i Nebi* Congress,[143] was held in Pakistan. The congress was organized by a Saudi Arabian institution called *Rabitat al-Alam al-Islami* (the Muslim World League). The *Rabitat* was founded in 1962, as a counterweight to Nasser's pan-Arabism, and aimed at propagating a strict religious fundamentalism in the Muslim world by publishing and distributing books, providing grants, subsidizing mosques, and paying the salaries of preachers (*imams*) in Western Europe as well as holding conferences and seminars.[144]

---

[137] Barlas, *Turgut Özal'ın Anıları*, 13; Hale, "Generals and Politicians in Turkey, 1983–1990," 2.
[138] Yeşilada, "Islamic Fundamentalism in Turkey and the Saudi Connection," 4; Ayata, "The Rise of Islamic Fundamentalism and Its Institutional Framework," 63. Turgut Özal became a parliamentary candidate from the NSP in 1977 after receiving the approval of Mehmet Zahit Kotku, the leader of the *Nakşibendi* brotherhood, İskenderpaşa congregation. Yet he could not win the elections. Turgut Özal's brother, Korkut Özal became an MP from the NSP, in the aftermath of the 1973 elections. See Nail Güreli, *Gerçek Tanık Korkut Özal Anlatıyor* [The Real Witness Korkut Özal Tells] (Istanbul: Milliyet Yayınları, 1994), 8, 126.
[139] Güreli, *Gerçek Tanık Korkut Özal Anlatıyor*, 132–3, 138. Korkut Özal met with General Evren in the aftermath of the military's warning letter of January 2, 1980.
[140] Ibid.
[141] Clement Henry Moore, "Islamic Banks and Competitive Politics in the Arab World and Turkey," *Middle East Journal* 44, no. 2 (Spring 1990): 247.
[142] Yeşilada, "Islamic Fundamentalism in Turkey and the Saudi Connection," 2.
[143] Sarıbay argues that *Siret-i Nebi* refers to the Prophet Muhammad's life and morality. Sarıbay, *Türkiye'de Modernleşme, Din ve Parti Politikası*, fn. 87.
[144] Oliver Roy, *The Failure of Political Islam* (Cambridge, MA: Harvard University Press, 1994), 116; Kepel, *Jihad*, 72.

The oil-exporting countries, mainly Saudi Arabia, were the real victors of the 1973 October war, which reduced the world supply of oil and increased the price per barrel. "In the aftermath of the war," argues Gilles Kepel, "the oil states abruptly found themselves with revenues gigantic enough to assure them a clear position of dominance within the Muslim world."[145] Saudi Arabia, having seen that its legitimacy was contested in the aftermath of the 1979 Iranian Revolution, extended its activities in 1980 with its campaign for a Wahhabite interpretation of Islam and its formation of fundamentalist networks targeting Muslim countries and Muslim immigrants in Europe.[146] In addition, Saudi Arabia used its petrodollars in an effort to establish its dominance among Sunni Islamist movements, including Afghan Hizb-i Islami, vis-à-vis pan-Arabism and Iran.[147] Oliver Roy notes the conformity of interests between Saudi Arabia and the United States during the cold war. According to Roy, the United States never regarded Islamism as an ideological enemy. Instead, the United States favored conservative fundamentalism (Saudi Arabia, Pakistan, General Numayri's Sudan) as a counterbalance to Iran and to Soviet expansion.[148] According to Kepel, the Saudi influence created a "notion of a worldwide Islamic domain of shared meaning transcending the nationalist divisions among Arabs, Turks, Africans, and Asians."[149]

Turkey's Minister of State, Hasan Aksay (a NSP parliamentarian in Süleyman Demirel's Nationalist Coalition government) represented Turkey at the First *Siret-i Nebi* Congress. The participant countries adopted the following goals and principles at the end of the conference:

1. The constitutional frameworks of the Islamic countries should be restructured according to Islamic principles and the Arabic language should be spread among the people.
2. Civil laws should be replaced by the *Sharia*.
3. Women should obey Islamic restrictions.
4. Necessary economic and political steps should be taken to establish modern Islamic states based on the *Sharia*.
5. At every level of educational training, Islam should be taught as a mandatory subject.
6. The five principles of Islam should be memorized by all primary school students.
7. Secondary school students must learn the entire Quran.
8. In order to promote these goals, Islamic educational institutions must be established in each country.
9. In order to recreate Islamic unity, all Muslim states should first recognize and accept their Islamic attributes and then establish

---

[145] Kepel, *Jihad*, 69.
[146] Roy, *The Failure of Political Islam*, 116; Kepel, *Jihad*, 70.
[147] Roy, *The Failure of Political Islam*, 108.
[148] Ibid., 130.
[149] Kepel, *Jihad*, 73.

a confederation under the guidance of a commonly elected Caliph.[150]

Thus, the Saudi-based *Rabitat* aimed at establishing a pan-Islamic federation based on the *Sharia*.[151] Because the *Siret-i Nebi* Congress was contrary to the secular character of Turkey, the Turkish chief prosecutor's office questioned Aksay's participation. But, because of the need to maintain the coalition government, "the issue was swept under the carpet in Turkey."[152]

During the Third Islamic Summit Conference in 1981, the Standing Committee for Economic and Commercial Cooperation (COMCEC) was established under the auspices of the Islamic Conference Organization. The COMCEC was funded by the *Rabitat*. It was one of three committees, along with the Permanent Committee for Scientific and Technological Cooperation and the Permanent Committee for Cultural and Informational Cooperation, that aimed at undertaking specific steps in order to realize the goals anticipated five years earlier at the *Siret-i Nebi* Congress. At the 1981 Islamic Summit Conference, the member states agreed to promote joint investments and cooperation in trade and industry, food and agriculture, transportation and telecommunications, science and technology, tourism, energy, labor, finance, social issues, population and health care, and information. The COMCEC would

1. Oversee implementation of the Islamic Conference Organization's decisions with respect to economic and commercial cooperation;
2. Find the necessary solutions to deal with potential difficulties in this regard; and
3. Promote programs directed at increasing member states' capacity for cooperation and to submit proposals to the Islamic Summit Conferences in this regard.[153]

Turkey's relations with Saudi Arabia were close enough to enable the military-backed government of former admiral Bülent Ulusu to issue a decree in 1981 allowing the *Rabitat* to pay the salaries of some two hundred government-employed Turkish religious functionaries serving Turkish migrant workers in Belgium and West Germany.[154] This arrangement was publicly reported for the first time by an investigative journalist, Uğur Mumcu, in 1987.[155] In response to criticism, General Evren argued,

---

[150] Yeşilada, "Islamic Fundamentalism in Turkey and the Saudi Connection," 2–3; Uğur Mumcu, "Türkiye'de Faisal Finans'ı kuran kişi Rabıtanın Türk temsilcisi: Salih Özcan" [Salih Özcan is the founder of the Faisal Finance, who is also the Turkish representative of the *Rabitat*], *Cumhuriyet*, March 13, 1987, 6.
[151] Lapidot, "Islamic Activism in Turkey since the 1980 Military Takeover," 69.
[152] Yeşilada, "Islamic Fundamentalism in Turkey and the Saudi Connection," 3.
[153] Ibid.
[154] Mumcu, *Rabıta*, 137–8.
[155] Retired General Bölügiray states that he learned the military's relationship with the *Rabitat* four years after he retired from the military from Mumcu's report in 1987. He notes, "while we were working [to curb the power of the Islamists], the military regime was making initiatives just on the opposite side." In Bölügiray, *Sokaktaki Askerin Dönüşü*, 218.

At that time, there was a shortage of foreign currency. We either would not send a religious functionary, or [by doing so] we would allow our citizens abroad [in Europe] to be poisoned [by Islamists]. For this reason, the government at the time chose the least bad choice. I do not accept this as a mistake and as a guilt. I would sign it again, [under] the same conditions.[156]

Evren went even further in describing the close relations between Turkey and the Muslim world in general:

improvement of our relations with the Middle Eastern and Islamic countries has gained a special political and economic content. We are in the endeavor of elevating our relations with the Middle East and Islam countries by developing and strengthening the existing historical, cultural, and spiritual ties and by achieving the productive cooperation in all areas that serves the interests of all sides. We see the positive results of various contacts both in dual-plan and in the framework of the Islam Conference.[157]

Another institution closely related to the *Rabitat* is the Islamic Development Bank (IsDB), which aims to foster the "economic development and social progress of member states and Muslim communities in accordance with the principles of the Shari'ah."[158] The chair of the IsDB, Ahmet Muhammet Ali, remarked in 1987, "We are in cooperation with the Rabitat. . . . We finance their projects, when our areas of interest coincide. We should work according to the Sharia order."[159] The chief counselor of the IsDB, Abdurrahman Nur Herzi, while noting the similarity of the goals of the IsDB and to those of the *Rabitat*, explained the division of labor between the organizations: ". . . we as the IsDB support educational projects in non-Muslim countries. Rabitat focuses more on projects of social content, like building mosques. For this reason, there could not have been IsDB financial support for the Rabitat's projects in Turkey."[160]

During the military regime, close relations were established with conservative Muslim countries like Saudi Arabia and the Gulf states. In 1982, at the meeting of the IsDB in Istanbul, General Evren defined Turkey as an "inextricable part of the Islamic Community." According to Hale, it was "hard to imagine that any President of Turkey could have made such a pronouncement in earlier decades, without provoking a storm of protest."[161] The military regime's understanding of secularism changed as it was altering the balance of political forces in the Turkish political scene in favor of the Islamists. The military was no longer pursuing its previous strict stand on secularism. This occurred because the military perceived that "if the state effectively told its citizens that religion played no part in official ideology, and neglected religious

---

[156] "Evren: Gene imzalardım," *Cumhuriyet*, March 28, 1987, 7.
[157] T. C. Başbakanlık, *T. C. Devlet Başkanı Orgeneral Kenan Evren'in Söylev ve Demeçleri (12 Eylül 1980–12 Eylül 1981)*, 411.
[158] MBendi Information Services, Islamic Development Bank, http://www.mbendi.co.za/cb16.htm (accessed October 12, 2004).
[159] *Cumhuriyet*, March 25, 1987.
[160] "Evren: Gene imzalardım," *Cumhuriyet*, March 28, 1987, 7.
[161] Hale, "Generals and Politicians in Turkey, 1983–1990," 14.

education, this left a moral void in the upbringing of the youth which had previously been filled by Marxism, fascism, and other anti-systemic doctrines."[162] The military continued to change its view during the post-1983 period.

Some of the manifestations of this change can be seen in a variety of cultural and educational policies. Under military rule, textbooks for secondary schools were rewritten with titles such as *National History*, *National Geography*, and *National Literature*. Special attention was given to the question of language – a controversial issue that dated back to the language reform of the Kemalist period. In contrast to that period, when modern Turkish was accepted, the Hearth offered to give more emphasis to an indigenous language based on old Ottoman forms.

In the post-1980 period, the state-owned television issued a long list of words that were banned from use over the network.[163] The state was not simply expected to promote a conservative understanding of national culture, but to discourage – or, as one document put it – to "extinguish" modernist movements in literature and the arts.[164] Since Islam was defined as the essence of the Turkish culture, the promotion of the national culture required that the state should plan religious and moral life in Turkey. This was regarded as essential not only for the intrinsic value of religious and moral teaching as a transmitter of culture, but also for the pedagogical value of such teaching in shaping the mind. It was the state's duty to create a culture that put man's spiritual needs at its center, thus guiding him to be obedient to authority. Even before the 1980 coup, Erbakan offered Islam as the solution to the anarchy problem in Turkey:

> The main reason why anarchy has become so widespread lies in not having emphasized religious education for a long time. . . . Because people who are afraid of Allah, and believe that they will definitely be giving an account for their acts, never are tools of internal and external traitor organizations; they never kill their brothers.[165]

In 1983, the WP stated in its party program that it regarded religious education for youth as an essential component for providing unity in the country against anarchy. Religious education was defined as the essence of the nation's spiritual (*manevi*) development.[166]

According to Erbakan, both left- and right-wing terrorism in Turkey were supported by Zionism, and foreign enemies were providing arms to both sides.[167] Even though the military's interpretation of the reasons for anarchy

---

[162] Ibid., 14–15.
[163] Toprak, "Religion as State Ideology in a Secular Setting," 12.
[164] Ibid.
[165] "Erbakan: Anarşinin bu derece yayılmasının sebebi din eğitiminin ihmal edilmiş olmasıdır" [The main reason why anarchy has become so widespread lies in the failure to emphasize religious education], *Milli Gazete*, August 12, 1980, 1, 11.
[166] Refah Partisi, *Refah Partisi Tüzük ve Programı* [The Welfare Party Program] (Ankara: Refah Partisi, 1983), 48.
[167] "MSP Genel Başkanı Prof. Dr. Necmettin Erbakan'ın 9.8.1980 günü düzenlediği Müslüman ülkelere yaptığı seyahat mevzuundaki basın toplantısının tam metni" [Press meeting of Professor Necmettin Erbakan regarding his visits to Muslim countries] *Milli Gazete*, August 12, 1980, 9. See also Refah Partisi, *Refah Partisi Tüzük ve Programı*, 46–9.

was not the same as that of Erbakan, the coup had changed the dynamics of the Turkish political scene permanently. In an interview with the author, a high-ranking Islamist foundation member argued, "The September 12th military cadre played a crucial role in the upbringing of a youth full of Islamic faith (*iman*). In the post-1980 period, students who took spirituality as their basis entered universities and violence between the right and the left at the universities diminished."[168]

The military, by regarding Sunni Islam as an effective counterforce to the rise of communism in Turkey and by eliminating the leftist movement, served the interests of Islamic groups who never regarded the secular-democratic character of the Turkish Republic as legitimate. The leader of the *Nurcus*' Fetullah Gülen congregation, Fetullah Gülen, commented that "Because General Evren introduced a mandatory religion course, he can go to heaven even if he does not have any other good deeds."[169] The military, by focusing primarily on the threat of communism, unintentionally created a POS for the political Islamists in Turkey. In the aftermath of the coup, the left and its organizations were physically eliminated. Furthermore, the ultranationalists' power was also diminished. The vacuum created by the decline of the left and the ultranationalists would be filled by the right-wing opposition (Islamists and nationalists who supported the TIS), which was obtaining increasing numbers of positions in parts of the state bureaucracy and the educational apparatus.[170]

TURKEY UNDER MOTHERLAND PARTY RULE (1983–1991)

The TIS continued under civilian rule, starting in 1983. General elections were held in Turkey on November 6 of that year. The military regime barred the Islamist WP, the center-left Social Democratic Populist Party (SDPP), and the center-right True Path Party (TPP) from the elections, and permitted three political parties to enter the 1983 elections: the MP, established with the military regime's encouragement; the Nationalist Democracy Party (NDP), led by a retired general, Turgut Sunalp; and the Populist Party (PP), led by a retired high-ranking procoup bureaucrat, Necdet Calp. The preference of the army was for the center-right NDP to win the elections and for a center-left party to become the opposition in the parliament.

When Turgut Özal informed General Evren that he wanted to establish the MP, Evren warned him not to admit people who belonged to the former NSP and NAP. Evren assumed that Özal would not admit leftists into his party; yet, Özal made clear that he was not prejudiced against any political ideas, and that his aim was to establish a political party that would unify diverse ideologies

---

[168] Author's interview with a high-ranking Islamist foundation member, Ankara, February 16, 2004.
[169] "Zorunlu din dersi Evren'in sevabı" [Mandatory religious education is Evren's deed], Mehmet Gündem's interview with Fetullah Gülen, *Milliyet*, January 17, 2005, 14.
[170] Margulies and Yıldızoğlu, "The Resurgence of Islam and the Welfare Party in Turkey," 149; Çakır, *Ayet ve Slogan*, 304.

under the same roof. He described the MP as "a nationalist, conservative, liberal (free market economy), and social democratic party."[171] The party was, indeed, an eclectic formation, in which liberal, social democratic, Islamic conservative, and ultranationalist factions were welded together.[172] Şevket Kazan, the vice-chair of the FP, regards Turkish politics as having been controlled by the United States and contends that "the Pentagon wanted the military to initiate the 1980 coup and the military permitted Özal to form his party in the aftermath of Özal's USA visit."[173] Kazan reported that, because the Islamist WP was not allowed to participate in the elections, the NSP's middle- and lower-tier Islamist cadres chose to join the MP as the best available alternative. This group formed an alliance (*Kutsal İttifak* – Holy Alliance) with the ultranationalist faction and constituted the conservative wing of the MP, which established a virtual monopoly over the Islamist vote.[174] Özal's former ties to the *Nakşibendi* order were useful for former NSP members. Korkut Özal, reporting one of his exchanges with Turgut, characterizes his brother's explanation of entering into politics as follows:

> I [Turgut Özal] have a lot of prescriptions that I believe can solve Turkey's problems. I could not implement them. Because I was not the man in charge, I could not have them accepted. I could not find a courageous governance. I have a feeling that if I enter the elections today, I can win and I can realize those [my projects]. Tomorrow, would not Allah ask, "My dear subject [*kul*], there was this opportunity, if you entered [the elections], you would win, you would realize your projects. Why did not you do that?" I am afraid that I will not be able to answer Allah's question.[175]

Thus, Turgut Özal perceived a political opportunity and consciously decided to exploit it.

Unlike the case of center-right parties like the Democrat Party (DP) and its successor, the JP, which the Islamic brotherhoods (*tarikats*) supported, in the MP the *tarikats* constituted a major wing of the party and were represented at the local, national, and parliamentary levels of the MP as well as at the cabinet level.[176] Sencer Ayata, a professor of sociology, observes that "this was not a typical relationship between a political party and pressure groups. This extensive network of religious groups in the MP partly explains why the influence of

---

[171] T. C. Başbakanlık, *Başbakan Turgut Özal'ın konuşma, mesaj, beyanat ve mülakatları (13.12.1985–12.12.1986)* [Prime Minister Turgut Özal's speeches, messages, statements, and interviews (December 13, 1985–December 12, 1986)] (Ankara: Başbakanlık Basımevi, 1986), 369.

[172] Barlas, *Turgut Özal'ın Anıları*, 28–9; Ersin Kalaycıoğlu, "The Turkish Grand National Assembly: A Brief Inquiry into the Politics of Representation in Turkey," in *Turkey: Political, Social and Economic Challenges in the 1990s*, eds. Çiğdem Balım et al. (Leiden, the Netherlands: E. J. Brill, 1995), 55; and Tünay, "The Turkish New Right's Attempt at Hegemony," 21.

[173] Author's interview with Şevket Kazan, the vice-chair of the FP, Ankara, February 16, 2004.

[174] Şevket Kazan, *Refah Gerçeği*, vol. 1 [The Reality of the Welfare] (Ankara: Keşif Yayınları, 2001), 10–11.

[175] Güreli, *Gerçek Tanık Korkut Özal Anlatıyor*, 141.

[176] Yeşilada, "Islamic Fundamentalism in Turkey and the Saudi Connection," 4; Ayata, "The Rise of Islamic Fundamentalism and Its Institutional Framework," 63.

Islamist groups in Turkey has become so overwhelming at the state level and in public life in general."[177]

Before the 1983 elections, Özal chose every MP candidate for member of parliament himself. The *Nakşibendis* were given privileged positions in the party, and this Islamic order emerged as "the single most important lobbying group in politics."[178] Later, the liberal wing on the one hand, and conservative and the nationalist wing (Holy Alliance), on the other, would engage in a power struggle among themselves to get the upper hand in the party. While the liberal wing emphasized the virtues of the market economy, the conservatives stressed the importance of the family, religion (Islam), and the national community. Thanks to the political leadership of Özal, the MP did not split in the 1980s, even though it contained these two opposing and irreconcilable ideological blocs: Western, liberal, and individualistic, on the one hand, and anti-Western, Islamic, and antiliberal, antiindividualistic, on the other.[179] Ayşe Güneş-Ayata and Sencer Ayata note, "The combination of economic liberalism with social conservatism in the neoright fashion was the cornerstone of Özal's politics who was personally close to both the globally oriented economic elite as well as the Islamic *tarikat* networks."[180] Korkut Özal suggested that Turgut Özal contacted conservative business circles when he decided to found the MP, and that there was a great demand in those circles for the establishment of such a party.[181] Yavuz describes the Özal era as follows:

One of the far-reaching legacies of the Özal years was the official legitimization of radically new perspectives on the role of Islam and the Ottoman heritage in contemporary Turkish society. He used the Sufi orders, kinship ties, and mosque associations to build dynamic bridges with society, resulting in the adaptation of these traditional networks to a modern urban environment. Özal also pursued a policy of Islamizing the educational system. His minister of education, Vehbi Dinçerler, a known Nakşibendi disciple, prepared a new curriculum focusing on rewriting the presentation of national history and culture. In the new curriculum, the term "national" (*milli*) was often used in a religious sense. The inner core of Özal's administration included leading members of the defunct pro-Islamic MSP [NSP] and a prominent disciple of Nakşibendi. Özal himself came from a religious Nakşibendi family.[182]

General Evren, in his preelection public speech on November 4, 1983, implied that the electorate should vote for Turgut Sunalp's NDP, instead of the MP.[183] Nonetheless, Hale notes that Evren "rapidly accepted Özal's election

---

[177] Ayata, "The Rise of Islamic Fundamentalism and Its Institutional Framework," 63.
[178] Ayata, "Patronage, Party, and State," 4.
[179] Ayşe Ayata, "Ideology, Social Bases, and Organizational Structure of the Post-1980 Political Parties," 38.
[180] Ayata-Güneş and Ayata, "Turkey's Mainstream Political Parties on the Center-Right and Center-Left," 94 (emphasis added).
[181] Güreli, *Gerçek Tanık Korkut Özal Anlatıyor*, 141.
[182] Yavuz, *Islamic Political Identity in Turkey*, 75.
[183] Barlas, *Turgut Özal'ın Anıları*, 52. According to Özal, the military envisioned that the MP could not even receive 10% of the votes in the elections. In ibid., 29.

victory with good grace, and seems to have enjoyed a cooperative relationship with him afterwards."[184]

Political Islamists had already started to infiltrate into the state bureaucracy[185] before the coup, when the NSP participated in coalition governments (1974–8). They continued to infiltrate during MP rule (1983–91).[186] Bülent Arınç, the former WP and current Justice and Development Party (JDP) member of parliament, as well as the parliament chair, declared that Özal, "without making any noise," did very good things to "destroy the bureaucratic-oligarchy" in Turkey by appointing "conscious Muslims" to the Constitutional Court, the Higher Education Board, and the presidency of universities.[187] Ayata suggests that "the Ozal [Özal] cabinets had at least three or four ministers of Naksibendi [Nakşibendi] persuasion. The parliamentary groups had even more MPs affiliated with various religious organizations, and the Islamists constituted the single most powerful faction in the party organization."[188] Korkut Özal reports that "Mr. Turgut took a lot of people on his side that trained and worked within state bureaucracy and politics. In other words, my political and bureaucratic heritage was left to my brother."[189] A number of people (Yıldırım Aktürk, Adnan Kahveci, Hüsnü Doğan, Hasan Celal Güzel, Mehmet Keçeciler, Ekrem Pakdemirli, Abdülkadir Aksu, Saffet Arıkan, Abdülbahri Koşar, Galip Demirel, and Vecdi Gönül), most of whom became MP parliamentarians, belonged to the group that Korkut Özal mentioned.[190] Yavuz characterizes the entry of large numbers of Islamists into the state bureaucracy under MP rule as a "drastic change . . . in the composition of the state elite." He argues that

> there has been a major break with the past Turkish political practice as a result of several factors. For example, the state elite is not as homogenous as it used to be. There is no single path to socioeconomic development as defined in the old ideology of "Westernization." Universal education and the expanding economy brought new recruits into state institutions who had a greater empathy for Islamic sentiments. . . . All of these

---

[184] Hale, "Generals and Politicians in Turkey, 1983–1990," 19. See also Barlas, *Turgut Özal'ın Anıları*, 28–9, 52; Marguilles and Yıldızoğlu, "The Resurgence of Islam and the Welfare Party in Turkey," 149.

[185] Sami Zubaida, "Turkish Islam and National Identity," *The Middle East Report* no. 199 (April–June 1996): 11–12.

[186] In the 1973 general elections, the NSP became the third largest party. It participated in the coalition government in 1974. Erbakan became a deputy prime minister under the RPP leader Bülent Ecevit. In 1975, Erbakan became minister in Süleyman Demirel's coalition government, which led the NSP to have more influence in areas including public education and communication. See Lapidot, "Islamic Activism in Turkey since the 1980 Military Takeover," 62; Ayata, "The Rise of Islamic Fundamentalism and Its Institutional Framework," 63.

[187] Yavuz Selim, *Yol Ayrımı: Milli Görüş Hareketindeki Ayrışmanın Perde Arkası* [Division in Road: Behind the Scenes in the Partition of the National View Movement] (Ankara: Hiler Yayınevi, 2002), 39–40.

[188] Ayata, "Patronage, Party, and State," 4.

[189] Güreli, *Gerçek Tanık Korkut Özal Anlatıyor*, 139.

[190] Ibid.

factors have made possible the emergence of a new "organic elite" – that is, an elite that identifies with society and is attuned for electoral reasons to public concerns.[191]

According to Turgut Özal, development had to be based on two indispensable factors: material (industrialization) and moral (protection of the cultural heritage), both of which would create a strong Turkish society.[192] He shared the Hearth's critical view of Westernization and development. Özal regarded Islam as a crucial component of the Turkish culture. For Özal, modernization (çağdaşlaşma) and Westernization referred to two different paths. While he regarded culture as a national issue, he viewed science and technology as an international one. Westernization meant a nation's resemblance to a Western nation with respect to culture, arts, lifestyle, and technology. Development referred to a nation's adoption of Western technology and science, while protecting its culture, as in the case of the Japanese. In Özal's view, Turkish people had to live and think like Turks, while benefiting from Western technology.[193]

Özal defined his party's understanding of conservatism as follows: "Our understanding of conservatism refers to our loyalty to our national, spiritual, and moral values, culture, history, customs, and traditions. We are never closed to new things. On the contrary, our foremost aim is a civilized, developed and great Turkey."[194] Thus, Özal's views clearly incorporated competing, if not outright contradictory or conflicting elements of social modernization and economic development associated with the West along with national-cultural conservatism, which insisted on preserving both the Turkish and the Islamic character of Turkey and its people.

Tünay argues that the "new right" in the post-1983 period tried to shape a new ideological system called "conservative nationalism," which aimed at harmonizing all contradictory elements of the traditional ideologies. Tünay notes that conservative nationalism "was a more refined and much more enriched form of the limited-appeal nationalism after the 1970s."[195] The basic political tenets of the conservative nationalism were as follows: first, because it discriminated only against the revolutionary left, it articulated the interests of different groups into a whole.[196] Second, it aimed at dissolving any mode of

---

[191] Yavuz, *Islamic Political Identity in Turkey*, 79.
[192] "Özal'ın Kültür Özel İhtisas Komisyonu'na Mesajı," in DPT, *Milli Kültür*, xxiii.
[193] "Başbakan Turgut Özal'ın Yankı Dergisi'nin Kültür Politikası Anketine Verdiği Cevaplar (4 Kasım 1985)" [Prime Minister Turgut Özal's Response to *Yankı* Magazine's Survey on Culture Policy (November 4, 1985)], in *Başbakan Turgut Özal'ın konuşma, mesaj, bayanat ve mülakatları (13.12.1984–12.12.1985)* [Prime Minister Turgut Özal's speeches, messages, statements, and interviews (December 13, 1984–December 12, 1985)], T. C. Başbakanlık (Ankara: Başbakanlık Basımevi, 1985), 710, 713.
[194] Turgut Özal, "19 Aralık 1983 TBMM'de Okunan Hükümet Programı" [The Government Program that was read at the parliament on December 19, 1983], in *Başbakan Turgut Özal'ın konuşma, mesaj, beyanat ve mülakatları (13.12.1983–12.12.1984)* [Prime Minister Turgut Özal's speeches, messages, statements, and interviews (December 13, 1983–December 12, 1984)], T. C. Başbakanlık (Ankara: Başbakanlık Basımevi, 1984), 24.
[195] Tünay, "The Turkish New Right's Attempt at Hegemony," 21.
[196] Ibid.

thinking based on class analysis. Thus, the Turkish "new right" raised certain concepts, like *ortadirek* (the central pole of the nomad's tent, which referred to "small agricultural producers, workers, government employees, craftsmen, and artisans, who symbolically constitute the center of Turkish society"). Third, a bias was shown in favor of religion and nationalism as an attempt "to mobilize different sections of society around a one nation hegemonic project, particularly with the power of Islam."[197] This effort to shape a new ideology represents a clear effort at "framing," designed to exploit the POS created by adoption of the TIS.

By the mid-1980s, the public had increasingly become receptive to appeals by the Islamists. Ronnie Margulies and Ergin Yıldızoğlu describe Turkey in this period as follows:

> The religious orders, particularly the Süleymancı and the Nakşibendi, were involved in a range of activities. Kuran [Quran] courses brought in the very young; university entrance examination courses, where students received free tuition and lived in hostels run by the orders, attracted the educated youth of the future; recruitment among students of the military academies was aimed at gaining influence within the armed forces. Mosques and their attendant religious associations represented direct channels of neighborhood organization and recruitment. All the *tarikats* were involved in these activities, often in competition with one another.[198]

Rise of the *İmam-Hatip* Schools, Quran Courses, and Mosques

Özal regarded strong faith in Allah as an essential factor for the public's solidarity. Thus, he believed that teaching essentials of the religion was beneficial. But this should not be a reason, he thought, for closing the country off to the world, or for lack of research, thinking, and discussion.[199] But at the same time, Özal was a critic of enforced secularism in Turkey. He suggested that

> I could not even learn how to worship at home. Because it was such a period. State employees had become the tools of the revolution. To sum up, my mother and father were state employees. They were the functionaries of the regime. Everything were applied to them in the first place. I remember that there were republic and new year celebration nights in towns, [and] cities. They would take people, [and] make them dance. . . . Today, such things cannot be done. . . . Today if someone wants to dance, he will dance, if he does not, he will not. Then, this was a top-down thing.[200]

It should be noted, however, that Turgut's brother Korkut Özal would later report that they were raised by their parents as very religious.[201] Turgut Özal's account of his family's experience under the revolutionary regime may, therefore, be an example of the conscious construction of an emotionally

---

[197] Ibid., 22.
[198] Margulies and Yıldızoğlu, "The Resurgence of Islam and the Welfare Party in Turkey," 149.
[199] Barlas, *Turgut Özal'ın Anıları*, 85.
[200] Ibid., 83–4.
[201] Güreli, *Gerçek Tanık Korkut Özal Anlatıyor*, 15–16.

powerful appeal designed to mobilize support for the Islamist educational agenda.

The Directorate of Religious Affairs (*Diyanet*) and the Ministry of Education were the two state institutions responsible for implementing the official state policy of the TIS. The MP emphasized the opening up of *imam-hatip* schools, Quran courses, and mosques. Özal emphasized increasing the quality and attraction of *imam-hatip* schools by opening up *Anadolu imam-hatip high schools* that provided instruction in English, and by increasing the branches of already existing *imam-hatip* schools.[202] Formally, the *Diyanet* supervises Quran courses, sermons in mosques, and publishes religious books and journals. In practice, however, the *Diyanet* has not been in control of all Quran courses and mosques. Even though the official curriculum of the *imam-hatip* schools has been determined by the Ministry of Education, a member of the divinity faculty in Ankara reported in an interview with the author in February 2004 that some schools, particularly those located in the countryside, remained under the influence of the Islamist orders.[203] The comments of a high-ranking FP member in an interview conducted in February 2004 suggest that the curriculum and practice of the *imam-hatip* schools is part of a coordinated Islamist strategy. The FP member reported that "in the *imam-hatip* schools students have been taught the meaning of independence and exploitation according to the National View." He went on to suggest that "because the students were already learning Islamic slogans, the Welfare Party, unlike in the pre-1980 period, was not using such slogans."[204]

The TIS also affected the Fifth Five Year Development Plan (1985-9). For the first time, the Turkish government officially defined culture as a value leading to "the consolidation of national integrity and solidarity" by protecting and developing national and moral values. According to the plan, "The strengthening of national integrity will be secured by conveying the common cultural legacy of the past to the young generations and developing in them a sound historical consciousness."[205] The plan gave a special emphasis to educating youth, in a way compatible with "national, moral, and cultural values," which was defined as the country's "guarantee for the future."[206]

Under MP rule (1983-91), approximately two thousand mosques were built in Turkey per year; by 1990, the total number of mosques in the country was 63,675. Formally, there is no relationship between mosques, which are under the control of the *Diyanet*, and the Islamist movement in Turkey. Yet, interviews with Turkish scholars of Islam conducted by the author in 2004

---

[202] Ruşen Çakır, İrfan Bozan, and Balkan Talu, *İmam-Hatip Liseleri: Efsaneler ve Gerçekler* [The İmam-Hatip High Schools: Myths and Realities] (Istanbul: TESEV Yayınları, 2004), 134. http://www.tesev.org.tr/etkinlik/imam_hatip_efsaneler_gercekler_kitap.pdf (accessed June 20, 2004).

[203] Author's interview with a divinity faculty member, Ankara, February 19, 2004.

[204] Author's interview with a high-ranking FP member, Ankara, February 16, 2004.

[205] DPT, *Fifth Five Year Development Plan (1985-1989)* (Ankara: Devlet Planlama Teşkilâtı, 1985), 218.

[206] Ibid., 165.

suggested that there are mosques beyond the control of the *Diyanet*, the exact number of which is impossible to determine.

Between the years 1983 and 1990, about 135 Quran courses were established on average each year. By 1990, the number of Quran courses was 4,998, nearly double (91.5% increase) the 2,610 in place in 1980 (there had been 3,047 in 1983).[207] Almost one million students (963,036) were educated at the Quran courses between the years 1984 and 1990. According to the Minister of State from the MP, Kazım Oksay, these courses aimed at teaching the religion and raising children who would be loyal citizens of the state, democracy, and the secular republic.[208] Yet, in the mid-1980s, President Kenan Evren[209] started to emphasize the antisecular nature of sermons in mosques and argued that there was a threat of *irtica* (Islamic reaction) in Turkey.[210]

The number of *imam-hatip* schools and students attending them also increased in the 1980s. While there were 48,900 *imam-hatip* students in the 1974 to 1975 academic year; this number had already reached 201,004 by the 1980 to 1981 academic year, an increase of 311 percent. By the 1990 to 1991 academic year, the number of *imam-hatip* students had increased to 309,553, an increase of 54 percent.[211] The curriculum for the *imam-hatip* schools at the secondary level was secular but included the teaching of the Quran at the elementary level for up to five hours per week. At the high school level, the curriculum included courses on the Quran, theology, Islamic jurisprudence, *hadiths* (the Prophet Muhammad's religious sayings), religious hermeneutics, preaching, and the history of world religions as well as history, geography, physics, mathematics, Turkish literature, and chemistry. The primary goal of the curriculum, however, is to train enlightened religious functionaries.[212] Yet, through a change in the *imam-hatip* schools' program, the students that attended these schools were given a greater chance to enroll in universities in departments other than theology.[213]

On average, 51,345 students graduate from the *imam-hatip* schools each year. Yet, the average annual demand for *imams* is only 2,288. In the year

---

[207] For yearly data on the number of courses and students, see Süleyman Hayri Bolay and Mümtazer Türköne, *Din Eğitimi Raporu* [Report on Religious Education] (Ankara: Türkiye Diyanet Vakfı Yayın Matbaacılık ve Ticaret İşletmesi, 1995), 128; *Cumhuriyetin 75. Yılında Türkiye'de Din Eğitimi ve Öğretimi İlmi Toplantısı* (Izmir, 4–6 Aralık 1998) (*Tebliğler*) [Scientific Meeting on Religious Education and Teaching in Turkey at the Republic's 75th Year (Izmir, December 4–6, 1998) (Presentations)] (prepared by Fahri Unan-Yücel Hacaloğlu) (Ankara: Türk Yurdu Yayınları, 1999), 409.

[208] Kazım Oksay, in Ergin, Bolay, and Yalçın, *Yeni Bir Yüzyıla Girerken Türk-İslam Sentezi Görüşünde Meselelerimiz*, vol. 1, 355.

[209] Evren retired from the army in 1983. He was acting president between 1982 and 1989.

[210] "Biz zamanımızı doldurduk diyen Kenan Evren: Camilerde yanlış konuşan vaizleri şikayet edin" [Evren, who stated that we fulfilled our time, argued that Islamist prayer leaders should be reported], *Milli Gazete*, January 9, 1987, 1.

[211] Çakır, Bozan, and Talu, *İmam Hatip Liseleri*, 64, 67.

[212] Ayata, "Patronage, Party, and State," 5.

[213] Halil Hayıt, "Hz. Peygamberin (s.a.v.) ilme verdigi önem ve imam-hatip liseleri" [Prophet Muhammad's emphasis on science and imam-hatip high schools], *Zaman*, October 6, 1992, 9.

1989, only 10 percent of *imam-hatip* graduates were employed by the *Diyanet*. As a result of *imam-hatip* graduates, who besides entering the divinity faculty, also enter the education, political science, and law departments as well as the police academy, and go on to find jobs in government and the private sector.[214] In the years 1986, 1987, and 1988, 18.31, 9.78, and 9.84 percent, respectively, of *imam-hatip* graduates attended theology departments at universities.[215] In 1987, 40 percent of Ankara University political science students were *imam-hatip* graduates; in 1992, they constituted 60 percent.[216] The military seems to be the most protected institution from the Islamist infiltration. The military rejects *imam-hatip* graduates who try to enroll in military schools. But Islamic brotherhoods, particularly the *Nurcus*, try to recruit students who are enrolled in military schools by providing them Islamic instruction in their homes on weekends.[217] As will be discussed in Chapter 6, by the mid-1990s, reports started appearing in newspapers regarding the Islamist infiltration into the military. In 1992, the Ministry of National Education's religious education chair, Halil Hayıt, argued for increasing the numbers of *imam-hatip* schools in Turkey, noting that the number of *imam-hatip* graduates who became lawyers, judges, prosecutors, managers, doctors, and engineers was quite high. Hayıt was hopeful for the future, as according to 1992 figures, 350,000 students were attending 389 *imam-hatip* schools under the guidance of 15,000 teachers. Seventy percent of the *imam-hatip* students were males.[218] Even though females cannot become prayer leaders or preachers, female students have been admitted to *imam-hatip* schools since the 1970s. By the 2003 to 2004 academic year, they constituted 41.89 percent of *imam-hatip* high school students.[219]

As the data presented in the table in the following text suggest, the proportion of all high school students in Turkey enrolled in *imam-hatip* high schools tends to reflect the relative power of Islamism in government (Table 3.3). Thus, the proportion of all high school students enrolled in these schools was highest from 1995 to 1996 (10.88%) on the eve of the electoral victory of the WP in December 1995. After the anti-Islamist education reform bill of 1997, enrollments began to decline, to only 2.37 percent of all high school students from 2003 to 2004.

[214] Briefing by General Çetin Saner on June 11, 1997 in *İrticaya Karşı Genelkurmay Belgeleri* [The General Staff's Documents on Reactionism], (prepared by Hikmet Çiçek) (Istanbul: Kaynak Yayınları, 1997), 46–7; Şevket Kazan, *Öncesi ve Sonrasıyla 28 Şubat* [February 28th Before and After], 6th ed. (Ankara: Keşif Yayınları, 2000), 56–7; and Hayıt, "Hz. Peygamberin (s.a.v.) ilme verdiği önem ve imam-hatip liseleri," *Zaman*, October 6, 1992, 9.
[215] Bolay and Türköne, *Din Eğitimi Raporu*, 150–2; Zekai Baloğlu, *Türkiye'de Eğitim* [Education in Turkey] (Istanbul: TÜSİAD Yayınları, 1990), 133.
[216] Salt, "Nationalism and the Rise of Muslim Sentiment in Turkey," 5. See also Nilüfer Narlı, "Islamic Alliance in the City," *Turkish Daily News*, April 7, 1994, B3.
[217] Yıldız Atasoy, *Turkey, Islamists, and Democracy: Transition and Globalization in a Muslim State* (London: I. B. Tauris, 2005), 156.
[218] Hayıt, "Hz. Peygamberin (s.a.v.) ilme verdigi önem ve imam-hatip liseleri," *Zaman*, October 6, 1992, 9.
[219] Çakır, Bozan, and Talu, *İmam Hatip Liseleri*, 75.

TABLE 3.3. İmam-Hatip *High School Students as a Proportion of Total Number of High School Students in Secondary* (Ortaöğretim) *Education, by Academic Year*

Year	High School Students in Secondary Education	İmam-Hatip High School Students	Percent
1989–90	1,329,010	92,585	6.97
1990–1	1,426,632	100,300	7.03
1991–2	1,582,347	117,706	7.44
1992–3	1,580,729	142,362	9.01
1993–4	1,954,750	162,828	8.33
1994–5	2,007,688	173,628	8.65
1995–6	1,716,143	186,688	10.88
1996–7	2,072,698	192,727	9.30
1997–8	2,065,168	178,046	8.62
1998–9	2,013,152	192,786	9.58
1999–2000	2,019,501	134,224	6.65
2001–2	2,316,832	71,742	3.10
2002–3	2,435,586	64,534	2.65
2003–4	3,587,436	84,898	2.37

Source: Ruşen Çakır, İrfan Bozan, and Balkan Talu, *İmam Hatip Liseleri: Efsaneler ve Gerçekler* [İmam Hatip High Schools: Myths and Realities] (Istanbul: TESEV Yayınları, 2004), 103.

Surveys of *imam-hatip* students show that nearly half chose on their own to attend *imam-hatip* high schools. According to one survey conducted in the years between 1993 and 1994, 50 percent of respondents said that they chose to attend *imam-hatip* high schools, while 26 percent claimed that their families wanted them to attend these schools. According to another survey conducted in the years between 1995 and 1996, 52.06 percent of respondents reported that they chose to attend *imam-hatip* high schools, while 33.27 percent claimed that their families wanted them to do so.[220] A survey conducted in 1993 revealed that 71 percent of *imam-hatip* students chose to attend *imam-hatip* high schools in order to get a better religious education, while 15 percent claimed they attended because their families wanted them to do so. Only 9 percent reported that they chose to attend these schools in order to be a prayer leader or preacher.[221]

Members of the Ankara divinity faculty suggested in separate interviews with the author in February 2004 that some conservative families, facing societal problems such as drugs, alcoholism, and prostitution, prefer to send their children to *imam-hatip* schools in order to protect their children's moral values.[222] Although there is no study that suggests that such children from secularized,

---

[220] Ibid.
[221] Ibid., 74.
[222] Author's interviews with Professor Nahide Bozkurt, Ankara, February 17, 2004; with Professor Hasan Onat, Ankara, February 19, 2004. According to a survey, the proportion of parents who said that they might think about sending their children to *imam-hatip* schools is the following: 62.7% for daughters and 63.5% for sons. This rate reaches to 77.4% (for daughters) and 79.1% (for sons) for the same question regarding the Quran courses. See Toprak and Çarkoğlu, *Türkiye'de Din, Toplum ve Siyaset*, 20.

modern families are converted to Islamism by the *imam-hatip* school experience, the treatment of these schools in the Islamist press of the pre-1980 period makes it clear that Islamists regard the *imam-hatip* schools as social networks that sustain and enhance their political power by educating the youth according to Islamic principles.[223] On November 29, 1996, Şevki Yılmaz, a parliamentarian from the WP, suggested that:

> In the parliament, there are 158 deputy members who were graduated from the *imam-hatip* [schools]. Our problem is not the distinction between high school [secular] and *imam-hatip* school, but to raise high-school students with the *imam-hatip* spirit. . . . The religion course is not enough for the people. A preparation for the *ahiret* [life after death] course should be provided. . . . In this country, the greatest terror, the greatest rebellion is initiated against Allah and His Prophet. Let's all together, from the Prime Minister to the Head of the Republic, make the people prepare for death and life after death. . . .[224]

At the Islamist Ensar Foundation's breaking-the-fast (*iftar*) dinner in December 1996, the former chair of the *Diyanet* and then parliamentarian from the TPP, Tayyar Altıkulaç reported that:

> the İmam-Hatip generation . . . became successful in all university departments that they entered. . . . İmam-hatip students, who did not know what to do after graduating from imam-hatip schools in the 1950s, today hold professorships at the universities.[225]

Ayata notes that these schools "have been important for the Islamist movement in terms of cadre-building: although education along fundamentalist lines is far from being part of the curriculum, factors such as classroom interaction, exchange of ideas among peers, and the collective religious identity conferred upon these schools make imam hatip school students highly responsive to all kinds of Islamist movements."[226]

Data on *imam-hatip* students suggest they are of modest origin and limited perspective. According to three different surveys regarding the profile of *imam-hatip* high schools students, an overwhelming majority of the parents of these students are elementary school graduates. Only a small proportion of parents are university graduates.[227] While nearly 70 percent of standard state high school students read mainstream newspapers, more than half of *imam-hatip* high school students read either Islamic or nationalist newspapers, and fully one-third appear not to read anything.[228] When asked in 1998 to identify their

---

[223] For the Islamists' views on the role the *imam-hatip* schools and Quran courses see *Milli Gazete* in the pre-1980 coup period.

[224] T.C. Anayasa Mahkemesi [The Turkish Republic Constitutional Court], *Anayasa Mahkemesi Kararı, Esas Sayısı: 1997/1 (Siyasi Parti Kapatma), Karar Sayısı (1998/1), Davalı Refah Partisi* [The Constitutional Court's Decision on the Welfare Party], 7 (Internet ed.).

[225] "Ensar en güçlü örgüt olmalı" [Ensar must be the strongest organization], *Yeni Şafak*, December 2, 1996, 4.

[226] Ayata, "Patronage, Party, and State," 5.

[227] Çakır, Bozan, and Talu, *İmam Hatip Liseleri*, 78–81.

[228] Ibid., 107. Left newspapers: *Cumhuriyet, Emek, Gündem*; liberal newspapers: *Radikal, Yeni Yüzyıl*; center newspapers: *Hürriyet, Milliyet, Sabah*; Islamic and nationalist newspapers: *Zaman, Türkiye, Akit, Yeni Şafak, Hergün, Ortadoğu*; magazines: *Akşam, Gözcü, Asabi*.

most-liked leader, 66.2 percent of *imam-hatip* high school students chose the Prophet Muhammad, and 9.6 percent identified Atatürk. In contrast, 77.6 percent of standard high school students chose Atatürk as their most liked leader, and 12.2 percent chose the Prophet Muhammad.[229]

Continuation of the Flow of Saudi Capital into Turkey

In the economic realm, as a government policy, the MP's emphasis was on liberal restructuring, aiming at diminishing the role of the state and opening Turkey to the world. Özal pursued an export-led growth strategy, which led to a search for foreign customers. Prominent scholars Sencer Ayata and Birol Yeşilada argue that the *Nakşibendi* networks in Turkey had ties to the oil-rich Gulf states, and these ties played a crucial role in promoting Turkish exports to the Middle East and maintaining steady oil supplies.[230]

Kepel argues that the Islamic financial system operated within two spheres: the first sphere was a partial redistribution of oil revenues among the member states of the Organization of Islamic Conference through the IsDB, which both strengthened Islamic cohesion and increased the interdependence among poorer member states and wealthy oil-exporting countries. The second sphere was controlled by Islamic private investors and depositors, which led to the creation of Islamic commercial banks starting in 1975 and of transnational holding companies such as Dar al-Maal al-Islami (the House of Islamic Finance, which was founded in 1981 by Prince Mohammed al-Faisal al-Saud, son of the assassinated King Faisal) and Al Baraka (Divine Blessing, which was founded in 1982 by the Saudi billionaire, Sheik Salih Abdallah Kamil). In the 1980s, the Islamic capital started to flow not only into Turkey, but also into Pakistan, Malaysia, Jordan, and Tunisia.[231]

Özal started the direct flow of Saudi and Kuwaiti capital into Turkey from the Al Baraka Group,[232] Dar al-Maal al-Islami,[233] and Faisal Finance,[234] with

---

[229] Ibid., 108.
[230] Ayata, "The Rise of Islamic Fundamentalism and Its Institutional Framework," 51–68; Yeşilada, "Islamic Fundamentalism in Turkey and the Saudi Connection," 1–11.
[231] The Islamic capital continued to flow in the 1990s. In 1995, there were 144 Islamic financial institutions worldwide, including 33 government-run banks, 40 private banks, and 71 investment companies. Kepel, *Jihad*, 78–9.
[232] The Al Baraka Group includes Al Baraka Inc. of Saudi Arabia, Al Baraka Inc. Co. in London, Al Baraka International Ltd. in London, Best Bank of Tunisia, Al Baraka Islamic Insurance Bank of Saudi Arabia, Al Baraka Islamic Insurance Bank of Saudi Arabia, Al Baraka Bank of Sudan, Arabian Thai International of Bangkok, Al Baraka Islamic Bank of Mauritania, Al Baraka Bank of Bangladesh, Jordanian Islamic Finance and Investment, and International Islamic Investment in Denmark. Yeşilada, "Islamic Fundamentalism in Turkey and the Saudi Connection," 6.
[233] Dar al-Maal al-Islami is the parent institution for 55 Islamic banks and maintains its headquarters in Geneva, Switzerland. The Maasaraf Faisal al-Islami in Bahrain, the Dar al-Maal Islami Trust, the Faisal Islamic Banks of Egypt and Sudan, and the Islami Tekaful Association are among the affiliates of the organization. Yeşilada, "Islamic Fundamentalism in Turkey and the Saudi Connection," 5.
[234] ARAMCO, a joint Saudi-American company, provided financial support for several Saudi-based international finance institutions that maintain investments in Turkey, including the *Rabitat*, Dar al-Maal al-Islami, the Al Baraka Group, and other Islamic Saudi-backed finance groups. *Cumhuriyet*, March 17, 1987, 11.

the cooperation of Islamists and of influential members of his own government. For example, Yusuf Bozkurt Özal, the prime minister's brother, was a founding member of the Al Baraka Türk. Salih Özcan, a former NSP parliamentarian was both on the board of directors of the Al Baraka Türk and the *Rabitat*. Ahmet Gürkan, a parliamentarian with the DP between 1950 and 1957 and with the JP between 1961 and 1965 as well as the chair of the Turkish-Saudi Arabian Friendship Association in 1987, was on the board of directors of the *Rabitat*. Salih Özcan, Ahmet Tevfik Paksu (a former NSP parliamentarian), and Halil Şıvgın (a former NAP parliamentarian who later became a MP parliamentarian) were the founding members of Faisal Finance in Turkey.[235] A number of Islamist foundations (e.g., the Bereket Foundation, the Özba Foundation, the Society to Disseminate Science [*İlim Yayma Cemiyeti*], the Foundation for Islamic Sciences Research [*İslami İlimler Araştırma Vakfı*], the Ensar Foundation, and the Aköz Foundation), which provided scholarships, financial assistance to Islamist publications, mosque building, and Quran courses, had ties to the Islamic finance institutions. Korkut Özal was among the founders of the Özba and Aköz Foundations, while Salih Tuğ, the former Intellectuals' Hearth chair, was on the board of directors of the Foundation for Islamic Sciences Research.[236]

Turgut Özal already had personal ties with Saudi Arabia. When he resigned from his post in July 1982, he served as the chairman of the Islamic Scientific Foundation in Saudi Arabia, until he became the prime minister in December 1983.[237] In the MP's election pamphlet in 1983 it was stated that capital flow into Turkey was possible from both Western and Middle Eastern countries.[238] The capital flow from the Middle East, particularly from Saudi Arabia, led to the emergence of a well-organized and wealthy Islamist bourgeois class called the Anatolian Tigers. They would provide financial support to the Islamist movement in Turkey. Under MP rule, Islamists' socioeconomic activity gradually

---

[235] Mumcu, "Türkiye'de Faisal Finansı kuran kişi Rabıta'nın Türk temsilcisi: Salih Özcan," *Cumhuriyet*, March 13, 1987, 6; Yeşilada, "Islamic Fundamentalism in Turkey and the Saudi Connection," 5; and David Baldwin, "Islamic Banking in a Secularist Context," in Wagstaff, *Aspects of Religion in Secular Turkey*, 25.

[236] Mumcu, "Dinsel amaçlı vakıflar Rabıta'nın gölgesinde adım adım örgütleniyor" [Religious foundations are step by step organized under the *Rabıtat*'s shadow], *Cumhuriyet*, March 15, 1987, 6; Mumcu, "Al Baraka Türkiye'de kurulurken iki isim buldu: Korkut Özal-Eymen Topbaş" [During its foundation in Turkey, Al Baraka found two names: Korkut Özal-Eymen Topbaş], *Cumhuriyet*, March 14, 1987, 6; and Yeşilada, "Islamic Fundamentalism in Turkey and the Saudi Connection," 5–6.

[237] Barlas, *Turgut Özal'ın Anıları*, 26. See also Yeşilada, "The Virtue Party," 77. "During the interim government that followed the military intervention, Özal occupied the post of the Deputy Prime Minister in charge of Economic Affairs. Özal stayed in this position for almost two years until the time of the 'bankers' crisis' in the summer of 1982. The fact that his Finance Minister, Kaya Erdem, was implicated during the crisis put pressure on him to resign." In Ziya Öniş, "Turgut Özal and His Economic Legacy: Turkish Neo-Liberalism in Critical Perspective," *Middle Eastern Studies* 40, no. 4 (July 2004): 116.

[238] Anavatan Partisi, *Anavatan Partisi Seçim Beyannamesi* [The Motherland Party's Election Declaration] (November 6, 1983), 90.

increased throughout Turkey. Özal, on his second day as a prime minister (even before his government received a vote of confidence in the National Assembly), signed a government decree allowing the establishment of the Faisal Finance and Al Baraka Türk finance institutions. These were provided special exemptions from the Turkish bankruptcy laws. In case of a bankruptcy, only 10 percent of those finance houses' current accounts and a mere 1 percent of their much larger participation accounts were to be blocked in the Central Bank, while other conventional banks would lose the use of 10 to 15 percent of their deposits.[239] Furthermore, by a second government decree, a tax exemption was extended to the IsDB. At that time, no other foreign company enjoyed such a wide range of exemptions from Turkish laws. Özal also provided legal grounds for charitable donations to be utilized for religious purposes in Turkey.[240] "It is interesting to note," argues Yeşilada, "that the second decision came soon after Korkut Özal, the younger brother of the Prime Minister, became a consultant for the Islamic Development Bank (IsDB). It should be noted, too, that Korkut Özal was a former parliamentarian of the fundamentalist NSP during the 1970s."[241] Along the same lines as Yeşilada, Clement Henry Moore finds that secular Turkey opened the door to Islamic banks and gave them special privileges vis-à-vis local conventional banks. Moore argues that possible personal ties can explain the presence of Islamic banks in Turkey. He also notes that "Al-Baraka and Faisal Finance both financed Turkish oil imports – in the respective amounts of $150 million and $50 million annually."[242]

The Islamists directed the flow of the Islamic capital into Turkey to create an opportunity for Turkish Islamist bourgeoisie to become a wealthy, industrial class that would provide economic support for the movement. In the mid-1980s, all Islamic finance houses were either from Saudi Arabia or Kuwait. Yet, in the 1990s, three Islamic finance houses were founded by Turkish Islamic businessmen. Furthermore, in 2001, Faisal Finance was transferred to one of the biggest Turkish conglomerates, Ülker. Islamic finance houses and holdings also received money from Turkish immigrant workers in Europe. Michael Rubin reports that "Between 1990 and 1996, Turkish workers in Germany remitted between $2 and $3 billion to Islamist holding companies."[243]

---

[239] Moore, "Islamic Banks and Competitive Politics in the Arab World and Turkey," 247.
[240] Yeşilada, "Islamic Fundamentalism in Turkey and the Saudi Connection," 3–4; Yavuz, *Islamic Political Identity in Turkey*, 89.
[241] Yeşilada, "Islamic Fundamentalism in Turkey and the Saudi Connection," 3. It should be noted that before Korkut Özal, Nevzat Yalçıntaş (the former chair of the Intellectuals' Hearth) was working for the same post at the IsDB. In Mumcu, "Al Baraka Türkiye'de kurulurken iki isim buldu: Korkut Özal-Eymen Topbaş," *Cumhuriyet*, March 14, 1987, 6. The *Nakşibendi* order played a unique role for the flow of the Saudi capital into Turkey. Korkut Özal, Minister of State and the prime minister's brother Yusuf Özal, and many MP parliamentarians had been members of the *Nakşibendi* order. The *Nakşibendi* order's powerful members had been key investment partners of the Saudi financial institutions in Turkey. Yeşilada, "Islamic Fundamentalism in Turkey and the Saudi Connection," 4.
[242] Moore, "Islamic Banks and Competitive Politics in the Arab World and Turkey," 248.
[243] Michael Rubin, "Green Money: Islamist Politics in Turkey," *Middle East Quarterly* XII, no. 1 (Winter 2005): 5 (Internet ed.).

Between the years 1985 and 2004, the special finance houses received $3.3 billion from the Turkish public.[244] In the 1990s and the first five years of the new century, the Islamic banking continued to grow (see Table 3.4). In 2005, the Islamic banking attained $250 to 300 billion worldwide, of which Turkey shared 3.04 percent.[245]

Between the years 1984 and 1986, the number of Saudi firms in Turkey increased from one to forty-six and that of Iranian firms from one to twenty-two.[246] In the 1990s, Islamic banks in Turkey increased their assets. For example, between 1985 and 1990, the total liquid assets of Islamic banks increased by some 600 percent.[247] By the mid-1980s, Turkey also increased its commercial relations with Islamic countries, from 23.0 percent of exports in 1980 to 42.8 percent.[248]

In the 1980s, the *Rabitat* continued to pay the salaries of Turkish religious functionaries in Western Europe. "I cannot understand what kind of a wrongdoing there can be," argued Amin El Attas, the co-general secretary of the *Rabitat*, in 1987, "if the Rabitat paid the salaries of the Turkish imams in Western Europe between the years 1980 and 1985."[249] As Attas stated, the *Rabitat* was still paying the salaries of the Turkish functionaries in 1985. This time, the payment was not made through the *Diyanet*, but through the *Rabitat* organization in Western Europe. Attas explained the aim and activities of the *Rabitat* as follows:

The Rabitat assists all Muslims in the world upon their wish. Our special area of interest is countries where Muslims are minorities.... The Muslims apply to us and request money for building up a mosque.... we [financially] assist them. Afterwards,... we send the imam [to the mosque].... the imams' nationality has no importance, it can be a Turk, a Pakistani as well.... We pay the salaries of 1,200 imams in the world. There are lots of organizations in the world that demand from us to send an imam. We want the imams not to interfere in the domestic affairs of the country to which they are sent. ... Sometimes we even do not know who the imam is.... We even do not come across with him, but we receive a report on his work. What is wrong with it? ... we only provide financial assistance. "Question: Yet, do you aim to make the Sharia widespread?" Yes, this is our goal. Allah says so. If you are a Muslim, you do what Allah

---

[244] *Yeni Şafak*, May 17, 2004.
[245] Malaysia shared 10.4%, Kuwait 22%, Egypt 22%, and Bahrain 8.4% of the world Islamic banking accumulation. Türkiye Katılım Bankaları Birliği, "Katılım Bankacılığının Türk Ekonomisi ve Finans Sektöründeki Yeri ve Önemi (21.12.2005)" [The Union of Turkish Participation Banks, Importance and Place of Participation Banking for Turkish Economy and Finance Sector (December 21, 2005)], http://www.ofkbir.org.tr (accessed February 2, 2006).
[246] Yeşilada, "Islamic Fundamentalism in Turkey and the Saudi Connection," 7.
[247] Türkiye Katılım Bankaları Birliği, "Katılım Bankacılığının Türk Ekonomisi ve Finans Sektöründeki Yeri ve Önemi"; Moore, "Islamic Banks and Competitive Politics in the Arab World and Turkey," 240–1. Katılım bank members are Albaraka Turkish Special Finance House, Asya Finance House, Turkey Finance House, and Kuwait Turkish Finance House.
[248] DİE, *Turkey and World Trade, 1950–1993* (Ankara: DİE, 1996), 58–9, 61, and 179.
[249] "İmamlara maaş ödememizde ne sakınca var, anlayamıyorum" [I do not understand what kind of a wrongdoing there is if we are paying the salaries of the imams], Nilay Karman and Enis Berberoğlu's interview with Attas, *Cumhuriyet*, March 29, 1987, 8.

TABLE 3.4. *Investment and Development Banks and Special Finance Houses in Turkey (as of November 2000)*

Special Finance Houses	Date of Establishment	Number of Branches	Nominal Capital Turkish Lira Billions	Paid Capital	Reserve Funds
Faisal Finance House[a]	1985	12	2,000	2,000	1,131
Albaraka Turkish Special Finance House	1985	22	20,000	20,000	1,998
Kuwait Turkish Evkaf Finance House	1989	23	21,630	21,630	1,194
Anadolu Finance House	1991	25	32,500	32,500	304
İhlas Finance House[b]	1995	35	10,000	10,000	14,740
Asya Finance House	1996	25	10,003	10,003	1,230
TOTAL		142	96,133	83,633	20,488

Source: Turkish Republic Central Bank, http://www.tcmb.gov.tr/ucaylik/ua5/a83.pdf (accessed December 2, 2005).

[a] In 2001, Faisal Finance was transferred to a Turkish conglomerate Ülker and became Family Finance. In January 2005, Anadolu Finance and Family Finance merged and became Turkey Finance Participation (*Katılım*) Bank.

[b] As of December 6, 2000, permission for banking operations has been terminated.

says. Propagating the Sharia should be the goal of all Muslims in the world. If you want to live according to the rules of Islam, your goal is to spread the Sharia.[250]

Thus, as Yeşilada notes, "the flow of Saudi capital into Turkey did not aim simply at economic payoffs. Rather, it brought with it some crucial political and social goals that could threaten the secular nature of the Turkish republic."[251] It is interesting to note the opinions of Turgut Özal and the then chair of the Directorate of Religious Affairs, Tayyar Altıkulaç, regarding the *Rabitat*. Özal asked, "Is the Rabitat a terrorist organization? The Saudi Arabia is governed by the Sharia. Yet, do we have relations or not? . . . I do not care, whether it is governed by the Sharia. Will we not have relations, if it is a Sharia state? This is same for Iran."[252] For Altıkulaç, the *Rabitat* affair was exaggerated by certain circles in Turkey that were disturbed by the improvement of religious services and religiosity in Turkey.[253] Bülent Ulusu, the prime minister

[250] Ibid.
[251] Yeşilada, "Islamic Fundamentalism in Turkey and the Saudi Connection," 2.
[252] Mumcu, *Rabıta*, 201; *Cumhuriyet*, March 21, 1987.
[253] "Rabıta'ya çarpanlar ve çarpılanlar," *Milli Gazete*, March 30, 1987, 12.

of the military junta, argued that he taught that the *Rabıtat* was an organization carrying for "good aims." Accordingly, he learned that the *Rabıtat* referred to the Muslim World League upon reading the journalist Uğur Mumcu's articles in 1987.[254]

The president of Turkey, Kenan Evren, became the director of the COMCEC at the Fourth Islamic Summit Conference (November 14–16, 1984).[255] It was a paradox that the most secular state in the Muslim world was actively participating in such an Islamic political network at the highest level. During the meeting in Istanbul, the COMCEC adopted the following decisions:

1. To establish a financial mechanism for medium-term foreign trade loans through the Islamic Development Bank.
2. To standardize trade regulations between members.
3. To create an information network for trade among members.
4. To establish a preference system for trade among members.
5. To promote joint investment ventures for the industrial development of member states.[256]

Turkey established close economic and political relationships with Muslim countries under MP rule. The Fifth Five Year Development Plan (1985–9) encouraged "investments of Gulf countries intended to develop the quality, technologies, and marketing capacity of the Turkish economy."[257] In 1985, Özal described Turkish relations with the Muslim world as follows:

Our government gives a great emphasis to developing our relations with the Islamic world. Recently, our President and I visited the countries in the region. Among those counties there are Saudi Arabia, Egypt, Iran, Iraq, Pakistan, Jordan, Algeria, United Arab Emirates, and Qatar. Some of the visits were for the first time in our history.... Turkey has become a center for developing political, economic, and trade relations.... Turkey's weight in the West rises, when the country's political, economic, and trade relations and influence increase in the Islamic world. Turkey's strengthened relations with the Islamic world are also in the interest of the West. The importance of the role that Turkey plays as a bridge between the West and East is understood in the West and in the Middle East everyday.[258]

Özal during another speech in 1986 stated,

Turkey discovered the Muslim brotherhood recently. Our relations with the Islamic countries are not only economic, but are a cultural, technological, and political whole.

---

[254] "Rabıta zinciri" [The *Rabıtat* chain], *Cumhuriyet*, March 19, 1987, 8.
[255] Yeşilada, "Islamic Fundamentalism in Turkey and the Saudi Connection," 3. The president of Pakistan, Zia Ul Hak, was elected director of the Permanent Committee for Cultural and Scientific Cooperation. The president of Senegal, Abdu Diuf, became director of the Permanent Committee for Cultural and Informational Cooperation. In ibid.
[256] Ibid.
[257] DPT, *Fifth Five Year Development Plan (1985–1989)*, 209.
[258] T. C. Başbakanlık, *Başbakan Turgut Özal'ın konuşma, mesaj, beyanat ve mülakatları (13.12.1985–12.12.1986)* [Prime Minister Turgut Özal's speeches, messages, statements, and interviews (December 13, 1985–December 12, 1986)] (Ankara: Başbakanlık Basımevi, 1986), 48–9.

Until the last five years, we lived like people having good sentiments toward Islamic countries, yet we could not express this.[259]

Economic relations with Saudi Arabia, which started under military rule, were further developed under MP rule, which led to the emergence of a wealthy and well-organized Islamist business class.

The 1980 coup aimed at bringing an end to the violence of extreme left-wing and right-wing groups as well as the threat of political Islam embodied in the NSP. Because of the ongoing global threat of communism, the military's foremost concern was the rise of radical leftism. The military's threat perception was influenced by the U.S. green belt project during the cold war, which was promoting Islam as a force to contain Soviet expansion toward the south. Thus, the 1980 military intervention was initiated primarily against the leftists. After the coup, the military eliminated the leftists and diminished the power of the ultranationalists. But the Islamist movement, which was a lesser threat in the eyes of the military at the time, continued to survive under the military regime. The TIS adopted and implemented by the military and maintained by the center-right MP opened the door to organizational and framing activities by Islamist forces. The TIS was a significant change from the past orientation of the Kemalist state and of the military. Islamist entrepreneurs successfully exploited this POS and changed the balance of political influence in Turkey in their favor.

The Turkish case is a good example of how movement entrepreneurs are able to seize upon an existing POS and construct a new one for movement mobilization. The first phase of the mobilization of the Islamist movement (1980–91) played a crucial role in strengthening the organizational network (formal and informal) of the WP and its successors. This enabled the party to frame the malfunctioning state as an additional POS, starting in the 1990s.

CONCLUSION

Islamist entrepreneurs exploited the TIS as a POS, which was created by the military as its inadvertent elite ally. Preexisting abeyance structures in the form of Islamic brotherhoods came to the fore by entering the MP, which ruled Turkey between 1983 and 1991, and becoming a major faction of the party. The post-1980 coup prime minister, Turgut Özal, opened the door to Saudi and Kuwaiti finance houses, which stimulated an Islamist business class, and laid one of the foundations for an Islamist political movement in Turkey. The MP pursued a strategy of establishing Islamic educational networks, creating thousands of Islamist cadre, and facilitating their entrance into secular universities and the state bureaucracy. In this way, the MP contributed to creating an Islamist elite. Islamist entrepreneurs both established Islamist social networks in an effort to Islamize the society from below, and backed the WP's organizational network, building the party's capacity to respond to the ills of the malfunctioning state starting in the 1990s.

[259] Ibid., 357.

4

The Malfunctioning State and Consolidation of the Islamist Social Movement

The malfunctioning state – characterized by massive corruption, unequal distribution of wealth, unemployment, and decay in moral values as well as deterioration in law and order – became a political opportunity structure (POS) in the second phase after 1991 of the mobilization of political Islam in Turkey. In the 1990s, the Welfare Party (WP) framed its mobilizational appeal in terms of a "Just Order," its slogan and critique of the Turkish political and social order, and thereby attracted the support of secular but disaffected voters. This chapter argues that the malfunctioning state, and the grievances it produced, did not by themselves create an Islamist social movement. In the pre-1980 coup period, one consequence of the malfunctioning state was de facto civil war. Yet there was no Islamist mobilization. The Islamist social movement did not arise until movement entrepreneurs seized upon the existing POS and framed a successful mobilizational appeal. It is this dynamic, the role of "agency" in the rise of the Islamist social movement in Turkey, that is the central focus of this chapter.

The Just Order fulfilled the three core framing tasks identified by Benford and Snow: it included diagnostic framing, which consists of identifying the problem and attributions; prognostic framing, which consists of the articulation of a solution to the problem; and motivational framing, or a call to collective action. WP activists, by appealing to both the material and the spiritual grievances of the public, tried to achieve a "consensus mobilization" among Turkish citizens with the argument that the source of their problems was the secular-democratic character of the state. The WP proposed replacing the secular state with an Islamist one.

The WP framed the failures of the secular-democratic state in terms of the global quest for democratization, freedom, and human rights in the post–cold war period. This enabled the party to frame an illiberal political agenda using a liberal vocabulary with appeal well beyond the traditional religious segments of the electorate. The organizational structure of the Turkish political system also was exploited by Islamist activists as an opportunity for mobilization and for penetrating the state. The existence of different electoral levels (national, provincial, and urban) in the Turkish political system allowed the WP to increase its vote share first in lower-level, local elections. The successful management of municipalities by WP governments convinced the electorate that the Just Order was not an empty slogan, but a viable alternative model to the malfunctioning state.

ORIGINS OF THE MALFUNCTIONING STATE

The malfunctioning state, which became evident in Turkey in the mid-1980s, has its origins in the economic policies that were pursued in the early 1980s. As a result of the International Monetary Fund's (IMF's) economic adjustment program in 1980, known as the January 24 Measures (24 *Ocak kararları*), Turkey ended its Import Substitution Industrialization (ISI) policy and adopted an outward-oriented growth strategy based on export promotion. Economic reforms aimed at restoring price stability, achieving viable growth, and increasing efficiency in resource allocation by increasing reliance on market forces.[1] The change in Turkish economic policy was "a turning point in Turkish economic history. For the first time in its recent history, the country aimed explicitly at making the economy more 'market oriented.'"[2] Sakallıoğlu defines the new economic policy as a "unique synthesis," in that "economic liberalism was promoted through a conservative-authoritarian political agenda as opposed to political liberalism."[3] Turgut Özal's economic strategy was to struggle against the problem of inflation by pursuing an export promotion strategy. The Turkish lira was devalued to maintain the competitiveness of Turkish exports. "The real effective exchange rate depreciated by about 29 percent in 1980, 6 percent in 1981, 13 percent in 1982, 6 percent in 1983 and 1984, 12 percent in 1986, and 4 percent in 1987 and 1988; it appreciated by 1 percent in 1985, 10 percent in 1989, and 35 percent in 1990."[4] While the Turkish lira was devalued, exports increased sharply in the 1980s. "Exports in current dollars increased by 62 and 22 percent in 1981 and 1982 respectively. During 1983 exports stagnated, increased again by 25 and 12 percent in current dollars during 1984 and 1985 respectively but slightly decreased in 1986 by 6.3 percent. During 1987 exports increased again by 36.7 percent."[5] Exports increased from $2.26 billion in 1979 to $10.19 billion in 1987.[6]

---

[1] Sübidey Togan, "Trade Liberalization and Competitive Structure in Turkey during the 1980s," in *The Economy of Turkey since Liberalization*, eds. Togan and V. N. Balasubramanyam (London: Macmillan Press, 1996), 6; Rüşdü Saracoğlu, "Liberalization of Economy," in *Politics in the Third Turkish Republic*, eds. Metin Heper and Ahmet Evin (Boulder, CO: Westview Press, 1994), 67.

[2] Togan, "Trade Liberalization and Competitive Structure in Turkey during the 1980s," 7.

[3] Ümit Cizre Sakallıoğlu, "Liberalism, Democracy and the Turkish Center-Right: The Identity Crisis of the True Path Party," *Middle Eastern Studies* 32, no. 2 (April 1996): 143. It should be noted that the Turkish case was not unique, in the sense that there were bureaucratic-authoritarian regimes throughout Latin America that promoted economic liberalism, while suspending democratization in the 1960s and 1970s.

[4] Saracoğlu, "Liberalization of Economy," 67.

[5] Togan, "Trade Liberalization and Competitive Structure in Turkey during the 1980s," 14.

[6] Ibid., 13.

Despite the economic measures aimed at establishing a self-regulating market economy, clientelistic relations between the state and businessmen continued to be dominant. Yet, unlike in the pre-1980 period, "decision-making power was centralized by the prime ministry, while the legislative, judiciary, and bureaucratic state institutions were weakened or undermined."[7] During the pre-1980 period, there was state intervention through routine bureaucratic procedures and "rents" arising from government policy were distributed to businesses on the basis of relatively impersonal criteria. In the post-1980 period, in contrast, "rents" were distributed highly selectively, on the basis of personalized criteria.[8] Özal's failure to establish the rule of law and develop a legal infrastructure, while making the economy more market oriented, was the weakest point in his economic approach.[9] In order to attract the flow of foreign capital into Turkey, Özal abolished the laws protecting the Turkish lira and requiring the declaration of personal wealth, which made it impossible to trace the flow of capital.[10] Mismanagement of taxation policy led the state to become dependent on debt for the financing of public spending. This worsened inflation and the unequal distribution of wealth in the country.[11]

Ziya Öniş, a professor of economics, suggests that "the successive crises that Turkey experienced over a short interval in 1994, 2000, and 2001 had their origins in key decisions implemented during the Özal era. . . . there is an essential line of continuity between the apparently more successful 1980s and the less successful and unstable era of the 1990s and beyond."[12] Even though the average growth rate was 2.6 percent between the years 1988 and 1994, there was instability in terms of gross domestic product (GDP). For example, the GDP increased by 9.1 percent in 1988, while decreasing by 5.4 percent in 1994. The rate of inflation, which was below 40 percent in the early 1980s, increased to nearly 70 percent in 1987 and to 120.7 percent in 1992.[13] In 1987, 20 percent of the population was sharing nearly half of the total household income (49.94%).[14] In 1994, 20 percent of the population was sharing more

---

[7] Haldun Gülalp, "Globalization and Political Islam: The Social Bases of Turkey's Welfare Party," *International Journal of Middle East Studies* 33, no. 3 (August 2001): 438.
[8] Ibid. See also Korkut Boratav, "İktisat Tarihi (1981–1994)" [History of Economics (1981–1994)], in *Türkiye Tarihi 5: Bugünkü Türkiye, 1980–1995* [History of Turkey 5: Today's Turkey, 1980–1995], ed. Sina Akşin (Istanbul: Cem Yayınevi, 1995), 173.
[9] Ziya Öniş, "Turgut Özal and His Economic Legacy: Turkish Neo-Liberalism in Critical Perspective," *Middle Eastern Studies* 40, no. 4 (July 2004): 114.
[10] "Köşe dönme yarışı başladı" [Contest for turning the corner started], *Zaman*, January 24, 2000, 2. According to the law of protection of Turkish lira, it was illegal to carry foreign currency in Turkey.
[11] Osman Altuğ, "Türkiye'de Uygulanan İstikrar Programı ve Başarı Şansı" [Chance of Success of Implemented Stabilization Program in Turkey], *Türkiye Ekonomisi ve IMF Paneli, 27 Nisan 2002 Tarihinde Düzenlenmiş Olan Panelin Bildirileri, Soruları ve Cevapları* [Turkish Economy and the IMF Panel (April 27, 2002)] (Ankara: Ankara Ticaret Odası, 2002), 79–80.
[12] Öniş, "Turgut Özal and His Economic Legacy," 115.
[13] Boratav, "İktisat Tarihi (1981–1994)," 185.
[14] DİE, *Statistical Yearbook of Turkey, 1991* (Ankara: DİE, 1992), 262.

Origins of the Malfunctioning State

than half of the total household income (54.9%).[15] The increase in the general consumer price index increased from 11.8 percent in 1970 to 101.4 percent in 1980. In 1983, it declined to 31.4 percent. But it nearly doubled in 1990 and its increase continued in the 1990s.[16] Increasing economic inequality created a POS that could be seized on by Islamist entrepreneurs.

The poor economic performance of the Turkish system in the 1980s supports the argument that grievances alone do not produce an Islamist social movement. Even though the economy was already malfunctioning in the pre-1980 coup era, the movement of political Islam could become an alternative to the malfunctioning state only in the 1990s, through successful framing activities of movement actors. Islamist entrepreneurs seized on the Turkish-Islamic Synthesis (TIS) as an opportunity to establish strong organizational networks and lay the foundation for gaining power in the 1990s.

Özal regarded the state bureaucracy as inefficient. For this reason, he preferred to rule in a top-down fashion by decree. This bypassed normal parliamentary procedures and constraints, and led to numerous corruption scandals. Özal pursued a relaxed policy with respect to penalizing economic crimes, mainly the misuse of export subsidies. Under Özal and the Motherland Party (MP) government, export subsidies in the form of export tax rebates were used to promote exports. Yet, Özal neglected to develop a strong institutional infrastructure that would enable an effective operation of a free-market economy. A large number of firms took advantage of export subsidies by overinvoicing.[17] As a result, scandals involving fictitious exports dominated the Turkish political scene in the mid-1980s.

Özal's export-oriented accumulation strategy and endeavors to control inflation turned out to be a failure. Only a limited number of enterprises benefited from the export promotion policy.[18] However, Özal's export-oriented economic policy did play a crucial role in the creation of a wealthy Islamic bourgeoisie in the 1990s. As will be argued in detail in the next chapter, an overwhelming majority of MÜSİAD (the Independent Industrialists' and Businessmen's Association) member enterprises – an important constituency of support for the Islamist social movement – were founded in the 1980s and 1990s.

Korkut Boratav, a professor of economics, calls the years between 1984 and 1988 the golden period for the MP, during which the party pursued clientelistic policies toward poor urban migrants. Following the 1984 local elections, the MP assumed control of the governments of most of the large provinces. The municipalities under MP governance issued decrees (*af yasaları*) that

---

[15] http://www.die.gov.tr/TURKISH/SONIST/HHGELTUK/071103.htm DİE, *Haber Bülteni*, no. 37 (February 27, 2006), (accessed March 3, 2006).
[16] Calculated on the basis of data in DİE, *Statistical Indicators (1923–1998)* (Ankara: DİE, 2001), 494; TÜİK (Turkish Statistics Institute), *Statistical Indicators (1923–2004)* (Ankara: TÜİK, n.d.), 533.
[17] Öniş, "Turgut Özal and His Economic Legacy," 122.
[18] Tünay, "The Turkish New Right's Attempt at Hegemony," 23–4.

legalized the establishment of shantytowns in large cities,[19] such as Istanbul. This worsened the already existing problem of rapid urbanization. Oğuz Işık and Melih Pınarcıoğlu, in their analysis of the shantytown problem in Turkey, argue that the decrees legalizing the establishment of shantytowns issued in the 1980s made the shantytown problem irreversible. In the 1980s, cities started to expand rapidly (see Table 4.1); as a result, shantytown areas, formerly located outside of cities, became neighborhoods inside cities, which increased the property value of shantytowns. Shantytown owners started to invade more state-owned lands and construct multiple-story buildings in order to earn money by selling or renting property.[20] Işık and Pınarcıoğlu call this the "commercialization of shantytowns" (*gecekondunun ticarileşmesi*).[21] But these trends also contributed to an important change in the composition of the electorate in Turkey's major cities and towns; a change that would be exploited by Islamist entrepreneurs in the 1990s.

The Turkish state did not have enough economic and social means to answer the demands of poor urban migrants.[22] Migrants experience problems in finding accommodations and jobs, and in adapting themselves more generally to urban life. Rapid urbanization, even though it led to the expansion of the informal sector and of the small manufacturing sector engaged in subcontracted work, did not result in an improvement in the economic welfare of the working classes; in the 1980s, there was a steady decline in their wages. Furthermore, "the share of urban wages and salaries in national income (GDP) declined from 32.7 percent in the late 1970s (1974–77) to 20.8 percent in the late 1980s (1988–91). In contrast, the increasing significance of 'rentier' earnings in national income during the same period could be seen in the growing proportion of 'interest' income to the GDP, which shot up from 1.9 percent in 1980 to 14.1 percent in 1988."[23]

There was also a decline in government salaries and wages. In the public sector, the civil service suffered the greatest absolute and relative declines in salaries, which was 50 percent since 1970. Meliha Altunışık and Özlem Tür, professors of political science, note that "There is an agreement among Turkish economists that the anti-wage policies have not been this severe in any other country, and that the decreases in purchasing power and real incomes of workers and state officials have not been as sharp as they were in Turkey during 1979–1988."[24] Thus, the 1980s saw a significant decline in the material well-being of important sectors of the population and the electorate.

---

[19] The first decree (#2805) was issued under military rule in March 1983; four other decrees were issued under MP rule, in March 1984 (#2981), December 1984 (#3086), May 1986 (#3290), and May 1987 (#3366). The March 1984 decree gave shantytown owners the right to construct buildings up to four stories high on state-owned land. Oğuz Işık and Melih Pınarcıoğlu, *Nöbetleşe Yoksulluk: Gecekondulaşma ve Kent Yoksulları Sultanbeyli Örneği* [Continuous Poverty: Shantytowns and the Urban Poor the Case of Sultanbeyli] (Istanbul: İletişim, 2001), 165.
[20] Ibid., 164–5.
[21] Ibid., 167.
[22] Boratav, "İktisat Tarihi (1981–1994)," 164.
[23] Gülalp, "Globalization and Political Islam," 441.
[24] Altunışık and Tür, *Turkey*, 80.

TABLE 4.1. *Shantytown Housing in Turkey, 1950–1990*

Year	Number of Shantytown Houses	Number of People Living in Shantytown Housing	Percentage of Urban Population Living in Shantytowns
1950	50,000	250,000	4.7
1960	240,000	1,200,000	16.7
1965	430,000	2,150,000	22.9
1970	600,000	3,000,000	23.6
1980	1,150,000	5,750,000	26.1
1990	1,750,000	8,750,000	33.9

Source: Ruşen Keleş, *Kentleşme Politikası* [Urbanization Politics] (Ankara: İmge Yayınevi, 1990), 369.

In the 1990s, problems in Turkish economics continued. For example, in the 1990s Turkey had the lowest value of its national currency relative to the U.S. dollar when compared with twenty-nine other Organization for Economic Cooperation and Development (OECD) member countries.[25] Between 1990 and 2002, Turkey had the lowest GDP per capita when compared with the other twenty-nine OECD member countries and the fifteen European Union (EU) countries.[26] Unemployment, which was only 0.3 percent in 1975, increased to 3.6 percent in 1980, to 4.7 percent in 1985, and to 9.0 percent in 1993. In 2004, the unemployment rate was 10.3 percent.[27]

In the 1980s and the 1990s the proportion of the population covered by social security schemes, including health services, increased steadily.[28] Yet, between 1980 and 1990, the number of public hospitals decreased by 0.67 percent, while the number of private hospitals increased by 38.8 percent. Between 1980 and 1995, the number of public hospitals increased by only 14.3 percent, while the number of private hospitals rose by 84.4 percent.[29] While still a relatively small share of the total number of beds,[30] the increasing number of private hospitals reinforced the emerging economic inequality in Turkish society.

---

[25] The thirty OECD member countries are Australia, Austria, Belgium, Canada, Czech Republic, Denmark, Finland, France, Germany, Greece, Hungary, Iceland, Ireland, Italy, Japan, Korea, Luxembourg, Mexico, the Netherlands, New Zealand, Norway, Poland, Portugal, Slovak Republic, Spain, Sweden, Switzerland, Turkey, the United Kingdom, and the United States.

[26] See OECD Web site http://ocde.p4.siteinternet.com/publications/doifiles/302005041P1T008.xl s (OECD Factbook, 2005), (accessed November 18, 2006).

[27] DİE, *2000 Census of Population* (Ankara: DİE, 2003), 54; DİE, *Statistical Yearbook of Turkey, 1994* (Ankara: DİE, 1995), 86; and DİE, *Statistical Yearbook of Turkey, 1979* (Ankara: DİE, 1979), 46.

[28] DİE, *Statistical Indicators (1923–1998)*, 117.

[29] Ibid., 54.

[30] See DİE, *Statistical Yearbook of Turkey, 2000* (Ankara: DİE, 2001), 124; DİE, *Statistical Yearbook of Turkey, 1971* (Ankara: DİE, 1973), 88; DİE, *Statistical Yearbook of Turkey, 1979*, 84; DİE, *Statistical Yearbook of Turkey, 1981* (Ankara: DİE, 1981), 86; and DİE, *Statistical Yearbook of Turkey, 1989* (Ankara: DİE, 1990), 95.

A particularly troubling indicator of the social consequences of the malfunctioning state was the increasing number of suicides between 1980 and 1998, and the growing proportion of these deaths attributed to economic problems and business failures. The latter rose from 2.8 percent in 1980 to 14.3 percent in 1991, to 17.1 percent in 1995, and to 20.7 percent in 1998.[31]

The WP received most of its electoral support from the urban poor. As the data in the next three tables demonstrate (Tables 4.2, 4.3, and 4.4), the urban poor had been the support base of the center-left Republican People's Party (RPP) in the 1970s, when it advocated a "fair order" (hakça düzen). The RPP proposed a welfare state for Turkey in line with many social democratic or socialist parties in Western Europe. The party was the voice of the underprivileged groups, who could not defend their own interests and rights.[32]

The Islamists were gaining electoral strength in the 1990s in most of the major cities. But they had not yet become the strongest party. The Democratic Left Party (DLP) also was gaining strength and enjoyed electoral support in the cities of Istanbul, Ankara, and especially Izmir, which is well-known for its secular-leftist electorate. However, the DLP could not sustain its growth because of two factors: first, it joined the coalition government after the 1999 general elections, and therefore became associated with the malfunctioning state in a period when social and economic conditions were in decline. Second, and even more important, the DLP did not have the strong organizational networks and entrepreneurial elites of the Islamist social movement. It was the WP and its successors that were supported by the Islamist social movement.

As a result of corruption scandals under the governance of the mainstream political parties, the WP started to be regarded by the public as the cleanest of all major political parties.[33] Furthermore, a new value structure, which was alien to the Turkish society, emerged during the Özal era. Ethics and close social and family relations started to decline. Instead, materialism, profit making, and mentality of "the ends justifies the means to become rich" began to be appraised in the society.[34]

The WP was the only party that analyzed the impact of the malfunctioning economy on the society. The party argued that the bad economic situation and the idea of materialism were leading to moral decay in the society, manifest in prostitution, alcoholism, drug addiction, mental illness, and corruption.[35]

---

[31] DİE, *Statistical Indicators (1923–1998)*, 45. In the year 2003, this rate is 19.7%. TÜİK, *Statistical Indicators (1923–2004)*, 40.

[32] Ayşe Güneş-Ayata, "The Republican People's Party," in Rubin and Heper, *Political Parties in Turkey*, 103–4. See also Cumhuriyet Halk Partisi, *Cumhuriyet Halk Partisi Programı* [Program of the Republican People's Party] (Ankara: n.p., 1977), 12.

[33] Gülalp, "Globalization and Political Islam," 438.

[34] Refah Partisi, *Birinci Büyük Kongresi, Genel Başkan Ahmet Tekdal'ın Açış Konuşması* (30 Haziran 1985) [The Welfare Party First Great Convention, the Chair Ahmet Tekdal's Opening Speech (June 30, 1985)] (Ankara: Refah Partisi, 1985), 35.

[35] Ibid., 36–7.

TABLE 4.2. *Party Support by Type of Urban Community (percent of total vote in community), 1973 General Elections*[a]

	Republican People's Party	Justice Party	All Other Parties
Istanbul	48.9	28.5	22.6
Shantytowns	47.5	26.7	25.8
Ankara	44.8	29.2	26.0
Shantytowns	45.9	27.7	26.4
Lower middle class	41.9	32.4	25.7
Middle class	62.6	21.8	15.6
Upper middle class	57.2	24.9	17.9
Izmir	44.6	40.9	14.5
Shantytowns	44.2	36.5	19.3
Lower middle class	44.1	41.9	14.0
Middle class	44.4	42.7	12.9
Upper middle class	50.4	37.8	11.8

Source: Micheal N. Danielson and Ruşen Keleş, *The Politics of Rapid Urbanization: Government and Growth in Modern Turkey* (New York: Holmes and Meier, 1985), 109.

[a] According to official electoral results, the JP received 27.8% of the votes in Ankara and 39.3% in Izmir in the 1973 general elections. The RPP secured 41.9% of the votes in Ankara and 44.1% in Izmir. These official statistics differ from those presented in the preceding text. But Danielson and Keleş's statistical data provide the only information regarding the distribution of votes according to wealth among the electorate.

TABLE 4.3. *Party Support in Major Cities in General Elections, 1969–1977 (percent)*

	Republican People's Party	Justice Party	National Salvation Party	Other Parties
Istanbul				
1969	33.9	47.8	–	18.3
1973	48.9	28.5	8.4	14.2
1977	58.2	28.4	6.6	6.8
Ankara				
1969	34.3	42.7	–	23.0
1973	41.9	27.8	9.3	21.0
1977	51.3	30.9	6.2	11.6
Izmir				
1969	35.1	53.2	–	11.7
1973	44.1	39.3	4.2	12.4
1977	52.7	39.7	2.9	4.7

Source: TBMM (Turkish Grand National Assembly) http://www.tbmm.gov.tr/kutuphane/elektronik_kaynaklar.html (accessed February 12, 2006).

TABLE 4.4. *Party Support in Major Cities in General Elections, 1983–1999 (percent)*

	Social Democratic Populist Party/ Republican People's Party	Democratic Left Party	Motherland Party	True Path Party	Welfare Party/ Virtue Party
Istanbul					
1983	–	–	45.5	–	–
1987	29.8	10.1	39.7	11.9	6.9
1991	18.9	17.6	27.5	18.8	16.7
1995	11.7	18.3	22.0	15.4	23.9
1999	9.6	29.7	15.8	5.4	21.3
Ankara					
1983	–	–	51.4	–	–
1987	29.6	6.1	39.6	14.5	4.2
1991	24.7	10.4	23.6	23.3	17.6
1995	16.9	14.2	21.6	13.1	20.9
1999	13.4	23.1	10.8	7.3	17.1
Izmir					
1983	–	–	34.5	–	–
1987	35.6	9.2	35.8	15.6	2.3
1991	24.5	15.4	25.6	27.6	6.0
1995	13.9	24.4	18.8	23.9	8.4
1999	9.8	40.3	15.8	9.6	4.9

Source: DİE, *Results of General Election of Representatives 18.04.1999* (Ankara: DİE, 2001), xvi–xvii, xxx–xxxi.

FRAMING THE POLITICAL OPPORTUNITY STRUCTURE: THE WELFARE PARTY AND THE JUST ORDER (*ADİL DÜZEN*)

In the 1990s, the WP, unlike the mainstream political parties, successfully exploited grievances arising out of the malfunctioning state to turn political Islam into a protest movement of disaffected citizens. By proposing a "Just Order," the WP responded to the secular but disaffected citizens' needs of daily life and grievances.[36] The WP's criticism, both of the Westernization of the country that had begun in the late Ottoman period and of the present secular-democratic character of the Turkish state, did not differ from that of the National Order Party (NOP, 1970–1) or the National Salvation Party (NSP, 1972–80). However, unlike its predecessors, the WP started to increase its vote

---

[36] Oliver and Johnston define framing as "a behavior by which people make sense of both daily life and grievances that confront them." In Pamela E. Oliver and Hank Johnston, "What a Good Idea! Ideologies and Frames in Social Movement Research," in *Frames of Protest: Social Movements and the Framing Perspective*, eds. Hank Johnston and John A. Noakes (Lanham, MD: Rownman and Littlefield Publishers, 2005), 190.

share in the municipal and parliamentary elections of the mid-1980s and the 1990s. The electoral success of the WP can be attributed to two factors: its ability to frame its critique of the malfunctioning state and its strong organizational networks, both formal and informal. The strong organizational networks of the WP will be examined in the next chapter. This chapter analyzes how the WP, unlike the mainstream political parties, framed the malfunctioning state so as to achieve mobilization of mass support.

The Welfare Party's Political Rhetoric in the 1980s

In the early 1980s, the WP's political message took the form of advocacy of "National Consciousness" (*Milli Şuur*), which was, like the "National View" (the NOP and the NSP), based on two factors: spiritual development based on Islam and material development based on industrialization. These would lead, in turn, to an independent foreign policy independent of Western influence. The party's emblem was composed of a crescent (*hilâl*) and wheat (*başak*): the former symbolized the country's independence; the latter symbolized welfare and the party's endeavor to elevate Turkey above the level of contemporary civilization (*muasır medeniyet*). This was presented in the party's program as its essential goal. The WP argued that material development would be incomplete without a prior achievement of spiritual development; and, like its predecessor parties, it regarded the Turkish people's conversion to Islam a thousand years ago as the starting point of Turkish history.

The "National Consciousness" rhetoric was a critique of Turkish Westernization attempts during the past two centuries. According to the WP, the dissolution of the Ottoman Empire was due to decay in national faith, traditions, and culture (Islam's power in the society) resulting from Westernization. The party regarded Western civilization and Zionism as the source of all evil and as the reason for the country's underdevelopment problem. According to this view, the West regarded Islam as an obstacle to its exploitation of the Muslim world. Hence, imperialism and Zionism had been working for two centuries to inject the idea of imitating the West (*Batı taklitçiliği*) into the Turkish people's minds. As a result, two types of perspectives emerged in the country: the National View (*Milli Görüş*), which was represented by the WP, and the imitators (*taklitçiler*) of the West, which were represented by all the other political parties.[37] The WP, in articulating its goals, called for an equal distribution of wealth among citizens; for protection of the family, which was defined as the essence of the nation; and for restructuring educational institutions in a way that would lead to the spiritual development of the country.[38]

The WP's use of the term *milli* (national) did not refer to the modern secular concept of nationalism. The term *milli*, referred to the Ottoman *millet* (national) system, wherein subjects of the empire were categorized according to

---

[37] Refah Partisi, *Birinci Büyük Kongresi, Genel Başkan Ahmet Tekdal'ın Açış Konuşması*, 7–11.
[38] Refah Partisi, *Refah Partisi Tüzük ve Programı*, 35, 38–9, 47.

their religion. Thus, in the WP's terms, *milli* referred to a religious community of Muslims (*umma*). The WP criticized the existing secular-democratic system of the country on the grounds that it was a top-down imposition, not representative of the nation's will. The party defined the establishment of a real pluralistic democracy and the representation of the national will in the country as one of its essential goals. Accordingly, democracy along with freedom of conscience, will, faith, and press were defined as the primary principles of the party.

The WP regarded all sorts of suppression of freedom of conscience, will, and faith as incompatible with secularism,[39] which it defined as follows: "Secularism is not an enmity towards religion. To the contrary, it is a principle that protects freedoms of faith and will from all sorts of violations."[40] Yet, the party's faith-based definition of "freedom of conscience" as "the right to live according to one's beliefs" led to conflicts with Turkey's secular legal system.[41] As a high-ranking Felicity Party (FP) member argued in an interview with the author in June 2004, "the Sharia refers to Islam."[42] This party member emphasized that "there is no forceful imposition in Islam and nobody's religion was interfered with under the Ottoman state, which was based on Islam."[43] But when asked, "What would happen to people who do not share the party's view on Islam, once the party's program is applied in Turkey?" he answered, "Religion commands people of reason (*din akıl sahiplerine hitap ediyor*). One who is out of his mind does not have a religion. Thus, Islam in this sense is a rational religion. In Islam, there is nothing that contradicts with reason. We do not have anything to do with insane people."[44] The FP member defined religion according to Islam as follows: "Religion is a sacred law (*ilâhi kanun*), which directs people of reason (*akıl sahipleri*) with their free will always to a right (*doğru*), beautiful (*güzel*), beneficial (*faydalı*), and just path."[45] Because the present secular-democratic character of the Turkish state does not conform to this path, it is not legitimate in the eyes of WP activists. Therefore, the nature of the state has to be redefined in Islamic terms.

According to Necmettin Erbakan, at this time chairman of the WP, there was neither democracy nor secularism in Turkey. More than 80 percent of the people, he argued, were living in a system they did not want. He attributed the low level of electoral support for the WP to the influence of external powers that did not want the strengthening of the National View in Turkey and to ignorance of the media about the party. The WP proposed to turn Turkey into a state of *hak* (godly, sacred, and just system of Islam). Erbakan also argued that Islam was a system of justice and *hak*. If a country wanted to apply Islam

---

[39] Refah Partisi, *Birinci Büyük Kongresi, Genel Başkan Ahmet Tekdal'ın Açış Konuşması*, 9.
[40] Refah Partisi, *Refah Partisi Tüzük ve Programı*, 37.
[41] Özbudun, "The Institutional Decline of Parties in Turkey," 251.
[42] Author's interview with a high-ranking FP member, Ankara, June 10, 2004.
[43] The Ottoman Empire was based on Islam; yet, the *Sharia* was not implemented under Ottoman Empire rule.
[44] Author's interview with a high-ranking FP member, Ankara, June 10, 2004.
[45] Ibid.

to its political system, it had to apply it in its fullest sense. Since the Quran and the *sunna* cannot be changed, there cannot be a reform in Islam in order to make it compatible with today's world.[46] But, this still left open the question as to how the state would be organized and by what principles. Islamic theologians acknowledge that Islam does not provide explicit guidance regarding the governance of a modern state.[47] As the former prominent NAP parliamentarian Nevzat Kösoğlu noted in an interview with the author, "there is no regulation in the Quran regarding the state structure and its governance."[48]

The WP criticized Turkey's Western-oriented foreign policy and emphasized instead worldwide Muslim unity. As a Muslim country, it was argued, Turkey had nothing to learn from the West. Ahmet Tekdal, the WP chair during the party's First Congress in June 1985, described the situation of the world as follows:

Humanity that needs peace, friendship, and welfare unfortunately faces again war, suppression, unfairness, even famine. Values that make a human being a human being, goodness, rightness, mercy, such great values have disappeared. A bold materialism dominated the entire world. An overwhelming majority of the people are in a spiritual abyss. Immorality, prostitution, cheating, alcoholism, [and] drug addiction have reached frightening levels. In every corner of the world, there is terrorism and anarchy. Wherever you look, humanity faces endless suppression, conflict and war. . . . If, in the world, the dominance of the hak and justice is not provided in its fullest sense, as long as it is not accepted that the hak has priority over power, humanity will face greater disasters.[49]

By the mid-1980s, the WP successfully framed the global agenda in Turkey in terms of a quest for more democratization, freedom, and human rights in order to appeal to a broad sector of the citizenry. Haldun Gülalp, a professor of political science, notes that the political conflict between the right and the left of the pre-1980 coup period was replaced by "identity politics" (religious and ethnic identity). This transformation in the rhetoric reflected an underlying strategy of the Islamists, acknowledged openly by Erbakan in 1985. "During the pre-September 12 period [i.e., before the 1980 military intervention]," he argued, "the country's primary concern was protection of lives and social peace. In the aftermath of 12 September, there had been changes in Turkey's issues. Today, primarily human rights, subjects about freedoms, and issues of how can we get rid of the nation's poverty problem gained more importance."[50] In its 1987 election pamphlet, the WP emphasized its demand for more democratization (freedom of faith and thought) [the headscarf issue][51]

---

[46] Hasan Hüseyin Ceylan, *Erbakan ve Türkiye'nin Temel Meseleleri* [Erbakan and Turkey's Essential Issues], 5th ed. (Ankara: Rehber Yayıncılık, 1996), 109–10, 121, 124, 181–3.
[47] Author's interviews with divinity professors, Ankara, February 17–18, 2004.
[48] Author's interview with Nevzat Kösoğlu, the former NAP parliamentarian, Ankara, February 17, 2004.
[49] Refah Partisi, *Birinci Büyük Kongresi, Genel Başkan Ahmet Tekdal'ın Açış Konuşması*, 4–5.
[50] Ceylan, *Erbakan ve Türkiye'nin Temel Meseleleri*, 117.
[51] The Turkish penal code prohibits the wearing of an Islamic headscarf (*türban*) in state institutions.

and for equal representation in the parliament (by changing the 10% threshold rule) followed by the problem of decay in ethical and moral values, as reflected in television programs and other media, nude beaches, gambling, corruption, drug addiction, alcoholism, and prostitution. The malfunctioning economy in the country was the last issue addressed in the election pamphlet. In "the solution of problems" section of the pamphlet, the WP focused on how it would solve economic problems and how the country would pursue an independent foreign policy with its faithful cadres. The problems of insufficient democracy and decay in moral values were not clearly addressed.[52] The slogans of the WP for the 1987 general elections included, among others, "first ethics and spirituality," "one who does not have a faith, fears the freedom of faith," "the WP protects the rights of the believers (*inananlar*)," "headscarf is our national dress," "imitators [of the West] produce only prostitution, gambling, alcoholic beverages," "we are different!," "abandon the imitators, look at the national view!," "enough! No to the rentier and the leftist," "neither the IMF, nor the EEC; the national view, the national effort (*milli hamle*)," "not a servant but a leading Turkey," and "we are coming with faith! We will complete our national view heavy industry effort."[53]

The Welfare Party Frames the Just Order as Its Political Rhetoric in the 1990s

The WP's primary emphasis on the adverse impacts of Westernization (religious and moral decay in the Turkish society), Western imperialism, and the "suppressive" character of the Turkish state received support from the Islamist segment of the electorate in the 1980s. Yet, it was impossible to become the ruling party by receiving only the traditional Islamist votes. Islamist leaders estimate their religiously committed support base to be only 11 percent of the electorate.[54] Thus, by the 1990s the WP, while keeping its Islamist staff and goals, put primary emphasis in its public rhetoric on socioeconomic problems, so that the party would appeal to the entire electorate and turn political Islam into a mass movement. According to Şevket Kazan, the vice-chair of the FP, the WP chose the "Just Order" (*Adil Düzen*) as its slogan in the 1990s as an explicit attempt to expand its electoral support. Kazan argued, "Elections are won by slogans. The National View leads you to win the electorate. Yet, it comes short in the next elections. Bahri Zengin, [a WP parliamentarian], formulated (*resimlendirdi*) the Just Order in a very beautiful way."[55] The Just Order, as a successful frame, had a great mobilization capacity, as social

---

[52] Refah Partisi, *Tek Çözüm: Refah Partisi* [The Only Solution: The Welfare Party] (Ankara: Refah Partisi, 1987), 4–15, 21–44.
[53] Ibid.
[54] Author's interview with a high-ranking FP member, Ankara, June 10, 2004.
[55] Author's interview with Şevket Kazan, the vice-chair of the FP, Ankara, June 9, 2004.

movement theory hypothesizes.⁵⁶ The Just Order, by covering a large range of problems, not only addressed a broad range of social groups, but also it "neutralized"⁵⁷ the frames of rival political parties.

The party announced its new slogan at its Third Congress in October 1990. Starting with the 1991 general election campaign, the WP utilized the Just Order as its slogan. The Just Order was a reformulation of the previous slogans, National Consciousness (*Milli Şuur*) and the National View (*Milli Görüş*) in the aftermath of the cold war. Erbakan, having realized the demise of the Soviet Union, initiated the effort to find a more attractive and systematic doctrine in 1987. The Just Order emphasized the necessity of an independent foreign policy, Muslim unity, democratization, freedom of faith, and human rights. It also aimed at establishing Islamism as a counterforce to U.S.-led capitalism and world order. Erbakan, during his election campaign in July 1991, declared the Just Order as a rival to "U.S.-led imperialism and capitalism."⁵⁸

Erbakan suggested the cooperation with the Muslim world called for by the Just Order would be realized by establishing five institutions: a UN organization representing Muslim countries, a defense organization like NATO, an economic union, a common currency, and a common cultural organization.⁵⁹ He predicted that once the WP came to power, a wave of revolution would spread throughout the Muslim world, and Western imitator governments would be toppled.⁶⁰

The Just Order, like the party's earlier political rhetoric, framed politics in terms of two rival groups: the imitators of the West and the Just Order. Erbakan continued to criticize all other political parties, on both the right and the left, on the grounds that they were pro-Western (pro–United States, pro-EC/EU, pro-IMF); damaged ethics; took materialism (*maddeci*) rather than spirituality as the basis of order in society; argued for a colonial type of development (*müstemleke tipi kalkınma*) under the tutelage of the West; pursued a dependent foreign policy; and suppressed the poorer classes by charging interest, devaluing Turkish currency, imposing unfair taxes, and distributing credits unfairly.⁶¹ Furthermore, the imitators were applying "enmity towards religion" and "the right to suppress (*zulüm*) Muslims" in the country. Thus, the imitator parties were antidemocratic and antisecular.⁶² Erbakan argued that the "illness

---

⁵⁶ Lyndi Hewitt and Holly J. McCammon, "Explaining Suffrage Mobilization: Balance, Neutralization, and Range in Collective Action Frames," in Johnston and Noakes, *Frames of Protest*, 33–52; Jürgen Gerhards and Dieter Rucht, "Mesomobilization: Organizing and Framing in Two Protest Campaigns in West Germany," *American Journal of Sociology* 98, no. 3 (November 1992): 555–96.
⁵⁷ Hewitt and McCammon, "Explaining Suffrage Mobilization," 34.
⁵⁸ Necmettin Erbakan's election speech in Muş (July 1, 1990), in Şevket Kazan, *Refah Gerçeği*, vol. 1 [The Reality of Welfare] (Ankara: Keşif Yayınları, 2001), 60.
⁵⁹ Necmettin Erbakan, *İslam ve İlim* [Islam and Science] (Istanbul: Furkan Yayınları, 1994), 68–71.
⁶⁰ Ibid., 72.
⁶¹ Ibid., 88.
⁶² Ibid., 78.

of imitation" was to be treated like cancer. The source of this illness, he argued, is imperialist and Zionist forces, which inject imitation into a nation that they want to exploit. If a nation cannot cure itself from this illness, it goes through a series of stages until it disappears: the first stage is the loss of national identity (*özbenlik*). This is followed by the second stage of economic and cultural exploitation of the nation. According to Erbakan, Turkey was already at the second stage of the imitation illness. In the third stage, the nation loses its independence. The last stage amounts to a loss of core identity, culminating in the nation's disappearance.

The vocabulary of the Just Order was designed to evoke Islamist sentiments. The WP continued to describe world affairs from the perspective of the Arab-Israeli conflict, combining anti-Western with anti-Zionist rhetoric. The party argued that the imitator parties ruled Turkey at all times and established a slavery system in the country by implementing pro-Zionist IMF's economic directives. Socioeconomic problems in Turkey were the result of the imitation of the West. The charging of an interest rate, unfair taxes, inflation, and fluctuating currency rates were defined as germs leading to the enslavement of Turkey (*köle düzeni*). While the Turkish public was suffering from this slavery system, which the party called the Pharaoh Ramses' slavery system in Egypt three thousand years ago, a few holdings in the country that collaborated with the system were getting rich. Furthermore, Turkey, by paying its foreign debts to "Zionist banks" abroad was contributing to Israeli military strength. This occurred, allegedly, because Israel was financing its armaments supply from the revenues of international debts. Israel was defined as an expansionist country trying to dominate the Middle East, including Turkey, to realize its goal of Zionism.[63] The Just Order emphasized that the nation's core identity did not lie in the West, but in the Muslim world. When Turkey enters the EC, Erbakan warned, the very next day Israel will enter. Since the EC was not an international agreement but aimed at becoming one state, Turkey and Israel will be made one state. This would mean the realization of Zionism's alleged ultimate goal of the establishment of the "Great Israel."[64]

The Islamists regarded capitalism as a system that makes people each other's slave by erasing all traditional values. The failure of capitalism's rival ideology, Marxism, led the Islamists to anticipate that humanity would not be looking for another ideology, but would be looking for faith.[65] The conflict between East and West during the cold war would now be taking place between the North and South. The South comprised underdeveloped countries many of which were Islamic; the North was led by the imperialistic United States – which, according to Erbakan, "lived like a Dracula." While the

---

[63] Refah Partisi, *Türkiye'nin Gerçek Durumu, Sebepleri* [Turkey's Real Situation, Its Reasons] (Ankara: Refah Partisi, n.d.), 8–9, 18–27, 32–5, 44–8; Necmettin Erbakan, *Adil Ekonomik Düzen* [The Just Economic Order] (Ankara: Semih Ofset, 1991), 1–98.
[64] Erbakan, *İslam ve İlim*, 51–3; Ceylan, *Erbakan ve Türkiye'nin Temel Meseleleri*, 169–70.
[65] Şükrü Karatepe, "İdeolojiden inanca" [From ideology to faith], *Zaman*, October 10, 1991, 2.

imperialist countries were becoming richer, the underdeveloped countries, suffering under the economic burden of huge foreign debts, were becoming poorer. According to Erbakan, the West, with the cooperation of Zionism, was exploiting the Muslim world through national and multilateral institutions and organizations (he mentioned the CIA [the Central Intelligence Agency], the MOSSAD [the Institute for Intelligence and Special Operations], the UN [the United Nations], NATO [the North Atlantic Treaty Organization] and universities and research centers in the United States) and by economic means (such as embargoes) and military means (the U.S. military force). According to Erbakan, with the end of the cold war, NATO was now targeting Islam, and both imperialism and Zionism were condemning antiimperialist Muslims as Islamic fundamentalists.

The WP argued that a Just Order based on Islam offered a political system for the emancipation not only of the Turkish people, but of all humanity.[66] For Erbakan, the entire political system of Turkey, which was irreparably corrupted, had to be changed. Turkey under the Just Order would lead the Muslim world, and as a result a new world order would be established, based not on repression but on felicity.[67]

The Just Order also focused on the malfunctioning state in Turkey. This attracted the ordinary citizens' votes. The WP argued that imperialism and Zionism were pursuing a conscious policy of "modern colonialism," which was causing socioeconomic problems in Turkey.[68] Özbudun argues, "The party combined religious and nonreligious appeals, as seen in its emphasis on industrialization, social justice, honest government, and the restoration of Turkey's former grandeur."[69] In economic terms the party resembled a social democratic party with its advocacy of a just economic order and its emphasis on equal income distribution as well as the moral obligation of improving the material position of the poor. Yet, it should be noted that the party differed from a conventional social democratic party in that it placed major emphasis on free enterprise and private capital as the principal source of growth, while downgrading the role of the state. The Just Order called for a free-market economic system, wherein demand would determine supply. The state would assist the private sector in planning and finance. The party defined the Just Order as "an order that is based on private entrepreneurship and purified from monopoly."[70] The WP called for the elimination of the interest rate, devaluation, artificially increased foreign currency rates, the establishment of a fair tax and credits system, the introduction of an Islamic banking system and

---

[66] "Refah Partisi Genel Başkanı Necmettin Erbakan'ın Aylık Basın Toplantısı" [The Welfare Party Chair Necmettin Erbakan's Monthly Press Meeting], *Milli Gazete*, November 6, 1990, 12–16; Erbakan, *Adil Ekonomik Düzen*, 12.
[67] "Adil Düzene Geçelim" [Let's Transfer to the Just Order], *Milli Gazete*, June 20, 1993, 6.
[68] Erbakan, *Adil Ekonomik Düzen*, 1–3.
[69] Özbudun, *Contemporary Turkish Politics*, 87.
[70] Refah Partisi, *Adil Düzen 21 Soru/21 Cevap* [The Just Order 21 Questions/21 Answers] (Ankara: Refah Partisi, n.d.), 1–3, 13–16, 40, 43; Erbakan, *Adil Ekonomik Düzen*, 3–4.

profit-sharing scheme, state ownership of basic services like public utilities and the infrastructure, and an increase in social security and welfare spending in the country. Erbakan argued, "these views were based on fundamental 'God-given' rights of the individuals found in the Quran and Hadiths."[71]

The Just Order criticized both capitalism and communism: whereas the former damages tranquility (*huzur*), freedom, justice, welfare, and respect; the latter, by abolishing profit, free-market economy, private ownership, and private investment, brought unhappiness to humanity. The WP regarded both capitalism and communism as being economic systems of Western civilization that gave priority to physical force (*kaba kuvvet*) rather than the *hak* (the godly, sacred, and just system of Islam). Capitalism and communism were like twins. The only difference was that in communism the repressing power was political, whereas in capitalism the repressing power was capital.[72] Like communism, capitalism was bound to come to an end one day. The WP argued that capitalism was causing the following illnesses: hunger, poverty, inflation, unemployment, exploitation, underdevelopment, unjust distribution of wealth, international imbalance, foreign debt, social crises, wars, terror, mafia, bribery, and moral decay.[73] The reason that capitalism was still alive today was that capitalist exploitative states imposed their system upon underdeveloped countries by force and pressure. One day the capitalist system would yield to the Just Order, beginning in Turkey and spreading to the whole world, as a result of which humanity would attain a permanent felicity system.[74]

The global quest for democratization, freedom, and human rights found an acceptable platform in Turkey, as elsewhere, in the aftermath of the cold war. Postmodern criticisms of the Western model of modernization, positivism, rationalism, and socialism were made. The WP found a political and social environment to present its political Islamist agenda in a nonexplicit way. The WP could frame state policies as treating the Muslim faithful unfairly, that is, unequally, and therefore frame its own position in terms of a fight for the equal rights of the people. In effect, the WP presented an illiberal political agenda by using a liberal vocabulary.

Erbakan argued that when the WP would establish the Just Order, it would provide the ground for the citizens to write a constitution that would be compatible with the nation's faith, customs, and traditions. There would no longer be any obstacles to freedom of faith and conscience; everybody would be able to live according to his or her belief.[75] Yet, Erbakan continued to offer a faith-based definition of the concept of freedom of faith and conscience, which was based on four factors: first, freedom of expression and freedom of spreading

---

[71] Yeşilada, "Realignment and Party Adaptation: The Case of the Refah and Fazilet Parties," in Sayarı and Esmer, *Politics, Parties, and Elections in Turkey*, 172–3.
[72] Refah Partisi, *Adil Düzen 21 Soru/21 Cevap*, 27–8.
[73] Ibid., 30.
[74] Ibid., 29.
[75] Ceylan, *Erbakan ve Türkiye'nin Temel Meseleleri*, 109–10, 121, 124, 181–3; Erbakan, *İslam ve İlim*, 79–80.

Framing the Political Opportunity Structure

one's thought and belief by all means; second, freedom to learn and teach one's faith; third, freedom of people from the same faith to organize and work together; and fourth, freedom to live one's faith.[76] While the WP frequently argued that once it would come to power, it would tolerate all religions and lifestyles, Erbakan divided the Turkish citizens into two groups: the Welfarists and people who were waiting to become Welfarists. Thus, Erbakan rejected pluralism in the society. He made his interpretation of Islam his starting point and argued if an Islamic society were established, then there would be democracy. Thus, Islam, not democracy, came first according to the party's ideology.[77] Furthermore, a high-ranking FP member acknowledged, in an interview cited earlier, that the Just Order basically referred to political Islam. Because the secular establishment of the Turkish state would not permit a party to make such an explicit argument, the FP member explained, the WP implicitly referred to the project of political Islam by explaining its content without naming it.[78]

Once the WP became the party of government, it maintained, it would replace imitation of the West with the Just Order, as a result of which there would be a change in national policy with respect to education, culture, and the arts; economics; and social issues.[79] Under the Just Order, youth, who would ensure the supremacy of the *hak* over unfairness, would be educated with a consciousness and spirit of the jihad and warriorship (*mücahit*).[80] The transition to the Just Order would not be a gradual one; it would take place as soon as possible.[81] Citizens would be "convinced" rather than "forced" when they transferred to the Just Order.[82] "We will demolish this slavery order by democratic means," stated Erbakan in a speech on December 17, 1991, "and establish the Just Order that emphasizes the primacy of God (*Hak*) and justice, while rejecting imperialism."[83] Ahmet Tekdal, in a speech delivered in 1993 when he was WP vice-chair, stated that he advocated installing a regime based on the *Sharia* in Turkey. Tekdal argued,

In countries which have a parliamentary regime, if the people are not sufficiently aware, if they do not work hard enough to bring about the advent of "hak nizami" [a just order or God's order], two calamities lie ahead. The first calamity is the renegades they will have to face. They will be tyrannized by them and will eventually disappear. The second calamity is that they will not be able to give a satisfactory account of themselves

---

[76] Necmettin Erbakan, *Kenan Evren'in Anılarındaki Yanılgılar* [Mistakes in Kenan Evren's Memoirs] (Ankara: Rehber Yayıncılık, 1991), 37.
[77] Tayfun Atay, "Türkiye Örneği," in Turan, *İslam ve Demokrasi Kutlu Doğum Sempozyumu*, 263–4.
[78] Author's interview with a high-ranking FP member, Ankara, February 16, 2004.
[79] Erbakan, *İslam ve İlim*, 53–4.
[80] Ibid., 88.
[81] Refah Partisi, *Adil Düzen 21 Soru/21 Cevap*, 35.
[82] Erbakan, *İslam ve İlim*, 94.
[83] "Erbakan: Biz demokratik devrim yapacağız" [Erbakan: We will make a democratic revolution], *Milli Gazete*, December 17, 1991, 6.

to Allah, as they will not have worked to establish "hak nizami." And so they will likewise perish. Venerable brothers, our duty is to do what is necessary to introduce the system of justice, taking these subtleties into consideration. The political apparatus which seeks to establish "hak nizami" in Turkey is the Welfare Party.[84]

Thus, the main tenets of the Just Order were not different from the party's previous political goal in the 1970s. Yet, the more the secular state started to malfunction in the 1990s, the more Erbakan's Just Order slogan appealed as an attractive alternative political project to disaffected citizens who had previously been voting for mainstream political parties.

THE WELFARE PARTY BECOMES A PARTY OF THE MASSES

The WP, which received only 4.4 percent of the vote in the 1984 local elections, became the leading party by securing 21.4 percent of the vote and 158 seats in parliament in the 1995 general elections. The party's framing of the malfunctioning state played a crucial role in its electoral success. As we have seen, the Turkish economy had been experiencing increasing problems of high inflation, corruption, inequality, and unemployment in the 1990s. In 1994 a serious economic crisis occurred, which caused the gross national product (GNP) per capita to decline by 27.3 percent, from $3,004 in 1993 to $2,184.[85]

Not surprisingly, the interviews conducted by the author for this study with a broad spectrum of public figures and academics suggest the primary concern of Turkish voters has been their social and material well-being. In the post-1980 period, the majority of the electorate first voted for center-right and center-left political parties in the hope these parties would solve the country's socioeconomic problems. In the 1983 general elections, voters supported the center-right MP. By the mid-1980s, however, the MP's vote share started to decline. This decline can be explained by several factors. First, even though Turgut Özal argued that his party was representing the interests of the "main pillar" (middle class) of the society (*Orta Direk*),[86] the MP's commitment to a free-market economy led to economic difficulties among the middle class, which constituted the bulk of the party's voting base. Second, with the removal in 1987 of the ban on political activities by former politicians of the pre-1980 period, Necmettin Erbakan took over leadership of the WP, Süleyman Demirel

---

[84] European Court of Human Rights, *Case of Refah Partisi (the Welfare Party) and Others v. Turkey (Application nos. 41340/98, 41342/98, 41343/98, and 41344/98)*, 10–11 (Internet ed.).

[85] Şeref Efe and Mustafa Rumeli, *Hükümetlerin Performanslarının Değerlendirilmesi* [Evaluation of Governments' Performances] (Ankara: Ankara Ticaret Odası, 2002), 10, 12, 28–30; Ekrem Pakdemirli, *Cumhuriyet Döneminin Ekonomik Büyüklükleri (1923–2002)* [Economic Indicators of the Republican Period (1923–2002)] (Ankara: Türkiye Odalar ve Borsalar Birliği Yayınları, 2002), 44.

[86] Kalaycıoğlu, "The Motherland Party: The Challenge of Institutionalization in a Charismatic Leader Party," in Rubin and Heper, *Political Parties in Turkey*, 45.

became the chair of the center-right True Path Party (TPP), and Alparslan Türkeş became the leader of the Nationalist Action Party (NAP). As a result, some Islamists who voted for the MP in 1983 transferred their support to the WP. At the same time, the TPP, as the heir of the Democrat Party (DP) and the Justice Party (JP) and under the leadership of the charismatic leader Demirel, became the major rival to the MP in the 1980s. While the MP advanced slogans of "transformation" and "leaping to a new age" by pursuing a free-market economy, the TPP pursued a populist political rhetoric championing egalitarianism, distributive policies, a paternalistic and protective state, and economic justice. A third factor explaining the decline in electoral support for the MP was the fact that the party, in terms of its organization, was closer to a cadre or caucus party model than to a mass party. It had only weak local networks. The TPP, in contrast, had a powerful, closely knit network of local party organizations with strong clientelistic ties.[87]

The majority of voters concluded that the MP would not solve their socioeconomic problems, and voted for the center-right TPP. The TPP's 1991 general election program, unlike that of the MP, was very comprehensive. In its election program, the TPP defined twenty unsolved problems facing Turkey, ranging from underdevelopment, threats against the unitary character of the state, and passive foreign policy to socioeconomic issues such as stable economics, unemployment, education, health, demography, environment, distribution of wealth, social security, investments, industrialization, agriculture and peasants, urbanization and housing, unequal taxation, debt problem, and clientelism. The party proposed detailed solutions to these problems.[88] While the MP declared that it believed in a "free market economy," based on competition,[89] the TPP emphasized that it was a party embracing all segments of the society: rich and poor; peasant, worker, and craftsman; young and old; the widow; the orphan; the abandoned (*kimsesiz*); the unemployed; the handicapped; and the retired.[90] Furthermore, TPP leader Demirel, during the 1991 election campaign, promised the public that once his party came to power, he would topple Özal from the presidency[91] and take him to court to give an account of corruption during his chairmanship of the MP[92] – which received public support.

---

[87] Sakallıoğlu, "Liberalism, Democracy and the Turkish Center-Right," 144; Frank Tachau, "An Overview of Electoral Behavior: Toward Protest or Consolidation of Democracy?" in Sayarı and Esmer, *Politics, Parties, and Elections in Turkey*, 37; Turan, *Türkiye'de Seçmen Davranışı*, 138; Özbudun, *Contemporary Turkish Politics*, 95; Ayata, "Ideology, Social Bases, and Organizational Structure of the Post-1980 Political Parties," 38, 40; and "Asiltürk: ANAP'ın oyları bize yöneldi" [Asiltürk: The MP's votes have been directed to us], *Milli Gazete*, September 2, 1991, 6.
[88] See DYP, *Seçim Bildirgesi, 21 Ekim Sabahı Yeni Bir Türkiye* [The TPP Election Pamphlet, On 21 October Morning, A New Turkey] (DYP, 1991), 45–320. See also Anavatan Partisi, *Anavatan Partisi Seçim Beyannamesi* [The Motherland Party Election Pamphlet] (October 20, 1991), 1–96.
[89] Anavatan Partisi, *Anavatan Partisi Seçim Beyannamesi*, 29.
[90] DYP, *Seçim Bildirgesi, 21 Ekim Sabahı Yeni Bir Türkiye*, 306.
[91] Özal was the president from 1989 until his death in 1993.
[92] "Cumhurbaşkanı adeta kaşınıyor" [The President seeks for a trouble], Ahmet Tan's interview with Demirel, *Cumhuriyet*, September 26, 1991, 6.

The TPP's slogan was "Democratic great Turkey and new Turkey." Demirel promised that once his party came to power it would solve all the economic problems of the country in five hundred days.[93] Tansu Çiller, then TPP vice-chair, promised that if the TPP were elected, everybody in the country would have two keys: one key for a house and another key for a car. Demirel, while emphasizing the unitary character of the Turkish state and the necessity to crush the Kurdistan Workers' Party (PKK) terrorism, argued for writing a more democratic constitution and for the establishment of a human rights ministry.[94] Turgut Özal had cheated the electorate since he had not fulfilled any of his promises; Demirel pledged that, if he were elected, he would provide the public with peace, safety, and jobs.[95]

The center-left, which was weakened as a result of the 1980 coup,[96] was represented in the 1990s by three parties, the Social Democratic Populist Party (SDPP), the RPP, and the DLP.[97] The end of the cold war led to a deflation of the left in politics throughout the world. In a June 2004 interview with the author, a prominent former DLP parliamentarian, Uluç Gürkan, suggested that "both the 1980 military coup and the egos of social democratic leaders led to the disintegration of social democracy in Turkey." Furthermore, he argued, "in the aftermath of the cold war, the left lost its reference point and started to pursue neoliberal policies. Social democracy in Turkey could no longer propose a viable program to solve citizens', particularly the poor classes', socioeconomic problems. The WP replaced the social democratic parties in Turkey."[98]

The center-left RPP parliamentarian Yakup Kepenek during an interview with the author in June 2004, explained the weakening of social democracy in Turkey in similar terms, but added two additional comments: first, he argued that an organized and self-conscious labor class, which would be the basis of left-wing politics, could not emerge in Turkey; and second, the left, in terms of political parties, trade unions, and foundations, has always been divided. In his view, the attitude of social democratic leaders played an important role in bringing about this division.[99]

---

[93] DYP, Seçim Bildirgesi, 21 Ekim 1991 Sabahı Yeni Bir Türkiye, 69–72, 305–20.

[94] "Özal, Çankaya'dan indirilecek" [Özal will be toppled from Çankaya], Cumhuriyet, October 2, 1991, 3; Erdal Şimşek, "Bugünkü koalisyonun ekonomik faciası, 2" [Today's coalition government's economic catastrophe], Akit, December 20, 1995, 7.

[95] "Demirel: Özal sirkatini söylüyor" [Demirel: Özal is not serious], Ahmet Tan's interview with Demirel, Cumhuriyet, September 27, 1991, 6; DYP, Seçim Bildirgesi, 21 Ekim Sabahı Yeni Bir Türkiye, 260–1.

[96] Unlike European social democratic parties, Turkish social democratic parties do not have strong links with organized groups, like trade unions. The 1982 Constitution created under the military rule set legal limits on establishing permanent and formal links between political parties and trade unions. Ayata, "Ideology, Social Bases, and Organizational Structure of the Post-1980 Political Parties," 43.

[97] Ibid.

[98] Author's interview with Uluç Gürkan, the former DLP parliamentarian, Ankara, June 10, 2004.

[99] Author's interview with Yakup Kepenek, the RPP parliamentarian, Ankara, June 11, 2004.

The demise of the Soviet Union suggested the exhaustion of state-led development models. In the aftermath of the cold war and the collapse of the Soviet Union, neoliberalism became a dominant ideology in Turkey (as it did elsewhere). The main tenets of neoliberalism are social and economic reforms that encourage the establishment of a market economy and provide for a diminished role for the state, along with depoliticization, pragmatism, and political centrism.[100] In the 1990s, the social democratic parties, while primarily emphasizing human rights, freedom, and democratization, did not propose viable solutions to the socioeconomic problems of Turkish citizens.[101]

Both Gürkan and Kepenek also noted that the Islamists, who are motivated by their ideology, are very diligent.[102] Kepenek argued that when compared with the Islamist parties, the RPP has deficiencies in its organization, particularly in contacting youth and women. Kepenek also noted that his party, unlike the Islamist parties, does not have anything to offer in the way of material benefits to shantytown residents.[103]

In the 1990s, the vote share of the leading center-left party, the SDPP, declined, for a number of reasons: first, a corruption scandal involving the party's Istanbul mayorship and the Istanbul Water and Sewage Agency (the İSKİ – *İstanbul Su ve Kanalizasyon İdaresi*) came as a great disappointment to the electorate as the leading social democratic party was not immune from corruption. Ayşe Ayata, a professor of political science, notes that a majority of SDPP party members regarded municipalities under their party's control "as a chance to obtain some tangible benefits, such as jobs, licenses for building houses, or legalization of buildings in squatter settlement areas" – what she calls "the embourgeoisement of local leadership in the 1980s." Furthermore, "there developed a list of contractors who were active party members with the ability to mobilize votes in local congresses. They demanded that mayors and cabinet ministers give them contracts in return for power. Thus, after 1991 there came a wave of corruption allegations."[104]

Second, the SDPP allowed candidates of the PKK-supported Kurdish separatist People's Endeavor Party (PEP – *Halkın Emek Partisi*) to enter the elections on the SDPP list.[105] After entering the parliament on the SDPP list, the PEP parliamentarians withdrew from the SDPP and established their own group. Many of the PEP parliamentarians were later charged with Kurdish separatism, and some were sent to prison.[106]

---

[100] Sakallıoğlu, "Liberalism, Democracy, and the Turkish Center-Right," 142.
[101] "Cem: Sağın değişimi karşısında şaşırdık" [Cem: We were surprised facing the change in the right], *Cumhuriyet*, November 20, 1991, 6; Şahin Alpay, "İnsiyatif sağ partilere kaptırıldı" [Parties on the right seized upon an opportunity], *Cumhuriyet*, November 21, 1991, 6.
[102] Author's interviews with Uluç Gürkan, the former DLP parliamentarian, Ankara, June 10, 2004; and with Yakup Kepenek, the RPP parliamentarian, Ankara, June 11, 2004.
[103] Author's interview with Yakup Kepenek, the RPP parliamentarian, Ankara, June 11, 2004.
[104] Ayata-Güneş, "The Republican People's Party," 117.
[105] Turan, *Türkiye'de Seçmen Davranışı*, 141.
[106] Ayata-Güneş, "The Republican People's Party," 114.

The SDPP's focus in the 1991 general elections was more on democratization and human rights, defined in terms of recognition of Kurdish identity in Turkey than on socioeconomic problems. The party campaigned on the premise that it would put more emphasis on education and health services. Yet, it did not offer a program for solving the problems of unemployment, inflation, corruption, and unequal distribution of wealth.[107]

Following the 1991 general elections, a TPP-SDPP coalition government was established. The SDPP became a coalition partner even though its vote share had declined by 8 percent since the 1989 local elections. The vote share of the center-left parties in major cities (Istanbul, Ankara, and Izmir) declined significantly in the 1991 general elections compared to the 1987 general elections.[108]

For the 1991 general elections, the WP formed an alliance with the Turkish nationalist Nationalist Work Party (NWP) and the Reformist Democracy Party (RDP, a mixture of the WP and the NWP) in order to pass the 10 percent threshold and gain representation in parliament. The Intellectuals' Hearth and the TIS intelligentsia organized around certain foundations played a crucial role in the formation of the alliance between these three parties. During the election campaign the WP proposed the Just Order. Public attention to the WP's political rhetoric started to increase in the 1990s. For example, between two hundred thousand and two hundred fifty thousand people attended the party's gathering, "*Büyük İstanbul Mitingi*" (Great Istanbul Political Gathering) during the 1991 election campaign.[109] In the 1991 elections, the WP ranked fourth, by winning 16.9 percent of the votes and sixty-two seats in parliament, a major improvement over the 7.2 percent and zero seats in 1987. The uneasy alliance between the WP, the NWP, and the RDP came to an end in the aftermath of the elections – primarily because the WP's ideology had been based on an Islamic *umma* or community of believers, and thus it rejected nationalism, whereas the NWP's ideology had been based on Turkish nationalism.[110]

The TPP-SDPP coalition government failed to fulfill any of the significant social welfare goals they articulated during the campaign. Furthermore, a major scandal, involving the Primary School Teachers Health and Social Aid Fund (İLKSAN – *İlkokul Öğretmenleri Sağlık ve Sosyal Yardım Sandığı*), revealed that the TPP, like the other mainstream parties (the MP and the SDPP), was not immune from corruption. In 1993, the İLKSAN, which is tied to the Ministry of Education, made a land purchase to build housing at a low price for

---

[107] "Güneydoğu'da işi silaha bırakmayacağız" [We will not leave the issue to be solved by arms], "Özal'ın Ortadoğu politikası yanlış" [Özal's Middle East policy is wrong], Ahmet Tan's interviews with Erdal İnönü, *Cumhuriyet*, September 23–4, 1991, 6.
[108] DİE, *Results of General Election of Representatives 18.04.1999*, xvi–xvii, xxx–xxxi.
[109] *Milli Gazete*, October 19, 1991, 3.
[110] Ruşen Çakır, "İttifak partileri için asıl bundan sonrası zor" [From now on it is difficult for the coalition parties], *Cumhuriyet*, October 5, 1991, 7; Maksut Mumcuoğlu, "Sonuç tek başına RP'nin değil" [The result is not of only the WP's making], *Cumhuriyet*, October 27, 1991, 5.

primary school teachers in Istanbul. But the land was extremely overvalued. Moreover, the fund did not have permission to build.[111]

As a result of the election of TPP leader Süleyman Demirel as president of the Republic in May 1993,[112] Tansu Çiller became chairman of the TPP and, therefore, prime minister. With the election of Çiller as the new leader in 1993, the TPP (the leader of the coalition) started to emphasize free-market orthodoxy, while neglecting social welfare policies. Çiller expected to achieve social improvement through tax reform and privatization.[113] Thus, the center-right political parties, like those on the center-left, failed to respond to the demands of the citizens.

The Turkish right in the pre-1980 period had always emphasized the importance of social welfare, sympathy for the poor, and egalitarian income distribution. Thus, communitarian egalitarianism (political, moral, and cultural) had priority over economic issues. This changed sharply in the mid-1980s. Turgut Özal regarded economics as just a matter of technical rules, that is, implementing the independent laws of economics properly. This may produce inequalities, but this is how a free-market economy functions.[114] Özal's statement "I like rich people" was a radical break from the traditional communitarian ideology of the center-right tradition.[115] Aside from the short interval under Demirel's rule (1991–3), Özal's economic policy dominated the Turkish center-right. As a result of this change, the center-right political parties started to lose their appeal to the voters.

Even though the political rhetoric of the mainstream political parties on both the right and the left changed in favor of a free-market economy, the public demand for communitarian egalitarianism did not. According to a poll that was conducted in 1991, 56 percent of the respondents considered it the state's responsibility to provide social welfare.[116] A further indication of alienation of voters from the center-right government was the fact that 50 percent of respondents claimed they did not trust the political system, and 42 percent claimed they did not trust the parliament. The most trusted institution was the military (91%), which was followed by religious organizations (67%) and the police (63%). Political scientist Yılmaz Esmer concludes from this lack of trust in democratic institutions that there was a problem with the country's political culture.[117]

---

[111] "İLKSAN'ın ucuz konut projesine yolsuzluk imajı nedeniyle ilgi yok" [There is no demand for the İLKSAN's cheap housing project because of the image of corruption], *Zaman*, November 29, 2004.
[112] Demirel served as president between 1993 and 2000.
[113] Sakallıoğlu, "Liberalism, Democracy and the Turkish Center-Right," 148, 153–5.
[114] Tünay, "The Turkish New Right's Attempt at Hegemony," 22–3.
[115] Ayata-Güneş and Ayata, "Turkey's Mainstream Political Parties on the Center-Right and Center-Left," 98.
[116] "Demokrat kurumlara güven az" [Trust in democratic institutions is low], interview with Yılmaz Esmer, *Cumhuriyet*, October 6, 1991, 12.
[117] Ibid.

In the 1990s, the WP, while proposing the Just Order, changed its traditional propaganda style by embracing all segments of the society (secular people; workers, the unemployed, and the retired; intellectuals suffering from human rights abuses; and Islamist women demanding more freedom of faith). Ayşe Öncü, a professor of sociology, calls the WP's television campaign in the 1991 general elections "a runaway success," which led to a dramatic shift in voting preferences in the short run, but more importantly, "it shaped a new public image for the party."[118] This time, the WP's constituents were everyday people of all walks of life and all ages, not just veiled women or bearded men. Öncü notes that of the seven female faces in the campaign – a migrant peasant, an environmentalist, a university student, a child, a "woman of life" (a prostitute), a human being, and a wife of a civil servant – only one was wearing an Islamic headscarf (*türban*). The *türbaned* young girl addressed the problem of prohibition of *türban* at universities by claiming that she was expelled from university during her senior year because of her headscarf, and promised that the WP, once it came to power, would solve the problem of discrimination against people on account of their beliefs and practices.[119] Öncü argues that the party launched an "image campaign," what the party activists called only "a change of method," aimed at transforming the party's "public identity from that of an inward looking, traditionalist, conservative religious party, to one of universal vision and future promise for everyone."[120] The party gave the message to the electorate that "we embrace all of you," "we know your problems," and "we are [all] the same."[121]

The WP further increased its vote share in the mid-1990s by engaging in diagnostic, prognostic, and motivational framing of the POS created by the malfunctioning state. The party skillfully framed the corruption scandals of the mainstream parties to strengthen its political argument that the source of the problem was the secular state (an example of diagnostic framing). Similarly, the WP attributed the dissolution of the Ottoman Empire to the abandonment of Islam and the emphasis on Westernization. Atatürk's revolution, the party argued, was Westernization in appearance only and did not elevate the country to the place that it deserved; the mainstream parties were utilizing secularism and Atatürk as protective shields to conceal their corruption and laziness. Westernization, according to the party, was the source of corruption and distanced the nation from its cultural roots.[122] The WP was careful not to alienate the electorate by overcriticizing the secular order and Westernization; instead, it focused on citizens' socioeconomic grievances – which, it argued, could be solved by only the establishment of a Just Order (an example of

---

[118] Ayşe Öncü, "Packaging Islam: Cultural Politics on the Landscape of Turkish Commercial Television," *Public Culture* 8, no. 1 (1995): 60.

[119] The WP used the word *headscarf* instead of *türban*, as the latter is regarded as a symbol of political Islam. In ibid., 61.

[120] Ibid., 60.

[121] Ibid., 61.

[122] Yavuz Kır, "Seçmenin Mesajı, 1–2" [The electorate's message], *Zaman*, April 11–12, 1994, 8.

prognostic framing). For example, the WP in its 1994 municipality election pamphlet commented that all other political parties, except the WP, were making fake promises in order to get citizens' votes. Problems such as poverty, exploitation, unemployment, unequal distribution of wealth, interest rate/usury, inflation, clientelism, bribery, an inefficient foreign policy, suppression, and terror remained unsolved. The election pamphlet addressed the source of the problem,

> Because those who have governed Turkey for fifty years do not know the source of the real problem. The WP knows very well the source of the problem. And in this historical moment, we as the WP give the assurance of a Just Order to our nation.[123]

The electorate was called on to take action to rectify the malfunctioning system by voting for the WP (an example of motivational framing): "The one that was already tried, is not retried. If the game stays the same and only the players change, elections are not beneficial (faydalı). Let's solve this problem in this election."[124]

For the 1994 municipality elections, the WP prepared a detailed and convincing plan for solving the problems of cities like Istanbul and Ankara. For example, Recep Tayyip Erdoğan, then WP mayoral candidate for the Istanbul municipality, prepared an emergency action plan (acil eylem planı), which explained in detail how he would solve the problems of corruption, air pollution, water scarcity, garbage collection, public transportation, and lack of infrastructure. The party also introduced projects that created opportunities for citizens' voices to be heard. It established consultation and complaint centers in neighborhoods, so that citizens would be able to contact the municipality. Their wishes would be recorded on computers, and the party would get back to them within forty-eight hours. A consultation assembly (danışma meclisi) would be established, wherein craftsmen and small business owners (esnaf ve sanatkar kuruluşları) as well as all civil society associations would be able to comment on the problems of Istanbul. The party also had a special project for children. The WP was the first party to establish children's assemblies. The party also wanted to transfer responsibility for education to local governments (municipalities). Children from shantytowns would attend municipality private schools (kolej). Day care centers, courses of foreign language, computer skills, and employment skills would be opened up in shantytowns.[125]

The successful management of municipalities under WP/VP (Virtue Party) governance[126] convinced the electorate that the Just Order was not an empty slogan, but a viable project that could answer the ills of the malfunctioning state. In the mid-1990s, the WP became a party of the masses. In 1991, Recep

---

[123] Refah Partisi, *Yerel Seçim '94* [The Local Election '94] (Ankara: Refah Partisi, n.d.).
[124] Ibid.
[125] Mehmet Terzi's interview with Recep Tayyip Erdoğan, *Milli Gazete*, March 20, 1994, 12.
[126] The WP/VP mayors were the same. Thus, the two parties can be treated as the same.

Tayyip Erdoğan, then WP Istanbul Province chair, proclaimed that "The WP is not a party that subordinates to subjects (*kul*). [Parties] that depend on subjects collapse. But [parties] that depend on Allah never collapse. We are a political party that is based on Hak/God. For this reason, we are powerful. We get our strength from God/Hak first, then from the public."[127] Şevki Yılmaz, a WP parliamentarian, stated during his 1991 election campaign that citizens, by having the right to vote, had a great weapon. "With this weapon," he declared, "either we will shoot ourselves or we will shoot the ones who have been shooting us for 60 years. This is the weapon of the vote."[128] In January 1995, then WP Istanbul mayor Recep Tayyip Erdoğan, declared that "the 21st century will be an era in which systems that are based on Islam will come to power in the world."[129]

The inability of the state to find a solution to the rising social problems of the 1990s led Turkish citizens to regard the Islamists as a potential antidote to the decay in moral values in the society. An important segment of Turkish society is conservative and emphasizes the protection of traditional values that are defined by Islam.[130] If secularism is not supported by law and order, religion becomes more appealing as a source of societal order. In a June 2004 interview with the author, Uluç Gürkan argued that atomized migrant citizens, who are initially conservative but not Islamist, become Islamists in shantytowns.[131] Similarly as Gürkan, a prominent professor of divinity, in an interview with the author in February 2004, suggested that participation in the Islamist movement has been widespread in shantytowns. The professor also noted that adoption of Western culture without eliminating its harmful sides led to degeneration in the society. For this reason, parents send their children to *imam-hatip* schools as a way of protection by providing a conservative education. Yet, the Islamists regard both *imam-hatip* schools and Quran courses as institutions to increase their political influence. The professor suggested that there would not be a demand for Islamism, if Turkey did not have socioeconomic problems.[132]

A high-ranking FP member also suggested a direct link between *imam-hatip* schools and the strengthening of Islamism.[133] Another prominent divinity professor, in an interview with the author in February 2004, argued that the Islamic brotherhoods had become protective shields among the migrant urban

---

[127] "Erdoğan: Refah Partisi yeni bir dünya düzeni kuracak" [Erdoğan: The Welfare Party will establish a new world order], *Milli Gazete*, September 2, 1991, 6.
[128] "İhaneti oylarınızla önleyin" [Stop the traitorship by your votes], *Milli Gazete*, October 4, 1991, 3.
[129] "Erdoğan: 21. yüzyıl İslam asrı olacak" [Erdoğan: The 21st century will be Islam's], *Beklenen Vakit*, January 9, 1995, 8.
[130] Toprak and Çarkoğlu, *Türkiye'de Din, Toplum ve Siyaset*, 21–3.
[131] Author's interview with Uluç Gürkan, the former DLP parliamentarian, Ankara, June 10, 2004.
[132] Author's interview with a divinity professor, Ankara, February 17, 2004.
[133] Author's interview with a high-ranking FP member, Ankara, June 10, 2004.

poor struggling with the consequences of rapid urbanization by providing social services to the needy, such as accommodation and financial assistance, that the state is supposed to provide.[134]

A segment of Turkish citizens who call themselves "secular" try to impose their "liberal" understanding of what constitutes a proper lifestyle on other people, just as the Islamists do. While the Islamists' interpretation of Islam distorts the religion, the "secularists'" interpretation of secularism leads to a misinterpretation of secularism among conservative citizens. The Just Order, by implicitly referring to the values of an Islamic society, successfully resonated with Turkish society's conservative values. As Hewitt and McCammon hypothesize, "For collective action frames to succeed in organizing potential recruits, they must strike the appropriate *balance* between resonating with the existing cultural repertoire and challenging the status quo."[135] The Just Order successfully established a balance between the existing conservative-Muslim value structure of Turkish society and criticism of the malfunctioning secular order.

In 1995, Turhan Tayan, the National Education Minister from the TPP, noted that the decay in traditional moral and religious values, particularly in metropolitan cities, had led to an increase in drug addiction among Turkish youth.[136] Erbakan, for his part, set forth what he perceived as the moral crisis of the West:

What is it that we call the modern world? Is it America? Is it the West? Do not those dissolve because of capitalism, as was the case of the Eastern bloc that suffered because of communism? What is the reality? Even though the U.S. has great global wealth, while exploiting millions of people through the monopoly and cartel of big holdings and multinational corporations, do not 3 million people live on the streets? ... Is not its youth going through a fast decay towards alcoholism, [and] drug addiction ... ? Do not gambling, alcohol, prostitution, and all sorts of immorality spread fast? Does not AIDS, which is one product of moral decay, spread like the illness of cancer, [and] threaten the entire society? What will you gain by imitating such societies, where all thinkers are shouting "Help! ... Is not there anyone who can save us?" Their situation looks like a bus with a bomb rolling from a cliff.[137]

The Islamists proposed to solve the problem of "crisis of morals"[138] in Turkish society by establishing an Islamic community based on the Quran and the *sunna*. The Islamists argued that the present Western orientation of the Turkish political regime was the reason for the rising problems of youth. Because the

---

[134] Author's interview with a divinity professor, Ankara, February 19, 2004.
[135] Hewitt and McCammon, "Explaining Suffrage Mobilization," 34 (emphasis in original). Hewitt and McCammon argue, "By balance, we suggest that if a frame either fails to draw adequately on dominant belief systems or mounts too great a challenge to them, it runs the risk of alienating potential recruits." In ibid.
[136] "Liseler korkutuyor" [High schools are frightening], *Zaman*, November 10, 1995, 11.
[137] Erbakan, *İslam ve İlim*, 74–5.
[138] Wickham, "Interests, Ideas, and Islamist Outreach in Egypt," in Wiktorowicz, *Islamic Activism*, 237.

state had not sufficiently emphasized Islam in education, youth were increasingly becoming unfaithful, pragmatic, individualistic, materialistic, brutal, covert, selfish, corrupted, and violent. The policy of Westernization had led Turkish youth to forget about their own national history and civilization. Texts in the public schools ignore the fourteen hundred years of contributions by Islam to the world. As a result, Turkish youth felt inferior to the youth of the West. They were interested in the "viruses of the West," such as drugs, disco, football, makeup, casual sex, and a bohemian lifestyle rather than in solving the problems of their own country. These developments, it was argued, reflected a tactic of the West: to pacify the youth in nations defined by the West as rivals. Such nations become colonies, unless the youth are organized through their own core culture. Yet, it was argued, the youth that give importance to Islam were being discriminated against in Turkey.[139] In June 2004 interviews with Felicity Party Women Commission workers, one party worker pointed out that the state did not sufficiently protect families and children in Turkey. Another party worker argued that moral values provide a self-correcting mechanism in a society, which eliminates crime and corruption. Thus, they suggested, "moral development should be the primary goal, which would create a moral society. Material development would follow the moral development anyway."[140] Thus, in the 1990s the WP became a mass party by reframing its appeal to the Turkish electorate in the form of the Just Order. The result was it became the single largest party, although in the 1990s by no means yet a majority party, in Turkish politics.

MUNICIPAL GOVERNANCE AS POLITICAL OPPORTUNITY STRUCTURE

Turkey, along with its modernization process, has been transformed by rapid urbanization. Mechanization of agriculture in the 1950s led to an unemployment problem among the rural population and their migration to urban areas in the 1960s.[141] But industrialization and development of the modern economic sector could not keep pace with urban population increases. As a result, unemployment in metropolitan areas exceeded the national average, starting in the mid-1980s.

Between 1950 and 1980, Turkey's urban population grew fourfold, from five million to twenty million, and from 25 percent to 44 percent of total population. Between 1980 and 1997, urban population increased from 44 percent to 60 percent of the total population. By the year 2000, 65 percent of Turkish citizens resided in urban areas. The Turkish state simply did not have the resources required to address the needs of this rapidly expanding urban

---

[139] Serdar Çelik, "Gençlik meselemize bakış 1, 2, 3, 4, 5, 6" [A view on our youth problem], *Akit*, November 27–30, December 1–2 1995, 7.
[140] Author's interviews with the FP Women Commission workers, Ankara, June 9, 2004.
[141] Orhan Türkdoğan, *Gecekondu, İnsan ve Kültür: İstanbul Örnek Olayı* [Shantytowns, Human Being, and Culture: The Case of Istanbul] (Istanbul: Genar, 2002), 12–13.

population for services: water, garbage collection, roads, housing, transportation, and jobs.[142]

In the 1960s, shantytowns began to emerge in large cities like Istanbul. Today, it is estimated that more than half the residents of large cities such as Istanbul, Ankara, Izmir, Adana, Antalya, Bursa, and Mersin live in shantytowns. Furthermore, more than 65 percent of the total urban population are shantytown residents.[143] The State Planning Organization's 1991 survey on shantytowns in Istanbul, Ankara, and Izmir acknowledged that the state was unable to provide basic urban services to shantytown residents, particularly roads and sewers.[144]

This rapid urbanization changed the nature of clientelistic politics in Turkey. The traditional form of rural clientelism declined, and patron-client relations started to take hold in shantytowns in the major cities.[145] How the WP utilized its strong organizational networks in the cities to expand its electoral support beyond the traditional Islamist segment of the society will be examined in more detail in the next chapter. It is important to note here that the WP's traditional support base, as discussed in Chapter 2, was in religiously conservative small cities and towns in Anatolia. The party, by responding to the demands of the urban poor, expanded its support base in the 1990s.[146]

Istanbul, Ankara, and Izmir are the most populated provinces in Turkey. These provinces only have a little more than 25 percent of eligible voters in general and municipal elections. Economic factors have been the main motive for migration to urban centers. According to the State Planning Organization's 1991 survey cited in the preceding text, nearly half of respondents argued that they migrated to Istanbul, Ankara, and Izmir in order to find jobs (48.6%, 57.4%, and 51.9%, respectively), which was followed by having a better income (*daha iyi geçinme*) (22.1%, 18.9%, and 16.5%, respectively).[147] According to sociologist Orhan Türkdoğan's survey on shantytowns in Istanbul, more than half of the respondents (54%) argued that they migrated to Istanbul because of economic problems.[148]

Yet, the unemployment problem among shantytown residents seems to be high. According to the 1991 survey, only between 35 and 40 percent of the respondents in Istanbul, Ankara, and Izmir (shantytown residents more than 12 years old) claimed that they were in the labor force the previous week (39.3%, 35.4%, and 39.3%, respectively). The labor force was overwhelmingly

---

[142] Ibid., 4, 7; TÜİK, *Statistical Indicators 1923–2004*, 6, 15.
[143] Türkdoğan, *Gecekondu, İnsan ve Kültür*, 12, 17.
[144] İstiklal Alpar and Samira Yener, *Gecekondu Araştırması* [Research on Shantytowns] (Ankara: Devlet Planlama Teşkilâtı, 1991), 84.
[145] Kalaycıoğlu, "The Turkish Grand National Assembly," 48–9, 51.
[146] Sabri Sayarı, "İslam, Laiklik ve Demokrasi: Türkiye Örneğinde Perspektifler" [Islam, Secularism, and Democracy: Perspectives on the Turkish Case], in TÜSES, *Türkiye'de İslamcılık* [Islamism in Turkey] (Ankara: TÜSES, n.d.), 63.
[147] Alpar and Yener, *Gecekondu Araştırması*, 174–6.
[148] Türkdoğan, *Gecekondu, İnsan ve Kültür*, 84.

composed of those between fifteen and thirty-nine years old, but significant proportions of the labor force in the shantytowns of Istanbul, Ankara, and Izmir were between twelve and fourteen years old.[149] An overwhelming majority of employed shantytown residents were either workers or were employed in the service sector.

According to a survey that was conducted in 1992 in shantytowns in sixty-two neighborhoods of Ankara, Istanbul, Izmir, and Gaziantep, 60 percent of the respondents were elementary school graduates.[150] According to the 1991 figures, an overwhelming majority of employed shantytown residents in Istanbul, Ankara, and Izmir had social security.[151] According to the 1992 survey, 30 percent of employed shantytown home-owners and 44 percent of shantytown tenants were not enrolled in any type of social security scheme.[152]

Various surveys on Istanbul's shantytowns conducted in 1990 and 2000 show that most shantytown residents owned a TV, washer, vacuum cleaner, refrigerator, radio, and phone.[153] However, Türkdoğan's survey of Istanbul shantytowns[154] revealed that 77 percent of respondents could not save any money.[155] Furthermore, 78 percent of the respondents claimed their monthly income was inadequate. Thus, 70 percent of the respondents claimed they were borrowing money.[156] According to the 1991 survey, between 70 and 80 percent of shantytown households in Istanbul, Ankara, and Izmir did not have any savings.[157]

Rural migrants to the cities experience problems in adapting to urban life. Migrants accustomed to living according to traditional norms of collaboration cannot find the same environment in the cities. This leads to the problem of their alienation from society and to the problem of atomization. This has been exploited by Islamist networks operating in shantytowns. When mass migration to cities started in the 1950s,[158] the cities were the places of modernizing republican elites. Rural migrants were expected to assimilate themselves into the Western-oriented urban society. But they often failed to adapt successfully. Moreover, in the course of time, the pace of rural migration to urban areas

[149] Alpar and Yener, *Gecekondu Araştırması*, 51.
[150] Tansı Şenyapılı, *1980 Sonrasında Ruhsatsız Konut Yapımı* [Illegal House Building after 1980] (Ankara: T.C. Başbakanlık Toplu Konut Dairesi Başkanlığı, 1996), 7, 10, 23–4.
[151] Alpar and Yener, *Gecekondu Araştırması*, 62.
[152] Tansı Şenyapılı, "Dar gelirli grupların kentsel konut mekanı" [Housing sites of the urban poor], (Unpublished study that was submitted to the Turkish Prime Ministry Community Housing Office Headquarters, 1993) (data collected in 1992).
[153] Türkdoğan, *Gecekondu, dnsan ve Kültür*, 101.
[154] Ibid.
[155] Ibid., 100.
[156] Ibid., 102.
[157] Alpar and Yener, *Gecekondu Araştırması*, 97.
[158] Mustafa Şahin, "Prof. Dr. Ruşen Keleş'le Kentleşme Üzerine" [Over urbanization with Professor Ruşen Keleş], *Zaman*, September 27, 1987, 9. "Over 3.3 million people were added to the urban population during the 1950s, more than twice as many as in the previous quarter century." In Micheal N. Danielson and Ruşen Keleş, *The Politics of Rapid Urbanization: Government and Growth in Modern Turkey* (New York: Holmes and Meier, 1985), 27.

increased so that the established urbanites became a minority of the urban population. Between the years 1945 and 1990, populations of the three largest cities (in order, Istanbul, Ankara, and Izmir) multiplied by 7.83, 11.26, and 8.89 times, respectively.[159] In the 1990s, because of a rise in PKK terrorism, there was an increased flow of migration from the southeast part of the country to the large cities.[160]

As a result of rapid urbanization, the migrants have not only made their presence felt in the city in physical and social terms, but have also become major actors in politics, particularly local politics.[161] For example, according to a survey that was conducted in 1993 regarding Ankara province's municipality assemblies, shantytown residents constituted an average of 30.4 percent of representatives in municipality assemblies. An average of 28.3 percent of these shantytown representatives were elementary school graduates.[162]

According to the 2000 population census figures, 64.9 percent of Turkish citizens live in cities. Istanbul, with a population of 9.1 million, ranks as one of the most populous cities in Europe. Ankara, Turkey's next largest city, has a population of 3.5 million, followed by Izmir, with a population of 2.7 million.[163] Together, these cities contained 28 percent of the eligible voters in the parliamentary and local elections held in April 1999.

Between 1980 and 1990, Istanbul's population increased by 54 percent, and the unemployment rate, which was 5.5 percent in 1980, increased to 6.2 percent in 1990. By 1990, many districts of Istanbul were among the most densely populated districts in the country. Between 1990 and 2000, both the population and unemployment rates in Istanbul continued to increase, the former by 37 percent, and the latter more than doubling from 6.2 percent in 1990 to 12.7 percent in 2000.[164] In terms of economic activity, more than half of the employed population in Istanbul works in the service sector, which is followed by the industrial sector.

Despite the increasing economic pressures on the rising immigrant population of the major cities in Turkey, in the 1970s, the NSP, the predecessor of the WP, was not the first-ranked party in elections, as the WP would be in the

---

[159] Aryeh Shmuelevitz, "Urbanization and Voting for the Turkish Parliament," *Middle Eastern Studies* 32, no. 2 (April 1996): 164.
[160] Işık and Pınarcıoğlu, *Nöbetleşe Yoksulluk*, 173.
[161] Tahire Erman, "Becoming 'Urban' or Remaining 'Rural': The Views of the Turkish Rural-to-Urban Migrants on the 'Integration' Question," *International Journal Middle East Studies* 30, no. 4 (November 1998): 542.
[162] Tansı Şenyapılı, "Bugün Değişene Bakmamak Geleceği Görmemektir" [Not Looking At Change Today Refers to Not Seeing the Future], in *Göç, Kent ve Gecekondu Kentte Mekanın Dönüşümü Sorunu ve Yaklaşımlar Üzerine Yazılar* [Articles on Migration, City, and Shantytown], eds. Yurdanur Dülgeroğlu Yüksel and Zeynep Kerem (Istanbul: Birsen Yayınevi, 1998), 155.
[163] DİE, *2000 Census of Population Social and Economic Characteristics of Population of Turkey* (Ankara: DİE, 2003), 28, 65. Bursa, Adana, Konya, and Gaziantep are cities with a population of more than 1 million.
[164] DİE, *2000 Census of Population Social and Economic Characteristics of Population, Istanbul* (Ankara: DİE, 2002), 50.

TABLE 4.5. *Rates of Increase in Cost-of-Living Index for Wage-Earners in Istanbul (percent)*

Year	General Index	Foodstuffs Total Index
1970	9.2	8.2
1971	17.1	11.9
1972	13.3	13.9
1973	14.3	17.2
1974	23.5	23.7
1975	21.7	26.8
1976	16.9	18.5
1977	30.6	27.1
1978	69.0	61.5
1979	76.3	59.8
1980	75.6	75.4
1981	35.9	41.7
1982	34.5	37.8
1983	28.1	24.1
1984	43.7	49.4
1985	43.2	39.5
1986	35.6	32.8
1987	44.9	47.5
1988	77.0	79.1
1989	71.0	69.5
1990	65.3	62.7
1991	67.9	67.6
1992	73.5	67.5
1993	75.6	64.8
1994	120.3	115.7
1995	94.3	93.9
1996	84.8	75.8
1997	91.8	84.5
1998	87.3	91.9

Source: DİE, *Statistical Indicators (1923–1998)* (DİE: Ankara, 2001), 492.

1990s. As the data displayed in the following text demonstrate, the cost of living for wage earners in Istanbul rose almost every year from 1970 to 1994 (Table 4.5). Despite an extraordinary rise in 1994, these data also suggest that economic grievances by themselves were not the determining factor in the rise of an Islamist social movement in Turkey in the 1990s. Similar trends in migration, growth of shantytown population, unemployment, and increasing cost of living, are evident in census and other data for Ankara, as well.[165]

[165] DİE, *2000 Census of Population Social and Economic Characteristics of Population, Ankara* (Ankara: DİE, 2001), 50; DİE, *Statistical Indicators (1923–1998)*, 482–3; DİE, *1990 Census of Population Social and Economic Characteristics of Population* (Ankara: DİE, 1993), 42–8; and Danielson and Keleş, *The Politics of Rapid Urbanization*, 166.

The large concentration of voters in urban areas facing significant social and economic problems has led political parties in Turkey to view local elections as a crucial opportunity to expand their electoral constituencies by increasing their political influence and visibility in the national political arena (see Table 4.6). Furthermore, control of municipalities enables a party to gain access to new sources of political patronage (such as municipal jobs and contracts for projects, like transportation and construction) that are useful for recruiting new activists and supporters.[166] In the years between 1984 and 1999, voter turnout in local elections was higher than what it had been in the 1960s and 1970s, and now it approximately equals the turnout for general elections.[167] Nihal İncioğlu, a professor of political science, suggests that rapid urbanization and the rise of major problems in cities increased urban voters' concern about the quality of municipal governance. Realizing that political control of the large cities could help increase their vote share at the national level, political parties have begun to assign more importance to the outcome of the local elections, leading to an increased voter interest in local elections.[168]

The support bases of the WP and its successor parties are located among the urban poor living in shantytowns. These are sectors of the electorate alienated from the mainstream political parties because of widespread corruption, mismanagement, and rising socioeconomic problems. The WP's successful governance of municipalities over which they gained control in the 1994 elections (e.g., Ankara and Istanbul) played a crucial role in convincing voters that the party's slogan of "Just Order" represented a credible promise to create an alternative to the present malfunctioning state. The party, as Erbakan argued, received most of its votes from the cities governed by the WP. Besides providing high-quality social services to citizens, the municipalities under WP governance solved the problem of corruption in local governance.[169]

The emphasis of the WP and its successor Islamist parties on face-to-face contact with voters and their offering of material benefits – food, shelter, clothing, health benefits, and jobs as well as financial contributions to social occasions, like weddings – to needy potential voters played an

---

[166] Nihal İncioğlu, "Local Elections and Electoral Behavior," in Sayarı and Esmer, *Politics, Parties, and Elections in Turkey*, 73.
[167] See data on turnout in TÜİK, *Statistical Indicators (1923–2004)*, 138–43.
[168] İncioğlu, "Local Elections and Electoral Behavior," 77–8.
[169] Konrad Adenauer Vakfı, *Refah Partisi Üzerine Bir Araştırma* [A Research on the Welfare Party] (Ankara: Konrad Adenauer Vakfı, 1996), 24; "İstanbul Büyükşehir Belediye Başkanı Recep Tayyip Erdoğan: Sorunları temizledik" [Istanbul Greater Municipality Mayor Recep Tayyip Erdoğan: We solved the problems], *Milli Gazete*, December 2, 1995, 16; "Belediyeler RP'yi iktidara taşıyor" [Municipalities carry the WP to the party of government], *Milli Gazete*, November 7, 1995, 8; and Nevzat Özpelitoğlu, "Refah'ın zaferi ezilmişlerin zaferidir" [The WP's victory is the suppressed people's victory], *Milli Gazete*, April 13, 1994, 2.

TABLE 4.6. *Party Vote in Municipal Elections, 1984–1999 (percent)*

Party	1984	1989	1994	1999
Center-Left				
Populist Party	8.8	–	–	–
Social Democracy Party	23.4	–	–	–
Social Democratic Populist Party	–	28.7	13.6	–
Democratic Left Party	–	9.0	8.8	18.7
Republican People's Party	–	–	4.6	11.1
Center-Right				
Nationalist Democracy Party	7.1	–	–	–
Motherland Party	41.5	21.8	21.0	15.1
True Path Party	13.2	25.1	21.4	13.2
Nationalist				
Nationalist Work Party	–	4.1	–	–
Nationalist Action Party	–	–	8.0	17.1
Kurdish				
People's Democracy Party	–	–	–	3.5
Islamist				
Welfare Party	4.4	9.8	19.1	–
Virtue Party	–	–	–	16.5

Source: DİE, *Results of Elections of Local Administrations, 18.04.1999* (Ankara: DİE, 2000), 2–3.

important role in increasing their vote share. In Sultanbeyli (a long-neglected shantytown in Istanbul) the WP had already gained power in 1989. The size of the electorate there increased from 8,937 in 1989, to 43,700 in 1994, a reflection of the massive immigration to the cities of Turkey, the resulting growth of shantytowns in them, and the corresponding increase in the size of the urban constituency available for mobilization by the Islamist social movement. In the 1989 local elections, the WP received 30 percent of the votes; in the 1994 elections, it secured nearly 60 percent of the votes. The WP's successful work in Sultanbeyli created a good reputation for the party, which led citizens in other districts in Istanbul (such as Üsküdar, Kartal, Ümraniye, and Eyüp) also to vote for the WP in the 1994 local elections.

The Sultanbeyli mayoralty (which is regarded as the gateway by which the WP gained control of Istanbul) addressed the problem of corruption by requiring applicants for employment (labor and staff) at the mayoralty not to accept bribes, and to pray five times a day. The WP mayor, Ali Nabi Koçak,[170] explained

---

[170] Ali Nabi Koçak graduated first from Yozgat *imam-hatip* high school and afterward from Istanbul High Islam Institute. He became a *mufti* of Kartal (a district in Istanbul) between 1976 and 1978. He withdrew from the *Diyanet* in 1984. In Işık and Pınarcıoğlu, *Nöbetleşe Yoksulluk*, 263.

this requirement as follows: "Because one who prays five times a day knows that he will give an account on the day of judgment. Thus, he will not receive a bribe and will not steal." The municipality put up a warning sign in the municipality building advising that "One who is bribed and who bribes is evil."[171] The WP mayors emphasized face-to-face contacts with citizens in their area of governance. During the religious fests (*bayram*), for example, WP mayors paid visits to nursing homes, student dormitories, abandoned children dormitories, hospitals, and prisons; during their visits, they distributed gifts of food and clothing.[172]

It is also important to note that the WP networks provide a sense of belongingness to shantytown residents. Erman's study on migrants in Ankara showed that the respondents in her study who resided in apartments in shantytowns considered themselves villagers despite having spent many years in the city. According to her survey, 49.5 percent of second-generation migrants still considered themselves people of rural origin, while only about one-fifth of respondents (20.2%) regarded themselves as urbanites. A few respondents (5.8%) regarded themselves as a villager on second thought.[173] The migrants in Erman's study simply could not become part of urban life.

Tahire Erman, a professor of political science, suggests that there are three conditions that help maintain and reinforce a rural identity among migrants: first, "when there is a significant discrepancy between rural and urban conditions, both in terms of practical reality and ideological constructs, and being an urbanite is defined and presented by urban elites in a way that excludes migrants, who are defined as inferior;" second, "when migrants are socially and economically insecure in the city and need the protection of their old environment (i.e., rural community);" and third, "when migrants lack economic, social, and political resources to take advantage of the opportunities and services in the city."[174]

In the 1980s, Turgut Özal introduced and promoted a new ethos based on individualism, competition, and acquisition of status on the basis of consumption and the display of wealth.[175] Ayşe Ayata suggests that "In the context of rapidly growing and differentiation cities, the rich, forming their own segregated communities, are increasingly isolated from the rest of the society."[176] Boratav argues that the nature of the Turkish upper class is highly

---

[171] "İstanbul'un yeni fetih kapısı Sultanbeyli" [Sultanbeyli is Istanbul's new conquest gate], Davut Yıldız's interview with Nabi Koçak, *Milli Gazete*, May 26, 1994, 12.

[172] "Kartal: Sekmen bayramlarda yaşlıları ve çocukları sevindirdi" [Kartal: Sekmen made happy the elderly and children] and "Bayram mutluluğu" [Happiness of a fest], *Milli Gazete*, May 26, 1994, 12; "Erdoğan Fatih Koleji öğrencileri ile" [Erdoğan is with the Fatih High School students], *Milli Gazete*, May 11, 1994, 12.

[173] Erman, "Becoming 'Urban' or Remaining 'Rural,'" 542, 544, 549, 552-4.

[174] Ibid., 556.

[175] Ayata, "Ideology, Social Bases, and Organizational Structure of the Post-1980 Political Parties," 97.

[176] Ibid., 98.

exclusive, despite the mobility between social strata as a result of economic growth and structural change.[177] Second-generation migrants, despite having higher education, most of the time cannot fulfill their expectations, and thus feel at a disadvantage. Ersin Kalaycıoğlu, a professor of political science, noted as recently as 1993 that "Primordialism is very much alive in Turkey. Kinship, even more remote blood relations, regional ties (e.g., *hemşehri* bonds), and service in the same military unit play an important role in establishing political links. . . . blood relations and *hemşehri* bonds are very strong bases for clientelistic politics."[178] But, as a result of the increased individualism (defined in terms of individual wealth and success) and competition in the society since the 1980s, *hemşehri* networks and tight kinship relationships in shantytowns are weakening and interest-based relationships are becoming more important. Today, Westernized urban elites who regard migrants as inferior are being challenged by Islamist elites, who propose an alternative way of life based on a politicized interpretation of Islam more familiar to immigrants from the more traditional countryside. In shantytowns, local communities organized around Sunni Islam have greatly increased.[179]

Erman argues that in some cases "migrants created their own communities with their own ways of life and values (communities which have often been criticized as the replica of the village in the city), and developed their own ways of dealing with the public sphere (such as *hemşehrilik*, clientalism)."[180] The implications of this for the Islamist movement are clear: elements of the Islamist constituency were migrating from rural areas to the major cities, creating a natural base of support and foundation for organization for the Islamists and the WP. The social alienation of these conservative migrants constituted yet another element in the POS created for the Islamist movement in the 1990s.

The WP tried to implement the Just Order in the municipalities under its governance as much as possible.[181] Unlike municipalities governed by the mainstream parties, those under WP rule provided free social services, including food houses (*aşevleri*), medical services, hospitals, elderly houses, parking places, cemetery services, dormitories, rehabilitation centers for handicapped people, mobile health services, scholarships, coal and food assistance, financial assistance to social occasions such as weddings and births, free public transportation for students, subsidized food and benefits at a cheaper price, such as bread, public transportation, courses for young females to develop their skills in handicrafts, municipality supermarkets that sell items at a very

---

[177] Korkut Boratav, *İstanbul ve Anadolu'dan Sınıf Profilleri* [Class Profiles from Istanbul and Anatolia] (Istanbul: Tarih Vakfı Yurt Yayınları, 1995), 28–30.
[178] Kalaycıoğlu, "The Turkish Grand National Assembly," 49.
[179] Erman, "Becoming 'Urban' or Remaining 'Rural,'" 557.
[180] Ibid., 541–2.
[181] Refah Partisi, *Adil Düzen 21 Soru/21 Cevap*, 34.

low price, dormitories for female students and working children (*çıraklar*), day care centers for children, nursing homes, and community housing (*sosyal konut inşaatı*).[182] In the year 2000, the VP mayor in Sultanbeyli, Yahya Karakaya, assumed the responsibility for the care of two physically impaired children who were abandoned by their parents. "Humanity has not died," he asserted.[183]

In the cities, public services could not keep pace with the enormous increase in the urban population. The SDPP was remarkably unsuccessful in providing basic public services, such as water, sewage disposal, and drainage. Furthermore, the corruption scandal in the Istanbul municipality under SDPP governance led to a negative image of social democracy in the eyes of the public. Under WP rule, there was no longer a problem of corruption in the municipalities.[184] Halil Ürün, the WP mayor of Konya, in central Anatolia, stated in 1994 that "Nobody can say that there is corruption in [the] Konya municipality.... Because we are people whose path is enlightened by the National View and aware of the fact that we will give account not only to courts, but also to the highest authority [God] one day. Our faith is our greatest power."[185] The WP's success in municipalities like Konya convinced voters that they should vote for the party in the 1994 local elections.

In Konya, four hundred families were provided with daily meals and two thousand families were supplied with food packages during Ramadan. In poor neighborhoods, citizens were provided free health services. Six thousand families were given free coal. The municipality also provided bread, drinking water, and public transportation at a very low price; built community housing, a municipal hospital, and a facility for abandoned pets; constructed roads and sewage systems; and opened a supermarket that sold low-price foods. The municipality also paid attention to cultural activities as well, repairing

---

[182] Kazan, *Refah Gerçeği*, vol. 1, 201, 210–11; "Sezal: Kahramanmaraş için yapacak çok şeyimiz var" [Sezal: We have a lot of things to do for Kahramanmaraş], *Milli Gazete* 2, March 22, 1994, 1; "Konya-Meram Belediye Başkanı Veysel Candan ile bir sohbet" [A conversation with Konya-Meram Mayor Veysel Candan], *Milli Gazete* 2, March 14, 1994, 6; "Hizmette yarışıyorlar" [They are competing in providing service], *Milli Gazete*, June 30, 1994, 6; "RP'den kömür atağı" [A campaign of coal from the WP], *Milli Gazete*, June 19, 1994, 1; "Adil Düzen'de müthiş gelir patlaması" [An incredible revenue boom in the Just Order], *Milli Gazete*, June 7, 1994, 3; "Siz de ekmeği 3 binden satın" [Then sell bread from three thousand], "10 Sebze marketi açılıyor" [Ten grocery markets will be opened up], "Pendik Belediyesinden yeni icraatlar" [New services from Pendik municipality], and "Hizmete devam!" [Continuation in service!], *Milli Gazete*, May 11, 1994, 12; *Milli Gazete*, May 9–10, 1994, 12; and *Milli Gazete*, May 3, 1994, 12; "Eyüpsultan Belediyesi ücretsiz balık dağıtıyor" [Eyüpsultan municipality distributes free fish], *Milli Gazete*, December 2, 1995, 16; "Halkımızı hizmete doyuracağız" [We will fulfill our public with service], *Milli Gazete*, November 12, 1995, 12; and "Keçiören'in bursları 17 Şubat'ta" [Keçiören's scholarships are on February 17th], *Zaman* February 10, 1998, 16.
[183] *Milli Gazete*, January 1, 2000, 4.
[184] Necmettin Erbakan, "Refah Partili Belediye Başkanlarının 1990 Mahalli İdareler Hizmetleri" [The WP Mayors' Services in 1990], in Kazan, *Refah Gerçeği*, vol. 1, 203–5.
[185] Muhtar Bedir's interview with Halil Ürün, *Milli Gazete* 2, March 18, 1994, 6.

historical sites, supplying mobile libraries (*gezici kütüphane*), and building parks and gyms.[186]

Another WP mayor explained the difference between the WP and other parties as follows: "We, unlike the other politicians, do not look over the public (*tepeden bakmak*) and regard them as vote depots. We came out of the public and came to this status by Allah's will and this public's support. We work with our public day and night. We contact everyone weekly and listen to their complaints and wishes; we also hold regular evening chats at neighborhoods. Moreover, we hold regular meetings and pay visits to small businesses (*esnaf*) in the bazaar."[187] The WP mayor of the Kartal municipality (a district in Istanbul), Mehmet Sekmen, argued that he established "the Just Order municipality in Kartal, where there will no longer be bribery and corruption. The citizen will immediately inform me regarding a municipality staff [member] who does not do his work and wants a bribe.... Our municipality's doors are open to our public everyday for 24 hours, including [on] weekends."[188]

In the WP Ankara municipality, in addition to construction of roads, sewage systems, and parks, the party provided numerous social services such as housing for children working on the streets, nursing and house-cleaning services and free transportation for old people, bread at a low price, meals for hundreds of thousands of people during Ramadan, free health care for one hundred fifty thousand people and free dental care for one hundred thousand people, in addition to the establishment of a children's assembly and the building of a library for children.[189] The WP municipality in Istanbul built municipal hospitals, parks, and community housing; repaired historical sites; constructed roads and sewage systems; provided scholarships to ninety thousand students and bread at a low price; and set up white tables in order to hear complaints and suggestions from citizens.[190]

The WP staff, unlike other political party workers, was very diligent. There were huge budget deficits in the municipalities that the party started to govern; the WP not only managed to balance the accounts, but also created a surplus. Erbakan reported in 1997 that the WP-governed municipalities inherited $16 billion of debt in 1994. But they generated a surplus of $1.2 billion in 1995, which increased to $2 billion in 1996 and $3.8 billion in 1997. The WP municipalities' revenues also increased from $150 million in 1994 to $390 million in 1995 and $1.87 billion in 1997.[191]

The municipalities governed by the WP also received financial assistance from the AMGT (*Avrupa Milli Görüş Teşkilâtı* – the National View Organization

---

[186] Ibid.; Kazan, *Refah Gerçeği*, vol. 1, 254–8.
[187] Muhtar Bedir's interview with Konya Karatay Mayor Mustafa Özkafa, *Milli Gazete* 2, March 15, 1994, 6.
[188] "RP'li Başkan Sekmen Belediyenin kapılarını halka açtı" [The WP mayor Sekmen opened the municipality's doors to the public], *Milli Gazete*, May 30, 1994, 12.
[189] Kazan, *Refah Gerçeği*, vol. 1, 259–66.
[190] Ibid., 267–83.
[191] "Hizmet Kervanı Yürüyor" [Service continues], *Milli Gazete*, March 28, 1997.

in Europe), which had ties to the party.[192] For example, the mayor of Ağrı went to Germany in 1994 to seek financial assistance for his municipality from the Turkish guest workers there.[193]

In the 1990s, the WP started to replace the social democratic parties in the municipalities in large cities. The WP was representing the disadvantaged masses who were suffering from the malfunctioning secular state. The replacement of the social democratic parties by the WP represented not only a transfer of power, but also a change in the balance of identity politics.[194] While the secular state was declining, the Islamist state model was rising.

Yael Navaro Yashin, in her study of the Istanbul municipality under WP governance, suggests that "In the 1980s, the Welfare Party officials incorporated the notion of 'civil society' into their discourse in a culturally specific manner. In fact, they obtained political power, initially in municipalities and eventually in the central government, by arguing that they were not representatives of 'the state,' but of 'civil society.'"[195] Erbakan put it this way: "Civil society is an expression of our core ideology's aspiration (özlem)."[196] WP officials defined the people's gathering around Islamist networks (Sufi orders, Islamist foundations, and charity organizations) as "civil society" challenging the "authoritarianism of secular elites and the state."[197]

Uğur Akıncı, in his analysis of the WP, defines the party as "a curious mixture of social-democratic populism and cultural radicalism."[198]

... Islamist municipalities have been "radical" in both senses of the term: they both supplied their followers with more pre-election incentives and post-election services than their secular competitors, and they also tried to inject a heavy dose of Islamic Ottoman (and clearly anti-secular and anti-Western) sensibility at a cultural level. Their rhetoric is replete with references to the good-old-Ottoman times as an era anchored firmly in Islamic morality, which in turn, they argue, brought wealth and power. Their commitment to radical activism, in both the above senses, is beyond any doubt.[199]

The WP social agenda in the cities under their control also included a strong Islamist element. The WP-governed municipalities banned the serving of alcohol in restaurants and public premises under their control both at the metropolitan and district levels.[200] One of the main problems of the secular state is

---

[192] Kazan, *Refah Gerçeği*, vol. 1, 204.
[193] "Gurbetçilerden Ağrı'ya 3,5 milyarlık yardım" [3.5 billion assistance from the migrants], *Milli Gazete*, May 30, 1994, 12.
[194] Gülalp, *Kimlikler Siyaseti*, 68–9.
[195] Yael Navaro Yashin, "Uses and Abuses of 'State and Civil Society' in Contemporary Turkey," *New Perspectives on Turkey* 18 (Spring 1998): 7.
[196] Ceylan, *Erbakan ve Türkiye'nin Temel Meseleleri*, 185.
[197] Yashin, "Uses and Abuses of 'State and Civil Society' in Contemporary Turkey," 9.
[198] Uğur Akıncı, "The Welfare Party's Municipal Track Record: Evaluating Islamist Municipal Activism in Turkey," *Middle East Journal* 53, no. 1 (Winter 1999): 76.
[199] Ibid., 76–7.
[200] "Kütahya: Belediye'ye ait yerlerde içki yasağı" [Kütahya: Banning of alcohol in municipality-owned places], *Milli Gazete*, May 3, 1994, 12.

lack of law and order to protect the lives of citizens and of the youth in particular. For example, it is quite common that pubs and restaurants stay open after midnight, serving alcohol to underaged youth, providing access to drugs, and disturbing residents nearby by playing loud music. Most of the time, the security forces that are supposed to enforce law and order are corrupt, and such businesses have become untouchables. These establishments hide behind secularism and Kemalism to legitimize their illegal activity.

The misuse of secularism and Atatürk for the purposes of such illegal activities, however, invites the citizens who are already dissatisfied with the malfunctioning secular state to reevaluate their views about modernization, secularism, and Westernization. Islamists who emphasize the protection of moral values are filling the gap that is left by the malfunctioning state.

The WP municipal officers in Istanbul legitimized the banning of alcohol by arguing that serving alcohol in public places was a means of excluding devout Muslims, whose convictions would not allow them to be present at places where alcohol was consumed.[201] The municipality also implemented some restrictive measures on pubs and restaurants that occupied sidewalk space with their tables and chairs, served alcohol, and played music at high volumes.

The antialcohol measures of local WP governments provide a good example of the framing efforts of the Islamists. The Islamists identified a grievance and used an appeal to liberal democratic and equal rights ethos in order to implement a conservative and Islamist response.

The WP was also the only party that took serious action against prostitution and for the protection of youth. Erdoğan argued that prostitution was a crime against humanity that demeaned a woman's honor. While pointing to the harmful effects of the media (*fuhuşa özendirici*) in encouraging prostitution, he could only suggest that the party would, instead, seek to encourage marriage by providing financial assistance to needy people.[202]

The WP municipalities have tried to increase the visibility of Islamism in public places, and to challenge the symbols of modernization with religious symbols, while providing high-quality services at a cheaper price. In 1995 the WP Istanbul municipality took over the Çamlıca Restaurant, which had been run by a contracting firm under whose management alcohol was served and prices were high. The municipality redecorated the restaurant, creating a nineteenth-century Ottoman atmosphere and a rural Anatolian ambience in the garden. Alcohol and all foreign beverages, including Coca-Cola, were removed from the menu. Traditional soft drinks, such as fruit juice (*şerbet*), were served. Prices were reduced by more than one-third.[203] In opening-ceremony remarks, the WP mayor of Istanbul, Recep Tayyip Erdoğan stated,

---

[201] Alev İnan Çınar, "Refah Party and the City Administration of Istanbul: Liberal Islam, Localism, and Hybridity," *New Perspectives on Turkey* 16 (Spring 1997): 37–8.
[202] Mehmet Terzi's interview with Recep Tayyip Erdoğan, *Milli Gazete*, March 9, 1994, 12.
[203] Çınar, "Refah Party and the City Administration of Istanbul," 30–1.

The Çamlıca premises have been renovated in accordance with the principles of national identity, national culture and national personality. No foreign beverages will be served here, whether with alcohol or non-alcohol. Our people will enjoy Turkish beverages and Turkish meals.[204]

In response to criticisms from the secular segment of society, the municipality argued that the restaurant was decorated and redesigned in an authentic way so as to attract tourists.[205]

When the WP Istanbul municipality insisted on building a mosque in front of the Atatürk statute in Taksim (the most famous square in Istanbul, in terms of artistic and social activity as well as nightlife, and hence symbolizing the republic's Westernization endeavors), it led to the criticisms and protests of the secular segment of society. In response, Erdoğan argued, "Tourists who come to Taksim do not even realize that they are in a Muslim country.... Symbols allow you to make a statement to the observers.... A tourist who comes to Taksim should be able to see what the art of a foreign country looks like."[206] Another symbol of the country's quest for modernization policy is the Cemal Reşit Rey Concert Hall, where Western classical music concerts were performed. Serving of beverages with alcohol at these concerts was cancelled. Turkish classical music and Turkish folk music were added to the repertoire. After the WP's assumption of power in Istanbul, a group of veiled women started to come to the concerts.

The visibility of Islamists (veiled women and men with Islamic beards) in public places started to increase.[207] The Islamists claimed that they wanted a real democracy in Turkey: in a real democracy, they argued, the state does not interfere with an individual's choice of clothing. Pious Muslims wear headscarves, veils, fez, and long robes. Devout Muslims, they pointed out, can tolerate women not wearing headscarves; wearing mini-skirts, tight jeans, and bathing suits; consuming alcohol; viewing pornography; and exhibiting behavior in public places that was incompatible with family values. Yet, those claiming to be secular, Kemalist, and Westernized could not tolerate that Muslims were covering themselves because of their faith.[208]

The Islamists interpreted the WP's success in the 1994 municipal elections as a reflection of the public's demand for a redefinition of the secular-democratic character of the Turkish state.[209] The Islamists argued that the secular segment of Turkish society was biased and antidemocratic for labeling *imam-hatip* schools and Quran courses as institutions that promote Islamist reactionism in the country, and asserted that *imam-hatip* graduates should be permitted to enter the military academy.[210]

---

[204] Ibid., 31. See also *Sabah*, July 23, 1995.
[205] Çınar, "Refah Party and the City Administration of Istanbul," 31.
[206] Ibid., 32.
[207] Ibid., 32, 34–5.
[208] Kır, "Seçmenin Mesajı 2," *Zaman*, April 12, 1994, 8.
[209] Ibid.
[210] Kır, "Seçmenin Mesajı 1," *Zaman*, April 11, 1994, 8.

Erdoğan also changed the name of a street in front of the İskendepaşa mosque where Zahid Kotku was *imam* in order to give the street his name.[211] Once the WP came to power in the Ankara municipality, it replaced the Hittite sun on the city emblem with an image of a mosque. The Hittite sun, argued the WP, was not a national symbol, as it belonged to a civilization from the pre-Islamic period.

The WP government of the Istanbul municipality organized conferences on issues such as "critiques of modernity," "the Islamic philosophy of science," and "Islam and aesthetics." The speakers were mostly Islamist intellectuals. These conferences were part of a WP effort to formulate an alternative high culture to replace that of the secular elites. WP officers argued that such cultural activities were a reflection of the "culture of the people" or "the voice of the civil society." Yet, at the conferences, the audience was often asked to sit separately according to their gender.[212]

The WP municipality under Erdoğan also organized veil fashion shows. According to Erdoğan, "If Pierre Cardin chooses the veil as fashion, the next day women will start to wear the veil."[213] Another activity that was held in the WP municipalities was "people's parliaments." One evening each week, the district mayor would visit the local coffeehouse to listen to citizens' demands from the municipality. WP officers called people's parliaments "direct democracy," which they regarded as "a right ordained up human beings by God."[214] As during his 1991 election campaign for parliament, Tayyip Erdoğan stated, "Give up becoming subjects of the subject, let's altogether become subjects of the God (*Hak*) and become saved." ("*Bırakın kula kulluğu, gelin Hakk'a kul olalım da hep beraber kurtulalım.*")[215]

Yashin, who observed the WP's activities in Kağıthane, a shantytown area of Istanbul, describes the people's parliaments as follows:

Before beginning the interchange, he [the mayor] always reminded neighborhood residents that these gatherings were in the model of Prophet Ömer's mode of governing in the early centuries of Islam.... Those attending the weekly "parliament," were almost exclusively men and mostly Welfare Party supporters, voiced their concerns about problems in the neighborhood: broken pipelines, uncollected garbage, traffic accidents, unpaved roads, lack of water, of electricity, etc.[216]

People's parliaments provided the appearance of transparency in governance, and citizens were pleased to see that the WP, unlike the other political parties responsible for the malfunctioning state, was listening to their problems. WP activists called themselves "servants of society." In the words of then

---

[211] "Vefatının 15. yılında İstanbul Büyükşehir Belediyesi'nden manidar değişiklik: M. Zahid Kotku Caddesi" [A meaningful change by Istanbul Municipality: M. Zahid Kotku Street], *Milli Gazete*, November 12, 1995, 12.

[212] Yashin, "Uses and Abuses of 'State and Civil Society,'" 9–10.

[213] Halise Çiftçi's interview with Süheyla Kebapçıoğlu, *Milli Gazete* 2, March 4, 1994, 1.

[214] Yashin, "Uses and Abuses of 'State and Civil Society,'" 12.

[215] Mehmet Metiner, "Erdoğanlar Mecliste" [Erdoğans are at the parliament], *Milli Gazete*, October 19, 1991, 6.

[216] Yashin, "Uses and Abuses of 'State and Civil Society,'" 12–13.

chair of the WP Ladies Commission, Süheyla Kebapçıoğlu, "In the municipalities under WP governance, there is the dominance of democracy, justice, equality, right, and law that our public has been looking for. For this reason, the WP governance, as a clean governance, gained the public's sympathy."[217] The WP also established children's assemblies in which children were taught to have responsibility and learn politics.[218]

In the 1995 general elections, the WP received 21.4 percent of the votes and emerged as the leading party in Turkey. From 1984 until 1995, the electorate approximately doubled, while the WP's vote share increased five times. Erbakan reflected on the importance of the WP's governance of municipalities for its performance in the 1995 general elections:

> If you analyze, you will see that all the provinces in which we reached great success are under the WP's municipality governance.... Our public sees [our] service. The SDPP came to municipality governance before, and as a result of bad governance it created a negative image of the RPP [the SDPP's successor party]. In contrast, the WP increased its vote-share to a great extent in provinces that are under WP municipality governance. Why? Because the WP does not speak empty words, but produces service.[219]

During the WP's youth meeting, held before the 1995 general elections, Erbakan noted that there were two hundred twenty thousand people in Turkey who had recently turned eighteen years old and thus would be voting in Istanbul for the first time. Of these, Erbakan reported, one hundred ten thousand were WP registered members, and the remaining were waiting to become Welfarists. "[M]any imam-hatip high schools and Quran courses were opened under the national view governance," observed Erbakan, "and newly rising generations had been added to the WP."[220]

Even though the news media in Turkey ignored the rise of the WP by not mentioning the WP's election campaign as often as they reported the campaigns of other parties, the increase in support for the WP was very visible. For example, the party's youth meeting in Istanbul, mentioned in the preceding text, drew twenty thousand people.[221] Corruption allegations against Prime Minister Çiller and concerns about the Islamist character of the WP dominated the 1995 election campaign. Çiller argued that her party was the only power that could stop the advance of the WP. The leading social democratic party, the RPP, under the leadership of Deniz Baykal, campaigned under the vague slogan "new left."[222] This approach proved unsuccessful. Parties of the left received the smallest vote share (25.3%).[223] While the mainstream parties both on the right and the left relied on criticism and "negative campaigning," the

---

[217] Halise Çiftçi's interview with Süheyla Kebapçıoğlu, *Milli Gazete* 2, March 4, 1994, 1.
[218] *Milli Gazete*, May 3, 1994, 12.
[219] Konrad Adenauer Vakfı, *Refah Partisi Üzerine Bir Araştırma*, 24–5.
[220] "Refah gençlerle başladı" [The WP started with the youth], *Yeni Şafak*, November 18, 1995, 3.
[221] Ibid.
[222] Turan, *Türkiye'de Seçmen Davranışı*, 145.
[223] Bülent Tanla, *Türkiye'nin Siyasal Haritası (1950–1995)* [Political Map of Turkey (1950–1995)] (Ankara: TBMM Basımevi, 1997), ix.

WP remained out of the malfunctioning system, calling all the parties corrupt and fake and offered a new political system to the voters.[224]

While the vote share of the TPP, the MP, and the RPP diminished, that of the WP and of Ecevit's DLP increased. As can be seen from the data displayed in Table 2.2, the 1995 election marked the lowest electoral points ever for moderate right and left tendencies, which had dominated Turkish politics to this point. The combined vote share of the center-right (the TPP and the MP) was 38.8 percent and that of the center-left (the RPP and the DLP) was 25.3 percent. The WP secured the largest single-party vote share with 21.4 percent of the vote. The nationalist NAP received 8.2 percent of the votes and the Kurdish separatist People's Democracy Party (PDP) received 4.2 percent.[225]

While the European social democratic parties retained their strength in the aftermath of the cold war, social democratic parties found it difficult to appeal to the electorate in Turkey. The defeat of the RPP, as the representative of Kemalism, in the 1995 general elections constituted a great success on the part of the Islamists, who argued that Kemalism was no longer able to solve the problems of the country. Kemalism had become marginalized, which could be utilized by the Islamists to redefine what it called the "antidemocratic" secularism in the country.

As a result of the rise of the WP in the mid-1990s, the RPP started to give more emphasis on the protection of secularism and defined itself as the guarantor of secularism in the country. Yet, this political rhetoric was not attractive for voters facing the effects of the malfunctioning state. The RPP's supporters were predominantly from economically satisfied and elitist strata of society. Thus, the RPP lost its social democratic identity in the 1990s. In 1995, the RPP's slogan "New left in the world, new RPP in Turkey" was not attractive to voters. Meanwhile, Necmettin Erbakan, declared, in November 1995, that the WP saved the municipalities from corruption and that the party, this time, would save Turkey in the elections.

The WP, while emphasizing the malfunctioning state, continued to appeal to Islamists. The mayor of Istanbul, Recep Tayyip Erdoğan, argued that once the WP came to power, youth would be raised who were attached to their national and moral values.[226] The WP Vice-Chair Musa Demirci suggested that the WP would come to power with its powerful cadre that was based on the masses. "Our nation's will," Demirci stated, "will end the yearning (*hasret*) of 100 years."[227]

In the aftermath of the 1995 elections, the WP, while becoming a party of the masses, tried to redefine the center according to a politicized form of Islam. According to the political process model (PPM), once a movement is underway, organizational dynamics come to occupy the center stage, while framing

---

[224] Turan, *Türkiye'de Seçmen Davranışı*, 146.
[225] Özbudun, *Contemporary Turkish Politics*, 78.
[226] "Refah gençlerle başladı," *Yeni Şafak*, November 18, 1995, 3.
[227] "RP iktidara hazırlanıyor" [The WP prepares to be the party of government], *Yeni Şafak*, November 12, 1995, 3.

processes continue to shape the development of the movement. The WP would not have been able to seize on the malfunctioning state as a POS, if it did not have a strong organizational network as a result of the TIS policy. The Islamist intellectual Ali Bulaç, just a few days before the 1995 general elections, described the state of the Islamist movement in Turkey, emphasizing its emergence through the exploitation of an opportunity by means of peaceful organizational activity:

> Everywhere people who give importance to their religious identity, who want to live their life with Muslim identity, are under great pressures. All political regimes want to remove Islam from everyday life; they are using all opportunities of state and government to secularize the Muslims. . . . As a response to this, Islamic movements, as reaction movements, utilize violence in most places, which results in doing harm both to themselves and their societies. For the first time, in Turkey, Muslims, while disregarding blood and violence, are pursuing a civil, peaceful way to make a demand for political leadership. At this stage, the WP represents the Muslims' demands. . . . The WP now has powerful and great societal support. This support is not just as a result of the active WP politicians. There are thousands and thousands of unknown heroes', diligent people's endeavors. In the last 20 years who made a step in the name of Islam, . . . this has been turned as support for the WP. Hundreds of foundations, associations, publishing houses, journals, congregational institutions, and people who spread the party's message (*tebliğciler*) that traveled Anatolia, they all worked for the WP. . . . They carried the WP to today.[228]

CONCLUSION

If the first stage of the mobilization of political Islam occurred as a result of political opportunities (the TIS), the second phase of the movement's development (since 1991) occurred due to both political opportunities (the malfunctioning state) and to organizational dynamics (the WP's strong organizational networks due to the TIS). The next chapter will analyze the organizational dynamics of the WP.

---

[228] Ali Bulaç, "RP'nin yakaladığı fırsat" [The opportunity that the WP seized upon], *Yeni Şafak*, December 21, 1995, 2.

5

Organizational Dynamics of the Islamist Social Movement

This chapter examines the second phase of the development of political Islam in Turkey, from 1991 to the present. According to the political process model (PPM), once a movement is underway, organizational dynamics come to occupy center stage, while framing processes continue to shape the development of the movement. As a result of the Turkish-Islamic Synthesis policy (TIS, the first political opportunity structure), the Welfare Party (WP) established a strong organizational network (formal and informal) in the 1980s that would enable the party and its successors to frame the malfunctioning state in a manner that mobilized the electorate against the secular-democratic state in the 1990s. By the 1990s, a parallel Islamic socioeconomic sector, comprising the Islamist business class and Islamist intellectuals, emerged next to the WP party apparatus.

In their study of the political framing process, Gamson and Meyer argue the media play a crucial role in "the construction of meaning and the reproduction of culture." Thus, the media's "openness to social movements is itself an important element of political opportunity."[1] Yet, in the Turkish case, it was not the openness of the media that allowed Islamist entrepreneurs to carry out a successful "framing" effort; it was the media's neglect of the Islamist movement that created space for Islamist entrepreneurial activities. The media did not pay sufficient attention to the WP's political rhetoric and activities until the mid-1990s. It was not until after the 1995 general elections, when the WP became the party of government that the media started to focus on the party's political goals and activities. The WP, Necmettin Erbakan argued, was at a disadvantage in advertising its program.[2] However, the WP successfully turned this disadvantage to an advantage by establishing a hierarchically organized network down to the level of electoral precincts and by pursuing a strategy of face-to-face contacts on the part of diligent party activists and volunteers to spread the party message of the "Just Order" by distributing selective material incentives

---

[1] Gamson and Meyer, "Framing Political Opportunity," 287.
[2] Ceylan, *Erbakan ve Türkiye'nin Temel Meseleleri*, 103.

(food, financial assistance, jobs, and the like) along with soft spiritual or emotional incentives intended to encourage feelings of solidarity and belongingness. The absence of mainstream, secular media attention also allowed the WP to push an Islamist agenda without drawing too much attention from the military guardians of secularism. By the time the media turned its attention to Islamism, popular support for the WP was too strong for the party to be suppressed.

The party activists embraced all segments of the society, without discriminating according to political, regional, or ethnic differences. This was an effective method for creating what Bert Klandermans and Bernd Simon call a "politicized collective identity"[3] among voters who were alienated from the malfunctioning state.

ISLAMIST PARTY ORGANIZATIONAL NETWORKS: THE WELFARE PARTY AND VIRTUE PARTY

The WP was distinguished from other political parties in Turkey by the hierarchical structure of the party and its indisputably authoritarian top-down decision-making style. WP members were divided into three groups: the founding fathers of the party, who had been working for their political cause since the establishment of the National Order Party (NOP) in 1969; youth who were influenced by the National Salvation Party's (NSP's) political rhetoric in the 1970s; and, people who joined the Islamist movement in the 1980s. While the founding fathers planned the strategy for the party, the second and third groups implemented the top-down policies of the founding fathers and provided a link and dynamism between the party's voters and the founding fathers.

The founding fathers (Necmettin Erbakan, Şevket Kazan, Oğuzhan Asiltürk, Recai Kutan, Fehim Adak, and Ali Oğuz) enjoyed undisputed authority and respect in the party; they controlled the party's headquarters and its group in the parliament. These individuals lost their high status only as a result of a conflict with Erbakan, or because of health reasons. Erbakan, as the party chair, made all important decisions regarding the party's governance. He determined the party's nominee list for elections to the party's General Governing Council (*Genel İdare Kurulu* – GİK), members of the party's congresses, and the party's group chairs in the parliament. Erbakan, who was called in public gatherings "*Mücahit* Erbakan" (Warrior Erbakan), enjoyed undisputed leadership in the party until 2001, when the movement split into two groups: traditionalists and reformists. At the party's Third Congress, held in October 1990, Erbakan was the only candidate for the party leadership and received 551 out of 552 votes. At the Fourth Congress in October 1993, Erbakan was again the sole candidate for the party leadership and received all 659 votes.[4]

The youth section of the WP was composed of people who were in their thirties and forties in the 1990s; they worked in the party's provincial organizations, and they governed municipalities. Those who joined the party in the

---

[3] Klandermans and Simon, "Politicized Collective Identity," 319–31.
[4] Çakır, *Ne Şeriat Ne Demokrasi*, 52–4.

1980s included people from various backgrounds and ideologies, women of all ages, Islamized students, young workers, and the young unemployed of the 1980s.[5]

The WP's networks, like the Islamist business class, grew stronger starting in the mid-1980s. For example, in the 1984 municipality elections, the WP's network was incomplete; due to financial constraints, the party could not participate in the elections throughout the country. Instead, the WP participated in 50 percent of provincial general assembly (*il genel meclisi*) elections, 16 percent of mayoral elections, and 17 percent of municipality assembly (*belediye meclisi*) elections. During general and local elections, the WP could not utilize the media to propagandize its appeal. Except for the party's informal press, *Milli Gazete*, the press did not pay attention to the party's political messages and activities.[6] In June 1985, WP Chair Ahmet Tekdal emphasized the importance of disseminating the party's message to citizens throughout Turkey, down to the level of neighborhoods and villages. He also stated the importance of establishing the party's organization in villages, neighborhoods, and electoral precincts (*sandıklar* – ballot boxes).[7]

As in the case of its predecessors, the NOP and the NSP, the WP was mainly financed by ideologically motivated Islamists. Between the years 1984 and 1987, the WP started to establish a widespread formal organization in which the Islamist business class played a crucial role. As a result of the TIS, the Islamist business class emerged as the wealthiest and best-organized segment of society, which had a positive impact on the WP's organizational skills and resources. By 1987, the WP had established party networks in all sixty-seven provinces and six hundred districts (*ilçeler*).

In the mid-1980s, regular province (*il*) meetings were initiated, both to control the activities of the party's networks and to determine new strategies for enhancing the party's relations with the electorate. Every month, there were district council (*ilçe divan*) meetings; afterward, province chairs and observers (province council) would hold a meeting at the party's headquarters, which was followed by a meeting of the General Governing Council of the party as a whole. These regular meetings kept WP staff members active and well-informed. Between 1985 and 1987, eighty-eight regular meetings were held for this purpose.[8]

The strengthened networks of the WP contributed to increasing its vote share starting by the mid-1980s. The return of Necmettin Erbakan into politics following the 1987 referendum that ended the ban on politicians who had served in the parliament in the pre-1980 period also contributed to the increase

---

[5] Ibid., 54.
[6] Refah Partisi, *Birinci Büyük Kongresi, Genel Başkan Ahmet Tekdal'ın Açış Konuşması* (June 30, 1985), 14.
[7] Ibid., 41.
[8] Selim, *Yol Ayrımı*, 78–9; Refah Partisi, *Büyük Kongresi* (30 Haziran 1985) [The Welfare Party, Great Convention (June 30, 1985)] (Ankara: Refah Partisi, 1985), 40–1; and Refah Partisi, *Refah Partisi İkinci Büyük Kongresi* (11 Ekim 1987) [The Welfare Party Second Great Convention (October 11, 1987)] (Ankara: Refah Partisi, 1991), 36, 38, 40.

in electoral support for the WP. Because of Erbakan's return, the Motherland Party (MP) started to lose its support from the Islamist sector of the electorate. In the 1984 municipal elections, the WP, led by Ahmet Tekdal, received only 4.4 percent of the vote; in the 1987 general elections, the party won 7.2 percent. Following the 1987 general elections, Erbakan placed special emphasis on strengthening the party's networks in Turkey. The WP continued to increase its vote share in the 1989 municipality elections, receiving 9.8 percent of the vote.[9]

By the 1990s, the WP had the most comprehensive party network in Turkey, starting from the provinces down to the level of electoral precincts. As a result, the WP approximated the model of a "mass party" or a "party of social integration."[10] Each electoral precinct was based on a single street; this makes clear the scope of the WP network and the extent of its penetration into mass society. A hierarchically organized network was necessary to enable the party to determine the socioeconomic problems and needs of society. According to the WP, a good network should provide planning (determining possible problems and goals, finding solutions to problems), organization (division of labor among party activists according to their capacities, and disciplined work by these activists), governance (all activists working in unity, and training each other so as to develop their skills), and control (by means of regular reports and coordination with the party's headquarters). Consistent with the Islamists' emphasis on morality, and in clear contrast to the widespread perception of party officials in Turkey as corrupt, all network activists were expected to work very hard, and to be patient, honest, knowledgeable, calm, trustworthy, kind, sympathetic, courageous, humble, energetic, and sincere.[11]

As displayed in Diagram 5.1, the WP networks consisted of a hierarchy of organizations, beginning at the top with the WP headquarters and the General Governing Council, which worked actively with party members. There were discussion commissions composed of experts and there was a special staff of teacher inspectors controlling the activities of the party staff. The provincial organizations were composed of province governing council regular and alternate members, province discussion commission members, province orators and teachers, an election headquarters chair and staff, a province finance committee, and a women's committee. The district (*ilçe*) organizations were composed of district governing council regular and alternate members, village and neighborhood staff, a district discussion commission, a district election headquarters chair and staff, district teachers and orators, a finance committee, and a women's committee. Subdistrict (*belde*) organizations were composed of subdistrict governing commission regular and alternate members, village and neighborhood

---

[9] European Court of Human Rights, *Case of Refah Partisi (the Welfare Party) and Others v. Turkey*, 5; Yeşilada, "The Virtue Party," 67; and Konrad Adenauer Vakfı, *Refah Partisi Üzerine Bir Araştırma*, 14.
[10] Özbudun, *Contemporary Turkish Politics*, 92.
[11] Refah Partisi, *Refah Partisi Samsun Merkez İlçe Teşkilâtı, Teşkilât Çalışma Modeli* [The Welfare Party Samsun Central District Organization, Organization Working Model] (Samsun: Refah Partisi, 1995), 8–9.

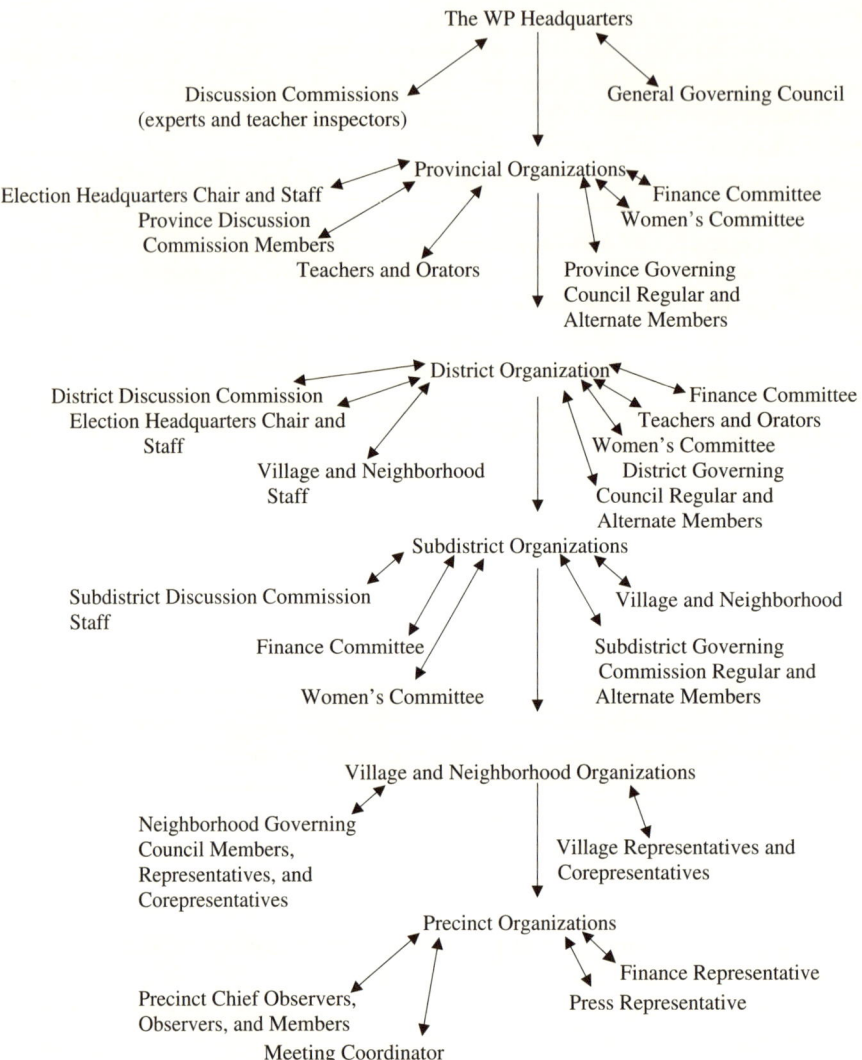

DIAGRAM 5.1. *The Welfare Party's Organizational Network*

staff, a subdistrict discussion commission, a finance committee, and a women's committee. Village and neighborhood organizations were composed of neighborhood governing council members, representatives and corepresentatives, and village representatives and corepresentatives. Precinct organizations were composed of precinct chief observers, observers, members, a finance representative, a press representative, and a meeting coordinator.[12]

---

[12] Ibid., 6–7.

Unlike other political parties in Turkey, the WP's organization relied on a tightly controlled network of ideologically motivated activists and volunteers down to the level of electoral precincts. The party had a council (*divan*) in every district comprising fifty regular and fifty alternate members. In neighborhoods, the party had a representative and a corepresentative. Under each neighborhood representative, there was one precinct chief observer (*başmüşahit*) and four observers who maintained a database of information on everyone living in the area, including the details of each family unit. In some areas, there were even representatives for each apartment building, who paid visits to households and spread the party's message. In 1991, Ali İbiş, then chair of the WP Istanbul Province Election Headquarters (*seçim karargâhı*), described the highly centralized organization of the party and how it functioned to deliver the party message:

> The WP's activities in Istanbul were coordinated and directed by one center. Strategies were determined at the Province Election Headquarters. Prepared advertisement material was transferred to province and district (*ilçe*) election headquarters. All these activities were carried out in a very organized and conscious manner. Too much attention was paid to the ripeness of time. Our view is based on the brotherhood of 60 million. For this reason, we specifically aimed at reaching out to all the citizens in this country [and] spreading our message by face-to-face contacts, if necessary. We sincerely believe that the majority of the citizens in this country do not think differently from us. Yet, they do not know us sufficiently. Unfortunately, the powers that control the media consciously do not want to spread the WP's message at all. Thus, we aimed at reaching out to all of our people regardless of their faith or gender.... We opened up 25 district chairmanships. We opened up 1,500 election communication offices and we prepared an army of volunteers composed of 60,000 people. Our ladies worked very hard on these tasks.... Besides our working group of 60,000 people, we also have other actively working members.[13]

According to Şevket Kazan, the establishment of a network down to the level of electoral precincts played a crucial role in the WP's success in the 1995 general elections. The WP had five observers for each ballot box: in Istanbul alone, for example, there were 16,974 ballot boxes, and the WP had five observers for each ballot box (meaning there were more than 90,000 WP activists deployed at this level of the electoral system alone). The party had an official cadre (*muvazzaf kadro*) of one hundred thousand workers for the elections – and as WP member Mehmet Ali Şahin reported, the party's volunteers numbered two or three times more than its official cadres. Furthermore, the party also had province and district governance as well as neighborhood discussion (*istişare*) councils, each composed of fourteen people.[14] Şahin described the party's mobilization of voters for the 1995 elections:

---

[13] Mehmet Metiner, "60 bin kişilik ordu" [An army of sixty thousand people], *Milli Gazete*, October 19, 1991, 3.

[14] "Refah'ın sırrı markaj" [The Welfare's secret is advertisement], *Yeni Şafak*, November 12, 1995, 3.

We completed all the work that has to be done during the election day at precincts months, even years ago. We registered all voters one by one. We directed our work accordingly. We determined people who were eligible to vote, but were not registered. We found them. We helped them to register to the district election councils.[15]

The WP utilized the latest technology for maintaining a database about its members and constituents compiled by the party's neighborhood representatives, and the data were used by the party staff to determine who was in need of help (e.g., on account of sickness, death, marriage, or other life-cycle events) in their area of control.[16] Fazlı Kılıç, the WP chair of the Election Coordination Center of Istanbul, Second Regional Center, suggested that the combination of technology and organization gave the WP a distinct advantage:

The WP works both with a very large cadre and utilizes the technology in the best sense. We can track the activities in districts through a network of computers and faxes and by having a large number of activists. I do not think that the other parties have such a large number of activists.[17]

The party targeted various segments of the society through a network of headmasters and teachers (*hatipler ve öğretmentler*). Headmasters and teachers engaged groups of housewives, government employees, university youth, *imam-hatip* students, teachers, unemployed people, retired people, and working people in discussions in local coffeehouses, in households, on university campuses, in pubs, and at local market places. All WP press conferences and speeches at political gatherings (*mitingler*) were recorded on videocassettes and distributed to the party's networks, down to the level of villages and neighborhoods. Thus, the voters were introduced to the "Just Order" (*Adil Düzen*) by a variety of means such as videocassettes, conferences, panels, and even by chats during the WP activists' household visits. The party, unlike the other political parties, emphasized the classical door-to-door canvassing by hundreds of thousands of highly motivated, devoted, and disciplined party workers – and their activity continued year-round, rather than being limited to election periods.[18] The party also gave importance to establishing good relations with the local press in order to disseminate its propaganda more widely.[19]

---

[15] Ibid.
[16] Konrad Adenauer Vakfı, *Refah Partisi Üzerine Bir Araştırma*, 45; Özbudun, *Contemporary Turkish Politics*, 84.
[17] "Refah Partisi'nin İstanbul Seçim Koordinasyon Merkezi'ndeki çalışmalar tam anlamıyla İktidarlık" [The WP Istanbul Election Coordination Center's work carries the party to leadership], İbrahim Aykut's interview with Fazlı Kılıç, *Milli Gazete*, December 14, 1995, 16.
[18] Özbudun, *Contemporary Turkish Politics*, 84–5.
[19] Kazan, *Refah Gerçeği*, vol. 1, 48, 63; Refah Partisi, *Refah Partisi Samsun Merkez İlçe Teşkilâtı, Teşkilât Çalışma Modeli*, 6–9, 12; Şevket Kazan, *Refah Gerçeği*, vol. 2 [The Reality of Welfare] (Ankara: Keşif Yayınları, 2002), 34; and Yeşilada, "The Virtue Party," 70. In August 1997, the WP had established its organization in all districts of Istanbul and in 24 counties out of 35. There were 472 representatives and 500 corepresentatives in all quarters of the province. There were 1,490 chief-observers and 2,137 observers overseeing the ballot boxes. See Yeşim Arat, *Political Islam in Turkey and Women's Organizations* (Istanbul: TESEV Yayınları, 1999), 22.

PARTY MOBILIZATIONAL EFFORTS

Since the party sought to redefine the secular-democratic political system in Turkey, it regarded elections as a means to realize that goal. Thus, the party regarded its voters as agents carrying out a special political mission: to turn the WP into a party of the masses. In the party's election pamphlets, voters were invited to learn about the current malfunctioning state, which the WP called a "slavery system" (*köle düzeni*) run by the "imitator" (*taklitçi*) political parties. Voters were made aware of what the WP believed to be the reasons behind the malfunctioning system in the country.[20]

For Erbakan, the WP had believers who voted for it, while other political parties merely had their electorate. Yeşim Arat, a professor of political science, argues, "Religion was the most effective means of political mobilization which could prompt intense sacrifice and commitment from the people who believed in the cause and the party they believed to be promoting this cause."[21] The WP had one million party activists in the 1990s, who regarded their work for the party as a special mission undertaken for God's sake (*Allah rızası için*); they did not expect material or worldly rewards.[22] This merger of the spiritual and the political was reflected in Erbakan's 1995 speech:

> This society is coming from the sufferings of 75 years by initiating jihad. You will work until there will no longer be left any unfaithful (*batıl*) in the world. There is no difference between the WP's candidate to be a candidate (*aday adayı*) and parliament member candidates. The only difference lies in if the candidates work with a great endeavor, they will gain the greatest will of God (*sevap*).[23]

The WP, while strengthening its network, changed its propaganda tactics as well, which is an evidence of framing in order to expand the party's electoral support base. In the 1980s, the WP's primary emphasis was on the protection of moral and religious values that would be embraced by the Islamist circles. Starting in the 1990s, the party focused on reaching out to disaffected secular voters by emphasizing socioeconomic and political problems in Turkey. Thus, in the 1990s, the WP changed its traditional propaganda style by including all segments of the society (secular people, workers, unemployed, and retired people, intellectuals suffering from human rights abuses, prostitutes demanding social justice, urban people demanding a clean environment, and Islamist students and women demanding more freedom of faith) in their election pamphlets.

The party's Public Relations Department played an important role in cultivating relations with, and extending ties to, different segments of the society. The party, through visits to hospitals, prisons, and housing for the elderly;

---

[20] Refah Partisi, *Teşhis: Türkiye'nin Gerçek Durumu, Sebepleri* [The Diagnosis: Turkey's Real Situation, Its Reasons] (Ankara: Refah Partisi, n.d.), 45–8.
[21] Arat, *Political Islam in Turkey and Women's Organizations*, 36.
[22] Ibid., 36–7.
[23] Şakir Bayramoğlu, "Milli Görüş'çü olmak bir sevdadır" [It is a love to belong to the National View], *Milli Gazete*, December 10, 1995, 2.

participation in celebrations of weddings and births; and offering condolences to citizens, gave the message that it was concerned with the problems of individuals and with associations like schools and unions.[24] The WP, unlike the mainstream parties, did not have specific ties to vocational organizations (*meslek*), such as labor, government employees, and employers. Instead, the party established ties to the chairmen of thirteen vocational organizations by holding regular monthly meetings with them.

The WP also made appeals to the Alevis, known as the secular sector of the society, attempting to give the message that "even Alevis vote for the WP; what are you waiting for?"[25] The WP's election pamphlets for the 1991 general election campaign included pictures of women who were not wearing headscarves, a clear effort to signal an inclusive rather than a sectarian orientation. During the election campaign, the WP's Ladies' Commission Chair Süheyla Kebapçıoğlu emphasized that there was an incorrect image of the party, as if it would only serve religious Muslims once it was elected. Kebapçıoğlu argued that the WP, although it was a salvation party, would nonetheless serve the entire public.[26]

Bahri Zengin, a prominent WP member of parliament and chair of the party's Advertising Department, played an important role in changing the party's propaganda tactics and developing its appeal to a broader public. Zengin suggested that the WP, in order to become the ruling party, had to secure the support of voters who did not belong to the traditional Islamic community; the party had to open itself to new segments of society. As part of this process, the WP established a dialogue with former socialist intellectuals, such as Murat Belge and Asaf Savaş Akat.[27] In fact, communism and political Islam, aside from holding quite divergent views on, for example, the role of religion in society and the right to own private property and make a profit, share some common points. Both communism and political Islam criticize Western imperialism and the free market economy as forms of "exploitation."

In the aftermath of the cold war, the social democratic left in Turkey was disoriented. The WP easily filled the political vacuum on the left by reframing its propaganda tactics. In the 1990s, the party particularly utilized the rhetoric of social democracy like justice, equality, freedom, and democracy to increase its vote share. During the 1991 election campaign, Erbakan defined the WP as a happiness (*mutluluk*) and felicity (*saadet*) party. Accordingly, happiness could be attained by felicity, freedom, justice, and respect (*saygınlık*). Erbakan, while arguing morality and spirituality (*maneviyat*) as the basis of felicity, suggested that it was necessary to adopt the U.S. federal system in Turkey. Once such a system was established, he asserted, people in Turkey would have the freedom to determine their own laws and to educate their children as they wished, along

---

[24] Arat, *Political Islam in Turkey and Women's Organizations*, 23–4.
[25] Çakır, *Ne Şeriat Ne Demokrasi*, 68.
[26] "Kebapçıoğlu: Bizi kasıtlı olarak yanlış tanıtıyorlar" [They are misrepresenting us on purpose], *Milli Gazete*, September 10, 1991, 3.
[27] Kazan, *Refah Gerçeği*, vol. 1, 64; Oral Çalışlar, *Refah Partisi Nereden Nereye?* (Istanbul: Pencere Yayınları, 1995), 56–7; and Selim, *Yol Ayrımı*, 78–9.

Party Mobilizational Efforts

with the freedoms of organization, faith, and speech.[28] Recep Tayyip Erdoğan, the WP Istanbul Province chair and candidate for parliament in the 1991 general elections, described how the party made an effort to appeal to a broader constituency in the elections:

> We opened up election coordination centers and election contact bureaus in neighborhoods throughout Istanbul. Furthermore, in all subdistricts and places that we thought important, lady contact bureaus continue their activities. Our Province Election Coordination Center that coordinates, controls, and determines strategies at the province level, has started to its activities. Regardless of faith, thought, and gender, to our entire public we will give the message of "Let's together establish a new world." Thus, we will send our message to everybody. With a very new rhetoric and propaganda technique, the WP can be a surprise first-ranked party. The WP's success will surprise everybody.[29]

The WP appealed to a broad segment of constituents: Islamists, poor urban migrants, businessmen, and upwardly mobile professionals. Their political interests ranged widely, from social and economic reform to replacing the secular state structure with one based on the *Sharia*.[30] Thus, the party's activities were divided between achieving long-term goals and engaging in short-term, election-oriented activities. The long-term activities aimed at making everyone a supporter of the National View Movement (*Hedef: Herkesi Milli Görüşçü yapmak*) by reaching out to every sector of the society and by means of continuous, well-organized hard work.

For the election period activities, the party devised a detailed strategy on how to convince the electorate to vote for the WP. In this context, the electorate was defined as a tool (*malzeme*).[31] As Erbakan stated, "there are two types of human beings: those that belong to the Welfare [Party] and those that are waiting to belong to the Welfare [Party]."[32] The party's activists were supposed to approach different sectors of the society (conservative, liberal, and Islamist) by utilizing appropriate propaganda tactics. Human beings were defined as creatures having weak and strong points. The network was supposed to find a way to convince the electorate. As was stated in the party's training pamphlet for party workers, "It is our business, we demand this person's vote. How can I receive this person's vote? A good marketing person is one, who sells his product to the door that he was expelled from previously. One who wants to get honey, does not destroy the behive (*arı kovanı*)."[33] For example, women orators in their visits to a liberal neighborhood would dress in a suit rather than in a long coat (*pardesü*), let alone a veil (*çarşaf*). They would greet with "good day" (*iyi günler*) rather than *selamunaleyküm* (let God's grace be on you). If they visited a shantytown, they would talk about the lack of services; whereas in a wealthy,

---

[28] "On mislini kazanacaksın" [You will earn tenfold], *Milli Gazete*, September 8, 1991, 6.
[29] "Erdoğan: İstanbul'da birincilik için çalışıyoruz" [Erdoğan: We are working to be ranked first], *Milli Gazete* September 10, 1991, 3.
[30] White, *Islamist Mobilization in Turkey*, 3.
[31] Refah Partisi, *Refah Partisi Samsun Merkez İlçe Teşkilâtı, Teşkilât Çalışma Modeli*, 10.
[32] Çakır, *Ne Şeriat Ne Demokrasi*, 81.
[33] Refah Partisi, *Refah Partisi Samsun Merkez İlçe Teşkilâtı, Teşkilât Çalışma Modeli*, 10–12.

conservative district they would emphasize social problems (drugs, alcoholism, prostitution, and the like). Party activists, after determining the problems in the area of their visit, would provide alternative solutions, such as providing material benefits – like food, clothing, jobs, and money – to the needy.[34] The party orators were advised to communicate to the electorate according to their constituents' capacity of understanding (*akıllarının kavrayabileceği ölçüde hitap*).

The electorate was divided into three groups: first, politicized people, who would definitely not vote for the WP. WP activists were advised to make sure that they would be aware of this group's harmful activities; second, neutral people, who were subdivided into three groups (sympathetic, negative, and unknowledgeable); and finally, the WP supporters. Party activists primarily focused on the second group: neutrals, who were regarded as people who might join the third group of WP supporters if they changed their political views – or who might simply be persuaded to just vote for the party. Party orators were trained at the party center to utilize appropriate tactics to convince a potential supporter. For example, activists were advised not to criticize the contacted person; and the constituent should not realize that the activists were smarter than him or her. Party activists were supposed to convince the electorate by creating a positive psychological atmosphere about the party. For example, if a voter argued that the WP could not win, then the activists would respond, "Yes, it may be the case. Yet, in the next elections, we will be the strongest party."[35] Party activists were also advised to pay attention to the ethnic, regional, historical, and political context of their dialogues with voters during their visits and to give a convincing message in a friendly manner without getting into divergent subjects. The primary advice of the WP to its activists was to give importance, value, trust, respect, and honor to the potential voter.[36]

Starting in the 1990s at the level of provinces, the WP emphasized its orators' and recruited members' education who would work in the party ranks. Activists were trained primarily about the principles that guided party activities, the organization of the party machinery to which they belonged, and the party ideology – the National Order. In August 1993, the party's Education Department started providing general training for its staff, controlled by the party's headquarters, through regular meetings on Fridays, Saturdays, and Sundays. Between the years 1990 and 1993, the WP trained seven thousand party activists. The party organized conferences, panels, and political gatherings (*mitingler*) covering a broad range of subjects such as human rights, current political problems, the concepts of independence and freedom, election laws, public relations, human psychology, and the environment in order to educate party members and/or the electorate throughout the country.[37]

---

[34] Arat, *Political Islam in Turkey and Women's Organizations*, 44–6.
[35] Refah Partisi, *Refah Partisi Samsun Merkez İlçe Teşkilâtı, Teşkilât Çalışma Modeli*, 10–12.
[36] Ibid.
[37] Refah Partisi, *Refah Partisi 4. Olağan Büyük Kongresi, Faaliyet Raporu (10 Ekim 1993)* [The Welfare Party Fourth General Great Convention, Work Report (October 10, 1993)] (Ankara: Refah Partisi, 1993), 30; Arat, *Political Islam in Turkey and Women's Organizations*, 24.

The party activists' emphasis on utilizing regular, face-to-face contacts to establish close and friendly relations with the electorate was especially effective in poor sections of cities (shantytowns), where residents needed a sense of solidarity as well as assistance in dealing with their socioeconomic and cultural problems – the latter involving adapting themselves to city life. The WP's networks became a source of social safety – affording a feeling of belongingness in an alien environment – for the migrant urban poor. The activists carried a message that the needy citizens were not alone.

Erman, in her study of the adaptation problem facing the migrant poor in the shantytowns of Ankara, points to the tension between the lower-class migrant youth "them" and the upper-class urban youth "the others" by quoting a migrant high school student:

Of course, we experience exclusion. Look at Çankaya (an upper-class district) youth who imitate Western culture. They definitely pretend that our people do not exist, they reject [us]. I cannot be friends with them. I cannot listen to the same music they listen to. Yet, I can live together with them if I am put in a room, but they cannot live with me. Why? Because they are conceited, they put on airs, they are inclined to look down on people like me.[38]

Another young, second-generation migrant woman who was a state employee and a committed leftist living on her own in a shantytown, argued in a separate interview that "she identified herself with the village because she did not want to be a part of the 'alienating' urban society." She described the contrast between village and city life that results in the atomization of the individual in the city:

There is sharing in the village; the relations are warm there. In the city, nobody knows anyone else, nobody asks how you are doing. This is because of the economic system – people have to work hard all day to make a living, and they get too tired or are short of time to see each other. On the other hand, in the village, they work together in the fields, helping one another.[39]

The WP responded to the opportunity inherent in the atomization of the urban poor. The WP, unlike the mainstream political parties, gave special attention to the needs of this population. The WP Istanbul Province Organization Election Coordination chair, Hasan Durmuş, argued, "The WP is the closest party to the electorate. Who died, who was born, who got married, we learn first before the state does. According to the situation, we visit for condolences, celebrations (*gözünaydın*), and congratulations."[40]

The WP had strong women and youth organizations. The WP Ladies' Commission (*Hanım Kolları*), as the most dynamic unit of the party, played a crucial role in increasing the party's electoral support base by paying weekly household visits. In a conservative society like Turkey, only a woman can establish a strong relationship with another woman. The former WP Istanbul

---

[38] Erman, "Becoming 'Urban' or Remaining 'Rural,'" 548.
[39] Ibid., 549.
[40] "Refah'ın sırrı markaj," *Yeni Şafak*, November 12, 1995, 3.

Province Organization chair and then WP member and candidate for parliament, Mehmet Ali Şahin, argued,

> ... the WP, unlike the other parties, relied on a faithful human force as its capital (*sermaye*). Within this human force, the party's ladies' commission was the main supporter. Like the party's headquarters, the ladies' commission was organized as province chair, district chair, and down to the voters.[41]

The Ladies' Commission was tied to the party's neighborhood organization. The commission's activities revolved around party organization, propaganda, and public relations units represented in the executive councils.[42] In the pre-1980 era, Islamist women were not actively involved in politics. In the 1970s, some of the NOP/NSP governors' wives spread the party's message by paying household visits. But it was not an organized and widespread activity. Starting in the mid-1980s, however, Islamist women started actively working to spread the message of political Islam (*tebliğ*). The Islamist women's activity became organized in October 1989. In January 1990, the party's Ladies' Commission's activities were coordinated through the party's Public Relations Chairmanship, as a result of which the commission's activities became planned, organized, disciplined, and regular.[43]

The WP Ladies' Commission pursued its activities by coordinating with the party's province (*il*), district (*ilçe*), subdistrict (*belde*), village, neighborhood, and apartment commissions. Women activists worked continuously throughout the year, seeking to increase the party's registered female membership. Women activists paid attention to be soft, convincing, respectful, and tolerant during their household visits. The orators' speeches were controlled by the party's provincial and subprovincial observers.[44]

In the 1990s, it was possible to see Islamist women in every sector of the society, including education, law, and the press. They organized panels, sport activities, and household visits; printed journals about women (such as *Mektup* – Letter and *Kadın ve Aile* – Woman and Family); and established associations and foundations, like the Foundation for Aid to Students' Parents. Their foremost aim was to reach all the citizens (housewives, working women, and government employees) and convince them that Islam was the right lifestyle. Ayşe Saktanber, a professor of sociology, attributes a religious motivation to the Islamist women's activities:

Muslim women, like any other dedicated *mümin* [believer], see this world as an essentially transitory phenomenon. Whatever they do in this world is directed towards winning

---

[41] Ibid.
[42] Arat, *Political Islam in Turkey and Women's Organizations*, 22.
[43] "Bu onurlu susuş, 29 Kasım günü sandıktan haykıracaktır" [This honest silence will shout at from the ballot box on November 29], *Milli Gazete*, November 11, 1987, 10; "İnsanlar arasındaki sevgiyi yok etmeyelim" [Do not erase brotherhood among people], Mustafa Kurdaş's interview with the WP Ladies' Commission Chair Süheyla Kebapçıoğlu, *Milli Gazete* 2, April 18, 1994, 1.
[44] Ibid.

God's favor in the other world. Hence the overall efforts they expand on leading their lives in accordance with Islamic ideals not only render Islam a living practice but also create its ethics of quotidian, which are designed above all to help Muslims prepare themselves for the other world and merit an eternal life in God's Heaven.[45]

The Islamist women pursued a patient and long-term strategy and paid special attention to the ignored, poor sectors of the society. The Islamist movement challenged the secular, modern lifestyle with the ethos of "living Islam as a conscious Muslim." In the long term, creating masses that would adopt an Islamist way of life would transform Islam from a private religious matter into "a living social practice." Since women were raising their children, they were "the crucial agents of everyday articulation and reproduction of Islamic ideologies."[46] Women confronted by Islamist women activists were taught how to raise their children according to Islamic rules and what an Islamic family should be.[47] The Islamist women utilized traditional social gatherings of women, like reception days or *kandil* (certain religious days in Islam) celebrations to talk about how to interpret Islam correctly. In time, such gatherings provided an emotional bond based on trust among the contacted women, along with a redefinition of the faith and lifestyle in an Islamist way. The Islamist women, while drinking tea, read passages from the Quran, answered questions about daily life, and organized small discussion groups to talk about women's rights in Islam or feminism, current political and socioeconomic issues affecting women and their families. As Saktanber argues,

> These creative and dedicated activities of Muslim women create an intellectually lively milieu intended to facilitate the consolidation of an alternative Islamic [way of] life style while at the same time strengthening their faith in Islam, bringing many Muslim women from different intellectual levels together around one ideal and perpetuating their sense of Islamic equality.[48]

The chairman of the WP Ladies' Commission, Süheyla Kebapçıoğlu, suggested that there was a significant difference between WP women activists and those of other parties.

> Other parties have ladies' commissions as well. . . . Yet, unlike us, they could not reach to our level of success and organization. Because we have essential differences. We work and advertise our party with a love of worshiping (*ibadet aşkı*). We are very close to the public and implement the principle of continuous work. We cannot see the same sacrifice in other parties. Generally, they focus on a small number of women in their actions, rather than embracing all segments of the society. Furthermore, they are eager to look for a materialistic interest and a price from all of their activities.[49]

---

[45] Ayşe Saktanber, "Becoming the 'Other' as a Muslim in Turkey: Turkish Women vs. Islamist Women," *New Perspectives on Turkey* 11 (Fall 1994): 123–4.
[46] Ibid., 111.
[47] "Müslüman kadınlar teşkilâtlanıyor" [Muslim women are getting organized], *Milli Gazete*, October 20, 1991, 10. See also "İzmirli hanımlar Adil Düzen için seferberlik başlattı" [Ladies of Izmir started a mobilization for the Just Order], *Milli Gazete*, September 1, 1991, 7.
[48] Saktanber, "Becoming the 'Other' as a Muslim in Turkey," 115.
[49] "İnsanlar arasındaki sevgiyi yok etmeyelim," *Milli Gazete* 2, April 18, 1994, 1.

The Islamist women activists provided material benefits (such as clothing, food) to poor people in shantytowns. The WP, unlike other parties, targeted the urban poor. As then WP chair of Social Assistance for the Yenimahalle Ladies' Commission, Kevser Karaman, stated, "Wherever there is a needy, abandoned, and poor; we have always been with them until now, and will continue to be with them."[50] It is important to note that besides providing material benefits to the voters, the party's women activists lead the voter's redefinition of herself. Turkish society is characterized by "classical patriarchy," that is, unlike in the case of modern societies, many norms and roles are based on gender. In conservative families, women are regarded as commodities belonging to their male kin. Thus, many Turkish women have a life that is organized around their families only. Migrant women, in particular, are expected to stay in their homes, so that they will be "protected" from "the dangers of the outside world."[51] Women, who were being suppressed in conservative families, emancipated themselves from their inferior status at home by being a member of the party network. The women activists, while teaching other women how to trust themselves by joining the network, also emphasize political education and indoctrination carried out by teachers. As Gülten Çelik, then chair of the Virtue Party's[52] (VP's) Women Commission emphasized the educational role of women activists:

The Virtue Party, by supporting and giving value to our women who have been suppressed for many years, convinces them to trust themselves. Women who trust themselves through their work in our network carry their mission to other members of the society. . . . The Virtue Party is an education hearth at the same time. All levels of people are merged together and they contribute to the network in terms of their knowledge and talent. Our women's commission is like a public university by its activities. Women who educate and improve themselves in our network become successful in every area of life.[53]

As Arat argues, "Women's organization and activism in the Welfare Party was an unprecedented phenomenon. No other party in Turkey could boast of a similar membership of women. Women of the Welfare Party registered close to a million members in about six years."[54] In 1994, Erbakan was congratulating the party's Women Commission for its tremendous success, as the commission was registering eight hundred members per month.[55] According to the WP's Istanbul Provincial Organization's progress report, between 1995 and

---

[50] "Ankara'nın ortayerinde bir avuç yardım sevinci" [A short happiness because of assistance in the middle of Ankara], *Milli Gazete*, March 21, 1994, 12.
[51] Erman, "Becoming 'Urban' or Remaining 'Rural,'" 550.
[52] In the aftermath of the closure of the WP, the VP succeeded the party.
[53] Fazilet Partisi, *Fazilet Partisi Genel Merkez 2000–2001 Faaliyet Bülteni, Kadın Kolları* [The Virtue Party Headquarters 2000–2001 Action Bulletin, Women's Organization] (Ankara: Fazilet Partisi, 2001), 9.
[54] Arat, *Political Islam in Turkey and Women's Organizations*, 8.
[55] "RP İl Hanımlar Komisyonları Ankara'da Toplandı: Hedef 1 milyon üye" [The WP Province Ladies' Commission met in Ankara: Target is one million members], *Milli Gazete*, May 5, 1994, 12.

1997, women members increased from 158,287 to 377,888. Women were also instrumental in persuading their husbands to register with the party: total party membership increased from 676,337 to 1,072,333 in the same period. Women members thus constituted approximately a third of the party's membership in Istanbul.[56] The reason behind such a great success was that the Islamist women activists utilized a nonpolitical setting – household visits – for spreading the party's message. The most productive results were achieved during the household chats for two reasons: first, the party's activists seized the most convenient atmosphere to spread the party's message during the household chats by establishing close relationships with the constituents. Second, since the present Turkish political and judiciary system do not allow talking explicitly about everything in public, household chats were places where the party activists could articulate the party's message freely and convince the constituents easily.[57]

The women activists strengthened feelings of solidarity, which led to a reinterpretation and reformulation of the concept of faith in the minds of the contacted people. After establishing close relations, the women activists recruited other women as members and co-workers. When the party established a new network in a quarter or a district, those women were given the task of institutionalizing the party, first by approaching the wives of the male elites from party circles. Afterward, they would determine the social fabric of the district, getting to know who was who. The women activists paid special attention to developing friendly relations with women who were liked and respected in the community and who were regarded as natural leaders concerned about the well-being of the community. The activists would ask such a woman leader to organize a tea party and invite her friends, so that the activists would be introduced to the community. Another tea party would follow at another friend's house.

During this process, the activists would avoid frightening the contacted women with religious propaganda or with alienating political discourse. The activists' goal was to implicitly give the message "we are the same," hence to convince the contacted women that Islamist women were not so different from them. The activists' foremost goal was to keep the political activity within the confines of the social.[58] Rümeysa Yazıcı, chair of Social Affairs for the VP Women Commission, suggested that freedom and democracy, human rights and the primacy of the law, development, protection of the balance between economic and social development, social justice, expanding equal opportunity, diminishing the differences among different sectors of the society and between regions, and respect for faiths were among the political messages of Islamist women activists.[59] Once a person was admitted to the party as a member, he or

---

[56] Arat, *Political Islam in Turkey and Women's Organizations*, 23.
[57] Fazilet Partisi, *Fazilet Partisi Tanıtım Başkanlığı, Tanıtma Rehberi* [The Virtue Party Advertisement Chairmanship, Advertisement Guidance] (Ankara: Fazilet Partisi, 1999), 21–2.
[58] Arat, *Political Islam in Turkey and Women's Organizations*, 40; Konrad Adenauer Vakfı, *Refah Partisi Üzerine Bir Araştırma*, 45–8.
[59] Fazilet Partisi, *Fazilet Partisi Genel Merkezi 2000–2001 Faaliyet Bülteni, Kadın Kolları*, 13.

she was expected to work for the party by attaching new members from his or her social status (e.g., student, worker, housewife).⁶⁰ The party's Women Commission utilized social gatherings as the tool for the party's mobilization in targeted neighborhoods.⁶¹

THE EMERGENCE OF "REFORMISTS"

The change in the party's propaganda tactics in the 1990s led to the perception that the WP changed its political rhetoric toward a moderate line. Two tendencies emerged in the party: the reformists (*yenilikçiler*) (the WP Istanbul Province Organization and its chair, Recep Tayyip Erdoğan, represented the reformist group) and the traditionalists (*gelenekçiler*). Çakır argues that the label of reformist does not refer to a change in the degree of commitment to political Islam. Reformist refers only to a change in tactics by using modern techniques to increase the vote share of the party. While the traditionalists wanted to keep the party as an ideological cadre party, the reformists wanted to transform the party into an ideological-mass party by opening its doors to everyone so long as they would agree on the tenets of the National View (*Milli Görüş*) and did not demand higher positions in the party structure. While the traditionalists admitted people into the party on the condition that they should adopt an Islamic way of life, the reformists argued that over time an admitted person would adapt an Islamic way of life as a result of participating in the party. Furthermore, it would be a good advertisement to show the public that the admitted secular people would find the right way of life by becoming Islamized in time. Thus, the wrong image of the party in the minds of the public would change.⁶²

The reformists' ultimate goal was to make the WP an ideological mass party by accepting secular as well as Islamist individuals and Islamizing the secular people over time.⁶³ All this suggests that reformists placed a greater value on electoral victory, which required a significant expansion of the party's constituency base, than on the religious purity of the membership. The goal of gaining power so as to be able to transform the state superseded the question of the means. The traditionalists, by contrast, were unwilling to employ means that compromised Islamic values to achieve the same goal (power to transform).

Recep Tayyip Erdoğan led the reformist group in the 1990s.⁶⁴ Erdoğan gave the following suggestions to the party's activists and workers during his Istanbul mayoral campaign in 1994: first, smile and be careful with regard to your behavior. Do not create an impression that will generate hatred toward you. Second, do not spit on the streets. Third, do not be frightening. It is not difficult

---

⁶⁰ Çakır, *Ne Şeriat Ne Demokrasi*, 55.
⁶¹ Arat, *Political Islam in Turkey and Women's Organizations*, 40.
⁶² Çakır, *Ne Şeriat Ne Demokrasi*, 76–7.
⁶³ Ibid., 83.
⁶⁴ Erdoğan, like Erbakan and Recai Kutan, was trained by Zahit Kotku and was raised according to the *Milli Görüş* tradition. Şaban Kalafat, "M. Zahid Kotku Caddesi" [The M. Zahid Kotku street], *Milli Gazete*, November 12, 1995, 12.

to be a Welfarist (*Refahlı*). A person can be drunk or may not wear a headscarf; if he or she accepts the WP's tenets, they are welcome. Fourth, do not be critical and judgmental. Fifth, you are not God (*ilâh*); you cannot label people as infidels and as evil (*münafık*). Finally, make your greetings widespread by using language that is appropriate to the contacted person. You cannot say *selamunaleyküm* to Hans (referring to a nonreligious person). There are such people in Turkey who do not understand *selamunaleyküm*. They say *iyi günler* (good day). The style of the greeting should be determined by the recipient.[65]

Although the party's political rhetoric changed toward a moderate line, there was no alteration in the party's goals. In 1995, during the party's youth meeting organized by the Istanbul province network, Erdoğan argued that a generation subordinated to Allah rather than to other subjects (human beings) was coming soon.[66] Even though the reformists were criticized by the traditional faction, the success of the new propaganda tactics led to an increase in the vote share of the party both in local and general elections in the 1990s.[67]

The WP's ties to various Islamic brotherhoods also brought an advantage to the party. For example, before the 1991 general elections, a prominent sheik of the İsmailağa congregation known as Cüppeli Ahmet Hoca called on his followers to vote for the WP and accused those who voted for other parties of being sinful (*vebal*). "Among the political parties," Ahmet Hoca stated, "only the WP produces solutions. This time we will say the 'Welfare.' Because the WP is the representative of a system that is based on God (*Hak*)."[68]

The change in the party's propaganda tactics, the establishment of a hierarchical network down to the level of electoral precincts, the presence of ideologically motivated party workers, and the support of the parallel Islamist sector (the Islamist business class and Islamist intellectuals) led to an increase in the party's membership[69] and vote share in the 1990s. In 1991, the WP had eight hundred thousand registered members and received 16.9 percent of the vote in the general elections,[70] up from 9.8 percent in the 1989 municipality elections. In 1993, the party's registered members numbered more than 1,600,000.[71] The real success for the WP was the 1994 municipal elections, when it not only received 19.1 percent of the votes, but also captured 327 municipalities,

---

[65] Çakır, *Ne Şeriat Ne Demokrasi*, 82–3.
[66] "Gençlik Refahı iktidara taşıyor" [The youth carries the Welfare to the party of governance], *Milli Gazete*, November 18, 1995, 12.
[67] Çakır, *Ne Şeriat Ne Demokrasi*, 79.
[68] "Cübbeli Ahmet Hoca: İnananlar Refah'ta toplanmaya mecbur" [Cübbeli Ahmet Hoca: Believers are obliged to get together at the Welfare], *Milli Gazete*, September 18, 1991, 1, 6.
[69] During interviews with the FP members and workers, I asked for the membership numbers. I was informed that because the party was outlawed twice, all the data were unorganized, thus, unavailable for researchers.
[70] The WP, the right-wing Nationalist Working Party, and the conservative Reformist Democracy Party formed an alliance in order to meet the 10 percentage threshold rule to enter the parliament. The alliance was disestablished following the 1991 elections.
[71] Refah Partisi, *Refah Partisi 4. Büyük Kongre, Genel Başkan Prof. Dr. Necmettin Erbakan'ın Açış Konuşması (10 Ekim 1993)* [The Welfare Party Fourth Great Congress, Chair Prof. Necmettin Erbakan's Opening Speech (October 10, 1993)] (Ankara: Refah Partisi, 1993), 11.

including Ankara and Istanbul as well as other sizeable cities, including Konya, Diyarbakır, Erzurum, and Kayseri. By 1995, the party had more than four million registered members[72] and three hundred thousand registered youth members.[73] In the 1995 general elections, the WP secured 21.4 percent of the votes.[74] The party formed a coalition with the center-right True Path Party (TPP) on June 28, 1996 and Erbakan became the prime minister of Turkey.

THE PARALLEL ISLAMIC SECTOR

The Islamist movement in Turkey seeks to replace the secular political, moral, and social order with an Islamic way of life. The movement required its own business class and intelligentsia to carry it from the periphery and transform it into a movement of the masses, and hence a powerful alternative to the existing secular order.[75] As a result of the TIS and Turgut Özal's antibureaucratic, export-oriented free-market policies,

a new urban middle class and business elite emerged whose members often originated from provincial towns. Their parents were often self-employed small traders, small shopkeepers, merchants, and agrarian capitalists. Some of them came from state employed families. Many provincial youngsters from this background moved to big cities where they had access to higher education. Since their graduation, many joined the urban middle class through employment in the modern economic sector, which expanded in the 1980s as a result of economic reforms that replaced the statist economic model with a liberal approach.[76]

Diane Singerman argues, "while several Middle Eastern countries, including Jordan, Morocco, Egypt, and Turkey, faced privatization pressures amid the growth of capitalism, they experienced a horizontal expansion of the military into the national economy."[77] In the Turkish case, however, the military never became an economic force. Thus, the country never experienced an expansion of the military into the national economy. Furthermore, in 1980 it was the military that encouraged the country to adopt the International Monetary Fund (IMF) austerity package that transformed the economy into a market-oriented one – and the more market-oriented the Turkish economy became, the stronger the Islamist business class grew, and the less power remained in the hands of the military.

Since the 1990s, the Islamists have become the best-organized group in Turkish society, by having a large number of associations, foundations, and

---

[72] Yeşilada, "Realignment and Party Adaptation," 173.
[73] "RP İstanbul İl Teşkilâtı tarafından düzenlenen Gençlik Gecesi büyük ilgi gördü" [The WP Istanbul Province Organization's youth night received a great interest], *Milli Gazete*, November 18, 1995, 12.
[74] Yavuz notes that "the main Sufi orders and Nurcu groups supported the WP because of its potential to form the government." In Yavuz, *Islamic Political Identity in Turkey*, 15.
[75] Saktanber, "Becoming the 'Other' as a Muslim in Turkey," 103–4.
[76] Narlı, "The Rise of the Islamist Movement in Turkey," 40.
[77] See Singerman, "The Networked World of Islamist Social Movements," 147–8.

holding companies; newspapers, periodicals, and publishing houses; TV and radio channels; Quran courses and university preparation courses; student dormitories; private schools; a pro-WP labor union (Hak-İş) and a pro-WP businessmen's association (MÜSİAD) as well as informal groups such as various Islamic brotherhoods. Most of these organizations and groups do not have formal, direct links to the WP. However, "they provide a comprehensive network that effectively encapsulates individual members and creates a distinct political subculture."[78]

The MÜSİAD

MÜSİAD (the Independent Industrialists' and Businessmen's Association) was founded by four young Islamist businessmen (Erol Yarar, Ali Bayramoğlu, Natık Akyol, and Abdurrahman Esmerer) on May 5, 1990. Erol Yarar was the chair of MÜSİAD until May 1999; he was then succeeded by Ali Bayramoğlu. It is commonly perceived that the first letter of its acronym "M" denotes "Muslim" rather than "*Müstakil*" (Independent).

Small- and medium-size enterprises proliferated in Anatolia as a result of export-oriented economic policies in the 1980s and 1990s. This new business elite, called the Anatolian Tigers (*Anadolu Kaplanları*), because it originated in Anatolian towns, wanted to stamp its provincial/Islamic identity on and preserve its values and traditions, shaped by Sunni Islam.[79] Yavuz describes the role of Islam in the Anatolian Tigers' economic activities:

In the enterprises of these Anatolian tigers, management is less rigid, and contact between workers and management has become more personalized. Social trust, solidarity, and loyalty are at the center of the regional economic development successes. The shared culture produced by communal ties, Sufi networks, and village connections ease conflict and facilitate economic activity.[80]

Gülalp argues that these enterprises "were open to exploitation by large capital through subcontracting links and left unprotected by the state. These employers were unable to find any representation in the Chambers of Commerce and Industry or in the Chambers of Craftsmen and Artisans."[81] MÜSİAD was founded to represent the interests of Anatolian businessmen against the dominance of TÜSİAD (the Turkish Industrialists' and Businessmen's Association), which represents Turkey's three hundred largest enterprises. It is an association of the Westernized big businessmen. TÜSİAD was established in 1971 by a group of big businessmen from the Western part of Turkey. TÜSİAD members were able to establish close relations with political authorities/the state, and thus enjoy special privileges. Erbakan seized on this as an opportunity to represent the interests of smaller, conservative businessmen with ties to

---

[78] Özbudun, *Contemporary Turkish Politics*, 92.
[79] Narlı, "The Rise of the Islamist Movement in Turkey," 40.
[80] Yavuz, *Islamic Political Identity in Turkey*, 88.
[81] Gülalp, "Globalization and Political Islam," 439.

various Islamic brotherhoods in Anatolia, and to start his political movement by founding the NSP. By the 1990s, a strong and wealthy Islamist business class had emerged that was able to compete with TÜSİAD.

The emergence and rise of the Islamist business class parallels the rise of the Islamist movement in the 1980s and 1990s. An overwhelming majority of MÜSİAD member enterprises were founded in this period. Companies formed before 1980 represent a small minority.[82] While most TÜSİAD member companies are large enterprises based in Istanbul, MÜSİAD member enterprises are from various Anatolian cities and towns. In 1996, Ali Bayramoğlu, then vice-chairman of MÜSİAD, explained the reason for the association's establishment:

Islamist circles were not included in the business world, and this was a deficiency. We determined that Muslim people were not effective in business life and, as a group of businessmen, we decided to coordinate our trade activities, build solidarity between ourselves, communicate, inform, and direct our businessmen to international markets and defend our beliefs.[83]

MÜSİAD gives importance to extending its organizational network in eastern and southeastern Turkey, an underdeveloped region that needs more investment (Kahramanmaraş, Gaziantep, Şanlıurfa, Elazığ, Diyarbakır, and Malatya). In 1997, then chair of MÜSİAD's Adana branch, Hüseyin Nuri Çomu, stated, "TÜSİAD is a closed box. You cannot count 10–15 names that are members of TÜSİAD from Anatolia. Industrialists in the east are looking for someone who represents their voice. Thus, we are born from this need."[84]

Ayşe Buğra, a professor of political science, argues that while TÜSİAD represents the economic, political, and social characteristics of the European model, MÜSİAD is based on the East Asian model, wherein "a certain interpretation of Islam is used as a resource to bind the businessmen whom it represents into a coherent community and to represent their economic interests as an integral component of an ideological mission."[85] While the Islamist business class does not want state intervention in the economy (they have been the main supporters of economic liberalization), they find "in Islamic symbols and ethics useful weapons for fomenting public opinion against state regulation of the economy and against the big industrialists who enjoy state patronage."[86] MÜSİAD aims at creating a market economy, which is regulated by Islamic principles in Turkey. Accordingly, economic activities should conform to Islamic principles, that is, trade should be conducted with a sense of responsibility that is defined by Islam.[87]

---

[82] Ibid.; Ayşe Buğra, "Class, Culture, and State: An Analysis of Interest Representation by Two Turkish Business Associations," *International Journal of Middle East Studies* 30, no. 4 (November 1998): 524-5.
[83] "MÜSİAD: Proving that business and faith do mix," Akif Beki's interview with Ali Bayramoğlu, *Turkish Daily News*, June 7, 1996.
[84] *Cumhuriyet*, April 12, 1997, 9.
[85] Buğra, "Class, Culture, and State," 522.
[86] Yavuz, *Islamic Political Identity in Turkey*, 89.
[87] "MÜSİAD: Proving that business and faith do mix," *Turkish Daily News*, June 7, 1996.

The Parallel Islamic Sector

The association regards earning money off interest as a "sin," not only because Islam bans it, but also because it is an instrument of abusing people. MÜSİAD aims at a gradual transformation of Turkish economics that will be in conformity with economic rules in Islam. Bayramoğlu explained how association members manage their trade activities in a liberal economic system by giving the example of the Prophet Mohammad's system at the beginning of the Islamic period:

> Two complementary periods overlapped in Mecca and Medina during the Prophet's time. I personally compare the present economic period to the first period of Islam, that is to say, that of Mecca. At that time many things which would be banned later were being employed; the Qur'an prohibited them step by step instead of cutting them off at once.[88]

Thus, MÜSİAD members "intended to make progress by taking one step at a time in order to achieve a planned economic system, but added that during this process they were aware they would inevitably get caught up in the faults of the capitalist system."[89] In addition to the association's commitment to a free-market economy, humanitarian, and egalitarian considerations are given emphasis in MÜSİAD's statement of its mission: "To support the righteous as if it is weak and to be against injustice as if it is [very] strong. To consider the needs of humanity and the sources of the country, to produce continuous, permanent and useful projects and to provide everything necessary to bring these projects to life."[90] In November 1995, then MÜSİAD Chair Erol Yarar, by recalling the coming 1995 general elections, argued that they would carry MÜSİAD's mission to the parliament.[91]

In the 1990s, MÜSİAD became the country's largest and most widespread businessmen's association. Unlike TÜSİAD, nearly half of MÜSİAD member companies were founded in the post-1980 period. MÜSİAD's membership consisted of 400 businessmen in 1991, which increased to 1,700 by 1993, 2,200 by 1996, and to 3,000 by 1998. In 1998, MÜSİAD was representing nearly ten thousand enterprises, which together employed roughly half a million people. The member enterprises' annual revenue in 1998 was $2.79 billion. Members are particularly active in manufacturing, textiles, garments, chemical and metallurgical products, automotive parts, building materials, iron and steel, and food products.[92] Some of these sectors were the chief beneficiaries of the export-oriented economic policies adopted by Özal, noted in Chapter 4. In 1999, the association had twenty-eight branch offices in Anatolia.

---

[88] Ibid.
[89] Ibid.
[90] MÜSİAD Web site, http://www.musiad.org.tr/english/about/mission.asp (accessed May 5, 2004).
[91] "Yarar: MÜSİAD misyonunu Meclise de taşıyacağız" [Yarar: We will also carry the MÜSİAD's mission to the parliament], *Milli Gazete*, November 2, 1995, 8.
[92] Narlı, "The Rise of the Islamist Movement in Turkey," 40; Gülalp, "Globalization and Political Islam," 439–40.

Gülalp criticizes some scholars who predict the decline of political Islam in Turkey as a result of further economic development and cultural secularization. While acknowledging that this view may have been correct for the 1970s, Gülalp notes the change in the power of the Islamist business class as a result of globalization. The Islamist businessmen were at a disadvantaged position vis-à-vis the big industrialists in the 1970s, when a traditional import-substituting industrial sector was developed in the protected environment of the statist period. However, with the wave of globalization, labor-intensive manufacturing in decentralized and small-scale enterprises that are located in the Third World and are linked to large, brand-name retailers based in advanced capitalist countries gained an advantage. As a result of globalization, the power of trade unions diminished, leading to the decline of traditional working-class politics. At the same time, the influence of small- and medium-sized manufacturing industries increased.

According to a survey conducted in five provincial Turkish towns, more than 80 percent of small- and medium-scale enterprises were founded in the post-1980 period, with almost half established after 1990. Nearly half of these firms are subcontracted manufacturers, with links to domestic and foreign companies. Thus, the Islamist business class thrives on free trade and open markets, as a result of which it becomes more powerful.[93] According to a survey that was conducted by MÜSİAD in 1997, 45 percent of its members reported they would like to trade with Muslim countries, 28 percent with Western Europe, 8 percent with the United States, 11 percent with the Commonwealth of Independent States (CIS), and 5 percent with Eastern Europe.[94] In 1996, Erol Yarar, then MÜSİAD chair, argued that even though the twentieth century was a sad century for the Muslims, this would change in the twenty-first century as a result of their increased wealth. "Muslims should do their best to become rich," he argued, "Without attaining economic independence, the *umma* of Islam [community of believers] will not be able to achieve their political independence. Muslims cannot stand for statism; they argue for free a market economy...."[95]

In the 1990s, interest in MÜSİAD's fairs has increased. MÜSİAD, unlike TÜSİAD, has been quite active in training its members, serving as a "socioeconomic school," as was defined by Ali Bayramoğlu. The association provides various services to its members such as organizing conferences and international fairs where MÜSİAD members can establish export-import links with foreign businessmen; publishing periodicals disseminating technology- and market-related information; preparing reports on countries with which MÜSİAD members might consider doing business; preparing reports on Turkish economics and making suggestions by contacting political authorities;

---

[93] Gülalp, "Globalization and Political Islam," 436–7.
[94] "İslam ülkeleri kazandırıyor" [Islam countries are profitable], *Milli Gazete*, August 2, 1997, 6.
[95] "21. yy. Müslümanların dönüm noktası" [The 21st century is Muslims' turning point], *Zaman*, January 29, 1996, 9.

The Parallel Islamic Sector

training its members in computer skills, management techniques, foreign trade procedures, foreign languages, and public speaking; and creating a feeling of solidarity among its members by emphasizing Islamic identity as the basis for cooperation in trade.[96] Bayramoğlu emphasizes that the goals of MÜSİAD differ from those of TÜSİAD:

> To establish an economic power, which belongs to people and to educate them has never been TÜSİAD's aim. They are only trying to be influential with authorities who are in power and to look out for their own interests in terms of new laws and decrees. On the other hand, MÜSİAD has always aimed to guide its members in their business activities, consult with them, develop their economic potential and form a system, which would also benefit the Turkish economy as a whole. When all of these points are taken into consideration, it can be seen that TÜSİAD's umbrella is too narrow for us.[97]

Unlike TÜSİAD, MÜSİAD provides social assistance to needy citizens. Thus, MÜSİAD is more than a business association that focuses only on profit making. On the contrary, it is an association that encourages social assistance and integrity to compensate for a malfunctioning state.[98] The association is also active in commenting on the politics of the Muslim world (such as the Palestinian problem) and on Turkey's political and economic problems (such as Kurdish separatism, the headscarf issue, democracy, secularism, and human rights). As an institution MÜSİAD defines itself as follows:

> MÜSİAD is a "businessmen['s] association" founded ... by concerned businessmen dedicated to the realization of a Turkey where human rights and supremacy of [the] law, justice and equality, peace and security and the welfare and happiness of the people are guaranteed; where community and universal values that are adopted historically by the people are protected; and where the country is effective in the region and respected in the world.[99]

The MÜSİAD leadership takes a global Islamic perspective. For example, during a breaking-the-fast (*iftar*) dinner organized by the association, the chair of MÜSİAD, Erol Yarar, pointed out that Muslims in Bosnia and Palestine were being massacred. He argued that foreign enemies, having injected the Turkish-Kurdish rivalry into Turkish politics, were now trying to introduce the even more dangerous threat of secular and antisecular conflict in the country.

MÜSİAD occasionally invited Erbakan and other WP deputy members and mayors to address its meetings[100] and supported Erbakan's D-8 (Developing 8) project of a Muslim union. In February 1997, Yarar argued that "Prime Minister Erbakan, by giving importance to paying visits to Islam countries starting with his first days of premiership, led to [the] development of this project.... The Christian world has the G-7 countries, now the Islam world has the D-8

---

[96] *Cumhuriyet*, April 12, 1997, 9; Gülalp, "Globalization and Political Islam," 439.
[97] "MÜSİAD: Proving that business and faith do mix," *Turkish Daily News*, June 7, 1996.
[98] "MÜSİAD özürlüye kucak açtı" [MÜSİAD opened its arms to the handicapped], *Milli Gazete*, February 5, 1997, 6.
[99] MÜSİAD Web site.
[100] "Tayyip Erdoğan: Önce İnsan" [Tayyip Erdoğan: Priority is human being], *Milli Gazete*, March 2, 1994, 6; "Adil Düzene Geçelim" [Let's transfer to the Just Order], *Milli Gazete*, June 20, 1993, 6.

countries: Malaysia, Indonesia, Nigeria, Turkey, Iran, Pakistan, Egypt, [and] Bangladesh."[101] Besides supporting the WP's political goals, observed Bayramoğlu, "MÜSİAD leads other Islamic civil associations in terms of activities. MÜSİAD has a place on the Administration and Coordination Council of the Voluntary Cultural Organizations Foundation, which was established by many civil organizations active in fields as diverse as the Hak-İş labor union, the Union Foundation, and the Organization to Spread Science [i.e., the Society for Expanding Science]."[102]

Regular weekly meetings at MÜSİAD headquarters in Mecidiyeköy-Istanbul are held "in order to keep the members informed about actual developments and to give theoretical views on behind-the-scene improvements. Speeches from experts are given during these weekly meetings. MÜSİAD has also established relations between its members and the public via periodic bulletins and other publications."[103] In addition, "Each MÜSİAD branch has to prepare at least one research report every year. Some of the subjects of these research reports have been domestic debt, the energy crisis, investment, export laws and regional problems."[104]

While the Islamist business class emerged in the 1980s and 1990s as a result of Özal's economic polices, the same economic polices (structural adjustment) led to a malfunctioning economic system in the country.[105] The wealthy Islamist business class established various foundations and associations to answer to the demands of Turkish citizens, while the secular state was declining in the 1990s. As Yavuz argues, "These charitable associations usually have a religious-social dimension that plays a key role by offering educational services, running printing houses, operating television and radio stations, and staffing health clinics. Thus a vibrant market freed from dependence on state subsidies and these associations have jointly carved out a larger space for voluntary activism and the externalization of Islamic identity."[106] During a speech before an April 1994 MÜSİAD meeting, Erbakan, while declaring the "Just Order" as the only solution to Turkey's problems, congratulated the association on its conscious efforts to create a great Turkey again.[107]

Islamic Organizations in Europe and the Islamist Movement in Turkey

The WP not only received financial support from the Islamist business class in Turkey, but also from Turkish migrant workers in Western Europe through the European National View Organization (*Avrupa Milli Görüş Teşkilâtı*, or

---

[101] "İslam Birliği hayal değil" [Unity of Islam is not a dream], *Yeni Şafak*, February 28, 1997, 7.
[102] "MÜSİAD: Proving that business and faith do mix," *Turkish Daily News*, June 7, 1996, 6.
[103] Ibid.
[104] Ibid.
[105] Korkut Boratav, "Inter-Class and Intra-Class Relations of Distribution under 'Structural Adjustment': Turkey during the 1980s," in *The Political Economy of Turkey: Debt, Adjustment, and Sustainability*, eds. Tosun Arıcanlı and Dani Rodrik (London: Macmillan, 1990), 224–5.
[106] Yavuz, *Islamic Political Identity in Turkey*, 96.
[107] "Tek Çare Adil Düzen" [The only solution is the Just Order], *Milli Gazete*, April 17, 1994, 6.

The Parallel Islamic Sector

AMGT). Necmettin Erbakan founded the AMGT in 1976 in Köln in order to create a financial support base for the NSP among Turkish migrant workers in Western Europe. Fikri Emanet, a former *imam* of the Turkish Directorate of Religious Affairs who worked for the AMGT for fourteen years after his retirement, argues that because the Turkish state ignored the religious needs of Turkish migrants in Europe, this gap was filled by the AMGT.[108] In 1987, Zihni Edis, then vice-chair of the AMGT Youth Branch, explained the motivation for founding the AMGT:

> When other countries such as Greece and Yugoslavia sent workers to Germany, they sent one preacher for every 60 workers. Unfortunately, even though we are Muslims who migrated to a Christian country, our state did not pay attention to our needs. As the National View Organization, we could not ignore such a situation.[109]

Edis argued that starting by the mid-1980s the AMGT was not only answering the religious needs of Turkish migrants in Europe, but also dealing with their problems in the workplace and providing them with social assistance as well as solidarity.[110] Another prominent former organization worker and a former *mufti* describes the collection of money for the WP through the AMGT:

> The WP Headquarters informs the National View center in Köln to "collect this amount of money." The [organization's] executive council meets. It determines this [the amount of money to be collected] according to regions and countries. Afterwards, this decision is announced to regions by the [organization] Chair. The region chairs determine the amount of money that mosques will pay. The mosque governing members determine the amount of money that the members will pay.[111]

The AMGT organization includes educational centers in 252 cities in Western Europe – located mainly in Germany, but also in the Netherlands, Austria, France, and Belgium – where a strict *Nakşibendi*-influenced teaching of Islam is provided. These educational centers were renamed the National View Organization of the Muslim Community (*İslam Toplumu Milli Görüş Teşkilâtı* – İTMGT). Yeşilada notes that each year, "over 14,000 students [in Europe] receive Islamic education that frequently attacks Atatürk's secular principles."[112] Some of the topics from the "Comparison of Islam, Capitalism, and Communism" course, which was offered during the 1991 to 1992 academic year at the Islamic Girls High School (*İslam Kız Lisesi*) in Austria, give some idea regarding the content of this education: "Religion cannot be separated from state; state serves religion;" "The lawgiver is Allah. And he wants the absolute (*ilâhi*) order. All sovereignty belongs to Allah;" "All sorts of interest

---

[108] Metin Gür, "Milli Görüş, İslam'ın neresinde?" [The National View, where is it in Islam?], *Cumhuriyet*, April 18, 1997, 10.
[109] Selahattin Altun, "Amacımız İslam Kardeşliği" [Our goal is the brotherhood of Islam], *Milli Gazete*, September 2, 1987.
[110] Ibid.
[111] Metin Gür, "Başarının ölçüsü para" [Measure of success is money], *Cumhuriyet*, April 17, 1997, 12.
[112] Yeşilada, "The Virtue Party," 73.

rate are sinful;" "In a capitalist system, religion is separated from state, [and] secularism is defended;" and "In a communist system, the state does not provide religious freedom."[113]

The İTMGT has 1,091 divisions with 2,317 centers employing 17,841 administrators, and more than 83,000 members.[114] Emanet argues that the organization was linked to the WP. Yet, he criticizes the organization, what he calls "a family firm," for its lack of democracy. Indeed, Erbakan made all appointments to prominent positions within the organization;[115] and the appointments of *imams* were also determined at the WP's headquarters in Ankara. During election periods, the *imams* were directed to give sermons arguing that Muslims had to vote for the WP, otherwise they could not be real Muslims, and urging the community to support the WP to come to power by all their means.[116] Erbakan and a number of WP members,[117] as well as representatives of various organizations from the Muslim world,[118] attended the İTMGT's Sixth General Convention in May 1990. During the convention, Erbakan was called "the commander," and an estimated twelve thousand participants swore "to do their best for the establishment of a Great Turkey and the Just Order."[119]

In 1997, the estimated value of real estate belonging to the İTMGT was more than 100 million German marks.[120] According to Yeşilada, Akgün Erbakan, the son-in-law of Erbakan's late brother, heads the European Construction Firms for Mosque and Community (*Avrupa Cemaat ve Camii İnşaat Firması*) and handles the İTMGT's finances.[121] According to another prominent former worker for the organization, the revenue of the National View in 1995 was 7 million German marks, which was earned from pilgrimage tours between Europe and Mecca and 2 million German marks from donations (*zekât*). Money was also collected from Turkish business owners in Europe to be sent to the WP, which was called "jihad money" or "cavalry debt." Those firms' products were sold within the Turkish migrant community in Europe. On a yearly basis, the WP was receiving 1.5 million German marks from such

---

[113] Metin Gür, "Din devletten ayrılmaz" [Religion cannot be separated from the state], *Cumhuriyet*, April 16, 1997, 12.
[114] Yeşilada, "The Virtue Party," 73-4.
[115] Gür, "Milli Görüş, İslam'ın neresinde?" *Cumhuriyet*, April 18, 1997, 10.
[116] Gür, "Başarının ölçüsü para," *Cumhuriyet*, April 17, 1997, 12.
[117] Temel Karamollaoğlu, Halil İbrahim Çelik, Halil Ürün, Fetullah Erbaş, Ali Sezal, Mehmet Ali Cengizgil, and the WP Istanbul Province Chair Recep Tayyip Erdoğan.
[118] Libya Call to Islam Association European representative Abdusselam Heribe, Saudi Arabian Embassy in Bonn Abdullah Galel, Islam Tekaful Institution General Manager Mehmet Erdoğan Segici, Afghanistan Hizbi Islam European Representative Abdussalam Ahtari, Hizbi Islam Political Committee Chair Karyab Abdullahkadir, Hizbi Islami Austrian representative Nakibullah Halak, Hizbi Islami Canadian representative Muhammet Hasan Nuri, and Kuwait Foundations General Manager Dr. Nadir Nuri.
[119] Metin Gür, "Şeriatın kalesi: Almanya" [The Sharia's castle: Germany], *Cumhuriyet*, April 14, 1997, 10.
[120] Gür, "Milli Görüş, İslam'ın neresinde?" *Cumhuriyet*, April 18, 1997, 10.
[121] Yeşilada, "The Virtue Party," 74.

firms.[122] For the 1995 elections, 700,000 German marks were collected from the organization's mosques in Berlin alone.[123]

Islamist Intellectuals

If the Turkish migrants in Western Europe and the Islamist business class in Turkey contributed financially to the WP, the Islamist intellectuals contributed to the party by helping to "frame" the political opportunity structure (POS). Turkish intellectual life, which had been dominated by secular thinkers since the establishment of the republic, was penetrated by Islamist writers beginning in the 1980s. As Michael Meeker argues, "In recent decades, the term 'intellectual' (*aydın*) has implied a secular writer. The intellectual was perhaps a humanist, a rationalist, a liberal, a Marxist, a nationalist, but he was certainly not an Islamist."[124] Since the 1980s, the number of Islamist publications and publishing houses has been increasing in Turkey.[125] Although the Islamists argue that this increase[126] is a result of increased consciousness among Muslims, the introduction of the TIS played a crucial role in achieving this result. Gülalp notes that the WP's relationship with Islamist intellectuals resembles the Republican People's Party's (RPP's) relationship with the Marxist intellectuals of the 1970s. As Marxist intellectuals contributed to the RPP's acquiring of a social democratic identity in the 1970s, Islamist intellectuals in the 1980s contributed to the development by the WP of a solid political Islamist rhetoric.[127] With the adoption of the TIS, political Islam started to fill the vacuum that was created by the suppression of the leftist movement.

Contemporary Islamist intellectuals in Turkey, such as Ali Bulaç (1951–), Rasim Özdenören (1940–), and İsmet Özel (1944–) publish books that are widely read in Islamist circles and columns in newspapers. They criticize the secularism, positivism, and humanism that emerged as a result of the Renaissance, Reform, and Enlightenment movements in the West, and point to the negative impacts on Turkey of modernization, technology, and Western lifestyle, and of Atatürk's policy of Westernization. They reject glorification of the Ottoman past, and seek, instead, a return to the era of *Asr-ı Saadet* (age of happiness). Meeker defines the portrait of a contemporary Islamist intellectual as follows:

He is somewhere between thirty and fifty years old and lives in Istanbul or Ankara. He was born to a family of provincial townsmen or officials and attended provincial primary and middle schools. Later, after coming to Ankara or Istanbul, he completed one

---

[122] Gür, "Milli Görüş, İslam'ın neresinde?" *Cumhuriyet*, April 18, 1997, 10.
[123] Gür, "Başarının ölçüsü para," *Cumhuriyet*, April 17, 1997, 12.
[124] Meeker, "The New Muslim Intellectuals in the Republic of Turkey," 191.
[125] Nilüfer Göle, "Secularism and Islamism in Turkey: The Making of Elites and Counter-elites," *Middle East Journal* 51, no. 1 (Winter 1997): 7 (Internet ed.).
[126] Ahmet Dinç, "İslamcı yayıncılıkta hamle" [A leap forward in Islamic publishing], *Zaman*, December 30, 1991, 7.
[127] Gülalp, *Kimlikler Siyaseti*, 69–70.

or more programs of secular higher education in Turkish universities. . . . He knows one or more European or Middle Eastern language other than Turkish. He has had a serious, long-standing interest in Western literature, philosophy, or social history, and there are more references in his work to Western writers and Western scholarship than to Islamic authorities or sources, although the latter are not infrequently mentioned and are sometimes discussed in detail.[128]

Contemporary Islamist intellectuals follow the earlier Islamist philosopher al-Ghazali's conservative interpretation of Islam. They argue that human reason cannot be the starting point for attaining the absolute truth. Thus, Islam cannot be reconciled with rationalism. The Islamist intellectuals regard the Quran and the *sunna* (the sayings and acts of the Prophet Muhammad) as the only source to reach absolute knowledge. According to their view, human reason and science should not contradict the Quran and the *sunna*, and human reason cannot replace faith. Thus, in the same way that al-Ghazali criticized philosophers who tried to reconcile Islam with Greek rationalism (such as Avicenna and Averroes) in the tenth century, contemporary Islamist intellectuals criticize the rationalism that has emerged as a result of the Renaissance, Reform, and Enlightenment movements in the West. Contemporary Islamist thinkers focus on such contemporary problems as the atomization of the individual resulting from modernization, societal decay in Western societies, Western imperialism, and environmental pollution. They argue that as a result of the failure of the modernization project (rationalism and positivism), the role of religion in society has started to increase once again. Islamist thinkers criticize political and cultural institutions that emerged as a result of the Turkish Revolution and call for re-Islamization in Turkey.[129]

Rasim Özdenören is an example of such an Islamist intellectual. He served as assistant general secretary in the State Planning Organization in the 1980s. In his widely read books *Essays on Thinking in a Muslim Way*, (*Müslümanca Düşünme Üzerine Denemeler*) and *Living in a Muslim Way* (*Müslümanca Yaşamak*), Özdenören argues that as a result of the Renaissance and Reform, which emerged as "atheistic" movements against Christianity, people started to think beyond a religious perspective.[130] Özdenören calls non-Islamic people (i.e., people who does not live in a Muslim way) a "*küfür* (impious) nation."[131] People of *küfür* take human reason instead of *vahiy* (God's orders) as their basis of thinking. Thus, they worship human reason, in accordance with rationalism and positivism.[132] According to Özdenören, "A human being should believe in religion just because it is a commandment of Allah."[133] Muslims obey Islam's rules because they are Allah's wishes, not because they think that

---

[128] Meeker, "The New Muslim Intellectuals in the Republic of Turkey," 190-1.
[129] Ali Bulaç, *Din ve Modernizm* [Religion and Modernism] (Istanbul: İz Yayıncılık, 1995), 9; Meeker, "The New Muslim Intellectuals in the Republic of Turkey," 189-90.
[130] Rasim Özdenören, *Müslümanca Düşünme Üzerine Denemeler* [Essays on Thinking in a Muslim Way] 5th ed. (Istanbul: İz Yayıncılık, 1990), 25, 63.
[131] Ibid., 36.
[132] Ibid., 37.
[133] Ibid., 46.

The Parallel Islamic Sector

the rules are rational. It is a *küfür* to believe in the religion because it is compatible with reason and philosophy; one must believe in the religion because it is the commandment of Allah.[134]

Since the West is dominated by rationalism and positivism, Özdenören argues, the West's understanding of democracy, and of freedom of religion, thought, and conscience is insufficient for Muslims who wish to live in a Muslim way,[135] because Islam does not have a secular structure.[136] Moreover, the West tries to impose its cultural, political, and economic values on the entire world in order to exploit poor countries. The West is aware of the fact that "Muslims are anti-imperialistic. This is not because of Muslims' political goals; it is just a result. A Muslim is anti-imperialistic because he rejects to resemble infidels (*kâfirler*)."[137] A Muslim, he asserts, should not adopt the Western way of thinking; a Muslim's mind should be purified from Western thoughts (what Özdenören calls the *cahiliye* era's mind), as a result of which he will be able to think about Islam on its own terms. Thus, an intellectual revolution is necessary in Muslim countries, particularly in Turkey.[138] Özdenören regards religion not as an issue that is related only to a person's private life, but as a problem of the community's lifestyle. He suggests that "Islam is not a fantasy of the mind, but it is a way of life."[139] Thus, in a secular system, the goal of a Muslim should be reaching the *Asr-ı Saadet*,[140] which Özdenören defines not as a time period in the past, but as a lifestyle. "*Asr-ı Saadet* does not belong to the past," he argues; "it is a discipline that should be lived today rather than yesterday."[141]

Contemporary Islamist intellectuals also criticize modernization and technology. Ali Bulaç, in his book *Religion and Modernism* (*Din ve Modernizm*), calls modernism "the Satan's imitation of Allah"[142] and argues that religion and modernism are incompatible with each other. Bulaç particularly focuses on the problem of the dominance of Western culture in the world and the atomization of the individual in modern societies. According to him, Western culture and economic system damage pluralism of cultures. This has occurred because the West regards the individual not as a "spiritual, intellectual, and metaphysical reality" but as a rational being. Western lifestyle and habits dominate the world.[143] As a result of modernization, one type of human being and one type of society emerge; thus, Bulaç argues, "the process of modernization kills intellectualism, cultures, and creativity."[144] Furthermore, he observes,

---

[134] Ibid., 47.
[135] Ibid., 64.
[136] Rasim Özdenören, *Müslümanca Yaşamak* [Living in a Muslim Way], 4th ed. (Istanbul: İz Yayıncılık, 1994), 53.
[137] Ibid., 34.
[138] Ibid., 32–3.
[139] Özdenören, *Müslümanca Düşünme Üzerine Denemeler*, 85.
[140] Özdenören, *Müslümanca Yaşamak*, 22–3.
[141] Ibid., 55.
[142] Bulaç, *Din ve Modernizm*, 9.
[143] Ibid., 26–7.
[144] Ibid., 48.

modernization led to the atomization of the individual that resulted in the modern society's spiritual inadequacy, sexual anomalies, destruction of families, prostitution, adultery, and alcoholism. To sum up, modernization, which promised happiness to humanity, has failed; "Modernism promised a world paradise, but it turned the planet to a hell."[145] Unlike modernism, he believes, religion regards the world as a home, where there is love, cooperation, family and relatives, and neighborhood. It is impossible for a person to become alienated in such a society.[146]

Like Bulaç, İsmet Özel notes that technology has led to the atomization of people and to a societal decay in modern societies.[147] Along the same lines as Özdenören and Bulaç, Özel argues that Western civilization emerged as a result of the dominance of humanism. Since the Quran regards human beings as incapable of creating a moral philosophy by themselves, it is "atheism" to think that human reason is capable of determining good and evil.[148] Humanism, by regarding the individual as the ruler of the world, led to the rise of technology, and the West dominated the world by utilizing technology.[149] Thus, science does not improve for the sake of science. Because Western people have a "brutal" and "selfish" lifestyle, the West, even though it is technologically improved, could not attain real civilization.[150] Özel regards technology as a tool of Western imperialism that constitutes a threat to an Islamic way of life; it is impossible to protect the values of Islam while utilizing the Western technology. Özel argues,

> Technology's logic forces the human mind to work in a very constrained way. Because technology has a logic that forbids going beyond the relationship of an object to another, it forces a person not to think about issues regarding the essence of an object. Mind cannot see the truth because it is occupied by seeing the reality. Yet, the relationship between the mind/reason and human existence can only be established by the truth. Technology does not give information about an object's truth; it gives information about an object's reality. Yet, the truth is without content.[151]

For this reason, Özel suggests that Muslims should reject Western civilization altogether, including its technology and science.[152]

Islamist intellectuals argue that as a result of the impact of Western thought (democracy and secularism that are defined according to Western values), Muslims currently live in a system that is an enemy to Islam.[153] The intellectuals suggest that Muslims should make a revolution in their minds first, that is,

---

[145] Ibid., 28.
[146] Ibid., 314.
[147] İsmet Özel, *Üç Mesele: Teknik, Medeniyet, Yabancılaşma* [Three Problems: Technique, Civilization, Alienation], 4th ed. (Istanbul: Çıdam Yayınları, 1992), 73-4.
[148] Ibid., 68, 80-1.
[149] Ibid., 123.
[150] Ibid., 45-6, 59.
[151] Ibid., 128.
[152] Ibid., 46.
[153] Ibid., 25; Özdenören, *Müslümanca Yaşamak*, 118-19.

they should adopt an Islamic way of life and refuse to understand Islam according to the Western way of thinking.[154] As Özdenören suggests, "Once Muslims' numbers increase and [they] form a congregation, they will implement the Islamic law [*Sharia*] among themselves. In such a case, [overtaking] the state will not be an aim, but [an Islamic state] will emerge as a result. . . . Once people implement the Islamic law for themselves, an Islamic state will follow."[155]

CONCLUSION

In the 1990s, WP entrepreneurs, unlike those in other parties, framed the malfunctioning state as an additional POS for the mobilization of Islamism in Turkey. The WP would not have been able to seize upon this opportunity, if it did not have the strong organizational networks, both formal and informal, that were established during the first phase of the movement's mobilization. WP entrepreneurs established a hierarchically organized network, down to the level of electoral precincts. The movement activists framed their tactics so as to increase the party's electoral support base. They provided both selective material incentives and emotional rewards through face-to-face contacts with the electorate that established close, friendly relations with their constituents, especially those who resided in shantytowns. The fact that municipalities exist, that the Turkish state is organized on multiple levels of governance, created a degree of inherent "openness" of the system to entry by new political actors. The Islamist movement exploited this structural opportunity. Having gained access, the successful performance of municipalities under WP control gave Islamists increased credibility on the national level as an alternative to parties tarred by the malfunctioning state. This contributed to the electoral victory of the WP in the 1995 general elections.

---

[154] Özdenören, *Müslümanca Yaşamak*, 115.
[155] Ibid., 129.

6

The Soft Intervention of 1997 and the Islamist Social Movement

This chapter analyzes how the narrowing down of a political opportunity structure (POS) forces movement entrepreneurs to frame new strategies for the movement's mobilization. In the 1995 general elections, the Welfare Party (WP) became the party of government by receiving the highest vote share. This led movement entrepreneurs to overestimate the movement's power vis-à-vis the secular-democratic state structure. Statements and activities of Islamist activists and WP members of parliament that contradicted the secular principles of the state led to the soft military intervention (countermobilization) on February 28, 1997 and the closure of the party by the Constitutional Court in January 1998.

Despite the military intervention, the Islamist movement, which had firmly established itself in the country in the years following the 1980 coup, could not be eliminated. The strong organizational networks established by the Islamist movement ensured its survival. Islamist entrepreneurs having realized the narrowing down of the POS after the events of 1997, reframed the movement under the banner of a new political party, the Virtue Party (VP). The VP dropped the political rhetoric of the "Just Order" in order not to be considered by the secular state as a continuation of the WP. The Islamist entrepreneurs within the VP, unable to call for a Just Order as a result of the countermobilization of secular state institutions, now attempted to exploit the issue of Turkey's possible membership in the European Union (EU) as a new political opportunity. However, this strategy also came to an end when the Constitutional Court outlawed the VP as well in June 2001.

The closure of the primary Islamist party four times since the 1970s (National Order Party [NOP] in 1971; National Salvation Party [NSP] in 1980; WP in 1998; and VP in 2001) led to a "framing contest" among Islamists, and a split of the movement between two parties in 2001. "Traditionalists" under the leadership of Recai Kutan, a longtime confidante of Necmettin Erbakan, established the Felicity Party (FP). "Reformists," under the leadership of Recep Tayyip Erdoğan, founded the Justice and Development Party (JDP). The reformist group determined there was no opportunity for change; all efforts at change, they believed, were futile. Indeed, insisting on changing the system might have perverse effects, by engendering a conservative, secular reaction and reversal of all the achievements already won. However, the political opportunity created by the still-malfunctioning state remained, as did the inability of the mainstream political parties to solve citizens' socioeconomic problems. Indeed, a serious economic crisis occurred in 2001, during the run-up to the 2002 general elections. By exploiting this opportunity, and reframing the EU membership issue, the JDP was able to create a more receptive environment for the Islamist movement in Turkey and secure the highest vote share (34.3%) in the 2002 elections and 363 of 550 seats in parliament, just short of a two-thirds majority. The FP, which attempted to reframe the traditional "National View" in its appeal to the electorate, received only 2.5 percent of the votes, and did not gain any seats in parliament.

The 2002 election thus confirmed the ability of Islamist entrepreneurs to frame otherwise secular issues in terms that enlarged the appeal for Turkish voters of the Islamist party and the social movement behind it. The results of this election, and developments since, suggest the balance of political strength between the well-organized Islamist social movement and the still fractured, disorganized, and ineffective secular political forces in Turkey may be tipping in favor of the Islamists.

THE WELFARE PARTY COMES TO POWER

The WP received the highest vote share (21.4%) in the December 1995 general elections[1] and emerged as the largest party in the parliament, with 158 out of 550 seats. Thus, a political Islamist party became the largest single party for the first time in the history of the Turkish Republic.[2] The WP's coming into power led the secular state elite (mainly the military) to undertake efforts to contain the Islamist movement. Since none of the political parties had a parliamentary majority, a coalition government had to be formed. The foremost goal of the secular establishment was to exclude the WP from government.[3] The pressures of the military, the pro-Western Turkish Industrialists' and Businessmen's Association (TÜSİAD),[4] and the media (e.g., the Doğan and Sabah conglomerates, the owners and operators of many of the newspapers and television channels in Turkey) pushed the two center-right parties, the True Path Party (TPP) of Tansu Çiller and the Motherland Party (MP) of Mesut Yılmaz to form a coalition government (*Anayol hükümeti* – the Mother-Path government) on March 3, 1996. The TPP controlled 135 seats, and the MP controlled 132,

---

[1] The elections were held on December 24, 1995.
[2] Jenkins, "Muslim Democrats in Turkey?" 49; Kepel, *Jihad*, 350.
[3] M. Hakan Yavuz, "Cleansing Islam from the Public Sphere," *Journal of International Affairs* 54, no. 1 (Fall 2000): 35.
[4] "The Turkish Industrialists' and Businessmen's Association (TÜSİAD) made its position on the Welfare Party very clear with an advertisement in the press, and asked the two center-right parties to ally their forces against possible Islamist involvement in the government." In Yavuz, "Cleansing Islam from the Public Sphere," fn. 34.

TABLE 6.1. *Percentage of Votes and Seats Won by Parties in 1995 General Elections*

Party	Vote	Seat
Center-Left		
Democratic Left Party	14.6	76
Republican People's Party	10.7	49
Center-Right		
True Path Party	19.2	135
Motherland Party	19.6	132
Islamist		
Welfare Party	21.4	158
Others	14.5	0
TOTAL	100.00	550

Source: DİE, *Statistical Yearbook of Turkey, 2002,* 200–1; DİE, *Results of General Election of Representatives (1983–1995)* (Ankara: DİE, 1998), 2–3.

giving the government only 267 (see Table 6.1). In order to rule, the coalition required the support of 276 out of the 550 seats. The Democratic Left Party (DLP), which held seventy-six seats in parliament, provided the necessary support, allowing the formation of the "Mother-Path" coalition government. Thus, even though the WP had a plurality of seats in the parliament, it was left as the main opposition party. This was a disappointment for the WP and its voters. As Yavuz argues, "The de facto closure of the system to the largest party in Parliament agitated a large segment of the electorate, and the RP [WP] deputies became excessively restive."[5] The primary goal of the WP "was to secure for itself a position in the center of Turkey's parliamentary politics."[6]

Because of the rivalry between the two coalition leaders, the anti-Welfare minority coalition government did not last long. Çiller and Yılmaz agreed on a rotating prime ministerial position, according to which Yılmaz would be the prime minister first and Çiller would assume the post in January 1997. Yet the rivalry between Çiller and Yılmaz, that is, their ambition to have absolute power over the government, continued. This rivalry opened a political opportunity that would be successfully seized upon by the WP.

Yılmaz searched for evidence of corruption allegedly carried out by the Çiller family in order to prevent Çiller from becoming prime minister, either by prompting her removal from the TPP chairmanship or by dividing her party. Yılmaz leaked some of the corruption documents related to Çiller to the WP. But instead of using these documents to attack Çiller, the WP utilized them to criticize the coalition government. And while the parliament was debating the corruption allegations, the Constitutional Court ruled in June 1996 that the

---

[5] Yavuz, *Islamic Political Identity in Turkey*, 240.
[6] Haldun Gülalp, "The Poverty of Democracy in Turkey: The Refah Party Episode," *New Perspectives on Turkey* 21 (Fall 1999): 46.

confidence vote that had allowed the MP-TPP coalition government to take office was invalid. In May 1996, the MP-TPP coalition was ended by the TPP's withdrawal from the government. The TPP then formed a new coalition with the WP. The WP, in return, agreed to support an end to the investigations in parliament of the corruption allegations surrounding Çiller.[7]

The WP-TPP coalition government (*Refahyol hükümeti* – "Welfare-Path" government) was formed on June 28, 1996, and Necmettin Erbakan became the prime minister of Turkey. Once Erbakan came into power, however, he faced a dilemma: on the one hand, he had an Islamist political agenda, which would have antagonized the military. On the other hand, if he maintained the secular status quo, this would have alienated the core WP supporters from the party. Erbakan's Islamist agenda was well-known. In a speech in January 1991, Erbakan had already called on Muslims to join the WP, stating that only his party could establish the supremacy of the Quran through a holy war (*jihad*) and that Muslims should therefore make donations to the WP rather than distribute alms to third parties.[8] Erbakan was even more explicit in April 1994 when he declared,

> Refah will come to power and a just [social] order (*adil düzen*) will be established. The question we must ask ourselves is whether this change will be violent or peaceful; whether it will entail bloodshed. I would have preferred not to have to use those terms, but in the face of all that, in the face of terrorism, and so that everyone can see the true situation clearly, I feel obliged to do so. Today Turkey must take a decision. The Welfare Party will establish a just order, that is certain. [But] will the transition be peaceful or violent; will it be achieved harmoniously or by bloodshed? The sixty million [citizens] must make up their minds on that point.[9]

Even though the WP aimed at establishing an Islamist political order in Turkey, the WP-TPP coalition government's program was "hardly distinguishable from the program of the previous center-right coalition." There was no mention of a Just Order. Even more striking, Erbakan signed a military agreement with Israel in September 1996 and dismissed a large number of military officers because of their alleged Islamist activities in December 1996, most likely in response to direct pressure from the Turkish military leadership.[10]

Nonetheless, while affirming his allegiance to secularism, Erbakan suggested that the ban on female students and civil servants wearing an Islamic headscarf (*türban*, a specifically Islamic headscarf, distinct from the traditional Turkish headscarf) should be lifted. He proposed that Turkish law should be restructured, calling for legal pluralism to allow for implementation of Islamic law. In January 1997, Erbakan hosted Islamic brotherhood (*tarikat*) leaders at his official residence, and he attempted to place a large number of their supporters in the state bureaucracy. He also proposed a project for constructing a grand

---

[7] *Zaman*, June 7, 1996; *Zaman*, May 25, 1996; and Yavuz, *Islamic Political Identity in Turkey*, 241.
[8] European Court of Human Rights, *Case of Refah Partisi (the Welfare Party) and Others v. Turkey*, 5–6 (Internet ed.).
[9] Ibid., 9.
[10] *Zaman*, September 6, 1996; Gülalp, "The Poverty of Democracy in Turkey," 46–7.

mosque in the middle of Taksim Square in Istanbul (an area that represents Atatürk's project of modernism) and proposed reconsecration of the Basilica Saint Sophia to Islam.[11] For the WP, these proposals were not new. The party had already proposed in 1992 making Turkish Radio and Television's (TRT's) broadcasts "just" and "compatible with moral values;" ending the ban on Islamic headscarves; reconsecrating the Basilica Saint Sophia to Islam; repairing foundation buildings (*vakıf eserleri*); prohibiting gambling; changing the law on political parties to permit parties based on religious or ethnic identity;[12] and admitting vocational (*meslek*) school graduates into the military academy (*harp okulu*).[13]

Erbakan also moved to shift Turkey's pro-Western foreign policy toward greater engagement with the Muslim world. Erbakan paid his first visit as prime minister to Iran, where he signed a $23 billion gas and oil agreement. However, Erbakan was humiliated during his subsequent visit to Libya. Muammar Qaddafi accused Turkey of being too pro-Western and of oppressing of the Kurds.[14] Erbakan hosted representatives of Palestinian Hamas, Egypt's Muslim Brotherhood, and Algeria's Islamic Salvation Front (FIS) at the WP political convention after becoming prime minister. Erbakan's hosting of the leader of Egypt's Muslim Brotherhood, the son of the late Hassan al-Banna, led Egyptian President Hosni Mubarak to pay a visit to Turkey to express his concern regarding Erbakan's "interference" in Egyptian politics.[15]

Several WP members of parliament and mayors also made statements and initiated activities challenging the secular character of the state. These played an important role in prompting the military's countermobilization and the Constitutional Court decision in 1998 to close the party down. In November 1996, for example, WP parliamentarian Hasan Hüseyin Ceylan suggested that the secular regime in Turkey had to be destroyed. Ceylan argued,

> Our homeland belongs to us, but not the regime, dear brothers. The regime and Kemalism belong to others.... Turkey will be destroyed, gentlemen. People say: Could Turkey become like Algeria? Just as, in Algeria, we got 81% [of the votes], here too we will reach 81%, we will not remain on 20%. Do not waste your energy on us – I am speaking here to you, to those ... of the imperialist West, the colonizing West, the wild West, to those who, in order to unite with the rest of the world, become the enemies of honor and modesty, those who lower themselves to the level of dogs, of puppies, in order to imitate the West ... it is to you I speak when I say: "Do not waste your energy on us, you will die at the hands of the people of Kirikkale."[16]

---

[11] The Basilica Saint Sophia was transformed into a mosque by the Ottomans in 1453 and converted into a museum by the Turkish Republic. Kepel, *Jihad*, 355.
[12] The current law on political parties does not allow a party to be founded based on a specific religion and/or ethnic identity.
[13] Refah Partisi, *Mecliste İlk 100 Gün* [The First 100 Days in the Parliament] (Ankara: Refah Partisi, 1992), 3.
[14] Yavuz, *Islamic Political Identity in Turkey*, 243.
[15] Ibid.
[16] European Court of Human Rights, *Case of Refah Partisi (the Welfare Party) and Others v. Turkey*, 10. Kırıkkale is a conservative province in Central Anatolia.

Also in November 1996, another WP parliamentarian, Şükrü Karatepe delivered a strong attack on secularism on Atatürk memorial day. His speech suggests the strength of the Islamist agenda of much of the WP membership:

> The dominant forces say "either you live as we do or we will sow discord and corruption among you." So even Welfare Party Ministers dare not reveal their world-outlook inside their Ministries. This morning I too attended a ceremony in my official capacity. When you see me dressed up like this in all this finery, don't think it's because I'm a supporter of secularism. In this period when our beliefs are not respected, and indeed are blasphemed against, I have had to attend these ceremonies in spite of myself. The Prime Minister, other Ministers and MPs have certain obligations. But you have no obligations. This system must change. We will wait a little longer. Let us see what the future has in store for us. And let Muslims keep alive the resentment, rancor and hatred they feel in their hearts.[17]

Such statements suggest that many WP members, despite the moderation of the party and the seeming adaptation of its leaders to secularism, still harbor a radical Islamist agenda.

The expulsion of allegedly Islamist-oriented officers from the military in December 1996 exacerbated the tension between the military and the WP. The breaking point was the "Jerusalem Night" (*Kudüs Gecesi*) incident on January 31, 1997, when the WP mayor of Sincan (a suburb of Ankara), Bekir Yıldız, organized a gathering with the support of Iranian diplomats. Slogans and banners demanding the application of the *Sharia*, as well as large posters of Hamas and Hezbollah leaders, were displayed. During his speech, the Iranian ambassador asked the Turkish people to obey the "precepts of Islam;"[18] and Yıldız stated that he would "infuse the *Sharia* into the intellectual sector"[19] in Turkey. As a response to this incident, the military sent tanks into the streets of Sincan the following day as a show of force. General Çevik Bir, who would lead the soft military intervention one month later, on February 28, characterized the military's show of force as "fine tuning in democracy." The Iranian ambassador was expelled, and the mayor of Sincan was jailed. The WP Minister of Justice, Şevket Kazan, visited the mayor in prison, a display of political sympathy that increased the tension between the military and the WP even further.

The WP's activities led not only to the countermobilization of the military, but also of the center-right and the center-left political parties (the MP, the RPP, and the DLP), the judiciary, some university faculty and students and even some presidents, TÜSİAD (a pro-Western businessmen's association), some media, and secular-oriented civil society associations such as the Association for Supporting Modern Life [*Çağdaş Yaşamı Destekleme Derneği*], the Pro-Atatürk Thinking Association [*Atatürkçü Düşünce Derneği*], the United

---

[17] Ibid., 11.
[18] Yavuz, *Islamic Political Identity in Turkey*, 243.
[19] T. C. Anayasa Mahkemesi, *Anayasa Mahkemesi Kararı, Esas Sayısı: 1997/1 (Siyasi Parti Kapatma), Karar Sayısı (1998/1), Davalı Refah Partisi*, 163; Kepel, *Jihad*, 356. During the investigation of Bekir Yıldız's house, a propaganda cassette of Cemalettin Kaplan was found. *Cumhuriyet*, February 7, 1997, 4.

Women Platform [*Birleşik Kadınlar Platformu*], the Mustafa Kemal Association [*Mustafa Kemal Derneği*], and the Faculty Members Association [*Öğretim Üyeleri Derneği*]. The chair of the MP, Mesut Yılmaz, compared the WP to the Nazis, arguing that the WP, like the Nazi Party, came into power by democratic means. According to Yılmaz, the WP, which was a threat to Turkey, regarded the state and its security forces as obstacles to its aim of establishing a totalitarian regime in the country.[20] Bülent Ecevit, then chair of the DLP, suggested that the WP was raising a militant cadre. According to Ecevit, Erbakan had close ties to the militants of Muslim countries, making the Erbakan government a threat not only to Turkey, but also to many Muslim countries.[21] Süleyman Demirel, then president of Turkey, also joined the anti-WP camp, emphasizing the importance of protecting the secular-democratic character of the Turkish state.[22] Demirel argued, however, that coups were not the solution to the problem. "The coups did not solve any of Turkey's problems," he pointed out, "The '80 military intervention is the factor most responsible for Turkey's current situation. You should pursue politics through political parties."[23]

THE "SOFT" INTERVENTION OF 1997 AND THE END OF THE WELFARE PARTY

In February 1997 the military carried out what is widely characterized as a "soft" intervention. Unlike the three previous interventions (1960, 1971, and 1980) described earlier in this volume, this time there were not any mass arrests, deployment of troops to the streets, and declaration of martial law. Past interventions included the seizure of state radio and television by the military as a means of securing mass communications, and therefore control over the country. Interviews by the author with several former military officers, including one individual who played a key role in the "soft" coup, make it clear that military leaders now thought "the era of military coups is *passé*."[24] In the present era of multiple and diverse means of mass communication, including especially the Internet and satellite-based television and radio with its global news networks reporting on events in real time, military leaders concluded that intervention along the lines of the past was now impossible. Interviews with the author also suggest that concern about potential negative reaction in the West, and among liberal sectors in Turkey, acted as constraints on military action. Thus, unlike 1980, when the military closed down all political parties and jailed many politicians, this time the government remained in place. After a legal process initiated by the public prosecutor, the WP eventually was banned,

---

[20] "RP'nin engeli devlet" [The WP's obstacle is the state], *Cumhuriyet*, February 14, 1997, 5.

[21] "Refah militan yetiştiriyor" [The WP raises militants], *Cumhuriyet*, February 11, 1997, 17.

[22] "Dini siyasallaştırmak suçtur" [It is a crime to politicize religion], *Cumhuriyet*, February 9, 1997, 3.

[23] "Darbeler çözüm değil" [Coups are not the solution], *Cumhuriyet*, February 6, 1997, 3.

[24] Author's interviews with Retired General Çevik Bir, July 21, 2003 and Istanbul, February 27, 2004.

The End of the Welfare Party

and Erbakan personally was banned from politics for five years. But the military took no direct action outside the law against any political figures. The military chose instead to present to Erbakan, while he was still prime minister, a bill of particulars against the Islamist social movement and what the military characterized as an effort to Islamize Turkish politics and society, and demand that the government take action against these activities.

The military already warned Prime Minister Erbakan, at a January 1997 meeting of the National Security Council (NSC), that he should take action, rather than only making statements, in order to stop antisecular activities and defend the secular regime. The NSC was founded in the aftermath of the 1980 military intervention. Until 2005, the NSC as a constitutional body was evenly divided between five civilians (the president, the prime minister, and the ministers of Defense, Internal Affairs, and Foreign Affairs), and five military officials (the chief of the General Staff, the commanders of the Land Forces, Air Forces, and Navy, and the general commander of the Gendarme). Its recommendations were assigned a priority in government legislation. Article 118 of the 1982 postintervention constitution states "the Council of Ministers shall give priority consideration to decisions of the National Security Council concerning measures it deems necessary for the preservation of the existence and independence of the State, the integrity and indivisibility of the country, and the peace and security of society." During the WP-TPP coalition government, all ministries represented in the NSC's regular meetings were governed by the TPP. Prime Minister Erbakan was the only representative from the WP at these meetings.[25]

The fact that no action was taken by the government against antisecular activities led to the soft military intervention of the NSC's military wing on February 28, 1997.[26] The military high command cited several incidents around the country as evidence of antisecular activity and declared political Islam as the number-one security threat to the existence of the Turkish Republic. The military presented an eighteen-point plan to curb the Islamist movement, which included the extension of compulsory primary education from five to eight years; closure of illegal Quran courses; monitoring the flow of Islamist capital; and restrictions on the Islamist media.[27] After some resistance, a sign of the Islamist movement's estimate of its power relative even to that of the military, Erbakan signed the plan on March 5, 1997, and asked the cabinet to implement it. But Erbakan also criticized the countermobilization of the secular sector of the society, throwing the earlier reference to Hitler by the leader of the MP back at the secularists:

It is wrong to target 70 million people by looking at a few organizations [İBDA-C, Aczimendis, and Kaplancıs] that are linked to terrorism. There is a leaning toward religiosity in Turkey as was the case of the world in the post-World War II period. There is

---

[25] Kazan, *Refah Gerçeği*, vol. 2, 149.
[26] Karmon, "The Demise of Radical Islam in Turkey," 11; Alan Makovsky, "Erbakan on the Ropes," *Policy Watch* no. 239, March 12, 1997; and *Milliyet*, February 15, 1997.
[27] Kepel, *Jihad*, 356–7; Gülalp, "The Poverty of Democracy in Turkey," 50.

nothing wrong with that. . . . There is not only extremism in the name of being Muslim, but also [Atatürkist] revolution fundamentalism (*devrim yobazlığı*), [and] leftist fundamentalism (*solcu bağnazlığı*). The number of leftist fundamentalists is a thousand times greater [than the number of Muslim extremists]. . . . There cannot be a war against religious people. The RPP [Republican People's Party] tried this; it did not work. Hitler [and] Stalin also tried this; it did not work either.[28]

In the spring and summer of 1997, the military held a series of briefings regarding the threat of political Islam in Turkey to which the press, the judiciary, public administrators, civil society associations, and academicians were invited. On April 29, 1997, General Çetin Doğan, during his briefing to the press, declared the new National Military Strategic Concept (MASK: *Milli Askeri Strateji Konsepti*). The military now declared Islamic reaction (*irtica*), rather than Kurdish separatism or external threats of interstate war, as the number-one threat to Turkey.[29]

Despite the soft military intervention, however, the Islamist movement was not eliminated. The Turkish-Islamic Synthesis (TIS) had created a POS that Islamists successfully exploited to build a strong organizational network and a significant political constituency capable of resisting suppression by the military. In 1997, the Islamist business class was already in control of half of Turkey's gross domestic product (GDP). In 1997, the Islamists owned 19 newspapers, 110 magazines, 51 radio stations, 20 TV channels, 2,500 associations, 500 foundations, more than a thousand companies, 1,200 dormitories, and more than 800 private schools and university exam-preparation courses.[30] Indeed, in an interview with the author conducted in July 2003, Retired General Çevik Bir observed that "the Turkish-Islamic Synthesis was a mistake."[31]

Only one of the NSC's declared points was implemented: namely, the extension of primary education from five to eight years (the education reform bill). The rest of the plan was not implemented. There was no transfer of private dormitories, foundations, and schools affiliated with Islamic orders to the Ministry of National Education; Islamic brotherhoods and their entities were not banned; religious facilities were not protected against political exploitation; and the infiltration of Islamists into the state bureaucracy and universities was not stopped. Nor was there any attempt to reorganize the licensing procedures with respect to short- and long-barrel weapons or monitor the financial activities of the Islamist bourgeoisie.

In the aftermath of the February 28 process, the military focused particularly on the *imam-hatip* schools to curb the Islamist movement, initiating an education reform bill designed to reduce the number of these schools. The military, during one of its briefings to the press, released a report, "The Concept of

[28] "Erbakan: Demokratlar görev başına" [Erbakan: Democrats go to duty], *Zaman*, March 8, 1997, 11.
[29] Çiçek, *İrticaya Karşı Genelkurmay Belgeleri*, 19.
[30] Briefing by General Çetin Saner, June 11, 1997, in Çiçek, *İrticaya Karşı Genelkurmay Belgeleri*, 41.
[31] Author's interview with Retired General Çevik Bir, July 21, 2003.

TABLE 6.2. *Comparison of Attitudes of* İmam-Hatip *High School Students and WP Voters*

	İmam-Hatip High School Students (percent)	WP Voters (percent)
Islamic regulations should be part of the legal system	80	61
Islamic regulations can be implemented without doing harm to democratic regulations	77	52
A woman who wants to wear the veil should be permitted to do so	83	73
Women and men should receive separate educations	65	65
Women and men should not sit together in public transportation vehicles	59	59
Beverages with alcohol should be banned	86	74

Source: Piar-Gallup public poll from *Cumhuriyet*, April 1, 1997, 3.

West Operation" (*Batı Harekât Konsepti*), which argued that there was a correlation between the rising number of the electorate graduating from the *imam-hatip* schools and the increase in the WP's votes. According to the military's estimate, if an election were to be held in 2000, a political Islamist party would become the governing party by securing 34 percent of the vote (they received 34.3% in the 2002 election); by 2005, with an anticipated additional *imam-hatip* graduate electorate of 6,506,479, the military estimated a political Islamist party would secure 66.94 percent of the vote (in 2007, the JDP secured 46.6% and the FP 2.3%).[32] In an interview with the author in June 2004, a high-ranking FP member, who was a minister during the WP-TPP coalition government, argued that the military was correct to regard *imam-hatip* graduates as an electoral base for the Islamist movement in Turkey. In his view, "the military's estimation for the coming general elections was correct."[33]

In 1997, a Piar-Gallup survey revealed that the views of *imam-hatip* high school students were closer to the Islamist way of thinking than those of WP voters in general (Table 6.2). The data shows *imam-hatip* high school students are somewhat more conservative socially than WP voters in general, but much more inclined to use state power to impose Islamic regulations on society. Furthermore, the survey also showed that an overwhelming majority of *imam-hatip* high school students regarded the *imam-hatips* not as schools for training

---

[32] Çiçek, *İrticaya Karşı Genelkurmay Belgeleri*, 60–1.
[33] Author's interview with a high-ranking FP member, Ankara, June 9, 2004.

TABLE 6.3. *Perceptions of the Function of* İmam-Hatip *High Schools*

	İmam-Hatip High School Students (percent)	Public (percent)
Training preachers	14.5	50.7
Raising a youth compatible with religious and moral values	63.9	30.1
Functioning like state high schools	13.4	7.9
No opinion/does not know	8.3	11.2

Source: Piar-Gallup public poll from *Cumhuriyet*, April 1, 1997, 3.

TABLE 6.4. *Sectors that* İmam-Hatip *High Schools Students Want to Work in the Future (percent)*

Preacher/Prayer leader	20.0
State/Public sector	37.7
Private sector	28.2
Other	4.5
Does not know/undecided	9.5

Source: Piar-Gallup public poll from *Cumhuriyet*, April 1, 1997, 3.

students to become prayer leaders or preachers, but for raising a youth who adhere to Islamic religious and moral values (Table 6.3). According to the survey, only 20 percent of respondents reported they wanted to be a preacher or prayer leader; nearly 66 percent of respondents reported they wanted to work either in the state or in the private sector (Table 6.4). The *imam-hatip* schools thus seemed not only to be expanding the Islamist electorate, but also to be functioning as training grounds for a new generation of Islamist entrepreneurs.

The education reform bill demanded by the military called for the extension of primary education from five to eight years. This led to the closure of all middle schools (in the Turkish system, these are referred to as secondary schools), including *imam-hatip* middle schools. This led to a storm of protest by Islamists in the spring and summer of 1997. Erbakan criticized the military's perception of *imam-hatip* graduates as potential participants in the Islamist movement and a threat to the secular order. He argued that it was the 1980 military regime that made the "religion and ethics course" compulsory in public schools, and emphasized the importance of the *imam-hatip* schools in providing proper religious education in Turkey.[34] But the reaction of Halil İbrahim Çelik, then a WP parliamentarian, to the attempt to close the *imam-hatip* schools is a better reflection of the depth of emotions behind the Islamist movement:

---

[34] "Erbakan'ın Evren Kozu" [Erbakan's Evren deal], *Yeni Şafak*, April 10, 1997, 4.

If you attempt to close down the *"Imam-Hatip"* theological colleges while the Welfare Party is in government, blood will flow. It would be worse than in Algeria. I too would like blood to flow. That's how democracy will be installed. And it will be a beautiful thing. The army has not been able to deal with 3,500 members of the PKK. How would it see off six million Islamists? If they piss into the wind they'll get their faces wet. If anyone attacks me I will strike back. I will fight to the end to introduce sharia.[35]

In May 1997, the pro-WP Islamist businessmen association, the Independent Industrialists' and Businessmen's Association (MÜSİAD), presented a declaration that was signed by 107 civil associations, foundations, and cultural organizations. The Islamists rejected the education reform bill on the grounds that the best age group for a child to memorize a given knowledge was between five and fifteen years old. If the reform was implemented, they argued, it would be too late for a child to become a *hafız* (a person who reads the Quran in Arabic) after receiving religious education beginning at fifteen years of age. Thus, according to Islamists, the reform was an ideological decision aiming at diminishing their power.[36] This argument was contradicted by the fact that students who completed the fifth grade (typically at age 12) were still allowed to receive Islam and *hafızlık* education during weekends and summer breaks. Moreover, as the data presented in the preceding text makes clear, the great majority of students who graduate from *imam-hatip* schools have no interest in becoming a *hafız*. Erol Yarar, then chair of MÜSİAD, defended *imam-hatip* schools and Quran courses by arguing that, contrary to the military's view of their students and graduates as sources of resistance to the regime, their students and graduates had never intervened in a protest or destructive action against the state. Yarar, then warned, and some might say threatened, the WP by making the following remarks,

If the uninterrupted eight-year [education reform] comes to the parliament as a governmental proposal, then it will be too late to reverse it. We are warning all ministers and MPs, including the Prime Minister Necmettin Erbakan. If they sign such a proposal, we will write their names on a blackboard, and brandish it over the doors of all closed down [*imam-hatip*] schools and [Quran] courses and we will never put it down.[37]

On May 11, 1997, Islamists took to the streets to protest the education reform bill. Hundreds of thousands of Islamists gathered in Sultanahmet Square in Istanbul under the slogan "Do not close down the İmam Hatips." During the protest, it was frequently announced that the protesters should not display any illegal banners; only the Turkish flag and *imam-hatip* school banners were allowed. Among those who participated in the protest were Yasin Hatipoğlu, the WP parliamentarian who was also parliament vice-chair;

---

[35] European Court of Human Rights, *Case of Refah Partisi (the Welfare Party) and Others v. Turkey*, 11.
[36] "MÜSİAD'dan RP'ye uyarı" [MÜSİAD's warning of the WP], *Zaman*, May 7, 1997, 11; Necdet Aral, "Kesintisiz-Kademesiz-Yönlendirmesiz sekiz yıllık temel eğitim programı" [Uninterrupted eight year education program], *Milli Gazete*, August 25, 1997, 2.
[37] "MÜSİAD'dan RP'ye uyarı," *Zaman*, May 7, 1997, 11.

Recep Kırış, vice-chair of the Great Unity Party; Hasan Celal Güzel, chair of the Rebirth Party; Nevzat Yalçıntaş, former chair of the Intellectuals' Hearth; İsmail Durak, a MP parliamentarian; WP parliamentarians and district mayors; members of the *İmam-Hatip* Graduates Association; Istanbul *İmam Hatip* High Schools Parents Association; and hundreds of Islamist associations and foundations, such as the Society to Disseminate Science (*İlim Yayma Cemiyeti*) and the Ensar Foundation. Orhan Tozbey, representing twenty-three *İmam Hatip* High School Parents Associations declared, "The state cannot be a parent. We are the parents. . . . We can educate our children in anyway we want. . . . The issue is not only closing down the imam-hatips, but raising a generation that is alien to national and moral values." İbrahim Solmaz, chair of the *İmam Hatip* Graduates Association; Recep Kırış; and WP parliamentarians Mehmet Ali Şahin and Yasin Hatipoğlu stated that the *imam-hatips* were the nation's schools and could not be closed down. It is important to note here that Islamists use the term *ümmet* (*umma*), which refers to the Islamic nation, instead of the ethnic Turkish nation. Both Mustafa Ergun, a trustee board member of the Society to Disseminate Science, and Ahmet Şişman, chair of the Ensar Foundation, suggested that "certain circles" were trying to bring the military and the *imam-hatips* into a conflict.[38] The *imam-hatip* high schools have continued to exist.

On May 21, 1997, the chief public prosecutor, Vural Savaş, responded to these developments by applying to the Constitutional Court for the closure of the WP on the grounds that "it was a 'center' (*mihrak*) of activities contrary to the principles of secularism."[39] Savaş, in support of his application, referred to the WP's advocacy of wearing Islamic headscarves in state schools and public administrative buildings;[40] Erbakan's and the WP members' call for the establishment of an Islamist regime in Turkey; WP Minister of Justice Şevket Kazan's visit to the WP mayor of Sincan in prison; Erbakan's hosting of Islamic brotherhood (*tarikat*) leaders at the prime ministry residence during Ramadan; the speeches of several WP members, including some in high office, calling for the establishment of an Islamist regime in Turkey and advocating the elimination of the opponents of this policy, if necessary by force; and the WP's refusal

---

[38] "İmam hatibe yakışır şekilde" [In a way that is compatible with an imam hatip], *Zaman*, May 12, 1997, 9; "Okulumu kapatmayın!" [Do not close down my school!], *Milli Gazete*, May 12, 1997, 8. Then WP mayor of Istanbul, Recep Tayyip Erdoğan, who was at an international conference, sent a fax message of support for the protesters. His name was chanted by "Istanbul is proud of you." In "Okulumu kapatmayın!" *Milli Gazete*, May 12, 1997, 8.

[39] European Court of Human Rights, *Case of Refah Partisi (the Welfare Party) and Others v. Turkey*, 5.

[40] Savaş, in support of his application, referred to the following statements of Erbakan: At the WP's Fourth General Congress on October 10, 1993, Erbakan stated, "when we were in government, for four years, the notorious Article 163 of the Persecution Code was never applied against any child in the country. In our time there was never any question of hostility to the wearing of headscarves." Erbakan in another speech of December 14, 1995 argued, "[university] chancellors are going to retreat before the headscarf when Refah comes to power." In European Court of Human Rights, *Case of Refah Partisi (the Welfare Party) and Others v. Turkey*, 8.

The End of the Welfare Party

to open disciplinary proceedings against those party members.[41] According to Savaş, the country was moving toward a civil war, and he declared that as long as he was public prosecutor, he would do everything he could to close down religious, separatist, sectarian, fascist, and communist political parties.[42]

Erbakan, facing the countermobilization of the secular state, attempted once again to reframe his party's view on secularism. He argued the WP was the guardian and the real assurance of secularism in the country, that it was only demanding secularism according to Western standards, that is, a complete separation of church and state. Yet, he also reminded that the WP was the greatest party of Turkey and democracy was made by the nation. "[I]f the party is closed down," Erbakan stated, "a new one will be founded on the very next day. The WP's votes will not go to anywhere."[43]

The WP parliament group chair, Salih Kapusuz, argued that Savaş's allegations were composed of newspaper clippings and were not based on solid grounds.[44] WP leaders denied that the party was exploiting religion for political purposes and suggested that secularism had to be redefined in Turkey. WP parliamentarian Abdullah Gencer attempted to reframe the issue of secularism:

Politics-religion, religion-politics cannot be separated from each other. If I am practicing Islam as a politician, this does not mean that I am exploiting the religion for politics. . . . The lived religion is never a tool. . . . Thus, we as parliamentarians from the WP never exploited the religion for politics; we found ourselves as Muslims, and lived like a Muslim. Today, we, as MPs, do not want to lose anything from our Muslim [identity]. We maintain our lifestyle today. . . . Why is Islam education a problem in Turkey? This, in my view, emerges from the wrong interpretation of essential principles that define the Turkish state in our Constitution. Particularly, the word "secularism" was not understood as living religions in the best way under the protection of the state. To the contrary, secularism was always understood as being an enemy of religion. . . . let's redefine secularism.[45]

In June 1997, General Çetin Saner, then the General Chief of Staff Intelligence chair, announced that the West Working Group (WWG) (*Batı Çalışma Grubu*) was founded to monitor the threat of Islamist reactionism in Turkey. General Saner declared the military, in accordance with its Internal Service Regulation (military code), could utilize force vis-à-vis the threat of Islamist reactionism.[46] It is interesting to note that the military during its briefing to the press commented that "the state watched the strengthening of the reactionist forces in the country since 1946." As a result of the transition to a multiparty

---

[41] Ibid., 6.
[42] "Refahı kapatma davası" [Case to outlaw the Welfare (Party)], *Zaman*, May 22, 1997, 11.
[43] "Erbakan: Biz Batıcı olduk" [Erbakan: We have become pro-Western], *Zaman*, October 9, 1997, 11.
[44] "Erbakan: Basit bir iddia" [Erbakan: A simple allegation], *Zaman*, May 22, 1997, 11.
[45] "Laiklik yeniden tanımlanmalı" [Secularism should be redefined], *Milli Gazete*, August 29, 1997, 16.
[46] "Orduda şeriat öfkesi" [The Sharia anger in the military], *Milliyet*, June 12, 1997, 14; Çiçek, *İrticaya Karşı Genelkurmay Belgeleri*, 34–5.

system, concessions were made to the Islamist segment in the country. Thus, the Islamists were able to organize themselves in the society under the umbrella of democracy. The military also suggested that the reactionary segment among Islamists started to enjoy an increased level of support under the WP-TPP government.[47] President Demirel, along the same lines as the military, argued that the country was successful vis-à-vis the separatist Kurdistan Workers' Party (PKK) terrorism: "Now the discussed threat is reactionism."[48]

General Fevzi Türkeri warned there was no control over religious affairs in the country. Because of the passivity of cadres in the Directorate of Religious Affairs (*Diyanet*), the Islamic brotherhoods (*tarikats*) and the National View Organization were organizing an Islamist movement. Islamist firms were given priority during the privatization process under the WP-TPP government, and the long-lasting Islamist infiltration into the state bureaucracy was still continuing. Regarding the foreign supporters of the Islamist movement in Turkey, the military identified Iran, Libya, Saudi Arabia, and Sudan as financial and/or military training supporters of Islamic fundamentalism in Turkey. The military now accused Saudi Arabia's *Rabitat* organization of financing political Islam in Turkey.

According to the military, there were one hundred wealthy Islamist businessmen who were supporting the Islamist movement in the country. These were quite wealthy individuals.[49] In addition to the Islamist business class in Turkey, there were also Turkish Islamist businessmen in Europe, particularly in Germany. There were more than a thousand Islamist firms – specializing in textiles, construction, and food – belonging to Turkish migrants in Germany, mainly in Berlin and Köln. The Islamist-owned companies in Germany had a close relationship with municipalities governed by the WP. WP mayors were paying frequent visits not only to the European National View Organization (AMGT), but also to these Islamist-owned companies in Germany. The military argued that the WP Istanbul mayor Recep Tayyip Erdoğan contacted Islamist companies during the general discussion meeting of MÜSİAD in Germany.[50]

Despite pressures from the secular state establishment, Erbakan continued to pursue a foreign policy that would strengthen Turkey's relations with the Muslim world. In June 1997, the D-8 (Developing 8) – consisting of Turkey, Malaysia, Nigeria, Iran, Bangladesh, Indonesia, Egypt, and Pakistan – was founded in Istanbul as a counterbalance to the G-8. Erbakan defined the D-8 as an organization "established in order to build tranquility, peace, and felicity in the world."[51]

---

[47] "Devlet irticaya seyirci kaldı" [The state turned a blind eye to reactionism], *Milliyet*, June 13, 1997, 14.
[48] "Demirel: Tartışılan tehtid irticadır" [Demirel: The discussed threat is reactionism], *Milliyet*, June 12, 1997, 15.
[49] "İrtica tehlikesi kamufle ediliyor" [The threat of reactionism is being camouflaged], *Milliyet*, June 12, 1997, 14.
[50] "Almanya'daki İslami sermaye" [Islamist capital in Germany], *Milliyet*, June 12, 1997, 15.
[51] Necmettin Erbakan, "Önsöz" [Foreword], in *D-8: Yeni Bir Dünya Düzeni* [D-8: A New World Order] Bülent Alan (Istanbul: Yörünge Yayınları, 2001), 15.

In justifying the foundation of the D-8 movement, Erbakan noted that the twentieth century witnessed two world wars and argued that in the aftermath of the cold war, "the Western leaders chose a way to maintain a world that is based on enmity, rather than establishing a new world that is based on peace."[52] Erbakan's evidence was a speech he attributed to British Prime Minister Margaret Thatcher. Erbakan alleged that Thatcher, in evaluating the future of NATO in the aftermath of the Soviet Union's dissolution stated, "An ideology that does not have an enemy cannot survive. For us to survive there should be an enemy. This new foe will be ISLAM."[53] Erbakan emphasized the wars that occurred in the Muslim world (the Iran-Iraq War, the Persian Gulf War); the massacres in Bosnia, Azerbaijan, and Chechnya; and the West's insensitiveness regarding the misery in Somalia and Rwanda as evidence that the West had chosen Islam as its new target. Thus, he argued, the West failed to bring peace into the world; the establishment of a new world order was necessary, and the D-8 would be a crucial step toward achieving this aim.[54] The main policy goals of the D-8 project were the following: "1. No war, but peace! 2. No conflict, but dialogue! 3. No double standard, but justice! 4. No priority, but equality! 5. No exploitation, but cooperation! 6. No pressures and subversion, but human rights, freedom, and democracy!"[55] The D-8 reflects an attempt to have solidarity among Muslim countries.

On June 18, 1997, the WP-TPP coalition government fell apart as a result of the pressures from the military high command, various members of parliament, and ministers from the TPP. Erbakan resigned from his post in the hope that the coalition would be maintained. However, President Demirel called on the chair of the MP, Yılmaz, to form a new coalition government that would stay in power until general elections were held in April 1999.[56] In July 1997, the DLP of Bülent Ecevit, the MP of Yılmaz, and the Democratic Turkey Party of Hüsamettin Cindoruk formed a new coalition government.

During the summer of 1997, that is, after the soft intervention and the ouster of the WP from government, the military continued its briefings regarding the Islamist movement in Turkey. During one such briefing the military described the infiltration of the Islamists into the state bureaucracy during the eleven-month WP-TPP coalition government. The WP purged top functionaries in the eleven ministries under its control[57] and replaced them with its own party cadres. According to the military, the WP appointed cadres mainly from its municipalities

---

[52] Erbakan, "Önsöz," 10.
[53] Ibid.
[54] Ibid.
[55] Ibid., 15.
[56] Kepel, *Jihad*, 357–8.
[57] The Ministry of Justice, the Ministry of Finance, the Ministry of Construction, the Ministry of Agriculture, the Ministry of Labor and Social Security, the Ministry of Energy and Natural Resources, the Ministry of Culture, the Ministry of Environment, and 11 State Ministries out of 21 were under the WP's governance. Kazan, *Refah Gerçeği*, vol. 2, 148–9.

in Ankara and Istanbul. This reflected the importance of the prior victories in municipal elections for building the Islamist movement organization. According to the military, during the WP-TPP coalition government, 170,000 Islamists infiltrated into the state bureaucracy.

Moreover, the Islamist capital's annual revenue reached $15 billion, and the Islamist bourgeoisie provided financial assistance to Islamist foundations for strengthening Islamist organizations and education.[58] The West Working Group, in its report regarding the Islamist bourgeoisie, announced a list of Islamist companies that provided financial assistance to the WP, including the thirty-six-company Kombassan conglomerate, Asya Holding, Bel-Çar, the Ülker biscuit company, the İhlas corporation, YİMPAŞ supermarkets, and SETAŞ. According to the West Working Group, Ülker had been providing financial assistance to Erbakan's National View Movement, the *Nurcu* Gülen congregation, and ultranationalists since the 1970s. The National View Organization of Muslim Community (İTMGT), which is under Erbakan's control, provided direct financial assistance to the WP and its municipalities as well as equipment such as vehicles and sound systems for the WP's election campaigns. The İTMGT also collected money from migrant Turkish Muslim pilgrims in Europe. For example, in the year 1997, the İTMGT received 750 German marks from each pilgrim, which amounted to 4.5 million German marks; the money was given to Erbakan during his pilgrimage in Saudi Arabia. The West Working Group report also noted that among the Turkish *tarikats*, *Süleymancıs* and *Nurcus* under the leadership of Fetullah Gülen were the best-organized Islamic brotherhoods abroad. The İTMGT, in addition to the pilgrimage tourism, received donations and membership dues, all of which were sent to the WP. Saudi Arabia, Iran, Kuwait, and Libya were identified as countries providing financial assistance for the WP's election campaigns. Several international organizations were identified by the military as providing financial assistance to the WP. These included the International Call for Islam Association and the Turkish-Libya Friendship and Fraternity Association in Libya; the *Rabitat* and Faisal Finance in Saudi Arabia; the World Islam Foundation, the Ministry of Avkat, and Beyt'uz Zekat in Kuwait; and the Islamic Republic of Iran.[59] The military also identified three banks established in the aftermath of the 1980 coup, Al-Baraka, Faisal Finance, and the Turkish-Arab Bank, as supporters of the Islamist movement in Turkey. The military also attacked certain newspapers such as *Türkiye*, *Zaman*, *Vakit*, and *Akit* as being Islamist, and urged that they not be read. According to the West Working Group's report on Islamist capital in Turkey, Islamic brotherhoods and congregations owned a total of 385 companies and were in control of 500 trillion Turkish liras (Table 6.5):[60]

---

[58] "İrtica Kadrosu 170 bin" [Reactionary cadre is 170,000], *Cumhuriyet*, August 2, 1997, 17.
[59] "RP'nin gizli kaynakları" [The WP's secret sources], *Cumhuriyet*, July 17, 1997, 1, 15.
[60] Çiçek, *İrticaya Karşı Genelkurmay Belgeleri*, 94–5.

TABLE 6.5. *Number of Companies Owned by Islamic Brotherhoods*

Tarikats and Congregations	Number of Companies Owned
Fetullahçıs (Nurcu order)	203
Nakşibendis	56
National View	47
Süleymancıs	29
Radical Islamists	31
Yeni Nesil (New Generation) Group[61]	6
Yeni Asya (New Asia) Group	6
Kadiris	7

Source: Hikmet Çiçek (prepared by), *İrticaya Karşı Genelkurmay Belgeleri* [The General Staff's Documents on Reactionism] (Istanbul: Kaynak Yayınları, 1997), 95.

The interim government established after the soft intervention, rapidly passed the military's education reform bill.[62] The Islamists continued their protests against the education reform bill during the summer of 1997. Protests took place in Istanbul, Ankara, Kayseri, Tokat, Gaziantep, and Konya, usually after prayers in mosques on Fridays. A group of Islamist associations and foundations declared the new education reform as "a great violation of democracy and human rights."[63] During the protests, the Islamists with beards, long robes, turbans, and veils shouted such slogans as: "The *imam-hatips* cannot be closed down;" "The Islamic movement cannot be hindered;" "Dishonest media;" "Do not touch my religion, the Quran, [and] the imam-hatip;" "Stop the devil of secularism in you;" "Hands that touch the imam-hatip and Quran courses should be broken;" "Even if our blood is shed the victory is Islam's;" "This is Turkey, not Israel;" "Warrior Ceylan;"[64] "Military, go back to the barracks;" "The Israeli servant, dishonest media;" "Hit hit [sic] to be heard, the military should hear;" "Sold media;" "The military cannot judge the police;" "Neither the military nor the state can discourage us;" "Hands that touch the Sharia should be broken;" and "Atheist government will give an account."[65] During a protest organized in Ankara in July 1997, some of the four thousand protesters made the gestures associated with the Hizbullah, the İBDA-C, the WP, and the right-wing Nationalist Action Party (NAP). When the police warned the protesters to end their protest, they directed their criticism at the military while praising the police forces. When the police attacked journalists who

---

[61] Both *Yeni Nesil* and *Yeni Asya* groups belong to the *Nurcu* order.
[62] Gülalp, "The Poverty of Democracy in Turkey," 51.
[63] "Bu ayıp size yeter" [This shame is enough for you], *Milli Gazete*, July 24, 1997, 8. The groups included MAZLUM-DER, the National Youth Foundation, the Ensar Foundation, the Birlik Foundation, the Association of Governing Economists and Accountants (*Yönetici İktisatçı ve Muhasebeciler Derneği* – YİMDER), and the Turkey *İmam Hatips* Foundation.
[64] Hasan Hüseyin Ceylan was a parliamentarian from the WP and participated in the protest in Ankara.
[65] "Camide siyaset" [Politics in the mosque], *Cumhuriyet*, August 2, 1997, 17; *Cumhuriyet*, July 28, 1997, 5; and *Cumhuriyet*, July 30, 1997, 17.

were taking photographs and videos of the protesters,[66] some of the protesters embraced the policemen. Erol Yarar, then MÜSİAD chair, argued during the association's regular Friday meeting that the education reform bill represented a totalitarian view, and hence was against human rights. According to Yarar,

> The eight-year uninterrupted education is part of a view along the same lines as Marx, Lenin, Mao, Hitler, Stalin, and Mussolini to raise a uniform type of human being. The Helsinki Human Rights Watch Commission ranked Turkey first in terms of human rights violations. This is a shameful picture for us.... The public will give their lesson [to the Ecevit-Yılmaz-Cindoruk coalition government] at the ballot box. The politicians cannot reverse the flow of this river. Let's give everybody freedom in education.[67]

Similarly, the WP parliamentarian Mustafa Baş argued, "the eight-year uninterrupted education is an ordered [imposed] system. One cannot reach to anywhere with this system. It is not only wrong scientifically, but also contrary to the constitution."[68] Despite the protests of the Islamists, however, the new education reform bill passed in the parliament on August 17, 1997, by a vote of 277 votes to 242. Besides the members of parliament from the WP, two parliamentarians from the MP, Cemil Çiçek and Ali Coşkun, and the independent parliamentarian Korkut Özal voted against the bill. Some TPP parliamentarians, including Tansu Çiller, absented themselves from the voting.[69]

The 1997 soft military intervention could not put an end to the Islamist movement in Turkey. Although the military is the most trusted institution in the eyes of the Turkish public, if a general election had been held at that time, the WP, according to an opinion poll that was conducted in January 1997, would have obtained 38 percent of the votes. The same poll estimated that the WP might obtain 67 percent of the votes in the general election to be held roughly four years later.[70] Furthermore, the Piar-Gallup opinion poll carried out in May 1997 revealed that only 9.4 percent of respondents regarded the threat of Islamic fundamentalism as the country's most important problem; an overwhelming majority identified socioeconomic problems as their main concern (Table 6.6).[71]

Islamist resistance to educational reform in speeches, demonstrations, and in the parliament even after the soft military intervention is evidence of the strength of the Islamist social movement organization and popular support. It is also a sign of confidence on the part of Islamist entrepreneurs, supported by polling data that showed the people were not worried about Islamism as much as by the economy, and that more voters were likely to support them in the future. These data were consistent with the basic understanding by Islamists of the opportunity structure in Turkey and the effectiveness of their framing strategies.

---

[66] "İrtica başkentte" [Islamic reaction is in Ankara], *Cumhuriyet*, July 30, 1997, 1, 17.
[67] "Kesintisiz eğitim tek tip insan yetiştirir" [Uninterrupted education raises a uniform person], *Milli Gazete*, August 3, 1997, 9.
[68] Ibid.
[69] "Artık sekiz yıl" [From now on eight-year], *Zaman*, August 17, 1997, 11.
[70] European Court of Human Rights, *Case of Refah Partisi (the Welfare Party) and Others v. Turkey*, 5.
[71] *Cumhuriyet*, May 7, 1997, 4.

TABLE 6.6. *Public Poll, 1997*

Poll: Most Important Problem Facing Turkey	Percent
Inflation and high living expenses	24.8
Unequal distribution of wealth/unemployment	12.6
PKK terrorism	9.6
Islamist reactionism/threat against secularism/the *Sharia* threat	9.4
Anarchy and terror	8.5
Political instability	6.7
Kurdish problem/the Southeast problem	5.6
Economic development	5.5
Violations of human rights and democracy	5.0
Corruption in state institutions	4.1
Implementation of Islamic values	1.5
Internal migration	0.5
Deterioration of moral values	0.4
Other	2.4
Does not have an idea/does not know	3.4
TOTAL	100.0

Source: Piar-Gallup public poll from *Cumhuriyet*, May 7, 1997, 4.

TABLE 6.7. *Public Poll, 1997*

Poll: How Can the Political Crisis Be Overcome?	Percent
By holding early general elections	42.1
By the WP-TPP government obeying NSC decisions	28.1
By establishment of a new coalition government	18.4
By military intervention	11.4
TOTAL	100.0

Source: Piar-Gallup public poll from *Cumhuriyet*, May 7, 1997, 4.

Regarding the question of how the political crisis in Turkey could be overcome in the aftermath of the NSC meeting of February 1997, an overwhelming majority of respondents argued for a democratic solution of the problem rather than a military intervention (Table 6.7).

Most of the high-ranking military cadres who initiated the 1997 coup retired. This was a reflection of the passing out of politics of a generation of Kemalists. General Teoman Koman, then commander of the Gendarme forces, emphasized during his farewell speech that the greatest threat to Turkey was reactionism, which had to be monitored. General Koman noted that the Islamic brotherhoods (*tarikats*) had become "religion holdings," which had exploited the sacred feelings of faith by politicizing the religion.[72]

---

[72] "Türkiye irtica felaketiyle karşı karşıya" [Turkey faces with the disaster of Islamist reaction], *Cumhuriyet*, August 30, 1997, 1, 15.

It is widely known that the military is the most protected institution from the infiltration of the Islamists. Yet, by the end of 1996, news regarding the infiltration of Islamists into the military started to appear in newspapers. According to a July 1997 report, some high-ranking retired and resigned generals entered the WP and the *tarikats*. According to a later analysis by a former police official, Islamists had been infiltrating the state bureaucracies for many years. And, a scholar published a similar analysis in 2003 and was assassinated shortly thereafter.[73] As early as 1993, during the WP's Fourth General Congress, six generals and twenty-eight colonels were already admitted to the WP.[74] This suggests a dramatic change has been taking place in at least some elements in the military, an institution known as monolithic in the defense of secularism. Thus, in May 1997, 160 commissioned and noncommissioned officers suspected of Islamist sympathies were expelled from the army, an action that received harsh criticism from the WP's Islamist constituency.[75] In March 1998, the NSC noted that "reactionism," the military's label for Islamic fundamentalism, was still present as a threat in Turkey.[76]

THE VIRTUE PARTY

By December 1997, activists in the WP came to understand the party would soon be outlawed by the Constitutional Court.[77] Therefore, on December 17, 1997, a group of parliamentarians from the WP close to Erbakan,[78] and under the leadership of Erbakan's lawyer, İsmail Alptekin, founded the VP. Later, Recai Kutan, a longtime confidante of Erbakan, became the party chair. On

---

[73] "RP'nin emekli asker kadroları" [The WP's cadres from retired military staff], *Cumhuriyet*, July 6, 1997, 15. See Necip Hablemitoğlu, *Köstebek* (Istanbul: Toplumsal Dönüşüm Yayınları, 2003); Zübeyir Kındıra, *Fetullah Gülen'in Copları* (Istanbul: Su Yayınları, 2001); Rachel Sharon-Krespin, "Fetullah Gülen's Grand Ambition: Turkey's Islamist Danger," *Middle East Quarterly* XVI, no. 1 (Winter 2009): 55–66; and Bill Park, "The Fetullah Gülen Movement," *MERIA Journal* 12, no. 3 (September 2008): 1–14 (Internet ed.) for the *Nurcus*' Fetullah Gülen congregation's infiltration into the state bureaucracy.

[74] Sadullah Özcan and Emine Dolmacı, "Bir davanın anatomisi" [An anatomy of a case], *Zaman*, June 22, 2001, 14.

[75] Ibid.; Kepel, *Jihad*, 357.

[76] "MGK bildirisinin tam metni" [The entire text of the NSC's declaration], *Cumhuriyet*, March 28, 1998, 17.

[77] Ahmet Necdet Sezer who served as president of Turkey between 2000 and 2007, became chair of the Constitutional Court on January 7, 1998, and voted in favor of the closure of the WP. Erbakan was banned from politics for five years. Özcan and Dolmacı, "Bir davanın anatomisi," *Zaman*, June 22, 2001, 14.

[78] The former WP parliamentarians – Oğuzhan Asiltürk, Abdullah Gül, İsmail Kahraman, Süleyman Arif Emre, Rıza Ulucak, Ömer Vehbi Hatipoğlu, Musa Demirci, Ertan Yülek, Temel Karamollaoğlu, Cevat Ayhan, Necati Çelik, Fehim Adak, Bülent Arınç, Bahri Zengin, Hasan Aksay, Aydın Menderes, Osman Yumakoğulları, Zeki Ünal, Lütfi Doğan, Hanefi Demirkol, and Mehmet Ali Şahin – became the VP's General Governing and Discipline Council members. T.C. Anayasa Mahkemesi, *Anayasa Mahkemesi Kararı, Esas Sayısı 1999/2 (Siyasi Parti Kapatma), Karar Sayısı 2001/2, Davalı Fazilet Partisi* [The Constitutional Court's Decision on the Virtue Party], 6 (Internet ed.).

The Virtue Party

January 16, 1998, the WP was outlawed by the Constitutional Court on the grounds that the party violated the principles of secularism and the law on political parties; Erbakan was banned from politics for five years.[79] Erbakan commented that "the Court's ruling had no historic value and would eventually rebound against those who had made it."[80] Following the party's closure, most of the WP's deputies joined the VP. As a result, the VP immediately obtained 144 seats in the parliament. The members of parliament from the MP who constituted the party's conservative wing (Cemil Çiçek, Abdülkadir Aksu, Ali Coşkun, and Nevzat Yalçıntaş) were admitted to the VP and served in the party's Chairmanship Council and General Governing Council. By admitting MP members to its governing councils, the VP thereby broadened its political profile and helped insulate itself against the charge it was merely the continuation of the WP under another name, and thus an Islamist threat to the secular state. Gareth Jenkins summarizes the dilemma of the VP leadership as follows: "if it appeared to be a continuation of the WP, it risked closure by the Constitutional Court; but if it distanced itself from the WP, it might alienate that party's former supporters."[81]

The Islamist movement reframed its strategy to project a more moderate image, as if it had moved to the center-right. The VP tried to distance itself from representing the Islamic identity. Instead, the party called its mission the "Virtue Movement" (*Fazilet Hareketi*), which was defined as a "nation movement" (*millet hareketi*).[82] Thus, the VP, rather than dividing citizens into "us" and "them," tried to create an image of a center-right party by focusing on the necessity of the promotion of human rights and liberal democracy in Turkey.[83] Within this framework, the VP abandoned the Just Order, emphasized its commitment to secularism and democracy, and appointed a number of well-educated secular women to its General Governing Council. The VP chose May 14, 1998 to hold its First Convention, which it called a "democracy celebration" (*demokrasi şöleni*). May 14 symbolized the electoral victory of the center-right Democrat Party (DP) over the center-left RPP on that date in the 1950 general elections. The VP thus sent a symbolic message to the electorate that it had moved to the center-right. The VP declared "the implementation of democracy at the highest level in the country" as its goal,[84] and Recai Kutan, the VP chair, asserted the party was open to dialogue in order to solve Turkey's problems.[85]

---

[79] Gülalp, "The Poverty of Democracy in Turkey," 53.
[80] Narlı, "The Rise of the Islamist Movement in Turkey," 43.
[81] Jenkins, "Muslim Democrats in Turkey?" 51.
[82] Faziet Partisi, *Türkiye'nin Öncelikleri ve Temel Görüşlerimiz, M. Recai Kutan'ın Basın Toplantısı 17 Aralık 1998 Bilkent-Ankara* [Turkey's Priorities and Our Essential Views, M. Recai Kutan's Press Meeting (December 17, 1998)] (Ankara: Fazilet Partisi, 1999), 3.
[83] Sadullah Özcan and Emine Dolmacı, "Fazilet Partisi: Geleneksel kader" [The Virtue Party: A traditional fate], *Zaman*, June 23, 2001, 12.
[84] Fazilet Partisi, *Türkiye'nin Öncelikleri ve Temel Görüşlerimiz, M. Recai Kutan'ın Basın Toplantısı 17 Aralık 1998 Bilkent-Ankara*, 9.
[85] Ibid., 5.

In the VP's election pamphlet for the 1999 general elections, the first issues discussed were the necessity of redefining the central/unitary state structure and the promotion of democracy, human rights, and secularism in Turkey, followed by socioeconomic problems. None of traditional anti-Western political sayings or slogans of the National View Movement (*Milli Görüş Hareketi*) were mentioned in the party's election pamphlet. The pamphlet defined three major political goals: "The state will be democratic, the governance will be uncorrupted, and the society will be free; Turkey will be a great power beyond the borders of a regional power; and the state will be a social state again."[86] In the 1999 general election campaign, the VP utilized such slogans as: "Leading and Great Turkey;"[87] "First-ranked democracy, First-ranked world power;" "The state's sole power is the nation;" "The judiciary will be both independent and unbiased;" "Whomever makes a mistake will be sent to the judiciary;" "The secret of successful governance: Honesty, being close to the public, openness, and transparency;" "Turkey will be a great world power;" and "Not a Turkey that takes place in history, but one that writes history: Strong army, Strong defense, Strong foreign policy."[88] Unlike the WP, the VP paid special attention to good relations with the West, affirming that "Our country's relations with the West, particularly with the EU and the U.S., are important."[89] In another VP pamphlet, the importance of having good relations with the Muslim world was mentioned only after relations with the West were discussed.[90] The party also emphasized the necessity of having good relations with the World Bank, the International Monetary Fund (IMF), and other international financial organizations.[91]

Thus, unlike the WP, the VP made a clear effort to look like other center-right parties. But closer examination of the VP's election pamphlets suggests that there was little difference between the demands of the WP and those of the VP with respect to changing the structure of the state in a way that would diminish the state's power vis-à-vis the Islamist movement. The VP framed its demands differently. It proposed that the state had to be restructured, and democracy and secularism had to be redefined, in order to "improve democracy" in the country. As Gülalp notes, "Democracy thus became the new platform by which political Islam redefined itself in Turkey."[92]

---

[86] Fazilet Partisi, *Günışığında Türkiye, 18 Nisan 1999 Seçim Beyannamesi* [Turkey in Daylight, April 18, 1999 Election Declaration] (Ankara: Fazilet Partisi, 1999), 6, 92.
[87] Fazilet Partisi, "Öncü Türkiye için Elele" [Hand in Hand for a Leader Turkey] (Ankara: Fazilet Partisi, n.d.), 2.
[88] Fazilet Partisi, *Günışığında Türkiye, 18 Nisan 1999 Seçim Beyannamesi*, 6, 42.
[89] Fazilet Partisi, "Öncü Türkiye için Elele," 35. See also Fazilet Partisi, *Türkiye'nin Öncelikleri ve Temel Görüşlerimiz, M. Recai Kutan'ın Basın Toplantısı 17 Aralık 1998 Bilkent-Ankara*, 54.
[90] Fazilet Partisi, "Öncü Türkiye için Elele," 36.
[91] Fazilet Partisi, *Türkiye'nin Öncelikleri ve Temel Görüşlerimiz, M. Recai Kutan'ın Basın Toplantısı 17 Aralık 1998 Bilkent-Ankara*, 37.
[92] Gülalp, "The Poverty of Democracy in Turkey," 53.

In the VP's election pamphlet it was stated, "The source of the state and its power is the citizen. The Virtue Party, for the sake of good state governance, argues for democratic participation, transparency, and having a governing cadre with responsibility and sensitivity regarding societal and national issues."[93] Within this framework the VP proposed the following: closure of the State Security Courts (*Devlet Güvenlik Mahkemeleri*); restructuring of the NSC in a way "compatible with democracy," that is, reducing the power of the NSC; changing the structure of the Higher Education Board (YÖK – *Yüksek Öğretim Kurumu*); making local governments autonomous from the central state; and promoting civil society associations and foundations.[94] This strategy of decentralization in effect called for shifting power to the levels of government where Islamists then held power. The VP made the same political demands in its proposal to change the constitution in November 1999. When this proposal is compared to the proposal of the WP for constitutional change, it becomes clear that these were the same demands. The only difference was the VP framed its demands as a step toward the greater liberalization and democratization required for Turkey's membership in the EU.[95] The VP declared that "From the perspective of Turkey's interests, we aim at completing the country's membership process in the EU. . . . We believe in maintaining our long-lasting strategic and defense relationship with the U.S. and improving this relationship to the level of economic cooperation and investment."[96]

Thus, after the 1997 military intervention, the Islamist movement started to regard the question of EU membership as a potential opportunity to be exploited in pursuit of the goals of changing the structure of the Turkish state. The pro-Western businessmen association TÜSİAD, while regarding the Islamist movement as a threat in Turkey, supported the idea of restructuring the Turkish state by diminishing the central authority's power vis-à-vis local governments for its own economic reasons. But TÜSİAD also justified its position in terms of promoting democratization. During TÜSİAD's meeting entitled "The Package of Elevating Democratic Standards" that was held in October 1997, both Recep Tayyip Erdoğan, then WP mayor, and Muharrem Kayhan, then chair of TÜSİAD, argued for strengthening the power of municipalities vis-à-vis the state. Accordingly, each municipality should be governed by its own constitution.[97]

The VP argued for making local governments autonomous from the central state. The VP's election pamphlet promised that

There will be a rapid transfer from a state where all powers are concentrated at the center toward a state in which local governments will have the power to govern. . . . The

---

[93] Fazilet Partisi, *Günışığında Türkiye, 18 Nisan 1999 Seçim Beyannamesi*, 7.
[94] Ibid., 23–9.
[95] Fazilet Partisi, *Fazilet Partisi'nin Anayasa Değişikliğine Dair Uzlaşma Metni Taslağı (11 Kasım 1999)* [The Virtue Party's Draft Proposal for a Constitutional Change (November 11, 1999)] (Ankara: Fazilet Partisi, 1999).
[96] Fazilet Partisi, *Günışığında Türkiye, 18 Nisan 1999 Seçim Beyannamesi*, 45.
[97] "Yerinden yönetim sağlanmalı" [Local governance should be provided], *Milli Gazete*, October 13, 1997, 6.

VP has an understanding of a state that takes freedom, participation, and human being as its starting point.[98]

Within this framework, defense, foreign relations, and justice would remain under the control of the central state. But all local governments would have control over the services that they provided, including health, education, culture, youth and sports, social aid and cooperation, tourism, environment, agriculture, forestry, construction, transportation, and infrastructure services. According to the VP's state model, principal service providers at the local level would be autonomous provincial governments (*il özel idareleri*), municipalities, and village executives (*köy yönetimleri*). Civil society associations would participate in the provincial general council, municipality council, and village governance. In this way, the public would participate directly in policy making at the local level. Local governments would finance themselves, and their financial activities would be monitored by a local inspector. Citizens' problems would be solved without resorting to the judiciary through the establishment of a public ombudsman.[99] In effect, large sectors of public policy making would be taken out of the hands of central state institutions, where secularism was still strong, and put into the hands of local government and civil society, where the Islamist social movement was strong, and growing.

A similar proposition to make local governments autonomous was proposed by the WP after the party's 1993 convention and was submitted to parliament as a constitutional amendment. As an alternative to Western democracy, the WP proposed a political order that was put into practice during the Prophet Muhammad's rule in Medina. Under its proposal, there would be a system of multiple legal orders, with each community having the freedom to live by the legal order that corresponded to its faith.[100] At a meeting on constitutional reform, Erbakan "suggested that the adherents of each religious movement should obey their own rules rather than the rules of Turkish law."[101] On March 23, 1993, Erbakan in a speech in the parliament stated,

> ... you shall live in a manner compatible with your beliefs. We want despotism to be abolished. There must be several legal systems. The citizen must be able to choose for himself which legal system is most appropriate for him, within a framework of general principles. Moreover, that has always been the case throughout our history. In our history there have been various religious movements. Everyone lived according to the legal rules of his own organization, and so everyone lived in peace. Why, then, should I be obliged to live according to another's rules? ... The right to choose one's own legal system is an integral part of the freedom of religion.[102]

The state's role "would be to guarantee the autonomy of each community, and the laws and conventions of each community would be binding for its own

---

[98] Fazilet Partisi, *Günışığında Türkiye, 18 Nisan 1999 Seçim Beyannamesi*, 9.
[99] Ibid., 11–13, 15–16.
[100] Gülalp, "The Poverty of Democracy in Turkey," 38.
[101] European Court of Human Rights, *Case of Refah Partisi (the Welfare Party) and Others v. Turkey*, 5.
[102] Ibid., 9.

The Virtue Party

members."[103] In another speech in October 1993, Erbakan argued for the plurality of legal systems in Turkey. He suggested,

> ... we shall guarantee all human rights. We shall guarantee to everyone the right to live as he sees fit and to choose the legal system he prefers. We shall free the administration from centralism. The State which you have installed is a repressive State, not a State at the people's service. You do not allow the freedom to choose one's code of law. When we are in power a Muslim will be able to get married before the mufti, if he wishes, and a Christian will be able to marry in church, if he prefers.[104]

Even though Islamist intellectuals argue that in such a political order, "civil society would have autonomy from the state and the minority would have autonomy from the majority,"[105] Gülalp notes the fact that "the notion of dividing society into communities of faith and building distinct legal orders that correspond to them violates the freedom of persons to live as they wish purportedly upheld by this model, because it treats persons not as independent individuals but rather as members of homogeneous communities." Although the model is portrayed as promoting civil society against the "oppressive" modern state, "there is a clear indication that the Islamists conceive of their envisaged order in totalitarian terms."[106] As Süleyman Karagülle, a WP parliamentarian, argued for affording local governments an autonomous status. Karagülle argued that even a federal state system based on existing administrative unites would be too large. He suggested creating smaller provinces and districts. He explained the WP's proposed political order for Turkey as follows:

> Each district will have its own law and regulate private and public law by itself. To a certain extent we can show the municipalities as an example of this. For instance, one subdistrict (*bucak*) can declare that it will not regard stealing as a crime. The other [subdistrict] can declare that it will cut off the arm of the pickpocket. Let it to cut off [his arm]. People will live in communities that they would like to be. Thus, the state will not determine how people will live. Instead, the public will live in the way that they choose. . . . The duty of the state, the military, the gendarme, and the police will be to guard each citizen's lifestyle that is based on the citizen's faith and thought. The state will not make any laws. It will not be an authority. It will be only a guardian. . . .[107]

The VP's discussion of human rights and democracy only in terms of the Islamic headscarf and the *imam-hatip* issues weakened the party's credibility in the eyes of the general public.[108] In the 1999 general elections, the VP received 15.4 percent of the vote – a 6 percent decrease from the vote share of the WP in the 1995 general elections. This decline in support for the Islamist political

---

[103] Gülalp, "The Poverty of Democracy in Turkey," 39.
[104] European Court of Human Rights, *Case of Refah Partisi (the Welfare Party) and Others v. Turkey*, 9.
[105] Gülalp, "The Poverty of Democracy in Turkey," 39.
[106] Ibid.
[107] "Türkiye'ye önce hukuk düzeni getirilmelidir" [First a legal system should be introduced to Turkey], Serpil Çelik's interview with Süleyman Karagülle, *Milli Gazete*, May 14, 1991, 12.
[108] Gülalp, *Kimlikler Siyaseti*, 13.

party can be attributed to the fact that the WP had been outlawed and its leader banned from politics, which demoralized its cadres and, presumably, alienated some of its voters. Nonetheless, the VP still ranked third in the 1999 general elections. As Şevket Kazan defined the VP period as the weakest era for the National View Movement.[109] Furthermore, in the 1999 local elections, which were held simultaneously with the general elections, the VP still ranked first in most of the municipalities including Istanbul and Ankara.[110] The strong organizational networks of the WP, now under the control of the VP, played an important role in this successful result. The party, within one year from its foundation, was organized in eighty provinces and all districts as well as in municipalities.[111]

The VP shared the same fate of the WP and its predecessors. Within the framework of the VP's endeavors to have a modern image, the party showed seventeen female candidates for the 1999 national elections out of which three female candidates entered the parliament. One of them, Merve Kavakçı, wore an Islamic headscarf. Kavakçı's insistence on entering the parliament and attending the swearing-in ceremony wearing her headscarf led the chief public prosecutor, Vural Savaş, to initiate a move to outlaw the VP at the Constitutional Court on May 7, 1999. Savaş argued that the party had become "a center of anti-secular activity" and that Erbakan was the party's shadow chair.[112] He also accused the party "of being vampires touring the country and gorging on ignorance."[113] During the swearing-in ceremony, Kavakçı faced an uproar from the mainstream parliamentarians, who prevented her from being sworn in; her parliament membership was annulled.[114] President Demirel called Kavakçı "an agent provocateur working for radical Islamic states."[115] VP Chair Recai Kutan characterized Savaş's allegation as "political rather than legal." Kutan added, "We are for the implementation of essential rights and freedoms in the broadest sense. We are always ready to make sacrifices with our nation in order to reach to this goal."[116] Bülent Arınç, then VP parliamentarian, called the case "unfair," on the grounds that the VP was not the continuation of the WP, but was a new party. He insisted that Islamism could not be suppressed.

> They cannot finish us by hanging, cutting, destroying.... we will not be finished. Our children are coming as our successors; they [the ones that try to finish us] should not be pleased.... If this country is a democratic state based on law, different opinions will live freely. One day this will come back to Turkey again.[117]

---

[109] Author's interview with Şevket Kazan, the vice-chair of the FP, Ankara, June 9, 2004.
[110] In Istanbul, Ali Müfit Gürtuna from the VP became the mayor by receiving 24.5% of the votes, while Melih Gökçek from the VP became the mayor of Ankara by getting 20.8% of the votes.
[111] Fazilet Partisi, *Türkiye'nin Öncelikleri ve Temel Görüşlerimiz, M. Recai Kutan'ın Basın Toplantısı 17 Aralık 1998 Bilkent-Ankara*, 3.
[112] "Yine kapatma davası" [Again a closure case], *Zaman*, May 7, 1999, 11.
[113] Yavuz, *Islamic Political Identity in Turkey*, 249.
[114] Jenkins, "Muslim Democrats in Turkey?" 52.
[115] Yavuz, *Islamic Political Identity in Turkey*, 249.
[116] "Hukuki değil" [It is not legal], *Zaman*, May 8, 1999, 10.
[117] "Arınç: Bizi tecrid edin" [Arınç: Isolate us], *Zaman*, May 8, 1999, 10.

The VP, having been weakened as a result of the countermobilization of the secular state institutions, framed the issue of Turkey's possible membership in the EU as a new POS. The Islamist movement, which had been opposed to seeking membership in the EU, started to argue for Turkey's admission. During his visit to Brussels in October 1999, for example, VP Chair Kutan argued that Turkey's membership in the EU would lead to the introduction of Western norms in the country.[118] The EU democratization reform packages for Turkey called for diminishing the power of the military, the main challenger of the Islamist movement. In October 1999, Jonathan Sugden, chair of Human Rights Watch Commission's Turkey section, while criticizing the closure of the WP and the pressures over the VP and the Kurdish separatist the People's Democracy Party (PDP), stated, "the headscarf issue is a human rights problem and the Human Rights Watch Commission is planning to pay a special attention to it."[119] This lent additional weight to the VP's own framing of the issue.

The VP also presented "the headscarf ban issue as a matter of human rights violation and suppression of personal liberties rather than as a matter of religion."[120] In various platforms, the VP parliamentarians criticized the "insufficient" democracy and secularism in Turkey. For example, Nazlı Ilıcak, then VP parliamentarian, argued during a Friday meeting of ASKON (*Anadolu Kaplanları* – Anatolian Tigers; an Islamist businessmen's organization), that Turkey was passing through "a fascist period" as a result of the cooperation between capital, the media, politicians, and the military. According to Ilıcak, for Turkey to be a livable country, the VP had to be the governing party.[121] VP Parliamentary Group Co-Chair Bülent Arınç argued that Turkey needed a new civil constitution.[122]

Although the countermobilization of the state's secular institutions led by the military after its February 1997 soft intervention compelled the Islamist movement to reframe its tactics, the secular countermobilization did not diminish the power of the Islamist movement in the long run. Adnan Demirtürk, then chair of the National Youth Foundation, in evaluating the impact of the postintervention era on the Islamist movement, remarked on the paradoxical effect of the intervention. "We work with a greater excitement, love, and effort," he declared. "Being under surveillance means being more transparent. Being more transparent results in acquiring more reputation and reaching out

---

[118] "Kutan: Türkiye'ye yazık ediliyor" [Kutan: This gives damage to Turkey], *Milli Gazete*, October 26, 1999, 11.
[119] "Başörtüsü insan hakları sorunudur" [Headscarf is a human rights problem], Mehmet Doğan's interview with Sugden, *Milli Gazete*, October 11, 1999, 4.
[120] Narlı, "The Rise of the Islamist Movement in Turkey," 44.
[121] "Ülke Fazilet ile kurtulur" [The country is saved by the Virtue (Party)], *Milli Gazete*, October 3, 1999, 19. To the ASKON's meeting, Istanbul University Law Department Professor Burhan Kuzu, the Chair of ASKON Ragıp Gültekin, and Kombassan Chair of Trustee Board Haşim Bayram participated.
[122] "FP: Önce Sivil Anayasa" [The VP: First a civil constitution], *Milli Gazete*, October 2, 1999, 10.

to new masses [people]."[123] Demirtürk argued, "We will conduct a comprehensive youth research. By this way, we will know our targeted mass."[124] The Islamist movement's adoption of a more moderate tone in the aftermath of the closure of the WP seems to be more of a tactical decision than a fundamental change. MÜSİAD Chair Ali Bayramoğlu, when asked in June 1999 whether "MÜSİAD has been changing or not," replied:

MÜSİAD may be changing in terms of conditions. But in terms of mentality and things that it will realize in the future, it does not change so easily. Because in terms of the rightness of principles that it presented and defended there is no possibility of change. This may be regarded (on the condition to be called together) as institutionalization and socialization. We could not realize the things that we targeted, at this point [we] can be seen as changing. Yet, the MÜSİAD community is behind all of its declarations to the public regarding issues for 9 years.[125]

Abdülkadir Aksu, the VP vice-chair, used the EU demands for abolition of the state security courts to reaffirm a long-standing demand of the Islamists. He stated,

Since the beginning, we have wanted the closure of the State Security Courts. We declared this in our election pamphlet [1999]. If our proposal were accepted at that time, we would not appear to be doing things because the Europeans want us to do so. Our wish is the total closure of the State Security Courts. Obstacles to human rights and freedoms should be abolished not as a result of the modern world's pressure, but because it is our nation's right. . . . Let's abolish all anti-democratic laws in the Constitution. Freedom of thought and expression should no longer be punished. Let's prohibit the suppression of people because of their thoughts and faiths. . . . People who govern the country should no longer imprison people who think and speak and should no longer concern with people's choice of clothing.[126]

The decision by Chief Public Prosecutor Vural Savaş to open a case to outlaw the VP led to a framing contest among the conservatives controlled by Necmettin Erbakan and the young reformists led by then Istanbul mayor Recep Tayyip Erdoğan. Erdoğan, having been sentenced to prison in April 1998, after his conviction for inciting religious hatred under Article 312 of the Turkish penal code, announced that he had changed his views. He contacted Western diplomats and journalists, and started to praise parliamentary democracy and Turkey's endeavors to enter the EU.[127] Because Erdoğan was banned from

---

[123] "Mercek altında daha çok çalışıyoruz" [We work more under supervision], Ebubekir Gülüm's interview with the MGV Chair Adnan Demirtürk, *Milli Gazete*, October 9, 1997, 16.
[124] "MGV'nin projesi insan" [The National Youth Foundation's project is the human being], Ebubekir Gülüm's interview with the MGV's Chair Adnan Demirtürk, *Milli Gazete*, October 8, 1997, 16.
[125] "TÜSİAD olmayız" [We will not be a TÜSİAD], Engin Şahin's interview with Bayramoğlu, *Milli Gazete*, June 20, 1999, 13.
[126] "DGM'ler tamamen kaldırılmalı" [The State Security Courts should be totally abolished], *Milli Gazete*, June 3, 1999, 11.
[127] Erdoğan, in one of his speeches, read Turkish nationalist Ziya Gökalp's poem, which stated, "The mosques are our barracks, the minarets our bayonets, the domes our helmets, and the believers our soldiers." In Jenkins, "Muslim Democrats in Turkey?" 52.

politics, Abdullah Gül represented the reformist wing at the VP's First Convention on May 14, 2000. The reformists lost the party leadership to the leader of the traditionalist wing, VP Chair Recai Kutan, by 521 votes to 631.

AFTER "VIRTUE": JUSTICE AND DEVELOPMENT

Internal competition for control of the VP was cut short by the June 2001 decision of the Constitutional Court to rule the party's actions incompatible with the secular character of the state and close it down. The closure of the primary Islamist party for the fourth time since the 1970s led the Islamist movement to split into two parties. The "traditionalists," under the leadership of Recai Kutan, established the FP. The "reformists," under the leadership of Recep Tayyip Erdoğan (the former founding member of the WP/VP and the mayor of Istanbul, who was at this time still banned from politics), founded the JDP. The JDP's traditionalists are understood by the majority of academics as reformists. Erdoğan previously made antisecular statements; in 1996, in a newspaper interview, he "admitted that democracy is not the goal but is an instrument for the WP." Similarly, Erbakan stated that "democracy is an instrument, not the aim; the aim is to establish *saadet nizamı* (order of happiness)."[128] In another interview, in 1994, Erdoğan affirmed, "Elhamdulillah [thank God] we are for the Sharia."[129]

The problem of the malfunctioning state and the inability of the mainstream political parties to solve citizens' socioeconomic problems continued. Gross national product (GNP) per capita declined from $3,255 in 1998 to $2,986 in 2000, an 8.3 percent decline, and to $2,143 in 2001, a 28.2 percent decline. The distribution of wealth became even more unequal, as 40 percent of the population shared only 16 percent of the annual GNP. The unemployment rate, which was 8.8 percent in 1994, increased to 10.6 percent in 2001.[130] The 2001 economic crisis was the deepest crisis in the history of the Turkish Republic. It adversely affected all segments of Turkish society – rich and poor, skilled and unskilled. While highly educated and skilled employees lost their jobs in large numbers, many small- and medium-sized businesses went bankrupt. The economic crisis further exacerbated the Turkish public's lack of trust in politicians.[131] Unlike the political parties that had already governed the country, the JDP, as a newly founded political party under the leadership of Recep Tayyip Erdoğan, a politician with a proven track record of dealing successfully with the socioeconomic problems of the population of Istanbul, seized on socioeconomic grievances in the national electorate as a political opportunity

---

[128] *Milliyet*, July 14, 1996. See also interview with Recep Tayyip Erdoğan, in Metin Sever and Cem Dizdar, 2. *Cumhuriyet Tartışmaları* [The Second Republic Discussions] (Ankara: Başak Yayınları, 1993), 419–32.
[129] *Milliyet*, November 21, 1994.
[130] Efe and Rumeli, *Hükümetlerin Performansları*, 12, 28–30.
[131] Ziya Öniş, "Domestic Politics versus Global Dynamics: Towards a Political Economy of the 2000 and 2001 Financial Crises in Turkey," in *The Turkish Economy in Crisis*, eds. Ziya Öniş and Barry Rubin (London: Frank Cass, 2003), 14–15.

during its 2002 election campaign. In the 2002 general elections, the JDP became the governing party by receiving the highest vote share (34.3%), while the FP received only 2.5 percent of the vote.

Islamists controlled an extensive network of private schools, dormitories, and university preparatory courses. The Islamist business class controlled interest-free financial institutions, many holding companies, and hundreds of enterprises, as well as capital measured in the billions of dollars. Hundreds of media outlets, as well as civic associations, foundations, and labor unions were under the control of Islamists. Moreover, thousands of Islamists had entered the state bureaucracies.[132] Thus, despite having banned two successive Islamist parties (the WP and VP), imposed constraints on the Islamist system of *imam-hatip* schools, and conducted a vigorous public campaign against Islamism as a threat to Turkish national security, the military failed, in the years following the soft intervention of February 1997 to stem the growing organization and resources of the Islamist movement, or weaken the electoral strength of the main Islamist party.

The JDP and the FP each have a strong and hierarchical organizational structure with motivated party activists.[133] Both parties are organized from provinces down to the level of electoral precincts and emphasize face-to-face contacts with the electorate (i.e., household chats) and provide selective material (such as food, clothing, scholarships, and coal) as well as soft incentives to the electorate.[134] Financially, the JDP seems to be stronger than the FP.

After the closure of the VP in 2001, the FP adopted the traditional rhetoric of the "National View" (*Milli Görüş*) that had been used by Erbakan in the 1970s. The FP Women Commission chair, Ayşenur Tekdal, in an interview with the author in June 2004, defined the "National View" as a "contemporary civilization project with the goal of having a livable Turkey, reestablishment of a strong Turkey, and a livable world."[135] As in the case of its predecessor parties, the FP women activists pay weekly household visits to the electorate. The FP has one neighborhood observer for each neighborhood, who holds face-to-face conversations. During the household chats, the party orators talk about Turkey's problems and distribute the party's message to the citizens. While some contacted people may reject the FP's political message, the women activists focus on commonalities (e.g., safety, freedom in education, and the like) rather than differences during their conversations. In time, some contacted constituents change their ideas and start to work for the party. In the words of Tekdal, "like a snowball, faith and love grow."[136]

[132] "Devlette 13 bin irticaci" [13 thousand Islamic reactionists are in the state], *Milliyet*, December 10, 2002.
[133] Adalet ve Kalkınma Partisi, *AK Parti Parti Tüzüğü* [The JDP Party Program] (Ankara: AK Parti, 2002); Saadet Partisi, *Saadet Partisi Teşkilât Rehberi* [The Felicity Party Organization Directory] (Ankara: Saadet Partisi, 2002).
[134] Author's interviews with high-ranking JDP party workers, Ankara, February 19, 2004 and June 8, 2004.
[135] Author's interview with Ayşenur Tekdal, the FP Women Commission chair, Ankara, June 9, 2004.
[136] Ibid.

The FP's women activists play a crucial role in spreading the party's message. Tekdal suggested, "since housewives affect their husbands and children, it is crucial to convince women."[137] She further suggested that, by the time the WP was banned it had had one million women members. By 2004, the FP had three hundred thousand women members.[138] The FP had more than one million members in total at this time, compared to the four million WP members.[139] The FP activists work for the party with the power of faith, believing that "spreading the party's message will lead to the establishment of a system that will lead people to have a perfect life with tranquility."[140] The FP activists assist citizens experiencing socioeconomic problems.

The JDP Women's Commission, like the FP Women's Commission, has neighborhood observers. The JDP, like the FP, emphasizes face-to-face contacts with the electorate. JDP Vice-Chair Murat Mercan, who is responsible for the media and advertising, explained that

> For us, the best way to have a healthy relationship with the society is to have face-to-face relations. Before the November 3rd [2002] elections, we did not have any newspaper ads. We did not utilize radios or the internet [for advertisement]. Instead, we emphasized two subjects: First, we effectively utilized billboards in all provinces; and second, mainly our Women Commission members visited neighborhoods and small business owners. No matter what you do, there is a certain judgment about you [the JDP]. You can change this judgment only by having a face-to-face conversation. Our parliamentarians go to their election areas and listen to citizens' problems and demands.[141]

The JDP has maintained its close contacts with citizens following the 2002 general elections. In order to have a sense of public opinion in determining its policies, the party regularly holds surveys conducted by its Women and Youth Commission members. The party has also a very effective organization called AKİM (*AK İletişim Merkezi – AK Communications Center*). There is an AKİM at the party's headquarters and in the offices of all province chairmanships, where all citizens are welcome to discuss their problems, complaints, and demands with party members.[142] Diligent and motivated AKİM party workers report citizens' complaints and demands to related state ministries and offices and follow up until a solution is reached.

The party's women members, who are trained at the party's headquarters about the party's political rhetoric of "conservative democracy" and propagation techniques, hold household chats. The JDP Women's Commission aims at women having an active role in politics. Commission Chair Selma Kavaf, in an

---

[137] Ibid.
[138] Ibid.
[139] Author's interview with Şevket Kazan, the vice-chair of the FP, Ankara, June 9, 2004.
[140] Author's interview with Ayşenur Tekdal, the FP Women Commission chair, Ankara, June 9, 2004.
[141] Adalet ve Kalkınma Partisi, *Türkiye Bülteni* [Bulletin of Turkey], no. 39 (Ankara: AK Parti, August 2006), 12–13.
[142] Ibid., 13–14.

interview with the author in June 2004, explained the motivation behind the party's women activists as follows: "Before the JDP came to power, the state and the nation were not at peace. There was a state-dictated structure over the nation. The nation always saw the state's cold face. The JDP emerged from the nation. The party by embracing the society, shows the state's warm face."[143] Kavaf defined conservatism "not as religiosity, but as the protection of faiths and sacred values;" and democracy "as being respectful to ones that are different from us."[144] Indeed, the JDP pays particular attention to reaching out to the secular segment of society. By 2004, the JDP had 516,000 women members. By 2006, the party had 2,800,000 members of which 721,000 were women.[145]

The party distributes selective incentives particularly to the urban poor residing in shantytowns. For example, under the leadership of Prime Minister Erdoğan's wife Emine Erdoğan the party started a "sister family project," through which needy families are provided with health care, jobs, and education by thirteen ministers and their wives. The party's Women Commission is also very active in distributing food packages, coal, and scholarships.[146] The Women Commission also established relations abroad – with, for example, the National Democracy Institute, the Norwegian prime minister, the German Christian Democrat Party, the German Greens Party, and various EU embassies.[147]

Since the JDP regards the youth as tomorrow's politicians, the party also established a network to reach out to university students. The JDP's Youth Commission, with well-educated and diligent members (most of them university graduates), regularly organizes educational seminars, conferences, youth festivals, and visits to nursing homes and orphans.[148]

The JDP, while providing financial assistance to needy segments of the population (e.g., handicapped people, free meals during Ramadan, scholarships for students, and assistance to people with no social security insurance), has also been quite active in dealing with social problems such as drug addiction and violence against children and women.[149] The JDP, by successfully responding to citizens' socioeconomic grievances, has played the role of a social democratic party.

---

[143] Author's interview with Selma Kavaf, the JDP Women Commission chair, Ankara, June 8, 2004.
[144] Ibid.
[145] "Erdoğan'dan 'Üye yapın' emri" [Erdoğan commands: "Register new members"], Yeniçağ, December 27, 2006.
[146] Adalet ve Kalkınma Partisi, AK Parti Genel Merkez Kadın Kolları Faaliyet Raporu [The JDP Headquarters Women Commission Work Report] (Ankara: AK Parti, 2003).
[147] Author's interview with Selma Kavaf, the JDP Women Commission chair, Ankara, June 8, 2004.
[148] Author's interview with Zelkif Kazdal, the JDP Youth Commission chair, Ankara, February 19, 2004; Adalet ve Kalkınma Partisi, Türkiye Bülteni, no. 33 (Ankara: AK Parti, February 2006).
[149] Adalet ve Kalkınma Partisi, Türkiye Bülteni, no. 41 (Ankara: AK Parti, October 2006); Adalet ve Kalkınma Partisi, Türkiye Bülteni, no. 39 (Ankara: AK Parti, August 2006); Adalet ve Kalkınma Partisi, Türkiye Bülteni, no. 30 (Ankara: AK Parti, November 2005); Adalet ve Kalkınma Partisi, Türkiye Bülteni, no. 27 (Ankara: AK Parti, August 2005); and Adalet ve Kalkınma Partisi, Türkiye Bülteni, no. 29 (Ankara: AK Parti, October 2005).

The main opposition party, the center-left RPP, while continuously arguing that secularism in Turkey is in great jeopardy; unlike the JDP and the FP, it does not have a strong organizational network with diligent and motivated party activists and remains very distant from the citizens. Yakup Kepenek, the RPP parliamentarian, during an interview with the author in June 2004, when asked what kind of a socioeconomic project that his party was offering to citizens, particularly those residing in shantytowns, replied, "We do not have anything to offer to them."[150]

Unlike the FP, the JDP rejects the National View Movement of Erbakan and defines itself as a "conservative democratic" party. However, unlike the center-right parties that emphasize protection of conservative values, both the FP and the JDP regard Turkey's present secular-democratic system as problematic. The JDP's prominent parliamentarians and party workers, like those of the FP, argue that the top-down definition of secularism does not fit Turkish society, which is shaped by Islam. The JDP, while emphasizing that the party is equally distanced from all faiths, regards the party's position on secularism and democracy as an expression of a demand coming from the public.[151]

The mainstream parties do not regard the JDP as a center-right party. Mehmet Ağar, then the chair of the TPP, in an interview with the author in June 2004, emphasized the importance of secularism in the governance of the state. Otherwise, he asserted, the state cannot treat all its citizens equally. Ağar, by arguing that under the JDP rule, the Islamic orders have become the determining factor in Turkish politics, did not regard the JDP as a center-right party.[152] Ayvaz Gökdemir, the former prominent TPP parliamentarian and former State Minister, in an interview with the author in June 2004, pointed out that the JDP's cadres come from the WP/VP. He, too, did not regard the JDP as a center-right party. Gökdemir commented, "there would be no JDP if Erbakan could have remained legally and politically active following the February 28th process."[153] In effect, he viewed the JDP as no different from the WP.

The JDP, unlike the center-right parties, tries to redefine the structure of the state according to a new interpretation of secularism and democracy. The party rejects ethnic, religious, and regional nationalism and tries to unify Turkish citizens under the umbrella of conservatism.[154] One prominent JDP parliamentarian, in an interview with the author in June 2004, argued that the public already knew the JDP's cadres and wanted more democratization, freedom of faith and thought, to have a better life, and to be treated equally by the state.

---

[150] Author's interview with Yakup Kepenek, the RPP parliamentarian, Ankara, June 11, 2004.
[151] Author's interviews with high-ranking JDP parliamentarians and party workers; and with FP members and party workers, Ankara, February and June 2004.
[152] Author's interview with Mehmet Ağar, the chair of the TPP, Ankara, June 9, 2004.
[153] Author's interview with Ayvaz Gökdemir, the former Minister of State and former TPP parliamentarian, Ankara, June 11, 2004.
[154] See Adalet ve Kalkınma Partisi, *Adalet ve Kalkınma Partisi 1. Olağan Büyük Kongresi, Genel Başkan Recep Tayyip Erdoğan'ın Konuşması (12 Ekim 2004)* [The JDP Chair Recep Tayyip Erdoğan's Speech at the Party's First General Convention (October 12, 2004)] (Ankara: AK Parti, 2004).

The electorate voted for the JDP in an attempt to realize these goals by a new method and rhetoric.[155] According to Şevket Kazan, the "reformists" in the VP realized that the goal of changing the secular state could not be realized by pursuing the National View line. Thus, they took Özal's MP of the 1980s as a strategic model for pursuing Islamization of the secular state without engendering a countermobilization. Kazan argues that the WP/VP's electorate voted for the JDP as a better choice than the FP for realizing Islamist goals. He criticizes JDP members for losing their motivation and abandoning their initial political rhetoric, and calls the party one "without an identity." Both FP and JDP activists interviewed by the author in 2004 vehemently rejected the term *moderate Islam* to describe their parties, arguing that "Islam is Islam; there cannot be a moderate Islam."[156]

THE JUSTICE AND DEVELOPMENT PARTY TESTS THE LIMITS

The JDP, despite the criticism of the FP, does seem to be on the way to becoming more moderate in time. The party has gradually started to define itself as a party of "conservative-democracy."[157] The JDP's proposals regarding democratization and freedom of faith and thought resemble the WP/VP's earlier proposals.[158] The party supports the goal of Turkey's entrance into the EU, and frames its calls for more democratization and freedom in Turkey in terms of implementing the EU reform packages based on the Copenhagen criteria, which are embraced by the majority of political parties, including the FP.

The JDP has successfully exploited Turkey's longtime quest for EU membership as a political opportunity to advance Islamist demands for change by utilizing a liberal tool kit. Both the EU and the JDP, for example, seek to reduce the role of the military in Turkish politics. As a high-ranking JDP parliamentarian remarked, in an interview with the author in June 2004, when asked what would happen if the EU does not admit Turkey as a member: "Even if the EU does not admit Turkey as a member, Turkey will be more democratic. Then, we will continue our way by means of the Ankara criteria instead of the Copenhagen criteria. Turkey should determine its geopolitical alternatives well. Turkey should not only count on the EU; there are Iran, Pakistan, the Turkic Republics for economic relations, the D-8 [Erbakan's project of Muslim union], and the Islam Development Organization, as alternatives."[159] In August 2005, Prime

---

[155] Author's interview with a prominent JDP parliamentarian, Ankara, June 8, 2004.
[156] Author's interviews with the JDP parliamentarians; and with FP members, Ankara, February and June 2004.
[157] See Yalçın Akdoğan, *Muhafazakar Demokrasi* [Conservative Democracy] (Ankara: AK Parti, 2003).
[158] See Refah Partisi, *Refah Partisi'nin Anayasa Değişikliği Uzlaşma Teklifi* [The Welfare Party's Agrement Proposal for a Constitutional Change] (Ankara: Refah Partisi, 1995); Fazilet Partisi, *Fazilet Partisi Anayasa Değişikliğine Dair Uzlaşma Metni Taslağı* [The Felicity Party Draft Agreement Proposal for a Constitutional Change] (Ankara: Fazilet Partisi, 1999).
[159] Author's interview with a prominent JDP parliamentarian, Ankara, June 8, 2004.

Minister Erdoğan, by pointing out the democratization reforms in Turkey as a result of the EU reform packages, commented that the JDP has initiated "a silent revolution" in the country.[160]

If the EU is an important international actor in the JDP's eyes with respect to the future of Turkey, the other crucial actor is the United States. The JDP supports the EU reform packages as a means of framing its efforts to change the definition of secularism and broaden the opportunities for Islamic religious activities in Turkey in terms of democratizing the country. The party also seems to support the U.S. "Greater Middle East Initiative (GMEI)," which focuses on exporting democracy and open market economics to the Muslim world. While the United States presents Turkey as a model secular democracy in the Muslim world, it also criticizes secularism in Turkey as being too strict for other Muslim countries. Both Turkish Islamists and U.S. analysts criticize Turkey's present secular character, and Kemalism, as incompatible with democracy.[161] Turkey has been presented by the United States as a model for the Muslim world because of its Muslim character, rather than its achievement in secularism. In April 2004, U.S. Secretary of State Colin Powell defined Turkey as a "Republic of Islam,"[162] which created discontent among the secular state establishment in Turkey. In response to the U.S. GMEI, then Turkish General Staff vice-chair, General İlker Başbuğ emphasized on numerous occasions that Turkey would maintain its secular-democratic character in the future, and did not seek to be a model of "moderate Islam" for the Muslim world. General Başbuğ commented, "A state cannot be based on both secularism and moderate Islam. . . Either the first one is present [as the basis of the state] or the other. Turkey is a secular, democratic, and social state based on the rule of law. Ideas other than this are not compatible with us."[163] Similarly, then President of the Turkish Republic Ahmet Necdet Sezer criticized the U.S. GMEI and the idea of defining the country as a "moderate Islam" by stating, "Neither Islam, nor democracy need each other in defining themselves. . . . Secularism is the best means to provide a balanced relationship between Islam and democracy."[164]

The change in U.S. policy manifest in the GMEI created great discontent among the secular state establishment in Turkey, and the secular segment of the population, who were already suspicious of U.S. intentions. Following the 2002 general elections, despite the fact that JDP Chair Erdoğan's eligibility for

---

[160] "4 yılda sessiz devrim yaptık" [We initiated a silent revolution in four years], *Yeni Şafak*, August 16, 2005.

[161] See Ömer Taşpınar, "An uneven fit? The 'Turkish Model' and the Arab World," *Analysis Paper* no. 5, *Brookings Project on U.S. Relations with the Islamic World* (August 2003); Graham Fuller, *The Future of Political Islam* (New York: Palgrave, 2003); and Yavuz, *Islamic Political Identity in Turkey*.

[162] "Powell'dan garip açıklama" [A strange statement by Powell], *Cumhuriyet*, April 3, 2004, 8.

[163] "TSK 'ılımlı Islam'a' karşı" [The Turkish Armed Forces is against 'moderate Islam'], *Cumhuriyet*, April 3, 2004, 8.

[164] "Cumhurbaşkanı Sezer'den önemli uyarılar" [Important warnings from President Sezer], *Milliyet*, October 1, 2005.

the prime ministership was being called into question for his having been banned from politics for earlier remarks hostile to secularism, U.S. President George W. Bush welcomed Erdoğan to the White House as if he were already Turkey's new leader.[165] This created the image in Turkey that the United States, consistent with the GMEI, had been backing the "moderate Islamist" JDP. For example, former TPP politician Ayvaz Gökdemir, in the June 2004 interview with the author cited in the preceding text, commented, "the U.S. embraced both Recep Tayyip Erdoğan and his party. While the reasons why the U.S. liked the JDP to that extent are unclear at this point, from the JDP leader's statements it is obvious that the JDP cadre has a very close relationship with the U.S. government."[166] On the relationship between secularism and Islam in Turkey, Gökdemir argued, "The secular Turkish Republic should get rid of its suspicions toward Islam. If secularism is indispensable, Islam is an indispensable reality of religion and culture. It is possible to be secular, democratic, Muslim, and civilized simultaneously. Today's government [the JDP government] may not represent this ideal synthesis, but Turkey [the Turkish public] has been living this synthesis."[167]

The JDP, which frames its efforts to redefine the present secular establishment in terms promoting more democratization, and conforming to EU statements, nonetheless advances, from time to time, proposals that reflect its Islamist agenda. For example, in May 2003 while passing Turkey's sixth EU reform package in the parliament, the party tried to introduce the establishment of chapels (*ibadethane*) in each residential building.[168] The proposal was withdrawn when it received high criticism from the secular sector of the society.[169] In August 2003, the seventh EU reform package transferred the General Secretariat of the NSC from military to civilian control; as a result, the NSC meets every two months instead of every month, unless otherwise suggested by prime minister or called for by the president.[170]

In November 2003, the party tried to open up the Quran courses and their dormitories year-round. Evening-time (*yatılı*) Quran courses would provide accommodation and food for working poor children. According to the proposal, an evening Quran course could be opened up with the application of ten people. This is a reflection of the strategy used by Islamists to draw people into their organizations and therefore, their influence. Nezih Varol, a professor at Marmara University Education Faculty, expressed his concern by pointing out that there were nearly one million working children in Turkey, and these Quran

---

[165] *Milliyet*, December 11, 2002; Yasemin Çongar, "Washington'dan tam not" [A full grade from Washington], *Milliyet*, December 12, 2002.
[166] Author's interview with Ayvaz Gökdemir, the former Minister of State and former TPP parliamentarian, Ankara, June 11, 2004.
[167] Ibid.
[168] *Milliyet*, May 31, 2003. In Islam, unlike in Christianity, there is no need to have a chapel to worship.
[169] *Radikal*, June 12, 2003.
[170] "AB'ye bir adım daha" [A one more step towards the EU], *Yeni Şafak*, August 8, 2003; *Milliyet*, August 7, 2003.

courses would be very attractive to them.[171] This proposal also was withdrawn as a result of criticism of the secular segment of the society.[172]

In February 2004, the JDP proposed a new law in the Turkish penal code, which would make it a crime, punishable by two to five years' imprisonment, to inhibit the right to educate and teach, the right to benefit from public services, and the right to organize massive religious prayers and rituals. The main opposition party, the RPP, rejected the proposal on the grounds that it would give a free hand to the Islamic brotherhoods and encourage Islamist activities challenging secularism.[173]

In May 2004, the party tried to establish control over the universities by tying their administrative and financial sources to the Ministry of Education. All appointments of university administrative and academic staff, as well as the selection of students who would be provided scholarships, would be determined by the Ministry of Education rather than by the universities. The party also tried to make it easier for *imam-hatip* graduates to enter universities. As a result of high criticism by the secular segment of the society[174] and President Sezer's veto, the proposal was postponed, to be taken up again in the future. In May 2004, along with the EU reform packages, the State Security Courts were closed down.[175]

In June 2005, the JDP government, despite President Sezer's veto, passed a new penal code, which reduced the number of years serving in prison as a punishment for opening up illegal educational institutions from a maximum of three years to one year. Furthermore, unlike the previous penal code, the clause calling for such institutions to be closed down was not included in the new penal code.[176]

To what extent Prime Minister Erdoğan has changed his ideas regarding political Islam has been questioned by the secular segment of Turkish society. In July 2003, a Turkish newspaper published a photograph of Erdoğan during his WP Istanbul province chairmanship, taken with the chair of the Hizb-i Islami Party in Afghanistan, Gulbeddin Hikmetyar. When asked his opinion about the picture, Prime Minister Erdoğan commented, "It is a photograph that was taken within the family."[177] In June 2006, Prime Minister Erdoğan

---

[171] *Cumhuriyet*, December 5, 2003.
[172] "365 gün din eğitimi" [Religious education for 365 days], *Milliyet*, December 6, 2003, 15; "AKP'den geri adım" [The JDP steps back], *Milliyet*, December 10, 2003, 14.
[173] *Cumhuriyet*, February 4, 2004.
[174] University professors peacefully protested in Istanbul, Ankara, and Izmir the JDP's proposal on universities. "Rektörlerden sessiz protesto" [Silent protest of university presidents], *Milliyet*, May 15, 2004; *Hürriyet*, May 14, 2004; and "Üniversiteler Anıtkabir'de" [Universities are at the (Atatürk's) mausoleum], *Cumhuriyet*, May 15, 2004.
[175] *Milliyet*, May 21, 2004; *Hürriyet*, May 21, 2004.
[176] "Kaçak eğitime AKP'den onay" [JDP's approval of illegal education], *Hürriyet*, June 30, 2005; *Milliyet*, June 30, 2005.
[177] *Star*, July 16, 2003. In December 2003, it was found out that Erdoğan during his Istanbul mayorship hosted members of the Islamic Brotherhood from Jordan and Egypt and members of the Islamic Salvation of Chechnyan Resistance Organization. *Cumhuriyet*, December 4, 2003.

made supportive remarks about Saudi businessman Yasin El Kadı, who is on the UN Security Council's list of those financing the Al Qaeda terrorist organization. Erdoğan defended his political adviser Cüneyd Zapsu's relationship with El Kadı, by stating, "I know El Kadı and I believe in him as much as I believe in myself. He is a benevolent lover of Turkey and has investments here. It is impossible that he is connected to terrorism."[178] The JDP government failed to comply with UN regulations regarding financiers of global terrorism by not freezing the property of El Kadı in Turkey. This failure led the United States to criticize the Erdoğan government.[179] Even after four years in office, Prime Minister Erdoğan stated, "I have never changed. Islamic ideas do not change."[180]

The tension between the JDP and the secular segment of the society once again rose following a terrorist attack on the Council of State (*Danıştay*, the high court in administrative affairs) judges in Ankara in May 2006. On May 17, lawyer Alparslan Arslan opened fire inside the Council of State, killing Second Criminal Bureau Judge Mustafa Yücel Özbilgin and wounding four more judges. Arslan was protesting against a ban on wearing the Islamic headscarf (*türban*) in state institutions. After his arrest, he declared "I am a soldier of Allah."[181] This was the first time a state official representing the secular Turkish Republic was targeted by an Islamist. Earlier, Prime Minister Erdoğan had declared that the issue of banning the Islamic headscarf in state institutions was an issue in the jurisdiction of the *ulema* (religious experts) rather than the Council of State. Parliamentarians from the main opposition party, the RPP, openly accused the JDP government of "emboldening religious extremists by voicing its opposition to the headscarf ban and through its frequent harsh criticism of court rulings."[182] Judge Özbilgin's funeral drew tens of thousands of Turkish citizens and became a bold message to the JDP of public support for Turkey's secular order. Protesters shouted, "Turkey is secular and will remain so," and called Prime Minister Erdoğan a "murderer;" they "demanded the government's resignation and booted and jostled senior ministers attending the service."[183] President Sezer issued a veiled warning to the JDP government by stating, "those responsible for the attack need to reconsider their behavior. No one is strong enough to redefine secularism and in turn harm democracy."[184] Despite the fact that Prime Minister Erdoğan complained there was a "conspiracy" against his government, then the chief of the General Staff, General Hilmi Özkök, urged Turkish citizens to persist with their demonstrations in the defense of the values of the secular republic.[185]

---

[178] *Milliyet*, July 14, 2006.
[179] *Milliyet*, September 22, 2006.
[180] Altemur Kılıç, "Uslub-u beyan, aynıyla Erdoğan (2)," *Yeniçağ*, December 20, 2006.
[181] *Turkish Daily News*, May 21, 2006.
[182] Ibid.
[183] Ibid.
[184] *Turkish Daily News*, May 19, 2006.
[185] *Milliyet*, May 19, 2006; *Yeniçağ*, May 20, 2006.

During the past decade, a division appears to have developed within the military regarding the definition of *secularism*. In an interview with the author in February 2004, the general secretary of the General Staff reported that the military was no longer monitoring the Islamists' activities in Turkey. The general secretary also denied the existence of the West Working Group, despite the fact that its founding and its report (cited previously) are matters of public record, and denied as well that there was an Islamic bourgeoisie in the country.[186] In an interview with the author in July 2003, Retired General Çevik Bir had suggested that military cadres did not see sufficient public support in response to the soft military intervention of 1997, and therefore predicted there would not be another military intervention to counter the Islamist movement in the future.[187] Chief of the General Staff, General Hilmi Özkök, who served between 2002 and 2006, had maintained close relations with Prime Minister Erdoğan. General Özkök suggested the military and the JDP "get along like a poem," and Erdoğan called General Özkök "*hocam*" (my teacher).[188] Both Özkök and Erdoğan later denied this exchange, which nonetheless, was seen by many television viewers throughout Turkey at the time.[189] The general was outspoken in his support for secularism following the murder of Judge Özbilgin.

The attitude of the military leadership seems to have hardened further with the appointment of General Yaşar Büyükanıt as chief of the General Staff following General Özkök's retirement in August 2006. During the summer of 2006, there had been a vigorous e-mail and cell phone text-message campaign against General Büyükanıt's promotion. Those behind the campaign suggested General Büyükanıt had a "secret Jewish heritage," and thus should not become the chief of the General Staff. The new military command under the leadership of General Büyükanıt made clear that the military was once again becoming concerned about an Islamist threat in Turkey. In September 2006, the commander of Land Forces, General İlker Başbuğ noted, "Unfortunately, today the threat of Islamist reactionism (*irtica*), despite the denial of certain circles [Islamists], has reached to a worrisome level." He asked, "Do all cadres of the Ministry of National Education comply with their duty of defending the Turkish Revolution? It is a fact that certain circles by pursuing a patient and planned strategy to erase the revolution have achieved an important distance in that direction."[190]

In October 2006, General Büyükanıt, speaking at the opening of classes at the Military Academy, defined Islamist reactionism as a still continuing threat for Turkey and reminded listeners that the military has a constitutional duty to

---

[186] Author's interview with the general secretary of the General Staff, Ankara, February 10, 2004.
[187] Author's interview with Retired General Çevik Bir, July 21, 2003.
[188] *Hürriyet*, "Erdoğan: 'Hocam' diye Atalay'a hitap ettim" [I called Atalay as my teacher], March 24, 2005; Emin Çölaşan, "Başbakanınız konuşuyor 1" [Your prime minister is speaking 1], *Hürriyet*, March 25, 2005.
[189] This included the author.
[190] *Milliyet*, September 26, 2006.

protect secularism.[191] With new military cadres taking the office, the military seemed to be playing a more active role in Turkish politics as the guardian of secularism. Secularists are still well-represented among the Turkish military elite, which leads to the conclusion that the military is divided between Islamist sympathizers and guardians of secularism. Following General Büyükanıt's speech focusing on the threat of Islamism, the former chief of the General Staff, Retired General Hüseyin Kıvrıkoğlu (1998–2002), commented, "The four-year silence has come to an end at last."[192]

The JDP's actions in office raise questions among secular people as to whether the party pursues a "moderate" Islamist/conservative-democratic line, or because of the secular military's harsh response to the WP and the VP, the JDP changed the movement's tactics, as they call it *takiyye* (a permitted behavior of disguise for the sake of promoting the cause of Islam)? While time will provide the answer to that question, it is clear that the JDP has successfully become a people's party by embracing particularly the urban poor segment of Turkish society, its determinacy in solving the problem of the malfunctioning state (comprising corruption, unemployment, the unequal distribution of wealth, and decay in moral values), and through its strong organizational networks with diligent parliamentarians and party workers.

The JDP presents itself as a moderate party. But the personal histories of its leaders and the policies it proposed and/or adopted in power both suggest the continuing strength of Islamism in the party. Moderation of the party is a response to the demonstrated willingness of the military to intervene and the increased weariness/watchfulness on the part of a military leadership that has reaffirmed its commitment to secularism. The soft coup and heightened vigilance on the part of new military leaders has narrowed down the POS for Islamists, but it has not eliminated it entirely. Social conditions in Turkey remain favorable for Islamist social mobilization, as demonstrated by the results of the most recent election.

THE JULY 2007 GENERAL ELECTIONS

On July 22, 2007, Turkey held early general elections, as a result of which the JDP secured an increased share of the vote (see Table 6.8). The success of the JDP must be attributed to the socioeconomic concerns of the Turkish public, particularly the poor segments of the population – and the JDP's strong organizational party networks, rooted in the Islamist social movement. The JDP secured its victory despite the party's mixed performance during its four-and-a-half-year rule. The party's record was especially poor in dealing with the PKK (also known as *Kongra-Gel*) and the threat and reality of terrorism. Its record in dealing with the high unemployment rate, the

---

[191] "Org. Büyükanıt, sert ve net konuştu" [General Büyükanıt spoke harshly and clearly], *Milliyet*, October 2, 2006.
[192] "Org. Kıvrıkoğlu ne demek istedi?" [What did General Kıvrıkoğlu try to say?], *Milliyet*, October 8, 2006.

TABLE 6.8. *Results of the July 2007 Turkish General Elections*

Party	Percentage of Vote	Seats in Parliament
Justice and Development[a]	46.6	341
Republican People's[b]	20.9	112
Nationalist Action[c]	14.3	71
Independents[d]	5.2	26
Democrat	5.4	–
Felicity	2.3	–
Other	5.3	–
TOTAL	100.00	550

Source: Turkish Statistics Institute Web site, http://www.tuik.gov.tr/secimdagitimapp/secim.zul (accessed September 10, 2007) and Turkish Grand National Assembly Web site, http://www.tbmm.gov.tr/develop/owa/milletvekillerimiz_sd.dagilim (accessed September 10, 2007).
[a] The JDP's seat declined to 338 on account of 1 JDP parliamentarian's death, 1 parliamentarian's expulsion from the party, and 1 parliamentarian's becoming a parliament chair.
[b] The RPP and the DLP formed an election coalition. Following the elections, the DLP with its 13 parliamentarians formed their own group in the parliament. Currently, the RPP has 98 seats in the parliament on account of 1 RPP parliamentarian's becoming an independent parliamentarian.
[c] The NAP's seat declined to 69 on account of 2 NAP parliamentarians' death.
[d] Following the elections, some independent parliamentarians gathered around their own political parties in the parliament. As of this writing, Kurdish separatist Democratic Society Party has 21 seats, right-wing Great Unity Party has 1 seat, liberal Freedom and Solidarity Party has 1 seat, and independent parliamentarians have 5 seats in the parliament. Currently, 4 seats in the parliament are empty.

increased crime rate, and Turkey's mounting foreign debt was also poor. The party's efforts to redefine secularism in Turkey proved controversial. But, the JDP was clearly successful in responding to the socioeconomic needs and demands of the poor. The social success of the JDP undermined the appeal of the center-right parties, such as the TPP, and thereby broadened the electoral base of the JDP beyond simple Islamism.

The 2007 general elections were originally scheduled for November 2007. But the crisis in parliament surrounding the election of Turkey's next president, which was originally scheduled for May, resulted in early elections. According to the Turkish Constitution, parliament needs a quorum of 367, or two-thirds of its members, to hold a presidential election. Once parliament votes, a candidate must receive the votes of two-thirds of all members (i.e., 367) in order to win election in either of the first two rounds of voting. But only a simple majority vote of 267 is needed if there is a third round. In April 2007, the JDP, in control of a 363-seat majority in the parliament, proposed to elect a "religious" president[193] – one who would represent Islamic values – without first securing the agreement of opposition parties whose support would be needed to obtain the four additional votes required. The nomination on April 24 of Foreign Minister Abdullah Gül as the JDP's candidate for the presidency by

---
[193] See parliament Chair and JDP parliamentarian Bülent Arınç, "Dindar bir cumhurbaşkanı seçeceğiz" [We will elect a religious president], *Milliyet*, April 16, 2007.

Prime Minister Recep Tayyip Erdoğan led to mass demonstrations by the secular segment of the population, protesting Gül's candidacy.

The first round of voting took place in parliament on April 27, but failed owing to the absence of a quorum; opposition parliamentarians had refused to attend. That same evening, the Turkish Armed Forces issued a strong statement on its Web site, noting that the military had been "the staunch defender of secularism. When necessary, it will display its attitudes and actions very clearly. No one should doubt that."[194] The next day, unlike its predecessor the WP in 1997, the JDP responded to the implied threat. Government Spokesman Cemil Çiçek declared, "A military warning against [the JDP] is democratically unacceptable. According to our Constitution, the military chief of staff is responsible to the Prime Minister."[195]

On May 1, the Constitutional Court annulled the first round of the presidential election following a petition submitted by the RPP, the main opposition party, to the effect that the quorum rule in parliament had been violated. The JDP, having seen that it would be unable to secure the votes required in parliament, cognizant of the fact that the constitution required new elections in the event parliament could not elect a president in four consecutive rounds, and facing pressure from secular state institutions, political parties, and civil society associations, called for early elections. On May 3, 458 members of the 550-member parliament voted to hold early elections on July 22.

The JDP's four-and-a-half-year performance was, as noted, decidedly mixed. To begin with, PKK terrorism dramatically increased since the 2003 Iraqi war – and, despite the military's demands, the JDP government refused to take strong measures to combat this threat. Second, unlike previous center-right and center-left parties, the JDP pursued controversial policies aimed at redefining secularism as represented by the secular state establishment, including the presidency, the Constitutional Court, the Council of State, the Higher Education Board, and the military. As noted earlier, the JDP persistently attempted to and sometimes successfully changed laws and regulations concerning the status of Islam in both education and public spaces to favor the Islamist movement. These efforts intensified the debate over Islamism versus secularism in Turkish politics.

Furthermore, persistent problems in the Turkish economy continued under JDP rule. Despite positive macroeconomic indicators, such as high GDP growth rates and the reduction of inflation to single digits during the JDP's tenure, the extent to which macroeconomic changes have trickled down to the microeconomics of the country is questionable.[196] Turkey's rapid growth rate was driven mainly by a massive inflow of foreign finance capital attracted by significantly high interest rates.[197] The relative abundance of foreign exchange led to overvaluation

---

[194] "Military issues harsh warning over secularism," *Turkish Daily News*, April 27, 2007.
[195] "Government lashes out at the military," *Turkish Daily News*, April 28, 2007.
[196] Author's interview with Professor Can Erbil, Brandeis University, Waltham, MA, September 17, 2007.
[197] Interest rates in Turkey are more than 10%, while they range between 3 and 4% in global markets. See Erinç Yeldan, "Patterns of Adjustment under the Age of Finance: The Case of Turkey as a Peripheral Agent of Neoliberal Globalization" (University of Massachusetts Political Economy Research Institute, *Working Paper Series*, no. 126, February 2007).

of the Turkish lira, which in turn led to an import boom in both consumption and investment.[198] This resulted in a dramatic increase in the country's external debt, from $130.1 billion in 2002 to $206.5 billion by the end of 2006 – the latter figure equal to half the total external debt that Turkey had accumulated during the previous eighty-three years.[199] Domestic debt, which was $91.7 billion in 2002, increased to $173.1 billion in 2006.[200] Turkey's increased dependence on the flow of foreign capital made the Turkish economy more vulnerable to fluctuations in global markets. Thus, macroeconomic growth did not automatically translate into socioeconomic development.[201]

The Turkish economy is also characterized by a persistent unemployment problem (more than 10%). Unemployment among urban youth is even higher, around 26 percent.[202] According to the Organization for Economic Cooperation and Development (OECD), long-term unemployment[203] in Turkey (39.6%) is higher than the total for the OECD (32.8%).[204] Turkey also has the lowest GDP per capita ($7,698), the lowest net national income per capita ($7,196), and the lowest health spending per capita ($586) among OECD members.[205] Despite some improvements, 20.5 percent of the population of Turkey lives under the poverty line (down from 26.9% in 2002),[206] and the distribution of wealth remains unequal (20% of the population of Turkey enjoys 44.4% of the country's income).[207] According to the Turkish Statistics Institute, only 30.1 percent of the population is satisfied with its household income.[208]

---

[198] The gap in Turkey's foreign trade balance increased from –$15.4 billion in 2002 to –$53.9 billion in 2006. Ankara Ticaret Odası, "Aylık Ekonomik Görünüm, Ağustos 2007" [Ankara Trade Chamber, Monthly Economic Profile, August 2007] (Ankara: ATO, 2007), 15.

[199] The Turkish lira appreciated by 40% in real terms against the U.S. dollar and by 25% against the euro. As of September 2007, Turkey's total external debt stock was $213.5 billion. See Yeldan, "Patterns of Adjustment under the Age of Finance," 4–7; Yeldan, "Turkey: Crisis and Beyond – A 'New' Government, with 'Old' Policies, and yet under 'Altered' Global Conditions" (Amherst College, September 2007, mimeographed). See also Undersecretariat of Treasury Web site, http://www.hazine.gov.tr/stat/ti87.htm (accessed September 7, 2007).

[200] As of September 2007, the domestic debt of Turkey was $192.2 billion.

[201] Yeldan, "Patterns of Adjustment under the Age of Finance," 14–16; author's interview with Professor Can Erbil, Brandeis University, Waltham, MA, September 17, 2007.

[202] Yeldan, "Patterns of Adjustment under the Age of Finance," 14. See also Turkish Statistics Institute, Household Labor Force Surveys.

[203] Defined as persons unemployed for 12 months or more as a percentage of total unemployed.

[204] *OECD Factbook 2007: Economic, Environmental, and Social Statistics* (OECD, 2007).

[205] These figures were as of 2005. See *OECD Factbook 2007*.

[206] The poverty line in Turkey was 26.9% in 2002. TÜİK, "2005 Yoksulluk Çalışması Sonuçları" [2005 Results of Poverty Study], TÜİK, *Haber Bülteni* no. 208 (December 26, 2006). For the year 2005, the Turkish Statistics Institute announced that the poverty line for per household of 4 persons was 487 YTL ($374.6).

[207] TÜİK, "2005 Yoksulluk Çalışması Sonuçları"; TÜİK, "2005 Gelir Dağılımı Sonuçları" [2005 Distribution of Income Results], TÜİK, *Haber Bülteni* no. 207 (December 25, 2006).

[208] Two percent are very satisfied, 28.1% satisfied, 25.5% neither satisfied nor not satisfied, 31.6% not satisfied, and 12.8% not satisfied at all. See ibid.

In addition to these persisting economic problems, the crime rate in Turkey significantly increased under JDP rule.[209] Given this record, the JDP's success in increasing its vote share in the 2007 elections was particularly surprising to some sectors of the Turkish public. The secular segment of the population, represented by the RPP,[210] and the nationalists, represented by the NAP, were especially shocked by the results.

However, the strong organizational networks of the JDP enabled it to respond to the demands of the Turkish poor, who were focused on their own socioeconomic problems. The JDP's ideologically motivated Islamist supporters were insufficient in number to carry the party to victory. It was the support the party received from poorly educated low-income voters, residing in shantytowns and in rural areas, that provided it with the requisite plurality.[211] Between the 2002 and 2007 general elections, the JDP increased its electoral base from nearly ten million votes to some sixteen million.

Nearly 65 percent of the Turkish population resides in urban areas.[212] Istanbul, Ankara, and Izmir accounted for one-third of registered voters in the 2007 elections.[213] In these cities, the JDP received most of its votes from districts that received migration, particularly since the mid-1980s, from rural Turkey. For example, in Istanbul the JDP received more than 50 percent of the vote in seven such districts. Similarly, the party drew most of its support in Ankara and Izmir from such districts. The JDP also secured significant vote support in a number of provinces in the rural areas of eastern, southeastern, and central Anatolia; the Mediterranean region; and the Black Sea region.[214] According to a poll conducted by the Istanbul-based A&G research firm in July 2007, 75.8 percent of respondents who intended to vote for the JDP said they were doing so because the party provided good constituent services during its governance.

---

[209] E.g., the Turkish Directorate of General Security reported that between the years 2005 and 2006, incidents of purse snatching (*kapkaç*) increased by 70%, particularly in big cities like Istanbul, Ankara, and Izmir. "Türkiye'nin asayiş raporu korkuttu" [Turkey's crime report is frightening], *Milliyet*, July 2, 2007.

[210] Meral Tamer, "CHP'ye oy veren seçmenin duyguları" [Feelings of the RPP's electorate], *Milliyet*, July 25, 2007.

[211] "A&G'nin Başkanı Adil Gür: Muhtıra olmasa da AKP bu oyu alırdı" [Chair of the A&G Adil Gür: The JDP would receive this vote share even if the military did not issue a warning], *Milliyet*, July 24, 2007.

[212] The eight most populated provinces in Turkey are, in descending order, Istanbul, Ankara, Izmir, Bursa, Adana, Konya, Antalya, and Mersin. Those cities made up only 44% (nearly 19 million) of registered voters in the 2007 elections. The JDP, except in Izmir and Mersin, ranked first by receiving the following vote percentages in the 2007 general elections: Istanbul, 45.2%; Ankara, 47.5%; Izmir, 30.5%; Bursa, 50.8%; Adana, 36.9%; Konya, 65.3%; Antalya, 34%; and Mersin, 27.2%. In the 2007 general elections, the RPP ranked first in Izmir by receiving 35.5% of the votes, while the NAP ranked first in Mersin by receiving 30.6% of the votes. See the Turkish Statistics Institute Web site, http://www.tuik.gov.tr (accessed September 10, 2007).

[213] The total number of registered voters in these 3 provinces was 12,855,150. See http://www.tuik.gov.tr (accessed September 10, 2007).

[214] Based on data available at the High Election Board Web site, http://www.ysk.gov.tr (accessed September 10, 2007).

Only 51.4 percent responded that they would be voting for the JDP because it was the party ideologically closest to their views.[215] These results provide further evidence of the expansion of the JDP's appeal beyond the Islamist movement.

Between 2003 and June 2007, the JDP government and its municipalities regularly distributed selective material incentives (food, clothing, and financial assistance; health services; scholarships and free schoolbooks) amounting to more than 3.3 billion YTL (new Turkish liras).[216] More than six million families regularly received food packages amounting to 322 million YTL, along with 4.4 million tons of coal.[217] The JDP also reformed the health care system and constructed 270,000 units of community housing for low- and middle-income people in eighty-one provinces. The party improved the conditions of public-sector workers by increasing their wages and by granting them full-time positions; it also increased scholarships to needy students by 200 percent. On the eve of the elections, the party postponed the rural sector's debt repayment to the state and increased the rates of state subsidies for certain agricultural products.[218] The JDP thus provided some selective material incentives for some rural voters.

The appeal of the JDP may also have been broadened, inadvertently, by the series of talks delivered during the election campaign by Necmettin Erbakan, honorary chair of the traditional Islamists' FP. He condemned the JDP as no longer being an Islamist party.[219] This may have convinced some secular, conservative, and disaffected voters that the JDP, despite its roots in political Islam, had by this time become a center-right party. Despite Erbakan's effort to deny the JDP an Islamist mantle, however, many Islamic brotherhoods and congregations declared that they would vote for the JDP.[220] In the end, as was the case in the 2002 general elections, a majority of the Islamist segment of the electorate voted for the JDP. Erbakan's FP received only 2.3 percent of the votes.[221] The JDP secured the support of Islamists, the urban poor, and more traditional rural populations in the 2007 general elections, thus achieving a significant increase in its vote totals.

---

[215] "Oylar kime, neden verildi" [To whom and why the votes were given], *Milliyet*, July 26, 2007.

[216] In August 2007, the dollar/YTL exchange rate was approximately 1:1.33.

[217] "Yaz ortasında kömür yardımı" [Coal assistance in the mid-summer], *Milliyet*, July 3, 2007; "AKP'den yardım yağmuru!" [Assistance shower from the JDP], *Milliyet*, July 16, 2007; and "İşte AKP yardımlarının faturası" [Cost of JDP's assistance], *Milliyet*, July 21, 2007.

[218] "AKP'nin 10 altın vuruşu" [The JDP's ten golden blows], *Milliyet*, July 24, 2007.

[219] Devrim Sevimay's interview with Necmettin Erbakan: "AKP seçilse de dağılır" [The JDP dissolves, even if it is elected], *Milliyet*, July 2, 2007; "Saadet'ten AKP'lilere: Beyaz imam hatipliler" [From the Felicity Party to the JDP parliamentarians: You are white imam-hatips], *Milliyet*, July 5, 2007.

[220] Ömer Erbil, "Tarikatlar, dini cemaatler ve 22 Temmuz 1-5" [The Islamic brotherhoods and congregations and July 22], *Milliyet*, July 10-14, 2007.

[221] The FP received 820,289 votes.

The success of the JDP in the conservative, Kurdish-populated regions of eastern and southeastern Turkey suggests that ethnic Kurdish nationalism was less important in influencing voting than Islamic brotherhoods and congregations, or local tribal families (*aşiretler*). The JDP's invocation of Islam as a basis for unity and stability in the country strongly attracted the electorate in the eastern and southeastern regions. The JDP, like its predecessors the WP and the VP, supports the idea of introducing a federal system in Turkey, which would make it easy to implement Islamist policies on a regional or provincial basis by eliminating centralized state control over the country. But the JDP's support for the idea of federalism also seems to have appealed to Kurdish nationalists who seek to establish a Kurdish federation in eastern and southeastern Anatolia. The appeal of the JDP in the eastern and southeastern regions was also strengthened by its efforts to construct roads and bring electricity, aimed at developing these economically backward regions.[222]

During its election campaign, the center-left RPP accused the JDP of posing "an Islamist threat." It also accused JDP ministers and parliamentarians, including Prime Minister Erdoğan, of corruption. But the RPP's elitist understanding of secularism – according to which Turkish society should entirely adopt a Western, liberal lifestyle, leaving only a minimal role for Islam – was at odds with the conservative Muslim value structure embraced by an important segment of Turkish society. The failure of the RPP to offer a convincing socioeconomic program further contributed to the party's electoral failure. It did not receive any significant support from poor voters. The RPP received 20.9 percent of the vote largely because of the election alliance it formed with the center-left DLP. In the July 2007 polls cited in the preceding text, 64.6 percent of respondents who declared their support for the RPP said they were doing so because they were worried about the republic and secularism, while 58.6 percent considered the party ideologically closest to their political views.[223] Although the RPP Chair Deniz Baykal argued that his party had been successful in the elections, a group of dissidents within the RPP sharply disagreed, pointing to the decline in the number of the party's seats in parliament, from 178 in 2002 to 99 in 2007 (currently 98 as the result of the defection of one parliamentarian who became an independent), and suggested that Baykal should not only resign from his post, but also leave politics.[224]

The right-wing nationalist NAP received 14.3 percent of the votes and reentered the parliament after a four-and-a-half-year absence. The party lost its traditional conservative/rural voter base in central and eastern Anatolia and the Black Sea region to the JDP, but improved its performance in comparison

---

[222] Taha Akyol, "Sandıktan çıkan mesajlar" [Messages that came out of the ballot boxes], *Milliyet*, July 23, 2007; Güneri Civaoğlu, "Baykal'ın bekleyiş nedeni" [Baykal's reason for waiting], *Milliyet*, July 24, 2004.
[223] "Oylar kime, neden verildi," *Milliyet*, July 26, 2007.
[224] "Sol ağır yenilgiyi tartışıyor" [Left discusses the heavy defeat], *Milliyet*, July 24, 2007; "Muhaliflerden sert çıkış" [Dissidents' firm opposition], *Milliyet*, July 25, 2007.

The Justice and Development Party Mobilizes

with the 2002 elections, when it received only 8.4 percent of the vote.[225] During the election campaign, the NAP clearly stated that, once it became the governing party, it would bring an end to PKK terrorism by taking necessary measures as suggested by the military (e.g., a possible cross-border operation against PKK camps in northern Iraq), and it unequivocally came out against the idea of federation in Turkey. The party also promised that Turkey would not grant any concessions with respect to Cyprus or the Armenian issue in return for EU membership. These positions attracted voters who were particularly concerned about the preservation of the Turkish state's unitary character. According to the July 2007 poll cited in the preceding text, 59.6 percent of respondents who intended to vote for the NAP reported they were doing so because it would solve the problem of PKK terrorism, while 56.6 percent asserted that the party was ideologically closest to their views.[226]

THE JUSTICE AND DEVELOPMENT PARTY MOBILIZES AGAINST THE SECULAR-DEMOCRATIC STATE

Following its electoral victory in the 2007 general elections, the JDP abandoned its policy of seeking consensus with liberals, mainly the pro-Western businessmen's association TÜSİAD and the secular-oriented media. And the party focused on two issues: first, preparing a new constitution, what the JDP called a "Civil Constitution;" and second, lifting the ban on female students wearing Islamic headscarf (*türban*) at universities. The JDP mostly kept what the new constitution would propose away from public debate. The party regarded the "Civil Constitution" as a means to lift the Islamic headscarf ban at universities, as it became clear in January 2008 that one of the propositions of the draft constitution was lifting this ban.[227]

While the Islamic headscarf issue became the center of attention of academicians, policy makers, and the media, it should be noted that following its electoral victory in the 2007 general elections, the JDP mobilized against the secular-democratic state by exerting its power in executive and legislative branches. The party was successful in some of its initiatives favoring the Islamist social movement's mobilization. The JDP-dominated parliament's election of Abdullah Gül as president in August 2007,[228] opened up an additional political opportunity enabling the party to mobilize the Islamist social movement. Unlike his prosecular predecessor Sezer,[229] President Gül approved most of the JDP's bills and

---

[225] "Oy depolarında hüsran" [Disappointment in ballot depots], *Milliyet*, July 23, 2007.
[226] "Oylar kime, neden verildi," *Milliyet*, July 26, 2007.
[227] "İşte sivil anayasa taslağı" [Here is the draft civil constitution], *Zaman*, January 3, 2008; "Anayasa taslağı Başbakan'da" [Draft constitution is at the prime minister], *Milliyet*, January 4, 2008.
[228] "Abdullah Gül 11. Cumhurbaşkanı" [Abdullah Gül is the eleventh president], *Hürriyet*, August 28, 2007. Gül received 339 votes out of 448 participated parliamentarians in the voting.
[229] *Hürriyet*, May 3, 2005; "Sezer'den mesajlı veto" [Sezer's veto is with a message], *Sabah*, March 30, 2007.

appointments of high-ranking bureaucrats into key state institutions.[230] Thus, under Gül's presidency, the JDP appointed *imam-hatip* (prayer leader and preacher) graduates and Islamic brotherhood members as high-ranking civil servants in public administration.[231]

The JDP also attempted at taking control of the judiciary. For example, in October 2007, the party, by mobilizing Ministries of International Affairs and Justice, tried to close down the Union of Judges and Prosecutors, an association that defends the judiciary's independence of the legislature and the executive. In fact, one of the propositions of the draft "Civil Constitution" was that freedom of judges and prosecutors to found an association could be restricted.[232] In December 2007, following President Gül's approval, the JDP amended the Law on Judges and Prosecutors, which required that all judicial candidates be interviewed by the Ministry of Justice.[233] The Union of Turkish Bar Associations protested the new law with the participation of more than ten thousand lawyers, prosecutors, and judges on the grounds that it would curtail the judiciary's independence by creating a JDP-controlled judiciary.[234]

The JDP successfully opened up new political opportunities favoring the Islamist media. For example, the JDP successfully utilized legal means to transfer Sabah-ATV, the country's second largest media conglomerate, to Ahmet Çalık, a pro-JDP businessman. In fact, Berat Albayrak, the prime minister's son-in-law, is chief executive of the Çalık conglomerate. In April 2007, Sabah-ATV owners' improper business practices led a national regulator to take control of the media conglomerate. In December 2007, the regulator sold Sabah-ATV to the Çalık conglomerate, which was the sole bidder at the auction. The Çalık conglomerate made the $1.1 billion purchase in April 2008 by receiving credits from two state-owned banks ($750 million) and from a Qatari company ($125 million) that gave it a 25 percent stake of

---

[230] "Sezer'in vetolu bürokratlarını, Gül atamaya başladı" [Gül has started to appoint bureaucrats who were vetoed by Sezer], *Milliyet*, September 18, 2007; "Sezer'in veto ettiği bir bürokrata daha atama" [Another appointment of a bureaucrat who was vetoed by Sezer], *Milliyet*, November 14, 2007; "Cumhurbaşkanı Gül hükümetten geleni onayladı" [President Gül approved all of the JDP's proposals], *Milliyet*, January 2, 2008; "Gül, 202 atama kararnamesi onaylamış" [Gül approved 202 appointments], *Milliyet*, January 17, 2008; "Gül, Sezer'in seçmediğini atadı" [Gül appointed people who were vetoed by Sezer], *Milliyet*, August 19, 2008; and "AKP'nin en rahat yılı" [The smoothest year for the JDP], *Cumhuriyet*, August 27, 2008.

[231] "Din adamları tıbbi etik kuruluna giriyor" [Religious experts are becoming members of medical ethics commission], *Milliyet*, December 26, 2007; Meral Tamer, "Bürokratları artık şeyhler mi belirliyor?" [Are sheiks determining bureaucrats?], *Milliyet*, December 29, 2007.

[232] *Milliyet*, October 17, 2007.

[233] "Tartışmalı yasa geçti" [The disputed law has been approved], *Milliyet*, December 2, 2007.

[234] "Avukat, hakim ve savcılardan protesto eylemi" [A protest gathering by lawyers, judges, and prosecutors], *Milliyet*, December 9, 2007. In March 2008, following the Union of Judges and Prosecutors' application, the Council of State overturned the new Law on Judges and Prosecutors. See *Radikal*, March 8, 2008.

Sabah-ATV.[235] Thus, the JDP during its second term as the party of government was quite successful in creating political opportunities for the Islamist social movement's mobilization.

The JDP's control over universities also started. In December 2007 President Gül appointed Professor Yusuf Ziya Özcan, who was criticized in secular circles for being pro-JDP, as chair of the Higher Education Board when his prosecular predecessor's term came to an end.[236] Professor Özcan, shortly after his appointment as the board chair, declared that all prohibitions at universities, including the Islamic headscarf ban, would come to an end.[237] The board chair created a pro-JDP cadre at the institution.[238] Thus, except for a number of prosecular board members, who were former President Sezer's appointees, the institution has no longer been playing its traditional role of guarding secularism at universities.[239]

In the winter of 2008, the JDP – having Professor Özcan and President Gül as elite allies – focused on lifting the Islamic headscarf ban. It should be noted that Prime Minister Erdoğan acknowledged that the Islamic headscarf is a political symbol by stating, "Can you accept that wearing of *türban* is a crime, even if it is worn as a political symbol? We will solve this problem in the shortest possible time."[240] In the JDP's quest for Islamic headscarf freedom at universities, the right-wing NAP, which appeals particularly to religious-conservative/Islamic and nationalist segment of the electorate, emerged as the main supporting political party in the parliament.[241] The NAP chair, Devlet Bahçeli, proposed to the JDP an amendment in the present constitution as a resolution of the Islamic headscarf issue instead of waiting for preparation of the new

---

[235] "TMSF ATV ve Sabah'a el koydu" [The national regulator took control of Sabah-ATV], *Hürriyet*, April 1, 2007; "Sabah-ATV Çalık grubuna satıldı" [Sabah-ATV was sold to the Çalık conglomerate], *Hürriyet*, December 5, 2007; "Sabah ve ATV resmen Çalık'ın" [Sabah-ATV officially belongs to the Çalık conglomerate], *Yeni Şafak*, April 26, 2008; and "Circulation wars," *The Economist*, May 8, 2008. Serhat Albayrak, Berat Albayrak's brother, became Sabah-ATV media groups' executive chief. The prime minister's media adviser, Ahmet Tezcan, resigned from his post and became Sabah-ATV media group executive board's adviser in September 2008. See *Vatan*, September 11, 2008. For pro-JDP media conglomerates see Mehmet Y. Yılmaz, "Başbakan'ın sevdiği gazeteler ve sahipleri" [Newspapers and their owners that the prime minister likes], *Hürriyet*, September 17, 2008.

[236] "İşte Gül ile yeni YÖK Başkanı arasındaki bağlantı" [The relationship between Gül and the new Higher Education Board chair], *Hürriyet*, December 10, 2007; "Bütün yasaklar kalkacak" [All prohibitions will be lifted], *Milliyet*, December 12, 2007. For the JDP's support for Professor Özcan during his chairmanship see "İki YÖK Başkanı arasındaki farkı bulun!" [Find the difference between two Higher Education Board Chairs!], *Radikal*, March 11, 2008.

[237] "Bütün yasaklar kalkacak," *Milliyet*, December 12, 2007; "Üniversiteler yasaklarla değil bilimle uğraşacaklar" [Universities will focus on science instead of prohibitions], *Yeni Şafak*, December 12, 2007.

[238] *Milliyet*, February 20, 2008.

[239] Since board members are appointed for 4 years, by 2011 there will be no President Sezer appointees left at the institution. See "YÖK Başkanı Özcan ekibini kuruyor" [Higher Education Board Chair Özcan is forming his own cadre], *Radikal*, February 20, 2008.

[240] "Yeni türban çıkışı" [A new rise for supporting türban], *Milliyet*, January 15, 2008.

[241] "MHP: Oyuncaklarını aldık" [The NAP: We got the JDP's political leverage], *Milliyet*, January 19, 2008.

constitution.²⁴² Erdoğan, having secured the NAP's support in the parliament, which provided a sufficient quorum to pass a bill on the Islamic headscarf, focused on lifting the ban at universities without waiting for the preparation of the "Civil Constitution."²⁴³ It should be noted that the JDP's quest for Islamic headscarf freedom at universities was only a first step in the party's ultimate goal of lifting the *türban* ban at state institutions. As Hüsnü Tuna, JDP parliamentarian, asserted, "When the time is ripe, our goal is lifting the ban on female state personnel wearing *türban* as well. I think that it is a shame to have such a ban."²⁴⁴

The JDP's Islamic headscarf initiative led not only the countermobilization of the judiciary, but also of the center-left RPP, some university faculty and presidents, some media, and some secular-oriented civil society associations. It is important to note that unlike during the February 28 process of 1997, when the military countermobilized against the WP, this time the military did not countermobilize against the JDP despite the party's endeavors to mobilize the Islamist social movement were bolder than those of its predecessor. The military, which has been harshly criticized mainly by Islamists and liberals for intervening in politics, seems to have refrained from commenting on the JDP's mobilizing of the Islamist social movement. Thus, unlike during the February 28 process, this time it was the judiciary (the Constitutional Court, the Supreme Court of Appeals, and the Council of State) representing the secular state sector that countermobilized against the JDP.

On January 17, Abdurrahman Yalçınkaya, chief public prosecutor, warned the JDP that "political parties cannot aim at changing the Republic's principle of secularism and they cannot initiate activities and make statements as such."²⁴⁵ Likewise, the Council of State declared that Islamic headscarf freedom would be incompatible with the constitution's principle of secularism.²⁴⁶

The JDP and the NAP agreed on a bill²⁴⁷ that provided Islamic headscarf freedom at universities except the police academy and military schools. Despite the judiciary's warnings²⁴⁸ and uneasiness of the secular segment of

---

[242] "Türbanın çözümü kolay" [Solution of the türban problem is easy], *Milliyet*, January 17, 2008.
[243] Ibid.
[244] "Tuna kişisel görüşümü söyledim" [Tuna: I stated my personal view], *Yeni Şafak*, January 26, 2008; "Hedef memura türban izni" [The goal is lifting the ban on türban for female state employees], *Milliyet*, January 26, 2008.
[245] "Yargıtay Cumhuriyet Başsavcısı Yalçınkaya'dan türbana izin uyarısı" [Chief Public Prosecutor Yalçınkaya's türban warning], *Milliyet*, January 17, 2008; "Yargıtay: Öneri laik üniter yapıya aykırı" [The Supreme Court of Appeals: The proposal is against the secular-unitary order], *Yeni Şafak*, January 18, 2008.
[246] "Danıştay da türban konusunda uyardı: Toplumsal barışı zedeler" [The Council of State warned as well regarding the türban issue: It harms the societal peace], *Milliyet*, January 18, 2008.
[247] "Erdoğan mutabakatı doğruladı" [Erdoğan confirmed the agreement], *Yeni Şafak*, January 24, 2008.
[248] "Yargıtaydan türban eleştirisi" [The Supreme Court of Appeals' türban criticism], *Milliyet*, February 4, 2008; "Yargıtay Başkanı Gerçeker: Türkiye ortaçağ karanlığına dönmeyecektir" [The Supreme Court of Appeals Chair Gerçeker: Turkey will not return to the darkness of the Middle Ages], *Milliyet*, February 7, 2008.

the society,[249] the parliament approved the bill on February 9 by 411 votes against 103 votes.[250] This led to the countermobilization of the judiciary against the JDP.

On March 14, the Chief Public Prosecutor Yalçınkaya filed a case with the Constitutional Court demanding to outlaw the JDP for being "a center of antisecular activities" and ban seventy-one of the party's members from politics for five years.[251] Yalçınkaya, in support of his application, referred to the party's Islamizing of the national education and its advocacy of illegal Quran courses and *imam-hatip* high schools; the JDP's establishment of a political Islamist cadre at state institutions by appointing Islamists to high-ranking positions; the JDP-controlled municipalities' banning of selling and consuming of alcohol under the guise of protection of the youth and public health; the party's Islamic headscarf initiative at universities; the party's advocacy of wearing of Islamic headscarf by female state personnel at state institutions; and the JDP's initiatives to undermine secularism by exerting its power in the executive and legislative branches as well as speeches and actions of several JDP members, including some in high office, against secularism.[252] Prosecutor Yalçınkaya asserted that the JDP was a continuation of the WP and argued that the Turkish Republic had never faced the threat of political Islam to this extent in its history.[253]

Prime Minister Erdoğan, having faced the countermobilization of the judiciary, successfully reframed his political rhetoric in order to turn the debate as a struggle between the public and the judiciary. On March 15, Prime Minister Erdoğan criticized the prosecutor by citing the Quran's *Araf* verse, which states that people who refuse to accept religion are like cattle. Erdoğan called the prosecutor's initiative "an act taken against the nation's will."[254]

On March 31, the Constitutional Court unanimously accepted Prosecutor Yalçınkaya's indictment to outlaw the JDP, while accepting the prosecutor's indictment to ban President Gül from politics for five years along with seventy JDP members by a vote of majority.[255] Prime Minister Erdoğan once again

---

[249] *Milliyet*, January 29–30, 2008; "Kadın dernekleri Anıtkabir'de" [Women's associations are at (Atatürk's) mausoleum], *Milliyet*, February 2, 2008; and *Yeni Şafak*, February 9, 2008.

[250] "Erdoğan: Milli irade tecelli etti" [Erdoğan: The national will was implemented], *Yeni Şafak*, February 9, 2008. In June 2008, the Constitutional Court overturned the constitutional amendments lifting the Islamic headscarf ban at universities by 9 votes to 2. See "Türban yargıdan döndü" [The judiciary overturned the türban amendment], *Milliyet*, June 6, 2008. Haşim Kılıç, Constitutional Court chair, and Sacit Adalı, Constitutional Court member, voted for the constitutional amendments that enabled *türban* freedom. As of this writing, 8 of 11 Constitutional Court members were appointed by prosecular former President Sezer. See "Sekiz üyeyi Sezer atadı" [Eight members were appointed by Sezer], *Radikal*, March 15, 2008.

[251] "AKP'ye kapatma davası" [Closure case for the JDP], *Milliyet*, March 14, 2008.

[252] T. C. Anayasa Mahkemesi, *Anayasa Mahkemesi Kararı, Esas Sayısı: 2008/1 (Siyasi Parti Kapatma), Karar Sayısı: 2008/2, Davalı Adalet ve Kalkınma Partisi* [The Constitutional Court's decision on the Justice and Development Party] (Internet ed.).

[253] Ibid.

[254] "Ayetle cevap verdi" [He answered by citing the Quran's verse], *Radikal*, March 16, 2008; *Yeni Şafak*, March 16, 2008.

[255] "İddianameye onay" [Approval for the indictment], *Milliyet*, April 1, 2008. Four Constitutional Court members voted against President Gül's ban from politics, while 7 members voted for the ban.

criticized the prosecutor by restating the Quran's *Araf* verse and asserted that given the JDP's high rate of electoral support, the party was representing the nation's will, which should be respected by everyone.[256] Minister of Justice Mehmet Ali Şahin argued that the case to outlaw the JDP was based on Yalçınkaya's "unserious allegations." Thus, Şahin stated that he was expecting the Constitutional Court members to make the right decision on the case.[257]

It is interesting to note that following when Yalçınkaya filed the lawsuit, a number of people including prosecular prominent figures, such as İlhan Selçuk, editor of leftist daily *Cumhuriyet* newspaper; Professor Kemal Alemdaroğlu, former president of Istanbul University; and Doğu Perinçek, chair of leftist Workers' Party, were arrested on March 21 as suspects of Ergenekon terror organization. The commonality of these three arrested people was that they were staunch prosecular JDP critics.[258]

The Ergenekon case is based on an allegation that a number of nationalist-oriented organized crime bosses, along with intelligence officers, retired generals, military officers, journalists, university presidents, professors, politicians, businessmen, civil society association members, and artists tried to initiate a coup against the JDP government by resorting to violence. Ergenekon suspects were arrested (and some of them were detained) without an indictment and were mainly interrogated based on their private phone conversations, which the police wiretapped. Arrests of prominent secular-oriented JDP critics within the framework of the Ergenekon investigation raised suspicions regarding the JDP government for trying to suppress its prosecular critics by arresting (and in some cases detaining) them together with possible real criminals.[259]

A scandal that erupted on May 13 further raised the secular segment of the society's suspicions regarding the JDP's intentions. Osman Paksüt, Constitutional Court vice-chair, complained that he was followed by a civil police car and was under surveillance for the past two months.[260] (Later, Paksüt's wife was called to give testimony within the framework of the Ergenekon investigation.)[261] Both the RPP and the NAP criticized the JDP government for establishing a dictatorial state based on fear.[262] In June 2008, it became clear that following the application of the General Directorate of Security's Intelligence Bureau, in April 2007 Ankara Heavy Criminal Court authorized the

---

[256] "Başbakan yine Araf suresiyle eleştirdi" [The prime minister criticized again by the Quran's Araf verse], *Milliyet*, March 31, 2008.
[257] "İddialar ciddi değil" [Allegations are unserious], *Milliyet*, April 4, 2008.
[258] Gözaltı depremi [An earthquake of arrests], *Milliyet*, March 22, 2008.
[259] For the Ergenekon case see Soner Çağaptay, "Turkey Versus Turkey," *Wall Street Journal*, July 8, 2008; Michael Rubin, "Erdoğan, Ergenekon, and the Struggle for Turkey," *Mideast Monitor, American Enterprise Institute for Public Policy Research*, August 8, 2008.
[260] "İşte Paksüt soruları!" [Here are the Paksüt questions!], *Milliyet*, May 16, 2008.
[261] "Ferda Paksüt ifade verdi" [Ferda Paksüt gave testimony], *Milliyet*, August 28, 2008.
[262] "Devlet röntgenci olamaz" [The state cannot monitor its citizens] and "AKP korku diktatörlüğü oluşturuyor" [The JDP has been establishing a dictatorship based on fear], *Milliyet*, May 21, 2008.

police to wiretap all citizens' phone and e-mail conversations throughout the country.[263]

The RPP Chair Baykal asserted that the JDP created an Islamic brotherhood-based and a pro-JDP monitoring organization within the police composed of five thousand people.[264] (Later, Hakkı Süha Okay, RPP parliamentarian, asserted that the monitoring organization within the police were members of the *Nurcus'* Fetullah Gülen congregation.[265]) Binali Yıldırım, Minister of Transportation, while stating that it was impossible to wiretap all citizens, noted that it was impossible to prohibit illegal monitoring.[266] Furthermore, two specialists from Telecommunications Directorate (*Telekomünikasyon İletişim Başkanlığı*), during their presentation at the Parliament Human Rights Investigation Commission, argued that wiretapping for intelligence purposes in Turkey was not done only by legal means, and the police had a technical capability to independently wiretap all communications, including area monitoring.[267]

It is important to emphasize that unlike during the closure cases of the WP and the VP, the United States and particularly the EU continuously criticized the Turkish judiciary and Prosecutor Yalçınkaya for opening the lawsuit to outlaw the JDP. For example, in March 2008, U.S. State Department Bureau of European and Eurasian Affairs Spokesman Chase Beamer, by implying that the prosecutor's initiative was against the Turkish electorate's will, stated that Turkish electorate's will had to be respected.[268] Likewise, in June 2008, U.S. Deputy Assistant Secretary Matthew Bryza argued, "outlawing the party [JDP] would be a great pity. But, we cannot issue an ultimatum; this is an issue of Turkey."[269]

In March 2008, Olli Rehn, member of the European Commission Responsible for Enlargement, criticized Prosecutor Yalçınkaya and the Turkish judiciary on the grounds that in the 2007 general elections the Turkish public made its choice by voting for the JDP, thus the case to outlaw the party meant that the Turkish judiciary was not respecting democratic principles. Rehn also warned that if the JDP was outlawed, the EU might see the necessity to hold Turkey's EU membership negotiation process.[270] Likewise, Javier Solana, high

---

[263] "Biri bizi gözetliyor!" [Somebody is watching us!], *Milliyet*, June 1, 2008.
[264] "Baykal: Cemaat kadrolu dinleme düzeni kuruldu" [Baykal: An Islamic brotherhood-based monitoring organization was established], *Milliyet*, June 4, 2008.
[265] *Cumhuriyet*, August 17, 2008.
[266] "Ulaştırma Bakanı: Konuşursanız dinlenirsiniz" [Minister of Transportation: If you speak, you will be monitored], *Milliyet*, June 4, 2008.
[267] *Milliyet*, June 26, 2008.
[268] "ABD Dışişleri Bakanlığı: Seçmenlerin iradesine saygı gösterilmeli" [United States Foreign Affairs Ministry: The electorate's will should be respected], *Milliyet*, March 15, 2008.
[269] "Talihsizlik olur" [It will be a pity], *Yeni Şafak*, June 26, 2008; "Parti kapatmak talihsizlik ama ültimatom veremeyiz" [Outlawing the party would be a great pity. But we cannot issue an ultimatum], *Milliyet*, June 26, 2008.
[270] "Rehn'den 'normal demokrasi' uyarısı" [Rehn warned about "normal democracy"], *Milliyet*, March 16, 2008.

representative for the Common Foreign and Security Policy, secretary-general of the Council of the EU, argued that outlawing the JDP would damage Turkey's EU membership process, thus he hoped that the Constitutional Court members would make the right decision.[271]

In May 2008, the EU representatives' statements regarding the ongoing JDP lawsuit led Sumru Çörtoğlu, Council of State chair, to warn the EU representatives to respect the Turkish judiciary's independence.[272] Yet, in June 2008, Parliamentary Assembly of the Council of Europe declared that the JDP's closure would be a "judicial coup."[273] Prime Minister Erdoğan supported the EU's involvement in the lawsuit as an international actor.[274] In fact, the United States and particularly the EU, by criticizing the Turkish judiciary, acted as international elite allies of the JDP by providing it legitimacy that the party successfully seized upon for its mobilization to defend itself to the Turkish public. Yet, the JDP Vice-Chair Dengir Mir Mehmet Fırat's statement regarding Atatürk's reforms revealed the JDP high cadre's view on the secular republic and society. Fırat argued, "Turkish society has been traumatized. Overnight they were told to change their dress, their language. Their religious ways were dismantled."[275]

While tension between the JDP and the judiciary continued, a public poll that was conducted by A&G firm in June 2008 revealed that 53.3 percent of the respondents opposed the closure of the JDP. Only 34.3 percent of the respondents supported the closure of the party, while 12.4 percent of the respondents declared no opinion. Furthermore, 30.3 percent of the respondents stated that they would vote for the JDP, if an election was held; 30.2 percent were undecided; and 12.7 percent would vote for the RPP and 11.7 percent would vote for the NAP. Thus, the JDP, despite its Islamist mobilization against the secular state, would still rank first if elections were held.[276]

It is interesting to note that on July 1 when Prosecutor Yalçınkaya presented his indictment at the Constitutional Court, within the framework of the sixth round of the Ergenekon investigation, a number of people, including prominent secular JDP critics, such as journalist Mustafa Balbay, *Cumhuriyet* newspaper Ankara bureau chief; Ufuk Büyükçelebi, editor of *Tercüman* newspaper; Retired General Şener Eruygur, chair of the Pro-Atatürk Thinking Society and former commander of Gendarme Forces; Retired General Hurşit Tolon, an active member of secular civil society associations and former commander of the First Army; and Sinan Aygün, chair of Ankara Chamber of Commerce were

---

[271] "AK Parti kapatılırsa AB ile kriz çıkar" [Closure of the JDP will lead to a crisis with the EU], *Yeni Şafak*, April 9, 2008.
[272] "Türban eğitim hakkı değildir" [Türban is not an educational right], *Milliyet*, May 11, 2008.
[273] "AKPM'den denetim tehtidi" [Parliamentary Assembly of the Council of Europe's regulation threat], *Milliyet*, June 27, 2008.
[274] "AB, Türkiye'ye kayıtsız kalamaz" [The EU cannot turn a blind eye to Turkey], *Milliyet*, May 14, 2008.
[275] Sabrina Tavernise, "In Turkey, Bitter Feud Has Roots in History," *The New York Times*, June 22, 2008. See also the JDP's defense in *Milliyet*, June 17–18, 2008.
[276] "Dava sürecinde toplum ne diyor?" [What does the public think for the judicial process?], *Milliyet*, June 30, 2008.

arrested and some were detained, without an indictment, for being a member of the Ergenekon terror organization.[277]

The JDP's and the Islamist media's visible support for the Ergenekon arrests and detentions should be noted.[278] The JDP along with the Islamist media, on the one hand, harshly criticized Prosecutor Yalçınkaya and the Constitutional Court members for opening up to outlaw the JDP; on the other hand, the party expressed its support for Prosecutor Zekeriya Öz for conducting mass arrests and detentions during the Ergenekon investigation.[279] Prime Minister Erdoğan even declared the JDP members as prosecutors of the Ergenekon case.[280]

The mass arrests and detentions of prominent secular JDP critics further raised uneasiness of the secular segment of the society. For example, the RPP Chair Baykal criticized the arrests by arguing that they reminded coup periods and totalitarian regimes of Hitler and Stalin. Baykal also asserted that secular people in Turkey were now targets of the JDP and the Islamist media.[281]

The Constitutional Court decided on July 30 that the JDP was a center of antisecular activities by voting ten to one; Haşim Kılıç, the Constitutional Court chair, voted against the decision that the JDP was a center of antisecular activities and voted for rejecting the entire case.[282] The court, instead of outlawing the JDP, issued a judicial warning and penalized the party to pay back half of funds that it received from state treasury in 2008. While six court members voted for the JDP's closure, four members voted for issuing a judicial warning and financial penalty.[283] Thus, the JDP was not outlawed by one missing vote, and the Constitutional Court for the first time did not ban an Islamist political party. The court's explanation of its decision on the JDP case was ambiguous: on the one hand, it acknowledged the JDP as an Islamist political party and stated the actions and statements of JDP members were incompatible with the secularism principle. On the other hand, the court also emphasized that the JDP did not resort to violence and applied its party of government power in order to elevate the country to civilized Western democratic standards within the framework of Turkey's EU membership. The court also stated that the majority of the

---

[277] "Ankara güne şok gözaltılarla başladı" [Ankara started the day by shocking arrests], *Milliyet*, July 2, 2008; "Ergenekon'da büyük gözaltı" [A great raid of arrests in Ergenekon], *Zaman*, July 2, 2008. The police had the court order for arrests on June 29, 2008. Retired Generals Tolon and Eruygur were detained without an indictment. After falling down, Retired General Eruygur lost his consciousness and he was released for medical treatment. Former JDP parliamentarian Turhan Çömez could not be arrested during the sixth round of Ergenekon investigation on the grounds that he was in the United Kingdom. In April 2008, the JDP expelled Çömez for criticizing the party. On March 6, 2009, Balbay was detained.
[278] See *Yeni Şafak*, *Zaman*, *Milli Gazete*, and *Vakit*.
[279] "İddianame adımı" [An indictment step], *Milliyet*, July 2, 2008.
[280] "Ergenekon davasında biz de savcıyız!" [We are the prosecutors of the Ergenekon case!], *Yeni Şafak*, July 15, 2008.
[281] "Başbakan'ın kişisel davası" [The prime minister's personal case], *Cumhuriyet*, July 2, 2008.
[282] Kılıç, as a Constitutional Court member, also voted against the closure of the WP and the VP. Kılıç was appointed to the Constitutional Court in 1990 by former President Özal.
[283] "AKP'ye 'ciddi ihtar'" [A serious warning to the JDP], *Milliyet*, July 31, 2008.

electorate voted for the JDP in the 2002 and 2007 general elections; and this meant that majority of the public regarded the JDP's actions as legitimate.[284]

The Constitutional Court's decision did not cease the mobilization of the Islamist social movement. In the fall of 2008, violent Islamist attacks on people who did not pursue an Islamic way of life started. For example, catering services of a number of state schools, municipalities, and teachers' locals were closed down during Ramadan, and some people who did not fast and shopkeepers who sold alcohol were beaten; the latter incident was initiated by JDP-governed municipality police, including in Ankara's Keçiören district where the prime minister resides.[285]

A comprehensive survey that was conducted by Binnaz Toprak between December 2007 and July 2008 revealed that as a result of Islamists' infiltration into state bureaucracy and Islamic brotherhoods' financial and organizational strengthening in Turkey under the JDP rule, secular-oriented people were under the JDP-backed Islamist pressure and were facing Islamists' discrimination in their daily lives and workplaces.[286]

The extent that the JDP is immune from corruption seems to be questionable. In the summer and fall of 2008, a number of corruption scandals related to the JDP erupted. For example, Şaban Dişli, JDP vice-chair, was compelled to resign from his post following allegations that he was bribed by a businessman with the amount of 1 million dollars.[287] Yet, the most important corruption scandal was a German court decision on a Germany-based Turkish Islamist the Light House Association (*Deniz Feneri Derneği*) case in which the court sentenced the association's chair and managers to prison for embezzling charity money raised from the Turkish community in Germany amounting to 14.5 million euros and illegally transferring it to pro-JDP businessmen and Islamist TV channel Kanal 7 in Turkey. German authorities alleged that a JDP-appointed RTÜK (Supreme Board of Radio and Television) chair along with Kanal 7 managers illegally funneled the charity money from Germany to Turkey.[288]

---

[284] "Neden odak oldu, neden kapatılmadı" [Why the JDP became a center of antisecular activities and why it was not closed down], *Milliyet*, October 24, 2008; "Şiddet yok, kapatılamaz!" [The JDP could not be closed down since there is no act of violence!], *Yeni Şafak*, October 24, 2008.

[285] "İşte Başbakan'ın Keçiören'i" [This is the prime minister's Keçiören], *Cumhuriyet*, August 21, 2008; "Avukata oruç dayağı" [A lawyer was beaten for not fasting], *Milliyet*, September 6, 2008; and "Çankaya'da içki dayağına soruşturma" [Investigation on the beating for selling alcohol in Çankaya], *Milliyet*, September 23, 2008.

[286] Binnaz Toprak, İrfan Bozan, Tan Morgül, and Nedim Şener, *Türkiye'de Farklı Olmak: Din ve Muhafazakarlık Ekseninde Ötekileştirilenler* [Being Different in Turkey: Being Discriminated in the Axis of Religion and Conservatism] (Istanbul: Boğaziçi Üniversitesi, 2008), 6, 13–14.

[287] "AKP'li Dişli'ye ağır suçlama" [An allegation regarding the JDP's Dişli], *Milliyet*, August 12, 2008; "Dişli istifa etti" [Dişli resigned], *Yeni Şafak*, September 3, 2008.

[288] "Deniz Feneri'nde RTÜK Başkanı da var!" [The RTÜK chair is also involved in the Light House case], *Milliyet*, August 30, 2008; "Kanal 7'ye Fener desteği" [The Light House Association's support for Channel 7], *Cumhuriyet*, September 10, 2008; "Deniz Feneri davasında karar açıklandı], *Hürriyet*, September 17, 2008; and "Alman Savcı Lötz: Asil failler Türkiye'de" [The German Prosecutor Lötz: The real criminals, who are responsible for the Light House corruption, are in Turkey], *Milliyet*, September 17, 2008.

The Justice and Development Party Mobilizes

The Doğan media group's informing of the public regarding corruption cases like *Deniz Feneri* led Prime Minister Erdoğan to harshly criticize the media group.[289] Erdoğan even called the public to boycott newspapers that "do not report correctly."[290] The JDP also pressure journalists who criticize the party. For example, the JDP did not renew some journalists' accreditation enabling them to report from the prime ministry on the grounds that the journalists were not reporting objectively.[291] Following the JDP's suppressive policy toward the press, chairs of World Association of Newspapers and European Newspaper Publishers Association wrote a letter to Prime Minister Erdoğan to renew accreditations of the journalists.[292]

As of this writing, creation of a pro-JDP cadre at universities also continues under the chairmanship of Professor Özcan. President Gül mostly appointed pro-Islamic headscarf professors as university presidents.[293] In January 2009, five pro-secular Higher Education Board members issued a statement criticizing Professor Özcan for changing the board to a pro-JDP institution and appointing pro-JDP and pro-Islamic headscarf professors as university presidents or board members.[294]

While Islamist infiltration into state institutions continues under the JDP rule,[295] the party's pressures over its prominent secular critics continues to rise. As of this writing, mass arrests and detentions of prominent secular JDP critics along with former and possible criminals within the framework of the Ergenekon investigation continue.[296] For example, among the tenth raid of Ergenekon arrests there were also former Higher Education Board chair, Professor Kemal Gürüz; Professor Yalçın Küçük; former National Security Council chair, Retired General Tuncer Kılınç; former War College chair, Retired General Kemal Yavuz; and former justice adviser of the General Staff, Retired General Erdal Şenel.[297] Even Sabih Kanadoğlu, honorary chief public

---

[289] See Soner Çağaptay, "Turkey's Media War," *Newsweek*, September 20, 2008.
[290] "Bu gazeteleri evlerinize sokmayın" [Do not purchase these newspapers], *Milliyet*, September 19, 2008.
[291] "Başbakanlıktan akreditasyon açıklaması" [The prime ministry's accreditation explanation], *Hürriyet*, November 12, 2008; "Başbakanlık 6 gazeteciyi akredite etmedi" [The prime ministry did not renew accreditation of six journalists], *Zaman*, November 12, 2008.
[292] "Akreditasyonları derhal iade edin" [Renew the accreditations immediately], *Milliyet*, December 18, 2008.
[293] "Üniversiteler ayakta" [Universities are concerned], *Cumhuriyet*, August 7, 2008; "Üniversitede istifa depremi" [Protest resignations at universities], *Milliyet*, August 7, 2008; "Türbanın rövanşı" [The türban revenge], *Milliyet*, August 8, 2008; and "YÖK'ten tartışılacak liste" [The Higher Education Board's list causes debate], *Milliyet*, August 14, 2008.
[294] "YÖK muhalif görüşleri sindiriyor" [The Higher Education Board suppresses its critical voices], *Milliyet*, January 15, 2009.
[295] *Cumhuriyet*, September 8, 2008; "Liselinin psikolojisi ilahiyatçıya emanet" [A divinity professor will determine high school psychology course curriculum], *Milliyet*, October 14, 2008.
[296] *Milliyet*, September 20, 2008; *Milliyet*, September 23–5, 2008; *Cumhuriyet*, September 24, 2008; and *Yeni Şafak*, September 24, 2008.
[297] Another Ergenekon terror organization suspect Bedrettin Dalan, founder of Yeditepe University and former mayor of Istanbul, could not be arrested during the tenth raid on the grounds that he was in the United States.

prosecutor of the Supreme Court of Appeals and former chief public prosecutor of the Supreme Court of Appeals, was among the suspects. It is interesting to note that Kanadoğlu was accused of being an Ergenekon terror organization member along with İbrahim Şahin, former special action bureau deputy of General Directorate of Security, who was sentenced to prison for establishing a crime organization within the police force as a result of then Prosecutor Kanadoğlu's investigation. As a reaction to the Ergenekon investigation, Kanadoğlu stated that Turkey would never be a country of a religious dictatorship or dictatorship of any sort.[298] Arrests of a number of retired generals, who had high positions during the soft military intervention of 1997, along with Professor Gürüz, who was the board chair during the same period, as Ergenekon terror organization suspects, raised secular segment of the society's suspicions toward the JDP whether the party was utilizing the Ergenekon case in order to eliminate its prosecular opponents by including them with former and possible criminals.[299] The RPP Chair Baykal called the Ergenekon case "the JDP's political revenge operation" and maintained that Turkey was going through a regime change under the JDP rule and, similar to the cases of Hitler's Germany and Khomeini's Iran, society's essential principles and respected figures have started to be replaced.[300] Oktay Vural, NAP parliamentary group co-chair, argued that the JDP was utilizing the Ergenekon case as a means to suppress its political opponents. Vural also maintained that the JDP created special intelligence units within the state institutions that provide information to the prime minister.[301] Independent member of parliament and former prime minister Mesut Yılmaz argued that he was informed by some members of the General Directorate of Security alleging that *Nurcus*' Fetullah Gülen congregation members infiltrated into the police force's intelligence department.[302] Ömer Faruk Eminağaoğlu, chair of the Union of Judges and Prosecutors, argued that the monitoring of seventy million citizens as (Ergenekon) terror suspects would only occur in a police state and dictatorships under Hitler and Mussolini.[303] The military under leadership of the Chief of General Staff General İlker Başbuğ[304] also expressed its disturbance regarding the way that the

---

[298] "Dinci dikta yerleşemez" [Religious dictatorship cannot establish itself], *Cumhuriyet*, January 8, 2009. Kanadoğlu was not arrested, but the police searched his houses and seized a number of documents for investigation. Şahin was detained after his arrest.

[299] Güneri Civaoğlu, "Dalga değil tsunami" [Not a wave, but a tsunami], *Milliyet*, January 8, 2009; Derya Sazak, "10. dalga" [The Tenth Raid], *Milliyet*, January 8, 2009; Murat Yetkin, "Ergenekon çözülüyor mu, giderek dolaşıyor mu?" [Is Ergenekon solved or further getting complicated?], *Radikal*, January 8, 2009; and Oktay Ekşi, "Devlet terörü" [State terrorism], *Hürriyet*, January 8, 2009.

[300] "İntikam kokusu alıyorum" [This is a revenge], *Milliyet*, January 8, 2009.

[301] "Özel birim oluşturdular" [They (the JDP members) created a special intelligence organization], *Cumhuriyet*, December 11, 2008.

[302] "İstihbaratın Gülenci olduğu iddiası var" [There is an allegation that the intelligence is pro-Gülen], *Milliyet*, January 15, 2009.

[303] "Bunlar dikta yönetiminde olur" [Such things occur under a dictatorship], *Cumhuriyet*, January 13, 2009.

[304] General Başbuğ became the chief of the General Staff in August 2008.

The Justice and Development Party Mobilizes 273

Ergenekon investigation has been handled. The military stated that essential human rights, the protection of personal immunity until proven as guilty, and the right to have a just trial were violated in the investigation.³⁰⁵

Despite the uneasiness of the secular segment of the society, arrests and detentions within the framework of the Ergenekon investigation continued. Among the eleventh raid of Ergenekon arrests there were also prominent JDP critics such as Mustafa Özbek,³⁰⁶ Turkish Metal Syndicate chair, one researcher, and one journalist. Police also searched and seized documents of a JDP critic, TV channel A.R.T. (Eurasia), and a number of research centers. Like the previous Ergenekon investigations, in the eleventh raid, arrests and detentions were done without an indictment.³⁰⁷

While time will reveal the content and result of the ongoing Ergenekon case, the way that the investigation has been handled and the arrests and detentions of prominent prosecular JDP critics along with former and possible criminals created a society based on fear in Turkey. Furthermore, illegal monitoring of JDP's political opponents continues. For example, an interception device was found at the RPP's headquarters in Ankara. The RPP Chair Baykal argued that he did not trust the police for the investigation of the incident.³⁰⁸ As of this writing, the JDP did not take any satisfactory action against wiretappings and monitoring of citizens. Even the military had to utilize a special device as a measure against a possible monitoring during General Başbuğ's courtesy visit to the NAP.³⁰⁹

Under the JDP rule, Turkey's establishment of close relations with political Islamist regimes like Iran, Hamas, Sudan, and Saudi Arabia should also be noted. This became even more visible during Israel's military operation in Gaza during the winter of 2009. The JDP successfully framed the Israeli-Hamas conflict as a political opportunity in order to galvanize the Turkish public's support for the party in the wake of March 2009 local elections.³¹⁰ As a reaction to the Israeli offense, Prime Minister Erdoğan stated that sooner or later Israel would be punished for transgressing the rights of innocents in Gaza by using unbalanced force and that Israel's actions would lead to its own destruction.³¹¹ A series of mass demonstrations were separately organized by the JDP and the FP with participation of a number of Islamist civil society associations throughout Turkey; for example one demonstration in Istanbul drew two hundred thousand people, while another in Kurdish populated Diyarbakır province

---

³⁰⁵ "Genelkurmay: Hukuk ihlali var" [The General Staff: Rule of law is not applied], *Milliyet*, January 17, 2009.
³⁰⁶ Özbek was detained.
³⁰⁷ "Şok baskınlar" [Shocking arrests], *Milliyet*, January 22, 2009.
³⁰⁸ "CHP Genel Merkezi'nde böcek bulundu" [An interception device was found at the RPP's headquarters], *Radikal*, December 31, 2008; "Fikret Bila: Baykal polise güvenmiyor" [Baykal does not trust the police], *Milliyet*, January 3, 2009.
³⁰⁹ "Org. Başbuğ, Bahçeli'yi ziyaret etti" [General Başbuğ visited Bahçeli], *Hürriyet*, October 10, 2008.
³¹⁰ For the March 2009 local elections, see Banu Eligür, "Turkey's March 2009 Local Elections," *Turkish Studies* 10, no. 3 (September 2009): 469–96.
³¹¹ *Hürriyet*, January 4, 2009.

drew fifty thousand people.[312] Rhetoric of mass demonstrations was designed to evoke Islamist sentiments; slogans of hundreds of thousands were the same: "Damn Israel," "Jews are cursed," and "Zionist Israel and imperialist USA will drown in massacred babies' blood."[313] There were billboards accusing Jews of civilian deaths in Gaza. Demonstrations were successful in creating anti-Jewish sentiments among the Turkish public. For the first time, the Turkish Jewish community issued a public statement expressing their concern regarding its physical safety.[314] This was followed by five American Jewish civil society associations writing a letter to Prime Minister Erdoğan regarding their concern about safety of Turkish Jews, while criticizing the anti-Semitic slogans during the demonstrations and the Islamist media's showing of Jews as targets.[315]

The uneasiness of the secular segment of the society once more rose as a result of arrests and detentions of prominent secular JDP critics, without an indictment, as Ergenekon terror organization suspects within the framework of the twelfth round of the Ergenekon investigation. The last raid of Ergenekon investigation particularly focused on secular-oriented civil society associations, such as the Association for Supporting Modern Life [*Çağdaş Yaşamı Destekleme Derneği*], Modern Education Foundation [*Çağdaş Eğitim Vakfı*], pro-Atatürk Thinking Association [*Atatürkçü Düşünce Derneği*], and '68 Foundation [*68'liler Vakfı*]. Among the arrests and detentions there were executive members and staff of these secular civil society associations, such as Professor Ayşe Yüksel; secular-oriented university presidents, such as President of Başkent University Professor Mehmet Haberal, President of Giresun University Professor Osman Metin Öztürk, former President of Ondokuz Mayıs University Professor Ferit Bernay, former President of Uludağ University Professor Mustafa Yurtkuran, and former President of İnönü University Professor Fatih Hilmioğlu; secular-oriented professors, such as Professor Erol Manisalı; and a number of students who received scholarship from the Modern Education Foundation.[316] It seems

---

[312] "İsrail'e öfke büyüyor" [Anger toward Israel is increasing], *Milliyet*, January 3, 2009; "Diyarbakır'da 50 bin kişi İsrail'i protesto etti" [Fifty thousand people protested Israel in Diyarbakır], *Hürriyet*, January 4, 2009. See also "İsrail'e öfke" [Anger toward Israel], *Milliyet*, January 5, 2009; Kadri Gürsel, "AKP diplomasisi ile artık daha Ortadoğuluyuz" [We are more Middle Eastern as a result of the JDP's diplomacy], *Milliyet*, January 22, 2009.

[313] "İsrail'e öfke büyüyor," *Milliyet*, January 3, 2009; "Filistin'le dayanışma mitingi başladı" [Solidarity with Palestine political gathering has started], *Milliyet*, January 4, 2009; "İsrail'e öfke," *Milliyet*, January 5, 2009; and "Her yer Filistin, hepimiz Filistinliyiz mitingi başladı" ["Everywhere is Palestine, we are all Palestinians" political gathering has started], *Milliyet*, January 18, 2009.

[314] "Museviler endişeli" [Jews in Turkey are worried], *Milliyet*, January 16, 2009.

[315] "Yahudi lobisi ayakta" [The (American) Jewish lobby is concerned], *Milliyet*, January 23, 2009.

[316] "Çağdaş Yaşam Derneği hedefte" [The Association for Supporting Modern Life is the target], *Milliyet*, April 14, 2009; "Çağdaşlığa darbe" [A coup against modernization], *Cumhuriyet*, April 14, 2009; "12. dalga sorgulanıyor" [The 12th (Ergenekon) round is being questioned], *Milliyet*, April 16, 2009; *Milliyet*, April 17–18, 2009; and *Cumhuriyet*, April 15–19, 2009. The Association for Supporting Modern Life Chair Professor Türkan Saylan was not arrested, but the police searched her house and seized a number of documents for investigation. Professor Saylan, who was a cancer patient, died in May 2009.

that the JDP during its second term as the party of government has successfully mobilized against the secular-democratic state.

CONCLUSION

The coming to power of the WP in 1996 represented a significant political success of the Islamist social movement in Turkey. The electoral victory of the WP was based on the strong organizational networks established by Islamist entrepreneurs; the space created for their organizing activities by the TIS as a de facto state ideology; and the successful framing of the malfunctioning state in a manner that appealed to grievances in certain sectors of the secular population. As a result, Islamists expanded their support base beyond merely Islamist constituencies. Even then, they were not invited to form the government until the secular center-right coalition government failed. Only then was the WP invited to join the government.

Once in power, the WP and the Islamist social movement behind it overestimated its own strength and underestimated the power and willingness of the military to act against the Islamist movement. Incautious behaviors of Islamist entrepreneurs led to the soft military intervention of February 1997, and the legal banning of the WP in January 1998 and of the VP in June 2001. However, these actions did not reduce the organizational and socioeconomic appeal of the Islamist social movement for the Turkish electorate. These actions did not redress the characteristics of the malfunctioning state, and the POS it created for Islamism.

Islamist entrepreneurs proved adept at framing new issues such as membership in the EU to their advantage, and in 2002 they entered the government under the banner of the JDP, the fifth in a succession of Islamist political parties competing for an electoral support in Turkey that have played by established rules of democratic competition for electoral support.

7

The Islamist Social Movement Today and Prospects for the Future

The question posed at the beginning of this study asked why Islamism, which has been present in Turkish politics since the 1970s, has achieved electoral success, and assumed the powers of government, only in the 1990s. This study demonstrates that the rise to power of the Islamist social movement in Turkey can be attributed to three factors: first, the emergence of a political opportunity structure (POS), created primarily by the adoption of the Turkish-Islamic Synthesis (TIS) by the military regime in the aftermath of the 1980 intervention; second, the presence of movement entrepreneurs with significant organizational and other resources; and, third, the successful framing of issues by entrepreneurs to expand the appeal of the Islamist social movement beyond the population of Islamists to secular but socioeconomically aggrieved voters.

The Islamist movement in Turkey is largely nonviolent. One of the major theoretical findings of this study is that political context constrains movement entrepreneurs' framing activities, even if the movement is antisystemic. In the Turkish case, the existence of a secular-democratic regime and its acceptance by the vast majority of citizens constrained Islamist entrepreneurs' strategies for mobilization. But it also created an opportunity to be exploited. Islamist entrepreneurs, while utilizing social networks to overthrow the secular order by Islamizing the society from below, also mobilized by forming a political party. The political process model (PPM) proposes that movement entrepreneurs do not determine their goals and strategies for mobilization in a vacuum. The political context – that is, the presence of a favorable political opportunity for mobilization – along with the movement's organizational dynamics and the framing of movement activists play a crucial role in social movement mobilization. The Turkish case thus suggests an important amendment to social movement theory.

The Islamist social movement in Turkey demonstrates that, given a democratic and open POS, social movement mobilization need not take the form of antisystem or extrasystemic social protest activity, even if the ultimate goal of the movement is to overthrow the system. Under these conditions, social movements can also mobilize by becoming a political party. Mobilization in the form of a political party is one of the underdeveloped areas in social movement theory. This study of Islamist mobilization in Turkey contributes to developing our understanding of this form of social movement mobilization.

During the first phase of the mobilization of political Islam in Turkey (1980–91), the secular military served as an inadvertent elite ally of the Islamist social movement by introducing the TIS – a mixture of Sunni Islam and nationalism – as the official state ideology, which opened up a social and political space for Islamist mobilization in Turkey. Following the 1980 coup, the military eliminated leftists and repressed ultranationalists. But the Islamist movement, which was a lesser threat in the eyes of the military at the time, continued to survive under the military regime (1980–3). The TIS represented a fundamental shift in state ideology away from the Kemalist understanding of secularism, which used state control to relegate religion to the private sphere.

Following the 1980 coup, the military no longer saw Islam as a force to be restrained; on the contrary, it was a useful tool that was to be encouraged as a means of countering the leftist threat. The military implemented the TIS by introducing Sunni Islam as a mandatory course in public schools (1982) and by permitting *imam-hatip* (prayer leader and preacher) graduates' entrance into all departments of universities. Adoption of the TIS as a de facto official ideology represented an important shift in the political opportunity for Islamists in the 1980s. The military opened the door to participation, influence, and organizational activity by Islamist intellectuals, clergy, activists, and politicians; in other words, the organizational and mobilizational activities of the Islamist entrepreneurs.

The center-right Motherland Party (MP), which ruled the country from 1983 to 1991, also acted as an elite ally of the Islamist social movement by maintaining the TIS through interpersonal ties and preexisting social networks, based in part on the *Nakşibendi* Islamic brotherhood. Under MP rule, Saudi capital flowed into Turkey through Saudi and Kuwaiti finance houses established with the cooperation of key members of the *Nakşibendi* brotherhood and influential MP members. This played a crucial role in the creation of a wealthy Islamist business class. The MP also conducted a program of *imam-hatip* schools, Quran courses, and mosques. These developments contributed to strengthening the organizational, financial, and human resources of the movement.

The Islamist movement in Turkey proselytizes an Islamic way of life, in the belief that the spread of Islamic piety will lead to an Islamic society and the transformation of Turkey into an Islamic state. Consistent with social movement theory, mosques, *imam-hatip* schools, Quran courses, and civil society organizations that belong to the Islamist business class serve as social networks facilitating the recruitment process. They provide an organizational network and reshape the identities of participants according to the Islamists' politicized interpretation of Islam. By the 1990s, a parallel Islamic sector, comprising the Islamist business class and Islamist intellectuals, emerged next to Erbakan's Welfare Party (WP) apparatus. Thus, during the first phase of the Islamist mobilization, Islamist entrepreneurs seized upon the social and political space provided by the military and by MP rule in order to strengthen the WP's organizational networks.

By the 1990s, the socioeconomic and political malfunctioning of the secular state had become a persistent problem, creating large segments of disaffected secular voters available for mobilization. Islamist entrepreneurs, having strong organizational networks, successfully seized upon the malfunctioning state as an additional political opportunity during the second phase of the mobilization of political Islam in Turkey (since 1991). Islamist entrepreneurs engaged in face-to-face contacts and distributed selective and soft incentives to spread the party's message of the "Just Order" in the 1990s. Islamist entrepreneurs used the global wave of democratization following the end of the cold war as an additional political opportunity to frame their political Islamist agenda utilizing a liberal tool kit to articulate the "Just Order," even though that appeal was deeply rooted in Islamism. The existence of multiple levels of governance, and therefore electoral competition, made Turkey an "open" system; that is, it constituted an additional dimension of the POS exploited by the Islamist social movement. The electoral victory of the WP at the municipal level, and the success of WP governance in the municipalities, convinced the urban electorate – which constituted 25 to 30 percent of the entire Turkish electorate – that the "Just Order" was not an empty slogan. Successful governance of major urban areas turned the Islamist movement into a viable alternative to the malfunctioning secular state. The Islamist social movement in Turkey thus demonstrates the dynamic relationship between movement entrepreneurs and their conscious framing of movement principles, on the one hand, and the existing POS, on the other, that is at the core of successful social movement mobilization. The Islamist social movement in Turkey is a clear demonstration of the centrality of "agency" to successful movement mobilization.

But, the Turkish case also illustrates the dangers of partial success, and an excessive orientation toward agency, for a social movement. The WP's emergence as the largest party and its entry into the government following the 1995 general elections led Islamist entrepreneurs to overestimate their power vis-à-vis the secular-democratic state structure. Persistent contradictory statements and activities by WP members and parliamentarians that challenged the secular establishment led to the soft military intervention (secular countermobilization) in February 1997 and the closure of the WP by the Constitutional Court in January 1998. Despite the 1997 military intervention, however, the Islamist movement had already firmly established itself in the country in the years since the 1980 intervention and could not be eliminated.

Islamist entrepreneurs recognized the narrowing down of the POS resulting from the 1997 soft intervention and simply reframed their appeal. Islamist entrepreneurs founded the Virtue Party (VP), dropping the political rhetoric of the "Just Order" in order not to be regarded as a continuation of the WP. This time, Islamist entrepreneurs exploited Turkey's longtime quest for European Union (EU) membership as a political opportunity to reframe Islamist demands utilizing a liberal tool kit. This strategy came to an end, however, when the

Constitutional Court also outlawed the VP in June 2001. Closure of the main Islamist party for a fourth time since the 1970s led to a split among Islamist entrepreneurs into two political parties in 2001, each of which pursued a different tactic for framing the Islamist agenda. The "traditionalists," under the leadership of Recai Kutan, a longtime confidante of Erbakan, formed the Felicity Party (FP); the "reformists," under the leadership of Recep Tayyip Erdoğan, founded the Islamist Justice and Development Party (JDP). The reformist group saw that, following the 1997 military countermobilization, there was no possibility to transform the secular-democratic polity in the short run. Indeed, there were clear indicators that military leaders had become aware of the mistake inherent in their adoption of the TIS and were reaffirming and strengthening their opposition to Islamism. The reformist leadership of the JDP realized that insisting on such change might risk all the achievements already won. Nonetheless, despite the military countermobilization, the malfunctioning state and the inability of mainstream political parties to solve citizens' socioeconomic problems continued to present Islamists with a POS. Under these conditions, the reformists of the JDP framed their appeal to voters in terms of social equality. The JDP became the governing party by securing the highest vote share in the 2002 general elections when it became the largest party in Turkey and the sole party of government. The party further increased its support in the 2007 general elections and, following the elections, placed its candidate into the presidency of Turkey.

Consistent with social movement theory, the Turkish case shows that grievance-based explanations (cultural and socioeconomic) alone are inadequate to explain social movement mobilization. Cultural explanations for Islamist mobilization are inappropriate in the case of Turkey. The Turkish Revolution, which introduced a secular nation-state, was a successful struggle against Western imperialism. Unlike the case of Arab countries, where there was simultaneously Western colonial domination and endeavors to install a Western type of state, in Turkey there was both independence and secularism. Thus, the secular Turkish state cannot be regarded as a political remnant of colonialism.

While the successful mobilization of political Islam can be attributed in part to the malfunctioning state and the structural conditions that it created, particularly since the 1990s, these factors alone do not explain how the Islamist movement could establish the well-organized and resource-rich networks that enabled it to address the ills of the state since the 1990s. For grievances to lead to successful social movement mobilization, two additional conditions must exist: a political opportunity and successful framing of that opportunity by movement entrepreneurs. Movement entrepreneurs must establish a dynamic relationship among movement networks, framing processes, grievances, and the POS. These four factors, while necessary for social movement mobilization, are insufficient by themselves. Movement entrepreneurs are also necessary for success.

The social movement literature has been conceptualized by analyzing cases mainly from Western Europe and the United States, where movements usually pursue goals compatible with the polity in which they mobilize. As a result, there is a positive normative bias in the literature. Social movements are assumed to share goals compatible with Western liberal ideas (promoting democracy and liberalism). This creates a problem for the analysis of Islamist mobilization in Muslim countries. The Turkish case demonstrates that a non-civil, peripheral, and resource-poor movement opposed to democracy can nonetheless exploit the opportunities available under a democratic system to become a political party, compete in elections, and mobilize the population in support of redefining the secular-democratic structure according to a politicized form of Islam.

There seems to be an emerging tendency in the treatment of Islamist mobilization to rely solely on grievances. Islamist movements are viewed as mobilizing in reaction against the lack of democracy in the Muslim world. This argument makes the literature on Islamist social movement contradictory to the foundations of social movement theory. The foundational literature criticizes solely grievance-based explanations for social movement mobilization by arguing that even under extreme conditions of human misery, movement mobilization is not assured. While not denying that the repressive political context of an authoritarian setting may itself trigger countermobilization, it is not the regime type, but the presence of a favorable political opportunity that is seized upon by movement entrepreneurs with strong organizational resources. It is this that determines a successful social movement mobilization. Whether the regime is authoritarian or democratic constrains movement entrepreneurs' strategies. The Islamist social movement in Turkey demonstrates that movement entrepreneurs play a critical role in social movement mobilization by seizing upon an existing political opportunity, whether it consists of grievances in the population or changes in the characteristics of the existing regime. The Islamist movement in Turkey exploited the TIS as a new opportunity, expanded existing "abeyance structures" and established new movement networks, and engaged in framing activities that addressed existing grievances. Thus, there is a dynamic relationship between the political opportunity (structure) and movement entrepreneurs (agency). When the political opportunity narrows down, movement entrepreneurs' successful framing efforts and the movement's strong organizational networks play a crucial role in the movement's mobilization. Social movement mobilization depends on the simultaneous presence of a political opportunity, movement entrepreneurs, organizational resources, successful framing processes, and grievances that can be created and exploited by movement activists. In the Turkish case, Islamist entrepreneurs, who came on the scene in the 1970s, made choices with goals in mind to create a movement. This enabled them to exploit a political opportunity that did not exist until the 1980s and 1990s.

This study thus underscores the importance of informal organizational networks in movement mobilization. The presence of Islamic brotherhoods acted as "abeyance structures" in the form of illegal Quran courses beyond state control. The Islamic brotherhoods, which were forced underground following the Kemalist Revolution of the 1920s, sustained Islamist movement aspirations, acted as the breeding grounds for creation of the Islamist elite that appeared in the 1970s, and provided the initial organizational resources for the movement.

The present study contributes to resolving the tautology problem surrounding the concept of POS. POSs have been defined only in terms of the existence of social movement mobilization. This view risks conflating opportunities with mobilization. POSs can exist for a long time without resulting in social movement mobilization. A POS is a set of structural conditions that can lead to social movement mobilization in the presence of movement entrepreneurs, organizational dynamics, and grievances. The problem of tautology in the concept of POS can be avoided by disaggregating the analyses of political opportunity, movement entrepreneurs, organizational resources, and grievances from each other. The causal sequence among these factors must be subjected to process tracing[1] in analysis of the development of a movement mobilization, as is done in Chapters 3 through 6 of this study.

Since the JDP came to power in 2002, there has been a continuous tension between the secular state establishment and the party. The JDP defines itself as a "conservative-democratic" party; unlike the center-right and center-left political parties, however, the JDP regards the secular character of the state as problematic. Thus, it tries to redefine the state structure according to a new interpretation of secularism and democracy; an idea that has been supported only by the Islamist segment of the population, including the traditionalist FP.

The JDP successfully exploited Turkey's longtime quest for EU membership as a political opportunity for advancing Islamist demands. The JDP reframed its Islamist agenda in terms of EU reform packages intended to democratize the country. These EU demands helped the Islamist movement diminish the power of certain secular state institutions, utilizing a liberal tool kit calling for democratization. The State Security Courts were closed down, and the National Security Council (NSC) is no longer headed by a general but by a civilian. Prime Minister Erdoğan, pointing to the democratizing reforms in Turkey resulting from the EU reform packages, declared that the JDP initiated "a silent revolution" in the country.

The JDP has been testing the limits of tolerance of the secular state establishment by trying to change regulations particularly in the area of education. Such changes are intended to open up political opportunities to further strengthen the organizational resources of the Islamist social movement. The JDP's persistent attempts to redefine secularism in Turkey in order to accommodate religion raise suspicions among the secular segment of the society that the party has a hidden Islamist agenda.

---

[1] "Chapter 10: Process Tracing and Historical Explanation," in *Case Studies and Theory Development in the Social Sciences*, by Alexander George and Andrew Bennett (Cambridge, MA: MIT Press, 2004), 205–32.

The JDP as the governing party following the 2002 general elections seemed to be in the process of adopting a more moderate line. However, having further increased its electoral support following the 2007 general elections, the JDP as the party of government seems to be in the process of abandoning its moderate line. As a response to the JDP's mobilization against the secular-democratic state, the Constitutional Court declared in 2008 that the party was a center of antisecular activities. Yet, the court instead of outlawing the JDP issued a judicial warning and a financial penalty. Thus, the Constitutional Court for the first time did not ban an Islamist political party. The secular state establishment's (the judiciary) countermobilization against the JDP did not cease the party's Islamist mobilization against the secular-democratic state. It seems that the JDP during its second term as the party of government has successfully mobilized against the secular-democratic state.

The JDP also benefits from U.S. advocacy of "moderate Islam" as a state model for the Muslim world. The U.S. government embraced the JDP and its leader following the 2002 general elections and presented Turkey as a model for the Muslim world because of its Muslim character rather than for its achievement in secularism. In effect, the U.S. government is repeating the mistake committed by the Turkish military when it adopted the TIS. The U.S. position has created discontent among the secular state establishment in Turkey and alienated the secular segment of society.

The persistent problem of the malfunctioning state and the inability of mainstream political parties to solve Turkish citizens' socioeconomic problems played a crucial role in the JDP's becoming the governing party following the 2002 general elections. Thus, it may be crucial for the JDP to achieve successful economic performance to maintain the electorate's support. The JDP, with its strong organizational resources with motivated and diligent party workers, has successfully become a people's party by embracing particularly the urban poor segment of the society by distributing selective incentives such as food, coal, and scholarships. It remains to be seen whether the party can be successful in its economic policies. If the JDP becomes successful in the economic realm, it is yet to be seen whether material well-being and modernization in the country will further increase the support for Islamism or for secularism. If it does not, the party may still succeed on the basis of its social support for the urban poor and its appeal to the traditionalist rural population.

Solving the country's persistent socioeconomic problems, however, is only one challenge the JDP government faces. Another challenge is the resurgence of Kurdish separatist Kurdistan Workers' Party (PKK) terrorism in Turkey since 2003. The JDP's soft relations with the military seemed to come to an end with the appointment of General Yaşar Büyükanıt as the chief of General Staff following General Hilmi Özkök's retirement in August 2006. The new military leadership under General Büyükanıt defined political Islam as a crucial threat, and declared its determination to combat Kurdish separatist PKK terrorism. Although it seemed that the military under the leadership of the new Chief of the General Staff General İlker Başbuğ maintained General Büyükanıt's policies, as of this writing, the military leadership no longer seems to pursue its traditional understanding and role in the defense of secularism. Reasons for this change in the military's policy vis-à-vis secularism remain to be seen: on the one hand, the balance of strength between Islamist sympathizer and guardians of secularism within the military might have tipped in favor of the Islamist sympathizers. On the other hand, the military, which has been harshly criticized mainly by Islamists and liberals for intervening in politics, might have been compelled to revise its traditional understanding of secularism. Whether the military will act as an elite ally and/or inadvertent elite ally of the Islamist social movement or it will play its traditional role in the defense of secularism remains to be seen. The renewed military offensive of 2007 against the PKK in Turkey and in northern Iraq has increased the salience of nationalism in Turkish politics.

The coming days may see increased tension between Islamism and Turkish nationalism with respect to defining Turkish society and its future. Islamism, unlike Turkish nationalism, does not accept the notion of a Turkish identity. Turkish nationalism, as a secular ideology, seeks to protect both the secular and the unitary character of the state. The Islamist movement is likely to have a hard time competing against the very foundation of the secular-democratic Turkish Republic: the Turkish nationalism of Atatürk. However, Islamist entrepreneurs may opt once again, as they have after each threat to the survival of their movement, to reframe their message to the Turkish people so as to neutralize the nationalist challenge and secure the power and appeal of the Islamist movement in Turkey.

Bibliography

Works in English

Acar, Feride. "Women in the Ideology of Islamic Revivalism in Turkey: Three Islamic Women's Journals," in *Islam in Modern Turkey: Religion, Politics and Literature in a Secular State*, ed. Richard Tapper. London: I. B. Tauris, 1991, 280–303.

Ahmad, Feroz. *The Turkish Experiment in Democracy, 1950–1975*. Boulder, CO: Westview Press, 1977.

Akıncı, Uğur. "The Welfare Party's Municipal Track Record: Evaluating Islamist Municipal Activism in Turkey." *The Middle East Journal* 53, no. 1 (Winter 1999): 75–94.

Akşin, Sina. "The Nature of the Kemalist Revolution," in *The Turkish Republic at Seventy-Five Years*, ed. David Shankland. Cambridgeshire, UK: The Eothen Press, 1999, 14–28.

Amenta, Edwin, and Michael P. Young. "Democratic States and Social Movements: Theoretical Arguments and Hypotheses." *Social Problems* 46, no. 2 (1999): 153–68.

Aminzade, Ronald. "Between Movement and Party: The Transformation of Mid-Nineteenth-Century French Republicanism," in *The Politics of Social Protest: Comparative Perspectives on States and Social Movements*, eds. J. Craig Jenkins and Bert Klandermans. Minneapolis: University of Minnesota Press, 1995, 39–62.

Amjad, Mohammed. "Rural Migrants, Islam and Revolution in Iran." *Research in Social Movements, Conflict and Change* 16 (1993): 35–50

Anheier, Helmut. "Movement Development and Organizational Networks: The Role of 'Single Members' in the German Nazi Party, 1925–30," in *Social Movements and Networks: Relational Approaches to Collective Action*, eds. Mario Diani and Doug McAdam. New York: Oxford University Press, 2003, 49–74.

Arat, Yeşim. *Political Islam in Turkey and Women's Organizations*. Istanbul: TESEV Yayınları, 1999.

Arıcanlı, Tosun, and D. Rodrick, eds. *The Political Economy of Turkey*. London: Macmillan, 1990.

Atasoy, Yıldız. *Turkey, Islamists, and Democracy: Transition and Globalization in a Muslim State*. London: I. B. Tauris, 2005.

Ayata, Ayşe. "Ideology, Social Bases, and Organizational Structure of the Post-1980 Political Parties," in *The Political and Socioeconomic Transformation of Turkey*, eds. Atila Eralp, Muharrem Tünay, and Birol Yeşilada. Westport, CT: Praeger, 1993, 31–50.

Ayata, Sencer. "Patronage, Party, and State: The Politicization of Islam in Turkey." *The Middle East Journal* 50, no. 1 (Winter 1996): 41–57.

———. "The Rise of Islamic Fundamentalism and Its Institutional Framework," in *The Political and Socioeconomic Transformation of Turkey*, eds. Atila Eralp, Muharrem Tünay, and Birol Yeşilada. Westport, CT: Praeger, 1993, 51–68.

———. "Traditional Sufi Orders on the Periphery: Kadiri and Nakşibendi Islam in Konya and Trabzon," in *Islam in Modern Turkey: Religion, Politics and Literature in a Secular State*, ed. Richard Tapper. London: I. B. Tauris, 1991, 223–53.

Ayata-Güneş, Ayşe, and Sencer Ayata. "Turkey's Mainstream Political Parties on the Center-Right and Center-Left," in *Turkey since 1970: Politics, Economics, and Society*, ed. Debbie Lovatt. New York: Palgrave, 2000, 91–110.

Balım, Çiğdem et al., eds. *Turkey: Political, Social, and Economic Challenges in the 1990s*. Leiden, The Netherlands: E. J. Brill, 1995.

Baumeister, Roy, Karen Dale, and Mark Muraven. "Volition and Belongingness: Social Movements, Volition, Self-Esteem, and the Need to Belong," in *Self, Identity, and Social Movements*, eds. Sheldon Stryker, Timothy J. Owens, and Robert W. White. Minneapolis: University of Minnesota Press, 2000, 239–51.

Benford, Robert D., and David A. Snow. "Framing Processes and Social Movements." *Annual Review of Sociology* 26 (2000): 611–39.

Berman, Sheri. "Islamism, Revolution, and Civil Society." *APSA, Perspectives on Politics* 1, no. 2 (June 2003): 257–72.

Brockett, Charles D. "The Structure of Political Opportunities and Peasant Mobilization in Central America." *Comparative Politics* 23, no. 3 (1991): 253–74.

Buğra, Ayşe. "Class, Culture, and State: An Analysis of Interest Representation by Two Turkish Business Associations." *International Journal of Middle East Studies* 30, no. 4 (November 1998): 521–39.

Burgat, François, and William Dowell. "Islamism as the Language of Political Reaction to Western Cultural Domination," in *The Islamic Movement in North Africa*, eds. François Burgat and William Dowell. Austin: Center for Middle Eastern Studies, University of Texas, 1993, 63–85.

Burstein, Paul, Rachel L. Einwohner, and Jocelyn A. Hollander. "The Success of Political Movements: A Bargaining Perspective," in *The Politics of Social Protest: Comparative Perspectives on States and Social Movements*, eds. Craig Jenkins and Bert Klandermans. Minneapolis: University of Minnesota Press, 1995, 275–95.

Çarkoğlu, Ali. "Religiousity, Support for *Şeriat* and Evaluations of Secularist Public Policies in Turkey." *Middle Eastern Studies* 40, no. 2 (March 2004): 111–36.

Clark, Janine A. "Islamist Women in Yemen: Informal Nodes of Activism," in *Islamic Activism: A Social Movement Theory Approach*, ed. Quintan Wiktorowicz. Bloomington: Indiana University Press, 2004, 164–84.

———. *Islam, Charity, and Activism: Middle-Class Networks and Social Welfare in Egypt, Jordan, and Yemen*. Bloomington: Indiana University Press, 2004.

Çelik, Yasemin. *Contemporary Turkish Foreign Policy*. Westport, CT: Praeger, 1999.

Çınar, Alev İnan. "Refah Party and the City Administration of Istanbul: Liberal Islam, Localism, and Hybridity." *New Perspectives on Turkey* 16 (Spring 1997): 23–40.

Danielson, Micheal N., and Ruşen Keleş. *The Politics of Rapid Urbanization: Government and Growth in Modern Turkey*. New York: Holmes and Meier, 1985.

Desai, Manali. "From Movement to Party to Government: Why Social Policies in Kerala and West Bengal are so Different," in *States, Parties, and Social Movements*, ed. Jack A. Goldstone. New York: Cambridge University Press, 2003, 170–96.

De Witte, Hans, and Bert Klandermans. "Political Racism in Flanders and the Netherlands: Explaining Differences in the Electoral Success of Extreme Right-Wing Parties." *Journal of Ethnic and Migration Studies* 26, no. 4 (October 2000): 699–717.

Diamond, Larry, and Richard Gunther, eds. *Political Parties and Democracy*. Baltimore, MD: The Johns Hopkins University Press, 2001.

Diani, Mario, and Doug McAdam, eds. *Social Movements and Networks: Relational Approaches to Collective Action*. New York: Oxford University Press, 2003.

Dumont, Paul. "The Origins of Kemalist Ideology," in *Atatürk and the Modernization of Turkey*, ed. Jacob M. Landau. Boulder, CO: Westview Press, 1984, 25–44.

Eisenger, Peter K. "The Conditions of Protest Behavior in American Cities." *American Political Science Review* 67, no. 1 (March 1973): 11–28.

Eligür, Banu. "Turkey's March 2009 Local Elections." *Turkish Studies* 10, no. 3 (September 2009): 469–96.

Emirbayer, Mustafa, and Jeff Goodwin. "Network Analysis, Culture, and the Problem of Agency." *American Journal of Sociology* 99, no. 6 (May 1994): 1411–54.

Entelis, John P., ed. *Islam, Democracy, and the State in North Africa*. Bloomington: Indiana University Press, 1997.

Eralp, Atila, Muharrem Tünay, and Birol Yeşilada, eds. *The Political and Socioeconomic Transformation of Turkey*. Westport, CT: Praeger, 1993.

Erman, Tahire. "Becoming 'Urban' or Remaining 'Rural': The Views of the Turkish Rural-to-Urban Migrants on the 'Integration' Question." *International Journal Middle East Studies* 30, no. 4 (November 1998): 541–61.

Esposito, John L. *Islam and Politics*. 3rd ed. New York: Syracuse University Press, 1991.

———. "Muslim Societies Today," in *Islam: The Religious and Political Life of a World Community*, ed. Marjorie Kelly. New York: Praeger, 1984, 197–225.

Fuller, Graham. *The Future of Political Islam*. New York: Palgrave, 2003.

Gamson, William A. *The Strategy of Social Protest*. 2nd ed. Belmont, CA: Wadsworth, 1990.

Gamson, William A., and David S. Meyer, "Framing Political Opportunity," in *Comparative Perspectives on Social Movements: Political Opportunities, Mobilizing Structures, and Cultural Framings*, eds. Doug McAdam, John McCarthy, and Mayer Zald. New York: Cambridge University Press, 1996, 275–90.

Ganz, Marshall. "Why David Sometimes Wins: Strategic Capacity in Social Movements," in *Rethinking Social Movements: Structure, Meaning, and Emotion*, eds. Jeff Goodwin and James Jasper. Lanham, MD: Rowman and Littlefield Publishers, 2004, 177–98.

Gellner, Ernest. *Encounters with Nationalism*. Oxford: Blackwell Publishing, 1994.

George, Alexander, and Andrew Bennett. *Case Studies and Theory Development in the Social Sciences*. Cambridge, MA: MIT Press, 2004.

Gerhards, Jurgen, and Dieter Rucht. "Mesomobilization: Organizing and Framing in Two Protest Campaigns in West Germany." *American Journal of Sociology* 98, no. 3 (November 1992): 555–96.

Glenn, John K. "Parties Out of Movements: Party Emergence in Postcommunist Eastern Europe," in *States, Parties, and Social Movements*, ed. Jack A. Goldstone. New York: Cambridge University Press, 2003, 147–69.

Goldstone, Jack A., ed. *States, Parties, and Social Movements*. New York: Cambridge University Press, 2003.

———. *Revolutions: Theoretical, Comparative, and Historical Studies*. 3rd ed. Belmont, CA: Wadsworth Cengage Learning, 2003.

Goodwin, Jeff, and James M. Jasper, eds. *Rethinking Social Movements: Structure, Meaning, and Emotion*. Lanham, MD: Rowman and Littlefield Publishers, 2004.
Göle, Nilüfer. "Islam in Public: New Visibilities and New Imaginaries." *Public Culture* 14, no. 1 (2002): 173–90.
———. "Secularism and Islamism in Turkey: The Making of Elites and Counter-elites." *Middle East Journal* 51, no. 1 (Winter 1997): 46–58.
Gülalp, Haldun. "Using Islam as Political Ideology: Turkey in Historical Perspective." *Cultural Dynamics* 14, no. 1 (2002): 21–39.
———. "Globalization and Political Islam: The Social Bases of Turkey's Welfare Party." *International Journal of Middle East Studies* 33, no. 3 (August 2001): 433–48.
———. "The Poverty of Democracy in Turkey: The Refah Party Episode." *New Perspectives on Turkey* 21 (Fall 1999): 35–59.
Hale, William. "Generals and Politicians in Turkey, 1983–1990." *The Turkish Yearbook of International Relations* XXV (1995): 1–20.
———. "Transition to Civilian Governments in Turkey," in *State, Democracy, and the Military: Turkey in the 1980s*, eds. Metin Heper and Ahmet Evin. New York: Walter de Gruyter, 1988, 159–75.
Handelman, Howard, and Mark Tessler, eds. *Democracy and Its Limits: Lessons from Asia, Latin America, and the Middle East*. Notre Dame, IN: University of Notre Dame Press, 1999.
Heper, Metin, and Ahmet Evin, eds. *Politics in the Third Turkish Republic*. Boulder, CO: Westview Press, 1994.
Hessini, Leila. "Wearing the Hijab in Contemporary Morocco: Choice and Identity," in *Reconstructing Gender in the Middle East: Tradition, Identity, and Power*, eds. Fatma Müge Göçek and Shiva Balaghi. New York: Columbia University Press, 1994, 40–56.
Hewitt, Lyndi, and Holly J. McCammon. "Explaining Suffrage Mobilization: Balance, Neutralization, and Range in Collective Action Frames," in *Frames of Protest: Social Movements and the Framing Perspective*, eds. Hank Johnston and John A. Noakes. Lanham, MD: Rowman and Littlefield Publishers, 2005, 33–52.
Hirschman, Albert. *The Rhetoric of Reaction*. Cambridge, MA: Harvard University Press, 1991.
Hobsbawm, Eric J. "Peasant Land Occupations." *Past and Present* 62 (February 1974): 120–52.
İncioğlu, Nihal. "Local Elections and Electoral Behavior," in *Politics, Parties, and Elections in Turkey*, eds. Sabri Sayarı and Yılmaz Esmer. Boulder, CO: Lynne Rienner, 2002, 73–90.
Jenkins, Gareth. "Muslim Democrats in Turkey?" *Survival* 45, no. 1 (Spring 2003): 45–66.
Jenkins, J. Craig, and Bert Klandermans, eds. *The Politics of Social Protest: Comparative Perspectives on States and Social Movements*. Minneapolis: University of Minnesota Press, 1995.
Jenkins, J. Craig, and Charles Perrow. "Insurgency of the Powerless: Farm Worker Movements (1946–1972)." *American Sociological Review* 42 (1977): 249–68.
Johnston, Hank, and John A. Noakes, eds. *Frames of Protest: Social Movements and the Framing Perspective*. Lanham, MD: Rowman and Littlefield Publishers, 2005.
Juergensmeyer, Mark. *The New Cold War? Religious Nationalism Confronts the Secular State*. Berkeley: University of California Press, 1993.

Kalaycıoğlu, Ersin. "The Motherland Party: The Challenge of Institutionalization in a Charismatic Leader Party," in *Political Parties in Turkey*, eds. Barry Rubin and Metin Heper. London: Frank Cass, 2002, 41–61.

———. "The Turkish Grand National Assembly: A Brief Inquiry into the Politics of Representation in Turkey," in *Turkey: Political, Social and Economic Challenges in the 1990s*, eds. Çiğdem Balım et al. Leiden, the Netherlands: E. J. Brill, 1995, 41–60.

Karpat, Kemal H. *The Politicization of Islam: Reconstructing Identity, State, Faith, and Community in the Late Ottoman State*. New York: Oxford University Press, 2001.

———. "Military Interventions: Army-Civilian Relations in Turkey Before and After 1980," in *State, Democracy, and the Military: Turkey in the 1980s*, eds. Metin Heper and Ahmet Evin. New York: Walter de Gruyter, 1988, 137–58.

Kayalı, Hasan. *Arabs and Young Turks: Ottomanism, Arabism, and Islamism in the Ottoman Empire, 1908–1918*. Berkley: University of California Press, 1997.

Kepel, Gilles. *Jihad: The Political Trial of Political Islam*. Cambridge, MA: Harvard University Press, 2002.

Khoury, Philip S. "Islamic Revivalism and the Crisis of the Secular State in the Arab World," in *Arab Resources: The Transformation of a Society*, ed. Ibrahim Ibrahim. Washington, DC: Center for Contemporary Arab Studies, Georgetown University, 1983, 213–36.

Kitschelt, Herbert P. "Political Opportunity Structures and Political Protest: Anti-Nuclear Movements in Four Democracies." *British Journal of Political Science* 16, no. 1 (January 1986): 57–85.

Klandermans, Bert, and Bernd Simon. "Politicized Collective Identity: A Social Psychological Analysis." *American Psychologist* 56, no. 4 (April 2001): 319–31.

Klandermans, Bert, and Suzanne Staggenborg, eds. *Methods of Social Movement Research*. Minneapolis: University of Minnesota Press, 2002.

Kramer, Heinz. *A Changing Turkey: The Challenge to Europe and the United States*. Washington, DC: Brookings Institution Press, 2001.

Kriesi, Hanspeter. "The Political Opportunity Structure of New Social Movements: Its Impact on Their Mobilization," in *The Politics of Social Protest: Comparative Perspectives on States and Social Movements*, eds. J. Craig Jenkins and Bert Klandermans. Minneapolis: University of Minnesota Press, 1995, 167–98.

Kriesi, Hanspeter, Ruud Koopmans, Jan Willem Duyvendak, and Marco G. Giugni. "New Social Movements and Political Opportunities in Western Europe." *European Journal of Political Research* 22 (1992): 219–44.

Kuçuradi, Ioanna. "Secularization in Turkey," in *Averroes and the Enlightenment*, eds. Mourad Wahba and Mona Abousenna. New York: Prometheus Books, 1996, 171–6.

Kurzman, Charles. *The Unthinkable Revolution in Iran*. Cambridge, MA: Harvard University Press, 2004.

———. "Structural Opportunity and Perceived Opportunity in Social-Movement Theory: The Iranian Revolution of 1979." *American Sociological Review* 61, no. 1 (February 1996): 153–70.

———. "A Dynamic View of Resources: Evidence from the Iranian Revolution." *Research in Social Movements, Conflict and Change* 17 (1994): 53–84.

Landau, Jacob M. *Pan-Turkism: From Irredentism to Cooperation*. Bloomington: Indiana University Press, 1995.

Landau, Jacob M., ed. *Atatürk and Modernization of Turkey*. Boulder, CO: Westview Press, 1984.

———. "The Nationalist Action Party in Turkey." *Journal of Contemporary History* 17 (1982): 587–606.

———. *Pan-Turkism in Turkey: A Study of Irredentism*. Hamden, CT: Archon Books, 1981.

———. "The National Salvation Party in Turkey." *Asian and African Studies* 11, no. 1 (1976): 1–57.

———. *Radical Politics in Modern Turkey*. Leiden, The Netherlands: E. J. Brill, 1974.

Lapidot, Anat. "Islamic Activism in Turkey since the 1980 Military Takeover," in *Religious Radicalism in the Greater Middle East*, eds. Bruce Maddy-Weizman and Efraim Inbar. London: Frank Cass, 1997, 62–74.

Lewis, Bernard. *The Emergence of Modern Turkey*. 3rd ed. New York: Oxford University Press, 2002.

Lichbach, Mark Irving, and Alan S. Zuckerman, eds. *Comparative Politics: Rationality, Culture, and Structure*. Cambridge: Cambridge University Press, 1997, 142–73.

Lovatt, Debbie, ed. *Turkey since 1970: Politics, Economics, and Society*. New York: Palgrave, 2000.

Lucardie, Paul. "Prophets, Purifiers, and Prolocutors: Towards a Theory on the Emergence of New Parties." *Party Politics* 6, no. 2 (April 2000): 175–85.

Maguire, Diarmuid. "Opposition Movements and Opposition Parties: Equal Partners or Dependent Relations in the Struggle for Power and Reform?" in *The Politics of Social Protest: Comparative Perspectives on States and Social Movements*, eds. Craig Jenkins and Bert Klandermans. Minneapolis: University of Minnesota Press, 1995, 199–228.

Mardin, Şerif. "The Nakshibendi Order of Turkey," in *Fundamentalisms and the State: Remaking Polities, Economies, and Militance*, eds. Martin E. Marty and R. Scott Appleby. Chicago: University of Chicago Press, 1993, 204–32.

Margulies, Ronnie, and Ergin Yıldızoğlu. "The Resurgence of Islam and the Welfare Party in Turkey," in *Political Islam: Essays from Middle East Report*, eds. Joel Beinin and Joe Stork. Berkeley: University of California Press, 1997, 144–53.

McAdam, Doug. "Conceptual Origins, Current Problems, Future Directions," in *Comparative Perspectives on Social Movements: Political Opportunities, Mobilizing Structures, and Cultural Framings*, eds. Doug McAdam, John D. McCarthy, and Mayer N. Zald. New York: Cambridge University Press, 1996, 23–40.

———. "'Initiator' and 'Spin-off' Movements: Diffusion Processes in Protest Cycles," in *Repertoires and Cycles of Collective Action*, ed. Mark Traugott. Durham, NC: Duke University Press, 1995, 217–40.

———. *Political Process and the Development of Black Insurgency, 1930–1970*. Chicago: University of Chicago Press, 1982.

———. "Revisiting the U.S. Civil Rights Movement: Toward a More Synthetic Understanding of the Origins of Contention," in *Rethinking Social Movements: Structure, Meaning, and Emotion*, eds. Jeff Goodwin and James Jasper. Lanham, MD: Rowman and Littlefield Publishers, 2004, 201–32.

McAdam, Doug, John D. McCarthy, and Mayer N. Zald, eds. *Comparative Perspectives on Social Movements: Political Opportunities, Mobilizing Structures, and Cultural Framings*. New York: Cambridge University Press, 1996.

———. "Introduction: Opportunities, Mobilizing Structures, and Framing Processes: Toward a Synthetic, Comparative Perspective on Social Movements," in *Comparative Perspectives on Social Movements: Political Opportunities, Mobilizing Structures, and Cultural Framings*, eds. Doug McAdam, John D. McCarthy, and Mayer N. Zald. New York: Cambridge University Press, 1996, 1–20.

McAdam, Doug, and Ronnelle Paulsen. "Specifying the Relationship between Social Ties and Activism." *American Journal of Sociology* 99, no. 3 (November 1993): 640–67.

McAdam, Doug, Sidney Tarrow, and Charles Tilly. *Dynamics of Contention.* New York: Cambridge University Press, 2001.

———. "Toward an Integrated Perspective on Social Movements and Revolution," in *Comparative Politics: Rationality, Culture, and Structure*, eds. Mark Irving Lichbach and Alan S. Zuckerman. Cambridge: Cambridge University Press, 1997, 142–73.

McCarthy, John D. "Constraints and Opportunities in Adopting, Adapting, and Inventing," in *Comparative Perspectives on Social Movements: Political Opportunities, Mobilizing Structures, and Cultural Framings*, ed. Doug McAdam, John D. McCarthy, and Mayer N. Zald. New York: Cambridge University Press, 1996, 141–51.

McCarthy, Justin. *The Ottoman Peoples and the End of Empire.* 2nd ed. London: Arnold, 2004.

Meeker, Michael E. "The New Muslim Intellectuals in the Republic of Turkey," in *Islam in Modern Turkey: Religion, Politics and Literature in a Secular State*, ed. Richard Tapper. London: I. B. Tauris, 1991, 189–219.

Meyer, David S. "Tending the Vineyard: Cultivating Political Process Research," in *Rethinking Social Movements: Structure, Meaning, and Emotion*, eds. Jeff Goodwin and James Jasper. Lanham, MD: Rowman and Littlefield Publishers, 2004, 47–59.

———. *A Winter of Discontent: The Nuclear Freeze and American Politics.* New York: Praeger, 1990.

Meyer, David S., and Debra C. Minkoff. "Conceptualizing Political Opportunity." *Social Forces* 82, no. 4 (June 2004): 1457–92.

Mische, Ann. "Cross-talk in Movements: Reconceiving the Culture-Network Link," in *Social Movements and Networks: Relational Approaches to Collective Action*, ed. Mario Diani and Doug McAdam. New York: Oxford University Press, 2003, 258–80.

Moore, Henry Clement. "Islamic Banks and Competitive Politics in the Arab World and Turkey." *Middle East Journal* 44, no. 2 (Spring 1990): 234–55.

Narlı, Nilüfer. "The Rise of the Islamist Movement in Turkey." *MERIA Journal* 3, no. 3 (September 1999): 38–48.

Oliver, Pamela E., and Hank Jonhston. "What a Good Idea! Ideologies and Frames in Social Movement Research," in *Frames of Protest: Social Movements and the Framing Perspective*, eds. Hank Johnston and John A. Noakes. Lanham, MD: Rowman and Littlefield Publishers, 2005, 185–203.

Oliver, Pamela E., and Daniel J. Myers. "Networks, Diffusion, and Cycles of Collective Action," in *Social Movements and Networks: Relational Approaches to Collective Action*, ed. Mario Diani and Doug McAdam. New York: Oxford University Press, 2003, 173–203.

Olsson, Tord, Elisabeth Özdalga, and Catharina Raudvere, eds. *Alevi Identity: Cultural, Religious, and Social Perspectives.* Richmond, UK: Curzon, 1998.

Öncü, Ayşe. "Packaging Islam: Cultural Politics on the Landscape of Turkish Commercial Television." *Public Culture* 8, no. 1 (1995): 51–71.

Öniş, Ziya. "Turgut Özal and His Economic Legacy: Turkish Neo-Liberalism in Critical Perspective." *Middle Eastern Studies* 40, no. 4 (July 2004): 113–34.

———. "The Political Economy of Islamic Resurgence in Turkey: The Rise of the Welfare Party in Perspective." *Third World Quarterly* 18, no. 4 (1997): 743–66.

Opp, Karl-Dieter. "Soft Incentives and Collective Action: Participation in the Anti-Nuclear Movement." *British Journal of Political Science* 16, no. 1 (January 1986): 87–112.

Özbudun, Ergun. "The Institutional Decline of Parties in Turkey," in *Political Parties and Democracy*, eds. Larry Diamond and Richard Gunther. Baltimore, MD: The Johns Hopkins University Press, 2001, 238–65.

———. *Contemporary Turkish Politics: Challenges to Democratic Consolidation*. Boulder, CO: Lynne Rienner Publishers, 2000.

———. "The Nature of the Kemalist Political Regime," in *Atatürk: Founder of a Modern State*, eds. Ergun Özbudun and Ali Kazancıgil. Hamden, CT: Archon Books, 1981, 79–102.

Özdalga, Elisabeth, ed. *The Naqshbandis in Western and Central Asia: Change and Continuity*. London: Curzon Press, 1999.

Parsa, Misagh. "Conversion or Coalition? Ideology in the Iranian and Nicaraguan Revolutions." *Political Power and Social Theory* 9 (1995): 23–60.

Passy, Florence. "Social Networks Matter. But How?" in *Social Movements and Networks: Relational Approaches to Collective Action*, ed. Mario Diani and Doug McAdam. New York: Oxford University Press, 2003, 21–48.

Redding, Kent, and Jocelyn Viterna. "Political Demands, Political Opportunities: Explaining the Differential Success of Left-Libertarian Parties." *Social Forces* 78 (1999): 491–510.

Robinson, Glenn E. "Hamas as Social Movement," in *Islamic Activism: A Social Movement Theory Approach*, ed. Quintan Wiktorowicz. Bloomington: Indiana University Press, 2004, 112–39.

Roy, Oliver. *The Failure of Political Islam*. Cambridge, MA: Harvard University Press, 1994.

Rubin, Barry, ed. *Terrorism and Politics*. New York: St. Martin's Press, 1991.

Rubin, Barry, and Metin Heper, eds. *Political Parties in Turkey*. London: Frank Cass, 2002.

Rubin, Michael. "Green Money: Islamist Politics in Turkey." *Middle East Quarterly* XII, no. 1 (Winter 2005): 1–11 (Internet ed.).

Rucht, Dieter. "The Impact of National Contexts on Social Movement Structures: A Cross-movement and Cross-national Comparison," in *Comparative Perspectives on Social Movements: Political Opportunities, Mobilizing Structures, and Cultural Framings*, eds. Doug McAdam, John D. McCarthy, and Mayer N. Zald. New York: Cambridge University Press, 1996, 185–204.

Salt, Jeremy. "Nationalism and the Rise of Muslim Sentiment in Turkey." *Middle Eastern Studies* 31, no. 1 (January 1995): 1–15 (Internet ed.).

Sakallıoğlu, Ümit Cizre. "Parameters and Strategies of Islam-State Interaction in Republican Turkey." *International Journal of Middle East Studies* 28 (1996): 231–52.

———. "Liberalism, Democracy and the Turkish Center-Right: The Identity Crisis of the True Path Party." *Middle Eastern Studies* 32, no. 2 (April 1996): 142–61.

Saktanber, Ayşe. "Becoming the 'Other' as a Muslim in Turkey: Turkish Women vs. Islamist Women."*New Perspectives on Turkey* 11 (Fall 1994): 99–134.

Saracoğlu, Rüşdü. "Liberalization of Economy," in *Politics in the Third Turkish Republic*, eds. Metin Heper and Ahmet Evin. Boulder, CO: Westview Press, 1994, 63–75.

Sayarı, Sabri, and Yılmaz Esmer, eds. *Politics, Parties and Elections in Turkey*. Boulder, CO: Lynne Rienner Publishers, 2002.

Schwedler, Jillian. *Faith in Moderation: Islamist Parties in Jordan and Yemen*. New York: Cambridge University Press, 2006.

———. "The Islah Party in Yemen: Political Opportunities and Coalition Building in a Transitional Polity," in *Islamic Activism: A Social Movement Theory Approach*, ed. Quintan Wiktorowicz. Bloomington: Indiana University Press, 2004, 205–28.

Shankland, David. *Alevis in Turkey: The Emergence of a Secular Islamic Tradition*. London: RoutledgeCurzon, 2003.

Singerman, Diane. "The Networked World of Islamist Social Movements," in *Islamic Activism: A Social Movement Theory Approach*, ed. Quintan Wicktorowicz. Bloomington: Indiana University Press, 2004, 143–63.

Smith, Christian. "Correcting a Curious Neglect, or Bringing Religion Back In," in *Disruptive Religion: The Force of Faith in Social Movement Activism*, ed. Christian Smith. New York: Routledge, 1996, 1–25.

Stirling, Paul. "Religious Change in Republican Turkey." *The Middle East Journal* 12, no. 4 (Autumn 1958): 395–408.

Stryker, Sheldon, Timothy J. Owens, and Robert W. White, eds. *Self, Identity, and Social Movements*. Minneapolis: University of Minnesota Press, 2000.

Tachau, Frank, and Metin Heper. "The State, Politics, and the Military in Turkey." *Comparative Politics* 16, no. 1 (October 1983): 17–33.

Tapper, Richard, ed. *Islam in Modern Turkey: Religion, Politics and Literature in a Secular State*. London: I. B. Tauris, 1991.

Tarrow, Sidney. *Power in Movement: Social Movements and Contentious Politics*. 2nd ed. New York: Cambridge University Press, 1998.

———. "States and Opportunities: The Political Structuring of Social Movements," in *Comparative Perspectives on Social Movements: Political Opportunities, Mobilizing Structures, and Cultural Framings*, eds. Doug McAdam, John D. McCarthy, and Mayer N. Zald. New York: Cambridge University Press, 1996, 41–61.

Taylor, Verta. "Social Movement Continuity: The Women's Movement in Abeyance." *American Sociological Review* 54, no. 5 (October 1989): 761–75.

Tessler, Mark. "Democratic Concern and Islamic Resurgence: Converging Dimensions of the Arab World's Political Agenda," in *Democracy and Its Limits: Lessons from Asia, Latin America, and the Middle East*, eds. Howard Handelman and Mark Tessler. Notre Dame, IN: University of Notre Dame Press, 1999, 262–89.

———. "The Origins of Popular Support for Islamist Movements: A Political Economy Analysis," in *Islam, Democracy, and the State in North Africa*, ed. John P. Entelis. Bloomington: Indiana University Press, 1997, 93–126.

Tibi, Bassam. *Islam between Culture and Politics*. New York: Palgrave, 2001.

Tilly, Charles. *From Mobilization to Revolution*. Reading, MA: Addison-Wesley, 1978.

Togan, Sübidey, and V. N. Balasubramanyam, eds. *The Economy of Turkey since Liberalization*. London: Macmillan Press, 1996.

Togan, Sübidey, Hasan Olgun, and Halis Akder. *Report on Developments in External Economic Relations of Turkey*. 2nd ed. Ankara: Foreign Trade Association of Turkey, 1988.

Toprak, Binnaz. "Islam and the Secular State in Turkey," in *Turkey: Political, Social, and Economic Challenges in the 1990s*, eds. Çiğdem Balım et al. Leiden, The Netherlands: E. J. Brill, 1995, 90–6.

———. "Religion as State Ideology in a Secular Setting: The Turkish-Islamic Synthesis," in *Aspects of Religion in Secular Turkey*, ed. Malcolm Wagstaff. Occasional Paper Series, no. 40. Durham, UK: University of Durham, Center for Middle East and Islamic Studies, 1990, 10–15.

———. "Islamist Intellectuals of the 1980s in Turkey." *Current Turkish Thought* 62 (Spring 1987): 2–19.
———. *Islam and Political Development in Turkey*. Leiden, The Netherlands: E. J. Brill, 1981.
Traugott, Mark, ed. *Repertoires and Cycles of Collective Action*. Durham, NC: Duke University Press, 1995.
Tünay, Muharrem. "The Turkish New Right's Attempt at Hegemony," in *The Political and Socioeconomic Transformation of Turkey*, eds. Atila Eralp, Muharrem Tünay, and Birol Yeşilada. Westport, CT: Praeger, 1993, 11–30.
Voss, Kim. "Collapse of a Social Movement: The Interplay of Mobilizing Structures, Framing, and Political Opportunities in the Knights of Labor," in *Comparative Perspectives on Social Movements: Political Opportunities, Mobilizing Structures, and Cultural Framings*, eds. Doug McAdam, John D. McCarthy, and Mayer N. Zald. New York: Cambridge University Press, 1996, 227–58.
White, Jenny B. *Islamist Mobilization in Turkey: A Study of Vernacular Politics*. Seattle: University of Washington Press, 2002.
Wickham, Carrie Rosefsky. *Mobilizing Islam: Religion, Activism, and Political Change in Egypt*. New York: Columbia University Press, 2002.
Wiktorowicz, Quintan, ed. *Islamic Activism: A Social Movement Theory Approach*. Bloomington: Indiana University Press, 2004.
———. *The Management of Islamic Activism: Salafis, the Muslim Brotherhood, and State in Jordan*. New York: SUNY Press, 2001.
Yashin-Navaro, Yael. "Uses and Abuses of 'State and Civil Society' in Contemporary Turkey." *New Perspectives on Turkey* 18(Spring 1998): 1–22.
Yavuz, M. Hakan. "Opportunity Spaces, Identity, and Islamic Meaning in Turkey," in *Islamic Activism: A Social Movement Theory Approach*, ed. Quintan Wiktorowicz. Bloomington: Indiana University Press, 2004, 270–88.
———. *Islamic Political Identity in Turkey*. New York: Oxford University Press, 2003.
———. "Cleansing Islam from the Public Sphere," *Journal of International Affairs* 54, no. 1 (Fall 2000): 21–42.
Yeşilada, Birol. "The Virtue Party." *Turkish Studies* 3, no. 1 (Spring 2002): 62–81.
———. "Realignment and Party Adaptation: The Case of the Refah and Fazilet Parties," in *Politics, Parties, and Elections in Turkey*, eds. Sabri Sayarı and Yılmaz Esmer. Boulder, CO: Lynne Rienner Publishers, 2002, 157–78.
———. "Islamic Fundamentalism and the Saudi Connection." *UFSI* no. 18 (1988–9): 1–11.
Zürcher, Erik J. *Turkey: A Modern History*. New York: I. B. Tauris, 1994.

Works in Turkish

Akçura, Yusuf. *Üç Tarz-ı Siyaset* [Three Kinds of Policy]. 3rd ed. Ankara: Türk Tarih Kurumu Basımevi, 1991.
Alan, Bülent. *D-8: Yeni Bir Dünya Düzeni* [D-8: A New World Order]. Istanbul: Yörünge Yayınları, 2001.
Aşıkoğlu, Nevzat Y. "Günümüzde Kur'an ve Hadis Öğretimi Üzerine" [On Today's Quran and Hadith Education], in Ankara Üniversitesi İlâhiyat Fakültesi ve TÖMER Dil Öğretim Merkezi, *Almanya, Fransa, İngiltere, İtalya, Japonya, ABD ve Türkiye'de Uluslararası Din Eğitimi Sempozyumu (20–21 Kasım 1997)* [Conference on International

Religious Education in Germany, France, England, Italy, Japan, the United States, and Turkey (November 20–21, 1997)]: 172–81.

Ayhan, Halis. *Türkiye'de Din Eğitimi (1920–1998)* [Religious Education in Turkey (1920–1998)]. Istanbul: Marmara Üniversitesi İlâhiyat Fakültesi Vakfı Yayınları, 1999.

Ayhan, Halis et al. *Kuruluşunun 43. Yılında İmam-Hatip Liseleri* [The Imam-Hatip High Schools at the 43rd Year of Their Foundation]. Istanbul: Ensar, 1995.

Baloğlu, Zekai. *Türkiye'de Eğitim* [Education in Turkey]. Istanbul: TÜSİAD Yayınları, 1990.

Barlas, Mehmet. *Turgut Özal'ın Anıları* [Turgut Özal's Memoirs]. Istanbul: Sabah Kitapları, 1994.

Baytok, Taner. *Bir Asker Bir Diplomat: Güven Erkaya-Taner Baytok Söyleşi* [One Soldier One Diplomat: Güven Erkaya-Taner Baytok Conversation]. 3rd ed. Istanbul: Doğan Kitapçılık, 2001.

Berkes, Niyazi. *Türkiye'de Çağdaşlaşma* [Modernization in Turkey]. 3rd ed. Istanbul: Yapı Kredi Yayınları, 2002.

———. *Teokrasi ve Laiklik* [Theocracy and Secularism]. Istanbul: Adam Yayıncılık, 1984.

———. *Türk Düşününde Batı Sorunu* [The Question of West in Turkish Thinking]. Ankara: Bilgi Yayınevi, 1975.

Bilgin, Beyza. "1980 Sonrası Türkiye'de Din Kültürü ve Ahlâk Bilgisi Dersinin Zorunlu Oluşu ve Program Anlayışları" [The Introduction of Mandatory Religious Culture and Ethics Course in Turkey after 1980], in T.C. MEB Din Öğretimi Genel Müdürlüğü [Ministry of Education, General Directorate of Religious Education], *New Methodological Approaches in Religious Education International Symposium Papers and Discussions (March 28–30, 2001, Istanbul)*. Ankara: MEB Yayınları, 2003, 671–93.

———. *Eğitim Bilimi ve Din Eğitimi* [Science of Education and Religious Education]. Ankara: Ankara Üniversitesi İlâhiyat Fakültesi Yayınları, 1988.

———. *Türkiye'de Din Eğitimi ve Liselerde Din Dersleri* [Religious Education in Turkey and Religion Courses in High Schools]. Ankara: Emel Matbaacılık, 1980.

Bolay, Süleyman Hayri, and Mümtazer Türköne. *Din Eğitim Raporu* [Report on Religious Education]. Ankara: Türkiye Diyanet Vakfı Yayın Matabaacılık ve Ticaret İşletmesi, 1995.

Bölügiray, Nevzat. *28 Şubat Süreci*, vol. 2 [The February 28th Process]. Istanbul: Tekin Yayınevi, 2000.

———. *Sokaktaki Askerin Dönüşü: 12 Eylül Yönetimi Dönemi* [Return of the Soldier on Street: The September 12th Governance Period]. Istanbul: Tekin Yayınevi, 1991.

Bora, Tanıl. *Türk Sağının Üç Hali: Milliyetçilik, Muhafazakârlık, İslâmcılık* [Three Situations of the Turkish Right: Nationalism, Conservatism, Islamism]. 2nd ed. Istanbul: Birikim Yayınları, 1999.

Bora, Tanıl and Kemal Can. *Devlet, Ocak, Dergâh: 12 Eylül'den 1990'lara Ülkücü Hareket* [State, Hearth, Dergâh: The Idealist Movement from September 12 to the 1990s]. 6th ed. Istanbul: İletişim Yayınları, 2000.

Boratav, Korkut. "İktisat Tarihi (1981–1994)" [History of Economics (1981–1994)], in *Türkiye Tarihi 5: Bugünkü Türkiye 1980–1995* [History of Turkey 5: Today's Turkey 1980–1995], ed. Sina Akşin. Istanbul: Cem Yayınevi, 1995, 159–214.

———. *İstanbul ve Anadolu'dan Sınıf Profilleri* [Class Profiles from Istanbul and Anatolia]. Istanbul: Tarih Vakfı Yurt Yayınları, 1995.

Bulaç, Ali. *Din ve Modernizm* [Religion and Modernism]. Istanbul: İz Yayıncılık, 1995.

Çağatay, Neşet. *Türkiye'de Gerici Eylemler (1923'ten Buyana)* [Reactionist Attempts in Turkey since 1923]. Ankara: Ankara Üniversitesi Basımevi, 1972.

Çakır, Ruşen. *Ayet ve Slogan: Türkiye'de İslamcı Oluşumlar* [Verse and Slogan: Islamic Emergences in Turkey]. 9th ed. Istanbul: Metis Yayınları, 2002.

———. *Ne Şeriat Ne Demokrasi: Refah Partisini Anlamak* [Neither the Sharia Nor Democracy: Understanding the Welfare Party]. Istanbul: Metis Yayınları, 1994.

Çakır, Ruşen, İrfan Bozan, and Balkan Talu. *İmam-Hatip Liseleri: Efsaneler ve Gerçekler* [İmam-Hatip High Schools: Myths and Realities]. Istanbul: TESEV Yayınları, 2004.

Çarkoğlu, Ali, and Binnaz Toprak. *Türkiye'de Din, Toplum ve Siyaset* [Religion, Society, and Politics in Turkey]. Istanbul: TESEV Yayınları, 2000.

Çelik, Recep. *Milli Mücadelede Din Adamları* [The Men of Religion during the War of Independence]. Istanbul: Emre Yayınları, 1999

Ceylan, Hasan Hüseyin. *Erbakan ve Türkiye'nin Temel Meseleleri* [Erbakan and Turkey's Essential Issues]. 5th ed. Ankara: Rehber Yayıncılık, 1996.

Çiçek, Hikmet, prepared by. *İrticaya Karşı Genelkurmay Belgeleri* [The General Staff's Documents on Reactionism]. Istanbul: Kaynak Yayınları, 1997.

Demirci, Mehmet. "Türkiye'nin Çağdaşlaşma Sürecinde Tarikatler" [Tarikats in the Process of Turkey's Modernization], in *Türkiye'nin Çağdaşlaşma Problemi ve İslam* [Turkey's Modernization Problem and Islam] (Sempozyum [Conference]: May 3–4, 1997, İzmir). Ankara: Türkiye Diyanet Vakfı Yayınları, 2000, 161–9.

Efe, Şeref, and Mustafa Rumeli. *Hükümetlerin Performanslarının Değerlendirilmesi* [Evaluation of Governments' Performances]. Ankara: Ankara Ticaret Odası, 2002.

Emre, Süleyman Arif. *Siyasette 35 Yıl* [35 Years in Politics]. 3 vols. Ankara: *Keşif Yayınları*, 2002.

Erbakan, Necmettin. *İslam ve İlim* [Islam and Science]. Istanbul: Furkan Yayınları, 1994.

———. *Adil Ekonomik Düzen*. Ankara: Semih Ofset, 1991.

———. *Kenan Evren'in Anılarındaki Yanılgılar* [Mistakes in Kenan Evren's Memoirs]. Ankara: Rehber Yayıncılık, 1991.

———. *Milli Görüş* [The National View]. Istanbul: Degâh Yayınları, 1975.

Ergin, Muharrem, Aydın Bolak, and Süleyman Yalçın. *Yeni Bir Yüzyıla Girerken Türk-İslam Sentezi Görüşünde Meselelerimiz: Milliyetçiler IV. Büyük İlmi Kurultayı* [Our Views on Turkish-Islamic Synthesis, While Entering a New Century: The Fourth Great Scientific Convention of Nationalists]. 3 vols. Istanbul: Aydınlar Ocağı, 1988.

Erkilet-Başer, Alev. "Sağ Siyasetin Payandası: Araçsalcı Dinsellik" [Commonality in the Right Politics: Tool of Religiosity]. *İslâmiyat* III (2000): 69–78.

Eroğul, Cem. *Demokrat Parti: Tarihi ve İdeolojisi* [The Democrat Party: Its History and Ideology]. Ankara: Sevinç Matbaası, 1970.

Evren, Kenan. *12 Eylülden Önce ve Sonra . . . Ne Demişlerdi? Ne Dediler? Ne Diyorlar?* [Before and After September 12 . . . What Had They Said? What Did They Say? What Do They Say?]. Istanbul: AD Yayıncılık A.Ş., 1997.

———. *Unutulan Gerçekler* [The Forgotten Realities]. Ankara: Tisamat Basım, 1995.

Gökalp, Ziya. *Türkçülüğün Esasları* [The Principles of Turkism], prepared by Mehmet Kaplan. Ankara: Kültür Bakanlığı Yayınları, 1990.

———. *Türkleşmek, İslamlaşmak, Muasırlaşmak* [Being Turkish, Islam, Modernized], prepared by İbrahim Kutluk. Ankara: Devlet Kitapları, 1976.

Gülalp, Haldun. *Kimlikler Siyaseti: Türkiye'de Siyasal İslam'ın Temelleri* [Politics of Identities: The Bases of Political Islam in Turkey]. Istanbul: Metis Yayınları, 2003.

Günay, Ünver. "Türkiye'de Toplumsal Değişme ve Tarikatler" [Social Change and Islamic Brotherhoods in Turkey]. *İslâmiyât* V, no. 4 (2002): 141–62.

Güreli, Nail. *Gerçek Tanık Korkut Özal Anlatıyor* [The Real Witness Korkut Özal Tells]. Istanbul: Milliyet Yayınları, 1994.

Güvenç, Bozkurt. *Türk Kimliği: Kültür Tarihinin Kaynakları* [Turkish Identity: The Sources of Culture History]. 5th ed. Istanbul: Remzi Kitabevi, 1997.

Güvenç, Bozkurt, Gencay Şaylan, İlhan Tekeli, and Şerafettin Turan. *Dosya: Türk-İslam Sentezi* [The File: The Turkish-Islamic Synthesis]. Istanbul: Sarmal Yayınevi, 1991.

İlhan, Atilla. *Hangi Batı: Anılar ve Acılar* [Which West: Memoirs and Pains]. Ankara: Bilgi Yayınevi, 1972.

İnan, Afet. *Türkiye Cumhuriyeti ve Türk Devrimi* [The Turkish Republic and the Turkish Revolution]. 4th ed. Ankara: Türk Tarih Kurumu Basimevi, 1998.

İnan, Arı. *Düşünceleriyle Atatürk* [Atatürk with His Thoughts]. 3rd ed. Ankara: Türk Tarih Kurumu Basımevi, 1999.

Işık, Oğuz, and Melih Pınarcıoğlu. *Nöbetleşe Yoksulluk: Gecekondulaşma ve Kent Yoksulları Sultanbeyli Örneği* [Continuous Poverty: Shantytowns and the Urban Poor the Case of Sultanbeyli]. Istanbul: İletişim, 2001.

Kafesoğlu, İbrahim. *Türk İslam Sentezi* [The Turkish Islamic Synthesis]. 2nd ed. Istanbul: Ötüken Neşriyat, 1996.

Kara, Mustafa. *Tasavvuf ve Tarikatlar Tarihi* [History of Sufism and Tarikats]. Istanbul: Dergâh Yayınları, 1999.

Kazan, Şevket. *Refah Gerçeği* [The Reality of the Welfare]. 3 vols. Ankara: Keşif Yayınları, 2001.

———. *Öncesi ve Sonrasıyla 28 Şubat* [February 28th before and after]. 6th ed. Ankara: Keşif Yayınları, 2000.

Keleş, Ruşen. *Kentleşme Politikası* [Urbanization Politics]. Ankara: İmge Yayınevi, 1990.

Kili, Suna. *Türk Devrim Tarihi* [History of the Turkish Revolution]. Istanbul: Türkiye İş Bankası Kültür Yayınları, 2002.

———. *Atatürk Devrimi: Bir Çağdaşlaşma Modeli* [The Atatürk Revolution: A Modernization Model]. Ankara: Türkiye İş Bankası Kültür Yayınları, 2000.

Kırkıncı, Mehmet. *Mektuplar, Hatıralar* [Letters, Memories]. Istanbul: Zafer Yayınları, 1992.

Kışlalı, Ahmet Taner. *Kemalizm, Laiklik ve Demokrasi* [Kemalism, Secularism, and Democracy]. 7th ed. Ankara: İmge Kitabevi, 2001.

Köker, Levent. *Modernleşme, Kemalizm ve Demokrasi* [Modernization, Kemalism, and Democracy]. 4th ed. Istanbul: İletişim Yayınları, 1999.

Kösoğlu, Nevzat. *Türk Milliyetçiliği ve Osmanlı* [Turkish Nationalism and the Ottomans]. Istanbul: Ötüken Neşriyât, 2000.

———. *Devlet: Eski Türkler'de, İslam'da ve Osmanlı'da* [The State: In Ancient Turks, Islam, and Ottomans]. Istanbul: Ötüken Neşriyât, 1997.

Kutay, Cemal. *Cumhuriyet'in 75. Yılında Onlara Saygı: Kurtuluşun "Kuvvacı" Din Adamları* [A Respect to Them in the 75th Year of the Republic: The Kemalist Men of Religion during the War of Independence]. Istanbul: Aksoy Yayıncılık, 1998.

Mardin, Şerif. "XIX. Yüzyılda Düşünce Akımları ve Osmanlı Devleti" [Ideologies in the 19th century and the Ottoman State], in *Türk Modernleşmesi: Makaleler*, vol. IV

[Turkish Modernization: Essays], ed. Şerif Mardin. Istanbul: İletişim Yayınları, 1991, 82–102.

Mumcu, Uğur. *Rabıtat*. 24th ed. Ankara: Uğur Mumcu Araştırmacı Gazetecilik Vakfı, 2000.

Onat, Hasan. *Türkiye'de Din Anlayışında Değişim Süreci* [A Process of Change in the Understanding of Religion in Turkey]. Ankara: Ankara Okulu Yayınları, 2003.

Ozankaya, Özer, ed. *Dünya Düşünürleri Gözüyle Atatürk ve Cumhuriyeti* [Atatürk and His Republic in the Eyes of World Thinkers]. 2nd ed. Istanbul: İş Bankası Kültür Yayınları, 2000.

Özdemir, Hikmet. "Siyasal Tarih, 1960–1980" [Political History, 1960–1980], in *Türkiye Tarihi 4: Çağdaş Türkiye 1908–1980* [History of Turkey 4: Modern Turkey 1908–1980], eds. Mete Tunçay et al. Istanbul: Cem Yayınevi, 1990, 191–264.

Özdenören, Rasim. *Müslümanca Yaşamak* [Living in a Muslim Way]. 4th ed. Istanbul: İz Yayıncılık, 1994.

———. *Müslümanca Düşünme Üzerine Denemeler* [Essays on Thinking in a Muslim Way]. 5th ed. Istanbul: İz Yayıncılık, 1990.

Özel, İsmet. *Üç Mesele: Teknik, Medeniyet, Yabancılaşma* [Three Problems: Technique, Civilization, Alienation]. 4th ed. Istanbul: Çıdam Yayınları, 1992.

Pakdemirli, Ekrem. *Cumhuriyet Döneminin Ekonomik Büyüklükleri (1923–2002)* [Economic Indicators of the Republican Period (1923–2002)]. Ankara: Türkiye Odalar ve Borsalar Birliği Yayınları, 2002.

Sarıbay, Ali Yaşar. *Türkiye'de Modernleşme, Din ve Parti Politikası: MSP Örnek Olayı* [Modernism, Religion, and Party Politics: The Case of the National Salvation Party]. Istanbul: Alan Yayıncılık, 1985.

Savaş, Vural. *Refah Partisi İddianamesi ve Mütâlâsı* [The Welfare Party Indictment and Its Comment]. Istanbul: Fast Yayıncılık, 1997.

Selim, Yavuz. *Yol Ayrımı: Milli Görüş Hareketindeki Ayrışmanın Perde Arkası* [Turning Point: Behind the Scenes of the Division within the National View Movement]. Ankara: Hiler Yayınevi, 2002.

Şenyapılı, Tansı;. *1980 Sonrasında Ruhsatsız Konut Yapımı* [Illegal House Building after 1980]. Ankara: T.C. Başbakanlık Toplu Konut Dairesi Başkanlığı, 1996.

Sever, Metin, and Cem Dizdar, eds. *2. Cumhuriyet Tartışmaları* [The Second Republic Discussions]. Ankara: Başak Yayınları, 1993.

Sitembölükbaşı, Şaban. "Türkiye'de İslam ve siyasal sisteme yönelik olumsuz tutumlar" [Islam in Turkey and Negative Attitudes Toward the Political System], in *İslam ve Demokrasi Kutlu Doğum Sempozyumu* [Islam and Democracy], ed. Ömer Turan. Ankara: Türkiye Diyanet Vakfı Yayınları, 1998, 267–84.

Tanla, Bülent. *Türkiye'nin Siyasal Haritası (1950–1995)* [Political Map of Turkey (1950–1995)]. Ankara: TBMM Basımevi, 1997.

Tezcan, Nuran. *Atatürk'ün Yazdığı Yurttaşlık Bilgileri* [Citizenship Information Written by Atatürk]. 2nd ed. Istanbul: Çağdaş Yayınları, 1994.

Timur, Taner. *Türk Devrimi: Tarihi Anlamı ve Felsefi Temeli* [The Turkish Revolution: Its Historical Meaning and Philosophical Basis]. Ankara: Sevinç Matbaası, 1968.

Toprak, Binnaz, İrfan Bozan, Tan Morgül, and Nedim Şener. *Türkiye'de Farklı Olmak: Din ve Muhafazakarlık Ekseninde Ötekileştirilenler* [Being Different in Turkey: Being Discriminated in the Axis of Religion and Conservatism]. Istanbul: Boğaziçi Üniversitesi, 2008.

Tunaya, Tarık Zafer. *Devrim Hareketleri İçinde Atatürk ve Atatürkçülük* [Atatürk and Atatürkism in Revolutionary Movements]. Istanbul: Bilgi Üniversitesi Yayınları, 2002.

Tunçay, Mete. *Türkiye Cumhuriyeti'nde Tek-Parti Yönetimi'nin Kurulması (1923–1931)* [The Establishment of a One-Party Rule in the Turkish Republic (1923–1931)]. 3rd ed. Istanbul: Tarih Vakfı Yurt Yayınları, 1999.

Turan, Ali Eşref. *Türkiye'de Seçmen Davranışı: Önceki Kırılmalar ve 2002 Seçimi* [Electorate Behavior in Turkey: Previous Breakdowns and the 2002 Elections]. Istanbul: Istanbul Bilgi Üniversitesi Yayınları, 2004.

Türkdoğan, Orhan. *Gecekondu, İnsan ve Kültür: İstanbul Örnek Olayı* [Shantytowns, Human Being, and Culture: The Case of Istanbul]. Istanbul: Genar, 2002.

Üçok, Bahriye. *Atatürk'ün İzinde Bir Arpa Boyu* [A Short Advancement in Atatürk's Path]. Istanbul: Cem Yayınevi, 2000.

Unan, Fahri, and Yücel Hacaloğlu, prepared by. *Cumhuriyet'in 75. Yılında Türkiye'de Din Eğitimi ve Öğretimi İlmi Toplantısı (Izmir, 4–6 Aralık 1998) (Tebliğler)* [Scientific Meeting on Religious Education and Teaching in Turkey at the Republic's 75th Year (Izmir, December 4–6, 1998) (Presentations)] (Ankara: Türk Yurdu Yayınları, 1999).

Yalçın, Süleyman. *Aydınlar Ocağı ve Türk-İslam Sentezi* [The Intellectuals' Hearth and the Turkish-Islamic Synthesis]. Istanbul: Uğur Ofset, 1988.

Yavuz, Ünsal. *Atatürk: İmparatorluktan Milli Devlete* [Atatürk: From an Empire to a Nation State]. Ankara: Türk Tarih Kurumu Basımevi, 1999.

Yirmibeşoğlu, Sabri. *Askeri ve Siyasi Anılarım, 1928–1956*, vol. 1 [My Military and Political Memoirs, 1928–1956]. Istanbul: Zafer Matbaası, 1999.

———. *Askeri ve Siyasi Anılarım, 1965–1999*, vol. 2 [My Military and Political Memoirs, 1965–1999]. Istanbul: Zafer Matbaası, 1999.

Yücekök, Ahmet N. *Türkiye'de Örgütlenmiş Dinin Sosyo-Ekonomik Tabanı (1946–1960)* [The Organized Religion's Socio-economic Basis in Turkey (1946–1960)]. Ankara: Sevinç Matbaası, 1971.

Primary Documents

Adalet ve Kalkınma Partisi. *AK Parti Parti Tüzüğü* [The JDP Party Program]. Ankara: AK Parti, 2002.

———. *AK Parti Genel Merkez Kadın Kolları Faaliyet Raporu* [The JDP Headquarters Women Commission Work Report]. Ankara: AK Parti, 2003.

———. *Adalet ve Kalkınma Partisi 1. Olağan Büyük Kongresi, Genel Başkan Recep Tayyip Erdoğan'ın Konuşması (12 Ekim 2004)* [The JDP Chair Recep Tayyip Erdoğan's Speech at the Party's First General Convention (October 12, 2004)]. Ankara: AK Parti, 2004.

———. *Türkiye Bülteni* [Bulletin of Turkey], no. 27. Ankara: AK Parti, August 2005.

———. *Türkiye Bülteni*, no. 29. Ankara: AK Parti, October 2005.

———. *Türkiye Bülteni*, no. 30. Ankara: AK Parti, November 2005.

———. *Türkiye Bülteni*, no. 39. Ankara: AK Parti, August 2006.

———. *Türkiye Bülteni*, no. 41. Ankara: AK Parti, October 2006.

Akdoğan, Yalçın. *Muhafazakar Demokrasi* [Conservative Democracy]. Ankara: AK Parti, 2003.

European Court of Human Rights. Case of Refah Partisi (the Welfare Party) and Others v. Turkey (Applications nos. 41340/98, 41342/98, 41343/98 and 41344/98).

Fazilet Partisi. *Türkiye'nin Öncelikleri ve Temel Görüşlerimiz, M. Recai Kutan'ın Basın Toplantısı 17 Aralık 1998 Bilkent-Ankara* [Turkey's Priorities and Our Essential Views, M. Recai Kutan's Press Meeting (December 17, 1998)]. Ankara: Fazilet Partisi, 1999.

———. *Fazilet Partisi Genel Merkez 2000–2001 Faaliyet Bülteni, Kadın Kolları* [The Virtue Party Headquarters 2000–2001 Action Bulletin, Women's Commission]. Ankara: Fazilet Partisi, 2001.

———. *Fazilet Partisi Tanıtım Başkanlığı, Tanıtma Rehberi* [The Virtue Party, Advertisement Chairmanship, Advertisement Guidance]. Ankara: Fazilet Partisi, 1999.

———. *Günışığında Türkiye, 18 Nisan 1999 Seçim Beyannamesi* [Turkey in Daylight, April 18, 1999 Election Declaration]. Ankara: Fazilet Partisi, 1999.

———. *Fazilet Partisi'nin Anayasa Değişikliğine Dair Uzlaşma Metni Taslağı (11 Kasım 1999)* [The Virtue Party's Draft Proposal for a Constitutional Change (November 11, 1999)]. Ankara: Fazilet Partisi, 1999.

———. *Öncü Türkiye için Elele* [Hand in Hand for a Leader Turkey]. Ankara: Fazilet Partisi, n.d.

Maarif Bakanlığı [Ministry of Education]. *Atatürk'ün Maarife Ait Direktifleri* [Atatürk's Directives on Education]. Istanbul: Maarif Matbaası, 1939.

Milli Eğitim Bakanlığı [Ministry of Education]. *Cumhurbaşkanı Kenan Evren'in Milli Eğitime Ait Direktif ve Sözleri* [President Kenan Evren's Directives and Speeches on National Education]. Ankara: MEB, 1984.

Milli Güvenlik Kurulu Genel Sekreterliği [The General Secretariat of the National Security Council]. *12 Eylül Öncesi ve Sonrası* [12 September in Turkey: Before and after]. Ankara: Türk Tarih Kurumu Basımevi, 1981.

Refah Partisi. *Refah Partisi Tüzük ve Programı* [The Welfare Party Program]. Ankara: Refah Partisi, 1983.

———. *Refah Partisi Birinci Büyük Kongresi, Genel Başkan Ahmet Tekdal'ın Açış Konuşması (30 Haziran 1985)* [The Welfare Party First Great Convention, the Chair Ahmet Tekdal's Opening Speech (June 30, 1985)]. Ankara: Refah Partisi, 1985.

———. *Tek Çözüm: Refah Partisi* [The Only Solution: The Welfare Party]. Ankara: Refah Partisi, 1987.

———. *Refah Partisi, Büyük Kongresi (30 Haziran 1985)* [The Welfare Party, Great Convention (June 30, 1985)]. Ankara: Refah Partisi, 1985.

———. *Refah Partisi, İkinci Büyük Kongresi (11 Ekim 1987)* [The Welfare Party, Second Great Convention (October 11, 1987)]. Ankara: Refah Partisi, 1991.

———. *Refah Partisi 4. Olağan Büyük Kongresi, Faaliyet Raporu (10 Ekim 1993)* [The Welfare Party Fourth General Great Convention, Work Report (October 10, 1993)]. Ankara: Refah Partisi, 1993.

———. *Refah Partisi 4. Büyük Kongre, Genel Başkan Prof. Dr. Necmettin Erbakan'ın Açış Konuşması (10 Ekim 1993)* [The Welfare Party Fourth Great Congress, Chair Prof. Necmettin Erbakan's Opening Speech (October 10, 1993)]. Ankara: Refah Partisi, 1993.

———. *Türkiye'nin Gerçek Durumu, Sebepleri* [Turkey's Real Situation, Its Reasons]. Ankara: Refah Partisi, n.d.

———. *Adil Düzen 21 Soru/21 Cevap* [The Just Order 21 Questions/21 Answers]. Ankara: Refah Partisi, n.d.

———. *Refah Partisi Samsun Merkez İlçe Teşkilâtı, Teşkilât Çalışma Modeli* [The Welfare Party Samsun Central District Organization, Organization Working Model]. Samsun: Refah Partisi, 1995.

———. *Refah Partisi Olağan Büyük Kongresi, Faaliyet Raporu* [The Welfare Party General Great Convention, Work Report]. October 10, 1993.

———. *Mecliste İlk 100 Gün* [The First 100 Days in the Parliament]. Ankara: Refah Partisi, 1992.

———. *Refah Partisi. Yerel Seçim '94* [The Local Election '94]. Ankara: Refah Partisi, n.d.

———. *Refah Partisi'nin Anayasa Değişikliği Uzlaşma Teklifi* [The Welfare Party's Agreement Proposal for a Constitutional Change]. Ankara: Refah Partisi, 1995.

———. *Refah Partisi ve Türkiye'de Demokrasi* [The Welfare Party and Democracy in Turkey]. Ankara: Bars Ltd., 1998.

———. *İktidarda Bir Yıl: RP-DYP Koalisyonu İcraatları* [One Year in Governance: The WP-TPP Coalition's Implementations]. Ankara: Refah Partisi, n.d.

Saadet Partisi. *Saadet Partisi Teşkilât Rehberi* [The Felicity Party Organization Directory]. Ankara: Saadet Partisi, 2002.

T. C. Anayasa Mahkemesi [The Turkish Republic Constitutional Court]. *Anayasa Mahkemesi Kararı, Esas Sayısı: 1997/1 (Siyasi Parti Kapatma), Karar Sayısı (1998/1), Davalı Refah Partisi* [The Constitutional Court's Decision on the Welfare Party] (Internet ed.).

———. *Anayasa Mahkemesi Kararı, Esas Sayısı 1999/2 (Siyasi Parti Kapatma), Karar Sayısı 2001/2, Davalı Fazilet Partisi* [The Constitutional Court's Decision on the Virtue Party] (Internet ed.).

———. *Anayasa Mahkemesi Kararı, Esas Sayısı: 2008/1 (Siyasi Parti Kapatma), Karar Sayısı: 2008/2, Davalı Adalet ve Kalkınma Partisi* [The Constitutional Court's Decision on the Justice and Development Party] (Internet ed.).

T. C. Başbakanlık [Turkish Republic Prime Ministry]. *Başbakan Turgut Özal'ın konuşma, mesaj, beyanat ve mülakatları (13.12.1983–12.12.1984)* [Prime Minister Turgut Özal's Speeches, Messages, Statements, and Interviews (December 13, 1983–December 12, 1984)]. Ankara: Başbakanlık Basımevi, 1984.

———. *Başbakan Turgut Özal'ın konuşma, mesaj, beyanat ve mülakatları (13.12.1984–12.12.1985)* [Prime Minister Turgut Özal's Speeches, Messages, Statements, and Interviews (December 13, 1984–December 12, 1985)]. Ankara: Başbakanlık Basımevi, 1985.

———. *Başbakan Turgut Özal'ın konuşma, mesaj, beyanat ve mülakatları (13.12.1985–12.12.1986)* [Prime Minister Turgut Özal's Speeches, Messages, Statements, and Interviews (December 13, 1985–December 12, 1986)]. Ankara: Başbakanlık Basımevi, 1986.

———. *Devlet Başkanı Orgeneral Kenan Evren'in Söylev ve Demeçleri (12 Eylül 1980–12 Eylül 1981)* [The Turkish Republic Head of the State General Kenan Evren's Speeches and Declarations (September 12, 1980–September 12, 1981)]. Ankara: Başbakanlık Basımevi, 1981.

———. *Devlet Başkanı Orgeneral Kenan Evren'in Söylev ve Demeçleri (12 Eylül 1981–12 Eylül 1982)* [The Turkish Republic Head of the State General Kenan Evren's Speeches and Declarations September 12, 1981–September 12, 1982)]. Ankara: Başbakanlık Basımevi, 1982.

———. *Gelişen Türkiye'de Hükümetin Yedi Yıllık İcraatı (1983–1990)* [The Governing Party's Seven Year Working Report in Developing Turkey (1983–1990)]. *Cilt: I Başbakanlık Bağlı ve İlgili Kuruluşları*. Ankara: T.C. Başbakanlık, 1990.

T. C. Başbakanlık Devlet Planlama Teşkilâtı (DPT) [The Turkish Republic Prime Ministry State Planning Organization]. *Milli Kültür: Özel İhtisas Komisyon Raporu Raporu* [The National Culture: The Special Commission's Report]. Ankara: Devlet Planlama Teşkilâtı, 1983.

———. *Fifth Five Year Development Plan (1985–1989)*. Ankara: Devlet Planlama Teşkilâtı, 1985.

Index

Abdülhamid II, Sultan, 40, 66
abeyance structures, 6, 17, 56, 135, 280
action mobilization, 30
Afghan Hizb-i Islami, 114. *See also* Gulbettin Hikmetyar
Ağar, Mehmet, 247
Ağaoğlu, Ahmet, 41
agency, 14–16, 18, 21, 30, 136, 278, 280
Ahmad, Feroz, 46n56, 89, 89n16
Akbulut, Ahmet, 110–11, 111n131
Akçura, Yusuf, 40–1
Akgönenç, Oya, 49n79
AKİM (*AK İletişim Merkezi* – AK Communications Center), 245
Akıncı, Uğur, 175
Akıncılar (Raiders), 69–70, 91. *See* Raiders organization (*akıncılar teşkilâtı*)
Akit (newspaper), 230
Aköz Foundation, 130
Aksay, Hasan, 66, 114, 234n78
Aksu, Abdülkadir, 121, 235, 242
Al Baraka (Divine Blessing), 129
Al Baraka Group, 129, 129n232, 129n234
Al Baraka Türk, 130–1
al-Banna, Hassan, 61, 218
Alemdaroğlu, Kemal, 266
Alevis, 71n203, 86, 86n3, 105, 190
al-Faisal, Muhammed, 113
al-Ghazali, 210
Alp, Tekin, 41
Al Qaeda, 252. *See* Yasin El Kadı
al-Saud, Mohammed al-Faisal, 129

Altıkulaç, Tayyar, 103, 128, 133
Altunışık, Meliha, 140
Amenta, Edwin, 18–19
American green-belt project (*yeşil kuşak projesi*), 91. *See* U.S. green-belt project
AMGT (*Avrupa Milli Görüş Teşkilâtı*), 69, 174, 207, 228. *See* European National View Organization
Aminzade, Ronald, 11
Anatolianists (*Anadolucular*), 98. *See* Azra Erhat Halikarnas Balıkçısı
Anatolian petty bourgeoisie, 65–6, 77
Anatolian Tigers (*Anadolu Kaplanları*), 130, 201, 241
antileftist Islamist circles in Turkey, 64
antileftist organizations in Turkey, 64
antinuclear movements in France, Sweden, the United States, and West Germany, 5, 18
Arab countries, 7, 279
Arab Islam, 47
Arab-Israeli conflict, 150
Arab nationalism, 40
Arat, Yeşim, 188n19, 189
Arınç, Bülent, 121, 234n78, 240–1
Armaner, Neda, 104–5
Aşıkoğlu, Nevzat, 109, 109n128
ASKON. *See* Anatolian Tigers
Asr-ı Saadet (age of happiness), 4, 209, 211

303

Association of *İmam-Hatip* Graduates, 31
Association for Struggling Against Communism in Turkey (*Komünizmle Mücadele Derneği*), 64
Association for Supporting Modern Life (*Çağdaş Yaşamı Destekleme Derneği*), 219, 274
Atatürk era, 41
Atatürk, Mustafa Kemal, 1, 5–6, 37, 41–3, 45–50, 54, 58, 88, 98, 103–6, 129, 160, 176–7, 207, 209, 218–19, 283
Atatürk Revolution of 1923–1938, 1, 43–4
Atay, Hüseyin, 103–4
authoritarian setting: countermobilization in, 11, 280
Averroes, 210
Avicenna, 210
Ayata-Güneş, Ayşe, 120, 157, 171
Ayata, Sencer, 62, 119–20, 129
Aygün, Sinan, 268

Bahçeli, Devlet, 263
Balbay, Mustafa, 268
Balkans: defeat of the Ottoman Empire in, 40
Başbuğ, General İlker, 249, 253, 272, 272n303, 273, 282
Basque separatists in Spain, 35
Baumeister, Roy, 32
Bayar, Celal, 50
Baykal, Deniz, 179, 260, 267, 269
Bayramoğlu, Ali, 201–6, 242. *See* MÜSİAD
Beamer, Chase, 267
Benford, Robert, 27, 27n111, 30, 136
Bereket Foundation, 130
Berkes, Niyazi, 38, 42
Berman, Sheri, 3n11, 27, 31, 31n122
Bernay, Ferit, 274
big industrialists and traders, 66
Bilgin, Beyza, 103–4
Bir, General Çevik, 48n74, 91, 219, 222, 253
Bölügiray, Retired General Nevzat, 90, 90n24, 91, 91n30, 92n42, 94, 94n52, 115n155
Bora, Tanıl, 64, 93, 100

Boratav, Korkut, 139, 171
Bozkurt, Nahide, 49, 127n222
Bryza, Matthew, 267
Buğra, Ayşe, 202
Bulaç, Ali, 181, 209, 211–12
Bush, George W., 250
Büyükanıt, General Yaşar, 253–4, 282
Büyükçelebi, Ufuk, 268

Çakır, Ruşen, 93, 198
Çakmak, Marshall Fevzi, 55, 55n102
caliphate, 6, 37, 42–3, 47
Calp, Necdet, 118
capitalism, 69, 149–50, 152, 163, 200, 207
Çarkoğlu, Ali, 4n12, 81
Catalan separatists in Spain, 35
Çelik, Halil İbrahim, 208n117, 224
Central Bank, 50, 131
Central Powers, 41
Ceylan, Hasan Hüseyin, 218, 231, 231n64
Chief Religious Office of the State, 37, 43
CIA (Cental Intelligence Agency), 62, 91, 151
Çiçek, Cemil, 232, 235, 256
Çiller, Tansu, 156, 159, 179, 216, 232
Cindoruk, Hüsamettin, 229, 232
Civelek, Sebahattin, 93
civil constitution, 241
civil rights movements, 8
civil society: definition of, 31n122
civil society associations: American Jewish, 274
    Islamists' utilization of (Egypt), 26–7, 31
    Islamists' utilization of (Turkey), 27, 31, 161, 175, 178, 237–9, 273, 277
    secular-oriented (Turkey), 219–20, 222, 256, 264, 266
civil states: civil movements in, 8–10
Clark, Janine, 26, 32–3
clientelism, 155, 161, 165, 172
clientelistic relations, 138
cold war: during, 62, 91–2, 114, 135, 150
    in the aftermath of, 29, 136, 149, 151–2, 156–7, 180, 190, 229, 278
collective action, 12, 14, 17n72, 18, 21, 29–30, 32, 136, 163

Index

collective identity: 6, 30, 33
 Islamic, 56
 Islamist, 4, 6
 Islamic politicized, 30
 politicized, 29–30, 33, 183
Çömez, Turhan, 269n277
communism, 22, 24–5, 56, 61–2, 64, 69, 91–3, 96, 100–1, 105, 118, 135, 152, 163, 190, 207
communists, 45, 67, 92, 92n42, 93
Comte, Auguste, 106
consensus mobilization, 30, 136
conservative Muslims, 51, 67
Constituent Assembly, 59
Constitution: in 1961, 59–61, 96
 in 1982, 101–2, 107, 156n96
Constitutional Court, 22, 34, 53–5, 60, 67n183, 68, 83, 121, 214, 216, 218, 226, 234, 234n77, 235, 240, 243, 256, 264–5, 265n250, 266, 268–70, 278–9, 282
conventional means, 9–10
conversational settings, 32–3
Copenhagen criteria, 248. *See* EU reform packages
Çörtoğlu, Sumru, 268
Coşkun, Ali, 232, 235
Council of State (*Danıştay*), 252, 256, 262n234, 264, 268
countermobilization, 11, 34, 214, 218–19, 221, 227, 241, 248, 264, 278–80, 282
coups. *See* military interventions
Çubukçu, İbrahim Ağah, 104–5
Cultural explanations, 5, 7, 279. *See also* grievance-based explanations
cultural nationalism (*kültür milliyetçiliği*), 97
culturalist paradigm, 15n64
Cumhuriyet (newspaper), 266, 268

D-8 (Developing 8), 205, 228–9, 248
Dalan, Bedrettin, 271n297
Dale, Karen, 32
Dar al-Maal al-Islami (House of Islamic Finance), 129, 129n233, 129n234
Darwinism, 106
da'wa (propagation of the faith), 33
Demirel, Süleyman, 63, 65, 65n167, 70, 70n200, 77, 90, 112, 114, 121n186, 154–6, 159, 159n112, 220, 228–9, 240
democracy, 4, 11, 21, 25, 27, 29, 31, 41, 51–2, 58, 62, 76, 82, 89, 125, 146, 148, 153, 177–9, 190, 197, 205, 208, 211–12, 219, 225, 227–9, 231, 235–9, 241–3, 246–7, 249, 252, 280–1
Democratic Left Party (DLP), 53, 61, 72, 74, 78–9, 82–3, 142, 144, 156, 170, 180, 216, 219–20, 229, 255, 260
Democratic People's Party (DPP), 53, 73, 75
Democratic Society Party (DSP), 53
Democratic Turkey Party, 83, 229
Democrat Party (DP), 50–2, 52n98, 53, 56–9, 59n128, 60, 63, 72, 74, 119, 155, 235
 DP rule, 57, 59
din u devlet (the unity of religion and the state), 38
Directive of Reactionism (*İrtica Direktifi*), 94
Directorate of Religious Affairs (*Diyanet*), 37, 47, 56, 59–60, 95, 103, 105, 124–5, 133, 207, 228
DİSK (*Devrimci İşçi Sendikaları Konfederasyonu* – Confederation of Revolutionary Trade Unions), 88
Dişli, Şaban, 270
Doğan conglomerate, 215
Doğan, General Çetin, 222
Doğan media, 271
Donuk, Abdülkadir, 96
Durkheim, 106
dynamic model, 18
dynamic statism, 21. *See* dynamic statist paradigm
dynamic statist paradigm, 21

EC (European Community), 150
Ecevit, Bülent, 77–8, 82, 90, 180, 220, 229, 232
education reform bill of 1997, 222. *See* soft military intervention of 1997
Egypt, 8–9, 26–7, 31, 132n245, 134, 150, 200, 206, 218, 228, 251n177
Eisinger, Peter, 13

elections: general elections (national elections): general elections (1950), 51, 55, 235
  general elections (1954), 52, 55
  general elections (1957), 52, 55
  general elections (1961), 56, 60
  general elections (1965), 60, 63
  general elections (1969), 63–4, 66
  general elections (1973), 68–71, 143
  general elections (1977), 71, 113
  general elections (1983), 25, 76, 118, 120, 154
  general elections (1987), 76, 78, 148, 158, 185
  general elections (1991), 76, 78, 158, 191, 199
  general elections (1995), 1, 33, 78, 82–3, 154, 179–82, 187, 200, 203, 209, 213–16, 239, 278
  general elections (1999), 82–3, 142, 236, 239–40
  general elections (2002), 1, 35, 83, 215, 244–5, 249, 258–9, 261, 270, 279, 282
  general elections (2007), 1, 35, 254–5, 258–9, 261, 267, 270, 279, 282
  local elections (municipality elections): local elections (1984), 78, 139, 154, 184–5
  local elections (1989), 158, 170, 185, 199
  local elections (1994), 78, 161, 169–70, 173, 177, 199
  local elections (1999), 167, 240
  local elections (2004), 83
  local elections (2009), 273
electoral base, 66, 71, 71n203, 77–8, 223, 255, 258
electoral precincts (ballot boxes), 31, 182, 184–5, 187, 199, 213, 244
elite alignments, 5, 12, 14. See also unstable elite alignments
elite allies, 12, 14, 19–20, 22, 263, 268, 283. See also inadvertent elite ally
El Kadı, Yasin, 252
Eminağaoğlu, Ömer Faruk, 272
Emre, Süleyman Arif, 66–8, 234n78
Ensar Foundation, 128, 130, 226, 231n63
Entente Powers, 41, 44n44, 45

Enver Pasha, 41
Erbakan, Akgün, 208
Erbakan, Necmettin, 4, 28, 33n133, 34n135, 56–7, 57n112, 66–71, 77, 83, 88, 90, 90n29, 94, 99, 117–18, 121n186, 146–7, 149–54, 163, 169, 174–5, 179–80, 182–5, 189–91, 196, 200–1, 205–8, 214, 217–18, 220–1, 224–6, 226n40, 227–30, 234, 234n77, 235, 238–40, 242–4, 247–8, 259, 277, 279
Erdoğan, Recep Tayyip, 34, 34n135, 35, 57n112, 161–2, 176–8, 180, 191, 198–9, 214, 226n38, 228, 237, 242, 242n127, 243, 246, 249–51, 251n177, 252–3, 256, 260, 263–5, 268–9, 271, 273–4, 279, 281
Ergenekon case, 266, 266n259, 269, 272–3
Erhat, Azra, 99
Erim, Nihat, 68
Erkaya, Retired General Güven, 92
Erman, Tahire, 171–2
Eroğan, Kadri, 65
Eruygur, Retired General Şener, 268, 269n277
Esmer, Yılmaz, 82, 159
etatism, 51
EU (European Union), 35–6, 141, 149, 214–15, 236–7, 241–2, 246, 248–9, 261, 267–9, 278, 281
EU reform packages, 35, 248–9, 251, 281
European Construction Firms for Mosque and Community (Avrupa Cemaat ve Camii İnşaat Firması), 208
European National View Organization, 69, 206–7, 228. See AMGT
European powers, 42
Evren, General Kenan, 86, 88–90, 92, 94, 101, 103, 105, 105n105, 108–9, 113, 115–16, 118–20, 125, 125n209, 134

Faculty Members Association (Öğretim Üyeleri Derneği), 220
fair order (hakça düzen), 142
Faisal Finance, 129–31, 133, 230
Felicity Party (FP), xix, 4, 23, 34–5, 45, 53–5, 67, 73, 75, 80–1, 83, 91, 100,

119, 124, 146, 148, 153, 162, 164, 199n69, 214–15, 223, 243–5, 247–8, 255, 259, 273, 279, 281
Fetullah Gülen congregation, 118, 234n73, 267, 272
fetva (religious orders), 38, 38n3, 42n30
Feyzoğlu, General Osman, 104
Fırat, Dengir Mir Mehmet, 268
First Nationalist Front, 70, 70n200
Foundation for Aid to Students' Parents, 194
Foundation for Islamic Sciences Research (*İslami İlimler Araştırma Vakfı*), 130
framing, xix, 3, 7, 12–13, 16–17, 27–31, 35, 85, 111, 123, 135–6, 139, 144, 144n36, 154, 176, 180, 182, 189, 241, 249, 275–6, 278–80
  diagnostic framing, 136, 160
  motivational framing, 136, 160–1
  prognostic framing, 136, 160–1
  reframing, 62, 164, 190, 215
framing consensus, 35, 35n137
framing contest, 214, 242
framing efforts, 16, 176, 280
framing processes, xix, 7, 12–13, 17, 23–4, 27–8, 30–1, 182, 279–80
framing strategies, 232
freemasonry, 69
Free Republican Party, 46n56, 48
Freudianism, 106
Fuller, Graham, 62, 91

Gamson, William, 9, 13, 21, 29, 35, 182
Ganz, Marshall, 15n64, 16
Gaza, 273–4
German Christian Democrat Party, 246
German Greens Party, 246
Germany, 5, 18, 32, 115, 131, 175, 207, 228, 270, 272
Gökalp, Ziya, 39, 41–2, 47n67, 97, 106, 242n127
Gökdemir, Ayvaz, 62, 247, 250
Gönül, Vecdi, 121
Goodwin, Jeff, 15, 15n64, 16, 25n100
Grand National Assembly, 37, 44, 46
Great Britain, 42n30, 44n44, 45
Great Israel, 150
Great Unity Party (GUP), 53, 226
grey wolf, 64

grievance-based explanations, 5, 8, 11, 279–80
grievances, xix, 2n7, 5, 7–8, 17, 29–30, 33, 55, 136, 139, 144, 160, 168, 243, 246, 275, 279–81
Gül, Abdullah, 33n133, 234n78, 243, 255–6, 261–3, 265, 265n255
Gülalp, Haldun, 147, 201, 204, 209, 236, 239
Gülen, Fetullah, 77, 118, 230, 234n73, 267, 272. *See* Fetullah Gülen congregation
Gulf states, 116
Gündüz, İrfan, 56
Güner, Arif Hikmet, 66
Gürgür, Nuri, 61
Gürkan, Uluç, 61, 61n141, 78, 156–7, 162
Gürüz, Kemal, 271
Güvenç, Bozkurt, 39, 97–9
Güzel, Hasan Celal, 102, 121, 226

Haberal, Mehmet, 274
hadiths (Prophet Mohammad's sayings), 101, 109–10, 125
Hak-İş, 31, 201, 206
Hale, William, 109, 116, 120
Halikarnas Balıkçısı, 99
Hamas, 24, 33n133, 218–19, 273
Hatipoğlu, Yasin, 225–6
Hayıt, Halil, 126
heavy industry leap forward (*ağır sanayi hamlesi*), 69. *See* NSP Necmettin Erbakan
hemşehri networks, 172
Herzi, Abdurrahman Nur, 116
Hewitt, Lyndi, 163, 163n135
Higher Education Board (*Yüksek Öğretim Kurumu*), 237, 256, 263, 271
Higher Education Law, 101
Higher Islam Institute, 105
Hikmetyar, Gulbeddin, 251
Hilmioğlu, Fatih, 274
Hizbullah, 4, 231
  in Lebanon, 33n133
Hizbu't-Tahrir, 4
Hobsbawm, Eric, 5
Holy Alliance (*Kutsal İttifak*), 119–20. *See* MP Turgut Özal

Human Rights Watch Commission, 232, 241

İBDA-C (Islamic Great Orient Fighters Front), 4, 221, 231
ideational factors, 8
identity politics, 2, 147, 175
identity reconstruction, 33
Ilıcak, Nazlı, 241
İLKSAN (*İlkokul Öğretmenleri Sağlık ve Sosyal Yardım Sandığı* – Primary School Teachers Health and Social Aid Fund), 158
imam-hatip graduates, 24, 108, 126, 177, 223–4, 251
İmam-Hatip Graduates Association, 226
imam-hatip high schools, 109, 109n128, 124, 126–8, 179, 226, 265
imam-hatip high school teachers, 109–10
imam-hatip schools, 25–7, 61, 63, 104–5, 123–7, 127n222, 128, 128n223, 162, 177, 222, 224–5, 277
imam-hatip students, 105, 110, 125–8, 188
IMF austerity package, 112, 200. *See* January 24 Measures
inadvertent elite ally, 11, 20, 22, 27, 135, 277, 283
İncioğlu, Nihal, 169
Independent Industrialists' and Businessmen's Association (MÜSİAD), 31, 139, 201, 225. *See* MÜSİAD
İnönü, İsmet, 49
institutional/conventional activities, 3
Intellectuals' Hearth (IH – *Aydınlar Ocağı*), 24, 65–6, 92, 96, 158, 226
International Monetary Fund (IMF), 112, 137, 148–50, 200, 236
Iran, 9, 34, 62, 85, 88, 91, 114, 132–4, 206, 218–19, 228–30, 248, 272–3
Iranian Revolution, 8, 33, 62, 91, 114
irtica (Islamic reaction), 94, 108, 125, 222, 253
Işık, Oğuz, 140, 140n19
İskender Pasha congregation, 63, 66–7. *See* Nakşibendi brotherhood/order
İSKİ (*İstanbul Su ve Kanalizasyon İdaresi* – Istanbul Water and Sewage Agency), 157

Islam, 98, 100–1, 146–7, 195, 202, 250n168
Islamic activism, 3
Islamic banking, 132, 132n245, 151
Islamic banks in Turkey, 131
Islamic brotherhood followers, 56
Islamic brotherhoods/orders/*tarikats*, 1, 1n1, 2–3, 6, 26, 45–8, 51–2, 56–9, 62–3, 77, 93–5, 108, 110–11, 119, 123, 126, 135, 162, 199, 201–2, 222, 228, 230–1, 233–4, 247, 251, 259–60, 270, 280
Islamic Development Bank (IsDB), 116, 129, 131
Islamic elite, 6
Islamic fundamentalism, 232
Islamic headscarf (*türban*), 147n51, 160, 160n119, 217, 239–40, 252, 261, 263–5, 265n250, 271
Islamic Jihad, 4
Islamic law (*Sharia*), 4, 213, 217
Islamic lifestyle, 30
Islamic orders. *See* Islamic brotherhoods
Islamic-oriented parliamentarians, 65
Islamic political party, 1
Islamic reaction (*irtica*), 108, 125, 222
   threat of, 125. *See* Islamic fundamentalism
Islamism
Islamist reactionism
Islamic revolts, 48
Islamic Revolution in Iran, 62, 85. *See* Iranian Revolution
Islamic Salvation Front (FIS), 218
Islamic state model, 30
Islamism, 2, 12, 26, 39–41, 61, 64, 93–4, 100, 114, 126, 128, 149, 162, 176, 183, 213, 232, 240, 244, 254–6, 275–6, 278–9, 282–3
Islamist: activists, 25, 136, 214
   bourgeois class, 130. *See* Anatolian Tigers
   business class, 23, 25, 27, 31, 85, 112, 135, 182, 184, 199–200, 202, 204, 206, 209, 222, 228, 244, 277
   elites, 111, 172
   entrepreneurs, 12, 17, 23–4, 28, 34–5, 93, 135, 139–40, 182, 214–15, 224, 232, 275–80, 283
   infiltration into military, 126, 234

infiltration into state bureaucracy, 63, 71, 121, 222, 228–30, 234n73

infiltration into state institutions, 121, 271

intellectuals, 2, 102, 178, 182, 199, 209–12, 239, 277

mobilization, 2, 4, 6, 9, 13, 16, 20, 24, 111, 136, 268, 277, 279–80, 282

political parties, xix, 4, 13, 55, 80–1, 275

reactionism, 177, 228, 233–4, 253

social movement, xix, 1, 136, 139, 142, 168, 170, 215, 221, 232, 238, 254, 261, 263–4, 270, 275–8, 280–1, 283

threat of, 227–8, 233, 253

women, 2, 160, 194–7

Israel, 24, 87, 150, 217, 231, 273–4

Istanbul *İmam Hatip* High Schools Parents Association, 226

İTMGT (*İslam Toplumu Milli Görüş Teşkilâtı* – National View Organization of Muslim Community), 31, 207–8, 230

Janissaries (*Yeni Çeri* – New Army), 38

January 24 Measures, 112, 137

Jasper, James, 15, 15n64

Jenkins, Craig, 10–11, 13, 25–6

Jenkins, Gareth, 235

Jerusalem Night (*Kudüs Gecesi*) incident, 33n133, 219

Jordan, 8–9, 129, 134, 200, 251n177

Justice and Development Party (JDP), xix, 1, 4, 34–6, 53, 55, 73, 75, 80–1, 83, 121, 214–15, 223, 243–4, 247–75, 279, 281–2

Women Commission, 245–6

Youth Commission, 246

Just Order, 3, 7, 29–30, 136–7, 144, 148–54, 158, 160–1, 163–4, 169, 172, 174, 182, 188, 206, 208, 214, 217, 235, 278

Justice Party (JP), 53, 56, 59, 63, 65–72, 74, 76–7, 89–90, 108, 119, 130, 143, 155

Kadın ve Aile (journal), 194

Kadiri, 77, 231

Kafesoğlu, İbrahim, 96–8

Kalaycıoğlu, Ersin, 172

Kamil, Sheik Salih Abdallah, 113, 129

Kanadoğlu, Sabih, 271–2

Kapusuz, Salih, 227

Karagülle, Süleyman, 239

Karakaya, Yahya, 173

Karatepe, Şükrü, 219

Karpat, Kemal, 40, 89–90

Kavaf, Selma, 245

Kavakçı, Merve, 240

Kayalı, Hasan, 39

Kazan, Şevket, 45, 51–2, 61–2, 66, 69, 91–2, 100, 119, 148, 183, 187, 219, 226, 240, 248

Kazdal, Zelkif, 246n148

Kebapçıoğlu, Süheyla, 179, 190, 195

Kemalism, 42, 89, 100–1, 176, 180, 218, 249

Kemalist regime, 45

Kemalist Revolution, 58, 281

Kemalist secularism, 85, 95

Kepel, Gilles, 114, 129, 129n231

Kepenek, Yakup, 156–7, 247

Khomeini, 62, 272

Kılıç, Haşim, 265n250, 269, 269n282

Kılınç, Retired General Tuncer, 271

Kırış, Recep, 226

Kırkıncı, Mehmet, 94

Kitschelt, Herbert, 5, 5n17, 18

Kıvrıkoğlu, Retired General Hüseyin, 254

Klandermans, Bert, 8, 10–11, 25–6, 29–30, 33, 183

Koçak, Ali Nabi, 170, 170n170

Koman, General Teoman, 233

Kongra-Gel. *See* PKK

Köprülü, Fuat, 51

Koraltan, Refik, 51

Korutürk, Fahri, 87

Kösoğlu, Nevzat, 45, 96, 98–9, 147

Kotku, Mehmet Zahit, 56, 56n110, 57, 63, 66, 113n138, 178, 198n64

Kramer, Heinz, 63

Kriesi, Hanspeter, 9, 13–14, 19–20, 20n86

Kubilay, 48

Küçük, Yalçın, 271

Kuçuradi, Ioanna, 45

Kudret (newspaper), 55

küfür (impiety), 56, 210

Kurdish separatism, 157, 222
Kurdistan Workers' Party (PKK), 86, 105, 254, 256. See PKK
Kurds, 78, 218
Kurzman, Charles, 33–4, 34n134
Kutan, Recai, 34, 183, 198n64, 214, 234–5, 240–1, 243, 279
Kuwait, 131, 132n245, 230
Kuwait Finance House, 113
Kuwaiti capital, 129
Kuwaiti finance houses, 25, 135, 277
Kuwait Turkish Evkaf Finance House, 133

Labor Party of Turkey (LPT), 53, 61–2, 62n150, 68
Lapidot, Anat, 94, 121n186
Lausanne Peace Conference, 45
Law on Giving Land to the Farmer, 50
Law on the Unification of Education, 43
leftist groups, 61, 87
leftist movement, 3, 24, 62–3, 65, 96, 98, 118, 209
Lewis, Bernard, 39, 43, 44n42, 46, 47n67, 48n70, 49
liberal democratic polities, 8, 10
liberalism, 29, 38, 46, 58, 61, 77, 137, 280
  neoliberalism, 157
Libya, 218, 228, 230
  defeat of the Ottoman Empire, in, 40
Light House Association (*Deniz Feneri Derneği*), 270
Light House Association case, 270
local governments, 29, 78, 161, 237–9. See municipalities

malfunctioning state, xix, 7, 27, 29–31, 81, 135–7, 139, 142, 144–5, 151, 160–1, 169, 176, 178, 180–3, 189, 205, 213, 215, 243, 254, 275, 278–9, 282
Manisalı, Erol, 274
Marxist, 61, 63, 209
  neo-Marksist, 86
Marxist intellectuals, 209
masons, 56, 66
materialism, 101, 106, 142, 147, 149
Mawdudi, Abu-l-'Ala', 62
mayorships, 78

McAdam, Doug, 2, 8, 10, 12, 14, 17, 21, 29, 35
McCammon, Holly, 163, 163n135
McCarthy, John, 26
McCarthy, Justin, 41
Meclisi Mesayih, 52
media, 3, 26–7, 31, 35, 95, 146, 148, 176, 179, 182–4, 187, 215, 219, 221, 231, 241, 244–5, 261–2, 264, 269, 271, 274
Mektup (journal), 194
Menderes, Adnan, 50, 58–9
Mercan, Murat, 245
Meyer, David, 3, 13–15, 15n64, 16, 21, 29, 35, 182
military-bureaucratic alliance, 59
military interventions: intervention of May 27, 1960, 59
  1960 military intervention, 59, 64n161
  1971 coup, 67–8, 92
  1980 coup, 11, 20, 24, 65, 76–7, 89–94, 98, 100–2, 113, 117, 119, 135–6, 139, 147, 156, 214, 230, 277
  soft intervention of, 1997, 35, 220, 229, 231, 241, 244, 278
military regime, xix, 3, 21, 25, 68, 76, 89–90, 91n30, 94–5, 103, 105, 107, 111–13, 115n155, 116, 118, 135, 224, 276–7
military rule, 11, 20, 59, 77, 88–9, 91, 102, 108, 117, 135, 140n19, 156n96
Millet (periodical), 55
millet system, 38, 145
Milli Gazete (newspaper), 67, 184
Ministry of Education/Ministry of National Education, 51, 103–4, 124, 126, 158, 222, 251, 253
Minkoff, Debra, 3, 13–14, 16
MİSK (*Milliyetçi İşçi Sendikaları Konfederasyonu* – Confederation of Nationalist Trade Unions), 88, 89n16
mobilizing structures, 12, 16
Modern Education Foundation (*Çağdaş Eğitim Vakfı*), 274
modernization, 7, 37–8, 40, 42–3, 45, 55, 122, 152, 164, 176–7, 209–12
modernization attempts, 7, 37–8

Index

Moore, Clement Henry, 131
moral values, 27, 29, 32, 82–3, 101, 122, 124, 127, 136, 148, 162, 164, 176, 180, 218, 224, 226, 233, 254
mosques, 25–7, 37, 47, 56–7, 60, 63, 94, 113, 116, 123–5, 207, 209, 231, 277
MOSSAD (Institute for Intelligence and Special Operations), 151
Motherland Party (MP), 3, 22, 24–5, 27, 53–4, 72, 74, 76–7, 79, 82–3, 85, 102–3, 107, 118–21, 124–5, 129–30, 131n241, 134–5, 139, 140n19, 144, 154–5, 170, 180, 185, 215–7, 219–20, 226, 229, 232, 235, 248, 277–8
movement activists, 3, 16–17, 30, 32, 35, 35n137, 213, 276, 280
movement entrepreneurs, xix, 3, 5, 7, 11, 15–17, 21, 28, 30, 33, 135–6, 214, 276, 278–81
movement mobilization, xix, 6–8, 11–12, 14, 16–21, 26, 30, 135, 276–81
movement participation, 9
Mubarak, Hosni, 218
Mumcu, Uğur, 4, 115, 115n155, 134
municipalities, 29, 78, 137, 139, 157, 161, 169, 172–6, 178–80, 183, 199, 213, 228–30, 237–40, 259, 265, 270, 278
Muraven, Mark, 32
MÜSİAD, 31, 139, 201–6, 225
Muslim brotherhood, 24, 134, 218. *See also* Hamas
Muslim Turks, 39
Muslim world, 4, 8–9, 11, 37, 61, 113–14, 116, 134, 145, 149–51, 205, 208, 218, 228–9, 236, 249, 280, 282
Mustafa Kemal Association (*Mustafa Kemal Derneği*), 202

nadwas (Quranic study groups), 26
Nakşibendi brotherhood, 25, 57, 66, 113n138, 277. *See Nakşibendi* order
Nakşibendilik
Nakşibendis
Nakşibendilik, 52
Nakşibendi order, 25, 48, 56n110, 63, 67, 113, 119, 131n241

Nakşibendis, 57, 63, 120, 231
Nasser, 113
National Consciousness (*Milli Şuur*), 145, 149
National Culture Report (NCR), 101, 105, 105n105, 106
National Democracy Institute, 246
National Military Strategic Concept, 222
National Order Party (NOP), 1, 4, 7, 22, 28, 53, 55–7, 66–7, 67n183, 68–9, 73, 75, 144–5, 183–4, 194, 214
National Salvation Party (NSP), 22, 25, 53, 55, 56n109, 68–70, 70n200, 71, 73, 75, 77, 87–8, 90–1, 94, 100, 108, 113, 113n138, 114, 118–21, 121n186, 130–1, 135, 143–5, 167, 183–4, 194, 202, 207, 214
National Security Council (NSC), 60, 68, 76, 89–90, 102–3, 221–2, 233–4, 237, 250, 271, 281
National View Organization of Muslim Community (İTMGT), 31, 207–8, 230. *See* İTMGT
National View Movement (*Milli Görüş Hareketi*), 66, 99, 191, 230, 236, 240, 247
National Youth Foundation, 50, 433, 481n63
Nationalist Action Party (NAP), 45, 54, 64, 70, 70n200, 71, 73, 75, 77, 82–3, 87, 90–4, 96–7, 99–100, 108, 118, 130, 147, 155, 170, 180, 231, 255, 258, 260–1, 263–4, 266, 268, 272–3
Nationalist Democracy Party (NDP), 54, 72, 74, 76, 118, 120, 170
Nationalist Work Party (NWP), 54, 72, 74, 77, 79, 158, 170
Nation Party (NP), 52–3, 55, 55n102, 61
networks, xix, 3, 6–7, 13, 16, 23–5, 25n100, 26–34, 61, 67, 69, 114, 120, 128–9, 135, 139, 142, 145, 155, 165–6, 171–2, 175, 181, 183–5, 188, 193, 201, 213–14, 220, 240, 254, 258, 275–80
New Nation Party, 65
New Turkey Party, 65
noncivil states: noncivil movements, in, 9
noninstitutional/unconventional activity, 3

non-Western case, 8
Numayri, General, 114
Nurcu brotherhood, 56, 94
Nurculuk, 52
Nurcus, 56n109, 57–8, 63, 118, 126, 230, 234n73, 267, 272
Nur faith movement, 26
Nursi, Said-i, 56–8

Öcalan, Abdullah, 86. *See* PKK
October war of, 1973, 114
OECD (Organization for Economic Cooperation and Development), 141, 141n25, 257
oil crisis of, 1973, 112
Okay, Hakkı Süha, 267
Oksay, Kazım, 125
Onat, Hasan, 48
Öncü, Ayşe, 160
Öniş, Ziya, 138
Opp, Karl-Dieter, 32
organizational dynamics, 3, 12–13, 17, 23–4, 27–8, 30, 180–2, 276, 281
organizational networks, 3, 13, 16, 23–4, 27, 30, 34, 61, 139, 142, 145, 165, 181, 183, 213–14, 240, 254, 258, 275, 278, 280
organizational resources, 12, 17, 280–2
Ortadoğu (newspaper), 98
Ottoman Empire, 37–41, 45, 55, 67, 97, 145, 146n43, 160
Ottoman era, 41–2, 45
Ottomanism, 39–41
Ottoman Muslims, 40
Ottoman nation, 39
Ottoman rule, 40, 48, 52
Ottoman Sultanate, 39
Ottomans, 39, 99
Özal, Korkut, 57n112, 113, 113n138, 119–21, 123, 130–1, 131n241, 232
Özal, Turgut, 25, 57n112, 76–7, 103, 112–13, 113n138, 118–24, 129–31, 133–5, 137–9, 142, 154–5, 155n91, 156, 159, 171, 200, 203, 206, 248, 269n282
Özal, Yusuf Bozkurt, 130
Özba Foundation, 130
Özbek, Mustafa, 273, 273n306
Özbilgin, Mustafa Yücel, 252–3
Özbudun, Ergun, 44, 49, 67, 151

Özcan, Salih, 130
Özcan, Yusuf Ziya, 263, 263n236
Özdenören, Rasim, 209–13
Özel, İsmet, 209, 212
Özkök, General Hilmi, 252–3, 282
Öztürk, Necati, 103
Öztürk, Osman Metin, 274

Pakistan, 113–14, 129, 132, 134, 134n255, 206, 228, 248
Paksu, Ahmet Tevfik, 56n109, 66, 130
Paksüt, Osman, 266
Palestine Liberation Organization (PLO), 24
pan-Arabism, 113–14
pan-Turkism/Turanism, 41, 61, 65, 97
pan-Turkists, 41, 65
parallel Islamic sector, 31, 200, 277
Passy, Florence, 30
People's Chambers (*Halk Odaları*), 48, 58, 58n121
People's Democracy Party (PDP), 54, 73, 75, 82, 170, 180, 241
People's Endeavor Party (PEP), 157
People's Homes (*Halk Evleri*), 48, 58, 58n121
perceived opportunities, 34, 34n134
Perinçek, Doğu, 266
Piar-Gallup, 223, 232
Pilavoğlu, Kemal, 58
Pınarcıoğlu, Melih, 140, 140n19, 170n170
PKK, 86, 105, 156–7, 225, 228, 233, 254, 261, 283
PKK terrorism, 156, 167, 233, 256, 261, 282
Polatkan, Hasan, 59
political Islam: in Muslim world, 4, 9, 61
 in Turkey, xix, 1–3, 5, 7–9, 20–2, 27, 30, 52, 76, 84–5, 92, 95, 112, 136, 182, 204, 222, 228, 277–8
 threat of, 88, 135, 222, 265
political Islamist agenda, 152, 278
political Islamist regimes, 273
political Islamist rhetoric, 209
political Islamists, 4, 6, 61, 95, 118, 121. *See* Islamists
political opportunities, 5, 12–17, 20–1, 33, 36, 181, 262–3, 281. *See also* perceived opportunities

Index

political opportunity structure (POS), xix, 3, 6–8, 11–22, 24–5, 27–30, 34–5, 85, 102, 118, 123, 135–6, 139, 144, 160, 164, 172, 181–2, 209, 213–4, 222, 241, 275–6, 278–81
political process model (PPM), xix, 2–3, 9, 12–17, 29–30, 180, 182, 276
political rhetoric, 3, 7, 28–9, 35, 62, 145, 148–9, 155, 158–9, 180, 182–3, 198–9, 214, 245, 248, 265, 278
poor urban migrants, 139
Populist Party (PP), 54, 72, 74, 76, 78, 118, 170
Powell, Colin, 249
positivism, 49, 105, 105n107, 106, 108, 152, 209–11
prayer leader and preacher courses, 51
prayer leader and preacher schools, 61
pro-Atatürk Thinking Association (*Atatürkçü Düşünce Derneği*), 219, 268, 274
Progressive Republican Party, 46n56, 48
Prophet Muhammad, 4, 101, 113n143, 125, 129, 210, 238

Quran, 26, 45, 47, 57, 60, 87, 93, 101, 108–9, 114, 123, 125, 147, 152, 163, 195, 210, 212, 217, 225, 231, 265–6
Quran courses, 3, 6, 25–7, 56–7, 63, 94, 108, 123–5, 127n222, 128n223, 130, 162, 177, 179, 201, 221, 225, 231, 250, 265, 277, 280
Quranic order, 45
Qutb, Sayyid, 61

Rabitat (Muslim World League), 113, 115, 155n155, 116, 129n234, 130, 132–4, 228, 230
Rabitat al-Alam al-Islami, 113. See *Rabitat*
radical leftists, 63, 85, 91
Raiders organization (*akıncılar teşkilâtı*), 87, 91
Ramadan, 173–4, 226, 246, 270
recruitment process, 27, 32, 277
Reformist Democracy Party (RDP), 73, 158, 199n70
Rehn, Olli, 267

religious education, 68, 102–5, 107–11, 117, 126–7, 224–5
religious instruction, 51, 57, 104, 107
religious values, 82–3, 163, 189
Republican Nation Party (RNP), 54–5
Republican Peasants Nation Party (RPNP), 54, 56, 61, 64–5
Republican People's Party (RPP), 46, 49–52, 54, 56, 58–60, 63, 68, 70, 72, 74, 76, 78, 82–3, 89–90, 142–4, 156–7, 170, 179–80, 209, 216, 219, 222, 235, 247, 251–2, 255–6, 258, 260, 264, 266–9, 272–3
RPP elite, 51
RPP under İnönü, 49
RPP's secularist policies, 49–51, 55, 65n167, 78, 260
Republican Reliance Party, 70, 70n200
resource mobilization, 30
right-wing nationalists, 78
riot behavior, 13
Risale-i Nur (The Epistles of Light), 58
Robinson, Glenn, 24
Roy, Oliver, 114
Rubin, Michael, 131, 266n259
Rucht, Dieter, 14, 30
rural conservative voters, 63
rural migrants, 166

Sabah-ATV, 262–3, 263n235
Sabah conglomerate, 215
Safa, Peyami, 97
Şahin, Mehmet Ali, 187, 194, 226, 234n78, 266
Sakallıoğlu, Ümit Cizre, 61, 108, 137
Saktanber, Ayşe, 194–5
Saltık, General Haydar, 86, 88, 90
Saner, General Çetin, 227
Saudi Arabia, 22, 25, 111, 113–16, 129n232, 130–1, 133–5, 228, 230, 273
Saudi capital, 23, 25, 85, 111–13, 129, 131n241, 133, 277
Savaş, Vural, 226, 226n40, 227, 240, 242
Saving Jerusalem rally, 87–8, 91n30
Saylan, Türkan, 274n316
Sebilürreşad (periodical), 55
Second Nationalist Front Government, 71

secular-democratic order, 12
secular-democratic polity, 3, 279
secular-democratic system, 29–30, 146, 247
secular disaffected votes, 29
secular elites, 175, 178
secularism, 4, 6–7, 29, 43–4, 46, 49–51, 57, 59, 62, 64, 69, 78, 83, 85, 87, 90, 93, 95, 101, 103–4, 107–9, 116, 123, 146, 160, 162–3, 176, 180, 183, 205, 208–9, 212, 217, 219, 226–7, 231, 233–6, 238, 241, 247, 249–56, 260, 263–5, 269, 277, 279, 281–3
secular military, 11–12, 20–2, 24, 27, 35, 254, 277
secular segment of society, 177, 246, 282
secular state, 7, 12, 30–1, 35, 38, 45–6, 51, 56, 83, 95, 107, 134, 136, 154, 160, 175–6, 191, 206, 214–15, 227–8, 235, 241, 248–9, 256, 264, 268, 278, 281–2
Sekmen, Mehmet, 174
Selçuk, İlhan, 266
Selçukis, 99
Selçuki Turks, 98
selective incentives, 31–2, 246, 282. *See* selective material incentives
selective material incentives, 32, 182, 213, 259
Şenel, Retired General Erdal, 271
sermons, 57, 60, 94, 124–5, 208
Şeyh (sheik) Sait, 48
Şeyh-ül Islam, 38n3, 42n30, 43, 44n42, 52
Sezer, Ahmet Necdet, 234n77, 249, 251–2, 261, 263, 263n239, 265n250
shantytown residents, 157, 165–7, 171
shantytowns, 2, 32, 140–1, 143, 161–2, 165–6, 169–72, 193, 196, 213, 246–7, 258
Sharia (Islamic law), 4, 27, 34n135, 43, 56, 70, 81–2, 87–8, 114–16, 132–3, 146, 146n43, 153, 191, 213, 219, 225, 231, 233, 243
Sharia courts, 43
Sharia rule, 56, 81–2
Sharia order, 87–8, 116
Sharia threat, 233

Silahçıoğlu, Retired General Doğu, 76
Simon, Bernd, 29–30, 33, 183
Sincan, 33n133, 219, 226
Singerman, Diane, 26, 200
Şıvgın, Halil, 130
Smith, Christian, 12
Snow, David, 27, 27n111, 30, 136
Social Democratic Populist Party (SDPP), 54, 72, 74, 78–9, 118, 144, 156–8, 170, 173, 179
social movement literature, 8–10, 10n36, 12, 17, 26, 32, 279
social movement mobilization, xix, 7–8, 11–12, 14, 16–17, 20–1, 276–81
social movements, 3, 5, 8–11, 13–15, 20–1, 25–6, 28–9, 61, 182, 276, 280
social movement scholarship, 8, 12
social movement theory, xix, 2n7, 5, 8, 10, 34, 276–7, 279–80
social networks: 3, 26–7, 30, 32, 128, 276–7
  Islamist, 27, 31, 135
  preexisting, 25–6, 277
  religious, 26
social religious movement, 8
Society to Disseminate Science (*İlim Yayma Cemiyeti*), 97, 130, 226
soft incentives, 23, 32, 244, 278
soft military coup of, 1997, 34
soft military intervention of, 1997, 55, 253, 272
Solana, Javier, 267
Soviet expansion, 91, 114, 135
Soviet Union, 149, 157, 229
Spain, 36
Staggenborg, Suzanne, 8
Standing Committee for Economic and Commercial Cooperation (COMCEC), 115, 134
state bureaucracy, 19, 37, 51, 59, 63, 65, 71, 85, 101, 118, 121, 135, 139, 217, 222, 228–30, 234n73, 270
State Planning Organization, 63, 105, 165, 210
State Security Courts, 237, 242, 251, 281
statist paradigm, 17, 17n72, 20–1
Stirling, Paul, 47
structuralist paradigm, 15n64
subaltern classes, 5
Sudan, 114, 228, 273

Sufi orders, 26, 120, 175, 200n74
Sugden, Jonathan, 241
Süleymancılık, 52
Süleymancı order, 57
Süleymancıs, 57, 63, 230-1
Sultanahmet Square, 225
sultanate, 6, 39, 42-3
Sultanbeyli, 170, 173
Sunalp, Turgut, 118, 120
sunna (the sayings and acts of the Prophet Muhammad), 147, 163, 210
Sunni Islam, 3, 24-5, 64-5, 76, 85, 93-4, 97, 103, 105-9, 114, 118, 172, 201, 277
Sunni Islamic orders, 93
Sunni Islamic religious education, 109
Sunni Islamist movements, 114
Sweden, 5, 18

Tachau, Frank, 82
Tamur, Galip, 45, 48n74, 100
Tanzimat era, 38-9, 42-3
Tapper, Richard, 95, 99
tarikats. See Islamic brotherhoods
Tarrow, Sidney, 2-3, 5, 8, 12-14, 15n64, 17-18, 18n77, 20-1, 25, 25n97, 29, 31-2, 35, 61
Tax on Agricultural Produce, 50
Tayan, Turhan, 163
Taylor, Verta, 6, 6n23
Tekdal, Ahmet, 147, 153, 184-5
Tekdal, Ayşenur, 244-5
Tercüman (newspaper), 268
third intervention (1980), 13
Third Islamic Summit Conference in 1981, 115
third military intervention. See 1980 coup
third intervention (1980)
"Three Kinds of Policy" ("*Üç Tarz-ı Siyaset*"), 40
Tijani order, 58
Tilly, Charles, 2, 8, 12-13, 15n64, 21
Tolon, Retired General Hurşit, 268, 269n277
Toprak, Binnaz, 37, 49, 49n79, 61, 70, 270
True Path Party (TPP), 54, 62, 72, 74, 77-9, 82-3, 118, 128, 144, 155-6, 158-9, 163, 170, 180, 200, 215-17,

221, 223, 228-30, 232-3, 247, 250, 255
Tuğ, Salih, 97n68, 103, 130
Tunahan, Süleyman Hilmi, 57
Tuna, Hüsnü, 264
Tünay, Muharrem, 94-5, 122
Turan, Osman, 65
Tür, Özlem, 140
Türkdoğan, Orhan, 165-6
Türkeri, General Fevzi, 228
Türkeş, Alparslan, 64, 64n161, 77, 90, 90n29, 97, 155
Turkification of Islam, 41
Turkification policy, 42
Turkish-Arab Bank, 230
Turkish Armed Forces, 87-8, 256
Turkish citizens, 7, 25, 28, 50, 90, 101, 136, 153, 157, 162-4, 167, 206, 247, 252, 282
Turkish Communist Party-Marxist/Leninist, 63
Turkish electorate, 55-6, 81, 164, 267, 275, 278
Turkish General Staff, 104, 113. See Turkish Armed Forces
military
Turkish Hearths, 45, 61, 100
Turkish Industrialists' and Businessmen's Association. See TÜSİAD
Turkish-Islamic Synthesis (TIS – *Türk İslam Sentezi*), xix, 3, 13, 22-4, 65, 76, 84-5, 93, 95-102, 105, 107, 118, 123-4, 135, 139, 158, 181-2, 184, 200, 209, 222, 275-7, 279-80, 282
Turkish Islamists, 11, 61, 88, 91, 96, 249
Turkish migrant workers, 69, 115, 206-7
Turkish national independence movement, 44. See War of Independence
Turkish nationalism, 39-41, 47n67, 64-5, 85, 93, 97, 100, 102, 106, 158, 283
Turkish nationalist ideology, 64
Turkish nationalist movement, 64
Turkishness, 45, 63-4, 96-100
Turkish political system, 29, 108, 136-7
Turkish Revolution, 7, 41-2, 44, 47, 97, 210, 253, 279
Turkish society, 1, 4, 28, 32, 35, 43, 45, 62, 76, 102, 106-7, 120, 122-3, 141-2, 148, 162-3, 177, 196, 200, 243, 247, 251, 254, 260, 268, 283

316   Index

Turkish youth, 101, 163–4
Turkism, 39–41, 63–4
Türkiye (newspaper), 230
TÜSİAD, 201–5, 215, 219, 237, 261

United Kingdom, 36
United States, 5, 8, 10, 18–19, 37, 92,
    114, 119, 149–51, 204, 249–50,
    252, 267–8, 279
ulema (the religious class), 6, 38, 38*n*3,
    46–7, 52, 252
Ülgenalp, General Refet, 68
ülkücü (ultranationalist) movement, 92,
    98
ülkü ocakları (ideas hearths), 92
ultranationalists (*ülkücüs*), 24, 61–4, 67,
    85–7, 90–2, 92*n*42, 93, 97–100,
    118, 135, 230, 277
Ulusu, Bülent, 89, 94, 115, 133
umma (Islamic community of believers)
    (*ümmet*), 6, 46, 107, 146, 158, 204,
    226
Union of Chambers of Commerce and
    Industry, 66. *See* Necmettin
    Erbakan
United Women Platform (*Birleşik
    Kadınlar Platformu*), 219–20
Unity of Education Law, 103–4,
    104*n*99
unstable elite alignments, 5
urbanization, 62, 86, 100, 140, 155,
    163–5, 167, 169
urban poor, 32, 76, 142, 165, 169, 193,
    196, 246, 254, 259, 282
Üruğ, General Necdet, 90, 94*n*52
Ürün, Halil, 173
U.S. cold war strategy, 62
U.S. green-belt project, 91, 135
U.S. Greater Middle East Initiative
    (GMEI), 249–50

Vahidettin, Sultan Mehmet VI, 44,
    44*n*44
Vakit (newspaper), 230
Varol, Nezih, 250
Vatan Cephesi (Fatherland Front), 58
Village Institutes (*Köy Enstitüleri*), 48–9,
    58
Virtue Party (VP), xix, 4, 22, 29–31, 34,
    54–5, 73, 75, 80–3, 144, 161, 170,
    173, 183, 196–7, 214, 234–44,
    247–8, 254, 260, 267, 275, 278–9
Virtue Movement, 235
voter alienation, 81
Vural, Oktay, 272

wage and salary earners, 50, 59
Wahhabite interpretation of Islam, 114.
    See Saudi Arabia
War of Independence, 6, 41–2, 42*n*30,
    44*n*42, 45, 47
weak state: movement mobilization in,
    19
Welfare Party (WP), xix, 1, 4, 7, 22–3,
    25, 27–33, 33*n*133, 34, 54–5, 73,
    75–84, 112, 117–19, 121, 124, 126,
    128, 135–7, 142, 144–56, 158, 160,
    160*n*119, 161, 161*n*126, 162,
    164–5, 167, 169–96, 198–99,
    199*n*70, 200–1, 205–9, 213–21,
    223–45, 247–8, 251, 254, 256, 260,
    264–5, 267, 275, 277–8
WP activists, 30, 32, 136, 146, 178,
    187–8, 192
WP entrepreneurs, 7, 213
WP Ladies' Commission, 193–5
Welfarists, 153, 179. *See* Welfare Party
Welsh nationalists
    in the United Kingdom, 36
Western civilization, 43, 100, 145, 152,
    212
Western colonial domination, 5, 7, 279
Western democracies, 8
Western Europe, 8, 10, 69, 113, 132,
    142, 204, 206–7, 209, 279
Western imperialism, 7, 28, 40, 100,
    148, 190, 210, 212, 279
Western liberal democracies, 9–10
Western liberal democratic settings, 11
Western liberalism, 38
Western type of state, 7, 279
West Germany. *See* Germany
Westernization, 28, 42, 101, 121–2,
    144–5, 148, 160, 164, 176–7, 209
West Working Group (WWG – *Batı
    Çalışma Grubu*), 227, 230, 253. *See*
    Soft military intervention of 1997
Wickham, Carry Rosefsky, 5, 26
Wiktorowicz, Quintan, 4, 10, 27
World Bank, 236

Index

World Values Survey, 81
World War I, 40–1
World War II, 50, 63
   in the aftermath of, 1, 221

Yalçın, Süleyman, 96–7, 97n68, 98, 100, 102
Yalçınkaya, Abdurrahman, 264–9
Yalçıntaş, Nevzat, 66, 97n68, 131n241, 226, 235
Yarar, Erol, 201, 203–5, 225, 232
Yashin, Yael Navaro, 175, 178
Yavuz, Hakan, 2n7, 25–6, 56, 56n109, 60n136, 70, 120–1, 200n74, 201, 206, 216
Yavuz, Retired General Kemal, 271
Yemen, 8–9, 26
Yeşilada, Birol, 113, 129, 131, 133, 207–8
Yıldırım, Binali, 267

Yıldız, Bekir, 219, 219n19.
   See 'Jerusalem Night' (*Kudüs Gecesi*) incident
Yıldızoğlu, Ergin, 71, 123
Yılmaz, Mesut, 215–16, 220, 229, 232, 272
Yılmaz, Şevki, 128, 162
Yirmibeşoğlu, Retired General Sabri, 76
Young, Michael, 18–19
Yüksel, Ayşe, 274
Yurdakul, Mehmet Emin, 41
Yurtkuran, Mustafa, 274

Zaman (newspaper), 230
Zapsu, Cüneyd, 252
Zengin, Bahri, 148, 190, 234n78
Zionism, 69, 117, 145, 150–1
Zionists, 67
Zorlu, Fatin Rüştü, 59
Zürcher, Erik, 44n44, 58, 68

BP 173.7 .E45 2010
Eligur, Banu, 1974-
The mobilization of
 political Islam in Turkey

JAN 21 2011